PRAISE FOR THE MOST FAMOUS MAN IN AMERICA

"Henry Ward Beecher was a phenomenon: the scion of an amazing family, the most renowned American preacher of his day, an anti-slavery stalwart—and the main protagonist in one of the most sensational sex scandals of the Victorian era. If you thought that the personalities and machinations surrounding the Clinton impeachment scandal were interesting, you will find the Beecher exposé riveting. More important, Debby Applegate has vividly brought Beecher and his entire era to life, in all of their piety, idealism, pomposity, and pride. I recommend her book highly to lovers of imposing historical figures and their tangled stories."

> —Sean Wilentz, winner of the Bancroft Prize for *The Rise of American Democracy*

"A wonderful portrait of a charismatic preacher with a deeply flawed private life, this biography vividly conveys the color and contradictions of 19th-century America. With a sure grasp of history, penetrating insights into religion, and many marvelous turns of phrase, Applegate brings to life a time that uncannily prefigures our own."

> —William Taubman, author of the Pulitzer Prize–winning biography *Khrushchev*

"At last, Henry Beecher receives the comprehensive treatment he is due, in this perceptive, engaging, and balanced study."

> —James MacGregor Burns, winner of the Pulitzer Prize and National Book Award for history and biography

"A lively narrative of 19th-century religion, power, passion, and politics, as well as a perceptive study of the elusive preacher who rode them to the top."

> —Joan Hedrick, author of the Pulitzer Prize–winning biography *Harriet Beecher Stowe*

"Historian Debby Applegate's *The Most Famous Man in America* is a brilliantly written, judicious, monumental biography of Henry Ward Beecher. The amount of new research material she unearthed is stunning. Chalk it up as a classic."

> —Douglas Brinkley, presidential biographer and author of *The Great Deluge*

"Debby Applegate brings to life 19th-century America's most influential preacher, who emerges in this full-blooded portrait as a fascinating tangle of all-too-human traits. Drawing off an impressive body of research, the author expertly weaves together biography and history in a riveting narrative that reads like a page-turning novel."

—David S. Reynolds, author of *John Brown, Abolitionist* and *Walt Whitman's America*

"The title is not misleading. Thoroughly researched, passionately written, and richly detailed, this book is *the* biography of America's greatest nineteenth-century preacher, Henry Ward Beecher. Through Applegate's discerning eye, the moral strengths and sexual vulnerabilities of the 'most famous man in America' come clearly into view. In the process, Applegate tells the larger story of nineteenth-century America's religious transition from a Puritan and theocratic past to a 'modern' liberal orthodoxy premised on happiness, love, and the banishment of original sin. Applegate's biography is must reading for serious nonfiction readers of American religion, politics, and culture in Victorian America."

—Harry S. Stout, Jonathan Edwards Professor of American Religious History, Yale University, author of *Upon the Altar of the Nation: A Moral History of the Civil War*

" . . . fast-paced . . . remarkably authentic. . . . [Applegate] accomplishes what every good biographer should: present a full-blooded portrait of her character in the context of his times. A rollicking good read."

—Ernest W. Lefever, *Washington Times*

"Beautifully written . . . An exceptionally thorough and thoughtful account of a spectacular career that helped shape and reflect national preoccupations before, during, and after the Civil War."

—*Kirkus Reviews* (starred review)

Not only is [Applegate] intimately acquainted with a wealth of primary sources, she writes in a fluid, captivating style that allows readers to feel that they know Beecher almost as well as she does . . . [She] offers a perceptive, engaging, and beautifully written account of one of the key figures of American religious history . . . Anyone interested in 19th-century religion, the roots of the theological view dominant in mainstream Protestantism today, or the thorny question of whether and how religious figures should enter the realm of politics owes Applegate a debt of gratitude."

—Andrew Stern, *The Christian Century Magazine*

The MOST FAMOUS MAN in AMERICA

THREE LEAVES PRESS

DOUBLEDAY

New York

The MOST FAMOUS MAN in AMERICA

THE BIOGRAPHY of HENRY WARD BEECHER

Debby Applegate

THREE
LEAVES

PUBLISHED BY THREE LEAVES PRESS

A hardcover edition of this book was originally published in 2006 by Doubleday.

Published in the United States by Three Leaves Press, an imprint of The Doubleday
Broadway Publishing Group, a division of Random House, Inc., New York.
www.doubleday.com

THREE LEAVES PRESS and its colophon are trademarks of Random House, Inc., and
DOUBLEDAY and its colophon are registered trademarks of Random House, Inc.

Book design by Terry Karydes

Library of Congress Control Number: 2005054842

ISBN 978-0-385-51397-5

PRINTED IN THE UNITED STATES OF AMERICA

3 5 7 9 10 8 6 4 2

Be true! Be true! Be true!
Show freely to the world, if not your worst,
yet some trait whereby your worst may be inferred.

Nathaniel Hawthorne.
The Scarlet Letter

THIS BOOK IS DEDICATED TO BRUCE TULGAN

Contents

The MOST FAMOUS MAN in AMERICA

Introduction

"HE WAS THE FAVORITE BY ALL ODDS; THE BEST LOVED MAN IN SUMTER THAT DAY"

For the first few days of the trip to Fort Sumter, the Reverend Henry Ward Beecher was in excellent spirits. Everyone aboard the ship was. They set off from New York City under a sunny April sky, sailing south past a gorgeous sunset. The moon was so entrancing that first night that most of the passengers stayed up late to enjoy it. The *Arago* was quite comfortable for a military steamship, more than adequate to host the Reverend Beecher and his distinguished guests. It was like staying in a first-class hotel, remarked one of the passengers.

When Beecher awoke the next morning the breeze was much warmer than it had been in New York, and the water unusually calm, so calm that Beecher did not complain of the chronic seasickness that plagued him on other ocean voyages he had taken. It was Sunday, so a regular religious service was scheduled. Because the passenger list was heavy with ministers, Beecher begged off delivering the sermon. He was saving himself for the main event at Fort Sumter.

They were an illustrious group, all invited guests of the federal government or of Beecher himself. Only a month earlier, in March 1865, the secretary of war, Edwin Stanton, sent an official order directing Brevet Maj. Gen. Robert Anderson and Henry Ward Beecher to choose a party of eighty people to attend a grand ceremony celebrating the Union army's recapture of Fort Sumter, South Carolina—the very spot where the Civil War had begun in April 1861. Anderson would raise the Union flag over the ruins, and Beecher would give a speech to com-memorate the occasion.

It was a bittersweet honor for General Anderson, who had surren-dered the fort under Confederate fire four years earlier. But for Beecher it was an unambiguous triumph—of all the great American orators, *he* was the one chosen to symbolize the newly reborn nation.

When news of the excursion leaked out, Beecher was besieged by both friends and strangers for a place on the *Arago*. Of course his wife, Eunice, would come, along with their young sons, Willie and Bertie, and their daughter and son-in-law, Harriet and Samuel Scoville. Then their close friends and Brooklyn Heights neighbors, John and Susan Howard, Chloe Beach, wife of the owner of the *New York Sun*, Theodore Tilton, Henry's old right-hand man at the *New York Independent*, and several of the wealthiest members of Beecher's Plymouth Church.

Besides Beecher's personal friends and patrons, the approved pas-senger list included a motley assortment of folks: military officers, politi-cians, wealthy merchants, intellectuals, and radical antislavery activists, including the renowned abolitionists William Lloyd Garrison and his English predecessor George Thompson. Reporters from many of the major New York newspapers claimed several more berths.

Space on the *Arago* filled up quickly, leaving hundreds of Beecher's parishioners still clamoring to witness their beloved pastor preside over this momentous occasion. Finally Henry Bowen, Beecher's ex-boss at the *Independent* and the biggest of bigwigs in Plymouth Church, took matters into his own hands, chartering a second private ship, the *Ocea-nus*, to carry those who could not be accommodated on the *Arago*. Half of Brooklyn and most of Plymouth Church seemed to be heading for South Carolina.

The lucky passengers of the *Arago* luxuriated in the balmy southern weather, treating the trip as if it were a tropical holiday. No one knew how long they would be gone, but no one seemed to care. Everyone was eager to mix and mingle, to put aside the stiff formality of everyday etiquette. They strolled the decks, played parlor games, and put on ama-teur theatricals and talent shows. Theodore Tilton, who fancied himself half poet, half radical agitator, recited verse, while others sang songs, acted in skits, or arranged themselves into dramatic tableaux. The more worldly folks could be found playing cards in the parlors.

Henry Ward Beecher was right in the middle of it all, a heavyset man with a wide smile, huge gray-blue eyes, and long graying brown hair tucked behind his ears. He was not handsome in any conventional sense, but he radiated youthful vigor. He moved with the freedom and energy of a big boy, perpetually joking, laughing, singing, and making introductions—he was the only one aboard who seemed to know everyone, and certainly the only one whom everyone aboard knew.

He talked constantly with everyone, joshing with the lowest cabin boy, flirting with the ladies, discussing matters of state with the generals and politicians. He was so full of fun that as they got closer to South Carolina, his friends on board began to wonder when he would have time to write his speech. After all, this was no average Sunday-morning sermon. The entire nation would be watching.

But Beecher showed no nervousness or concern. This wasn't procrastination. It was his habit to wait until the last minute so his ideas would be fresh for the audience. "Some men like their bread cold," as he liked to say. "I like mine hot."[1]

Finally Sam Scoville, Beecher's kindhearted son-in-law, became so anxious on his father-in-law's behalf that he felt forced to say something. With all due respect, shouldn't Mr. Beecher take some time to prepare his oration? After all, Sam reminded him, Beecher had many vicious enemies—in both the South and the North—who would rejoice if his speech was unequal to the magnificent occasion.

"What do you mean by coming around trying to scare a man to death?" demanded Beecher jovially. "I'll have something to say when the time comes."[2]

IN FACT BEECHER WAS NERVOUS, much more so than he let on. He hadn't felt this way for many years. Not since he was a shy, chubby little boy with a speech defect, teased for talking, as he put it, as if he "had pudding in my mouth."[3] Not since, as an immature fourteen-year-old, he froze with stage fright when asked to say a prayer at a school meeting.

Since that humiliating moment in high school, Beecher had more than mastered the art of public oratory. By now, at the age of fifty-one, he had given thousands upon thousands of speeches—from entertaining his school chums by standing on a haystack and imitating his father's preaching to leading rowdy open-air camp meetings on the western frontier to delivering high-priced orations in the most luxurious halls of New York, Boston, Philadelphia, and London. In this era before movies or television, when the theater was scorned by many respectable people, he was one of the best-paid entertainers in the country. He commanded the princely sum of $125 for an hour-and-a-half lecture, giving well over fifty lectures a year on subjects like "Patriotism" or "The Beautiful in Nature and Art."

In addition to his public lectures, Beecher preached twice on most Sundays at his own Plymouth Church in Brooklyn, a cavernous building that could hold a standing-room-only crowd of three thousand people—which it did whenever he was slated to give the sermon. His congregation was among the largest in the nation, with approximately two thousand members. His volcanic preaching was so widely celebrated that tourists by the hundreds took the Sunday ferries, nicknamed "Beecher Boats," from Manhattan to Brooklyn to hear the flamboyant preaching at "Beecher's Theater." His exuberant knack for controversy made him the darling of the popular press, and his every word was printed and reprinted in even the most remote corners of the country.

Anyone would have thought that by now Henry Ward Beecher would have been so jaded by the attention of strangers that he would have grown past the eager desire to please that drives most public performers. But Beecher's need for an adoring audience seemed insatiable.

Even now, in the spring of 1865, his wife, Eunice, was begging him to turn down the invitations to lecture that poured through their mail slot. He'd just been offered a book contract to write his first novel for the unheard-of sum of twenty-four thousand dollars, more than three times what he could make on the road that season. If he would refuse the constant deluge of lecture engagements and stay in Brooklyn, she reminded him, he could write the book *and* stay with her and the children. "Come home and let me shut you up in the study two weeks, 'til you write that story," she beseeched him. "And then we'll burn all the lecture letters, snap our fingers at all the committees—pay off all debts and be a happy darling home all the rest of our days."[4]

Eunice had common sense on her side, as she usually did, but her husband was not tempted by visions of hearth and home. The silence of the writer's study was terrifying compared to the glory of a standing ovation. He was addicted to the adulation, to the testimony of being wanted, to the love that overwhelms the man standing alone onstage, surrounded by laughing, weeping, cheering crowds who want nothing but more of him. Beecher had sought this adulation his whole life, and he found it. Yet still he was not sated.

Now the invitation of a lifetime had arrived. Surely this would ensure his place in the history books: the first official speech by a Union man on Southern soil, marking the approaching end of four bloody years of civil war. As newspapers as far away as the London *Times* noted, choosing Beecher as the national orator would show the world that the United States had waged war on its own people not merely in defense of what may "be called Union, or Empire, or integrity of territory" but in defense of liberty and morality.[5] Beecher's presence would prove that this was a war for the emancipation of the slaves, not merely the subjugation of the South.

It was impossible to turn down this opportunity. Still, there was good reason for Beecher to feel nervous. "To be called to be the orator of a nation upon such a day was an honor which might have oppressed any man," observed the editors of *Harper's Weekly* magazine, but for Beecher the stakes were even higher.[6] To put it bluntly, Henry Ward Beecher was one of the most hated men in the Confederacy. Many Rebels loathed him almost as much as they did Abraham Lincoln, the Great Tyrant himself.

Over the last fifteen years Beecher had built a national reputation by attacking the "peculiar institution" of slavery, calling for its abolition in the pulpit, on the public platform, and in newspaper columns. At a time when many churches were silent on the subject, and prominent ministers cited Scripture as evidence that God approved of slave owning, Henry Ward Beecher convinced many thousands of Americans that slavery was ungodly and unchristian. The nation's soul, he warned, would be destroyed if it did not purge itself of this monstrous sin.

Beecher was not among the most radical of the abolitionists—he left that to men like William Lloyd Garrison and George Thompson—but he was their equal in audacity. Radical abolitionists like Garrison denounced the founding fathers for legalizing human bondage, and condemned the United States Constitution as a "covenant with death and an agreement with hell."[7] They excoriated the mainstream churches for betraying humanity, calling for a revolt against any form of Christianity that did not condemn slavery as a sin.

In contrast, Beecher took a more moderate tack. He insisted that it was possible to respect the founding fathers while admitting that they had made a terrible mistake. He maintained that the Christian Church need not be rejected wholesale, it merely needed to be reformed. Beecher's determination to negotiate his way to liberty for all Americans without ripping apart the bonds of loyalty to the past appealed to a generation of Americans searching for a resolution that would not destroy their cherished but flawed founding myth.

But if Beecher was more of a reformer than a revolutionary in substance, his methods of persuasion were considered radical. It might be better to describe them as pyrotechnical. He had a talent for dazzling imagery and oversize emotional gestures. "I never hear, of the experience of others who are troubled, or struggling, or groping their way, that their condition does not instantly present itself as a drama before my eyes and I do not *think* of it but *see* it," he often observed. With his vivid visions and "flaming enthusiasm," Beecher "stirs you up in all sorts of queer intentions utterly contrary to those of your whole life; he exhorts sympathy and emotion and tears from his bitterest opponents," observed the essayist Adam Badeau.[8]

Beecher leveraged his personal charisma for the cause, turning his massive church into a powerful antislavery institution, reputed to be a stopping place for runaway slaves on the Underground Railroad. He held infamous mock "slave auctions," imitating the call of an auctioneer as he raised the money to free beautiful women from bondage. He publicly promoted plans to send boxes of Bibles and rifles—"Beecher's Bibles," they were nicknamed—to the settlers fighting the proslavery forces in Kansas. In 1863, when it seemed as if Great Britain might ally with the Confederates, Beecher delivered a course of speeches in England that helped turn international sympathy against the Rebels.

As the most famous preacher in the land, he made the antislavery movement respectable to mainstream Americans. Lincoln himself personally chose Beecher to speak at Fort Sumter, saying, "We had better send Beecher down to deliver the address on the occasion of the raising of the flag because if it had not been for Beecher there would have been no flag to raise."[9]

But with this international fame came an ugly backlash. Beecher became a pariah in the South, in danger of being lynched if he set foot below the Mason-Dixon line. Even his huge popularity in the North was marred by deep pockets of revulsion. Most Northerners did not care much about the plight of the slaves, and they blamed him and people like him for inciting the Rebellion. Indeed, it was a toss-up whom they blamed more: Henry Ward Beecher or his meddling sister, Harriet Beecher Stowe, whose blockbuster novel *Uncle Tom's Cabin* swept a tidal wave of public opinion into the antislavery camp.

Both proslavery Southerners and their Northern sympathizers (nicknamed Copperheads, evoking the venomous southern snake) lashed out at him for polluting the church with politics, for stirring up a peaceful people to bloody internecine conflict. Beecher was the target of a constant smear campaign. He was regularly denounced as a "nigger-lover" or "nigger-worshipper," as a warmonger and a charlatan who was exploiting the race issue to gain attention and political power. The *New York Herald* regularly called for Beecher to be hanged for treason, a sentiment echoed by many of its readers.

The mudslinging climaxed in the fall of 1864, during the campaign to reelect President Lincoln. A deluge of obscene cartoons, broadsides, and articles poured from Copperhead printing presses, claiming that he advocated "the amalgamation of the races" through black and white intermarriage. Other threats were more violent. Plymouth Church was threatened several times by local hooligans, and Beecher's house in upscale Brooklyn Heights was vandalized with black paint.

Beecher felt the tide of public opinion beginning to turn as the Union army kicked off a string of victories in early 1865. Charleston fell to Federal troops at the end of February, Union forces then retook Fort Sumter, and Sherman began steamrolling across the South in his historic march to the sea. By the end of March it was clear that the Confederate army was running out of steam. Then came the telegram from Secretary Stanton asking Beecher to preside over the flag raising.

This would be his very first speech on Southern soil. For Beecher this trip to Fort Sumter was more than an act of patriotism; it was a matter of personal pride. For years jeering enemies had called him a hypocrite and a coward for not daring to take his message directly to the Southern slave owners. Now he would show them all. He was heading to the heart of the Confederacy, to South Carolina, where the anti-Union forces were so fierce they were dubbed "the Fire-eaters." Here in the very birthplace of secession, Beecher would show himself not as a warmonger but as a man of peace. He would make them love him.

AS THE ACTUAL DEPARTURE from New York loomed closer, Beecher expressed unusual anxiety about the task ahead. When the invitation first arrived, he'd been exhilarated. But "as the thing itself draws near, it comes with a solemn shadow to me," he confided to his congregation the Sunday before he left; "the greatness of the mission seems to me such that, though I am unaccustomed to tremor, my soul trembles within me."[10]

He was under enormous pressure politically to sound just the right note between celebrating the Union triumph and promoting the national reconciliation that President Lincoln had called for only a month before, in his second inaugural address: "With malice toward none, with charity for all, with firmness in the right as God gives us to see the right, let us strive on to finish the work we are in, to bind up the nation's wounds." Beecher knew that his critics, both South and North, would pick apart his words, some searching for signs that he was abandoning the cause, others looking for veiled insults, treachery, or evidence of a hidden political agenda.

As the ship rounded Cape Hatteras and approached the archipelago of islands that surround Charleston Bay, his nervousness grew. It had been years since he'd written out an entire speech. He usually spoke extemporaneously, limiting his preparation to brainstorming the topic an hour or so before he was scheduled to go on, and scrawling a few notes to remind himself of his key points as he spoke. This spontaneity was the source of some of his most electrifying performances. But it also made it easy for him to get carried away by the moment, throwing caution to the wind and saying things that seemed injudicious or openly inflammatory when they appeared in print.

This time he was determined to deliver an oration that would stand close scrutiny on paper as well as thrill a live audience, a speech that would please everyone and offend no one, and that would begin the process of healing the wounds of war. He maintained his breezy, devil-may-care air, but when the revelers on the *Arago* stopped in Hilton Head to do some sightseeing, he sneaked away by himself. Finally he sat down and in his long, loose handwriting wrote out the whole speech word for word.

The night before the ceremonies the *Arago* set sail from Hilton Head for Charleston, anchoring just before dawn at the bar of the harbor. The bay was too shallow for the ship to navigate, and so General Quincy A. Gillmore, the chief officer in charge of this captured district, was sending a special craft to ferry them to the fort.

The next morning, Good Friday, April 14, the passengers awoke to a hot sun and a strong northeasterly breeze. By the time General Gillmore's transport, a low, long converted blockade runner commandeered from the Confederates, hove into view, the decks of the *Arago* were packed with people taking the warm morning air. As the blockade runner pulled up alongside, the passengers were surprised to see the sailors dancing on the deck of the transport, waving their arms and shouting the stunning news: "Lee has surrendered!"

They could hardly believe their ears—but it was true! The Confederate commander, Robert E. Lee, had surrendered to General Ulysses S. Grant at a courthouse in Appomattox, Virginia. The Rebellion was crushed! The decks of the *Arago* exploded with joy. In that glorious moment, "Every man was my brother, and every woman my sister," as Beecher recalled. The omens could hardly have been better for this historic day.

After a hasty breakfast Beecher's party boarded the transport for the fort, wending their way through the same waterways where Rebel torpedoes had sunk Union ships only a short time before. Now the harbor was swarming with Union sea craft commandeered from the conquered South Carolinians—ferryboats, steamships, fishing rigs, submersibles, skiffs—every one of them covered from stem to stern in a rainbow of flags and banners. It was a remarkable scene. Every boat he'd ever seen before "looked stark naked compared with these," Beecher remarked.

As the steamer surged forward, Fort Sumter rose up out of the water before them. Gazing on it, Beecher said he was beset by a "strange trembling." He had, he said, that "sense of being almost petrified, with which one looks upon a long desired sight, and, from very excess of feeling, has no feeling."[11]

They pulled up to a makeshift dock clinging to the edge of the battered island. After years of bombardment Fort Sumter was in ruins. It looked, Beecher thought, like a huge brick kiln tumbled over on its side. The base was littered with cannonballs, rusted and cankered by the salt seawater, and surrounded by huge mounds of rubble and broken brick. The parapets along the top of the one wall left standing were ragged as a saw edge.

They disembarked and entered the demolished fortress by a flight of wooden steps, which led over the brick walls and down through the debris into the central parade ground. In the well of the fort almost four thousand people stood waiting in the sun. On one side were marines, sailors, and infantrymen, some serving as an honor guard. On the other were several brigades of African American soldiers, including one commanded by Henry's brother Colonel James Beecher, who had led his troops into Charleston under a banner designed by Harriet Beecher Stowe, consisting of a rising sun framed by the word "Liberty" in huge crimson and black letters and the inscription "The Lord is our Sun and Shield." Milling around were clusters of Brooklynites from the *Oceanus*, as well as a contingent of freed slaves come over from the mainland.

One by one the distinguished politicians, generals, and dignitaries made their way up the stairs to the crest of the wall and descended onto the parade ground, accompanied by the sound of the drum and fife. Each was met with huge cheers as they made their way to a rough platform, decorated with bunting, boughs of myrtle, and wreaths of flowers, standing next to a barren flagpole. The ceremonies were running late, of course. As the crowd waited there were impatient murmurs from the black sections of the crowd: "Where's Beecher? Where's Beecher?" Finally someone shouted: "There he is, in the white hat."[12]

Everyone looked up, and there he was, as one observer put it, "the great expected," his white felt hat looming over the top of a parapet, and then bobbing down the stairway into the center of the fort. Both black and white erupted into wild cheers, far surpassing the reception greeting those who had come before—"a fitting welcome for the great champion of the rights of man," as the *New York Times* reporter wrote.[13] "He was the favorite by all odds; the best loved man in Sumter that day," remarked his friend and comrade in arms Theodore Tilton.[14]

Now the ceremonies could begin. The army chaplain read some verses from the Bible, and Beecher's colleague from Brooklyn, the Reverend Richard Salter Storrs, Jr., gave the prayer. There was a huge burst of applause when the tattered flag came out of the leather bag in which it had been kept since the surrender of the Union garrison at Sumter four years earlier. General Anderson made a few brief remarks, then began to hoist it slowly up the pole. "I dissolved," Henry said as he watched it climb, "and cried like a child, like a woman, or rather like a *man*. I had company, for tears were falling on every side."[15] Soldiers saluted, men clasped each other in emotion, several women fainted, and many people prayed.

When the Stars and Stripes reached the tip-top of the pole, a one-hundred-gun salute let loose. In return cannons boomed from every ship and every barricade in the harbor, including those that had fired on the Union forces four years earlier. The bay thundered as if the battle for Charleston were on again, and clouds of smoke enveloped the fort until the sky was black.

An hour of joyous clamor passed before the crowed calmed down. Finally Beecher walked to the front of the platform, taking off his hat and pulling out his carefully worded manuscript. A cold wind caught up the pages, flapping them madly and drowning out his strong voice. His long hair flew into his eyes and whipped around his head. A cry rose up from the crowd: "Put on your hat, Mr. Beecher."[16] He plunked his hat firmly back on his head, took hold of his manuscript with both hands, and began to read his speech word for word.

His speech was a stirring history of the long buildup and great conflagration of the Rebellion, but after all the fiery rhetoric it ended on a surprisingly generous note: "I charge the whole guilt of this war upon the ambitious, educated, plotting political leaders of the South," he shouted. *"But for the people misled, for the multitudes drafted and driven into this civil war, let not a trace of animosity remain.* The moment their willing hand drops the musket and they return to their allegiance, then stretch out your own honest right hand to greet them."[17] With liberty secure, now mercy and love could reign.

For more than an hour Beecher struggled with the wind, the papers, and his own overwhelming sense of the occasion. The conditions were not the best. The audience was tired of standing for so long and unable to hear well in the wind, so their attention wandered. Whether out of concern for the audience or for his strained voice, he was forced to stop in the middle to rest, letting the band recapture the audience's attention by playing a patriotic tune—something he never did.

Moreover, Beecher's unusual caution stripped the speech of his typical pyrotechnics. "Mr. Beecher's speech reads well," wrote one Brooklynite, but "In its delivery it lacked the electricity of an off-hand effort. It was received tamely[.]"[18] Another listener noted that "it lacked the peculiar magnetism of his less studied efforts," and that he seemed intimidated by "the consciousness that he was speaking, at least, semi-officially, and that his utterances would be regarded, not only as the voice of the authorities at the Capital, and of all the nation, but would pass from that hour into history."[19] Indeed Beecher was so eager to take the role of national healer that he seemed rather too magnanimous toward the Rebels, leaving the audience hungry for the feeling of partisan triumph they felt due them after four years of pain and sacrifice.

Although it was not his most brilliant performance, the effect would be the same as if it were: The newspapers would report it and the history books would record it. The Union soldiers could write home to parents, wives, and sweethearts, telling how they'd heard the famous Mr. Beecher speak. The newly freed slaves could say they had seen the great defender of liberty in the flesh. Of course many folks, given their druthers, might have preferred to see his sister, the great authoress Harriet Beecher Stowe, up on stage—but this was more than good enough.

HENRY WARD BEECHER acquired the mantle, and onus, of Christian leadership from his father—the Reverend Lyman Beecher, the last great

Puritan minister in America. In the early decades of the nineteenth century, Lyman Beecher's skill as a preacher and reformer made him one of the most famous, and most controversial, men in the nation.

Lyman Beecher possessed a passion for saving souls and saving the nation, which he passed down to every one of his twelve children. He adored his children, insisting that they were special, that they were endowed with great gifts of intelligence, compassion, and self-discipline. He instilled in them his sense of divine mission—and, many critics would add, his hubris. They were his own personal band of apostles.

Even more than his sermons and reform projects, which were influential enough to secure his place in history, Lyman Beecher's greatest claim to fame was his children. He was renowned, even by his foes, as "the father of more brains than anyone in America." Under Lyman's influence, the Beecher children yoked the Puritan legacy of a strong social conscience to a modern mastery of persuasion and public opinion. For nearly a century they defined morality in America, keeping their fellow citizens riled up, inspired, and entertained. Each new controversy seemed only to enhance their unique reputation. As one family friend famously phrased it: "This country is inhabited by saints, sinners, and Beechers."[20]

Lyman Beecher insisted that all seven of his sons become ministers, and each brought his own idiosyncrasies to the calling. Edward was a highly respected scholar and editor, Thomas was an innovator in the field of social services, and James went to China as a missionary and commanded an African American army regiment. Lyman's daughters were even more remarkable. Catharine Beecher was a pioneering educator of women and author of more than a dozen books. Isabella Beecher Hooker was a women's rights activist. But the celebrity of his daughter Harriet outstripped them all. Harriet Beecher Stowe was the most famous woman in the English-speaking world, having sold millions of copies of her novels in dozens of languages.

Of all the Beecher children, Henry's success was the most surprising. He was a classic middle child, surrounded by siblings who seemed brighter, more ambitious, and more disciplined than he. Frankly, no one expected much from him as a boy. He was bashful and garbled his words when he spoke. He skipped school and spent much of his time looking for fun and finding trouble. Even when he entered college he could not be bothered to study subjects that didn't interest him; his grades were so poor that he was one of the few students in his class at Amherst College not invited to speak at graduation.

The great scourge of Henry's childhood was religion—his father's religion. Like many Yankee children of that age, he was brought up to believe that the devil roamed the earth, and that wicked little boys would burn forever in the fires of hell. "I do not recollect," Beecher later said, that "one word had been said to me, or one syllable had been uttered in the pulpit, that led me to think there was any mercy in the heart of God for a sinner like me."[21]

Many Americans would be scarred by such teachings, but for Henry and his siblings the psychological effects were especially harsh. These fiery visions came from their very own father, who was so loving in deed and so ferocious in doctrine. Lyman left his children a complex legacy. They basked in his extraordinary love even as they quailed under his terrible theology. Some of his children thrived in this polarized environment, but others were irreparably damaged by it. Two of his children would climb the highest peaks of fame and accomplishment. Two of his children would commit suicide.

Henry's career was shaped by the conflict between his powerful longing for Lyman's love and his instinctive rebellion against his father's unforgiving religious dogma. The high expectations Lyman expressed for his children added to the fearsome pressure. God and his father stood shoulder to shoulder in Henry's young mind, and their approval seemed equally unattainable.

It was only when he began to liberate himself from his childhood fears and depressions, and to reject his father's insistence on religious conformity, that Henry's career began to take off. As he broke free of these childhood bonds, he made a remarkable discovery. The less he preached of God's wrath, and the more he emphasized the pleasures of God's love, the more people came to listen.

Instead of the Rule of Law touted by Lyman, by midcentury Henry was offering the Gospel of Love. "It is Love the world wants," he thundered from his pulpit in the 1850s. "Higher than morality, higher than philanthropy, higher than worship, comes the love of God. That is the chiefest thing."[22] God, he insisted, was not an exacting judge but a loving parent. Do as Lyman did, not as he preached, was Henry's new message. In essence he transformed the Puritan God into an omnipotent version of his own affectionate father.

Henry embraced the new with all the enthusiasm that his father had employed in defending the old. He knocked down the stifling solemnity endemic to churches in that era, adding lively music, flowers, and jokes. He criticized some of the most established institutions as hypocritical and backward, with a cheerful irreverence that sent shock waves through America. "What is Orthodoxy?" Beecher asked his followers. "I will tell you. Orthodoxy is *my* doxy, and Heterodoxy is *your* doxy, that is if your doxy is not like *my* doxy."[23]

His iconoclasm blew through the stuffy Victorian culture like a tempest. Soon people were flocking to hear this remarkable man. He was like no minister anyone had ever seen. Young Beecher was bold and funny, a natural actor who made his ideas come alive. He behaved more like a jovial farmer than the somber, starchy clergymen of the day. "Did I, when I became a minister, cease to be a man or a citizen? No! A thousand times no!" he insisted. "Out upon this idea that a minister must *dress* minister, *walk* minister, *talk* minister, *eat* minister and wear his ministerial badge as a convict wears his stripes."[24]

There was not a trace of "holier than thou" about him. He spoke plainly and with an air of candid personal confession that made him seem at once endearingly sensitive, admirably virile, and completely trustworthy. "It is important to have this fact, of the native and habitual outspeaking sincerity of the man, thoroughly stated; for on it stands his life," wrote one friend; "he was always natural, always himself, always giving forth his own interior condition, honestly and frankly[.]"[25]

In contrast to the staid leading men of the day, Beecher's sermons, speeches, and newspaper columns were filled with funny, poignant stories about his personal fortunes and foibles, inviting even those readers who would never set eyes on him to feel a sense of identification with this poor soul of a preacher. As the great Oliver Wendell Holmes wrote, "Wherever Mr. Beecher goes, everybody feels, after he has addressed them once or twice, that they know him well, almost as if they had always known him; and there is not a man in the land who has such a multitude that look upon him as if he were their brother."[26]

Henry Ward Beecher promised a generation scarred by the hellfire and damnation of the old orthodoxy that it was possible to have happiness here on earth as well as after death. "Abraham Lincoln emancipated men's bodies; Henry Ward Beecher emancipated their minds," as one admirer wrote. "The one delivered them from injustice; the other, from superstition."[27] If he could find happiness so could they, he assured his audiences, for he was just like them. "I always feel most for those who are farthest from grace," he confessed, "perhaps because I see in them some likeness to myself."[28]

Yet stories of generational backlash, of sons finding success by rejecting the ways of their fathers, are never quite so simple. Every son—from angry rebel to devoted mama's boy—shapes his life based on how he first saw himself mirrored in the eyes of the adults who raised him. Henry's balancing act—striving to win the love and respect of his father while simultaneously seeking his own happiness, even when it meant rejecting Lyman's most cherished values—was projected onto the culture, larger than life. As people followed Henry's success story, they worked through their own generational conflicts.

Henry's approach to religion was the same as his approach to slavery. He insisted that he was not rejecting his father or his father's faith; instead he was simply clarifying and improving the old-time religion for a fresh era. Henry Ward Beecher had a genius for putting "new wine in an old bottle," as one journalist wrote after visiting Plymouth Church.[29]

This technique worked as well spiritually as it did politically, reassuring Americans that they could embrace healthy change without burning their bridges to the past. "He was one of those men," as the writer Edward Eggleston noted, "who connect the past with the future, and make of themselves a bridge for the passage of multitudes."

Unfortunately Henry's slippery path between old and new only inflamed the ire of his conservative critics. To his enemies he seemed all the more dangerous because, as a Beecher and a Christian minister, his corrupting influence came from within the very heart of orthodoxy. Yet even many of his staunchest foes found him so goodhearted and sincere, so warm and intelligent, that they couldn't help liking him personally. "He was phenomenal in his ability to make people love him," as one observer put it.[30]

AFTER THE CEREMONIES AT FORT SUMTER, Henry went ashore to visit his brother James's headquarters, and then he joined the rest of the *Arago* passengers at the Charleston Hotel for a grand congratulatory dinner, followed by a ball in one of the old Charleston mansions commandeered by General Gillmore. After supper, around eight o'clock, everyone gathered to watch the harbor as the flagship, and every man-of-war, transport, and underwater monitor became "a skeleton pyramid of flame."[31] Lanterns were strung along the rigging to the top of the mainmasts, the reflection from the water doubling the brilliant lights of red, white, blue, green, pink, purple, and gold and the long columns of smoke. Rockets screamed from every deck, bursting into fantastic tints, then splashing into the sea. The boom of a single gun from the flagship capped off the show, leaving the harbor suddenly dark and silent.

After the fireworks and the final speeches of the dinner, the ball commenced. Some of the Plymouth Church people were likely a little scandalized by the very idea of a ball; many respectable Christians in their circle did not hold with dancing. Some went home early, perhaps out of discomfort. But when asked why they left the ball so soon, they replied that their hearts weren't in it—that they had been disturbed by strange feelings of foreboding.

Just as the fireworks began, five hundred miles away in Washington, D.C., President Abraham Lincoln and his wife, Mary, were settling into a private box at Ford's Theater to watch a production of *Our American Cousin*. As the last lights were burning in Charleston Bay, a shot rang out in Ford's. Chaos erupted as an actor named John Wilkes Booth jumped from the balcony onto the stage and dashed out the door. Suddenly Mrs. Lincoln screamed. The president had been shot in the back of the head. By the next morning "Father Abraham," as the newly freed slaves dubbed him, was dead.

In Charleston, though, they danced through the night and went to bed without an inkling. The next morning reports of Lincoln's assassination raced across the country via telegraph, newspapers, and word of mouth. It was said that no news had ever moved so fast before in American history. But down south, where the railroads and telegraph lines were cut, only Union officers had access to the outside world, and they were keeping a tight lid on it. No one knew if this was the first step in a coup d'état or the signal for a new Rebel revolt.

The next day Beecher and his family and friends went sightseeing among the ruins of the burned-out city, buying worthless Confederate money as keepsakes and picking up souvenirs from the junk lying in the streets: papers, books, statuary, manacles, plants, whatever they could carry. It was quite a sight to see, some of the greatest reformers of the last twenty years—Beecher, Garrison, George Thompson, Massachusetts senators Charles Sumner and Henry Wilson—jolting along the rutted roads in donkey carts because all other vehicles had been commandeered by the Union army. After this Beecher and his party intended to head south to tour Savannah, Georgia, and then Florida.

The morning they were scheduled to leave Charleston, a crowd of former slaves followed them to the wharf to see them off. They surged around Beecher, Garrison, and the other abolitionists, pressing on them whatever gifts they had been able to find or make—flowers, wreaths, small cakes, and treats scrimped from their scant food rations. One black man stood waving the flag with one hand and holding two children with his other arm, saying, "O men of the North, now you see why I love this flag: because it makes my children mine, who never were mine before!"[32] His arms loaded down with flowers and gifts, Beecher staggered up the gangway. As the boat pulled out, the black man knelt at the wharf's edge holding the Stars and Stripes in one hand and silently pointing at it with the other. It was their last vision of the ruined city.

Their first stop was back at Hilton Head, to visit the wealthy resort of Beaufort. As they waited to go ashore, Beecher was hanging around on deck, joking and talking of their holiday plans, when a boy passed by with a telegram from General Gillmore for Senator Wilson. Ever the wiseacre, Henry teased the messenger, asking him what was in the telegram, what could be so very important? After a long moment Senator Wilson came out of his cabin, his face dark with agitation. "Good God!" he cried. "The president is killed!" As Wilson read the dispatch aloud, Beecher remembered, "It was not grief, it was sickness that I felt."

They stood there for a moment silent and dazed. "It's time all good men were at home," Beecher finally said quietly. The ship spun 180 degrees and sailed back to Hilton Head, where they boarded a steamer for New York. All the way home they were drenched by a cold unpleasant rain, as if the God who made the weather shared their grief. "But, oh, the sadness of that company, and our nights' and days' voyaging back!" Beecher recalled. "We knew nothing but this: that the President had been assassinated. All the rest was reserved for our coming into the harbor." There were no amateur theatricals, no poetry readings, no sunlit strolls on the return voyage. They filled the time talking anxiously among themselves, fearing the worst: an uprising of traitors in New York, a coup d'état in Washington, D.C.

As they approached the bay of New York, the suspense grew excruciating as dense fog and stormy weather delayed their docking. Onshore all of New York was shuttered and draped in black bunting, consumed by grief and uncertainty. A few newspapers had printed brief, complimentary accounts of Beecher's speech at Sumter, but his great historical moment was swallowed up by the coverage of Booth's treason and Lincoln's long funeral procession back to Illinois.

Finally the *Arago* docked. Henry had hoped for a huge gala reception at the pier to celebrate their triumphant return. But, he said, "instead of that, on a dreary morning, drenched, chilled, and seasick, we came creeping up the bay under a cloudy sky, a fit symbol of our nation's loss, and betook ourselves to our several homes."[33]

Chapter 1

"Damned If You Do, and Damned If You Don't"

One evening in late December, sometime around 1820, Henry Ward Beecher trudged through the snow, returning home from running an errand for his parents. Exactly how old he was he couldn't say, but he was still a chubby little boy, with wide gray eyes set above apple red cheeks. As he passed up the long town common in the center of the village, he was surprised to see Litchfield's little brown Episcopalian church lit up like a beacon in the early darkness.

Henry was far too young to follow the fine theological distinctions his father used to separate the good Protestants from the bad Protestants, but of this he was sure: The Episcopalians were on the bad side. He needed no other proof than the fact that they didn't attend the white-steepled church where his father, the Reverend Lyman Beecher, preached every Sunday. In truth, God and Lyman Beecher were so intertwined in the little boy's mind that he did not quite grasp that Episcopalianism was a rival religion, he later recalled, "for I supposed there was no other religion except that which my father looked after."

Henry was irresistibly drawn to the open door of the church, and as he peered in he was shocked to find candles blazing at every window; boughs of spruce, pine, and arborvitae twined around the pews; and a choir singing blissfully about the birth of Christ. He had never seen such a spectacle, certainly not in his father's austere meetinghouse, and he could not imagine what it meant.

Although he did not know it then, this dazzling vision would be Henry's only taste of Christmas as a child. Christmas "was not known in the house of my father, for he was a Puritan of the Puritans," Henry said years later. "I never heard of Santa Claus when I was a boy. I never hung up a stocking. I feel bad about it to this day."[1]

When Henry was a boy, his faith in his father was so deeply ingrained that it never occurred to him to ask why they did not celebrate Christmas. If he had, Lyman's answer would have been unequivocal. As an orthodox Calvinist, Lyman Beecher interpreted the Bible literally, as solid fact, and there was nothing in the Scriptures to suggest that Christ was born on December 25. And even if there were, the day would be an occasion for solemn prayer, not sensual frivolity. Why, the Beechers didn't even celebrate their own birthdays.

If the Episcopalians chose to delude themselves about Christ's birth that was one thing, as far as Lyman was concerned, but this business of filling the church with decadent appeals to the senses—with music, gaudy decorations, and gifts—was a sneaky attempt to lure the good Christians of Connecticut from the true faith of the Puritan fathers. Lyman had no patience for newfangled notions of religious tolerance or the separation of church and state. Episcopalians, Unitarians, Catholics—Lyman lumped them together with atheists, drunkards, thieves, and Jeffersonian Democrats, declaring each one a force of deviltry to be fought tooth and nail.

Despite his harsh dogma, Henry's father was not a cruel man. Those who knew the famous Reverend Beecher only by rumor or from reading his sensational fire-and-brimstone sermons were often surprised to find that in person he was warm and witty, fiercely intelligent, and deeply compassionate. When he invoked the terrors of the devil and the terrible judgment of God's law, it was not out of perversity but because he was truly heartbroken that, as he saw it, so many "immortal souls are sleeping on the brink of hell."[2]

Lyman's devotion to God was rivaled only by his devotion to his children, and like any good parent, he wanted them to be happy. But in this age before modern medicine, when many families in New England lost at least one child to the grave, he was tortured by the fear that his children would be suddenly swept away by death before he could bring them to God. If they felt deprived by missing such pleasures as Christmas, Lyman was more than willing to trade their happiness on earth to secure their eternal happiness in heaven.

That cold Christmas Eve, Henry's small heart swelled with conflicting emotions as he "stood wistful, and with a vague curiosity, looking in, and wondering what sort of folks these Episcopal Church people were." He would have liked nothing better than to be in the middle of such gaiety and excitement. Yet even at this young age, he found it impossible to shake his father's teachings. He turned away from the church and headed home, with a "feeling of mixed wonder and pity" for those people who dwelled so far outside his father's sphere.[3]

This complex constellation of feelings colored every corner of Henry's childhood. He idolized his father and yearned desperately for Lyman's love and approval, yet every natural impulse in him craved forbidden pleasures. He longed to be like his older brothers and sisters, who seemed so easily to meet the high standards of Lyman and his fearsome God. But no matter how afraid he was of hell and how hard he tried to get into heaven, his desire for earthly happiness kept getting in the way.

Twenty-five years would pass before Henry would begin to question seriously his father's opinion on this or any other matter. When he did, however, he quickly made up for lost time, tossing out his father's beliefs by the bushel. By then Henry was becoming a wealthy, worldly man who shamelessly indulged his newly acquired tastes for European travel, velvet jackets, sumptuous rugs, and expensive art, spending enormous sums of money on gifts for his family and friends. Before long he would even give up his belief in hell itself.

But even when he succumbed to the Victorian craze for Christmas, celebrating it at home and in his church with all the merry trimmings, the holiday never really took hold in him. What he had yearned for all those years ago was not toys or Santa Claus, he recalled in old age—"A little love was what I wanted[.]"[4]

LYMAN BEECHER HAD GOOD REASON to fear for his son's soul. Henry Ward Beecher was born in the summer of 1813, in the midst of one of the most terrifying, tumultuous periods in American history. From the distance of two centuries, we have mythologized the decades after the War for Independence as an Arcadian idyll of happy farmers and wise founding fathers. But the American Revolution was a genuine, bloody revolution, and, like all revolutions, it left a long wake of social, economic, and political upheaval. The future of the young Republic was still very much up in the air in 1813, creating an atmosphere of tremendous exhilaration and profound anxiety—a potent combination that would shape the emotional core of Henry Ward Beecher and his generation.

Relations between the United States and England had remained strained and murky since the end of the war, growing even more complex as the French Revolution of 1789 and then the invasion of Europe by Napoleon Bonaparte's armies tore up old diplomatic alliances. Tensions peaked when England attempted to cut off sea trade between the United States and the Continent by attacking American ships and impressing almost a thousand American sailors, in essence kidnapping them and forcing them to work on British ships. Finally, in the summer of 1812, President James Madison declared war on the United Kingdom—the War of 1812 or the Second American Revolution, as it came to be known.

Eager to retake their former colony, the British invaded from all sides, from the Great Lakes in the north to the Gulf of New Orleans in the South. In the spring of 1813 eight British warships sailed into the waters of the Connecticut Sound, blockading the ports, burning wharves and trading ships, and forcing the city of New London to evacuate when the fleet tried to sail up the Connecticut River. By the summer of Henry's first birthday, the Redcoats were marching into Washington, D.C., where they burned the Capitol to the ground and pushed the Republic to the edge of bankruptcy.

If any state should have stood firm in the midst of this chaos, it ought to have been Connecticut, the Land of Steady Habits, where clocks, granite, and schoolteachers were its chief exports, and the specter of Puritanism still stalked every crevice of its rocky hills. Long after the new federal constitution of 1788 guaranteed the separation of church and state at the national level, Connecticut proudly remained a theocracy, in which every household was taxed for support of the state-sanctioned Congregationalist Church. For more than two hundred years the same aristocratic network of merchants and ministers—"the Standing Order," as it was known—controlled both politics and society. Federalist in their politics and Calvinist in their religion, the Standing Order considered themselves the last bulwark against the "forces of innovation and democracy," which had led the country once again to bloodshed. So great was their animosity toward "Mr. Madison's war" that Connecticut seriously considered seceding from the Union—an idea that the citizens of the South would revive forty years later.

But with the state's stony, overfarmed soil, burgeoning birthrate, and dependence on European trade, no place was hit harder than Connecticut by the anxiety and turmoil of the post-Revolutionary period. So many young people were fleeing the state for the rich bottomland of the Ohio frontier that the region was designated the "Western Reserve of Connecticut." A dangerous discontent was rising among those who remained at home. Out-of-wedlock births were skyrocketing, and drunkenness was a genuine epidemic, with the average citizen now drinking up to five gallons of cheap hard liquor a year. To top it off, a coalition of Jeffersonian Democrats, attorneys, atheists, workingmen, and "unofficial" religious sects was starting to agitate for an end to the old Standing Order. To many folks it seemed as if Lucifer was loose upon the land.

But Connecticut Yankees were a wily, peculiar breed, according to early American folklore, with a slippery shrewdness that could confound even Satan himself. They were filled with contradictions—in turn slyly funny and profoundly grave, aggressively innovative and doggedly conservative, "a rare combination of philosopher and fighter," as Frederick Law Olmsted once remarked.[5] At the same time, they were absolutely, infuriatingly, convinced of their own superiority, and obsessed with converting the world to their way of thinking. In a contest of wit and will, the devil and the Connecticut Yankee were considered nearly an even match. If there was any truth in this stereotype, it was sure to be found in Litchfield, Connecticut, and in the Beecher clan.

Perched high up in the Berkshire hills, the village of Litchfield gloried in its paradoxical reputation as a bastion of both progressive intellectual culture and staunch religious orthodoxy—"half Hebrew theocracy, half ultra-democratic republic," as Lyman's daughter Harriet described it.[6] It possessed two claims to national fame: its outspoken minister, the Reverend Lyman Beecher, and its pioneering schools, Miss Sarah Pierce's Litchfield Female Academy, one of the nation's first serious schools for girls, and Judge Tapping Reeve's Litchfield Law School, the country's first school devoted solely to the study of the law. Together the two institutions attracted students from as far away as Ohio, South Carolina, Canada, and the West Indies, graduating scores of future congressmen, ambassadors, cabinet secretaries, and political wives, who extended the town's reputation to London and Paris.

In June 1813 Litchfield looked much as it does today, laid out along four broad tree-lined streets that crossed to form a long, grassy town common. In its habits, however, it was more akin to an English colony than to contemporary America. Indeed, Litchfield clung more tightly to the old ways than most New England towns. Villagers still rose with the sun and shut their houses up tight with the tolling of the nine o'clock bell. Many of the clothes were still homespun and homemade, and children went barefoot all days but Sunday. The older "respectable" men of the town still strolled the streets in outdated colonial garb, clad in short breeches buckled at the knee, tricornered hats, cutaway coats, and the occasional powdered wig. Only Democrats and infidels, it was said, wore pantaloons, or trousers as they came to be called. With deliberate symbolism the Congregational meetinghouse stood in the dead center of the common at the very summit of a hill, and from its old-fashioned swallow's-nest pulpit the Reverend Beecher ruled over the manners and morals of the town.

Most folks here took religion seriously. From hardscrabble farmers to the town gentry, they lingered at Buell's general store or on the steps of the courthouse, debating Parson Beecher's Sunday sermon, or whether it was God's will to install a woodstove to warm the meetinghouse in winter. Surely, some argued (out of piety or stinginess it was hard to say), such an indulgence would send them down a slippery slope to decadence. After years of fruitless debate seven progressive young men finally purchased a stove on their own and, after more wrangling, were allowed to install it on a trial basis. It made its debut on an unusually warm November day. As they entered the meetinghouse, the townspeople stared suspiciously at the contraption, sitting smack dab in the broad middle aisle.

Old Deacon Trowbridge, a firm opponent of the stove, scornfully gathered up the tails of his long coat as he passed it, as if the devil himself would send out a spark to singe it. Uncle Noah Stone, a wealthy farmer, scowled and muttered about the uncomfortable heat. Mr. Bounce, editor of the village paper and a stove advocate, warmed his hands over the stove with a satisfied air, tucking the skirts of his coat safely between his knees.

The climax of the conflict came during the sermon, when the Reverend Beecher began warning of hell's "heaping coals of fire." Pious Mrs. Peck, wife of an antistove deacon, felt so overcome by the unfamiliar heat that she fainted dead away. Mrs. Peck quickly recovered her wits, if not her dignity, when the young men, barely containing their laughter, informed the congregation that because the day was so warm they had not lit a fire. The stove stayed, a small victory for progress.

The Reverend Lyman Beecher was an eccentric, contradictory character, the spitting image of the canny Connecticut Yankee. At Sunday services strangers to his church were often startled to see a short, wiry man clad in a shabby black tailcoat, his shoulder-length gray hair tied in a simple ponytail, bound down the aisle of the sanctuary, toss his dusty hat on a chair, and leap up the steps of the pulpit. With his tattered clothes, brusque manners, and thick country accent he was often mistaken for an uneducated farmer, but when he spoke listeners quailed before his aggressive arguments and maddening self-assurance.

In theory Lyman viewed the world through the fatalistic lens of Calvinism—believing that sin and corruption lurked around every corner, and that human fate was preordained by God's plan. But in practice Lyman was an irrepressible enthusiast and an instinctive pragmatist who believed that well-motivated human willpower could accomplish nearly anything. Lyman's passion often made him overzealous and intolerant of other views, but it was also his greatest gift, sending him careening from dry-as-dust logic to ecstatic emotion, forcing his audience to think and feel in equal measure. *"Eloquence is logic on fire,"* as Lyman liked to say.[7]

Lyman was enraged by the tide of rebellion he saw rising all around him, but in typical fashion he read it as an urgent sign from God: Surely this was the promised darkness just before the new Christian millennium, when Jesus Christ would return to earth. To Lyman his mission was clear: He would personally lead the crusade to turn not just Connecticut but all of America into God's kingdom, in preparation for the return of Christ. This was a true culture war, and as Lyman noted with satisfaction, "I was built for war."[8]

His crusade was two pronged, employing a curious combination of modern organizational skills and old-fashioned emotional appeals. In the months before his son Henry was born in 1813, Lyman led a "missionary tour," crisscrossing lower New England on horseback, attacking the places "where Satan had long held control."[9] In front of the state legislature in May he announced the formation of the Connecticut Society for the Suppression of Vice and Promotion of Good Morals, a new form of voluntary charitable organization that quickly spawned a network of associations dedicated to stamping out various social disorders—the Great Benevolent Empire, as it came to be known.

Believing that virtue was meaningless without faith, however, Lyman was also determined to spark a popular wave of religious conversions, a religious revival, as it was called. He turned up the emotional heat at home, preaching his millennial message as many as nine times a week, speaking personally with scores of potential converts and leading daily public prayer meetings. His efforts began to pay off not long after Henry's birth, when an epidemic of cholera whipped through Litchfield, killing six people. Strained by grief and panicked by the possibility of sudden death, villagers now poured into the church, desperate to save their souls and appease God's terrible wrath. Soon the revival was spreading across Litchfield County and western Connecticut, driven by Lyman's ambitious network of ministers. The kingdom of God seemed just around the corner.

HAD SHE BEEN LIKE OTHER WOMEN in the village, Roxana Foote Beecher might have found plenty of reasons to complain about her peripatetic husband. Nine months pregnant, with six young children to feed and clothe, she could easily have regarded her husband's unstinting devotion to God as neglect of his earthly duties. But Roxana Beecher was not like other women.

In an age when few women possessed formal education, Roxana was a skilled artist and a genuine intellectual, fluent in French, with a passion for history, math, and science, and whose most treasured possession was an imported English encyclopedia. Roxana's piety equaled Lyman's, but in contrast to her high-strung husband, she was by nature "calm and self-possessed," with an "easy and gentle temperament that could never very strictly enforce any rules," as her eldest daughter recalled; "at the same time, in sudden emergencies she had more strength and self-possession than my father."[10]

"I cannot describe your mother in words," Lyman said later. "It was not the particular this or that put together would describe Roxana, but a combination such as I never met with but in her."[11] But in one important way, Roxana was typical of her time: she had give birth to seven children in the last thirteen years: Catharine, born in 1800, William in 1802, Edward in 1803, Mary in 1805, George in 1807, Harriet in 1811, and a little girl who died before her third birthday.

Henry Ward Beecher was born in his mother's bed on June 24, 1813—"the fourth, fifth, sixth or seventh child, somewhere thereabouts," he later joked, not altogether humorously. The labor was uncomplicated, and Henry was a healthy, good-natured baby, just the sort of circumstances that made it easy for him to get lost in the domestic whirlwind. After her delivery Roxana's only observation was that her eyes felt unusually weak, making it difficult to sew while she recovered—"rather an inconvenience," she observed mildly, "considering how requisite the use of the needle is where there are so many girls and boys as we have here."[12] If the birth of a first child is poetry, as Henry's sister Harriet quipped, the birth of the eighth is decidedly prose.

The Beechers lived in a rambling white house set on an acre and a half of land around the corner from the Congregational meetinghouse. It was a typical Yankee hodgepodge, a plain two-story main building with rooms and wings added on, helter-skelter, over time. Outbuildings clustered around the yard, including a woodshed, a drafty old barn that housed the horse and chaise and a menagerie of animals, and a privy that served as the family toilet.

This was the era of "plain living and high thinking," as Ralph Waldo Emerson dubbed it. Even for the well-to-do, cash was scarce and luxuries limited in rural New England, especially with the wartime trade embargoes. Almost everything a family needed had to be wrested from the hardscrabble soil by someone's broad back and bare hands. "Duty" was the watchword for adults and children alike, in an era when discipline and self-sacrifice were all that stood between survival and ruin. "Any amusement is a sinful waste of time that does not prepare us for a better discharge of duty," as Catharine Beecher characterized the philosophy of the time.[13]

For the Beecher family this stern way of life was exacerbated by the genteel poverty of the ministry. It was a constant strain to support seven children on Lyman's meager salary of eight hundred dollars a year plus an annual load of firewood from each family in the parish. By the time Henry was three years old, the family circle had swelled to include an orphaned cousin, two indentured black servant girls, and a never-ending stream of visiting ministers and extended family. To eke out their provisions, they planted every inch of the parsonage yard with fruit trees and vegetable gardens. To bring in more hard cash Roxana rented rooms to students attending the law school or the female academy, although feeding the extra mouths ate up much of their profit.

In these circumstances, privacy was an entirely different concept from ours. Everyone shared a bed, at times with several people. Trundle beds were tucked under the tall bedsteads and pulled out at night to fit even more sleepers. When guests stayed over, they piled into any bed that had room for them. When it was too cold to visit the privy out back, slop jars in the bedrooms served as toilets, to be emptied out the window or slid under the bed until morning. Washing up was done around a water basin in the kitchen; on lucky winter days the basin wasn't filled with ice, on even luckier days there was a little warm water left in the kettle. Soap was homemade and saved for laundering clothes. Humans were expected to scrub the dirt off with a coarse towel. More than one of the genteel city girls who rented rooms at the parsonage abandoned her books and returned home, unwilling to live under such ascetic conditions.

Adding to the physical hardships of life in the Beecher household was the heavy weight of orthodox religion. Every day began and ended with family prayers, Bible reading, and hymn singing. Every child past the age of seven attended a heavy schedule of prayer meetings, lectures, and religious services in the drafty meetinghouse, as well as regular religious instruction at school. Undue frivolity was discouraged, so they did not celebrate Christmas or birthdays. Dancing, theater, and all but the most high-toned fiction were forbidden. Sundays were spent in quiet contemplation—a special torment for fidgety children.

But this dour picture tells only half the story. Although the Beechers were plain and pious, they were not stuffy or stodgy. They brimmed with high spirits, quick enthusiasm, and an almost eccentric disregard for social conventions. "There is," as Lyman's youngest daughter noted, "the strangest and most interesting combination in our family of fun and seriousness."[14]

Lyman was a truly rare father. Impulsive and emotional, he was blessed with a "passionate love of children," as Catharine put it, treating his children with "all the tenderness of a mother and the untiring activity and devotedness of a nurse, father and friend."[15] He loved to romp with the kids, and had a knack for making hard work fun—telling stories as they peeled apples on autumn evenings, making a game out of stacking firewood, and leading them on expeditions into the woods to pick berries or collect nuts or catch fish.

On Sunday evenings, after the last church service, Lyman would gather the children as he took up his beloved fiddle to "run down" from the day's work. On a good night he might even indulge in a little "double shuffle" from his youth, defying his own disapproval of dancing. On nights like this he "was lively, sparking, jocose," Harriet Beecher recalled; "and loved to have us all about him, and to indulge in a good laugh."[16]

Yet for all Lyman's natural charisma, Roxana was the emotional anchor of the family. In contrast to Lyman, she was an easygoing optimist, whose tendency, as she put it, to "make all nature wear the face of hope and joy," eased the endless round of work, and the stern demands of duty. Writing to her sister when Henry was a year old, Roxana offered a snapshot of her warm, unpretentious parenting: "I write sitting upon my feet, with my paper on the seat of a chair while Henry is hanging around my neck and climbing on my back, and Harriet is begging me please make her a baby."[17] Harriet's wish was soon granted with the arrival of their ninth child, a little boy they named Charles.

Even when the toddlers, Harriet and Henry—in the mistaken belief that they were some sort of onions—ate the rare Dutch tulip bulbs that had been sent to her at great expense from New York, Roxana did not scold. "My dear children, what you have done makes mamma very sorry," she said quietly, and then spun such a vivid picture of the beautiful red tulips that the children were nearly as disappointed as she was.

Henry's first memory was of his mother's calm, consoling arms. He was trying to crawl down the steep center staircase by himself, when all at once the "sudden sense of being alone frightened me, and I gave one shriek," he remembered; "and then the echo of my voice scared me worse, and I gave another shriek that was more emphatic," and Roxana rushed in from the kitchen, scooping him up.[18] He couldn't remember how her face looked at that moment, but he would never forget the feeling of relief and comfort as she pressed him against her soft, warm bosom.

Then one cool July night, just as Henry turned three, his mother disappeared into her bedroom and did not come out. Suddenly the house that had been brimming with high spirits was now hushed with fear. The older children moped around, red eyed and morose, occasionally bursting into tears, and his father's face was strained and bleak. Baby Charles, only nine months old, was sent to stay with friends, the boarders from Miss Pierce's school abruptly dispersed to other houses, and Judge Reeve's wife, always a close friend of the family, was now at the parsonage almost around the clock.

Little Harriet and Henry were only dimly aware of what was happening. They were allowed to see their mother only once a day now, as she sat up in bed wanly eating gruel. Her skin was pale, almost transparent, except for a bright red spot on each cheek. Her breathing was labored, and a constant cough choked her lungs—all the telltale signs of late-stage tuberculosis.

One evening, just as summer was fading into fall, Lyman called the children to gather around their mother's bed one final time. In a weak voice she expressed no fear or regret, only joyful anticipation. She whispered that she had seen such glorious views of heaven that she was almost overwhelmed. Roxana then dedicated her sons to God as ministers and missionaries. She tried to speak to the children directly but could barely be heard above their sobbing. She consoled them by whispering that God would take better care of them than she ever could, and that they must trust Him. She said a special prayer for Henry and Charles, the youngest of all.

Too little to comprehend what was happening, Henry had only a strong impression of great fear and pain, and of being distracted by Charles, dressed in a long white baby dress, as he was handed into the arms of Mrs. Reeve. His mother fell silent as if she were drifting off to sleep, as his father began to usher the children out of the room. Suddenly Mrs. Reeve called out: "Lyman, she is reviving!"

"I went to the bedside," Lyman recalled, "and she opened her eyes and smiled and I said, 'Dear wife, we have had much blessedness together in life, much joy in Christ's work and kingdom'—she said 'yes!' "

Then, abruptly, she was gone. It seemed, Mrs. Reeve observed with bleak optimism, like "a victory over the grave."[19]

The bustling parsonage was now shuttered and silent, as the children absorbed not only their own pain but their father's terrible despair. In Puritan fashion the mirrors in the parsonage, as well as Roxana's artwork, were draped in white cloth, mimicking the shroud that wrapped her body. Harriet, five years old at the time, remembered Henry frolicking like a kitten in his golden curls and black frock, too young to go to the funeral or to understand the explanations of the adults.

A few days later Catharine found him digging a hole in the dirt under her window. What was he doing? she asked. "I'm going to heaven to find ma," he explained. Harriet understood. "They told us at one time that she had been laid in the ground, at another that she had gone to heaven; whereupon Henry, putting the two things together, resolved to dig through the ground and go to heaven to find her."[20]

Lyman's spinster sister, Esther Beecher, came to help take care of the older children, while the youngest were sent to stay with others who, it was presumed, could take better care of them than a grief-stricken widower. Of the little ones, only Henry remained at home, bringing a measure of unrestrained joy to a house otherwise filled with sadness. "Henry is a very good boy, and we think him a remarkably interesting child and he grows dearer to us every day," his sister Catharine wrote several months after Roxana's death; "he is very affectionate and seems to love his father with all his heart—His constant prattle is a great amusement to us tho' sometimes it is tiresome."[21]

Yet even the uncomprehending little boy registered his family's grief, developing a mysterious "thickness of speech." "When Henry is sent to me with a message," his Aunt Esther said at the time, "I always have to make him say it three times. The first time I have no more manner of an idea than if he spoke Choctaw; the second, I catch now and then a word; by the third time I begin to understand." Various explanations were suggested—an "enlarged palate," swollen tonsils, bashfulness—but no real medical cause was ever found. As with many children so afflicted, it was likely a manifestation of the stress that surrounded him.

"The last success that ever would have been predicted for him," his sister observed years later, "would have been that of an orator."[22]

ONE MORNING IN LATE SEPTEMBER, almost a year to the day after Roxana's death, Lyman was scheduled to give his weekly lecture on religion to the students of the female academy, just as he did every Saturday. But this day was special, Miss Pierce told the girls, admonishing them to "pay particular attention" to Reverend Beecher, "as he was not going to be here but two or three Saturdays more." He was going on a long journey, she explained, and would not be back for a while.

A wave of girlish giggles rolled across the classroom. "I suppose," one of the girls noted in her diary, "it was because he was going to Boston to buy him a wife."[23]

Officially Lyman was going to deliver an important sermon to the illustrious Park Street Church in Boston. But the gossip of the young ladies was prescient. A little more than a month later, Lyman made a second trip to Boston, this time in his battered one-horse chaise. He was going, he told the children, to bring home their new mother.

At a time when mothers frequently died in childbirth and wives were crucial economic resources, such a rapid remarriage was not as shocking as it might now seem. As a widower with eight children, a house full of boarders, and a parish full of obligations, it was natural that Lyman Beecher would remarry as soon as possible. Although still grieving deeply, Lyman threw himself into courtship with typical gusto, setting his sights on Miss Harriet Porter, the twenty-seven-year-old daughter of a prominent physician from Portland, Maine.

Harriet Porter was beautiful, cultured, and connected to some of the finest families in New England, including the governor of Maine and a United States senator. The Porters were appalled at their daughter's intention of marrying a poor country parson, nearly twice her age, whom she barely knew. But unlike her worldly parents, Harriet Porter was an ardent born-again Christian who shared Lyman's fundamentalist zeal. "He is to be considered a messenger from the court of Heaven," she insisted.[24] In the face of such divine opposition, her parents were forced to relent.

Four-year-old Henry was elated by the prospect of a new mother. "I had rather an indistinct idea of how a *new* mother looked—or *any* mother," he said, "but I had a feeling that it was going to be something very good." It had only been a year since Roxana's death, but already his memory of her was fading. Finally one day, just as dusk fell and the three little ones were climbing into their trundle bed upstairs, the word came: When they awoke their new mother would be here. Although the older children were apprehensive, Harriet, Charles, and Henry could hardly sleep with excitement. Just as he was drifting off, Henry remembered, "we heard a racket downstairs; and every mother's son and daughter of us began to halloo; 'Mother! *Mother!* MOTHER!'"

They heard the tread of footsteps on the stairs and the creak of the door, Henry recalled, and then "we saw a dim shadow pass into the room, and somebody leaned over the bed and kissed me, and kissed Charles, and said: 'Be good children, and I will see you more to-morrow.' I remember very well how happy I was. I felt that I had a mother. I felt her kiss, and I heard her voice. I could not distinguish her features, but I knew that she was my mother."[25]

The next morning they tumbled down the stairs, eager to see her in daylight. Their new mother was a beauty, slim and pale with soft auburn hair and bright blue eyes. Her hands were soft and uncallused by hard work, with sparkly rings adorning her slender fingers. It was as if, Harriet said, "she were a strange princess rather than our own mamma." Little Charles clung fearfully to Aunt Esther, but Henry eagerly climbed into her lap, babbling happily of how he had dreamed of her last night.

Arriving in Litchfield, the new Mrs. Beecher was delighted by the cultivated social life, the cozy house, and her remarkable new family. "I have never seen a finer family of children or more agreeable," she marveled a few weeks later. They loved to read, she noted, and "some of them are of uncommon intellect." About Harriet and Henry their step-mother was especially warm. The two were so close they seemed almost like twins—"always hand-in-hand. They are as lovely children as I ever saw, amiable, affectionate, and very bright."[26]

For a brief moment it seemed that Harriet Porter might heal the gaping wound left by Roxana's death. But after a few months it became clear that, in temperament, Harriet Porter had little in common with Roxana. Unlike Lyman's sanguine first wife, the new Mrs. Beecher was an anxious perfectionist, "a woman of profound veneration, rather than a warm and loving nature," Henry recalled, who "looked at everything from a very severe point of view." Harriet Porter suffered from what was then diagnosed as melancholy (what we would now call depression), which was exacerbated by her devotion to the grim teachings of Calvinism. She treated life on earth as an unpleasant duty, a cross to be borne until one reached the joyous gates of heaven. Her life teemed with crosses, Henry remembered with resentment. "She took them and carried them herself, and put them upon her children."[27]

Young and privileged, Harriet Porter was unprepared for the harsh reality of her new role as the wife of a poor, overworked pastor and stepmother to eight lively children. Making matters worse, within a year of her wedding, Harriet Porter entered the exhausting cycle of childbearing, quickly adding four more children to the Beecher brood: Frederick in 1818, Isabella in 1822, Thomas in 1824, and James in 1828. Henry's first, brief letter, written at the age of five, caught the barnyard logic of breeding in the days before modern birth control. "Der Sister," he wrote, "We ar al well. Ma haz a baby. The old sow haz six pigs."[28]

Soon she was spending more time cloistered in her room, praying intently and suffering from vague maladies. All the children found their new stepmother forbidding and gloomy, but little Henry was particularly intimidated by her. "I was afraid of her," he said. "It would have been easier for me to lay my hand on a block and have it struck off than to open my thoughts to her." Lyman genuinely loved his new wife, but even he was forced to admit that Henry "would have had no need for that feeling if it had been his first mother."[29]

The towheaded little boy was, by all accounts, unusually lovable, with an irrepressible cheerfulness. "I was born so that it is easy for me to be joyful," as he later put it.[30] But beneath the surface of Henry's happy-go-lucky personality a deep, inchoate yearning took root. As he got older, listening to stories and reading old letters from the mother he barely remembered, Henry fantasized more and more about Roxana. In his imagination she became a paragon of unconditional love, his own guardian angel. Filled with unquenchable longing, he sought substitutes in the sympathy of softhearted females who seemed less likely to judge him.

When he was desperate for comfort or burdened with guilt, he ran to Aunt Esther, to his sister Harriet, or to Aunt Sarah Chandler, the warmhearted black woman who cooked and washed for the Beechers. In particular, "Aunt Chandler took the place of a mother to me"; she was Harriet Porter's alter ego, soothing his hurt feelings and sneaking the lad bread and cheese when he was sent to bed without supper.

From them "I neither got a cuff, nor a scolding, nor exposure," Henry remembered; "they would hide my faults and shield me. And I recollect distinctly that with such persons it was easy for me to be frank."[31] This potent triangle of influences—an idealized absent mother; a distant, critical stepmother; and a bevy of smart, strong-willed sisters and aunts who doted on the boy but had little time to spoil him—bred in him a lifelong craving for the affection of attractive, intelligent women.

"I needed nothing but a little attention," Henry concluded years later, as he described his relationship with his father and stepmother. "Although I was longing to love somebody, she did not call forth my affection; and my father was too busy to be loved."[32]

BY THE 1850S, when Henry was eclipsing his father as the most famous minister in America, it became fashionable to speculate about the relationship between the two men. Some people argued that Henry was a chip off the old block, the natural heir to Lyman's charisma, brains, and ambition. Others took the view of Robert Ingersoll, the notorious American agnostic: "Henry Ward Beecher was born in a Puritan penitentiary, of which his father was one of the wardens."[33]

There was much truth in both interpretations. Lyman Beecher was the polestar of Henry's childhood, a loving, heroic figure who stood only slightly below God himself in the boy's eyes. Yet, like the Lord of the Old Testament, Lyman often seemed capricious in the way in which he wielded his great power. Henry was never sure if he'd run into the lenient, affectionate side or the wrathful, authoritarian side of his father, and this uncertainty shadowed his childhood.

Like all the Beecher children, Henry adored his father and would do anything to please him. "My father was one who was calculated to draw out a demonstrative affection," he later recalled. "Down on his hands and knees he has given us many a ride, and great has been our exultation, when after a prodigious show of wrestling, we flung him full length upon the grass."[34] The suspicion that Lyman let him win never lessened the thrill of victory.

Even in old age, Henry remembered the rush of joy and relief he felt when, "unable to sleep and crying down the dark stairs where pain and fear strove with each other, I went into my father's room, and he put his hand upon my head, and with tones of great kindness and love said, 'You have got the toothache, my dear boy! Come get in with me and cuddle down by my side,'—how that filled me with affection, and such gladness that I forgot the toothache!" It was, he said, like the "rest of God."[35]

Lyman loved his boy with the same ardor. To the end of his life, he told of how, as a toddler, Henry would run out to the gate to meet him as he returned home from work, crying, "Oh, Papa, Papa!"

"I have never forgotten that, never shall," Lyman said.[36]

But in the wake of Roxana's death these playful moments grew less frequent. Preoccupied by his lingering grief and his expanding evangelical empire, Lyman left the day-to-day tasks of childrearing to his wife, intervening only to deliver the occasional spanking or cuff on the head. In the custom of the day, affection was understood rather than spoken, even in this unusually expressive family. "I never said to him, 'I love you, father'; and he, as near as I can recollect, never said to me, 'I love you, Henry.'" Still, Henry noted with typical irony, "I knew that my father loved me. He told me so every time he whipped me."[37] In truth, the boy was a little afraid of his father.

But the greatest barrier between Henry and his father was religion. Before her death Roxana's cheerful piety had calmed her husband's deep-seated anxiety and lightened his morbid theology, but under Harriet Porter's chilly influence the dark, authoritarian aspects of Calvinism permeated the parsonage. The endless round of religious rituals that had once seemed merely gloomy now became utterly bleak.

"Sunday was the dreadful day of the week to me," Henry remembered—the day of "Thou shalt not, thou shalt not." From sunset on Saturday to sunset on Sunday, playing, working unnecessarily, reading anything but the Bible or religious literature, even laughing was forbidden. Happiness itself seemed to be a sin on the Sabbath, from Henry's point of view. He remembered vividly the "mortal terror" he felt as a very small child on waking up one morning, "merry as a cricket, singing almost before I was awake, and full of rogueries," when suddenly, "I thought, 'It is Sunday, and I am pulling cotton wool out of the blanket

and playing with it?' I had such a horror of the wickedness which I supposed I was committing that I hid myself under the bed clothes, creeping out as I found I was not dead[.]"[38]

Coming down to breakfast on a Sunday, he was met with the dreaded
question: "Do you know your catechism?" After breakfast the conscientious Harriet Porter quizzed the children in the Westminster Catechism,
a long series of questions and answers that laid out the Calvinist creed.
This was a special misery for the bashful, thick-tongued boy, and even
when he stammered out a correct answer, he barely understood its big
words and tortuous logic. Adding injury to insult, if he did not know
his lesson he got no dinner—a painful punishment for the perpetually
hungry lad. Following catechism, two long church services dominated
the middle of the day, meaning hours of sitting in a scratchy Sunday
suit on stiff wooden pews, his head bobbing with sleepiness. After supper, before twilight, Harriet Porter gathered all the little children in her
bedroom to pray and talk about their obligations to God.

"It seemed to me that there was nothing so lazy as the sun on
Sunday," Henry recalled resentfully. As sunset approached Henry and
Charles would perch impatiently in the west window of the sitting
room, watching the sun graze the top of the cherry tree, then sink behind its branches, then down, down to the last glimmer on the horizon.
"And the moment it was down, we would give utterance to an outcry
of joy."[39]

It does not take a huge leap of sympathy to understand the feelings
of a boisterous boy suffering through a long, dull Sabbath day. It requires
far more of the modern imagination to picture the way the Calvinist
obsession with death could shape the personality of a sensitive child.

New England, it has been said, is the child of a superstitious mother
and a philosopher father. This fusion of the supernatural and the hy-
perlogical is at the heart of Lyman Beecher's theology. In seeking to
impose the rule of divine law on an unruly universe, Calvinism takes
the great unanswerable questions of life—Why is there so much pain
in the world? Is there a higher power in the world? What happens when
we die?—and poses them, as Harriet later observed, "with the severest
and most appalling distinctness."[40] Lyman and his fellow divines merci-
lessly drilled their parishioners in these impenetrable questions, casting
a morbid pall over the culture in general and over the Beecher house
in particular.

While the children were young, much of what Lyman preached was
too abstruse for their meager understanding. Only one of their father's

beliefs stood out in ghastly, vivid detail: If God did not choose to save their souls, then they would burn forever in the everlasting fires of hell.

"Is eternal punishment a reality?" Charles asked Henry many years later, then answered his own question. "Father thought so. He never doubted. Strike that idea out of his mind and his whole career would be changed, his whole influence on us modified."[41]

From earliest childhood Henry was urged to prepare for death. Even casual conversation was peppered with vivid threats of hell, faint promises of heaven, and concern over the treacherous state of his soul. The first trauma he could remember in his young life came from listening to the cautionary tales of a visiting minister: "He told me how a bad boy fell sick and how he saw the Devil coming after him, and how he cried, 'O mother, mother! there is the Devil! There he is as far as that onion-bed! There he is coming through the gate! Here he is inside the door!' " After that, he said, "I saw forty devils in the air. I dreamed of them. I did not for years shake off the feeling of terror which that conversation produced in my mind."[42]

Deaths were announced in the village by the tolling of the meetinghouse bell. One weekday when Henry was so little that his bare feet couldn't touch the floor of the old family chaise, he was riding along with his stepmother on an errand when suddenly the bell began to boom. Harriet Porter turned to the boy and asked, "Henry, what do you think when you hear a bell tolling like that?" Caught off guard by this rare inquiry into his thoughts, Henry blushed and could think of nothing to say. "I think," she went on solemnly, scarcely noticing his silence, "was that soul prepared? It has gone into eternity."[43]

The indoctrination into Calvinism took a heavy psychological toll. In today's culture parents consider it a prime duty to build up their child's self-esteem, but prior to the 1830s most Christian parents took the opposite view, believing that their task was to tame their child's strong ego and natural willfulness, to make him humble before God. "Henry, do you know that every breath you breathe *is sin?*" Lyman asked as soon as the boy was old enough to speak. "Well, it is—every breath."[44] It was a crushing thing for a little boy to hear, especially from the mouth of his own father.

And why was he was born so sinful? According to the catechism, the answer was clear: Because Adam and Eve disobeyed God, forever corrupting all human beings. This concept of "original sin," as it is known, was one of the first sentences a Yankee child learned to read, printed in every school primer: "In Adam's fall, we Sinned All." The cruel logic of original sin was enough to turn any child away from religion, Henry's sister Harriet later remarked in disgust:

> Tell a boy God loves him, and religion has a chance to take hold. Tell him he is under God's wrath and curse, and so made liable to all the miseries of his life, to death itself, and the pains of Hell forever, because somebody ate an apple five thousand years ago, and his religious associations are not so agreeable—especially if he has the answers whipped into him, or has to go to bed without his supper for not learning them.

The burden of original sin was compounded by the capriciousness of salvation. In the Calvinist universe, salvation was considered a supernatural act, a testament to God's sovereignty and mercy, not merely a reward for good behavior. So how would a person know if he or she had been saved? Of course no one could be certain of their fate until they caught sight of the pearly gates, but revivalists like Lyman Beecher believed that the saving grace of God would descend like a lightning bolt, in a moment of intense visceral revelation. If you did not experience the anguish and the crisis, if God did not choose to make you one of his special "elect," then it didn't matter how good or faithful you had been; chances were you were going to hell. A famous jingle neatly captured the paradox:

> *You can and you can't,*
> *You shall and you shan't;*
> *You will and you won't.*
> *You're damned if you do,*
> *And damned if you don't.*

"Thus was this system calculated, like a skilful engine of torture," Harriet concluded, "to produce all the mental anguish of the most perfect sense of helplessness with the most torturing sense of responsibility."[45]

Some pockets of people—the Baptists, Unitarians, and Universalists, among others—were beginning to object to the strict doctrine of original sin and "limited salvation," arguing that an all-benevolent God would never be so heartless as to punish a child arbitrarily for the crimes of his parents. Twenty-five years later Henry would take up this argument himself, but as a child his father's ideas were planted so thoroughly that he never questioned their cruel, convoluted logic.

Instead he assumed that if he was not saved it must be his own fault, that he must be a terribly wicked boy. "My innumerable shortcomings and misdemeanors were to my mind so many pimples that marked my terrible depravity," he remembered; "and I never had the remotest idea of God except that He was a Sovereign who sat with a scepter in His hand and had His eye on me, and said: 'I see you, and am after you.' So I used to live in perpetual fear and dread, and often wished myself dead."[46]

Henry did not quite understand that death was the portal to hell, but he knew he didn't want to go there. Yet he couldn't muster much enthusiasm for heaven either. From everything he'd been told, heaven sounded like a dull place where all the angels stood around in white robes, singing hymns and telling God what they thought of him. "I did not like it; and I thought I was a miserable wretch because I did not."[47]

For all the talk of heaven and hell, death remained an abstraction to the boy until his seventh birthday. That summer Frederick, Harriet Porter's firstborn child, not yet two years old, was struck by the dreaded "black canker," later known as scarlet fever. The fever quickly seized Harriet Porter, and then one child after another. Miraculously, Henry remained untouched. Lyman walked the floor with the baby night after night as the poor child choked from his infected lungs. "It has seemed for a while here as if God was about to sweep us away with a stroke," Lyman wrote in desperation to Edward, now away at Yale College.[48]

But God was merciful. The fever burned out almost as quickly as it ignited. Everyone began to struggle back to health. Except for Frederick. The day before Henry's seventh birthday the terrible tidings came: "He is *dead!*" Henry wept until no more tears would come. "It was the first initiation into anguish uncontrollable."

Everything about the funeral was ghastly: The little body laid out in the "cold stiff parlor," the somber service, "the screwing down of the coffin lid." Worst of all was "the horror of the intermittent toll of the church bell," as it announced the death of his brother, accompanying them on the long ride to the graveyard. There the bell's lament was replaced by the sickening thud of dirt clods striking the lid of the coffin as the words "Dead, *dead*, DEAD!" echoed in Henry's head.[49]

When they returned home he fled to the barn to find relief among the silent animals. In the family's grief, no one spoke to the boy to explain or comfort him. For years afterward he was haunted by the boom of the church bell. "It was a vague terror," Henry said later. "I felt that the whole air was full of a sensitive, jealous spirit that was ready to smite me down, I knew not when, or how, or where."[50]

Frederick's death sent Harriet Porter into a tailspin of depression from which she never fully recovered. Meanwhile Lyman's anxiety for his remaining children's souls spiraled out of control, spilling out in every prayer, every letter, every conversation with his children. For Henry the constant reminders of the horrors awaiting him, the stark specter of the grave without salvation, burdened the normal foibles of a little boy with an almost unbearable weight.

"I don't remember a year of my life, after I was seven or eight years old," Henry recalled bitterly, "that I did not go about with a feeling of sadness; a feeling that I was in danger of exile from Heaven—all because I was a sinner, and I didn't want to be."[51]

LIFE IN LITCHFIELD WAS NOT all melancholy, however. Henry spent many contented hours mucking around the ponds and forests of Litchfield, hunting for squirrels, fishing with a hook made from a bent sewing pin tied to a piece of string, climbing trees with his father to harvest nuts in the fall. "I was a better boy for a week after one of those nutting expeditions," he said. "The devil did not tempt me half so much then as at other times."[52] The key to happiness, Henry figured, was to keep out of the way of adults as much as possible. At home this wasn't hard. The only serious snag was school.

Formal schooling was a haphazard enterprise in this era. Attendance was not yet compulsory, even in New England, "the land of schools." Almost no training was required to be a teacher, especially in the "dame schools," run by spinsters, widows, or wives as a way to earn money in their home. Children attended whenever and wherever they could, usually in the winter after the harvest and the summer after planting. All grades were taught in the same room, adding to the confusion.

Barefoot, wearing the checked cotton smock and long blond curls of a toddler, Henry was about four years old when he was enrolled in a dame school run by Deacon Collins's daughter. His memories of his time there were dim but cheery: the kindly face of the young teacher, a long, tall bench so high his feet dangled in the air. Unfortunately this idyll ended abruptly when he and Harriet were switched to a school run by the Widow Kilbourne out of her house on West Street.

Widow Kilbourne taught as everyone did in those days, by sheer, rote repetition. Children learned their letters by looking at them in the spelling book and then stepping to the front of the class and repeating them from memory. With her nearly photographic memory, Harriet thrived under the system of rote recitation, but it was a disaster for Henry. Each time he stood up to recite, his thick speech humiliated him. The other children ridiculed him "for talking as if I had pudding in my mouth," and the impatient widow treated him as if he were stupid and stubborn.[53]

Here his memories were vivid and painful: dozing with his head on the hard desk, a sharp pinch on the ear from the teacher, and, he recalled, a "rousing slap on the head for some real or putative misdemeanor, and a helpless rage inside in consequence."[54] By the time Henry was six years old, his speech defect began to fade naturally, but it left him with a hair-trigger sensitivity to insult or embarrassment, and a strong antiauthoritarian impulse.

Around this time Connecticut began to enforce a controversial new policy of providing public "district schools." So, off Henry went to the "boy-trap," as he named it. The school's single room, crowded with hard wooden benches, scarred desks, and a little tin stove, was frigid in the winter, roasting in the summer, and miserably dull in all seasons. Like the rest of the smaller students in this culture of usefulness, Henry brought a brown towel or a blue-checked apron to hem as he sat dreading his turn to recite. He did master a few new skills, however. "We could make a cat's cradle under the bench unseen," he remembered. "We learned how to make paper spit-balls, and to snap them across the room with considerable skill."[55] His handiest new talent was the ability to read answers from a crib sheet tucked in his hat without getting caught.

In his loathing of school Henry was no different from most of the boys in the village. But it set him starkly apart from the rest of his bookish family. "There was a great deal of intellectual oxygen in the air we breathed," Charles was to write of their childhood years. A constant stream of visiting ministers, politicians, and law students made the modest Beecher house "substantially a debating society," as his brother Tom later described it, animated by "long, long discussions, lasting till past midnight and resumed at every meal."[56]

"The law of his family was that, if any one had a good thing, he must not keep it to himself," remembered Charles; "if he could say a funny thing, he was bound to say it; if a severe thing, no matter—the severer the better, if well *put;* everyone must be ready to take as well as give." As they debated, Lyman would often stop the children in midsentence, to point out those arguments that might get the best of him. The legendary "rhetorical and emotional friskiness of the Beechers," as one critic characterized it, was nurtured in that drafty Litchfield kitchen.[57]

All Lyman's children—the girls as well as the boys—were encouraged to join the debates and to do their best to shine. Although Lyman was no feminist by today's standards, he was the rare father who delighted in his daughters' intelligence, encouraging them to discuss, study, and write, and later to have careers. By his own example at home, he encouraged all his children to develop what would have been considered a masculine approach to ambition and conflict as well as a feminine sensitivity to emotion.

Most of the children thrived in this intense, competitive ethos, but it didn't suit Henry one bit. Children in large families are often pigeonholed into distinct roles that, whether accurate or not, define their identities for years to come. Among the Beecher children the roles were early and firmly established. Catharine was the boss. Edward was the perfect student. William was a sickly boy, to put it bluntly, more pitied than admired. Mary was the good girl. George was marked by what might be called an "artistic temperament." Harriet was a brilliant bookworm, and Charles was nearly as bright and musically gifted to boot.

Henry had all the classic tendencies of a middle child; he was easygoing, eager to please, hungry for attention. From an early age he felt awkward and insignificant among all these strong personalities and high achievers. Of all his siblings, Henry was closest to Harriet. She was his only true confidante, and, like him, she wore her longing for love on her shirtsleeve. Yet even Harriet could make him feel inferior, simply by making him seem so ordinary in comparison. "Harriet is a great genius," as Lyman wrote to his brother-in-law when Harriet was eight and Henry six. "I would give a hundred dollars if she was a boy and Henry a girl. She is as odd as she is intelligent and studious. Henry is Henry—grown older and learning some bad things from bad boys—but on the whole a lovely child."[58] But being a lovely child was not enough to stand out among the Beechers.

By the age of ten Henry seemed more like a farm boy than a preacher's kid; strong and stocky, with ruddy cheeks, callused hands, and a husky voice. Despite his poor grades and bashfulness around adults, he was obviously as intelligent as any of his brothers or sisters. But while they had also inherited Lyman's mental discipline and earnestness, Henry seemed heir only to his father's wit and emotional enthusiasm.

Unlike his serious siblings, Henry was a natural cutup, with an infectious sense of humor and a special talent for mimicry. While his older brothers were emulating their father by memorizing Bible verses and studying their catechism, he imitated the Reverend Beecher by dressing up as a minister, wearing huge "blue goggles" he had scavenged for eyeglasses. Mounting a pile of hay for a pulpit, he would, as one friend remembered, "begin his sermons to his school-mates; he used no articulate words, but a jargon of word sounds, with rising and falling inflections, wonderfully mimicking those of his father. The rotund phrasing, the sudden fall to solemnity, the sweeping paternal gesture, the upbrushing of the hair, were all imitated perfectly by the son." For his grand finale Henry would take off the goggles and somersault dramatically down the haymow as his friends roared with laughter.[59]

But the admiration of his friends came at the expense of his parents' approval. Henry's irreverent humor and impulsiveness waged constant war with his fear of disgrace, despite the fact that his boyish desires seemed so normal, so harmless, that it was often hard for him to see the crime in them. In the logic of his Calvinist upbringing, there were no distinctions between reasonable or unreasonable rules, no room for experimentation or negotiation—obedience was in itself the divine goal. As Henry later lamented, "I supposed myself to be a sinner in the very fact that I did not feel sinful."[60] For the Beecher children in particular their father's zealotry, his tendency to split the world into friends or foes, made the natural rebellions of youth seem inconceivable. At best Lyman would be heartbroken. At worst Henry feared that his father might cast him out, lumping him with all the other enemies of godliness.

In his darker moods Henry fell into a cycle of shame and self-loathing, which, in turn, bred discouragement, skepticism, and secret resistance. "I remember thinking, 'Well, it is no use for me to try to be a good boy,'" he recalled. "'I may as well go by the wholesale as by the retail.'"[61] In this rudderless state, if "I commenced going wrong I went on going wrong. When I did an improper thing, or performed my duty unfaithfully, I was afraid of being found out, and then I prevaricated a little. That made that matter worse," since lying only stirred up his fear and disgust, making it easier to be tempted again.

As his conscience grew heavier, Henry would avoid his stepmother and anxiously scan his father's face when he came home from work, to see if he'd been caught in the lie. After a week or two of mounting guilt and anxiety, the situation would reach a breaking point—"a reckoning," he called it—a catharsis that usually came by way of a whipping behind the woodshed. But after the whipping his conscience was wiped clean. "Then I was free again; and O, how happy I was!" Until the next temptation came along, and the cycle began again.[62]

The New England conscience, it has been said, doesn't stop you from doing what you shouldn't, it just stops you from enjoying it.[63] Trapped by his conflicting desires for independence and approval, seeing no way to be himself and also be loved, Henry learned to fib a little, to make excuses, and bend rigid rules in favor of emotional impulses, acquiring a taste for secret rebellion and surreptitious risk taking that would last his entire life. This conflict would also become the source of many of his greatest gifts and most penetrating psychological insights—but that would come much later.

For the moment, however, no one quite understood how to motivate Henry. As he put it, "what I needed was something to let me up, and not to press me down."[64]

WHEN HENRY WAS TEN his oldest sister, Catharine—talented, witty, and fun-loving—became engaged to Alexander Metcalf Fisher, a brilliant young professor of mathematics at Yale. They would marry when Fisher returned from a year-long tour of the great European universities to collect scientific apparatus for the laboratories at Yale.

Fisher was the ideal son-in-law, but Lyman could feel nothing but anxiety for the young couple, since neither Catharine nor Alexander Fisher had experienced "a saving change." That spring, Lyman pressed his daughter harder than ever to feel her great guilt and repent of her sins. Carefree, sensible Cate dutifully examined her soul, growing increasingly agonized and depressed. Yet try as she might, she simply could not feel that she was the most loathsome of sinners. And if she was, she asked her father defiantly, was it not God who, in His great plan for the world, created her so? If she was born to sin, then how was she to blame?

Her resistance only intensified Lyman's hectoring. "Catharine had been sick three days, the first in acute distress," Lyman wrote to the newly converted Edward, with some sense of triumph. "I had been addressing her conscience not twenty minutes before. She was seized with the most agonizing pain. I hope it will be sanctified."

That very same weekend Alexander Fisher boarded a ship in Boston Harbor and began the long, dangerous voyage across the Atlantic. In Litchfield anxiety mounted as weeks passed without a word from Fisher. Rumors were whispered of a shipwreck. By the end of May their worst fears were confirmed. A tempest had overtaken the ship, ripping off its rudder and sending it crashing into the western cliffs of Ireland. Alexander Fisher had drowned.

Lyman heard the terrible tidings first and broke the news to Catharine in a letter. With a callousness that could come only from great faith, Lyman informed her that there was no evidence that Professor Fisher was converted before he died. Although he was a pious, upright man, filled with natural goodness, it seemed likely that her fiancé was now forever damned. "And now, my dear child, what will you do?" he wrote. "Will you turn at length to God, and set your affections on things above, or cling to the ship-wrecked hopes of earthly good?"

Catharine's grief over Fisher's death was magnified tenfold by her father's insistence that there was no hope for his soul. As spring passed into summer, Catharine prostrated herself in prayer. Yet neither relief nor grace came. "I feel greatly afflicted," she wrote to Edward. "I feel no realizing sense of my sinfulness, no love to the Redeemer, nothing but that I am unhappy and need religion; but where or how to find it I know not."[65]

The longer she reflected, the more it seemed that her inner convictions did not square with her father's doctrines. She had been given too much strength of mind, too much self-esteem, too much logic, to abase herself before such a capricious God. "I feel all the time as if there was *something wrong*—something that is unreasonable," Catharine protested to Edward. "I feel that I am guilty, but not guilty as if I had received a nature pure and uncontaminated. I can not feel this; I never shall by any mental exertion of my own."

Marshaling her years of kitchen-table theological training, Catharine now argued with her father and brother. She gave voice to the questions that were just beginning to percolate in Henry's young mind. How could God condemn one of the most devout men she knew and yet save others not half so good? If she was born a sinner, how could a just God punish her for what she could not help? If God is merciful why would He turn away from her now, when she wanted Him most?

All summer long they went back and forth. As Lyman admitted to Edward, "she is now handling edge-tools with powerful grasp." At times he was at his wit's end, he confessed. All Lyman could do was repeat:

This is God's law. "In other words, I answer objections and defend the ways of God."[66]

Ten-year-old Henry followed the debate between Catharine and Lyman with hushed awe and alarm, although he only half understood what it meant. He remembered sitting outside his father's study listening to his oldest sister, her face swollen from days of crying, argue with his father. The mercilessness of Lyman and his God "took the form of breaking up and destroying all the religious teachings of her life," Henry later said. "The doctrines she had learned did not sustain her, and she went into rebellion against them."[67] If they could not help Catharine, the favored first child, then how could they possibly help him?

Never before had the cruel contradictions of Calvinism been so dramatized in their house. Never before had Lyman's ideas of God come into such stark conflict with the needs of his children. Yet not once did Lyman doubt his dogmatism. He saw no inconsistency—it was his great love that made him browbeat her so. But for the children it was the first crack in the infallibility of their father and his Calvinist creed.

That winter Catharine escaped for a long, cathartic visit to Fisher's parents. When she returned she was no longer a lighthearted girl. Over the years she would become increasingly domineering, querulous, and eccentric, brimming with schemes to right the world. Catharine would never marry. Lyman interpreted Fisher's death as a sign that in God's divine plan, his daughter had a special mission on earth. Within a year they decided that she would start a school for girls in Hartford, which she hoped would outshine even the Litchfield Female Academy. Over the next five decades she forged a remarkable career as an educator, reformer, and writer. Her spectacular ambition was thwarted only by her deep-seated conservatism, another bitter paradox learned at her father's knee.

Nor would Catharine experience a Calvinist conversion. She retained a fierce loyalty to Lyman and to the facade of New England orthodoxy. But her mind was beginning to seek its own explanations. Even as she strove to make her father proud, she struck a path of surreptitious rebellion. After Lyman died she would convert to her mother's original Episcopalian faith. Her example would not be lost on Henry.

IN JANUARY 1825, WHEN HENRY WAS ELEVEN, Harriet Porter suffered what seemed to be a stroke, paralyzing her on one side. Although she improved somewhat, she was left with severe pain in her head. She was only thirty-four years old and would never feel really well again. With his stepmother bedridden, it was decided that Henry should go to Hartford, where Catharine had recently founded her school for girls. Nineteen-year-old Mary served as a teacher, and thirteen-year-old Harriet both studied and helped out with some of the teaching duties. There would be plenty of family supervision.

Here, surrounded by so many lively girls, Henry was finally in his element. The "Hartford family annex," as they nicknamed it, was the ideal place to perfect his skills as a class clown and entertainer of the less serious sex. He was a "small specimen of perpetual motion, perpetual prank, and perpetual desire to give wrong answers to every sober grammatical rule," as one of his teachers recalled.

The stories of Henry's wit were legendary. When kept in from recess one rainy day to study grammar, he spent the entire "play-spell," as it was called, opening every umbrella in the school and stacking them on the vestibule stairs so they would pour out onto the head of the next person to open the door. His classmates could not contain their glee. His sisters were not at all amused. Henry kept up a running commentary of wisecracks that Harriet later attributed to an insatiable need for attention. Catharine sat him near her elbow to keep an eye on him, but that only put him more squarely at the center of things. Occasionally even she was swept up by his sense of humor. During a natural history class he offered his own explanation of the theory of tides.

"Well, you see," he said confidently, "the sun, he catches hold of the moon and pulls her, and she catches hold of the sea and pulls that, and this makes the spring tides."

"But what makes the neap tide?" asked the teacher, curious to see where this would lead.

"Oh!" he replied, "that's when the sun stops to spit on his hands."

The most frequently repeated story from his days in Hartford came from one of the many occasions when his sister pulled him aside to offer him grammar and syntax help. It is too convenient to be accepted as literally true, but it well illustrates how he was remembered by his contemporaries.

"Now, Henry, *a* is the indefinite article, you see, and must be used only with a singular noun," coaxed the teacher. "You can say *a man* but you can't say *a men*, can you?"

"Yes, I can say *amen* too," Henry retorted. "Father says it always at the end of his prayers."

"Come, Henry, now don't be joking! Now decline *he*. Nominative, *he*, possessive, *his*, objective, *him*. You can see *his* is possessive. Now, you can say '*his book*' but you can't say '*him book*.'"

"Yes, I do say *hymnbook*, too," shot back Henry.

"But now, Henry, seriously, just attend to the active and passive voice. Now 'I strike' is active, you see, because if you strike you do something. But 'I am struck' is passive because if you are struck you don't do anything, do you?"

"Yes, I do—I strike back again!"

Henry lasted only six months before Catharine packed him up and sent him home. As his sister summed up the situation, "it was the opinion of this class that there was much talent lying about loosely in him, if only he could be brought to apply himself."[68]

In desperation Lyman sent Henry to the neighboring town of Bethlehem to study with a Reverend Langdon, who boasted of his "extended, minute, and reiterated drilling." He boarded in a roomy old farmhouse owned by the kindly Widow Ingersoll. In the logic of a young boy, it was as if he had been banished from his family as punishment for his being stupid. "I used to feel very sorry for him, he seemed so homesick," said the widow's daughter. "He liked to be off by himself, wandering around in the woods, and I don't think he studied much." There was something, she said, that seemed "a little off" about the boy.[69]

The village was buzzing with excitement when Henry came home from Mr. Langdon's that autumn for Thanksgiving. Litchfield was in the grip of the biggest religious revival anyone had ever seen in those parts. It began in the summer with Lyman skillfully heaping coals on the fire, scheduling prayer meetings every night, bringing in guest speakers, and raising the urgency of his pleas. Soon the excitement was spreading to villages throughout the county.

For Lyman it was an especially glorious harvest. One by one his children were touched by God's grace and reborn as Christians. Already Edward and William were well on their way to the ministry, and Catharine had joined a church in Hartford. Just before Thanksgiving Mary and Harriet returned from Hartford to be baptized in their father's church, and George, even now, was spending his nights shut up in his room, praying and sobbing in anguish as he laid bare his sins and begged for the Lord's mercy.

Twelve-year-old Henry was quickly caught up in the excitement—becoming "serious," in the lingo of revivalism—and began to harbor hope that he too would experience God's saving grace. Perhaps now he would join the rest of his family in the sacred circle of God's elect, the chosen "saints," rather than languishing forlornly with the sinners outside. But by the time he returned to school, the revival was cooling down, and Henry felt no different. God had not chosen him.

When word came of George's ecstatic conversion, Henry was bereft: "It seemed as though a gulf had come between us, as though he was a saint on one side of it while I was a little reprobate on the other side. If there had been a total eclipse of the sun I should not have been in more profound darkness outwardly than I was inwardly," he recalled. "I did not know whom to go to; I did not dare go to my father; I had no mother that I ever went to at such a time; I did not feel like going to my brother; and I did not go to anybody. I felt that I must try to wrestle out my own salvation."[70]

Finally, tentatively, he reached out to George. Mr. Langdon's drilling had not done much to improve his writing skills, but Henry was clearly already well versed in the buzzwords of orthodoxy.

Dear Brother,
I write to you this evening to tell you how I feel. You have I suppose heard that I was serious. I have been seeking after god but have not found him as yet. I wread his holy word but find no relief but bring heavier curses on my head. I wred and pray but instead of getting out of the swamp I get further [in.] I have a new Hymn book which I wread before [I became] serious and felt no harm, but now the more I wread the more I feel. I have seen your letter that you wrote home. I have been a little wretched before but never felt my lost condition before.*

He concludes on a note of forced optimism: "I can't write to you much this evening but at a more convenient season I hope I shall have some more important news about my soul. From your affectionit Brother H. W. B., written in a hurry. P.S. please to Answer it quick as possible."[71] George's response has been lost, but whatever he said, it did little to ease the boy's suffering.

Decades later Henry claimed that his only positive religious memories from childhood came from two African Americans, Aunt Chandler and Charles Smith, a jack-of-all-trades who worked as the Beechers'

The author has retained original spelling, punctuation, capitalization, and italics in quoted material except where changes are indicated by brackets.

occasional handyman. Charles Smith and Henry shared a room, as was the custom in those crowded New England houses. Every night as the boy lay on his narrow cot, the man sat in the candlelight, reading his Bible and praying as if he were holding a conversation with an old friend, smiling, chuckling, and breaking out into snatches of song as he traced out the words. Sometimes he talked to the boy about his soul, but with an intimacy and interest that Henry had never felt from his family.

Henry had never seen religion inspire such joy, such sensual pleasure, and he had certainly never seen anyone laugh while they prayed. "How that man does enjoy it!" he wondered in envy. "It was a revelation and an impulse to me," he remembered—although he didn't understand it at the time.[72] Twenty years later the idea that religion could make a person happy here on earth, not only in heaven, would become the cornerstone of Henry's career.

Chapter 2

"I Shall Have the Boy in the Ministry Yet"

enry was twelve years old and still drilling away unhappily at Mr. Langdon's school in Bethlehem, Connecticut, when shocking news arrived: His father had a new job, and they were all packing up and moving to Boston, Massachusetts.

Immediately Henry rushed into the widow's house where he was boarding and began packing up his meager belongings. He thrust the bundle into the hands of his bewildered landlady, asking her to send it on to Litchfield when the next stagecoach came by. The boy then lit out on foot, "in a perfect panic of apprehension and homesickness," the widow's daughter recalled—in his hurry leaving behind both his hat and his Bible.[1]

"Here's Henry!" his brother Charley cried out in surprise, as Henry strolled into the yard after his nine-mile trek. What brought him home without warning? He was afraid, Henry explained, that when the family left for Boston they might forget and leave him behind.[2]

FOR SOME TIME NOW LYMAN BEECHER had been quietly mulling over the possibility that the family might have to leave the place they had called home for the past sixteen years. These last few years had brought irreversible, unwelcome changes to the staid society of Litch-field. In particular, Lyman's heart was broken when a coalition of lawyers, "Sabbath-breakers, rum-sellers, tippling folk, infidels and ruff-scuff generally," as he called them, forced Connecticut to abolish or "disestablish" state-sponsored religion, stripping him of much of his political and social influence.[3]

Just as important was what had not changed. Lyman's annual salary had not grown in those sixteen years, while his family had doubled in size. He now had the expense of putting two sons through college, with more coming fast on their heels. If he did not receive a raise, George would have to withdraw from Yale College.

Massachusetts was now the only state in the Union to retain state-sponsored religion. It was the last official bastion of Congregationalism, the religious denomination established by the New England Puritans. But there too, change was afoot. In Boston the liberal elite were cultivating what they saw as a more enlightened form of Calvinism, which they called "Liberal Protestantism" but their foes called "Unitarianism."

They attacked the harsh doctrines of original sin and arbitrary salvation as cruel, superstitious, and slanderous of God's good name. Surely the Lord is not a tyrannical king, the Unitarians argued, but an enlightened republican. A man may be a sinner deserving of punishment, but that is due to his own free will rather than some spurious inheritance from Adam and Eve.

With God unwilling to weigh in personally on this doctrinal controversy, the combatants turned to secular law to adjudicate. In 1821 the Congregational monopoly in Massachusetts was effectively overturned by the courts; the upshot of the ruling was to give the people in each parish the right to choose the theological orientation of their ministers. Eighty churches in the Boston area joined the Unitarian movement, turning the Congregational ministers out on their ears. On his Connecticut hilltop Lyman was infuriated by this treachery. "It was a fire in my bones," he said; "my mind was all the time heating, heating, heating."[4]

It seemed like a call from God, then, when Lyman received an offer from a newly founded Congregational church in the North End of Boston, at a salary of two thousand dollars a year. At the age of fifty, when many men were contemplating retirement, Lyman Beecher announced that he was retaking Massachusetts for the Puritans.

"Well, Dr. Beecher," asked one of his admirers, "how long do you think it will take you to destroy Unitarianism in Boston?"

"Humph!" Lyman replied with brusque confidence. "Several years, I suppose,—roots and all."[5]

Boston was a much smaller place in 1826, before its rocky hills were excavated to fill in the bays and coves of its scalloped shoreline. With a population of nearly fifty thousand, the city was the hub of New England. It was the nation's major intellectual center and an important seaport, with a naval base and a harbor overflowing with the world's goods. The upper end of society was dominated by old-money merchant families and the Unitarian elite, who sent their sons to Harvard College and indulged a cosmopolitan taste for balls, cardplaying, fancy dress, and fine wine. At the bottom end were sailors, laborers, and a slowly rising tide of immigrants, who contributed to the city's rowdy street life.

The Beecher family settled into a small rented house at 18 Sheafe Street in the North End of Boston, a stone's throw from the old Copp's Hill burying ground. A sense of decay now clung to the ancient brick houses and crooked alleyways, once the neighborhood of the colonial aristocracy. Construction sites pocked every street, as the crumbling old mansions were being replaced with tenements designed to house the Irish, German, and English immigrants pouring onto the wharves. Sheafe Street remained a last haven of the old upper crust, but most well-to-do townspeople were fleeing south to Beacon Hill and Bowdoin Square.

There were now only four children living at home, plus loyal Aunt Esther: Henry, nearly thirteen, Charles, ten, Isabella, four, and Thomas, a two-year-old toddler. James, the last of Lyman's children, would be born two years later. Edward also rejoined the family, taking a job as the minister of the prestigious Park Street Church on the corner of Boston Common.

"A green, healthy, country lad, with a round, full, red-cheeked face, at about 13 years of age, we entered this city of marvels," Henry recalled. "We were dazed and dazzled with its sounds and sights." In Litchfield his father had dominated the village, just as the stately belfry of his father's church ruled over the landscape, and the tolling of the lone bell commanded the air. Henry took it for granted that his father's way was the way of the world, and those who refused it were infidels who stood outside of respectable society. But here the skyline was filled with steeples of all kinds. No one, no matter how powerful, could rule over all of them.

Before the family left Litchfield, a well-traveled man told Henry in jest that "the churches in Boston were so thick that the bells on Sunday morning would almost play a tune." The very first Sunday after they arrived, Henry was astonished by the symphony of bells, saturating the air with their calls to worship. He ran into their little backyard to listen closer and was dumbfounded to recognize the song "Greenville." This must be what the man had meant!

When the melody changed to the slow, sad tune of "Saint Martyn's," he rushed inside, red-faced and breathless, to find Charles. Charles followed him out back and "opened his eyes with a look of amazement as utter and implicit as if he had been a young devotee witnessing his first miracle." With the casual authority of an older brother, Henry explained how God commanded the town's bells to sing a hymn. Unfortunately the moment was ruined by the family's new cook, eavesdropping from the kitchen, who laughingly explained that the music came from Old North Church's "*chime* of bells"—a tuned set of bells that could play different notes.

"Of course, we were wiser and less happy," Henry said. "But never in forty years, has that chime of bells sounded in my ears without bringing back, for a second, the first electric shock of wonder and pleasure."[6] It was a thrilling introduction to wider vistas of adolescence.

The North End was a boy's paradise. Tar-blackened wharves jutted into Boston Harbor, lined with every kind of sailing vessel imaginable, from rickety skiffs to full-rigged clipper ships. Mysterious places of sin, unheard of in Litchfield, were everywhere: boardinghouses, brothels, gambling dens, back alleys where cockfights and rat baitings were held. Local boys insisted that British blood still stained the paving stones of Prince Street.

Henry and Charles were brawny, bold kids, who plunged headlong into the rough-and-tumble street life. Two-year-old Thomas Beecher idolized his older half brothers. "Edward was a man, like father," Tom remembered. "But Henry and Charles were heroes, doing things." In the summer the boys swam from the wharves, and watched the militia train on Boston Common. In the winter they ice-skated on the town millpond and coasted on down Snowhill Street, bursting out onto Prince Street, one of the busiest intersections in the city. While Tom shivered with fright in his trundle bed at the sound of the fire bell, they dashed out of bed to chase fires in the middle of the night. This was, Henry remembered, an enchanted time of life, "sometimes turbulent with passions, but always throbbing with excited feelings, led on and fed by tantalizing fancies."[7]

The all-season entertainment was brawling. Henry threw himself into street fighting and local turf battles with the same enthusiasm that his father had for theological skirmishes. These city kids were sharper and savvier than those of the village but, Henry noted with pride, "few of them could wrestle or hold their own in a footrace against the hearty country boys."

As residents of Sheafe Street, Charles and Henry counted themselves among the "Salem-Streeters," a loose gang of boys named for the local main street. "When nothing else was on hand small scrimmages were gotten up between ourselves—Sheafe Street vs. Bennett Street, etc.; but we all united against Prince Street," Henry recalled. "Yet, when the West-Enders came over in battle array, yelling, throwing stones and driving in the timid lads caught out of bounds, all the North-Enders rose, forgot their local feuds, and went forth in awful array to chastise the wretches that lived at the West End."

Henry was fearless in the face of physical challenges. In a legendary game of Follow the Leader, he led a dozen boys on a winding route, trying to lose them by tricks, fear, strength, or stamina. They chased Henry through a construction site, up ladders, down ropes, through the old burying ground, leaping from tombstone to tombstone, then sliding down the steep hill to the causeway below, down the wharf, onto a ship, and along the deck. One by one the boys dropped off in exhaustion or fear, until there were only two left. Finally they had him trapped out on the bowsprit of the ship, with no place left to go. Henry paused for a moment and then plunged straight into Boston Harbor. When he swam up to the surface of the water, there were the two boys, standing on the bow of the ship. "They did not dare!" Henry crowed. "That day's work established our reputation!"[8]

But Henry's moods could shift abruptly between audacity and insecurity. He was determined to swim across the Charles River, a great feat of bravery and strength by any standards. He steeled his nerves and set out, easily making it halfway across, when he was suddenly struck with fear. What if he should get a cramp and drown? In panic he turned and swam back to shore, "forgetting that it was just as far to one side as to the other!"[9] It was the perfect emblem of Henry's budding adolescence.

Lyman Beecher's relentless combativeness and his self-righteous reforms irritated nearly everyone, from North End immigrants to Beacon Hill Brahmins. Genteel Bostonians mocked his provincial accent, shabby clothes, and unsophisticated manners. Less genteel Bostonians sent vicious hate mail to his house, targeted him with angry pamphlets and sermons, and passed along disparaging jokes and rumors. A caricature of Beecher began appearing in shopwindows, showing the minister with a double profile, like the Roman god Janus. On one side his face was twisted into a violent scowl, with thunderbolts and forked lightning clutched in his hand. On the other his expression was pale and gentle, and with this hand he offered an olive branch.[10] The broadside was spiteful, to be sure, but it perfectly captured Lyman's contradictory personality.

For the first time Henry was seeing his father outside the cocoon of family life. "I never thought in Litchfield of his being a great man," Henry recalled, but here in Boston where "his name was in everybody's mouth, I had the vague impression that my father was a man of a great deal of public renown"—a villain to some and a hero to the zealous young evangelicals of Boston. He didn't understand all the details of these battles, but the attacks only made him more loyal to his father. What choice did he have? "Remember that neutrality is treason," as Lyman liked to say, "and if persisted in, is fatal."[11] Had he given the critics a fair hearing, Henry would have been surprised at how closely they reflected his own troubled feelings toward his father's demanding doctrines.

Unfortunately this constant public sparring kept his father even busier than in Litchfield. Most of the time Henry was left unsupervised and adrift. As usual school was his nadir. Every morning after prayers and breakfast, Henry and Charles now strode off to the Boston Latin School. Founded in 1635, Boston Latin was the premier preparatory school in the county. Ancient languages were the core of the curriculum. With his halfhearted prior education, Henry was ill prepared for its rigors. He struggled mightily with Latin and made his first, feeble attempts at Greek, but he was barely keeping his head above water.

Henry's rough rural training served him well in other ways, however. He earned a reputation as one of "the brave boys that showed heroism when punished." He could take, as he said, "ten, fifteen, twenty, or thirty blows on one hand and an equal number on the other, until the flesh swelled up like pulp, it was my pride to stand and take it without flinching, and look around at the boys who sat admiring my pluck." Of course this only stoked his resentment toward his teachers. Oh, afterward, Henry recalled with relish, "didn't I snap spit-balls at him when he wasn't looking!"[12]

LYMAN BEECHER'S RISING REPUTATION as the "great gun of Calvinism" preceded him to the City of Pilgrims.[13] Lyman Beecher was what Alexis de Tocqueville called, with some derision, "a political priest." Much as he loved theology, he was by instinct more of a doer than a thinker. Lyman firmly believed that the best fisherman was he who caught the most fish, regardless of the bait used. He helped found the American paradox of "activist conservatism"—in their defense of traditional values, Beecher and his fellow evangelical crusaders were constant innovators in the arts of mass persuasion and organization building.

Here in Boston, Lyman began to tailor his message to suit a more sophisticated audience that had been raised on the republican ideology of natural rights, human liberty, free will, and humanitarian concern. The harsh orthodox insistence that God had predetermined everyone's damnation was turning away those who regarded such ideas as superstitious and inhumane. As Lyman noted, doctrines like infant damnation made it hard "to treat converts as reasonable beings."

He began softening these ideas to fit a more progressive, self-empowered culture, maintaining that God endowed humanity with a predetermined plan for the world, but He also gave free will. Surely God was not sadistic, Lyman insisted. God would not be so unfair as to punish man if he did not have the ability to avoid sin. He maintained that Adam's descendants did not inherit the original sin itself but instead inherited a natural tendency to sin that would inevitably result in actual, voluntary sins deserving of God's punishment. Infants, thus, could not be damned because they had not yet had time to commit any sins. As for adults, they should not wait passively for salvation to descend from on high, but should immediately and totally cease their sinning and devote themselves to the Lord's work so as to be worthy of His grace.

When combined with his fiery preaching style, Beecher's attempt to modernize and soften the harshness of hyper-Calvinism was a decided hit. From the first, curiosity seekers came to the Hanover Street Church, drawn by the notoriety of "Brimstone Beecher." But, as Lyman gloated, "Many that came to scoff remained to pray."[14] Lyman's message of "immediatism"—his insistence that anyone could stop sinning immediately and build a new life—was inspiring for the city's middling folk, the clerks, journeymen, and workers come to seek their fortunes in the city, who lived in the cheap roominghouses of Hanover and Ann streets and were searching for their own identity between the squalid lower rungs and snobbish upper tiers of Boston society.

While Lyman was softening theologically, however, he was becoming more of a militant in other spheres. Lyman channeled the new converts into his own evangelical army—"a disciplined moral militia"—devoted to building God's kingdom brick by brick. Committees, charities, and benevolent societies proliferated, including the Hanover Street Church Young Men's Association, a prototype for what would become the Young Men's Christian Association, or YMCA. Lyman was an acute politician, and under his direction, these zealous young men became a political powerhouse. By fine-tuning the techniques Lyman had helped to pioneer in Connecticut—especially cheap, mass-produced newspapers and tracts, and a coordinated distribution system of ministers, missionaries, and lay volunteers—they laid the groundwork of modern mass media.

"I didn't set up for a reformer any more than this: when I saw a rattlesnake in my path I would smite it," Lyman protested, but he was soon spearheading a reform movement.[15] They ended the popular Sabbath-day steamboat excursions, passed laws against lotteries, and campaigned tirelessly against liquor, gambling, cotillions, and other devilish diversions. They funded missionaries to convert the heathen lands, they blanketed the countryside with thousands of religious tracts and Bibles, and helped establish libraries, debating societies, and public lecture series known as "lyceums."

SURROUNDED BY NEW PRESSURES AND TEMPTATIONS, and experiencing the natural turbulence of a teenager, Henry "grew gloomy and moody, restless and irritable," his sister Harriet recalled. He was falling behind in school and into wild ways after school. "I cannot see how, if I had remained much longer in Boston, I could have escaped ruin," Henry said later.[16]

The answer to his problems seemed to lie in Boston Harbor. Henry's first sight of the harbor, bristling like a pincushion with the masts of tall ships, left him almost delirious with delight. Every afternoon the boys played on the ships of the merchant marine docked at Long Wharf, and in the men-of-war in the navy yard just over the bridge in Charlestown. He spent hours climbing on the long rows of cannons, still facing out to sea from the War of 1812, and "just waited for some Britisher to dare to come in sight!"

Hoping to encourage his son in some way, Lyman took advantage of Henry's interest in seafaring, giving him naval histories and biographies of Captain James Cook and Admiral Lord Horatio Nelson. But Lyman's plan backfired. "The adventure fever that often seizes boys took hold of me," Henry said, and he began fantasizing about running away to sea, the age-old way for a young man to make a fresh start and leave his landlocked troubles behind. Why, look at Lord Nelson, the great hero of Trafalgar: He was a restless parson's son who ran away to the sea at the tender age of twelve, becoming an admiral while still in his twenties. "At last I could stand it no longer," Henry declared.[17] He bundled up some clothes and made his way to the wharf.

Once there, however, he couldn't bring himself to actually sign on to a voyage. In desperation he returned home and wrote a letter to one of his brothers announcing that he could no longer remain in school and was becoming a sailor. Of course, he added, he wanted his father's permission but he would go without it if necessary. Henry then dropped the note where his father was certain to find it.

When Lyman happened upon the confession he said nothing of it. Instead he invited Henry to come saw wood with him—a flattering sign that he wanted to talk to his son man-to-man. At the woodpile Lyman casually turned the subject to Henry's future.

"Let us see," said Lyman. "Henry, how old are you?"

"Almost fourteen!"

"Bless me! How boys do grow!" his father responded. "Why, it's almost time to be thinking of what you are going to do. Have you ever thought?"

Henry said that he wanted to go to sea.

"Well, well! After all, why not?" Lyman asked slyly. "But not merely as a common sailor, I suppose?"

"No, sir; I want to be a midshipman, and after that a commodore."

"I see," said the preacher. "Well Henry, in order for that, you know, you must begin a course of mathematics and study navigation and all that."

"Yes, sir; I'm ready," Henry replied with surprise.

"Well then, I'll send you up to Amherst next week, to Mount Pleasant, and then you'll begin your preparatory studies, and if you are well prepared, I presume I can make interest to get you an appointment."

Within a week Henry found himself on a stagecoach heading west toward Mount Pleasant Classical Institution in the landlocked village of Amherst, Massachusetts.

"I shall have the boy in the ministry yet," Lyman predicted.[18]

WHEN HENRY STEPPED OFF THE STAGECOACH from Boston, he was deep in the Connecticut River Valley. Mount Tom and Mount Holyoke loomed to the south, and Sugar Loaf to the north, with lush old-growth forests on every side. The southeastern view was the most impressive, especially at sunset, when the jagged notch of the Pelham Hills glowed a deep royal purple.

The village of Amherst was perched halfway up into the hills, scorning the swampy bottomlands of the valley but too modest to aspire to the peaks. This was a place of few pretensions, a small "untidy and huddled" cluster of brick and clapboard buildings with a slightly sunken look, as if they were slowly sliding downhill.[19] The long town common was still used as pastureland, with each family in town allowed to pasture one cow apiece during the summer season. At one end of the common was a weed patch of thistle and burdock, at the other a marshy, muddy frog pond, home to a population of geese, peepers, and various amphibians. A dirt path led to the top of a steep, treeless hill dominated by the spare, square brick buildings of Amherst College.

Like Litchfield, Amherst embodied the Yankee vision of the good life: The town meeting determined politics, the Congregational Church governed morals, and farmers and local craftsmen led the economy. As with Litchfield, the town was saved from the narrow-minded dullness endemic to small-town life by a passion for higher education. Through the efforts of zealous townsmen, the village now boasted the Amherst Academy, considered one of the best schools in western Massachusetts, as well as the fledgling Amherst College and the newly established Mount Pleasant Classical Institution.

As the name suggests, the Mount Pleasant Classical Institution aspired to something grander than its plain and pious sister institutions. It stood at the summit of a hill half a mile out of the center of town, surrounded by a large kitchen garden, deep groves of oak and chestnut trees, and the finest vistas in the valley. The large new building was of far greater architectural pretension than any other in the village, with massive white Doric columns fronting the main house, and two long wings with double verandas.

Experimental education was a hot topic in the 1820s—reflecting a new interest in all kinds of progressive social reforms—and the idealistic young founders of Mount Pleasant were determined to be at the forefront of the movement. They drew their curriculum from a hodgepodge of models: the military discipline of West Point; an emphasis on manual labor from the famed Institut d'Éducation in Hofwyl, Switzerland; the practical commercial training of the German gymnasiums; the scientific method of analysis associated with Francis Bacon; and the ancient languages of traditional classical academies as well as a new interest in modern languages, all resting on the firm foundation of evangelical Christianity.

The annual bill for this ambitious program topped $250—more than twice the cost of the local Amherst Academy, even more than Amherst College. This fee included tuition, room, board, furniture, fuel, lights (in the form of candles or oil), and mending and washing of clothes. Books, paper, and school uniforms were extra.

Two hundred fifty dollars was an astronomical sum for a poor parson with three sons in school, but Lyman struck a deal. In exchange for the renowned Reverend Doctor Beecher's patronage, amounting to a promotional quote in the school catalog and good word of mouth, Henry paid one hundred dollars a year. The air of grateful relief in Lyman's blurb sounds as personal as it is professional. Mount Pleasant, he wrote, "awakens my gratitude to God as a merciful provision for children and youth at the most critical period of their lives."[20]

HENRY ARRIVED IN AMHERST as a healthy, slightly plump fourteen-year-old with blue-gray eyes and long, dark brown hair. "He was a good-looking youth," one teacher remembered, with "a frequent smile upon his face." If he was homesick, it didn't last long. "I enjoy myself *pretty* well," he told Harriet not long after he arrived. Mount Pleasant didn't offer the first-class education of the Boston Latin School, but it gave him the chance to be an ordinary boy, and he seized it with relish.[21]

Mount Pleasant ran on a rigorous schedule, with classes in Latin, Greek, English grammar, mathematics, elocution, and the Bible as well as unusual subjects like bookkeeping and Italian. The boys practiced military drills in the morning and marched in formation to chapel, meals, and Sunday church. His afternoons were free until teatime (as the evening meal was then called). Every evening ended with religious services at eight and the boys tucking into bed at nine.

Scholastically Henry was determined to make a fresh start. "I formerly indulged myself with the habit of letting my thoughts wander and letting my imagination build towers etc., now I am trying to break myself of the habit, but find it very difficult," he lamented to Harriet. With Latin, he assured his sister, "all I have to do is study straight ahead. It comes pretty easy," but Greek was "rather hard," with its queer foreign alphabet.[22]

He struggled along in a haphazard way, but he was falling behind fast. As the end of his freshman year approached, it began to look as if Henry might not be promoted into the sophomore class. Mathematics would be his Waterloo—"algebra was my master and it rode me like a nightmare," Henry recalled with a shudder.[23]

It was fitting, then, that his math instructor was a military man, William P. N. Fitzgerald, a twenty-four-year-old former West Point cadet with a genius for numbers. Fitzgerald's promising military career had been cut short only the year before, after an excessive Christmas celebration that left the young man drunk, disorderly, and expelled. After his disgrace, and presumably his reformation, Fitzgerald hired on at Mount Pleasant as a teacher of math, philosophy, and drawing.

Henry was assigned to share a room with Fitzgerald for part of that first year. He longed to impress his dashing new roommate but had no idea how. The first time Fitzgerald called Henry to the blackboard to work a problem in front of the class, the boy almost whimpered aloud with dread and self-pity. He struggled with the chalk for a moment and then gave up with a whine.

Fitzgerald cut short his excuses and evasions. *"That lesson must be learned,"* Fitzgerald said in a low, intense voice. "I don't want any reasons why I don't get it."

"I did study it two hours," Henry protested.

"That's nothing to me; I want the lesson. You need not study it at all, or you may study it ten hours—just to suit yourself. I want the lesson. Underwood, go to the blackboard!"

"Oh! yes," Henry retorted, "but Underwood got somebody to *show* him his lesson."

"What do I care *how* you get it? That's your business. But you must have it."

When Henry next returned to the blackboard, Fitzgerald was even more intimidating. As Henry wrestled with the figures, the teacher suddenly called out, "No!" in a cold, calm voice.

Henry stopped, erased his work, and began the problem over again.

Again he heard the teacher say, "No!" In embarrassment and confusion, Henry retreated to his seat.

The next student went to the board and began the problem. This time, when Fitzgerald interrupted the problem, the boy at the board continued to work it out and when he sat down was rewarded with the phrase "Very well."

"Why," whined Henry, "I recited it just as he did, and you said No!"

"Why didn't you say *Yes*, and stick to it?" Fitzgerald asked. "It is not enough to know your lesson," he added. "You have learned nothing till you are *sure*. If all the world says *No*, your business is to say *Yes* and to *prove it!*"[24]

The encounter made a huge impression on Henry. The experience of rising to a challenge, however hesitantly, was new to him and he took it as a turning point. "In less than a month I had the most intense sense of intellectual independence and courage to defend my recitations," Henry recalled with satisfaction. Algebra was "the hour when I was delivered from the bondage of *I can't*, and born into the glorious liberty of *I can*; and it has never left me since."[25] In losing the skirmish, Henry had won his first battle.

Henry never became much of a mathematician, but that only made William Fitzgerald's achievement all the more impressive. By August 1829, the end of his junior year, Henry wrote to his brother Edward of his plan to stay at Mount Pleasant for another year, "almost for no other purpose than to learn mathematics, it is taught so well here!"[26]

BEFORE BOARDING SCHOOL, Henry had found most of his companionship within the fraught confines of his family, with Harriet and Charles as his closest comrades. Left on his own, he discovered that he had inherited his father's "genius for friendship." He "talked a good deal," recalled one roommate, "and was full of life and fun." Like his father he loved to tease and be teased, and he had a fondness for practical jokes. He was a thorough good sport—a hail-fellow-well-met, as they used to say. "He was whole-souled and hearty, humorous in the extreme but without a particle of viciousness," testified another classmate.[27] With the innate empathy of a younger brother, he was especially kind to the littler boys.

What a wonder it was to live among a mob of boys! After school he and his pals rambled in the woods, swimming and fishing in the local ponds, climbing trees and roasting chestnuts and green corn in ovens built of stones. Henry played football, learned the flute well enough to play in a ragtag marching band, and took over a little patch of ground, planting a flower garden. He didn't even seem to mind the military marching.

As with most teenagers, his moods swung across the spectrum, from insufferable insecurity to noble ambition, romantic melancholy to boyish boisterousness. "I used to look across the beautiful Connecticut River valley, and at the blue mountains that hedged it in, until my heart swelled and my eyes filled with tears; why, I could not tell," he said later. "Then I would push out into the woods and romp with the wildest of them."[28] His favorite retreat was a tree house he built near campus where he could be alone.

Henry's imagination was fed in ways that it never had before. At Mount Pleasant there were boys from Greece, Turkey, Colombia, Cuba, Canada, Brazil, England, and the Southern states, as well as a fair share of homegrown Roman Catholics. While Boston had opened his eyes to the existence of a world outside his own village, it was Mount Pleasant that gave Henry his first taste of the world beyond New England.

In the early 1820s Greece was invaded by the Turkish army, a far-off war that captured the imaginations of the Western World when the legendary Romantic poet Lord Byron set off to fight for the Greek cause. Fleeing the turmoil, a number of young Greek refugees ended up in Amherst, where several Christian philanthropists paid for their educations.

It was among these exotic newcomers that Henry found Constantine Fontellachi Newell, his first truly close friend. In 1822, when Constantine Fontellachi was nearly eight years old, his home, the Aegean island of Chios, was attacked by the Turks. His parents were killed in the battle, but the little boy somehow survived. Constantine escaped the invaders by hiding along the rocky shoreline until he was discovered and taken aboard by a coasting vessel. Somehow he made his way to Boston, where he was adopted by a Mrs. Newell of Amherst, who enrolled him in Mount Pleasant.

Constantine immediately captured Henry's eager imagination. He was literally tall, dark, and handsome, a dashing figure who commanded one of the student divisions in military drill, a living replica of Lord Byron, who had met his death near the battlefields of Greece only two years after Constantine's daring escape.

Perhaps it is not surprising that the two boys became best friends: Constantine, a foreigner who had only recently learned English, and Henry, who had spent his life feeling like a perpetual outsider. With the grateful awe of a gawky, plump boy more distinguished for his wit than his looks, Henry adored Constantine. "He was the most beautiful thing I had ever seen," Henry said. "He was like a young Greek god. When we boys used to go swimming together I would climb out on the bank to watch Constantine swim, he was so powerful, so beautiful."[29]

Such romantic language was quite common between friends—among young men as well as young women. This was an era in which men regularly shared beds with each other, often talking deep into the night, in which deep male intimacies were honored and envied rather than discouraged as an alarming sign of unmasculine weakness or homosexuality. Yet even in a culture where close male friendships were common, what they shared seemed rare and special to them.

This young Greek god gave Henry his first taste of real intimacy. It is no coincidence that Constantine was an orphan with no family ties to bind his loyalties. This was the first time that Henry came first in someone's life, and it was exhilarating. He had finally found a soul mate.

When Henry returned for his sophomore year he encountered the second teacher who would shape his future: John E. Lovell, the instructor in elocution and public speaking. Elocution was an integral part of a quality education in the nineteenth century. Oratory played a central role in American culture as a form of information, education, and entertainment. First-rate speakers were true celebrities, akin to being a television star in the twenty-first century. Lawyers and politicians like Daniel Webster, Henry Clay, and John C. Calhoun could keep an audience of thousands standing spellbound for hours at a time, without the aid of microphones. A fiery revival preacher like Charles Finney could draw crowds from miles around, just for the sheer excitement of his sermons. Boys with any ambition longed to join the ranks of the immortal orators, the way later boys might aspire to play professional baseball or become an astronaut.

Like William Fitzgerald, John Lovell was an inspired teacher who demanded success. Lovell demystified eloquence, showing that it is not a God-given gift but the product of disciplined practice. Public speaking is a very physical skill, and Lovell made his students drill endlessly in all aspects of it: accent, tone, pronunciation, gesture, facial expression, posture, voice projection. Lovell would first recite a piece, and then the students would memorize it and repeat it again and again, imitating every inflection, movement, and glance until it was a perfect replica of the original speech. "It was drill, drill, drill," Henry said, "until the motions almost became second nature."[30]

At first Henry was timid and halting, afraid of his own voice. But it didn't take long for him to fall in love with the art of oratory. For the first time in his life, Henry showed real discipline, spending hours practicing precise arm gestures or experimenting with the inflection of a single phrase. Like a tennis player practicing serves or a musician playing scales, he developed a kind of vocal muscle memory that made his later speaking style seem uniquely spontaneous and natural.

In oratory Henry finally found his métier, and a way to be like his father without repressing his own personality. If he would never surpass his siblings academically, here was a subject in which bookishness and dry-as-dust erudition were drawbacks rather than assets. Finally his natural emotiveness, his desire for attention, and his drive to perform were not handicaps but advantages. And, unlike his other classes, here the reward for excelling was applause.

From this point on Henry seized any chance to speak in public. He helped found a debating society and became its most ardent member. The first time he astonished the other boys with a perfectly timed, original illustration off the top of his head, he experienced a rush of adrenaline unlike any he had ever felt. Suddenly his tendency to get carried away by the moment was working to his advantage. He envisioned even greater turns of phrase for the next debate, supposing "that it would come again just by calling." Unfortunately, without preparation, "I found to my sorrow that it would not come for the calling any more than a wild bird would sing again today in the same tree because he sang there yesterday."[31]

He also discovered that he was a natural actor, often starring in school performances. Were it not for the fierce evangelical disapproval of the theater, Henry might have had a triumphant career as an actor, many of his friends noted. But at that time theaters were considered by most devout Christians to be dens of iniquity, places where well-to-do dandies, prostitutes, and the working class mingled freely. As a career, acting ranged somewhere in prestige between prostitution and rum selling—popular with some folks but decidedly déclassé in Beecher circles.

Decades later both Harriet and Henry wrote novels that were adapted into successful plays. But Henry did not attend a single performance. By that time Henry's scruples were relaxed enough that he would have gladly gone to the theater, but he said, "it would take months of explanation and years of weary controversy to explain the why and the wherefore, so I say to myself it is not worth while[.]"[32]

Sometimes when the world was saying *"No,"* he simply found it easier to agree than "to say *Yes* and to *prove it."*

HENRY HAD NOT SEEN MUCH OF HARRIET since she moved to Hartford and he went off to boarding school, but their emotional affinity carried their relationship through the long absence. He was far more candid with her than with anyone else, yet even with her his letters reflect the acute self-consciousness he felt among his family. They are stiff, righteous little notes, calculated to impress with his newfound seriousness and sophistication. "I do not like to read the Bible as well as to pray," he told Harriet with deliberate nonchalance, "but I suppose it is the same as it is with a lover, who loves to talk with his mistress in person better than when she is far off."[33] It was a surprisingly suggestive sentiment for a sheltered fifteen-year-old, and a sign of his growing awareness of the world.

For the most part, however, his sentiments ran to pious boilerplate. It seemed to be the only way he knew to communicate with his family, with his religious anxiety growing most acute when he was afraid of failing in school. Even with Charles, who was now attending boarding school at Groton Academy, he could never simply chat about his personal life. "In order to make it profitable as well as interesting," Henry informed Edward, "we have in every letter some difficult [Bible] passage for one another to explain."[34] More complex religious problems required letters to George and Edward, since, as Henry noted plaintively, he was sure that his father was too busy with more important matters to answer his questions.

Henry's notebooks from the time are full of that odd combination of dry logic and lurid imagery that characterized Calvinism. On his father's advice he began keeping a scattershot diary, filled mostly with doodles, bits of homework, pithy sayings, and the name "Nancy" scribbled over and over again in dreamy loops of ink. His first serious entry was a "Proof of Hell": "I prove first that there must be a hell, and then it will appear evident that there must be a judgment." This is followed by six pages of proof texts, with neatly numbered arguments, leading to the next puzzle: "Who will enjoy heaven most?"

That question was more easily answered. But it led to his final inquiry, rehearsed here before being sent off to one of his brothers: "I wish to ask you, not as a question, but for my own information, what do you think about the devil? Now, this of itself is quite a curious question, but what I wish to ask in this particular is, Do you think that he is at all under the divine direction we are?"[35] An excellent question, one that has stirred much debate among theologians. But neither God nor the Devil was very inspiring when shoehorned into an algebraic equation or a geometric proof—especially for a boy who hated math.

In spiritual matters, Henry confided to his siblings, Mount Pleasant left something to be desired. Some of the boys hid out in the woods to play cards, and even those who dared not defiantly claimed that there was no more harm in it than in playing chess. It wasn't uncommon, he said, to hear even little boys "swearing most shockingly. . . . By far the greatest part of the boys disregard the Sabbath entirely, and if things go on at this rate much longer this institution will become as bad as the Unitarian one at Northampton," Henry told Harriet.

Overall, however, Henry's letters convey more wishfulness than genuine piety. His yearning to join the mischief makers was apparent even in his denunciations. "When I mix with the boys I do talk and act unworthy of a disciple of Christ," he wrote wistfully to Harriet. "I find this to need much watchfulness and prayer, for I believe that I take to light trifling more than people generally do."[36]

The summer of his fifteenth birthday, the state of his soul seemed to take a turn for the better. For years religious revivals had been regularly popping up around the country, a movement that came to be known as the Second Great Awakening. With the recent proliferation of roads and newspapers, news of these religious outbreaks was traveling faster and farther than ever before. Accounts of these rich spiritual harvests spread the inspiration like wildfire. The movement was now building to a new climax, with the red-hot center of it burning just over the Massachusetts border in upstate New York. Inevitably the virtuous village of Amherst caught the fever.

Schools were often the site of mass religious revivals, where strong, ever-present peer pressure intensified the natural emotional ferment of adolescence. Many ministers, including Lyman Beecher, warned against school revivals. They could be dangerous for impressionable teenagers. The angst of the conversion process, added to the stress of studying long hours in dark rooms and the poor food available on the average student's budget, often led students to nervous and physical breakdowns.

The most sensitive scholars lost weight, became feverish and bedridden, strained their eyes into temporary blindness, or grew agitated to the point of fits.

But many schoolmasters were willing to assume these risks, since becoming known as the site of a religious "awakening" boosted the reputation of any Christian school. The headmaster of Mount Pleasant was now doing everything he could to create an atmosphere of powerful spiritual suspense designed to "awaken" the students to God's call. Besides the regular chapel services, he scheduled twice-daily prayer meetings and special sermons, calling for the boys to scrutinize not only their own souls but each others'.

For years Henry had sat through his father's exhortations, often getting swept up in the emotional fervor. "I feel when in meeting or when reading any book, as if I should never cease serving Christ, and could run with patience the race which is set before me," he told Harriet. But once the book was closed, the meeting ended, he forgot his vows and lost himself again in more worldly pleasures. "About half the time I lived under conviction of sin, and the other half of the time I was getting over it," as he later put it.[37]

This revival promised to be no different. The first time Henry was asked to lead the prayer in one of the school prayer meetings, he was so stricken by stagefright he thought he would suffocate. "I gasped, literally, and said, 'No sir,' " he remembered. "I felt awfully, I was perfectly paralyzed." When Henry refused, William Fitzgerald, his math teacher, was asked to pray instead. "I will try," the ex-cadet replied humbly.

"I said to myself," Henry recalled, " 'Here is a minister's son, who has all his life long been under Christian instruction, and he is asked to pray and he won't; and here is a poor boy that never had any Christian instruction in his early days and he turns round and makes it!' It almost killed me." His pride piqued, Henry arrived at the next meeting tight with nervous tension but determined to acquit himself. " 'If they ask me to pray, I will pray,' " he vowed. "I was acutely sensitive to conscience, to praise and blame, to shame, to pride, and all of them were running wild in my mind, like so many colts in an open pasture-lot," he said later.[38] But when he finally began to speak, he found that he had a flair for public prayer. In fact he rather enjoyed exhorting his friends.

This boost to his confidence filled Henry with pious aspiration, sweeping him up into one of his "mushroom hopes." It seemed that the day of his salvation had finally come. "I do not know how or why I was converted. I only know I was in a sort of day dream," he said; a dream "in which I hoped I had given myself to Christ." Exhilarated and bursting with holiness, Henry wrote to his father with the good news.

Lyman was overjoyed. Unfortunately, as always, within three or four weeks the boy's conviction began to ebb. "I was beginning to feel quite jolly again," Henry said when his father's warm response arrived in the mail. Lyman wanted Henry to come home even before the upcoming vacation began, so he could join the Hanover Street Church at the next Communion Sabbath. His conversion had been a long time coming, and Lyman was eager to close the deal.

Communion Sabbath was the sine qua non of church membership. In this ritual, confessed Christians consume a portion of bread and sip of wine as a symbolic memorial of Christ's last supper. It was a grave privilege, reserved only for the baptized "saints" of the church. To partake of the communion without being anointed by God was a sin far worse than mere wickedness. Henry panicked when he received his father's letter, but in the end, "pride and shamefacedness" kept him from confessing that he was pretty sure he was not officially a Christian by his father's standards.[39]

With a leaden heart, Henry returned to Boston to be examined by the church committee about the authenticity of his "hope" and the "evidences" of being saved. Sitting in front of his father's friends and colleagues, he was struck "cold and almost paralyzed" by their questions. In the end the committee approved him based less on his testimony than their certainty that "the son of such a father ought to be a good and pious boy." But Henry's feeling of relief was short-lived. Having fooled the deacons was one thing, but he could not fool God.

On the morning he was to take communion, Henry was almost blinded by anxiety. The poor boy sat guilt stricken in his pew while his father radiated pleasure and pride. Fear choked his throat as the roll call of "saints" admitted to communion was read. When his name was announced, Henry, "rose up with every emotion petrified" to take the communion offering.

The experience was so traumatic, so otherworldly, that even years later, he described the scene in the third person, as if watching himself in a dream. He swallowed the bread, sipped the wine, and then returned to his seat in a stupor. Numbly he stared up at the ceiling, counted the spots on the carpet, listened to the rustle of the women fanning themselves. He was grateful even for the irritation of a "fly that lit on his face, as if something familiar at last had come to break the awful trance," all the while wondering bleakly "whether he should be struck dead for not feeling more—whether he should go to hell for touching the bread and wine, that he did not dare to take nor to refuse," he said.

After the service ended, Henry walked home alone, crying with shame and confusion, "wishing he knew what, now that he was a Christian, he should do, or how he was to do it." He had always thought that Christians were the happiest people on earth. Why then was he so wretched?

Miserable as it was, Henry's counterfeit conversion brought some advantages. As a born-again Christian and a son of the Reverend Beecher, he was treated as an expert and a model by his fellow students when he returned to school. Now some of the boys were coming to him to ask him to explain hard theological concepts like "predestination." He did his best, although, he confided to Edward, "I never could do it to my own satisfaction."[40]

Soon Lyman Beecher claimed his ultimate victory. At the end of his sophomore year, Henry wrote to his father that he was giving up the sailor's life to enter the clergy. Lyman was jubilant. Henry's feelings were more ambivalent.

"How did I come to be a preacher?" Henry asked years later. "It was fate, I suppose; that's all. I do not think that I can honestly assign any other reason. I took to preaching, as did my brothers simply because nobody ever dreamed of my father's boys doing anything else. That's all there is to it."[41]

DURING HIS TIME AT MOUNT PLEASANT, Henry developed from a shy, untamed boy into a promising young man of seventeen. The school had given him his first taste of self-mastery and, to use his own word, "self-esteem." Yet even after three years, he lagged behind many of the boys, especially in Greek and mathematics. As final exams approached, Henry grew morose and self-pitying as he strove to make up the difference. His problems, he protested, were not due to "want of study," but to the unfairness of his teachers. "I do not think that my instructors do right by me; for although they know that my lessons are double those of any other boy still they scold and ridicule me during recitation," he complained to Harriet.

His only fortification, he told Harriet, was to remind himself that he was studying not for himself ("if I was studying for myself alone I should have given up long ago") but to better serve God. "Nevertheless," he concluded dutifully, although without much conviction, "if it will do me any good, if it will break down my proud spirit, if it will make me depend more upon help from above than earthly help, I will suffer it—yes, rejoice in it."[42]

To Henry's great relief he did graduate, cutting quite a picture at the graduation ceremonies. He played roles in three of the day's performances—an old sea dog in a comic scene and the Earl of Warwick in a dramatic dialogue. He capped off the ceremonies by reciting the apocalyptic revelations of the biblical prophet Joel.

Constantine graduated alongside Henry, impressing the audience by reciting the speech of Catiline before the Roman Senate and taking part in an Italian dialogue—surely the first time most Amherst folks ever heard the Italian tongue. After graduation Henry and Constantine remained close friends. Then, in April 1832, after several years at Mount Pleasant and another two living in Amherst, Constantine made plans to go into business in Boston, leaving Henry behind to finish his college degree.

Before parting, the two pals drew up a remarkably formal five-point covenant of friendship, longer, more contractual, and tenderer than most marriage vows. They pledged themselves "to be real, lawful, and everlasting brothers," with a passion and candor that Henry never expressed to his brothers by blood. They swore to write each other once every two months if both were in the United States (or every three months if one was in a foreign land) and to defend and forgive each other's faults. "As formerly we were connected by nothing save voluntary friendship which could be broken off," they concluded, "so now we are connected by a love which cannot be broken." As a token of their bond, Henry signed the pledge "H. C. Beecher," taking "Constantine" as his new middle name.[43]

After Constantine went to Boston, the intimacy of their friendship dwindled, as even the strongest childhood bonds sometimes do. If the promised letters arrived, they were lost along with many others. For several years Henry signed his name Henry Constantine Beecher. Near the end of college, as manhood approached, he reverted to his given middle name.

In 1842 Constantine returned to Greece, where he died suddenly of cholera. Henry was heartbroken. Not long after, he named his third-born son William Constantine Beecher.

～　～

The question of where Henry should go to college was a problem. Lyman's heart lay with his beloved alma mater, Yale College, and he longed to have all his boys follow him there. William, a slow student, had skipped college to go straight on to the seminary at Andover, but Edward had graduated from Yale, and George was enrolled there now. But he was dubious about whether it would suit Henry.

Forgetting his early enthusiasm for Mount Pleasant, Lyman was now "exceedingly dissatisfied with the results of three years' study there and an expense of more than 800 dollars"—overlooking the fact that the advantage of Mount Pleasant was that he had not actually had to pay eight hundred dollars for his son's education. Henry, Lyman thought, "has been taught carelessly and has formed a habit of getting his lessons (I speak of the languages specially) superficially." At Yale, where large classes were taught by young, inexperienced tutors rather than full professors, Henry was sure to slip through the cracks.

Lyman was also worried about the rowdy atmosphere of New Haven, where the boys engaged in elaborate pranks, brawled openly with the townspeople, and revolted against the faculty—at one point several students went so far as to explode a makeshift bomb in Yale's chapel. There was also a large contingent of students from the South at Yale, Lyman noted, bringing with them the "Southern influence" of "honor and spirit," which often led to dueling, gambling, and other dangerous hobbies that could easily corrupt his impressionable boy.

Reluctantly Lyman decided to send Henry to Amherst College, the small, newly established school just down the road from Mount Pleasant. Founded in 1821 by Congregationalists as a bulwark against the Unitarian menace that had overtaken Harvard, the college was dedicated to preparing indigent young men for the ministry. "I shall regard his safety greater in Amherst than in New Haven," Lyman concluded.[44]

But money was probably the largest part of the equation. Tuition at Amherst College was forty dollars a semester, with board at a dollar and a half a week, notably cheaper than Yale. The school also possessed a large charity fund devoted specifically to scholarships for needy students. Even with this aid, the Beechers had no idea how they would keep Henry in school. Lyman was eager to get his boys into the ministry, but with George at Yale and Charles rushed into attending Bowdoin College in Brunswick, Maine, the next year, they were strained beyond limit.

One evening, not long after Henry entered his freshman year of college, the money finally ran out. Lyman expressed no doubt that the Lord would take care of them as He always had, and went to bed in peace. But his poor wife, Harriet Porter, lay awake crying, not only in despair of making ends meet but because her husband was blessed with faith and she seemed cursed with none.

The next morning, a Sabbath day, a messenger knocked at the door bearing an anonymous note and the miraculous sum of one hundred dollars. Much later the money was revealed to be a gift from Harriet Porter's well-to-do brother-in-law, in gratitude for Lyman's help in converting one of his children. Whether Uncle Homes got wind of their plight through earthly channels or was moved by divine inspiration, Lyman considered it Providence just the same.

Now, little Tom remembered, at morning prayers Father began to pray for "our boys at college: 'May they become good ministers of our Lord Jesus Christ!' "[45]

Chapter 3

"IF YOU WISH TRUE, UNALLOYED, GENUINE DELIGHT,
FALL IN LOVE WITH SOME AMIABLE GIRL"

*J*t was 10:00 P.M. and the streets of Boston were dark when
Henry set off for his freshman year of college in the summer
of 1830. It would be an uncomfortable night, sleeping sitting
up on the stiff stagecoach seats, swaying with every rut and pothole as
the horses raced along at the miraculous rate of one hundred miles in
fifteen hours. But by midday he would be ensconced at his sister's house
in Hartford, Connecticut, indulging in a rare, brief visit before heading
on to Amherst, Massachusetts.

Henry had scarcely seen his older sisters since he went off to boarding school. In the intervening years the Beecher sisters had become
prominent citizens in the city of Hartford. Catharine's school for girls,
the Hartford Female Academy, now boasted a national reputation, and
she was publishing her first book, *Suggestions on Education*, to critical
acclaim. Nineteen-year-old Harriet continued to teach at the academy,
but Mary had taken a different path, marrying Thomas Clapp Perkins,
a leading local lawyer, and retiring forever from public life. Mary now
had two small children, several servants, and one large house, which she
managed with the help of good Aunt Esther.

Not long after noon the next day, Mrs. Thomas C. Perkins was called
downstairs by a knock on the front door. There, gazing up at her, stood
a lanky, smooth-faced young man clad in an old suit patched at the
knees and elbows and accompanied by a battered horsehair trunk. After

a moment of confusion the stranger finally introduced himself—in this era before photography, before the railroad made travel commonplace, Henry had simply grown beyond Mary's recognition. Canny Catharine did better, but Harriet, his old boon companion, had no idea who he was. "She could not think what to make of it when I went up and kissed her," Henry chuckled.[1]

At the age of seventeen Henry had matured physically, but emotionally and mentally, to quote his sister, "it was difficult to say which predominated in him most, the boy or the man."[2] The next day Catharine insisted that he come to a "levee" she was hosting at her boardinghouse—after three years in a single-sex school this would be his first "boy-girl party." Arriving early that evening, Henry hid by the pianoforte, paralyzed by adolescent embarrassment until Harriet rescued him. He basked happily in her attention until she began to urge him to come meet some of the girls.

In a panic Henry bolted for the hallway as soon as Harriet turned her back, nearly knocking over one startled gentleman. Red faced, he grabbed his hat, sneaked past the parlor, then dashed for the front door, picking up speed when he realized that half a dozen young ladies were sitting on the hall stairs watching him in amusement. He whipped out the door and hightailed it to his sister's house, where Mary and Aunt Esther consoled him.[3]

The next day was more to his liking. For fun Harriet and Catharine dressed their pliant baby brother in a woman's cloak, bonnet, and scarf, while Harriet put on a man's cloak and hat, and then called in some of the girls to look. Everyone swore that Henry was Harriet, and Harriet, he thought, looked exactly like Charles! It seems safe to say that when Henry finally departed for college he was still much more boy than man.

THE EARLY 1830S WERE A REMARKABLE TIME to be a college student—more akin to the late 1960s than other eras. The average age of the population was sixteen in 1830, the result of a baby boom following the War of 1812, and the number of colleges had quintupled from nine to nearly fifty. The old generation of founding fathers was dying, symbolically passing the revolutionary mantle to this rising generation. A delicious sense of "Newness," as one contemporary called it, pervaded the culture. "There was a breath of new air, much vague expectation, a consciousness of power not yet finding its determinate aim," Ralph Waldo Emerson recalled forty years later.[4]

This "go-ahead" spirit had many origins. It was drifting in from Europe, where Romantic writers were challenging the staid hierarchies of the classical tradition and the rationalism of the Enlightenment, and scientists were demystifying the natural world in every field from physics to physiology. It was stirred by homegrown technological inventions that harnessed iron, water, and steam to accomplish fantastic things that mere men never could. It was fed by the opening of the western frontier, where cheap land inspired even the poorest Americans to dream of reinventing themselves, and by a surge of democratic populism in government, as many states eliminated property qualifications and other barriers to mass political participation for white men.

In religion 1830 was the "Year of the Great Revival." The religious revivals that had dotted the landscape for the last fifteen years suddenly massed into a tidal wave, washing tens of thousands of souls up to the shores of heaven, and unleashing a powerful optimism and energy upon the land. "Universal Education," "Universal Reform," and "Progress" were becoming the great rallying cries of the thinking classes.

Amherst College perfectly captured the zeitgeist. The campus was painfully plain, as even its admirers admitted. Johnson Chapel, with its mammoth white pillars, housed the classrooms and laboratory. Flanking the chapel were three unadorned brick boxes, student dormitories named simply South, Middle, and North colleges. A water well, privy, and woodshed rounded out the official architecture of the school. There was no dining hall, so students took their meals in town. The college had only six full professors, most of them ordained ministers, and a minuscule endowment, yet students were pouring in so fast that it was rapidly becoming the second largest college in New England.

Amherst had a different ethos than Harvard or Yale, where the prerogatives of tradition, wealth, and aristocratic bloodlines dominated. Here most of the students were from the hardscrabble hill towns of western New England and upstate New York, the pious sons of farmers and parsons, often the first in their families to go to college. Nearly half the students received financial aid from various charitable funds, and most supported themselves through odd jobs and schoolteaching. Many were recently converted older students, and a majority were heading for the ministry. They were "Country graduates," to use Nathaniel Hawthorne's phrase: "rough, brown-featured, schoolmaster-looking, half bumpkin, half-scholarly figures, in black ill-cut broadcloth,—their manners quite spoilt by what little of the gentleman there was in them."[5]

But what these boys lacked in poise they made up in ambition. They were a brainy, intense lot, the vanguard of America's growing obsession with self-improvement. Amherst College was "an infant Hercules," Emerson wrote in admiration after visiting the campus. "They write and study in a sort of fury, which, I think, promises a harvest of attainments."[6] Their religious zeal was so notorious that their Unitarian foes dubbed Amherst "the priest factory." Temperance societies, in which students pledged to avoid hard liquor, were common on many campuses, but Amherst was famous for adopting the radical "cold water" requirement that members abstain from beer, wine, opium, and tobacco as well.

In the twentieth century, evangelical Christians came to be characterized as reactionary and anti-intellectual, but in the 1830s they were the nation's most ardent advocates of education, believing that ignorance and sin went hand in hand. Amherst was deeply influenced by the new German vision of liberal education, with its emphasis on independent thinking over rote recitation, and scientific observation and experimentation over a priori reasoning. It was among the first schools to use blackboards—an innovation that seems small today but that changed the very nature of teaching. The faculty's attempt in 1828 to introduce the study of modern languages and literature fell apart for lack of support, but in 1831 they successfully scraped together four thousand dollars to send a professor to Europe to purchase the latest scientific books and equipment. Amherst in 1830, as one of Henry's professors recalled, "was regarded as pre-eminently the *live* College and the progressive Institution of New England."[7]

IF ANY PLACE SHOULD HAVE FELT FAMILIAR to Henry, then surely Amherst was it. Yet his transition to college was miserable. To save money he rented a room a mile from campus in a private home, sharing with a Boston Latin boy two years younger than himself, and several seniors who took no notice of the bashful freshman, leaving him lonely and isolated. At the same time, as the son of the notorious Lyman Beecher, Henry was "a marked man" on campus, as one classmate recalled (one fellow student was actually named Lyman Beecher Harkin). Everyone was judging his every move.

Perhaps the problem was that Amherst was too much like home, with its combination of high expectations, sharp scrutiny, and benign neglect. "I went through another phase of suffering which was far worse than any I had previously experienced," he said years later. "It seemed as though all the darkness of my childhood were mere puffs to the blackness I was now passing through."[8]

As usual schoolwork was the wellspring of his despair. The first-year schedule was full of his worst subjects: Latin, Greek, algebra, geometry, and English grammar. Like many a freshman, Henry felt in over his head, certain that his classmates were far better prepared than he was. He was disorganized in every way. Clothes and books were strewn around his room, as one friend put it, "in utter confusion—some upon the floor, others in chairs, or the windows, and others under or upon the bed."[9] As Henry said, quoting his freshman roommate, "I had a place for everything and *everything* in its place—that is on the *table*."[10]

"I have not fixed a plan of study or anything else hardly. I have tried to form them so many times and failed that I begin to distrust my own self," he lamented to George a few months into the first semester. He lived in dread of disapproval and was shattered by the smallest setbacks. "I *feel* every day that I am blown about by every little circumstance, all at loose ends,"[11] he wrote; "and so I seek conversation etc. to keep myself from my own thoughts—and if they trouble me now I don't know what they will do when I grow older."

Like his father, Henry laid the blame for his suffering on Mount Pleasant. "My going to Mt. Pleasant cut me all up as to being *thorough*," he complained.[12] Perhaps, he suggested, he should leave college and study for a year with Catharine and Harriet in Hartford. Or maybe he should become a farmer. But those ideas went nowhere.

In typical fashion Henry's anxiety erupted into a spiritual crisis. He hit bottom in February of his freshman year, just as a new wave of religious revivals was sweeping through the colleges and academies of the Northeast. Hoping to join the trend, the faculty tried to spark their own revival with a "concert of prayer." But none of their efforts took hold until one of the senior boys was suddenly struck down with a mysterious illness. Shocked and frightened by the death of their classmate, several seniors became "serious," as the Calvinists liked to say, and experienced dramatic conversions, sending a domino effect through the rest of the school.

Night after night prayer meetings filled the classrooms, and morning after morning the names of new converts were announced at chapel. Once again Henry was "prodigiously waked up" by the spiritual commotion around him. Given that he was already ostensibly a Christian, however, this new emotional turmoil sent him into a spiral of uncertainty that, he later confessed, "came near wrecking me." He tried attending "an inquiry-meeting" for those with spiritual hope, but when young Beecher walked in, the professor leading the meeting stopped dead, saying: "My friends, I am so overwhelmed by the consciousness of God's presence in this room that I cannot speak a word."

What he meant was not entirely clear, but Henry didn't wait to find out. In the sudden silence the lad shamefacedly got up and left the room. "There was no humiliation that I would not have submitted to ten thousand times over if thereby I could have found relief from the doubt, perplexity, and fear which tormented me," he said years later.[13]

After weeks of misery Henry went to see President Heman Humphrey for guidance. President Humphrey was an upright man of exemplary character, but even his admirers found him inflexible and uninspiring. Like all the authority figures in Henry's life, he failed to help the poor boy. "I am without hope and utterly wretched, and I want to be a Christian," Henry moaned as he sat down in the president's study.

"Ah! it is the spirit of God, my young man," President Humphrey responded solemnly, "and when the Spirit of God is at work with a soul I dare not interfere."

"I went away in blacker darkness than I came," Henry said.[14]

Ultimately aid came from a very different quarter. Moody Harrington, an earnest senior who at the age of thirty-two was older and more mature than most of his classmates, noticed Henry's distress. At first Henry was intimidated by the upperclassman. "I remember that my poetic temperament, alongside of his rigorous, logical temperament, used to seem to me mean and contemptible," he recalled. "I thought he was like a big oak-tree, while I was more like a willow, half-grown and pliant, yielding to every force that was exerted upon it."[15]

But as Moody took the freshman under his wing, offering him sympathy and encouragement, Henry began to blossom. "I wanted someone to brood me," Henry said later, and he did.[16] It was a new kind of relationship. Moody did not treat him like a peer or a peon, but like the attentive, nurturing older brother Henry had always longed for. No one—certainly no one in the Beecher fold—had ever responded to his needs with such empathy.

Henry's stories about how he emerged from this and other religious crises are always fuzzy. "The precise time of my conversion I cannot tell," he later confessed. Over and over he describes epiphanies that turn out to be merely high points in an ongoing cycle of anguish and elation. Still, there was hope of progress. His earthly friendship with Moody inspired Henry to stumble, half blindly, toward a new vision of God. In one version of the story, his catharsis came as he was tramping through the woods after class, when "there arose over the horizon a vision of the Lord Jesus Christ as a living Friend, who had the profoundest personal interest in me, I embraced that view and was lifted up."[17]

In another version, he was kneeling by the fireplace in his room, where he had been studying and praying, when he was struck by this thought: "Will God permit the devil to have charge of one of his children that does not want to be deceived?" Suddenly there arose in him "such a sense of God's taking care of those who put their trust in him that for an hour all the world was crystalline, the heavens were lucid, and I sprang to my feet and began to cry and laugh; and feeling that I must tell somebody what the Lord had done for me, I went and told Dr. Humphrey and others."[18]

These moments of relief and ecstasy came and went, but for the first time they were leading Henry in a new direction. This concept of Christ as personal friend and mentor—a divine version of Moody Harrington—stood in stark contrast to the legalistic theology he'd grown up with, in which God was a stern judge and Christ was the sacrificial scapegoat who would atone for mankind's crimes. For the first time Henry glimpsed a new path to salvation based on acceptance rather than judgment.

AS IT DOES WITH MOST homesick freshmen, Henry's unhappiness evaporated as soon as he discovered the pleasures of college social life. In no time at all he was one of the popular boys of the class. Official extracurricular activities were few in the 1830s, but he played flute in the college band, was a zealous member of the College Temperance Society, and undoubtedly shone in the Society for Inquiry, the school's religious club. The boys loved Henry's sparkling sense of humor and practical jokes, and he could often be found lounging on the steps of Johnson Chapel, regaling a crowd with his wit. "Nobody could be gloomy or desponding near your father," one classmate, S. Hopkins Emery, told Henry's son years later. "He made us all cheerful and happy."[19]

By the time his freshman year drew to a close, Henry was brimming with newfound self-assurance. Over the summer break he intended to get a job as an agent for one of the voluntary societies, traveling around to small towns distributing Bibles or religious tracts, "or something like that, or do something or other," he told Harriet. "I shall in a month or two be eighteen years old," he said, "and I think that is old enough to begin to do something."[20]

Finally the last day of school arrived. To save the cost of coach fare, Henry decided to walk the hundred-odd miles from Amherst to Boston, along with two of his new college friends, including one of his roommates, Ebenezer Bullard. It was too long to walk in a single day, so Ebenezer invited the fellows to stop overnight at his family's farm in West Sutton, Massachusetts.

That evening the boys arrived at a big rambling white farm-house. The kindly Mrs. Bullard fed the ravenous teenagers a raft of old-fashioned Yankee delicacies. Even in old age Henry remembered her home-churned butter spread on snowy white bread, bowls of thick cream poured over crumbled coarse brown bread and whortleberries, tangy homemade cheeses, and steaming fruit pies. But what really caught Henry's imagination was Ebenezer's sister Eunice.

MUCH HAD CHANGED in the nine months since that embarrassing evening in Hartford. Henry was no longer the bashful boy who stammered and blushed and ran away from the gentler sex. To speak plainly, Henry was girl crazy.

Perhaps this was not surprising. Even as a little boy Henry longed for female attention and seemed to feel, at least subconsciously, that the way to replace his long-lost mother was to find a wife of his own. When he was only eight or nine years old, Henry surprised his stepmother by declaring: "I am never going to get married."

"Ah, why not, Henry?" she asked.

Blushing violently, he replied, "Well, I never could ask a girl, 'Will you have me?' "[21]

It was an odd thing for a boy in short pants to worry about, but on this subject Henry was precocious. Years later he recalled infatuations with not one but two "older women." At the age of twelve the object of his adoration was Mary Peck, a friend of his sisters; when she married he expressed his sorrow by copying into her keepsake album a maudlin poem about life's disappointments and the consolations of Christ. In high school he developed a crush on Nancy, a classmate's older sister. Home on vacation in Boston, he spiffed up his shabby clothes and screwed up the courage to visit Nancy's house. As he lingered in the parlor with his family before he left, the transformation was obvious.

"Lyman," Harriet Porter said slyly, without looking up from her lace knitting, "Mount Pleasant is an excellent school. Henry is improving very much. He has grown tidy, blacks his boots and brushes his hair, and begins to pay a proper attention to his clothes." Charles exploded with laughter, and Henry turned red.

"Oh! it is the school, is it?" Lyman said, peering over his paper. "Humph! I guess the cause is nearer home."

Unfortunately his social calls went no further than leaning against the window and watching Nancy sew—"she had such little pink fingers," he said, "how I wanted to take hold of them!" Whenever the girl would glance up, however, "I would be covered with hot and awkward confusion." But Nancy was also too old for him, and soon married someone her own age.[22]

Now a college man, he was determined to become "a complete gentleman," turning to Harriet for help in improving his *manners, conversation,* and propriety." "I wish that you would tell me everything in which you think I need to improve and I will try to correct it," he wrote his sister.[23] He threw himself into the task with gusto, forcibly conquering any last shyness and discovering a natural gift for flirtation.

Soon his pals were complaining that Henry spent too many evenings taking tea and trading confidences with the young ladies of Amherst: girls like Lucy Humphrey, daughter of President Humphrey, or Catharine Dickinson, daughter of one of the college's founding fathers and aunt to a newborn baby girl who would one day become the poet Emily Dickinson. He took a special shine to a young charmer he identified only as Susan.

Among girls Henry was at his best: sweet, attentive, witty, confident. In turn feminine friendships offered a cozy haven for his easily battered ego. When he was downhearted or discouraged, he was sure that marriage would solve all his problems, including his battle with the books. "I sometimes wish that I was married to one who could have enough influence over me to keep me *thorough,* in *all my* studies," he confided to George. "I believe it would make another man of me."[24]

EUNICE WHITE BULLARD was a handsome girl with rosy, clear skin, a curvy figure, and thick auburn hair styled in fashionable ringlets. Like

Henry, Eunice was a middle child among a brood of nine children and was accustomed to the hard work required of even a well-to-do farm girl. The Bullards were devout Congregationalists, from old-line Puritan stock on both sides. Two of her brothers attended Amherst with Henry, and three joined the ministry. Intense and intelligent, she had recently graduated from an academy near Amherst and was now teaching school.

Eunice's father, Dr. Artemas Bullard, was a prominent physician and the squire of Bullard Hill, one of the largest farms in the area. He was a tall, taciturn man, overbearing and notoriously cheap. Dr. Bullard loved his children, but he was often strict to the point of severity. When Eunice and her sister once dared to appear at the dinner table in relatively low-cut dresses, Dr. Bullard hurled a bowl of hot soup at them, remarking that they must be cold and the soup would warm them.

As a child of an orthodox, well-to-do doctor, forbidden from joining the other kids in such dubious pastimes as dancing lessons, Eunice grew up feeling isolated and socially awkward. As a little girl she was teased for her prissiness—"teasing, they called it—I called it tormenting me," she remembered. One day some children from the village cornered her by the village gristmill, egging her on to swear and say wicked words. When she refused they picked her up and dangled her over the waterwheel, threatening to toss her into the churning stream if she didn't "show the Doctor that his children could be just as bad as they were."

Poor Eunice protested that if she cursed and took the Lord's name in vain, "I should go to 'the bad place' when I died." They pushed her head under the flume of water, then pulled her out, as she described it, "strangled and gasping for breath when in my great fright I cried out 'By God!'—and wild with a great horror of what I had said I fell into convulsions in their hands."

She lay there apparently unconscious until the miscreants finally ran for help. Eunice was bedridden for several weeks after her trauma. "Father was surprised and alarmed that I remained so long ill, but I dared not tell *why*," Eunice remembered, "but young as I was I brooded over my *great sin*—sure that death was near and I should be forever lost." The only consolation was that her mysterious illness brought her the undivided attention and open affection of her parents.

Eunice was close to her mild-mannered mother, Lucy White Bullard. Still, Eunice, like Henry, often felt neglected and misunderstood. She envied her brothers' advanced educations, and resented that so much of her time was spent sewing and cooking for them. Surrounded by seven teasing brothers and a critical father, she could be oversensitive and insecure. But she also shared the Bullards' sharp wit and could hold her own in any conversation.

Eunice was not overwhelmed by her first impression of Henry. He looked no older than fifteen, with his smooth boyish face, wide mouth, and saucer-size blue-gray eyes. "Truth to tell," she confessed, he "was an exceedingly homely young man." But his gawky looks were mitigated by "the roguish mouth, the laughing, merry eyes and the quaint humor and quicker repartee"—true, he was "not an Apolo for Beauty. But in youth or old age, who, after spending an hour with him, ever thought of that, or *believed* it?"[25]

After supper the family gathered in the cheery "home room." Dr. Bullard was out on a house call to a patient, but the boys chatted and joked with Mrs. Bullard, while Eunice sat down to darn a coat that Ebenezer had brought home for mending. As she began to wind a skein of homespun thread into a ball for darning, Henry gallantly offered to hold the skein. Somehow, however, he managed to make a mess of the thread ("A badly tangled skein, is it not?" he asked innocently), requiring half the evening to untangle it. He filled in the time entertaining Eunice and her family with funny stories. His lively, clever talk and flattering attentions were a marked contrast to the dreary routine of farm life, and Eunice's opinion of Henry was rising dramatically. "Before the first evening was past none of the family felt him to be a stranger," said she.

Her father returned just as they were all laughing uproariously at one of Henry's anecdotes. Dr. Bullard stood in the doorway, surprised and rather disapproving at the tumult, but by the end of the evening he found himself laughing and swapping stories with "*young Beecher*," Eunice remembered, "as cheerfully as if they had been boys together."

"He's smart," Dr. Bullard said approvingly. "If he lives, he'll make his mark in the world."[26]

The next day his companion left for Boston, but Henry decided to stay on through the weekend. His interest in Eunice was unmistakable. Like many farmers, the Bullards made their own cheese and Henry spent most of his time with the girl in the dank, sour-smelling milk-cellar room, helping her churn butter and rub down the rows of yellow cheeses aging on wooden shelves. He did his own buttering up of Dr. Bullard, roaming the farm with him, asking questions about planting, harvests, and husbandry. He flirted sweetly with Mrs. Bullard, who loved him from the first. "Henry always brings sunshine and makes me feel young," she often said. He paid her the compliment of eating voraciously from her packed larder.[27]

By the time he left, Henry had a full-blown crush on Ebenezer's "kind, amiable and beautiful sister." As he wrote to his college friend Howard Chauncey, he now "put her on the list of those to be 'tho't more of' "—at the head of the list, in fact, replacing the unsuspecting Susan. Those days at Bullard Hill were the highlight of his vacation, fueling his fascination with the *"important and interesting* topic" of courtship.[28]

LITTLE TOM BEECHER, only seven years old, waited "in an agony of delight that could not be endured" for his big brother to come home from college. When Henry finally rattled the door latch, Tom dashed under his mother's bed to savor the joy of being sought and found and "tossed above the clouds by great, strong brother Henry." Tom's joy was shared by his father, whose morning prayer was now one of thanks: "Thou hast brought back our boys in health."[29]

Things were not going well for the Reverend Beecher. His plan to wipe out Unitarianism was stalled, and his crusade against the liquor trade and Sunday recreations had enraged the working classes, especially the Catholic immigrants, who resented his Protestant bigotry. But no one guessed the depth of their opposition until one frigid winter night in 1830, when the fire bell rang in the North End, signaling that the Hanover Street Church was ablaze. The firemen—a rough, rowdy lot with many Catholics among them—rushed to the scene, but when they realized it was "Old Beecher's" church, they refused to put out the fire.

Bystanders joined the firemen standing in the snow, watching flames climb the steeple, when a series of blasts burst through the basement. The cellar had been rented to a local merchant who was, ironically, using it to store jugs of rum that were now exploding from the heat. The gathering crowd roared with laughter when they realized that Boston's temple of temperance was spouting liquor. The firemen shouted jokes about "hell-fire" and Beecher's "broken jug." "Only smell the brimstone!" called out the rowdies. "I wonder what 'Old Hell-fire' will do now that his shop is burned?" Some began chanting a spontaneous little ditty, punning on the old rhyme about Christ's offering of forgiveness, "While the lamp holds out to burn the vilest sinner may return":

While Beecher's church holds out to burn
The vilest sinner may return.[30]

By two in the morning there was little left to save. Lyman wore a brave face, declaring the next day that they would rebuild, but his feelings about the city were never quite the same.

Far more bitter was the growing schism within his own ranks. The church he loved so much was beginning to splinter, and he was at the center of the divide. On one side stood the ultraorthodox ministers of Andover and Princeton, who feared that Beecher's efforts to make Calvinist doctrine more palatable to his Boston audiences were treading close to heresy. On the other flank was a new, radical group of freelance revivalists headquartered in upstate New York, a region so thoroughly evangelized it was nicknamed the "Burnt-Over District." Led by the legendary lawyer-turned-preacher Charles Grandison Finney, this "holy band" accused Beecher of being too conservative, of caring more for respectability than saving souls.

The conflict between Beecher and Finney was one of style, not theology. These itinerant preachers—modeled after Christ's apostles—rode from town to town holding extended mass meetings that often went on for days, employing a barrage of psychological tactics to create a frenzy of emotion. Alarming tales were told of women breaking the taboo against speaking in mixed gatherings, of men and women fainting, weeping, and shaking with an almost erotic passion until they broke down, sobbing with repentance and ecstatic relief. Lyman was appalled by Finney's "New Measures," as they were called, and was certain that such unruly, unregulated behavior would undermine the traditional authority of the ministry and torpedo his cause with the Boston Brahmins and other self-styled sophisticates. "Satan as usual," Lyman declared, "is plotting to dishonor a work which he cannot stand."[31]

Beecher swore that Finney's band would not set foot in New England, but as rumors spread of Finney's power, Lyman's own congregation clamored to see this fantastic phenomenon with their own eyes. Finally Beecher capitulated, inviting the great revivalist to Boston near the end of Henry's freshman year. Finney stayed most of the summer, awakening a revival so powerful that many considered it the peak of the Second Great Awakening. Unfortunately Lyman's new alliance with Finney only inflamed his "hyper-Calvinist" enemies.

Disheartened, Lyman was turning his mind to a fresh battleground:

the western frontier. For years he had denounced the Yankees who headed west as shiftless malcontents, too foolish to stay at home. As a child Henry had hidden under his bed when wagons full of dusty migrants passed through Litchfield, terrified by rumors that the pioneers kidnapped little boys to take with them.

But Lyman's tirades went unheeded. With the opening of the Erie Canal in 1825, the vast valleys of the Ohio and Mississippi rivers were filling up with adventurous young men, landless farmers, and impoverished immigrants. When an 1828 landslide sent the roughneck Democrat Andrew Jackson to the White House and the legendary Tennessee frontiersman Davy Crockett to Congress, it was a clear sign that the West would no longer be an appendage to the Northeast but a force all its own.

Now Lyman began to believe that the moral destiny of America lay out West. "If we gain the West, all is safe; if we lose it all is lost," he told his children; "the competition now is for that of preoccupancy in the education of the rising generation, in which Catholics and infidels have got the start of us."[32] Edward was the first Beecher to go, accepting a job as president of the newly established Illinois College. Soon Lyman was mulling over an equally enticing offer: the presidency of a new theological seminary in Cincinnati, Ohio. Nothing could be decided, however, until his Boston church was rebuilt.

For Henry it was a restless summer. Nothing came of his plan to peddle Bibles, so he spent the summer attending his father's revival meetings, leafing through Sir Walter Scott's adventure novels, and idly roaming the streets of Boston. He was surprisingly removed from his father's battles. After years of training he could recite every theological argument against Unitarianism, "just like a row of pins on a paper," but clearly his heart wasn't in it.[33]

Charles Grandison Finney made a stronger impression on him. Finney was so personal, so emotional, in contrast to the dry formality of most orthodox preachers, that he seemed almost irreverent. Henry was shocked the first time he heard the revivalist pray for "Dr. Beecher" instead of "the pastor of this church," and praying by name for sinful, sick, or suffering congregants.[34] Instead of splitting theological hairs, Finney made God's case with the simple, straightforward logic of a prosecuting attorney. Soon the boy was won over by his vibrant style. The famous Finney was "truly a grand preacher," he declared to Chauncey Howard, "a man after my own heart."[35]

But love was Henry's primary preoccupation. As the beginning of the fall term neared, Henry decided to cut his vacation short a week early so he would have time to visit Ebenezer Bullard's sister on the long walk back. "Bullard declared that before he tried to travel on foot again he would get in love," Henry later chuckled to Chauncey, "for he found it improved the pedestrian powers most wonderfully."[36]

SOPHOMORE YEAR MARKED a new phase in Henry's life. His confidence was growing by leaps and bounds, both socially and intellectually. He embarked on a program of self-improvement, beseeching Harriet for advice on how to refine his manners and conversational skills, and keeping a notebook of "outlines of the lives who have made themselves or have attained any great end by decision of character." He was determined to refute his father's snobbish Boston critics, proving that a fellow could be both an evangelical Christian and a cosmopolitan gentleman.

Henry's summer dalliance with Eunice Bullard only whetted his romantic ambitions. He spent Thanksgiving with a classmate's family in the nearby village of South Hadley, where he fell hard for yet another sister, with the prim name of Mindwell Gould. "*Dear Mindwell*, Mrs. *Mindwell* Beecher!! How would that sound?" he asked Harriet with glee. Henry swore he was heeding President Humphrey's warnings to the boys against early engagements, but he cited Humphrey's one exception: " 'I've no objection to your *thinking* of it,' " the president told the boys. After all, Humphrey added, " 'if a man is going through a woods, and sees a good young *sapling* he may mark it and come back afterward and get it, if *he can*.' "

"At any rate I am determined to 'mark her,' " Henry declared.[37]

But by the end of the fall semester Henry's longings overpowered both President Humphrey's advice and Mindwell's charms. Whether it was true love or the fact that Ebenezer's sister was the first girl to reciprocate his interest, Henry turned his attention back to Miss Bullard.

When Ebenezer mentioned to Henry that his sister would be spending the winter at her Aunt Fletcher's home in Whitingsville, Massachusetts, Henry slyly found a position teaching school in the neighboring village of Northbridge over the long January vacation. He even arranged to board with Eunice's aunt. Schoolteaching was hard, dull, poorly paid work, but Henry had a plan, and, as he said prophetically, "I possess real Beecher blood in the matter of *planning*."[38]

On the way to his new job he dropped by Bullard Hill to share his good news. Eunice's parents were pleased, and Henry seemed innocently surprised to hear that he and Eunice would be boarding in the same house. Dr. Bullard suggested that since his daughter had been hoping to continue her education, this would be a perfect opportunity for Henry to tutor her in Latin. Quite rightly Eunice didn't think Henry had much to teach her in Latin—"*I* who have been a school-ma'am for three terms!"—but she made no objections to the plan.

On January 2, 1832, the very first evening he arrived in Whitingsville, Henry found Eunice in the parlor. Conveniently her aunt and uncle were out on errands, but her young cousin lingered by the fire. Henry helped her cousin with his lessons while she wrote letters, until impatience got the better of him and he struck up a conversation. So how were her Latin studies coming along? Did she know all the grammar? Could she conjugate all the verbs?

"Oh! yes," she replied. "I think so."

"Suppose you try some of them, and let me see how well you understand them."

"I respectfully conjugated the verbs as he gave them out," Eunice recalled, until at last he asked her to conjugate the verb *amare*, "to love." She did so perfectly, and then turned back to her writing desk. Another hour passed. Finally Henry could wait no longer. Just before bedtime he slipped a note onto her writing desk: *"Will you go with me as a missionary to the West?"*

Stunned, Eunice didn't know what to say, and she certainly wasn't going to answer with her cousin in the room. After a long, excruciating silence, the cousin went off to bed and Henry pounced, urging Eunice to give her answer. The surprised girl demurred. But as he noted, she was halfheartedly saying no with her mouth, but saying yes with her eyes. She tried to deflect him by saying he must speak to her parents, but Henry pressed to hear how *she* felt about his proposal. Young Beecher was not the most subtle of suitors.

There was much to say against such a hasty engagement. They had known each other for only six months, and it would be years before they could marry—at least two and a half years of college and another three of seminary for Henry. But they were both sensitive souls, united in their romantic visions and their eagerness for undivided approval, loyalty, and love. Eunice was eighteen years old, with no other suitors in sight, and she was flattered by Henry's passionate persistence, his gregarious charm, and his prominent family connections. She could hardly help but fall head over heels in love.

Eunice said yes then and there.

The next Saturday, Henry went to West Sutton to ask the Bullards for her hand. Naturally they were horrified, and her father was furious at "being outgeneraled by a boy." This was clearly not the "mark" he'd meant Henry to make.

"Why, you are a couple of babies! You don't know your own minds yet, and won't for some years to come," Dr. Bullard protested over and over again. A seven-year engagement was more risky for a woman than for a man, for if it was broken she could well end up a spinster. "But *only a boy*' as they thought him, who could resist Henry when he pleaded in earnest?" Eunice recalled with satisfaction. By the end of the day they were convinced that he was truly devoted to their daughter.

"Boy as he seems, he will be true to Eunice," the doctor admitted to his wife, after Henry left. "I have no fear on that score."[39]

In the end, it may be that Dr. Bullard's doubts were well founded. But just then nothing could dim their enthusiasm for each other. "If you wish true unalloyed, genuine delight, fall in love with some amiable girl," Henry exulted to his friend Chauncey. "It surpasses other pleasures as the golden grain does the dry chaff and husk!"[40]

THE LOVEBIRDS TRIED TO KEEP their engagement hush-hush, knowing his family would worry that Henry was throwing away his education, but he gushed so about his good fortune that he quickly tipped his hand. But love also gave Henry a newfound defiance. "I am not anxious to vindicate myself," he responded to a scolding from his eldest brother, William. Nonetheless, he protested, "It is all false, as false as can be. No term since I have been in college have I studied so much as the last term; no year accomplished so much as the last."[41]

Henry spoke the truth. After a dozen years of lackadaisical efforts, he was blossoming intellectually. His transformation did not occur in the classroom, though, but in a dusty little room cluttered with books and journals on the second floor of North dormitory: the home of the Athenian Society.

This was the heyday of the literary club in America. At Amherst the two main literary societies, the Athenians and Alexandrians, dominated intellectual and social life on campus. The Athenian Society met every week to read and write poetry, essays, and anonymous satires, and to debate the hot topics of the day. They sponsored guest speakers, held public-speaking exhibitions and intramural debates, and pooled their money to buy books. At a time when many college libraries amounted to several shelves of dreary textbooks and religious volumes, the literary clubs provided almost all outside literature, competing with their rivals to build the biggest collection. By the time the Athenians assembled a catalog in 1836 they owned 2,440 books, representing the full spectrum of contemporary writing in America, and subscribed to dozens of newspapers and journals from across the country.

Here Henry was exposed to the latest ideas in literature, philosophy, politics, and current events—all the modern movements ignored by the classical curriculum. The club room was the antithesis of the classroom: democratic, spontaneous, and cutting edge instead of hierarchical, formal, and conservative. The Athenians owned almost all the major works of European Romanticism, from the eminently Christian English poets and orators to the speculative German philosophers, even the radical French novelists and social theorists who were shunned by most orthodox Christians.

For the earnest young men of the 1830s, these Romantic writers represented a rebellion against the tyranny of tradition and a soul-deadening culture obsessed with money, propriety, and material comfort. They emphasized imagination over reason, spontaneity over formality, spirituality over religion, self-expression over social convention, nature over society, and individual conscience over the rule of law. Their manifesto was summed up by the English poet and critic Samuel Taylor Coleridge: "Deep thinking is attainable only by a man of deep feeling."

There were scandalous aspects to the European Romantics, of course. Foes accused the worst of them of promoting irreverence, libertinism, and the dangerous politics of the French Revolution. But there also were many instinctive connections between American evangelical Christianity and European Romanticism: the emphasis on sublime inspiration and obsessive introspection, the repudiation of worldly concerns in search of the divine, and an abiding faith in the individual's ability to transform himself and his world.

Henry took to this new ethos like a fly to honey. Always a slow reader, he absorbed most of it secondhand through journals and reviews (he would always prefer grazing periodicals to plowing through treatises), and he did not master all its philosophical complexities. But, having spent his youth struggling to shoehorn his own effervescent personality into starchy social conventions, he understood the Romantic impulse intuitively.

He loved the iconoclasm—the repudiation of old forms to get at fresh truths—the exaltation of the imagination, the fascination with beauty and nature, and the insistence that human passion was a subject worthy of exploration rather than suppression. He was enthralled by the idea of the Poet as a natural aristocrat whose self-expression was a conduit between heaven and earth. After years of probing his motives and moods and always falling short, suddenly his sensitivity, suffering, and self-doubt were no longer signs of sinfulness, but of his superior sensibility.

"I never have performed so much real *mental labor* as within six months past," Henry enthused to Harriet in the spring of 1832. "I am beginning to learn to *think, write* and *debate.*" Forced for the first time to write regularly and read his compositions aloud, he quickly discovered that his father's kitchen-table training gave him a leg up over the other boys. In Athenian meetings he spoke fluently on topics like "the importance of the three professions: medicine, law, and theology" and "the tendencies of society toward perfection," and debated such questions as whether it was "desirable for students in college to enjoy female society" (arguing in the affirmative). "In mere recitation of mathematics or languages many of us could surpass him," one classmate recalled, "but in extemporaneous debates he could beat us all."[42]

He became an avid reader, picking up a passion for books that would drain his pocketbook and fill his shelves. No one on campus was better read in current events, poetry, and belles lettres. He read a great deal of English poetry: Spenser, Milton, Byron, and Burns, as well as lesser versifiers. He filled up notebooks with his own heroic couplets and blank verse, usually on themes of noble self-sacrifice and the glories of nature, and published his poems and essays in the college literary magazines, which he also helped edit.

Now Henry burned with a new aspiration: to be a Man of Letters. Among the boys he became renowned for his originality and eloquence. "He had always something to say that was fresh and striking and out of the beaten track of thought," said his classmate Thomas Field, "something, too, that he had not gotten from books, but that was the product of his own thinking."[43] It was a sign of his stature that when the great statesman and presidential candidate Henry Clay visited the college, Henry had the honor of presenting Clay with a memorial Bible.

Henry was the quintessential sophomore, taking juvenile delight in his new sophistication, solemnly dedicating himself to Truth and Light and then merrily tossing out Latin puns and cracking in-jokes about professors, classes, and books. He was always on the lookout, as he put it, for the "opportunity of exhibiting the analogy between Conic sections and Comic sections."[44] He cultivated a reputation for eccentricity, building an odd doughnut-shaped desk for himself out of a circle of wood with a hole cut in the middle for a chair. Ensconced in his nest, surrounded by books, his room was the natural hangout for the late-night bull sessions he loved.

His schoolwork finally fell into a rhythm, based mostly on neglect. "I studied what I liked and didn't study what I didn't like," he said flatly.[45] Henry's idiosyncratic approach to homework verged at times on insolence, saved only by his obvious good nature. He informed Ebenezer Snell, the round-faced, sweet-tempered young professor of mathematics, that he should not have to study math since it would be of no use to a minister. When Snell insisted that math would discipline his mind, he replied, "If that's all, I shan't go to class any more. My mind gets enough discipline inventing excuses for not being there."[46] By the end of his junior year, Snell had generally given up calling on him—a tacit admission of defeat.

But the most momentous event of Henry's sophomore year was the arrival of a letter from home announcing that Lyman and Catharine were traveling to Ohio to survey the scene. Henry "fairly danced" with delight when he heard the news. "I sang, whistled, flew around like a mad man. Father's removal to the West is my 'heart's desire,' " he wrote to Harriet. "Edward went to see and was caught—Eve went to see and ate some apples—father I trust will go to see and come back and let us go and see."[47]

For the last few years Henry had toyed with the idea of becoming a foreign missionary in some exotic land, China, say, or the Sandwich Islands. Now his imagination was gripped by the Wild West. In typical fashion he read everything he could find on the western territories, pouring out poems and essays ("I have a book full of blank verse, all fixing for the West!" he boasted) and founding a club—"the society of Western Inquiry." As he read, his sister Harriet recalled, it suddenly seemed possible to fulfill both his father's wishes and his own dreams of glory, honor, and "knightly daring" that he had once pinned on the navy.[48] He would be a home missionary, as they were called, dedicated to bringing the Yankee God to the uncivilized frontier.

By autumn it was definite. Everyone, from Aunt Esther to the sisters of the Hartford Annex, was pulling up stakes and heading to Cincinnati. Only Mary intended to stay settled with her family in Hartford. Charles and Henry would join the family after graduating, and study for the ministry at their father's new theological seminary. The arrival of the Beecher clan, Henry declared with biblical hubris, "will make the people of the west think that Jacob and his family are again going down to Egypt."[49]

Although Eunice tried to share his enthusiasm, her heart sank when Henry told her the news. From Ohio to Massachusetts, she observed sadly, "was too long a walk for vacation."[50]

By now it seemed to Henry that his real life took place at school, surrounded by his chums; visits home were mere tours of duty. " *'There is no place like home!'* No thank fortune—for there is no one to talk with, no one to walk with and nothing to do but eat gingerbread and stroll around the streets," he wrote to Chauncey Howard only a few days after his summer vacation began; "it will take me weeks to throw off the stupor acquired while stagnating here."[51]

Returning for his junior year, Henry's mind was primed to make another major intellectual leap. That fall the long-awaited crates of new scientific books and equipment—"philosophical apparatus," as they called it—finally arrived from Europe. Suddenly scientific inquiry was all the rage on campus, inspiring the boys to found a new Society of Natural History with its own library and cabinet of natural curiosities.

The architect of the new science curriculum was the Reverend Professor Edward Hitchcock. A nationally prominent geologist as well as an ordained minister, Professor Hitchcock was doubly blessed with profound religious faith and a voracious curiosity about the natural world. Early in his geological expeditions across Massachusetts, Hitchcock was confounded by evidence suggesting that the earth was much older than biblical calculations—evidence such as ancient geological sedimentation and fossils of unknown, long-extinct animals. But unlike later generations, he refused to choose between abandoning the Bible and denying the physical evidence. Instead he sought a middle path, dedicating his career to reconciling rational observation and analytical rigor with biblical revelation—to proving, in his words, that "the principles of science are a transcript of the Divine Character."[52] For Hitchcock and his like-minded colleagues, the natural world was like a language or set of symbols by which God communicated with humanity. Natural Theology, they called it.

The study of cause and effect was Hitchcock's passion. Instead of examining God's creations one by one, he taught the boys to study nature's mechanisms and interrelationships. He pushed them to see analogies and connections where they perceived only contrasts and antitheses, to observe closely and hold their presumptions until the evidence began to suggest theories and conclusions. He insisted that they develop the moral courage to question ideas that flew in the face of conventional wisdom.

Henry showed no special interest in science until the day he watched the normally shy and stammering Professor Hitchcock grow rapturous as he described his discovery of a new species of flower. It was just a plain little white flower, as far as Henry could see, but that only made his teacher's enthusiasm more curious and compelling. He found that Hitchcock's insistence on linking divine cause to earthly effect, and logical extrapolation to emotional inspiration, resonated strongly with his Beecher training. Soon the boy's tramps in the woods were no longer devoted to catching flying squirrels and stealing apples but to collecting geological and botanical specimens. It was considered a tremendous honor when he was invited to join the Society of Natural History late in his junior year.

That same autumn a German scholar named Johann Spurzheim embarked on a tour of the United States to promote a new science called "phrenology." Phrenology—a word taken from Greek to mean "discourse on the mind"—promised to demystify human behavior by breaking down the mind into approximately thirty different features, each one residing in a different "organ," or section, of the brain. Spurzheim argued that the way the brain shaped the surface of the skull revealed information about one's emotions, character, and intelligence. By interpreting the bumps and ridges of the skull, one could tell which characteristics dominated an individual's personality. Armed with this knowledge, one could then exercise and strengthen the weak parts of his mind or character, just as one might build up a bicep.

Two months into his popular lecture tour, Dr. Spurzheim abruptly died, but in that short time he kindled a craze that lasted for years. Suddenly it seemed that every man in America was doffing his hat to have his skull examined. At Amherst the most ardent convert to phrenology was Orson Fowler, a solemn young man from a poor, orthodox farm family who was headed for the ministry. Looking for a good laugh, several skeptics invited Fowler to debate his case in Beecher's room, with young Beecher leading the opposition.

The plan was to flummox poor Fowler with unanswerable objections. The more Henry researched phrenology, however, the more persuasive he found it. Finally a friend asked him point-blank: "What is your estimate of the real logical validity of these objections to Phrenology?"

"Why," said Henry, "I was thinking if these objections were all that could be alleged I could knock them to pieces."[53] From that day forward, phrenology was Henry's great passion.

To Henry the physiology of the skull was less compelling than the way phrenology illuminated human nature. "I suppose I inherited from my father a tendency or intuition to read man," Henry noted.[54] But in contrast to the Calvinist tendency to see human nature in black and white—natural/supernatural, body/soul, saint/sinner, saved/damned—what he loved about phrenology was the way it broke down the mind's faculties into an array of motives, instincts, and attributes that combined to attain various ends. With its emphasis on complex "mixed motives" and therapeutic growth, phrenology was not physiology, as the experts claimed, but an early, practical version of psychology.

Henry immediately formed a "club for physiological research," filling his room with pamphlets and charts, even a model of the human head with each "organ" traced and labeled. In Athenian meetings he debated phrenology's scientific merits and lectured on it to the Natural History Society, taking Professor Hitchcock's methods for categorizing and classifying natural phenomena like minerals or plant species, and using them to identify and classify the various elements of "human nature."

He and Fowler began performing around campus as a duo, with Henry lecturing on the "fundamental principles" of phrenology and Fowler reading the boys' skulls, charging two cents a head. As word spread they were invited to speak in several local villages. Flushed with their success, after graduation Fowler abandoned his plans to join Henry in attending Lyman Beecher's new seminary in Ohio, instead embarking on a wildly successful career running his own "Phrenological Institute" in New York City. Although phrenology was eventually discredited as an independent science, its insights would have a huge impact on American culture over the next two decades, due largely to Orson Fowler.

As for Henry's own skull, Fowler diagnosed "an impassioned temperament . . . a strong social brain," with "very large Benevolence" (kindness toward others) and "Amativeness fully developed" (meaning sexual or romantic love). Speaking frankly, from the shape of Henry's

head—"small brow and big in the lower part of his head, like a bull"—
he was "not likely to be a saint."[55] No doubt this was a helpful warning
to the skull's owner rather than a fatal prophecy.

HENRY GOT HIS FIRST TASTE of the ministry over winter vacation,
while working as a schoolmaster in the district schools he had once despised. His first job passed without much excitement, but in his junior
year he took a position in the village of Hopkinton, near Eunice's home
in eastern Massachusetts, where the Unitarians and Congregationalists
were locked in a fierce battle. The Hopkinton school committee was
split between those who thought it a coup to hire a Beecher and those
who thought the devil's spawn was coming to teach their children.

As soon as Henry arrived, several older, bigger students, sons of
staunch Unitarian families—"the enemies of Godliness," as Henry
described them—began acting up, vowing, in his words, "that young
Beecher should not stay in town a week." Such rebellion wasn't unusual
in this haphazard educational system. Teachers were often the same age
or size as their older students, and it was common for the bigger, rougher
boys to challenge the authority of the new, usually transient schoolmasters—often through physical intimidation. It was, however, more
specifically Beecherish to attribute his discipline problems to a divine
conflict between the Unitarians and Congregationalists.

The disruptions continued until Henry finally kicked the ringleader
out of class. The next morning the troublemaker returned "full of fight
and with a huge goliath to back him," to exact vengeance. Henry sought
out the town school committee for help, but they told him to deal with
the matter himself, suggesting that he just force out the misbehaving
boy. So, Henry wrote to Chauncey, "I took my rod and struck at him."
The boy hit back.

> A battle commenced. I parried his blows (you know I *box* a little)
> and beat him still over shoulders, arms, side and finally broke the
> ruler over his head. I then seized a club of wood which lay upon
> the floor and smote him again *hip and thigh*. The school was all in
> an uproar. The girls screamed, little boys cried. Some boys went to
> help me, some to fight me.

As shrieking children poured out of the one-room schoolhouse,
townspeople rushed in to break up the fight. Henry resigned his posi-

tion on the spot. The school committee begged him to stay on, but Henry refused. Finally some of the local parents asked him to open a private school for the rest of the term, which he did with great success. He still heard whispers that several boys were waiting to jump him as he walked home from late-night church meetings, but, he declared breezily, "I do not feel in the least troubled that God will overrule all things for good."[56]

A brawl with his students was hardly a sign of maturity, nonetheless he was excessively proud of his sensational stand against the Unitarian menace. "To be reviled while one is trying to do good, is honorable—a privilege I have never deserved—but which I prize," he wrote righteously to his brother William.[57] Stirred by the adrenaline of battle, he threw himself into religious activities, helping the local minister, teaching Sunday school, and speaking at various church meetings five or six nights a week—"between you and me," he bragged to Chauncey, "the good folks of Hopkinton are somewhat pleased with this schoolmaster."[58]

Returning to Amherst, Henry now jumped at any chance to speak in public, leading prayer meetings, conducting a Bible class for the young ladies of the village, and delivering lectures on phrenology and temperance in the surrounding villages.

Temperance was the hot topic of the moment, with each speech ending in a dramatic call for everyone in the audience to sign "the pledge." The instant feedback was exhilarating. "I was addicted to going out and making temperance speeches," recalled Henry.[59]

Eunice came to as many of these speeches as she could, and her admiration for "My great Henry" was boundless. He used his first, unusually generous, lecture fee of five dollars to buy Eunice a gift: a copy of Richard Baxter's classic religious treatise *The Saint's Everlasting Rest*, a meditation on the heavenly bliss awaiting good Christians—"not a usual love-token," she remarked dryly.[60]

The summer after his junior year, Orson Fowler arranged for Henry to give a major temperance lecture on the Fourth of July in Brattleboro, Vermont. It was a rousing success, and his delighted hosts promised him the magnificent sum of ten dollars to cover his expenses. Elated, he returned to school "no longer a mere student, but a public man, one who had made speeches, one who determined to be modest and not allow success to puff him up," he remembered.

But vanity quickly overwhelmed his halfhearted humility. For a perpetually poor boy, who had to borrow cash to pay for the postage on his letters, the arrival of the ten-dollar bill in the mail was a red-letter day. "O that bill!" Henry recalled. "How it warmed me and invigorated me! I looked at it before going to sleep; I examined my pocket the next morning early, to be sure that I had not dreamed it. How I pitied the *poor* students, who had not, I well knew, ten dollars in *their* pockets."[61]

The money did not linger long in his trousers. Walking into the local bookshop, he spied the works of the English orator Edmund Burke. "With the ease and air of a rich man I bought and paid for them," Henry said, and then arranged them artfully on his desk, hoping to inspire whispers of envy among his friends. "After this I was a man that owned a library!" he recalled with fresh pleasure. Now "every penny I could raise or save I compelled to transform itself into books!" By the time he graduated his little library numbered almost fifty volumes.[62]

With his last eighty-five cents he bought a plain gold engagement ring for Eunice.

Theirs was a deeply romantic relationship, and if blushing hints of kisses, carriage rides, and covered bridges are reliable, it was also very sensual. Henry put his fiancée on a tall pedestal. "She is as I should think Mother was—and is in *some* respects like *Mary*," he told Harriet.[63] Eunice did share many characteristics with the female Beechers. They were all intelligent, affectionate, and strong willed, with a keen sense of humor and the ability to sacrifice and work hard. But Eunice had more in common with the public sisters—Catharine, Harriet, and Isabella—than with the modest, soft-spoken Mary and Roxana. Eunice's inbred ethic of female self-sacrifice concealed potent, if unformed, ambitions.

Nonetheless Eunice differed from his family in crucial ways. Her drives and desires were as strong as any of theirs, but it was the rare woman in the nineteenth century who was raised to express herself as openly as a Beecher, male or female. While Henry was an optimist who channeled his insecurity into jokes, Eunice was a pessimist who expressed insecurity through hypochondria, false modesty, and jealousy. Thirty years later she could name every rival for her fiancé's affection, marking *"Mindwell Gould"* in particular.[64]

Illness was her most common response to feeling neglected, disrespected, or socially awkward. For a young woman growing up in a physician's family, sickness, guilt, and attention were all closely linked. She joked openly that any Bullard brother who was ill was the brother most loved at the moment. At a time when even minor maladies could lead to death, illness was a way to wrest the spotlight away from her siblings and to get her family's unconcealed love.

At heart Eunice was a profoundly lonely young woman who fished for compliments or complained of aches and pains because she knew no other way to reassure herself that she was truly loved. "I know I'm a fretful girl *sometimes* but if others would only give me kind *words and looks* always, I'm very sure I should never fret whatever else might be my lot in life," said Eunice.[65] Nowadays we might say she lacked self-esteem. Yet even in that more sentimental era, it was unwise to put oneself at the mercy of a world filled with hard looks and unkind words.

In June 1833 the lovers set out separately to visit Henry's brother William, who was preaching in Middletown, Connecticut, and his new wife. Henry and Eunice described the holiday in very different but characteristic ways. For Henry it was a triumph, an opportunity to show off his smart, pretty fiancée to his oldest brother. For Eunice it was a miserable trip alone on a crowded stagecoach in which no one spoke to her, except for a young lady with motion sickness who asked to switch seats.

Once the two were reunited in Middletown, she was again struck by illness. Walking to church on a rainy Sunday, her shoes became worn down and hurt her feet, creating blisters. Overnight the pain worsened in her foot and leg, until at length she began to feel spasms in her neck and jaw—the telltale signs of lockjaw, or what we now know as tetanus. The local doctor administered a poultice to the sores and gave her a drink of "fermentations of hops" (presumably some sort of beer), which eased her symptoms. Eunice was sure she had narrowly cheated death.

No one speculated openly that the spasms might have come from the tension of meeting her new relatives (which would explain why beer—no longer considered a remedy for tetanus—might help). William and his wife left no recorded opinion of the visit, but it is notable that the trip ended early, as Henry reported, when Eunice, "at the urgent request of my brother and sister returned me to school."[66]

But if others did not always see Eunice's charms, to Henry she offered the loyalty, attention, and affection he had always lacked in his own family. He had good reason to feel neglected. When the older children left home, Lyman plied them with long letters brimming with affection and advice. By contrast, Henry rarely heard from his preoccupied parents or older siblings. After the family left for Ohio, Henry was crushed when he did not receive a letter from his family for almost six months.

Finally a letter arrived from Harriet, delayed by the long, slow trip east. As he sat by the fire in his dorm room reading it, the old insecurity and self-pity welled up, now bolstered by the image of himself as the Romantic loner. "I began your letter in mighty good spirits, but am almost a mind to cry now I've finished it," he began his reply to Harriet:

Mail after mail was come and wildly disappointed my eager expectations. I will not trouble you with complaints again—and for a long time to come will not pester you with letters. Dear sister in sober truth I find no place with so little sympathy as home, and I must say it—I almost always feel that my friends despise me. I know I don't deserve it—tho' they think I do. I don't—for I am not deceitful as mother has said. I *am careless* and I never found freedom in telling my plans. I shrink from my own kindred for it always seemed they looked coldly upon me. I ought not to have written this—but I could not help it, for it swelled as it often does till it seems as tho' my heart would burst. I never tell Eunice of it. I find there a home for all I want and am not unkindly thought of by her who is indeed very dear to me and will be to you. Don't you show this to *anybody*, I don't want father to know I feel bad, ever, for he is *always* kind to me—but I think he feels a *sorrowful* kindness and that is what *cuts* me more keenly.

In this jumble of emotions, it isn't clear what he means by deceit, but one thing is obvious: In Eunice, Henry finally found the unconditional love and admiration he longed for.

HENRY ENTERED HIS SENIOR YEAR of college very much the big man on campus. He was elected president of both the Athenian Society and the Society of Natural History, had several pieces coming out in the literary magazines, and the college band had just acquired snazzy new white-and-black uniforms. He had a room on campus surrounded by all his friends. *This* was the year, he assured Chauncey, that they would have some fun.

Academically he was finally free of Greek and was taking subjects that genuinely interested him: political economy, anatomy, rhetoric, and moral philosophy. By now Henry seemed to care little for what his professors thought ("Indeed to be honest I have not looked at a lesson this term until in the recitation room," he confessed to a friend[67])—but occasionally his touchy pride overwhelmed his easygoing nature, making him defensive and defiant.

"To some my college course has seemed a shameless waste of time and money," he wrote to Chauncey just before classes began. Such criticism, he declared, came from uninspired grinds who were content to regurgitate the worn-out rhetoric of old men. If they prefer "drowning their meager ideas in those of others—or be versed in the whole system of argumentation by cramming with x & y's—+ & ='s, let them." He, for one, had loftier goals. "I court a place not among great geniuses merely—but among the great benefactors of mankind," he told Chauncey.

> For this reason poetry—beautiful writing have been my delight. Mathematics, etc. have been of little esteem. Reasoning and splendid logic have been like spirits which possessed me. I do not mean with their efficiency but with deep admiration of them. I long to see some theological tenets exploded—to get up out of labyrinths which the whole creation have stumbled together in till now—to untwist many fallacious modes of reasoning which have no more foundations in the Bible than in the stars—views of God—of man—of doctrines.[68]

Yet, for all Henry's noble protests, his iconoclastic ambitions warred with his Beecher breeding. He now had enough education and confidence to question the old orthodoxies and traditional social conventions, but not enough to repudiate them completely or to craft his own conclusions. In his own words, he had "strength enough to row out, but not enough to fight the tide to get back to shore."[69] Most of the time he simply trod water, waiting for a wave of conviction to wash him ashore.

As in the 1960s, the exhilarating spirit of "Newness" on campus soon spilled over into aggressive rebellion. Over the course of his senior year, the college was bedeviled by conflicts between the administration and the student body. The faculty infuriated the boys by banning anonymous essays in the literary clubs after their satires grew too nasty. They expelled several seniors for "gross immorality," including drinking, cardplaying, stealing college property, and a hint of fornication.[70] Complaining that their education ought not be tainted by coarse competition, a group of students petitioned to abolish the system of honorary speaking appointments at graduation and other public performances. When the trustees refused, the boys boycotted their speaking appointments in protest. But one issue towered above all these controversies: the battle over slavery.

Slavery was not a common topic when Henry entered college. The last time it had dominated public debate was in 1820, when Congress deadlocked over whether slavery would be legal in the new western states. The conflict grew so rancorous that, for a time, it seemed that the fragile bonds of the United States might snap. Disunion was narrowly averted by the Missouri Compromise, which preserved the federal balance of power by admitting Maine as a free state and Missouri as a slave state, and confined slavery below the latitude of 36° 30' (excepting Missouri itself), which separated North from South. While many Northerners disapproved of human bondage, nearly all viewed it as a dangerous political quagmire, best left alone.

But this new generation, born after the upheaval of the Revolutionary era and mere children during the Compromise debates, was less fearful and more idealistic. Inspired by men like Lyman Beecher and Charles Grandison Finney, with their thundering insistence that *now* was the time to repent and immediately cease sinning, many genuinely saw themselves as their brothers' keepers, duty bound to emancipate the world from sin.

As they threw themselves into a variety of humanitarian and moral reform campaigns, it was inevitable that they would eventually turn their attention to the enforced bondage of more than two million dark-skinned Americans. Reared to view all the world through the lens of evangelical religion, they did not see slavery as a question of political compromise but of religious principle. As such, they must act. "Young gentlemen," the Reverend Beecher often insisted, "anything can be done that ought to be done."[71]

On the slavery question, however, Lyman Beecher was not in the vanguard. "Never a conservative and never quite a radical," as one family friend described him, Lyman viewed moral reform more as a means of restoring traditional social order than a path to democratic liberation.[72] He regarded slavery as evil and encouraged efforts to end it. Yet, like many Christians, his sympathy for the slave was offset by inbred bigotry. Born when slavery was still legal in the North and raised in a culture of strict social hierarchies, Lyman had, as his future son-in-law observed, "without being conscious of it, not a little of the old Connecticut prejudice about blacks."[73] Lyman himself had held two black teenage girls as indentured servants for a number of years.

As with Finney's controversial "New Measures," Lyman feared that this volatile issue would taint his wider religious crusade. Instead he advocated gradual emancipation, supporting the American Colonization Society, which proposed to end slavery by purchasing and then deporting slaves back to Africa. It was a scheme that put as much emphasis on ridding America of free blacks as on ridding it of slavery.

In 1829, a balding, bespectacled twenty-six-year-old printer named William Lloyd Garrison called on the preacher, announcing that under Beecher's influence he had come to believe that human bondage was a heinous sin and that Christians should demand that slaveholders immediately repent and free their slaves. Following Beecher's example, he wished to start a national organization and a newspaper to awaken the conscience of Americans. He was asking for Beecher's help.

To Garrison's surprise, Lyman put the young man off, saying, "I have too many irons in the fire already."

"Then you had better let all your irons burn than neglect your duty to the slave," he retorted brazenly.

Lyman softened but did not relent. "Your zeal is commendable, but you are misguided. If you will give up your fanatical notions and be guided by us (the clergy), we will make you the Wilberforce of America," referring to the legendary statesman who led the movement to ban slavery in the English colonies.[74] Garrison left unsatisfied. Once more he appealed to Beecher by letter, but he received no answer.

Undaunted, Garrison went around to the other Boston churches, but every clergyman echoed Lyman's response—they sympathized with his arguments but the issue was too explosive to touch. Finally Garrison decided to go it alone. When he published the first issue of the *Liberator* in January 1831, his masthead was a deliberate rebuke to these stodgy churchmen: "I do not wish to think, or speak, or write, with moderation. . . . I am in earnest—I will not equivocate—I will not excuse—I will not retreat a single inch—and *I will be heard*."[75]

Garrison's newspaper might have languished in obscurity had it not been for an astonishing turn of events. In the summer of 1831 a Virginia slave named Nat Turner led a band of fellow bondsmen in an armed revolt, slaughtering several white families before being caught and hanged. Suddenly people who had never thought twice about slavery were gripped by a terror of murderous slave uprisings. Overnight the nascent abolition movement was thrust into the spotlight, as Garrison and his ilk were denounced as pernicious, violent agitators.

True to his word, Garrison did not retreat. In 1832 he published *Fiery Thoughts on African Colonization*, a watershed pamphlet denouncing the American Colonization Society as "the scurvy device of men stealers," in his famous phrase. Colonization was not only impractical, he argued (estimating that in fifteen years fewer than fifteen hundred blacks had been sent to Liberia, while the population of slaves was increasing at an annual rate of 150,000), but it was immoral, rationalizing Northern bigotry while pandering to Southern slave owners. When Lyman defended the Colonization Society, Garrison charged him with hypocrisy for refusing to endorse the immediate abolition of slavery while demanding that everyone immediately cease all other sins.

Garrison's stand electrified the righteous young men of Amherst, prompting vigorous public debate and private soul-searching. Radicalized by his arguments, ten bold students quit the College Colonization Society and made Amherst one of the first schools in the nation to establish a College Antislavery Society. Within a year the society grew to seventy members, nearly one-quarter of the student body. These were not troublemakers, but the most mature and pious students in the school, more than half of them bound for the clergy. So they were surprised when the nervous faculty asked both the Colonization and Antislavery societies to disband voluntarily, saying that they were injuring the cause of religion and threatening the prosperity of the college. The colonizationists quickly complied, but the abolitionists refused on principle.

In many ways it was a classic generation gap, with the older generation hoist by its own petard. After years of cultivating the moral consciences and religious passions of these boys, the faculty were startled when they turned their well-sharpened scruples against traditional authority. Steeped in a potent mixture of strong emotion, unyielding idealism, and social activism, these young "Romantic radicals," as they came to be known, were equally startled by the stodginess of their elders.

On the slavery question, as in virtually all of these squabbles, both petty and profound, we find Henry hewing to the moderate middle, stranded awkwardly between the generations. By training and temperament he was a natural recruit for the Antislavery Society. He took a lively interest in various reform movements, and several of his closest friends were among its founders. Privately he referred to himself as an abolitionist.

But much as Henry admired cultural iconoclasm, he inherited his father's political temperament. He shied away from the grand revolutionaries, leaning instead toward the conservative gradual reformism of the famed English Whig Edmund Burke, whom he deeply admired. And when facing disapproval, Henry instinctively mouthed the cant of conventional Christianity, often echoing his father's opinions verbatim. Taking a stand for immediate abolition would have been a public betrayal of his father in his skirmish with William Lloyd Garrison. Instead Henry avoided official debate on the topic, his literary magazine reviewed Garrison's *Thoughts on Colonization* unfavorably, and he declined to add his name to the Antislavery Society's rolls. When the faculty forcibly shut down the society, he did not protest.

Many years later, when public opinion had shifted, he would forget all this, recalling that he took the side of immediate emancipation against colonization in the Athenian club debates. But that was simply rewriting history.

FOR EUNICE THIS LAST YEAR of college was one of mounting anxiety. As each day passed, she became more miserable at the prospect of Henry's leaving for Ohio without her. She begged her father to let her go west as a schoolteacher, but he refused, and in the weeks before graduation Eunice spiraled into depression.

The Amherst College Commencement was the high point of the year for both town and gown. Not long after dawn on August 27, 1834, peddlers and farmers with wares to sell began to stake out spots on the green. As the morning air grew heavy and hot, the road outside the Congregational Church filled with carriages of every type, from lowly oxcarts to elegant four-in-hands. By nine o'clock the pews were overflowing, and perspiring young men jammed the back of the church. On the front platform the trustees and visiting dignitaries sat in stiff formality, and a choir perched in the center gallery.

President Humphrey opened the ceremonies and then introduced the first student speaker. Another speaker followed, then another and another. On and on the young orators droned, but Henry was not among them. Graduation speakers were chosen based on academic grades, and of thirty-nine students graduating, he was one of only thirteen who had no role in the commencement exercises.

Undoubtedly Henry's pride was stung, but he hid his feelings with humor. He later liked to say that the only time he stood next to the head of his class was when they were all arranged in a circle. There were other disappointments as well. No family or far-flung friends were in the audience except for Harriet, who made the arduous ten-day trip from

Cincinnati to Toledo by stagecoach, to Buffalo by steamboat, to Albany by canalboat, arriving by stage in Amherst. Lyman and Catharine had come east as well, but were too busy with fund-raising to attend the ceremony. But Henry could boast of one source of distinction. There, printed in the commencement program next to his name, where other boys listed commonplace Yankee villages, was his exotic new hometown: Cincinnati, Ohio.

When the ceremony ended, nearly three hundred graduates and guests trooped across the common to enjoy a celebratory dinner. The food was abundant but there was not a drop of liquor to be seen, recalled an astonished English visitor. Without the lubrication of liquor, the virtuous diners cleared out quickly to promenade the common. "Yet there was no sport, no show, no merrymaking of any kind," the Englishman marveled. "But there was, as remarkably characteristic, in the midst of this bustle, a Yankee auctioneer resolved to improve the occasion. He was mounted in a cart and selling, or trying to sell, books, prints, harness, and carriages—the very carriage he came in."[76]

After commencement Henry spent a final few days with Eunice. As he lit out for the West, she bade him farewell knowing that she might never lay eyes on him again.

Chapter 4

"IT WAS A FEARFUL THING TO PULL UP A
NEW ENGLAND OAK BY THE ROOTS AT A RIPENED AGE
AND TRANSPLANT IT TO THE SOIL OF THE WEST"

*C*incinnati was in the grip of a heat wave when Henry stepped out onto the city's famous Public Landing, a wide limestone quay extending three hundred feet along the Ohio River. For the last two years he had read everything he could find on Ohio, but nothing could have prepared him for the sight of his new home in August 1834.

The first surprise was the pigs. Swine were everywhere, rooting through the gutters, blocking the roadways—visibly earning the city's nickname of Porkopolis. Then there was the startling array of vehicles. Along the cobblestone bank, wagons, carts, and coaches of every kind jockeyed for space among the crates and barrels, pigs and passengers. Down below, hundreds of boats such as he'd never seen were slowly making their way down the river or vying for a place to dock: double- and triple-decked steamboats, low-lying canalboats, rough-hewn canoes, and flat-bottomed riverboats weighed down with lumber, coal, or livestock.

And the people! The streets were a kaleidoscope of accents, complexions, and customs—tough Kentucky roustabouts and threadbare German and Irish immigrants, aristocratic New Orleans cotton merchants and high-toned Virginia planters, stiff-backed Yankee lawyers and stolid Pennsylvania Dutch farmers, mulatto grog-shop keepers and wary former slaves.

This was no frontier outpost. With a burgeoning population of thirty thousand, "the Queen City of the West," as locals proudly dubbed it, was a place of tremendous ambition and plenty of hubris. Geographically it was the hub of the West, a trading center linked in all directions by the Ohio and Mississippi rivers. The fame of the city extended across the Atlantic, attracting European travelers curious to see this New World metropolis. Cincinnati was a truly "singular spectacle," observed Alexis de Tocqueville when he visited in 1831. "All that there is of good or of bad in American society is to be found there in such strong relief, that one would be tempted to call it one of those books printed in large letters for teaching children to read; everything there is in violent contrast, exaggerated; nothing has fallen into its final place: society is growing more rapidly than man."[1] It was just the place for an independent-minded young man to make a name for himself.

The town was constructed on a series of terraces rising up from the river into an amphitheater of thickly forested hills. Walking up from the landing, past the warehouses and stores of Front Street, it began to feel more like New England. Elegant wood-framed shops and trim brick houses surrounded by flower gardens lined the wide, paved streets. The familiar feeling was no illusion. There on Vine Street stood the graceful mansions of John and Samuel Foote—the brothers of Henry's mother, Roxana—who had settled in Cincinnati some years earlier. Here too were General Edward King, Harriet Porter Beecher's prosperous cousin, and many old friends from Litchfield Law School.

As Henry climbed the hill heading out of town, up the winding dirt road that led to Lane Theological Seminary, the trepidation of the new gave way to a very different sort of anxiety. After seven years away at school, he was returning to the bosom of his family. For the next three years he would live under his father's roof and study theology under his father's watchful eye. As he made his way through a grove of ancient beeches and buckeyes, past a clearing of fresh stumps and the raw log cabins that housed the seminary students, up to the new president's house, Henry was even less prepared for what he found. The campus was nearly deserted.

TWO YEARS EARLIER the arrival of the Beecher family had been heralded as a divine coup by all the "best people" of Cincinnati. Luring America's most famous preacher away from Boston was indisputable proof of the city's rising stature. A cadre of transplanted Yankees and other "intelligent, New England sort of folks," as Catharine Beecher called them, offered them a warm welcome.[2] They invited the family to their literary clubs and evening soirees, donated money to Beecher pet projects, and sent their daughters to Catharine's newly founded Western Female Academy. Within six months of opening, Lane Seminary was thriving. It had an enrollment of one hundred students and the generous financial backing of Arthur and Lewis Tappan, wealthy New York silk merchants turned evangelical philanthropists. Soon, boasted the locals, Lane Seminary would be the Princeton of the West.

Nonetheless the move was difficult for the Beechers. "It was a fearful thing to pull up a New England oak by the roots at a ripened age and transplant it to the soil of the West," observed a family friend.[3] It required great adjustments. The women of the family were heartbroken at leaving the family ties and creature comforts of the East. In compliance with a complex interdenominational agreement, Lyman had to switch his religious denomination from Congregationalism, the relatively democratic version of Calvinism that ruled in New England, to the more rigid ecclesiastical hierarchy of Presbyterianism that dominated everywhere else.

Religion in general was different out West. There were no settled religious traditions there, only a bustling spiritual marketplace, with dozens of sects vying for public attention. Commerce was the one true religion of Cincinnati. Anything that rocked the boat or restricted an individual's freedom to strike a good bargain was considered a secular sin. Personal liberty was the great lure of the West, and no one was less popular here than those meddling, holier-than-thou Yankee immigrants, who made it their mission to "Puritanize, Yankeeize" everyone into being just like them.[4]

It was only a matter of time before Beecher zeal ran up against Buckeye boosterism. Within a year of his arrival Lyman had affronted so many of the working class and Roman Catholics that a local newspaper referred to him as "The Right Reverend and Awful Lyman Beecher, D.D.—The wily political priest."[5] His impolitic essay, A Plea for the West, which called for eastern missionaries to civilize the wild western infidels, outraged the city's elite, who regarded Cincinnati society as the height of sophistication. Just as Henry was setting out for Ohio, the national press was excoriating Lyman for delivering a series of anti-Catholic sermons in Boston, accusing him of inspiring a mob to burn down an Ursuline convent in Charlestown, Massachusetts. But these were minor squalls compared to the tempest brewing over slavery.

The force behind Lane's antislavery fracas was a student named Theodore Dwight Weld, whose piercing eyes, thick black beard, and powerful charisma conjured the image of a wild bear. Like many activists of his generation, Theodore Weld was converted to Christianity by Charles Grandison Finney, and to abolition by William Lloyd Garrison. At the age of thirty-three Weld was older than many of the other divinity students and had already earned some fame as an orator and evangelical reformer. His influence helped persuade the Tappans to join the antislavery cause and to donate the money that paid Lyman Beecher's salary. Weld also recruited many of the pupils who poured into Lane that first year.

That first class of theological students was the cream of the radical generation of 1830. Brilliant and disciplined, they were unusually zealous, even by Beecher standards. They were, as Charles Beecher described them, "a noble class of young men, uncommonly strong, a little uncivilized, entirely radical, and terribly in earnest." The students adored Weld. "In the estimation of the class, he was president," Lyman remembered with some bitterness; "they thought he was a god."[6] They were the perfect soil for Weld's antislavery seed.

FROM THE DISTANCE OF 150 YEARS it is difficult to understand how Americans could have tolerated slavery. Thousands of books have explored the complex social factors that kept the "peculiar institution" alive for so long. Boiled down to its essence, however, there were two primary obstacles to the emancipation of the slaves:

The first was the Constitution. The second was the Bible.

Surely, one might protest, both the Bill of Rights and the Golden Rule establish revolutionary democratic principles that prohibit slavery: equality under the law and equality under God. But the Sermon on the Mount and the Bill of Rights were manifestos, not covenants and contracts. The devil, as they say, is in the details.

The apostles of Christ and the founding fathers of the Republic were pragmatic revolutionaries. Few converts would be won by calling for the wholesale destruction of old social institutions, no matter how inequitable. Instead they found more success applying Christian and democratic principles to improve and regulate the social institutions that already existed—including slavery. Neither the Constitution nor the Bible required slavery to exist, and neither explicitly endorsed slavery as a social good. But both documents enshrined slavery as a normal, legal, even godly, fact of life.

In the Constitution slavery is subtly but deeply entrenched. The founding fathers explicitly recognized the legal status of slaves, describing them as "three fifths of all other Persons," for the purpose of allotting congressional representatives, in Article one, section two. Article four, section two, requires that all persons "held to Service or Labor in one State, under Laws thereof, escaping to another"—that is, runaway slaves—must be returned to their owners. If individual states wished to abolish slavery they could, but the federal government could do nothing without amending the Constitution by national consensus.[7]

Slavery figures far more prominently in the Bible. It makes its first appearance in the book of Genesis, and plays a prominent role throughout the Old Testament and in the lessons of Christ's apostles. Indeed, some of the Lord's most favored subjects were slaveholders—including Abraham, the recipient of God's original sacred covenant with humanity. At no point does the Bible explicitly call for the abolition of slavery or for the exclusion of slaveholders from the church, even in the most egalitarian teachings of the New Testament. At best the Bible describes how to make bondage more consistent with God's laws. At worst the words of Leviticus 25:44–46 seem like a solid endorsement of African American enslavement:

> Both thy bondmen, and thy bondmaids, which thou shalt have, shall be of the heathen that are round about you; of them shall ye buy bondmen and bondmaids. Moreover of the children of the strangers that do sojourn among you, of them shall ye buy, and of their families that are with you, which they begot in your land; and they shall be your possession. And ye shall take them as an inheritance for your children after you, to inherit them for a possession; they shall be your bondmen forever.

In favor of the idea that Jesus Christ commands us to treat everyone as equals, antislavery Christians cited New Testament verses like Colossians 3:11: "Where there is neither Greek nor Jew, circumcision nor uncircumcision, Barbarian, Scythian, bond nor free: but Christ is all, and in all." On slavery specifically, however, Christ was silent.

Until the 1830s slavery in the United States was conceived primarily as a constitutional issue—an approach that always ended in political impasse. The genius of these early evangelical activists was to reframe it as a matter of personal morality. If slaveholding were declared "a sin *per se*," and unrepentant slaveholders barred from spiritual communion and respectable Christian society, they might be persuaded or shamed into emancipating their slaves, thus avoiding political upheaval.

So the first, formidable order of business for the antislavery activists was to persuade the churches to reinterpret the Bible, with less attention to the letter and more to the spirit of Christ. Together Theodore Weld and his patrons, Arthur and Lewis Tappan, were determined to make Lane Seminary the leader in this revisionist theological movement and the western headquarters of the antislavery crusade. Unfortunately they did not inform President Beecher of their plans.

When Weld arrived at the seminary in Walnut Hills, he was surprised to find that President Beecher shied away from the slavery question and that most of the students shared his conservative views. "I suppose there was a general consent in the institution that slavery was somehow wrong and to be got rid of," as one student put it. "There was not a readiness to pronounce it a sin."[8] As for the immediate abolition movement, as Weld wrote to Lewis Tappan, it "was regarded as the climax of absurdity, fanaticism and blood."[9] Undeterred, Weld set out to win the students to the antislavery cause one by one. By the end of the fall term Weld had assembled enough supporters to propose a public debate.

Weld arranged the event like an extended revival meeting rather than a traditional debate. For eighteen nights "Prayer Hall" was packed with students, faculty, and townspeople come to watch the fireworks. In contrast to the literal reading of Scripture taught by the hyperorthodox, Weld and his team took a more liberal, openly interpretive approach to the Bible. Noting that there were many acknowledged wrongs the Bible did not specifically name as sins (drunkenness was a prime example), they argued that Christ's command to treat the poor and oppressed as one would treat oneself superseded all other Scripture. Several Southern students testified to the horrible conditions of slaves in their home states, and James Bradley, Lane's only black student, told the heartrending tale of how he had purchased his own freedom from bondage. The debate concluded with an overwhelming vote in favor of immediate emancipation.

Straightaway the eager students formed their own Antislavery Society, and began putting their principles into action, establishing Bible classes, free schools, and a library in "Bucktown," Cincinnati's black slum. Arguing by example, Weld and his band socialized freely in the black community, attending prayer meetings, weddings, and funerals, and even boarding in black homes.

This was dangerous business. Cincinnati, it was often said, stands in the North but turns its face to the South. The city lay directly across the river from the slave state of Kentucky, serving as a regional market for Virginia planters, Kentucky farmers, and Louisiana merchants, as well as a fuel stop for steamboats hauling gangs of shackled blacks to the slave market in New Orleans. It was also the first Northern stop for runaway slaves and boasted one of the largest free black populations in the country. When word got out of the students' doings, President Beecher was swamped by complaints from local leaders. Some were motivated by commercial cowardice, fearing that Southerners would take their business elsewhere. But it was the social intermingling that set off the most visceral anger.

Instead of promoting tolerance, the visible presence of so many free blacks drove white Cincinnatians to magnify the privileges of white skin. Official "Black Codes" forbade African Americans from testifying in court and attending public schools, and custom barred them from all but the lowest jobs. Even white paupers in the poorhouse wouldn't carry water for their own use, leaving it to the black paupers. Yet despite the obsession with segregation—and the fact that most mixed-race "mulattoes" were the fruit of white masters forcing themselves on female slaves—racist fears of "amalgamation" were not unfounded. In Cincinnati one antebellum census counted fourteen mulattoes for every ten blacks, compared, for example, to New York City, which had three mulattoes for every ten blacks. The vision of thousands of newly freed slaves pouring across the river, competing for jobs, and intermarrying with whites was too much for most Ohioans to bear.

These local fears were inflamed by the shocking news stories flooding in from across the country. Everywhere the emerging abolition movement was provoking a violent backlash. In July 1834, as Henry was preparing for his college graduation, white rioters raged through New York City, burning down the home of Arthur Tappan's brother Lewis before heading into an armed standoff with the dry-goods clerks who were standing watch at Arthur's silk warehouse. In September, Prudence Crandall, a Quaker schoolteacher who dared start a boarding school for black girls in Connecticut, was literally burned out of her home, then driven out of the state. Cincinnati's newspapers picked up the savage drumbeat, warning darkly that such things could happen here.

Under pressure from Lane's trustees, Lyman pleaded with Weld and his followers to be more discreet, insisting that "true wisdom consists in advocating a cause only so far as the community will sustain the reformer."[10] The students were outraged that Dr. Beecher, of all people, would ask them to compromise their religious principles for fear of public opinion. It was the defining paradox of Lyman's style of leadership, as his daughter Harriet noted: "People who thus set the example of free and independent thinking in one or two respects, and yet hope to constrain their disciples to think exactly as they do on all other subjects, generally reckon without their host."[11]

If Lyman misjudged his students, he also mistook his new hometown. At the end of 1834's spring term he departed on a long fundraising trip through the eastern states, assuming that the controversy would die out over the summer vacation. Instead tensions mounted as an oppressive heat wave settled on the valley, sweeping in a deadly epidemic of cholera. They climaxed in August with the rumor that a group of young black women had been seen riding up to Walnut Hills for a picnic with the students. Around town it was whispered that a mob was planning to march on the seminary.

Only days before the fall term was to begin, the trustees, infuriated by the unrepentant "niggerism" of the students, voted to ban the school's Antislavery Society, to outlaw all discussion of slavery even in private, and to fire the one openly abolitionist professor. They also made plans to expel Theodore Weld. All they needed was for the president to return and ratify their vote. Until then, they announced, they were shutting down the campus entirely.

WHEN HENRY WARD BEECHER ARRIVED in Walnut Hills, the humid air was thick with anxiety. The students were dispersed, and his father still had not returned from the East. The trustees and students were locked in furious brinksmanship, and there was talk of raising a mob to clear out the whole damned nest of abolitionists. Word of the crisis at Lane had spread quickly through the religious and reform newspapers, and was picked up by the mainstream press. This was now a national spectacle, with all eyes on Lyman Beecher, watching to see which side he would take. Oliver Johnson, a former Boston parishioner, remembered the cascade of prayers pleading for the great Reverend Beecher to defy the bigotry of public opinion, just as he had once stood against the liquor trade.

When Lyman finally returned in early October, he was besieged by both sides to resolve the standoff. But he could not fathom the intense passions on each side. Lyman's sympathy for the students' cause was growing, but he also saw the very real peril in challenging the racial and political status quo. When he asked the students to compromise their principles for the sake of the school, they declared that they would rather withdraw altogether. Lyman begged them to stay, but it was too late. Their faith had been shattered.

The Lane imbroglio was a crucial turning point for both the antislavery movement and the Beecher family. Lyman's very presence in the Lane fiasco focused the nation on the relationship between slavery and religion with new intensity. Many observers were convinced that the early leadership of a man like Dr. Beecher might have unified Christian sentiment behind the antislavery movement, possibly averting the Civil War. "I verily believe," Oliver Johnson wrote fifty years later, "that if Lyman Beecher had been true to Christ and to liberty in that trying hour, the whole course of American history in regard to slavery would have been changed, and that the slaves might have been emancipated without the shedding of blood."[12]

Instead no one was pleased with his choice. In some circles Beecher was tarred as a hypocrite and a tyrant. "He was a trimmer, and had less respect to the means than the end," Lewis Tappan observed of Lyman, using contemporary slang for an unprincipled compromiser. "He believed in the doctrine of expedience to a criminal excess, I thought."[13]

Editorializing in the *Liberator*, William Lloyd Garrison announced that Lane Seminary "is now to be regarded as stricktly a Bastille of oppression—a spiritual Inquisition," a sentiment Arthur Tappan paid to have widely reprinted in pamphlet form.[14] In Cincinnati and among the vast majority who were revolted by abolition, the seminary was considered a cauldron of radicalism and race mixing. When the smoke cleared, only seven pupils remained enrolled—including Henry and his brother Charles—and the school was teetering on the edge of bankruptcy.

For the Beecher children it was strange and upsetting to watch their mighty father beseeching these young men, many no older than Henry, to stay with him. "I can see him now, joining them in the little log house just opposite ours—pleading, remonstrating, with tears and almost with groans," Isabella, Lyman's eleven-year-old daughter, recalled. "I was but a child, but was in such sympathy with his distress that I never could forgive the young men for departing from such a loving guide and friend."[15]

Henry's feelings were more ambivalent. "I tell you one thing, Chauncey, I look back with more regret and longing on the old house and friends than ever the Israelites did to the leek dishes and boiled onions," he wrote to his college pal that fall. "But here I am and can't help myself." It was embarrassing to know that his college friends were reading the rumors and accusations, and he could not help being defensive. "You have heard all sorts of stories I suppose about Lane Seminary but it is not a Devil's den after all but a right down comfortable place—which I shall love . . . well," he insisted to Chauncey.[16]

Yet in these humiliating circumstances, it would be emotional treason to take any side but his father's. So Henry parroted Lyman's prejudices, blaming the fracas on the students' arrogance and extremism rather than Cincinnati's bigotry or his father's leadership. They "were ultra abolitionists—denunciators, self-congratulating and rash," and "when to their other follies they added that of walking with blacks—boarding with them, inviting them to the seminary, etc.," well, it was only natural that the community would condemn them. "Chauncey," he concluded, "you have no idea of ultraism till you have felt and seen it and its effects."[17]

But the age of ultraism was just beginning. Only six weeks after the term started, just as the campus was settling down and Henry was settling in, the other apple dropped. In November one of the founders of Lane Seminary, the Reverend Doctor Joshua Lacy Wilson, filed charges accusing Lyman Beecher of heresy, hypocrisy, and slander. The ecclesiastical trial was scheduled for the following May.

JUST AS IT HAD IN COLLEGE, Henry's natural buoyancy soon conquered his homesickness. The West suited him, with its free and easy manners, wide-open opportunities, and unashamed pursuit of happiness. Transplanted into this new culture, the old family patterns turned on their heads. After years of feeling like the family underdog, Henry was the one who was thriving.

Life in Ohio was difficult for the older Beechers. An unpredictable climate, frequent outbreaks of malaria and cholera, and sheer misery ate away at Harriet Porter's fragile health, piling more work on Aunt

Esther's long-suffering shoulders. Lyman was anxious and distracted by his upcoming heresy trial and the near-collapse of the seminary. As she entered her mid-thirties, the oldest child, Catharine, was growing frustrated and cantankerous. She quarreled with her sister Harriet over the administration of her new school, leaving Harriet overwhelmed and depressed by the drudgery of teaching. Twenty-seven-year-old George was now embarking on his first job in Batavia, Ohio; for him the normal challenges of a novice minister were exacerbated by wild mood swings.

Henry blew through this hothouse atmosphere like a cool breeze. He was, Isabella said, "so cheerful and funny that it kept us all good natured."[18] Henry and Harriet now reversed their old roles, with Henry providing inspiration and consolation; "he is more angel than brother," as Harriet told a friend "—he is too good for me."[19]

Even school, his old foe, had lost its menace. With four professors teaching only a handful of students, the seminary was a homey, informal place. Already absentminded by nature, Lyman was far too distracted to be a close disciplinarian or a rigorous teacher. Instead he treated all the students like sons, running classes like a boisterous kitchen-table debate, with everyone expected to pitch in with questions and arguments. "Theological students need a mustard plaster all over the body to wake them up, and to stimulate them to intense animation!" as Lyman liked to say. It was ironic that Lane now had a reputation for censoring free speech, as Henry observed. "The students after each lecture are full at questioning every nook and corner of the arguments until they get their belly full (excuse it, such a word!) of Abolition and everything else," he told Chauncey.[20]

Debate was so vigorous that Lyman occasionally found himself cornered. He once dug himself into a logical hole so deep that his only solution was to toss out a non sequitur, befuddling the boys just long enough for him to grab his hat and race out the classroom door. Lyman's unsystematic methods were perfect for Henry, and for the first time in his life he was his father's prodigy. Emotionally they were closer than they'd ever been.

Intellectually, however, the teacher who made the greatest impact was Calvin Stowe. Professor Stowe was Lane's one great scholar, a brilliant linguist who was fluent in a half dozen languages and a leader in the new field of historical biblical research. Tall and stocky, with a round face dominated by bushy eyebrows, Stowe was an eccentric, sensitive man of thirty-three—young enough to be part of the Romantic generation but old enough to be a good influence.

The two shared a room that first year, making poor Stowe the butt of Henry's pranks. Every morning the punctual professor had repeatedly to shake the sleepy-headed young man awake for early prayers. Finally one day Stowe simply left in disgust, abandoning Henry to his bed. As the door clicked shut, Henry somehow summoned the gumption to spring up, dress himself, and cut through the forest at a run so that, to Stowe's "almost frightened amazement," Henry was found "sitting directly under the Professor's desk, waiting for him, when he entered to conduct prayers."[21] No doubt it was a relief to the poor professor when he and Harriet Beecher fell deeply in love—with the happy prospect of replacing his bedfellow.

In November, Stowe began a weekly public lecture series on the Bible that turned everything Henry knew of Scripture on its ear. Unlike the preachers Henry grew up with, Stowe did not treat the Bible as if it were "a treatise written in the English language by New-Englanders, and in which every word must bear the exact sense of a New England metaphysical treatise," in Harriet's words.[22] Instead he drew on recent German scholarship, which treated the Bible as both divinely inspired literature and a complex historical document, translated from ancient languages and reflecting the mores of foreign cultures. "Read it simply for the sake of enjoying it; read it as a glowing description of a series of magnificent pictures which were passing before the eye of the writer," Stowe counseled in his introductory lecture on the Book of Revelation; "and remember while you read, that it is an Oriental, an Asiatic, and a Hebrew book."[23]

While Lyman referred to the Bible "as a code of laws," focusing on the binding covenants and punitive wrath of the Old Testament, Stowe drew Henry's attention to the parables of the New Testament. He turned the Gospels of Christ into a thrilling tale of twelve young apostles and their valiant leader, relying only on wits and eloquence to save the world. Instead of viewing Scripture "as a carpenter does his nail-box, going to it only to find screws and nails to hold together the framework of a theological system," now Henry imagined Jesus as a living, breathing man striding through the streets of Jerusalem, as real as any of the heroes he'd read about in books.[24]

Stowe's spiritual seeds would not bear fruit for several more years, but they rooted deeply in Henry's fertile imagination. As the end of the spring term approached, traditional analytic theology returned with a vengeance, as the entire school focused its attention on Lyman's heresy trial.

LYMAN BEECHER'S NEWEST NEMESIS was the Reverend Doctor Joshua Wilson, a tall, stone-faced man born on the Kentucky frontier in the late 1700s. For twenty-four years Dr. Wilson was the standard-bearer for Calvinism in Ohio. It was said that he was so rigid that he refused to hang pictures in his house because to do so violated the biblical prohibition against graven images, and so belligerent that his critics once set fire to his church. He was such a doctrinaire Presbyterian, Harriet joked, that he ranked the Bible as "the *next best book* to the Catechism."[25] Clearly threatened by this eastern interloper, Wilson began plotting against Beecher the moment the preacher set foot in Ohio. In the wake of the Lane rebellion, Wilson seized on Lyman's weakened state to root him out of the seminary and, if possible, out of the Presbyterian Church.

It is hard for modern minds to understand the rancor of this heresy trial. "To us the whole controversy seems so like tweedledum and tweedledee that it is impossible to take it seriously," as Lyman's own great-grandson observed. "But to them it was not only a matter of life and death, but one of eternal life and eternal death."[26] At issue were the same conflicted teachings on original sin and God's sovereignty that bewildered Henry as a child and drove the wedge between the Congregationalists and Unitarians in Boston.

This dispute seemed arcane even in 1835, but the conflict reflected a widening cultural divide in America. Ministers of all stripes were fighting to maintain their influence in a society growing ever more secular and diverse. Looking for a larger piece of shrinking pie, the Calvinists turned against one another. On one side were those who were attracted to rational liberalism, which emphasized free will, the dignity of humanity and its potential for progress, and a more openly interpretive approach to the Bible that tried to make it relevant to contemporary problems. On the other side were those who clung to an older form of fatalism, emphasizing mankind's subservience to a willful God and to traditional church authority, enforced by a strict and literal reading of Scripture.

Ever the politician, Lyman dealt with this impasse by what some considered a philosophical and psychological sleight of hand. The doctrine of original sin, as he and his New School brethren interpreted it, did not mean that humans were doomed to sin by Adam's fall from Eden, but that humans had an irresistible natural tendency to sin. Lyman even changed that cornerstone of Calvinism, the Westminster Assembly Catechism, so that when Henry and his siblings came to the line "No mere man since the fall is able perfectly to keep the command-ments of God," they were made instead to recite, "No man since the fall is willing to keep the commandments of God."

Henry put it plainly: "My father was tried for believing that a man could obey the commandments of God."[27]

This slick "Yankee answer," according to Dr. Wilson and his Old School supporters, was simply not supported by Scripture. To preach that God was bound by human laws of rationality was to lead people directly to the gates of hell. Wilson also charged Lyman with hypocrisy, claiming that he skipped from pulpit to pulpit, switched denominations in bad faith, and altered divine doctrines to suit different audiences.

No one who knew Lyman would ever accuse him of deliberate false-hood, but even his friends admitted that he had blind spots that might seem hypocritical. His rash pronouncements in the heat of battle often undermined him, his reasoning could be slippery and self-serving, and he preferred subtle strategizing to sweeping stands on principle. None of this was lost on Henry. "I know you're plagued good at twisting," he teased his father. "But if you can twist your creed onto the Westminster Confession you can twist better than I think you can."

"All my boys are smart," Lyman shot back, "and one of them is impudent."[28]

The news that the "great gun of Calvinism" was on trial for heresy quickly spread through the newspapers. Cincinnatians were torn among sympathy, exasperation, and displeasure that once again the Rever-end Beecher was making their city the center of national controversy. When the trial opened on June 9, 1835, in Lyman's Second Presbyterian Church in the center of town, the pews were packed. Calvin Stowe was appointed moderator, with the local church elders serving as justices.

The whole family turned out in support, but Henry was more "of a spectator than a partisan on either side," as Harriet put it delicately. More plainspoken, Isabella recalled him sitting in the choir gallery en-tertaining the young folk with a stream of sarcastic jokes about her fa-ther's opponents. In fact there was a juvenile air to the proceedings. "It is all—'I say you did' and 'I say you didn't' 'Joe begun at me first,' " Cal-vin Stowe later admitted.[29] In a match of wits and rhetoric, however, few could best Lyman Beecher, and on the eighth day he was acquitted by 23 votes to 12. Furious, Wilson appealed the decision to the next level of authority, the Presbyterian Synod in Dayton, forcing a retrial the following October.

After seven years on his own, it was a shock to be thrown back into his father's endless battles. "I went from my college life immediately to the West and there I fell into another fuliginous Christian atmosphere," Henry recalled years later. "How I despised and hated this abyss of whirling controversies that seemed to me to be filled with all manner of evil things, with everything indeed but Christ."[30]

Henry gave no outward sign of any spiritual distress, however. On June 27, 1835, three days after his twenty-second birthday, he opened a new leather-bound ledger book, picked up his goose quill pen, and began a journal. He made no mention of his father's recent trial; instead he was happily absorbed in a novel by Sir Walter Scott.

But then it is hard to know Henry's true feelings, for, as he confessed in his very first entry, his earlier efforts to keep a diary had been hampered because "I never could be *sincere*; the only use which I distinctly know that I have derived from it, is a knowledge of my being very averse to saying first what my feelings were—I could not help feeling: '*this* will perhaps *be seen.*' "

The lifelong conflict between Henry's desire for freedom and for approval was reaching its zenith. Perhaps it was simply the sincere insincerity of youth, as they say, or perhaps he was inspired by Lyman's deft exercise of mutually opposing ideas. Whatever the cause, Henry stumbled on a simple resolution to his dilemma. In this diary, he concluded, he will not "tell *all* my feelings." Instead "in mental *dishabille* I will stroll thro' my mind and do as I choose."[31] It was an odd and disarming form of sincerity—this frank declaration of one's own evasiveness—and over time it would become Henry's stock-in-trade.

Two weeks after Lyman's acquittal, another bitter blow fell on the family. After a decade of ill health and deepening depression, Henry's stepmother, Harriet Porter, passed away at the age of forty-five. A few days later a cryptic obituary appeared in the *Cincinnati Journal*, damning the dead woman with faint praise. Unlike the serene Roxana, when Harriet Porter approached death the memory of her lifelong failings "brought such anxiety and dismay that her spirit died within her, and it was not until after the most contrite acknowledgement of all she deemed her failings in duty to others [. . .] that her spirit found peace."[32] Signed only C, the obituary was likely authored by the increasingly sharp-tongued Catharine. No matter how she may have repented, Harriet Porter's stepchildren never forgave her for not being their mother.

Not one word of her death appears in Henry's diary.

~ ~

HENRY DID NOT LET his father's quarrels interfere with his lively social life. Nearly every afternoon after class he walked the two miles
into town, where he paid social calls and stopped by the post office,
courthouse, and newspaper offices to pick up the latest gossip. He made
friends with the city's workmen, mechanics, and steamboat captains,
who let him ride the river for free—a habit he would retain for the
rest of his life. He joined the church choir, the Young Men's Temperance Society, and the local phrenological club, and delivered speeches
wherever he could wangle an invitation. But his chief ambition was to
become a writer.

Cincinnati was the literary capital of the Mississippi Valley, boasting an impressive array of newspapers, magazines, print shops, and literary clubs. In contrast to the more genteel literary culture of the East, in
the West the newspaper was king. Here newspaper editors were men of
influence, equal in power to politicians and ministers. Opportunities to
publish abounded, and the Beechers quickly took advantage of them.
Catharine had already written two books on religion and education,
and Harriet produced a popular geography textbook and a number of
short stories, winning a fifty-dollar prize from Judge James Hall's prestigious *Western Monthly Magazine*.

Under Calvin Stowe's influence, Henry was reading more deeply
than he had before, developing a passion for Sir Walter Scott, Lord
Byron, Robert Burns, and George Crabbe, as well as for German literary criticism. He discovered Shakespeare, who initially struck him
as stiff and unrealistic but soon became his great idol. His opinions
were decidedly conventional, with a strong moralistic strain, but in the
West, where most people looked on "book learning" with suspicion, he
counted as an intellectual sophisticate.

Spurred by his sisters' example, Henry began contributing to the
local papers, especially the *Cincinnati Journal*, a Presbyterian paper that
covered the Beecher family's doings so thoroughly and sympathetically
that Harriet referred to it as "our family newspaper."[33] He reported on
debates and contributed occasional essays, most of which recapitulated
his father's views, including several attacking Catholicism and another
denouncing "Ultraism." He was immensely flattered by an invitation
to write on phrenology for the *Western Monthly Magazine*. Newspaper

editor wouldn't be a bad job, he began to think; perhaps he could be like Thomas Brainerd, the editor of the *Journal*, who was also a licensed minister.

Socially his father's Second Presbyterian Church was the center of Henry's world. It was the most upscale of the city's churches, boasting prominent members of the bar like Judge Jacob Burnet, Nathaniel Wright, and Edward Mansfield; large landowners like John H. Groesbeck; and many ambitious young men like Salmon P. Chase, who would go on to become chief justice of the U.S. Supreme Court.

But here as elsewhere, women were the true pillars of the church. Cincinnati's young women were a bit wild by eastern standards—socializing without chaperones, attending dances, reading questionable novels. "I reckon," wrote one shocked Lane student, "they would not answer for ministers' wives. Perhaps they would suit lawyers better."[34] But they were catnip to Henry. In fact, he reported to Chauncey, his new friends were "all among the softer sex."[35]

He began teaching a popular evening Bible class that quickly drew the daughters of the city's most influential men—Margaret Groesbeck, Mary Wright, Catharine Dickinson, Abbe Hall, Caroline Burnet. Henry was a rare commodity out West, high-minded but funny, boyish yet emotionally expressive, happy to pick flowers along the riverbank and take picnics up into the hills, or to sit for hours in a dim parlor talking about poetry, books, and relationships.

In spite of his engagement to Eunice, he embarked on a series of extravagant flirtations. He rejoiced in Margaret Groesbeck's company, "for I love her tho' I am not 'in love with her'"; he was fascinated by the hint of sin, remarking how "beautiful everything *external* is about Caroline. But what a work has grace to do within!" and he gallantly hid his disappointment about Catharine Dickinson's upcoming marriage, explaining to her: "You know how deeply I love all when I love at all."[36]

Henry had no sense of being unfaithful to Eunice. "Nothing I have ever dreamed of could better my real choice," he insisted.[37] But others did not see it that way. Henry was spending so much time visiting Nathaniel Wright's lovely daughter that the Wright house was nicknamed "Beecher's tavern." Not only was fourteen-year-old Mary Wright one of Isabella Beecher's best friends, she was intelligent, pretty, and obviously infatuated with Isabella's gallant older brother. When Harriet warned him of Mary's crush, Henry dismissed it as the babble of "Ma'am scandal." Why, he was also rumored to be engaged to Margaret Groesbeck, and if that wasn't proof of his innocence, then what was? When Mary's parents finally asked him to stop calling, he was shocked. Lesson learned: The next evening he called on Margaret Groesbeck instead.

Incidents like this revived his old insecurities. Not long after this, he was shaken when Margaret joked that he was too irreverent to be a minister. That night he lay awake stewing over her words. "Is it possible that I am regarded generally as a light, trivial, worthless jester?" he wrote to her the next day. "God knows, that if I have a good deal of mirth, I can compensate for it in secret," but really, he insisted, that was not necessary.

"If a minister were made to wear a lachrymose face and never to enjoy or make mirth, you said truly that I was not born to it," he wrote to Margaret. But there are three kinds of ministers, he maintained, "the ascetic, the neuter and the sunshiny." Clearly he had no aptitude for asceticism and too much personality to be neuter. Instead he took a prophetic stand: He intended to be one of the "glorious sunshiny ones," the type "who think there is a time for relaxation and elegant enjoyment." After all, he concluded piously, "To be mirthful is part of our constitution and I believe God never gave us that which it is sin to exercise."[38]

By contrast, Henry's brother Charles was growing more lachrymose every day. Constitutionally the two were polar opposites. Intensely serious and ruthlessly honest, Charles shared Henry's growing theological skepticism. But unlike his blithe older brother, Charles was incapable of papering over his doubts. Unable to follow his father's path, he announced that he was leaving the seminary to become a musician.

Henry was irritated rather than sympathetic. Charles's determination to either untangle the dense web of doctrine or turn away from religion altogether struck him as immature and impractical. "Can I construct an irrefutable argument vs. fatality from facts upward?" Henry asked in exasperation. "If I had no vexation to earn money—I would certainly try."[39] For his part Charles seemed both envious and contemptuous of his brother's easygoing conscience.

The simmering friction between the two brothers boiled over when Charles fell in love with the bewitching Mary Wright. Mary, unfortunately, remained smitten with Henry. The two brothers nearly came to blows one evening after church, when Charles wanted to walk Mary home and Henry insisted on doing it. Not long afterward Charles fled downriver to New Orleans, where he struggled to support himself as a church organist. The family organized regular prayer circles for his salvation, but in the end it would be Henry who brought him back to the fold.

Lyman's second heresy trial consumed the autumn of Henry's second year. Lyman marshaled his boys into a traveling campaign team, fanning out across southern Ohio on horseback to lobby the country deacons who would decide the case. "Dr. Beecher and his sons, it was soon found, could race and chase and ride like born Kentuckians, and that 'free agency' on horse-back, would go through mud and fire and water as gallantly as ever 'natural inability' could," Harriet recalled with amusement.[40]

A few days before the trial, Henry and Lyman boarded a steamboat for Synod in Dayton, Ohio, where they were joined by George and Edward Beecher. Again the proceedings lasted a week, with Lyman giving a virtuoso performance of logic chopping and hairsplitting. Increasingly abolition was the not-so-secret subtext of the conflict, with many antislavery men torn between their loyalty to traditional orthodoxy and their attraction to the New School's more liberal, activist interpretations of Scripture.

This time Henry was more mature, dutifully disparaging his father's opponents and recording Lyman's arguments and advice, but his boredom and disrespect were obvious. "I never saw so many faces of clergymen and so few of them intellectual faces," he wrote to the family at home. He took his cues from his father, who in private was increasingly dismissive of the Presbyterian Pharisees and their rigid regulations.

Once again Dr. Wilson was bested, but this time Lyman's exoneration was more grudging. The hypocrisy and slander charges were not proved, Synod decided, but warned that Dr. Beecher "has indulged a disposition to philosophize" instead of simply teaching pure Scripture.[41] Again Wilson appealed the verdict, this time to the national General Assembly to be held in Philadelphia the following summer.

Up in Walnut Hills, the year 1836 began on a happy note, with the marriage of Calvin Stowe and Harriet Beecher. Their quiet wedding stoked Henry's desire for a wife of his own—"patience—patience!" he counseled himself. Harriet became pregnant immediately after the wedding, and when Stowe left a month later on a long book-buying trip to Europe, she moved back home. It was the first time she and Henry had lived together since she was twelve years old, and their relationship blossomed with the new intimacy.

Down in the city, however, the slavery question was again rearing its ugly head. The abolitionists had grown bolder. In the summer of 1835, the American Antislavery Society, backed by Arthur and Lewis Tappan, launched what became known as the "Great Postal Campaign." Within a year more than a million pieces of antislavery propaganda—pamphlets, graphic etchings, newspapers, printed handkerchiefs, medals, and emblems—were sent to ministers, elected officials, and newspaper editors across the country, in an effort to persuade the nation's opinion makers. Theodore Weld spearheaded a campaign to build a network of antislavery societies throughout the rural hinterlands, which then deluged Congress with antislavery petitions. In five years the number of antislavery societies shot from zero to two thousand.

The success of the abolitionists provoked howls of rage and violence. Southern mails began refusing to deliver antislavery material and appealed to Northern legislatures to outlaw abolitionist agitation. Sympathetic politicians, newspapermen, and ministers in the North began to echo the demands of the South, proposing a gag rule in the U.S. Congress and the suppression of radical pamphlets and newspapers. Hostile newspapers carried advertisements offering bounties for the heads of William Lloyd Garrison and Arthur Tappan. James Thome, one of the leaders in the Lane Debates, was lynched in Georgia, and his fellow seminarian, Amos Dresser, was given a mock trial and whipped, naked, in Tennessee. Major antiabolitionist riots swept through Washington, Philadelphia, Baltimore, and a number of smaller cities, and in October 1835 William Lloyd Garrison was seized by a Boston mob and dragged through the streets by a rope. His life was saved only when he was locked up in protective custody. The struggle against Southern negro slavery was increasingly becoming a battle for Northern white liberty of speech.

So far Cincinnati had escaped bloodshed. Then, in the winter of 1835–36, James G. Birney, a former slave owner–turned–abolitionist, announced that he was bringing his antislavery newspaper, the *Philanthropist*, to Cincinnati in the spring. The *Philanthropist* was far more moderate and religiously orthodox than Garrison's *Liberator*. That made no difference to the mobs that had already run him out of several smaller towns.

Birney's timing was particularly bad. Local businessmen were working to bring the first railroad line to Cincinnati, creating a link to the Carolina coastline. Any hint of anti-Southern sentiment might sour the deal. A meeting was called on January 22 to head off the problem, led by the city's richest and most respected citizens, and many members of the Second Presbyterian Church, including Judge Burnet, John Groesbeck, and Henry's uncle John Foote. Judge Burnet was deputized to warn Birney that if he came to town, a mob would sack his press forthwith.

Birney refused to back down. Tensions simmered until he started publishing in April. Local hooligans responded by burning down one of the city's mixed-race bawdy houses, threatening to castrate the men inside as a large crowd gathered to enjoy the flames. Sated for the moment, the mob dispersed. Still, Birney stood his ground.

A few weeks later Henry was granted his great wish. Thomas Brainerd, the editor of the *Cincinnati Journal*, was accompanying Lyman to his final heresy trial in Philadelphia. He asked Henry to edit the paper in his absence. Henry soon found it not as easy as he'd anticipated. "I am not cut out for an Editor of a newspaper," he lamented only a few weeks into his tenure, "but it brings me $40 a month which is much to my finances."[42] He celebrated by buying himself an elegant overcoat and a plain pocket watch.

His first issue came out on May 26, loaded with boilerplate editorials condemning the evils of the theater, the unrestrained liquor trade, and traveling on the Sabbath. His only mention of slavery was an odd clip from the antislavery paper the *Emancipator*, citing a rumor that Lyman Beecher and his sons were coming around to immediate abolition.

There was some truth in the story. George joined the Antislavery Society in 1836 and in 1837 reeled in William as well. In Illinois, Edward was converted to the cause when his close friend, the antislavery editor Elijah Lovejoy, was killed by a sniper during an antiabolitionist riot in 1837. On the other hand, Catharine was even now working on a book rebuking female abolitionists.

Henry remained somewhere in between. Privately he told Chauncey, "I'm an abolitionist yet, strong as ever but not one all afire, full of brimstone and *damnation* for all of other opinions, proud as Lucifer and inflexible as a mountain[.]"[43] But publicly he was in a bind. Besides his loyalty to Lyman, there was the fact that nearly every girl he knew had a father who was staunchly antiabolition. One thing Henry refused to be was a social pariah. But as the summer wore on he found it increasingly difficult to balance conscience and popularity.

In June surprising news arrived from Philadelphia: Joshua Wilson had been persuaded to withdraw his charges of heresy, finally freeing Lyman. The Old versus New School battle was increasingly bound up with the slavery question, with many Southern congregations allying with the stodgy literalists of the Old School, and Northern congregations veering toward the liberal activism of the New School. In such a volatile climate, it seemed impolitic to pursue a man like Lyman Beecher, who straddled the center.

July brought the semiannual influx of Southern buyers, bringing scores of influential fat cats and rowdy young men into the city, at the same time as the Southwestern Railroad Convention was meeting in Tennessee to decide on the new rail routes. Suddenly the presence of Birney's "abolition rag" seemed intolerable to the men of Cincinnati.

The first attack came at midnight on July 12, 1836, when a mob broke into the print shop that produced the *Philanthropist*, damaging the press and type, and threatening worse if Birney would not stop publishing. Most of these men were not Southern riffraff or working-class thugs, but "mobocrats"—Northern-born members of some of Cincinnati's wealthiest and most prominent families, acting with the tacit approval of the city's "respectable" citizens. In defiance Birney and his printer patched up the press and put out a new edition.

Henry felt emboldened now that the nettlesome slavery issue was transformed into a question of law and order. He responded with an editorial that condemned mob violence as an attack on the sanctity of private property and "the first, the highest, the most sacred, the last deserted right of freedmen, the right of free discussion." He wrote virtually nothing on slavery itself in the coming weeks, but he recognized the unintended benefits of martyrdom. "One may doubt after all whether these men are not friendly to Abolitionists," he concluded. "They are laboring more busily than anybody else to make them."[44] At Henry's urging Harriet wrote a lengthy anonymous letter to the editor, complementing his editorial and defending democratic debate.

After a tense, sweltering-hot week, a citizens' meeting was called to consider whether to take further action against Birney. More than a thousand men turned up. Citing the Boston Tea Party as their precedent, they "in so many words voted a mob," as Harriet put it. A committee of thirteen, led by Judge Burnet and including many good Presbyterians, delivered an ultimatum: If Birney did not cease publication, a mob would be raised of at least five thousand people, including two-thirds of the property owners of the city. They gave Birney until noon the next day to make his decision.

Again Birney refused. The next night the committee's predictions came true. When darkness fell, a mob, drunk on cheap corn whiskey and riled by the heat, again set upon the printing office. Across the city, blacks fled in fear. The mob smashed the press, scattered the type, and threw it in the river, all under the eye of the mayor, who told them to go home when they were done. Beyond the call of reason, they instead headed to the boardinghouse where Birney lodged. Birney was gone. Instead they found the young lawyer Salmon P. Chase barring the door, refusing to let them pass. His quiet courage took some of the wind out of their sails. Frustrated and at loose ends, the mob headed to Bucktown, destroying the nicest of the black-owned houses, scattering furniture and ripping up mattresses until feathers filled the streets.

The rioting subsided around dawn but resumed the next day. Now the mayor tried to calm the hooligans, to no avail, and many pillars of the community who had incited the mob began to fear for their own homes and property. Switching sides, the mayor swore in an ad hoc posse to patrol the streets. Henry was no Salmon Chase, but by now his heroic impulses were thoroughly aroused, and he volunteered for the patrol. Harriet was shocked to find him bustling over the kitchen stove, pouring melted lead into a mold.

"What on earth are you doing, Henry?" she asked.

"Making bullets, to kill men with, Hattie!" he replied.

"I never saw Henry look so terrible!" Harriet later recalled. "I did not like it, for I feared he was growing blood-thirsty."[45]

There was talk that the rioters might head up the hill to the seminary. "For a day or two," Harriet wrote Stowe, "we did not know if there would actually be war to the knife, as was threatened by the mob, and we really saw Henry depart with his pistols with daily alarm, only we were too full of patriotism not to have sent every brother we had, rather than not have had the principles of freedom and order defended." Finally, after several terrifying days, the mob, "unsupported by a now frightened community, slunk in their dens and were still," in Harriet's words.

Throughout the weeks of violence Henry—with Harriet's help—printed a full array of pro- and antislavery letters and news. He found he had a taste for the adrenaline of public controversy, but on slavery itself he remained equivocal. In his penultimate editorial, titled "Mobs!!" he reminded his readers that he carefully refrained from taking either side except that of law and order.[46]

The effect of the riots on Henry and Harriet was not as dramatic as it was for others, like Salmon Chase, who risked both his life and his legal career, and came away an ardent abolitionist. Nevertheless the experience finally gave Henry his entry into the great debate of the century. In the principle of free speech, he found a safe, solid platform from which to survey the rest of the field.

WITH GREAT RELUCTANCE Henry gave up the *Journal* when Brainerd and his father returned in the autumn. In the hope of staying on, he'd overestimated his finances, and was mortified to find himself forced to return his new overcoat and pocket watch when he couldn't make the payments.

On his way home from the East, Lyman stopped once more in the "Boston marriage mart," carrying home his third and last wife. Lydia Jackson was a forty-seven-year-old widow, a member of the Hanover Street Church who kept a kind of ministerial boardinghouse nearby. Lyman must have had her in his sights from the outset, because he headed directly to her house as soon as he came to the city and proposed almost immediately upon his arrival.

Lydia Jackson turned out to be Lyman's "most efficient and practical wife," as one friend testified, and she ran him with a firm hand. She brought two of her six children with her, but they never became part of the family, and she herself never got along well with Lyman's children. Easygoing Henry had no particular problem with Lydia, but he laughed as only a young man can at his father's infatuated depiction of her as a pretty young thing. "Oh father," he marveled to William, "to think of *youth* and *beauty* in the *region* of forty-seven!"[47]

Henry was now nearly finished with his ministerial training. As he told the story years later, the closer he got to graduation the stronger his religious doubts grew. For three years he had lived on arcane doctrines, petty ecclesiastical politics, heresy hunting, and constant sectarian warfare waged in the name of God. "I had been stuffed with these things. I had eaten and drank them. I had chopped and hewed them. I had built up from them every sort of argument. I had had them ad nauseam."[48]

"I had about made up my mind to go into some other profession," Henry later said, but he did not have his brother's courage or moral conviction.[49] He could not bear to face his father's disappointment, especially in the wake of Charley's defection. As Henry later told it, that spring he spiraled into another religious crisis.

If this was true, however, Henry hid it well. For the first time since he began keeping a diary, the pages began to fill with long, technical theological proofs, practical notes on potential sermons, and professional tips. Any hints of doubt are less about religion per se and more about the all-or-nothing nature of Calvinism. "I cannot think of God without great emotion—a stirring up within my bosom, a glow of feeling, tenderness and tears—yet it does not command the will," he wrote in March. "I do not find that it produces in me such entire strong determinations to give up all for him, to live entirely for him."[50]

Once again Henry was saved by an epiphany, much like the one that pulled him out of his spiritual quagmire in college. As at Amherst, his accounts of this revelation differ, so it is impossible to know what actually happened. Perhaps it was the stark contrast between Henry's heady explorations into the world of romance and his father's humiliating theological battles. Perhaps it was, as Harriet said, "a period of spiritual clairvoyance."[51] Perhaps it was nothing more than his old cycle of depression and elation, but Henry later named it the great turning point of his life.

One "blessed morning of May," he was walking outdoors near the seminary, preparing a talk for his young ladies' Bible class on "Jesus as a Conversationalist," when something struck him. Just as in college, the vision that arose was a powerful projection of his deepest personal longings.

> There rose up before me a view of Jesus as the Saviour of sinners— not of saints, but of sinners unconverted, before they were any better—because they were so bad and needed so much; and that view has never gone from me. It did not at first fill the whole Heaven; it came as a rift along the horizon gradually, little by little, the cloud rolled up. It was three years before the whole sky was cleared so that I could see all around, but from that hour I felt that God had a father's heart; that Christ loved me in my sin; that while I was a sinner He did not frown upon me nor cast me off, but cared for me with unutterable tenderness, and would help me out of sin; and it seemed to me that I had everything that I needed.[52]

In that moment it felt as if a heavy weight was lifted from his heart. "I went like one crazed up and down through the fields half crying, half laughing, singing and praying and shouting," he said later. "One might have thought that I was a lunatic escaped from confinement; how I ran up and down through the primeval forest of Ohio, shouting, 'Glory, glory!'"[53]

In his retellings sometimes this new vision of God was one who "felt toward me as my mother felt toward me"; at other times, it was "a God deals with his creatures as a father deals with his children." Occasionally this new God was "a great-hearted gentleman, who is never inquisitive, who never takes advantage of me, who never domineers over me, even by implication, but who always makes me happy, and makes me happy so that happiness makes me good."[54] In each case the paradigm was the same—God's nature was parental, not governmental; medicinal, not punitive; and salvation came from love rather than obedience to the law.

It is said in the Bible that God made man in His own image. While we have no proof of that proposition, it is unarguable that man fashions God into a mirror of himself. "The god of the cannibals will be a cannibal, of the crusaders, a crusader, and of the merchants, a merchant," as Ralph Waldo Emerson observed.[55] In Henry's case there was nothing he wanted more than to be treated with the courtesies of a gentleman, to have a mother to comfort him and a father who loved him unconditionally. After a lifetime of believing that being good and being happy were incompatible, it was intoxicating to think that happiness might lead to goodness and that Christ was sent to make mankind happy rather than vice versa. Most notable, perhaps, is the transposition of his God and his father. For years he had seen his father in the image of the stern Calvinist God; it was an act of both rebellion and resolution to turn God into the loving image of father. The problem was that this sunshiny vision was heresy.

On June 5, 1837, Henry graduated from Lane Seminary. "It was hot as mustard" that day, but the chapel was brimming over with young people, as Henry's admirer, the winsome young Mary Wright, described it in a letter to Isabella. Lyman opened the ceremonies with a prayer, some hymns were sung, and the oratory began:

> The speeches were so dull and the weather so hot that I began to be afraid that the audience would not be pleased, when your father called out Mr. Beecher—and in came the second Dr. Beecher (Now Isabell, as he is going to be married I can say what I please) and as he opened his mouth every one seemed to wake up, his manner is so impressive, and his voice so deep and commanding—His subject was regeneration, and as it has been so much talked upon it requires a great deal of talent to make it original and interesting, but your brother did both, he struck out a new path and every word was so forcible and went so directly to the point and every idea was

clothed in such flowing and elegant language, that I don't know what, only it was first rate.

"Isabel—Isabel, what shall I do, he is going to be married," Mary concluded mournfully. "Oh dear me."[56]

That same summer nearly nine hundred miles to the east, a young Ralph Waldo Emerson got his first taste of notoriety while delivering his landmark "American Scholar" address to the students of Harvard College. In it, Emerson called for a new sort of minister for the coming age, indeed a new sort of man—one who rejects the "timid, imitative, tame," and instead cultivates originality, courage, and, above all, "self-trust." The orator who offers his own "frank confessions," predicted Emerson, will find that audiences "drink his words because he fulfills for them their own nature; the deeper he dives into his privatest, secretest presentiment, to the wonder he finds, this is the most acceptable, most public, and universally true."

"Our intellectual Declaration of Independence," as Dr. Oliver Wendell Holmes described Emerson's oration, was so iconoclastic that it shocked even the liberal Unitarians of Cambridge and Boston. Not a soul under heaven would have associated a son of Lyman Beecher with such heterodox sentiments. Yet, already Henry was taking his first, tentative steps toward the Emersonian ideal. Pinned under the watchful eye of his father, he was simply taking a little longer than Brother Emerson to find his way to self-reliance.[57]

Chapter 5

"HUMPH! PRETTY BUSINESS!
SON OF LYMAN BEECHER, PRESIDENT OF A
THEOLOGICAL SEMINARY, IN THIS MISERABLE HOLE"

*O*ut West, folks used to say that you could tell who had settled a town just by glancing around. If you saw a Congregational church and a college, you knew it was settled by New Englanders. If it had a Presbyterian church and a distillery, you could be sure it was established by Virginians. When Henry stepped off the steamboat onto the rough wharf of Lawrenceburgh, Indiana, in the spring of 1837, there was no question about it: He was in a Virginian town.

Lawrenceburgh (later spelled Lawrenceburg) was a slovenly little settlement carved out of the junction of the Ohio and Miami rivers twenty miles west of Cincinnati. A makeshift jumble of shops, taverns, and warehouses clustered around the wharf, and rangy, long-legged hogs roamed the muddy streets. Most of the houses were only one step above log cabins, built right up to the road, without a plant or shade tree in sight.

The town was a central exchange point for Kentucky, Ohio, and Indiana. Only fifteen hundred people called it home, but the streets were swollen by an endless tide of travelers—farmers and businessmen coming to trade, crews of transient day laborers working on the Whitewater Canal and the Lawrenceburgh & Indianapolis Railroad, and a stream of restless pioneers passing through on their way somewhere else. Taverns outnumbered churches, and grog shops and bawdy houses were the primary entertainment. It was, as Henry said, a town "with two distilleries and twenty devils in it."[1]

Henry was welcomed to Lawrenceburgh by Martha Sawyer, a strong-willed Yankee woman of nineteen. Martha had discovered Henry that spring, speaking in a small hall across the border in Covington, Kentucky. She was immediately smitten by the young preacher and campaigned to bring him to the tiny, struggling Presbyterian Church of Lawrenceburgh. Almost a hundred people turned out to see Henry's trial sermon, drawn by the Beecher name. The unexpected throng made the young preacher so nervous that the sermon fell flat. But the indomitable Miss Sawyer was so pleased with Henry's performance that she insisted he return the next Sunday.

Lawrenceburgh was "a destitute place indeed," Henry wrote in his diary after his first visit, and the congregation was a shabby collection of impoverished spinsters and laborers' wives.[2] But by the time he got home to Walnut Hills, he'd made up his mind: If they offered him the post, he would accept it.

Henry's family and friends were appalled by his decision. No one with any ambition would go to Indiana. Of all the new western states, Indiana was considered the most backward and undeveloped, filled with land too swampy to farm and rivers too shallow to navigate, a place to pass by on the way to Illinois, Michigan, or more promising vistas. Why, everyone knew that native Indians still roamed the woods! (That is, until the autumn of 1837, when the U.S. militia drove the remaining tribes across the Mississippi River to Kansas.) Lyman Beecher vigorously advised Henry to wait for a better offer.

But Henry had his own motives. There was still a possibility that he might be offered a job as permanent editor of the *Cincinnati Journal*, and Lawrenceburgh was close enough for him to commute regularly to Cincinnati by steamboat (a prospect that didn't pan out). He liked the freedom of starting in a young church with few expectations to bind him. Besides, the sooner he had a job, the sooner he could marry.

Just before his twenty-fourth birthday, he received the call from Lawrenceburgh—"a very flattering call it was and did my heart good," he said with delight. The "vote for me unanimous, blank filled for $250, with but one dissenting voice 'he voting for double that sum.' "[3] With an additional contribution from the Home Missionary Society, his final salary was set at three hundred dollars annually—not much more than the seventy-five cents a day earned by the day laborers working on the

Whitewater Canal. It wasn't enough for him to rent his own home, but Martha Sawyer arranged for him to board with the local doctor, Jeremiah Brower, a staunch Old School Presbyterian. "Won't grow rich, not much left to end year to lay up," Henry wrote to his old friend Howard Chauncey, but there was plenty of room to rise in a town "growing in population and sin."[4]

A few days after his graduation from Lane Seminary, Henry left his father's house for good, taking with him only some hand-me-down clothes, his beloved books, and his journal. All he needed now was a wife. Like Jacob in the book of Genesis, he had waited—none too patiently—for seven years. Now his happy ending was at hand.

THE LAST SEVEN YEARS had been difficult for Eunice Bullard. Bound by her engagement but with no home of her own, Eunice lived the life of a spinster, drifting among the limited occupations open to women. Schoolteaching had never been to her taste, so she tried earning money by sewing clothes for her sisters' families and weaving straw braid to be stitched into summer hats—exhausting, poorly paid work. Eventually she moved in with her older sister, Maria, and her brother-in-law Ira Barton, a well-to-do attorney in Worcester, Massachusetts. In exchange she tended her sister's children, sewed, and kept house, an arrangement she soon came to resent. Eunice was merely biding time until Henry came to rescue her from her humdrum life and give her the right to her own happiness.

Yet her faith in Henry's saving grace was clouded by anxiety. Their long-distance engagement was fraught with mysterious difficulties, only hinted at in Henry's diary and various family letters. Illness was a constant threat—both the Bullards and the Beechers were constantly announcing their imminent deaths, only to find themselves miraculously recovered. Garbled rumors of Henry's flirtations surely filtered back to Eunice, if only through teasing comments from her brothers living in Ohio. With her father's warnings about broken engagements and old maids ringing in her ears, Eunice could hardly help but be distressed.

Eunice had her own problems with gossip and tale-telling. At one point Catharine and Eunice—neither of whom could be called easygoing—found themselves in a fracas after Catharine's most recent trip East. The family spent an entire day resolving the matter, with Lyman and Calvin Stowe adjudicating and Henry leading Eunice's defense. At the end of this odd proceeding, Henry—who always enjoyed drawing up official-looking documents—wrote a long, formal agreement signed by Henry and Calvin, which acquitted Eunice of any "suspicion of constitutional weakness or imprudence," and of a general disposition to tattle and gossip. The "whole story," Henry concluded in triumph, "shews her to be a young lady of strong mind, ardent feelings, great firmness of purpose and nice sense of honor, and sensibilities almost morbidly acute."[5]

Unfortunately we have no record of Eunice's side of the matter. Just before his graduation from Lane, Henry burned all her letters to him, putting them permanently "out of danger."[6] His love letters to her were lost in one of their moves. But Eunice left her own record, in the form of a fictionalized memoir. Published in 1859, *From Dawn to Daylight, or the Simple Story of a Western Home* was inspired by the rising popularity of women novelists, particularly the spectacular success of Harriet Beecher Stowe. But unlike the sentimental plots churned out by most women writers, *Dawn to Daylight* is a bitter exposé of the hardship and personal abuse suffered by the young wife of a western minister. Names and a few details were changed, but she insisted that the story was "literally true," and independent evidence bears out her claim. The novel's rare combination of sentiment and shrewishness draws a vivid emotional portrait of their early life together.

By Eunice's account the most dramatic threat to their engagement came from her miserly father and his "increasing love of wealth."[7] Several times over the past seven years Dr. Bullard offered Eunice sums of money, from five to a hundred dollars, as tokens of his affection, only to withdraw the money just as she was reaching out to claim it. While the stern old man liked Henry personally, the fact that he was a poor home missionary did not stand in his favor.

The reader enters this dense thicket of oedipal tensions in the first pages of *Dawn to Daylight*. As the story opens, Eunice's alter ego, Mary Leighton, is engaged to George Herbert (the combined names of Eunice's two favorite sons), a young divinity student in the West, when suddenly her father, Dr. Leighton, accepts on her behalf another proposal of marriage from an obnoxious but wealthy local man. Delighted by the prospect of a rich son-in-law, the doctor insists that his daughter break her engagement to George. Like any good sentimental heroine, Mary refuses to deny her true love, but her father hounds her for months, insisting that she marry the loathsome suitor. After a final fight with her father, the heartsick girl falls ill with scarlet fever. The prospect of her death, brought on by his own greed, sends the doctor to his knees at her sickbed, begging forgiveness. She emerges from her feverish delirium only when he admits that he was a fool to sell his daughter's happiness.

But here Eunice's tale departs dramatically from the standard romantic plot, suggesting the unaccountable hand of truth. Mary is not rescued by her father's change of heart, for despite his show of regret the doctor has not entirely relinquished his plans. She escapes only when Dr. Leighton discovers that while Mary was sick, old "money-bags" ran off and married a wealthy lady from Boston. Mary, of course, makes a speedy recovery and joins George out West.

It is a peculiar, rather comic story that flatters no one—the heroine was publicly dumped and her father made a fool. Yet it unconsciously captures the emotional equation that ruled Eunice Bullard's life. Although she was a remarkably strong woman, she was always eager to cast herself as a victim, even when it was unflattering or humiliating. Her painful need for sympathy outweighed—and impeded—her desire for happiness. Her grudges were as raw in 1859 as they were in 1837.

Henry was not averse to playing for sympathy, but unlike his fiancée, he was acutely aware of how he seemed to others. During their engagement he regularly kept his feminine confidantes sitting up late into the night while he recounted the tribulations of his courtship. But when Henry cast himself as victim, he burnished his image until it glowed. "I sit and think over all his sorrows, all the *injustice* that was at one time done him—all his gentle childlike tenderness of heart, till I think it cannot be that heaven will not claim its own and take him to the world where alone he will find those like him," Harriet Stowe wrote of her brother, after one of these late-night sessions. "I thought all the time that I wanted to thank him for *being so good [.]*"[8]

His sister Isabella, younger and more impressionable, offered even more gratification than Harriet. "Had a long, long talk with Bella about dear E. Rehearsed some of our vicissitudes, trials etc.," Henry confided to his diary. "Poor girl—she did as everybody has done who ever heard it truly told—*wept.*"[9] While Eunice's *fiction* burns with the acrid smell of reality even twenty years later, Henry *lived* as if he were the hero of a fascinating romantic novel.

After only two weeks in Lawrenceburgh, Henry's patience finally ran out. One bright July morning he sat down and wrote Eunice her final love letter. If all went well he would be ordained in August, he told her, and would come to marry her at the end of October. Sealing up the letter, he rushed down to the post office.

Walking home to his little room through the dusty streets, however, his excitement faded as he contemplated four more months of waiting. "Why wait to be ordained?" he suddenly asked himself. "Why not go East at once and bring my wife back with me—to the ordination? I will do it."

Henry strode directly to the church trustees to tell them of his intentions. He hopped on a steamer for Cincinnati that very evening, stopping only long enough to borrow his brother George's good black suit for the wedding ceremony. Had it not been for that small concession to vanity, he might have beaten the letter to Bullard's Hill.

Henry's letter arrived on the morning of July 29. That evening Eunice retreated to her room to compose an answer to Henry and to make up an invitation list. "While I sat thinking to whom I should write I heard some little commotion and excitement at the front door," Eunice recalled, "and then flying up stairs to my study, Mr. Beecher appeared!"

Breathlessly Henry tumbled out his story. And now, he concluded, they must be married at once. "Now Eunice I *must* start for the West— the last of next week. Will you be ready to go then?"

"Why, Henry. No! It will be impossible to get ready!"

"What do you need to get ready?" he asked naively.

There was a wedding dress and trousseau to sew, a cake to bake, plus a million other chores, she protested.

"Dress just as you are now. Who will mind it?" Henry replied. "Next week is August third. I *must* be in Worcester that evening, and in Boston the following day, on important business, which I have promised to transact and from Boston go to New York, and thence direct, and as quickly as I can, to my people."

"But Henry! Tomorrow is Sunday—the last day of July—and that leaves me not quite three working days."

It is a testament to the depth of their love that she did not object more heartily to his insensitivity. She agreed to hold the ceremony the following Thursday afternoon, August 3. But Henry had other advantages. As she sewed her dress, he wrote up wedding invitations, beat the eggs, and stoned the raisins for the wedding cake that Eunice baked, and kept her in good spirits. "Did he not ever make hard things easy—and crooked places straight," Eunice marveled.[10]

Their wedding took place on one of those steamy summer days native to eastern Massachusetts, where the muggy air thickens until the middle of the afternoon, when it is washed clean by a sudden, magnificent downpour. Henry was uncharacteristically sober as the ceremony approached. "This afternoon at about three I am to be married to E.W. Bullard," he wrote in his diary. "We are both dressed and waiting for the company."[11]

A little after two o'clock, as the guests began arriving, the sky erupted with thunder and lightning. The rain was still raging at three o'clock. Eunice had seen her sisters married during storms, and took this as a bad omen. "I had always said I would not be married in a storm and refused to go down," she said defiantly. "I had yielded to all else, but here I was deaf to expostulation." The guests were growing restless, thinking of the feeding, milking, and dinners awaiting them at home. But, after seven years Eunice could wait a few more minutes, and so would they.

A little before four the storm rolled out as suddenly as it had rolled in. Henry, in his borrowed black suit, and Eunice, in her plain mull gown, were ushered into the steaming parlor. As the couple entered a huge, glorious rainbow—"the most brilliant I ever saw," Eunice said—suddenly lit up the room. The guests murmured that it looked as if the couple was being married under its arch. The clergyman uttered a prayer that "the bow of peace and promise ever rest upon them thy servants."[12]

As soon as the guests cleared out, the new Reverend and Mrs. Beecher traveled to the nearby town of Worcester to visit her sister and brother-in-law. Henry preached in Worcester, and then they went on to Boston, where he spoke at his father's old church on Sunday morning and his brother Edward's old church in the evening. It must have felt as much like a victory tour as a honeymoon.

CONTINUING THE PATTERN of their engagement, the honeymoon was more difficult for Eunice than for Henry. In a daze of pride and happiness, Henry seemed strangely blind to his beloved bride. Hurrying to the church in Worcester, he was certain he'd forgotten something but could not think of what it was until he mounted the steps of the pulpit and realized that it was Eunice.

Once they left the familiarity of her sister's home for Boston, Eunice became anxious and ill, fearing that she might have contracted the deadly cholera morbis. She was just well enough to escape Boston by boat to New York City, where they stayed at the home of her other sister and consulted a doctor, who suggested that her discomfort might have come from eating too many cucumbers and leeks, both summer delicacies. That is to say, she was simply suffering from diarrhea and perhaps some nervous indigestion.

Whatever the cause of Eunice's illness, she was plainly unnerved by her new life. She had never been to a major city and had rarely socialized outside of her own family circle. And then there was the looming prospect of sex. Undoubtedly both bride and groom were virgins at their wedding, and they had laid neither eyes nor lips on each other for four years. Plunged into the boisterous streets of Boston and New York, with a man she barely knew anymore leading her to the far end of America— who can blame Eunice for taking to her bed?

But if the big city was intimidating, the journey westward was downright frightening. When the newlyweds arrived at the train station in New York to board the cars for Pittsburgh, it was the first train she had ever ridden and perhaps ever seen. The "rail way" was still in its infancy, but already it was *the* symbol of modernity. Yet to see the great locomotive for the first time—belching soot, smoke, and red-hot cinders; huffing like a huge, hungry animal; the steam whistle and iron wheels on iron tracks shrieking as if in unearthly pain—it resembled nothing so much as a massive black dragon.

Eunice was understandably nervous about riding the "iron horse," but she tried to mask her lack of sophistication. When they pulled into the station to change trains, the platform was chaotic with passengers and porters rushing to and fro. Henry set her beside the ticket window while he looked after the luggage, instructing her to stay put until he came to collect her to board the next train. She was waiting apprehensively when she spied a man who looked just like her new husband hop aboard the car and settle into reading his newspaper. Still Eunice did not move, assuming that Henry would come get her.

She stiffened with alarm when the final bell rang. Porters quickly loaded the last bags, husbands hurriedly gathered their wives and children, but Henry remained calmly reading his paper. Unable to endure a moment longer, Eunice rushed to the door and called out. He started up in shock, bounded across the platform, and, with the conductor's help, swung her on board as the train began moving.

Again Henry apologized profusely for forgetting her. "*He* says it was *absent-mindedness,*" she wrote.[13] Nonetheless Henry's remarkable insensitivity to his new wife is surprising, when only weeks before he was quaking with desire for her. Eunice had lived so long in his imagination that in one sense their wedding was merely a way of stamping his dreams with the emotional authority of fact. He didn't need her presence to feel loved, he needed only her consent. Yet his behavior was so obviously—and so unconsciously—hurtful that it suggests that the reality of his marriage was already disappointing to him. Henry smoldered with the pent-up passions of a twenty-four-year-old man, fanned by years of flirtations and fantasies. To be held at arm's length by fretfulness, illness, and Eunice's own (not unreasonable) disappointment must have been a terrible blow to his ego. Perhaps there was a part of him that did, indeed, want to leave her behind.

In Pittsburgh the couple left the railroad and boarded a canalboat, one of the ubiquitous flat-bottomed boats pulled by pack animals that walked along the shoreline. It was a slow, uncomfortable trip through low-lying water, so slow that travelers occasionally got off and walked alongside the boat to stretch their legs. Several times their boat got tangled in the dense canebreaks and thickets of alder saplings that lined the shore, forcing everyone to disembark while the boatmen cut through the swamp. The railroad had not brought them to a glorious future, it seemed, but to an almost primordial past.

The last leg was by steamboat, far faster than canalboat but equally crowded, dirty, and uncomfortable. A full gamut of western characters could be found crammed on the decks and in the parlors of the steamer—professional gamblers and pickpockets, rough boatmen with bowie knives strapped to their sides and shabby Methodist missionaries clutching their Bibles, dark-skinned slaves and calico-clad mothers shushing their wailing children. There was a constant stream of profanity, tobacco juice, and the easy intimacies that marked travelers in the West. Passengers ate at long wooden trestles, bathed at a couple of tin basins abetted by a common towel and comb, and slept in triple-decker bunks hung by ropes along the walls, with unlucky passengers stretched out on tables, floors, and benches. The danger of the steamboat equaled its discomfort. The shoreline and sandbars were littered with the wreckage of overheated boiler explosions and boats run aground.

After ten days of hard travel, the newlyweds arrived in Cincinnati, with eighteen cents remaining in their pockets. Up in Walnut Hills, the Beechers gave a warm welcome to Henry's pretty, clever bride. "I thought you were the most of a beauty of anybody we had ever seen," Harriet later told Eunice. Eunice put her best foot forward for her in-laws. "She has won the hearts of all that have seen her," Charles wrote to Isabella. "And they are as happy as after so many trials I think they fully deserve to be." Even Henry's young admirer, Mary Wright, admitted petulantly that Eunice "seems farther from suspicion in every point than any of my friends. She is very pretty, sensible, and any thing but ill natured—she is very economical and cheerful—just the one to make your brother happy."[14]

AS THEY BOARDED THE STEAMBOAT for Lawrenceburgh several days later, Henry warned Eunice to lower her expectations for their new home. But as they "picked their way from the wharf to the house *through mud and over pigs,*" in Eunice's words, she was appalled by how crude and ugly the town was. She was openly relieved to arrive at Dr. Brower's pleasant two-story clapboard house. It was not as genteel as she would have expected for a physician, which seemed odd, she observed, since Mrs. Brower had had the benefit of an "eastern education." Still, it felt like an oasis.[15]

Eunice's dismay resurged that evening, on her first encounter with the great scourge of the West: the mosquito. In these muggy, low-lying western river valleys, tall tales were told of mosquitoes so large they could carry off a cow, and swarms so thick they would block the sun. Mosquitoes were far more dangerous than the story spinners knew: Mosquitoes carried malaria, or what the settlers called "chills and ague"—a combination of high fevers and chills so intense that the entire body shook. Once contracted, malaria stayed in the body forever and could recur at any time. For longtime Hoosiers the periodic "shakes" simply became second nature. But, as Eunice was quick to notice, the chills often led to pneumonia and other more serious illnesses, which could easily kill off a body weakened by high fevers. She knew nothing of all this that evening, but by the next morning Eunice's face, arms, and throat were swollen by mosquito bites.

The First (and only) Presbyterian Church of Lawrenceburgh was a homely, low-slung building, one of those plug-ugly country meeting-houses that were designed not so much to please God as to frighten the Devil, as the saying went. A rough wooden platform served as the pulpit, a single small stove provided heat, and the only light came from the windows. Henry did everything himself: sweeping, dusting, and cutting firewood on Saturdays, opening the church, building the fire, and closing up on Sundays. His first successful act was to beg money from his friends in Cincinnati for lard-oil lamps, which he installed, filled, and lit each Sabbath. "I was, literally, the light of that church,"

Henry laughed. "I did all but come to hear myself preach—that they had to do."[16]

The contrast between Cincinnati and Lawrenceburgh was much starker than that between Boston and Cincinnati. Unlike Ohio, which had a large Yankee population, Indiana drew most of its citizens from the upland South, especially the backcountry of Kentucky, as well as the tidal basin of Virginia and Delaware. Most were hardscrabble farmers chased by poverty and lured by cheap land and plenty of elbow room. Hoosiers had no tolerance for anything that struck them as pretentious or conceited. Indiana was a place where it was thought better not to wear fine clothing, if a traveler wished to avoid comments, stares, or a well-aimed dollop of tobacco juice; a place where the future governor, James Whitcomb, almost got off on the wrong foot when it was discovered that he wore a nightshirt to bed. Corn liquor, homemade peach brandy, and tobacco—"chawed" or in a pipe—were the primary indulgences, even among the women (who usually preferred smoking to chewing their tobacco).

Indiana put little stock in formal education, resting contentedly at the bottom of the free states in literacy, public education, and number of newspapers. In the southern counties where Lawrenceburgh lay, more than 40 percent of the population was illiterate. Most people held to the Methodist belief that too much education was a liability for a minister, and that a preacher who read a sermon from notes was, by definition, untouched by the Holy Spirit. Even lawyers and newspaper editors worried that being too grammatically correct would be seen as being "stuck up" or "puttin' on airs." But if Hoosiers had a reputation for being brusque and parochial, they also retained the Kentuckians' open-hearted warmth, lively hospitality, and colorful wit.

With her pretty face swollen and bespeckled by mosquito bites, Eunice was now doubly anxious about her debut as the minister's new wife. "They will not accuse their pastor of marrying for beauty, that's certain," she said gamely. As they entered the plain wooden church on Sunday, Henry stopped at the door to introduce her to his patron, Martha Sawyer. Intimidated and flustered, Eunice replied, "How do you do, Mrs. Beecher!" Henry laughed and moved the conversation along, but Eunice was mortified.[17]

As he mounted the platform that morning, the young Reverend Beecher did not cut a fancy figure. His wardrobe consisted almost entirely of hand-me-downs. With his smooth cheeks, unkempt hair (now cut by Eunice), and exuberant voice he did not bring much gravity to the pulpit. "How vividly I recall that first Sabbath! How young, how boyish he did look!" Eunice remembered years later. "And how indignant I felt, when some of the 'higher classes' come in out of simple curiosity, to see the surprised, almost scornful looks that were interchanged."[18]

"Higher classes" was a relative term. Eunice was aghast at the odd parade of characters who came up to shake the new Mrs. Beecher's hand after the service. "The most grotesque styles of dress," she exclaimed; "the funniest and most uncouth modes of expression!" The settlers looked as weathered and sinewy as beef jerky, clad in cheap calico and homespun linsey-woolsey. They spoke in the peculiar dialects of their native regions, with a bluntness born of harsh, lonely lives. Eunice had never seen such a queer hodgepodge of people. What they had in common, she noted, was a uniformly pale yellow complexion and the aura of a hard-used life.

As they crowded around her, suspiciously eyeing her good dress, reserved Eastern manner, and robust good health, they were as leery of Eunice as she was of them. In a place where malaria left the skin sallow and drawn, they were so unaccustomed to seeing rosy cheeks that Eunice was asked several times "if I had not a 'fever spell' upon me, because my cheeks were so red!"[19]

Those first few weeks, Eunice's homesickness was allayed only by her affectionate husband and her kind Yankee hosts. Just as she was beginning to adjust, Henry took a brief trip to Cincinnati on church business. Bad news arrived as soon as he left: Dr. Brower's mother had died, and his widowed father would now have to move into Henry's room.

In times of genuine hardship Eunice—with her unyielding practicality and bred-in-the-bone work ethic—truly shone. Unencumbered by the Beecher faith in divine financing, she immediately sat down and tallied up their money situation, something that Henry, with his resistance to math, had never really done. They could afford no more than thirty dollars a year for rent, a paltry sum even in such a poor place. Eunice clapped on her shawl and bonnet and began to scour the town.

"Oh! the search for that $30 house!" After two discouraging days of knocking on doors she abandoned that hope and began looking for four rooms, then lowered her sights to three rooms, and then two. Finally she swallowed her disgust and settled on two filthy rooms above a warehouse near the wharf, overlooking a backyard filled with old junk and sewage.

With the help of family and friends they cobbled together a home. Henry sold his gold college pin, and Eunice sold her new woolen cloak, a wedding present from her father, for thirty dollars. Lyman preached a rousing sermon on the duty of supporting the young clergy to his wealthy Cincinnati congregation, eliciting donations of linen, utensils, and furniture. Henry's brother George, newly married to a well-to-do Ohioan named Sarah Buckingham, gave them the magnificent gift of a cookstove and oil lamps. To their everlasting pride, a family friend, Mrs. William Henry Harrison—the wife of the old Indian-fighting general who would soon be elected ninth president of the United States—gave them a sturdy bureau and the heavy brass andirons, shovel, and tongs with which she had begun housekeeping forty years before. A friendly steamboat captain agreed to ship the whole lot back to Lawrenceburgh for free.

Those two weeks of setting up housekeeping were one of the high points of their marriage. Clad in a sturdy gray apron, Henry worked side by side with her, scouring the tobacco-stained walls and floors with soap, water, and sand, mending the castoff furniture, and lightening the load with constant jokes—"making a frolic of those three days" of scrubbing. The newlyweds nearly burst with satisfaction as they arranged their worldly goods, with a new corn-husk mattress on the bed, a closet fashioned from a strip of four-cent calico taped to a wire string, and Henry's saddle, bridle, and buffalo robe hanging from a hook above the door (the horse itself had to be borrowed). The crowning glory was his "library," lovingly displayed in a bookshelf rigged from old packing crates.

Henry marked the day in his journal: "At housekeeping with this same dear wife. Began Oct. 17, 1837." He hummed to himself as he strolled the dingy streets of Lawrenceburgh, contentedly quizzing the world: "Was there ever a man so happy as I am?"[20] Neither knew on that joyful October day that after only two months of marriage Eunice was pregnant.

THIS WAS THE "AGE OF THE COMMON MAN," as the pundits of the day dubbed it—when the populist impulses of 1776 truly began to find their footing in American culture. The opening of cheap land in the West, the extension of voting rights to all white men in the western states, and the expansion of common education were sweeping out the old colonial habits of deference to elites and replacing it with a new faith in the vox populi. In politics, this movement was marked by the presidency of Andrew Jackson, who was given a landslide victory by

eastern workingmen and western farmers attracted by the antiaristocratic rhetoric of the Democratic Party. In religion it was found in the
remarkable rise of the Methodist Church.

Methodism was a deeply populist religion, which held that salvation was open to any sinner who sought the open arms of Jesus. Methodists had no interest in metaphysical debates. Instead they emphasized
the power of God to bestow happiness, and the dignity of individual religious feeling—the more fervent the better—even among poor people,
women, and blacks. It was a theology made easy for the average man
to understand, emphasizing love and free will rather than exclusionary
tests of faith and esoteric logical proofs. Methodists were famous, above
all, for their passionate preaching, lively singing, and flamboyant emotional expressiveness.

This defiant antielitism shaped everything about the sect. In the
West the Methodists developed an extraordinarily successful system of
itinerant ministers who rode in regular circuits from one isolated settlement to another, ministering to small congregations that were run by
lay leaders until the next time the preacher returned months later. In
warm seasons they would get up camp meetings that lasted for days,
drawing hundreds, even thousands of people. These circuit riders were
young, uneducated men, some barely literate—graduates of Brush College, as they proudly proclaimed. Henry recalled one prominent Methodist elder who "knew so little, had so little culture, that he had to
count the chapters to tell what chapter it was, and then count the verses
to tell what verse it was." Yet these men "were real preachers," Henry
admitted years later. "Their personal experience was very strong, and
their feelings were outspoken, demonstrative."[21]

In New England the Methodists were still a minority, but they were
fast taking over the rest of the country, especially the rough western
states like Indiana, where Methodists outnumbered Presbyterians nearly
4 to 1. By midcentury Methodism was the single most popular denomination in the United States. With success, however, came the yearning
for respectability, exerting pressure to curb the excessive emotionalism
of the revivals and camp meetings—the hysterical sobbing and "holy
laughter," the involuntary physical responses like "the jerks," in which
worshippers began to twitch and turn until they fell convulsing into the
straw, or the "barking exercise" (also known as "treeing the devil"), in
which they began barking and baying. By the time Henry began preaching, the only place where such wild frontier emotions were still common was among the settlers of Indiana and Illinois.

Most Presbyterian clergy were both competitive with and contemptuous of the Methodists. Yet they had to be careful in their criticism. Remember, Henry wrote in his diary, "you can gain men easily if you get round their prejudices and put truth on their minds. But *never* if you attack *prejudice*. Look well at this."[22]

Nothing in Henry's education had prepared him to preach to this hard-bitten audience, who held Methodist emotionalism as the gold standard of religion. But he tackled his new job with all the professionalism that he could muster. He laid out his goals and strategies, he carefully composed and numbered all his sermons, and kept an elaborate journal with notes on what he preached, who came, and how it went over. For most of that first year, the young parson cribbed from his father's themes and volumes of old Calvinist sermons. He preached at least one sermon of heavy-going biblical analysis a week, and tried his hand at some fire and brimstone.

"I had just come out of the Seminary," Henry later recalled, "and retained some portions of systematic theology which I used when I had nothing else; and as a man chops straw and mixes it with Indian meal in order to distend the stomach of the ox that eats it, so I chopped a little of the regular orthodox theology, that I might sprinkle it with the meal of the Lord Jesus Christ."[23] Unsurprisingly, this was not very gratifying to him or his congregation. Threatening his people with the lake of eternal fire left him especially depressed, Eunice recalled. "I preached a great many sermons," Henry claimed, "which, after six months, I would not have preached again."

At first the new preacher attracted quite a few curiosity seekers, but after a month or two it was obvious that Henry's efforts weren't amounting to much. "I remember distinctly that every Sunday night I had a headache," he recalled. "I went to bed every Sunday night with a vow registered that I would buy a farm and quit the ministry." Just as in school, he berated himself for his procrastination and laziness. "I made many promises," he said, "that, if God would help me, I would make my sermons a long time beforehand."[24] He asked his brother-in-law, Calvin Stowe, to come help him get up a revival, but Stowe refused, saying that he had to face this challenge by himself.

Soon Beecher lost even the advantage of novelty, however, when the Methodist church in town acquired an energetic new pastor. To Henry's chagrin the new minister managed to spark his own revival within the first six months by sponsoring a camp meeting, a huge outdoor gathering of constant preaching, prayer, and exhortation that lasted for ten days. By the end of that year the Lawrenceburgh Methodist Church had taken in two hundred new members. Beecher, in stark contrast, added only eight people to his own congregation (including his own wife) over his entire term.

Still, Henry plugged away. By the time George Beecher and his new wife, Sarah, came to visit in the spring of 1838, Henry was making great strides as an orator. George was considered the rising star among the Beecher sons, and after receiving two new prestigious job offers that winter, he was about to leave for a prosperous church in Rochester, New York. Before he departed, the two brothers took turns preaching that Sunday.

"When George preached the first sermon, I came home, and said to my wife: 'I never felt as much indisposition to go into the pulpit again as I do now,'" Henry remembered. "The next night I preached, and George came home and said to his wife: 'Well, Sarah, since I have heard Henry preach I feel as if I had not been called to the ministry.' "[25] It was high praise indeed, and he counted it as a milestone.

WHILE HENRY RETAINED HIS Presbyterian pretensions in the pulpit, after church he tossed aside the gentlemanly ambitions he had so carefully cultivated in Cincinnati and threw himself into the local scene. "I could have said: 'Humph! Pretty business! Son of Lyman Beecher, president of a theological seminary, in this miserable hole,' " Henry recalled, but that would have been absurd. Young and poor as he was, he had no airs to put on with his neighbors.

Before long the young Reverend Beecher seemed to know everyone, high and low. "He was universally popular," testified the pastor who succeeded him. "He would hunt and fish with men not used to the society of clergymen, and spent much time down on the river" loafing and chatting with the constant flow of people coming on and off the boats.[26] For the first time since college he was spending most of his time with other men, hanging around the general store talking politics or debating religion for hours with everyone from an old infidel shoemaker to the rival Baptist minister.

But Eunice hated life in the West. She found nearly everything about Lawrenceburgh to be crude, ignorant, and dirty. Raised in a culture in which ministers topped the social ladder, she resented the infor-

mal familiarity with which the town treated her husband—a Beecher,
no less!—and the way westerners treated the clergy like objects of reluctant charity.

For all their education and eastern refinement, there was no way
around it: The young Beechers were dirt-poor. It was no small task to
keep house, even in two rooms. All their firewood and all their drinking, cooking, and washing water had to be hauled from the backyard up
a flight of steep stairs. It was a constant battle to subdue the mud and
manure that made its way up from the road. They were far too poor to
hire a servant to help. Too poor even to receive mail—at a time when
postage was extremely expensive *and* paid by the recipient rather than
the sender, they often left letters sitting in the post office until they had
the money to pay for the stamps.

The Beechers—long experienced in the ways of pious poverty—offered Eunice what help they could. As a way to eke out extra income
and escape the overwhelming drudgery of housework, Henry's equally
impoverished sister Harriet had begun to write stories, Sunday-school
tracts, and essays, and she urged Eunice to follow her example. "If you
can make money by sewing and it hurts you to wash and iron and do
those things why not hire the latter with the avails of the former?"[27]
Eunice, a highly skilled seamstress, did try, earning nearly two dollars a
week by sewing for a few hours a day. But she hated it—it was exhausting, demeaning work, and nearly impossible once the baby was born.

There were good times in Lawrenceburgh, too, Eunice later admitted. She and Henry were never so close as in those two small rooms.
Henry would work on his sermons in the bed-sitting room, surrounded
by books at his new work desk, purchased at the expense of Eunice's
winter cloak. Six feet away his wife sewed, kneaded bread, or washed
dishes until Henry whistled for her help. She would drop her work, her
hands still covered with dough or soapsuds, to sit at Henry's knee to
listen to him read from his sermon-in-progress. Reciprocating the favor,
Henry could be mildly helpful around the house, occasionally frying a
steak or making a pot of coffee, and once, to his great pride, kneading
and baking a loaf of bread when Eunice was suddenly overcome by an
attack of the chills.

Soon Eunice's health began to fail under the influence of the harsh
climate, hard work, and pregnancy. The prospect of a child filled her
with fear and anxiety. She confessed to George and Sarah that during her pregnancy, "often I had felt that it would be no great trial to

me—and release me from a load of responsibility, which I felt unfit to sustain, should the babe be stillborn."[28]

For three weeks she suffered from false contractions, before heading into labor around midnight on May 15, 1838. It was a hard birth, lasting eight hours. "The child was presented wrong," Henry wrote to his mother-in-law, "its hand being on its head and it was *two hours* before it could be remedied, which so exhausted the child that we thought at first that it was dead—but after a few moments it shot forth from its mouth very satisfactory evidence of breath and breath well used."

They named their healthy eight-pound girl Harriet Eliza—just as his sister Harriet had named her first boy Henry. The new father was besotted by his daughter, whom they nicknamed Hattie. "It's a real *Beecher baby*," he crowed, "and I shall be much mistaken if everybody does not say '*Oh how exactly like its father!*'" Eunice's feelings were more complex. "Henry makes a dear, fond father," she told George and Sarah. "The only trouble about it is a wee bit of *jealous* fear, lest he should love *me less*, as he loves his babe more. Jealous of my own daughter!"[29]

That summer was lovely. Eunice recovered quickly, and Henry had reason to believe that his congregation might soon offer him a raise in salary. Various Beechers came to help with the baby, and Harriet Stowe brought her own baby Henry for a heartwarming visit. The proud father so enjoyed loafing with his happy little family that he made not a single entry in his diary for three months.

BY NOW HENRY SHOULD HAVE BEEN officially ordained as a minister, but he was waylaid by ecclesiastical backbiting and the Beecher baggage. For the last several years the annual Presbyterian General Assembly had nearly broken up over the bickering between the Old and New School factions. When the General Assembly met in Philadelphia in May 1837, the meeting degenerated into an angry riot of clergymen standing on their pew seats howling at one another.

At that same moment, just across town, Angela Grimké—a Quaker reformer who was once a pupil of Catharine Beecher's and now the bride of the abolitionist Theodore Weld—was giving an impassioned speech against slavery in Philadelphia's newly erected Abolition Hall. A woman onstage speaking to a mixed-race audience was too much for the antiabolitionists to stomach. When a black man was seen entering the hall arm in arm with a white woman (in fact, a light-skinned former slave), a mob arose with sudden, terrifying force, smashing the windows and doors and returning the next day to burn the hall to the ground. The city's firemen, sheriff, and mayor stood watching as the reformers fled.

By the end of the week Abolition Hall was a smoldering rubble, and the Presbyterian General Assembly was in shambles. The Presbyterian Church was now officially split in two. Theology was the ostensible cause, but everyone whispered that the real reason was slavery, with rumors of a secret alliance between the Southern slaveholding churches and the Old School orthodoxy.

If "theology is but another name for the politics of the universe, or the Kingdom of God," as Charles Beecher observed with typical Beecher bias, then this corrupt bargain between hyperorthodoxy and slavery was inevitable. "Old School theology enthrones a great slave-holder over the universe," Charles argued, while the "New School enthrones a great Emancipator."[30]

After the schism at the General Assembly, Presbyterian synods across the country were given the choice of affiliating with either the New or the Old School organizations. As a Beecher, Henry was a well-known New Schooler, but his church was part of the presbytery of Oxford, Ohio, a staunch Old School outpost where many of the churchmen had supported the heresy charges against his father. His ordination exam was an all-day oral interrogation, and his hyperorthodox examiners would be looking for any chance to trip him up. But after a lifetime of drilling Henry was ready. "I knew all their proofs, all their digging cuts, all their ins and outs."

The exam was to be held sixty miles away, in Eaton, Ohio. When he arrived, the board of examiners was packed with his father's Old School enemies. The room was tense as the moderator, "Father" Archibald Craig, a tall, lean man of fifty or sixty, with a "shrill, ringing voice," called them to order. "There he sat," Henry crowed in the sarcastic account he sent to his brother George, "the young candidate begotten of a heretic, nursed at Lane; but, with such a name and parentage and education what remarkable modesty, extraordinary meekness and how deferential to the *eminently acute* questioners, who sat gazing upon the prodigy! Certainly this was a bad beginning! Having predetermined that I should be hot, and forward and full of confidence, it was somewhat awkward truly to find such gentleness and teachableness!"

As the examiners warmed up "the questions came like hail," Henry said. "Some of them I answered directly, some ingeniously, some intelligently, and others somewhat obscurely." But in all cases he told them essentially what they wanted to hear. The board was shocked to find that just "when they thought they were going to get heresy they got a perfect avalanche of orthodoxy."

Some might accuse Henry of hypocrisy, or even lying, that day. Retelling the story years later, Henry would describe it as a natural gift for persuasion. "Somehow I have always had a certain sympathy with human nature which has led me invariably, in my better moods, to see instinctively, or to perceive by intuition, how to touch the right chord in people, how to reach the living principle in them; and that faculty was awakened on this occasion," he recalled. After a full day of questions the panel unanimously declared Henry orthodox and eligible for ordination. They would set the date of the ceremony when they met the following day.

The trouble was, as Henry put it, "that then they slept on it." Lyman's Old School enemies were galled at once again being outfoxed by a Beecher. So in the first order of business the next morning, they voted to postpone setting the date for Henry's ordination while they debated several resolutions designed specifically to confound him.

First they passed a motion declaring that the Presbytery of Oxford align itself officially with the Old School National Assembly—the very same one that had expelled Lyman and his New School supporters in Philadelphia the year before. Then they passed a motion requiring all candidates for ordination to swear allegiance to the Old School Assembly. Only then did they return to Henry's case, demanding that he take the oath.

"I refused" on the spot, Henry said, even after Father Craig generously offered him six months to think on it. So "they turned me out—and gave me my papers back again."

"I felt as big as forty men," Henry recalled, without even a hint of irony. "I simply said: 'Well, brethren, I have nothing to do but to go back to my father's house.' "[31]

Before leaving, Henry asked about the status of his post in Lawrenceburgh. The board replied that in light of his decision, it was declared officially unfilled. "Just what they *had to* say, and just what I wanted them to say and moreover just what I determined they should say," Henry told his brother with some bravado. "I drove home forthwith, got back on Saturday. On Sunday recounted from the pulpit the doings of the [Presbytery] and declared them vacant if they continued under Oxford."

The story infuriated Beecher's congregation, just as he hoped it would. Under the young minister's not-so-subtle guidance, the members held a meeting two days later, and by "a unanimous vote they withdrew from Oxford and declared themselves an *Independent Presbyterian Church.*"[32] It was the first time, but not the last, that his congregation would defy a higher authority out of loyalty to Henry.

News of Henry's crisis spread like prairie fire, throwing the entire western Synod into an uproar. Oxford's decision to ally themselves with the Old School as a way to force Henry's hand effectively forced the hand of every Presbyterian minister in the western territory, requiring each church to declare its allegiance one way or another. There was no more room for hedging.

Within several weeks of Henry's debacle the Synod convened in Cincinnati for a vicious fight to the finish. Henry rode up to Cincinnati to watch the debates. Now that he was personally involved, he took an unusual interest in the dry ecclesiastical proceedings. But as the meeting degenerated into open hostility, his usual boredom hardened into deep disgust, and he left for home before they cast the final, acrimonious vote to split the western territory into two separate synods, one Old and one New School.

Lyman's dreams of a western religious empire now lay in shards around his feet. His beloved church was nearly destroyed, not by its enemies but through its own internal contradictions and petty jealousies. When asked years later if he regretted leaving Boston for this godforsaken country, Lyman replied, with a hint of sadness, that he preferred not to think about the past.

But the younger Beecher was exhilarated. It was just as well to have these men of "mad ambition and madder jealousy" out of their camp, he told a friend. With their underhanded tactics, "there *was not one moment's safety for character or standing to any New School man.*" With his dramatic display of loyalty, Henry earned his father's approval and found his first intoxicating taste of fame. He could not help gloating about his newfound notoriety. "My case may stand for many," he exulted. "A graduate of Lane (that propaganda of heresy)—the son of the Arch Heretic—has received the imprimatur of Orthodox Oxford!"[33] There was something deliciously funny and deeply satisfying to Henry in gaining renown as an *orthodox rebel.*

On November 9, 1838, Henry was ordained by his father and Calvin Stowe, establishing him as minister of the Independent Presbyterian Church of Lawrenceburgh within the newly created New School Presbytery of Cincinnati. The symbolism was ideal. He began his career by simultaneously swearing allegiance to his father, fulfilling the deathbed dream of his mother, and declaring his independence. But just as Henry was celebrating his triumphant outmaneuvering of the Old School enemies, he was hit with the first big blow of his career.

THAT AUTUMN THE UNITED STATES was gripped by a major financial depression. It began in the spring of 1837, when the bottom dropped out of the international cotton market, igniting a financial panic that shut down the banking system of New York. This in turn plunged the supply of money to a new low, crippling the overextended and under-regulated western banks. Eastern commerce ground to a halt, and now the paralysis was spreading to the agricultural regions of the West. In Cincinnati, Catharine Beecher's Western Female Seminary failed in May 1838. Uncle Samuel Foote was bankrupted by generosity when many of his friends defaulted on personal loans. In New York, the Tappan Brothers' dry-goods business went under. Arthur Tappan's checks to Lane Seminary were suddenly worthless, leaving President Beecher and Professor Stowe nearly penniless.

In Lawrenceburgh, the government-backed canal and railroad projects had kept the depression at bay, but in the fall of 1838 the Ohio River—the great commercial highway of the region—began to dry up, making it almost impossible to carry goods in or out of town. Wages tumbled and prices skyrocketed. Coffee, butter, and sugar were going for the exorbitant price of fifty cents a pound. Only corn and its two subsidiary products, pork and whiskey, could still be bought for a pittance.

Henry's little family was bowled over by the sudden contraction of the economy. In anticipation of his upcoming raise, they had gone into debt to fix up their rented house. Now his congregation could no longer meet even his current salary, and the coffers of the American Home Missionary society were practically empty. Henry's income from all sources for 1838 would amount to far less than three hundred dollars, not including the potatoes and corn given by farmers in lieu of money, and the regular plates of tenderloin sausage sent over by "the gentleman who does pork business."[34]

Squeezed by stress, the constitutional differences between Eunice and Henry began to emerge, especially relating to money. Eunice had inherited "my father's dread of living in *debt*," as she admitted, while Henry possessed *his* father's almost reckless faith in Providence. "God only knows how we are to get along," he confessed to George that fall, "and I leave it cheerfully to him."[35] In one year Henry had run up credit all over Lawrenceburgh.

His parishioners were happy to support him when he was attacked by outsiders in his squabble with the Presbyterians, but in exchange they tightened their claims on him. The day after the church declared its independence from the Old School Presbyterians, one of Henry's parishioners came to scold the young pastor for a variety of sins. They were unhappy with his rising debts around town, laying the blame on his weakness for "fine living"—a claim that surely outraged Eunice. They were put off by his failure to make regular pastoral visits among the congregation over the summer, and several members had been insulted by a sermon that had seemed to attack them personally. His summer of pleasure had a steep price.

The local critics also had harsh words for his wife. Henry's parishioners were offended by Eunice's frequent absences from church and by her failure to accompany Henry on his rare pastoral visits. The matrons of the town thought she put on airs, with her fancy manners and Yankee habits, and they sniped at her lax housekeeping. In her defense, Eunice was plainly overwhelmed by work. But why then, the ladies gibed, did she keep the pretentious habit of serving the family's daily meals on a *tablecloth?*

"It has depressed me exceedingly. Told wife of it," Henry wrote ruefully. "I was becoming too much elated and too independent. Tho' painful I can truly say it has done me good. It has given me *Experience*. It will be my fault if I am not a better man, and don't preach better for it, than before." Not for the first time, and certainly not for the last, Henry vowed to take a crash course in humility: to avoid all debt, to visit more, to "abate my desire for *fine living*," and to "diminish self-estimation."[36]

To earn badly needed cash, Eunice began sewing for hire, and Henry tried to follow Harriet's example by writing Sunday-school books and articles, but that didn't amount to much. As their troubles mounted, their home life began to show the strain. Like most twenty-five-year-olds, Henry had no taste for calling on old ladies, shut-ins, and poker-faced respectables, to talk gravely about their souls or to comfort the grieving or ill. But he found plenty of time to go fishing with his new pals or to loaf around the cracker barrel in the general store. Eunice developed a poisonous jealousy of his time away from home, which festered until it became, in her mind, the central conflict of her marriage. Within a year of their wedding they embarked on the classic marital cycle of neglect and nagging. Unfortunately to outsiders henpecking is more obvious than stealthy emotional neglect. The more shrill Eunice became, the more sympathy flowed to Henry. There was, as his brother Charles quipped, "No terror like the terror of Eunice."[37]

Although it was a subject of discussion among his family and friends, Henry himself said very little about the friction at home. As 1838 drew to a close he began to recover his health and optimism. His first day back in the pulpit after a month's illness, he preached from John 14:27: "Peace I leave with you, my peace I give unto you; not as the world giveth, give I unto you. Let not your heart be troubled, neither let it be afraid."[38] He spoke movingly of how to cope with trouble, sickness, and despair. Afterward the congregation buzzed with approval, noting that the autumn's harsh lessons seemed to be giving him a new power in the pulpit. Perhaps they were right.

WITH THE NEW YEAR Henry determined to make a fresh start. After several friends (and potential converts) surprised him by joining the Methodists, he began to study his competitor's tactics. Finally he decided to visit the Methodist church himself. He was astonished by what he saw.

The sermon was plainspoken and sensational, skillfully pulling the audience onto an emotional seesaw, alternately issuing vivid warnings of impending doom and impassioned pleas to flee to the glorious bliss of God's love. Lively hymns, adapted from popular folk tunes (in marked contrast to the gloomy Puritan dirges sung in a perpetually minor key) sung not by a professional choir but by the entire congregation, punctuated the passionate prayers and exhortations. He watched in amazement as their "low" methods drove the otherwise "sober and unextravagant" townspeople into a frenzy of feeling, groaning with misery and fear, crying and shouting with joy and fervor, filling the air with "Amen!," "Mercy! Mercy!," and "Come to Jesus!" This "contagion of example," Henry noted, awakened an "animal excitation or magnetism" that saturated the room, creating the "*extraordinary zeal* of members, to increase their ranks."

Just as important was the contrast between the long, arduous Presbyterian conversion experience and the easygoing Methodist belief that anyone could join the church if they took Jesus Christ as their savior. It was difficult to compete, he noted in his diary, when "I am opposing a church which lets into full communion *any who choose* without any change of heart or preparation whatsoever, except *seriousness* and desire to be better."[39]

Yet even as he continued to rail against the "excess and absurdity" of the Methodists, Henry began quietly, deliberately to imitate them. He put more emphasis on "regular and attractive" music, eventually making it his personal signature. He began to cultivate, in his words, "More spirited preaching."[40] To make his sermons seem spontaneous, he trimmed his notepaper to fit unobtrusively inside his pulpit Bible, so that no one could see that he was speaking from notes. That spring he seemed to be on fire.

Suddenly opportunity landed in his lap. Samuel Merrill, an early Yankee settler who was now a wealthy landowner in Indianapolis and the president of the Indiana State Bank, began attending Henry's church whenever he was in town to inspect the local branch bank. That spring, as Merrill was riding by coach into Lawrenceburgh, a box of coins fell and broke his leg, forcing him to remain in town for six weeks while the leg healed. Over those six weeks Merrill and the young pastor hit it off, discovering a mutual love of books and ideas. (Sam Merrill would later found the famous publishing firm the Bobbs-Merrill Company.)

As the Old and New School rivalry came to a head in late 1838, the small Presbyterian church of Indianapolis was one of the casualties. Led by Samuel Merrill, a circle of well-to-do businessmen split off from the Old School church to establish a more liberal New School church. The new Second Presbyterian Church promised a generous salary, but they were having a devil of a time breaking through the common prejudice against settling in Indiana. After the job was refused by six ministers, including his own brother, Samuel Merrill turned to young Beecher, asking him to come preach a trial sermon in Indianapolis.

Indianapolis was two days of hard riding from Cincinnati, more than forty miles of rough tracks cut through an ancient forest of maple, walnut, oak, and ash trees. Indianapolis was not much larger than Lawrenceburgh, but as the newly designated state capital it had higher aspirations. A grand new domed capitol building gleamed in the center of town, and the streets swarmed with judges, legislators, land speculators, entrepreneurs, and bankers, buzzing with schemes to bring highways, canals, and railroads to the young capital.

Here, Henry was treated like a VIP, sleeping in the town's finest hotel and dining with some of the town's most prominent men, including the former governor, Noah Noble. After his sermon the committee plied him with flattery, telling him that the "young men not generally attached to any church are favorably impressed with me. My manners win them," Henry confided to his diary. "They think I have the right kind of mind."[41]

By his second visit Henry was nearly decided. He drew up lists of pros and cons, leaning heavily toward the pros. All his reasons for leaving boiled down to ambition, both godly and personal. He saw boundless opportunities for influence in the fledgling church, the raw new capital, and the rich but unformed state. He dutifully noted how much good he could do for the New School cause in Indiana, but the capping motive was his desire for a more stimulating intellectual environment, where he would finally find "Gratification of all literary appetites."[42] Then there was the money. The founders were committed to paying the minister enough to live within their own range of comfort, a tempting promise to a man in perpetual debt.

The official call came on May 13, 1839, by unanimous vote, offering an annual salary of six hundred dollars. Henry had no hesitation. It was his duty to go, he told his bereft parishioners.

Eunice was harder to convince. For all her complaints she was reluctant to leave the friends they'd made in Lawrenceburgh and the close proximity of Walnut Hills. But Henry played on her anxiety about baby Hattie, who was sickly and losing weight. He reassured her that Indianapolis's climate would be gentler and healthier. With Eunice's consent, they made plans to leave by the end of July.

Henry's first two years as a minister had been a mixed bag. He'd improved vastly as an orator, but as a spiritual pastor he left much to be desired. As the Reverend Joseph Tarkington, his Methodist rival, put it, "Mr. Beecher could outpreach me, but I could outvisit him, and visiting builds up a church more than preaching."[43]

"I had been discontented for two years," Henry later admitted, but now everything was looking up. For the first time his father was asking for *Henry's* help with a revival in Oxford, Ohio. "I know he will come if he can," Lyman told his new wife, Lydia, for he is "so like-minded with his father."[44]

Just before they left for Indianapolis, Henry delivered the Independence Day oration, a national tradition on the Fourth of July and a great honor. It was declared "a rich treat" by the editor of the *Lawrenceburgh Political Beacon*, who asked if he could print a copy of the speech.[45] Surprisingly Henry refused, explaining that it would take more time to write up his notes than he could spare. The Reverend Beecher was shaking the dust of Lawrenceburgh from his shabby coat and moving on.

Chapter 6

"I Am a Western Man"

*J*ulia Merrill never forgot the first time she laid eyes on Henry
Ward Beecher. She was only twelve years old when her father,
Samuel Merrill, brought her to what she called "that Godforsaken town of Lawrenceburgh." While her father finished his business at the state bank, he left her to wait for Beecher in a dingy local
tavern, staring out the fly-specked window, trying to ignore the dank
smells drifting from the kitchen. "All at once I saw a gentleman fly
down a pair of stairs and cross the street," Julia remembered. "He did
not look like the preachers of the Old School Presbyterian church to
whom I had been accustomed. Instead of being tall, thin, sallow and
grave looking—this man was small, ruddy, spry, and jolly in appearance;
his head was surmounted by a white plug hat!"[1]

The jolly little man introduced himself with such warmth that Julia's shyness melted away, and she happily took his hand and crossed the
street to meet Mrs. Beecher. The Merrills were appalled by what they
found. There was not a dollar in the house, and the Beechers' hand-
me-down clothes were worn into rags. Worst of all was little Hattie,
teething and fretful in the high summer heat, her skin sallow and her
weight only a few pounds more than when she was born more than a
year earlier. Samuel Merrill insisted that they take his own private carriage to Indianapolis, leaving Julia to help them, while he continued on

his rounds by public coach. Eunice would always remember that generous journey as a small miracle of happiness. As they stopped to pick blackberries along the road, the very taste of the fruit seemed to bring Hattie back to health.

After four days of travel they rolled through the dusty yellow streets of Indianapolis up to the Merrills' splendid house on New Jersey Street. Julia led Eunice and Hattie through the wood-paneled central hall into a sitting room to meet her mother, Jane Merrill, while Henry lingered outside taking care of the horses.

At the threshold Eunice stopped dead in horror. There, wrapped in blankets despite the August heat, lay a wan woman, two blue-skinned children, and an older girl, each one shaking visibly with the chills. A moment later, Henry entered the room, Eunice burst into tears and turned sharply upon him. "Oh! Henry, they are all sick with 'chills,' and you were told no one ever had them here!"

Mrs. Merrill was taken aback by Eunice's outburst. "You must be mistaken, Mrs. Beecher," she said mildly, "everyone has 'chills and fever' more or less constantly." The swampy, low-lying city was notorious for its malarial air, and anyone in Indianapolis for even a day would find that out.

"No!" declared Henry, "we were emphatically told that it never came here."

His words were met with a tense, puzzled silence. No one spoke as they were led to a guest room. "I was astonished that he said no more," Eunice said, "but, on looking at the stern eyes, the pale and closely-sealed lips, a part of his character I had never seen before was revealed; the perfect silence and power of self-control, under what he felt was a wrong done to himself but which he saw it was too late to prevent."[2]

It was a look that she would come to know well over the years, whenever Henry was caught in circumstances he did not like and could not get out of. Like Eunice, his sister Harriet attributed that stony response to anger: "When he is angry he doesn't say anything; he shuts his mouth and stays still."[3] But Henry's close friends would later concede that it often had more to do with avoidance than anger.

Henry never seemed to "prevaricate, to give a shifty, double-sensed answer," as more than one friend observed, but he "could be silent; no man more utterly so. And at times, when pursued by questions that he did not wish to answer, he would pass into silence, not only, but an impossibility of countenance that gave no more sign of understanding or of repose than the face of the Sphinx." As another friend noted, "He could conceal, when concealment was necessary, only by maintaining an absolutely impenetrable reserve."[4]

The confrontation with Mrs. Merrill made Henry seem like either a fool or a liar. But if Henry noticed the tension he took it in stride. His diary offers only this placid account: "*Indianapolis. Arrived with my family Thursday eve., August 4, 1839. Came to Mr. Merrill's.*"[5]

Eunice's worst fears quickly came true. Both Henry and Eunice were quickly struck down by malaria. A "spell" began with chills, heralded by yawning and stretching, blue fingernails, and exhaustion, then little pricks of cold that spread until the victim's teeth began to chatter. After an hour or so warmth would slowly come back, and rise to a raging heat, accompanied by searing pain in the head and a dull backache. The spell ended with a drenching sweat. Home remedies were plentiful, but until the discovery of quinine nothing helped except building up an immunity over time.

For almost a month Henry and Eunice were so sick they could not leave their bed in the Merrills' house. When his strength returned, Henry found inspiration in his suffering. "The very sickness leaves such a mark of love, that I hardly know how to admire it enough and my eyes fill with tears when I think of it," he wrote in his diary. "I was so cold and formal and *doctrinal*; so *vain glorious*, man fearing and worldly. It is all—God came and cast me down and rebuked and led me to thinking and more serious efforts at a spiritual life."[6]

But for Eunice it was a bitter beginning, laying the foundation of a resentment that would only grow.

ONE COULD SAY THAT INDIANAPOLIS was a city founded on a mistake. In 1821 the leading men of Indiana decided to move the capital to the dead center of the state, to make it easily accessible to all citizens. They chose a densely forested site on the banks of the White River. Unfortunately the river turned out to be too shallow to navigate and the land too swampy for easy road-building. Isolated by its topography, Indianapolis retained the harsh habits of the frontier long after most western towns had shed them. Fresh tree stumps, weeds, and axle-deep ruts cluttered the streets, and mud-chinked log cabins stood next to ambitious half-built buildings stranded by the economic depression.

With a little less than three thousand citizens, the town was flavored by the rough-edged culture of Kentucky. "The whole city was given over to politics and money making," Henry observed, with flourishing side industries in gambling, corn liquor, horseracing, and whores.[7] Clerks, farmers, congressmen, army officers, artisans, and judges all played cards and drank together, argued politics, and bragged about business. Speculation was shifting from canal building, which shut down with the depression, to railroads, although that was still a distant dream.

The founders of the Second Presbyterian Church were shrewd self-made men, the type of civic boosters who believed the conventional wisdom that a bank's bonds were more valuable within sight of a church steeple. They were, said Samuel Merrill, exceedingly pleased with "getting a son of Dr. Beecher for our pastor."[8]

The small congregation boasted some of the leading families of the town, including bank officers, lawyers, and politicians. The congregation held services on the second floor of an all-purpose civic building, surrounded by open pasture. To enter the makeshift sanctuary they climbed up a crooked wooden staircase, under which stray sheep often gathered to rest. At first the sheep, hearing the feet of churchgoers leaving services, would politely rise and walk, one by one, from the front of the stairs. After a few Sundays, however, the sheep stopped bothering to move, leaving their sister flock to push through *them*. The little congregation didn't mind—they thought it looked rather biblical.

But the bucolic scenery belied a hostile environment. Henry's first service was packed with curious Hoosiers, including several Methodists and Old School churchmen who were girding themselves for doctrinal battle. But anyone looking for a fight was disappointed. In his very first sermon Henry declared his independence from sectarianism, speaking from 1 Corinthians 2:1–5: "I am determined to know nothing but Christ." His subsequent sermons were equally unexpected, taking up unusual topics like penal reform and why religion should not be gloomy. Every week more people trickled up the stairs to see this odd sort of Presbyterian.

Henry's new ecumenicalism began as a calculated strategy to broaden his appeal and preempt potential critics but soon became heartfelt. Still, in this age of heresy hunting, it paid to be cautious. As 1839 drew to a close Henry set out his new resolutions in his diary—he might be dropping his father's sectarian zeal, but he retained his father's canny political pragmatism.

I am resolved never to become a disputant or champion on any of those points which *divide truly evangelical Christians*. If I feel it a duty ever to speak of such topics I will strive to do it so as to soften and win the feelings and promote charity rather than bitter sectionalism.

2. Resolved that I will strive to cherish *secret feelings* of love to all other Churches beside my own;—to say nothing evil of them, nor to desire their members; nor their decline.

3. Resolved that in public and private I will give my life to bring all Christians to work of preaching the *true* power of Gospels—the love of Christ.[9]

The Beechers were delighted by Henry's sudden success. Within months of his arrival in Indianapolis he was hearing the kind of praise he had longed for as a child. "I think in *one year* my brother Henry will make his influence felt all over the state of Indiana," his sister Catharine predicted. "I have never seen persons improve as fast *morally and intellectually* as my brother since they commenced the duties of their mission." Isabella seconded her older sister's confidence. "I think he is going somewhat in father's track and will perhaps one day come somewhere near him in eminence—tho' I fear as a domestic character he will not be his equal."[10]

ISABELLA BEECHER'S INSTINCTS were correct. While Henry's career was taking off, his home life struggled. At first he and Eunice and little Hattie lived with the Merrills and their bevy of bookish daughters. In January 1840 they borrowed enough money to purchase a small cottage near the outskirts of town. On one side was pastureland, on the other a "swale," or shallow ravine, which ran between his cottage and the mansion owned by Harvey Bates, Indianapolis's leading citizen. It was a heavy mortgage, requiring him to pay one hundred dollars a year out of his six-hundred-dollar salary, but they were eager to be settled for, once again, Eunice was pregnant.

The little wooden frame house was just ten feet across, with enough yard to keep a small garden and a few chickens. "One room was to serve for entrance into the house, for parlor study and bedroom. The bedroom was so small that I was obliged to make the bed on one side first then go out on the veranda, raise a window, reach in, and make the bed on the other side," recalled Eunice. "The little kitchen—partitioned off from the veranda—was just large enough to allow a passage between the cooking table and stove into the dining-room without burning my dress; and my kitchen table was only divided from Mr. Beecher's study by the partition."[11]

Between the grind of work, recurring fevers and chills, and pregnancy, Eunice was laid low through most of the long, damp winter. In March, Eunice again spent three weeks suffering false labor pains, lying in their tiny little bed pushed up against the window. The contractions persisted until Tuesday, March 10. In tiny, uncharacteristically controlled handwriting Henry recorded the event in his journal: "My wife today, after a horribly protracted labor of a whole day (three weeks of false pains preceding) brought forth a dead son. She was very quiet and easy afterward."

The next day Henry described the heartbreaking funeral: "Buried the little boy. Dr. M. and myself alone in graveyard. At the last day, may not this little spirit give triumph to its body, above hundreds who lie beside it—cut down in manhood?" It was their first real taste of death.

Temperamentally Henry and Eunice dealt with loss in opposite ways. Eunice was openly distraught, while Henry slipped into stony silence. In his diary, after his brief account of the burial, Henry changed the subject abruptly, writing in the next line: "Began my garden. I wish to keep a little record of progress of things. Rose bushes, honeysuckle, willow trees have been in leaf for some days."[12] Consciously or not, he turned the tasks of digging and death into a scene of sowing and rebirth.

From that day forth in Henry's diary, all personal commentary, all mention of wife and children, disappears. Except for occasional notes on his reading and sermons, his journal is entirely devoted to gardening, including minute notes on his plantings, cultivation, harvests, and eating, as if nature itself were the antidote for death. He filled his yard with vegetables, flowers, and fruit trees, taking on further foolish debt to buy two more plots of land. He became a mainstay of Indiana's horticultural society and an avid collector of plants, introducing a host of new species to the region, and winning many prizes at the state fair. He scoured the state library for books on farming, gardening, and husbandry and soothed himself to sleep by reading seed catalogs. "If I have said it once, I have said it five hundred times, that I spoilt a good farmer to make a poor minister," he liked to say.[13]

Flowers were his greatest passion. He gave away so many bouquets, slips, and seeds that he nicknamed himself the Bishop of Flowers, even among grizzled farmers who had little use for a plant that couldn't be eaten. More than half a century later old women still tended with pride the rosebushes and fruit trees the Reverend Beecher had given them as young brides. "Flowers," Henry liked to say, "are the sweetest thing that God ever made and forgot to put a soul into."[14]

In the wake of the stillbirth, Eunice's in-laws offered what consolation they could. "I cannot on the whole regret that Providence saw fit to deny the gift of life to another little one at a time when your extremely reduced and enfeebled health must have made the charge of it an extremely trying and laborious if not dangerous one," Harriet Stowe wrote to Eunice with bleak pragmatism.[15]

Poverty compounded their grief. Within the course of six months they had racked up more than five hundred dollars of debt, only one hundred dollars less than Henry's annual salary. They were forced to take in a boarder to help pay their bills, adding to the strain of overwork and frequent malarial attacks. "I have been shaking and burning alternately with remarkable vehemence," Henry wrote to Walnut Hills. "Between both operations a man is left well nigh stultified." Eunice made no effort to conceal her discontent. "I had never seen such a woman; she could be as beautiful as a princess, and as plain and homely as possible. So she could be sparklingly bright and bitterly sarcastic," recalled one of Sam Merrill's girls.[16] Adding to her unhappiness, she was soon pregnant again.

Finally Henry decided to send her and two-year-old Hattie home to Massachusetts for a long visit. The three departed for West Sutton in November 1840, leaving behind a swirl of unkind gossip about Eunice and the state of the Beechers' marriage. "Mr. Beecher left us on Monday to take his wife to New England who is in very bad health and who is strongly suspected here to be as *ill disposed* as indisposed. Mr. Beecher is still popular but his wife is a great weight on him whether from mere ill health or something else I cannot say," his friend Samuel Merrill wrote.[17]

It was a bittersweet homecoming for Eunice. Henry was a model of attentiveness on the long journey, but her pleasure was shattered by the misbegotten kindness of a fellow traveler when Henry rose to find her a cup of tea. "I was very pale and sick and he looked very young, beside me then," Eunice recalled with chagrin. "While he was gone, one lady whose little boy was very troublesome, said, 'How proud you must be of such a *kind and helpful son*. I wish I could hope that my boy would grow up half as good.'"[18]

When her beloved mother met her at the door of Bullard's Hill, Eunice's joy again turned to bile. "You want to see the Doctor?" Lucy Bullard asked the gaunt, sallow-faced woman who greeted her, without even a hint of recognition. "The Doctor is out, but will be in soon. Won't you sit down?"

Eunice was only twenty-nine years old, but after three years out West, she looked easily a decade older. No matter what the gossips of Indianapolis might say, her suffering had taken a genuine toll.[19]

WITH HIS WIFE AND DAUGHTER GONE, Henry found it too laborious to live alone, so he rented out their cottage and moved into the grand home of one of his patrons, Harvey Bates. Harvey Bates was a founder of the city's first insurance and gas companies, and an early backer of the railroad—the sort of man crucial to every successful western city, who combined wheeling and dealing with civic boosterism. In exchange for the hospitality, Henry offered to tutor Elizabeth Bates, the lovely, dark-haired daughter of his host, and her best friend, Julia Merrill, Sam Merrill's girl, along with several of their thirteen- and fourteen-year-old friends. In that year Henry forged a deep bond with Julia and Elizabeth, and in return the girls developed passionate crushes on their dashing young teacher.

In their adolescent enthusiasm, Julia and Betty were expressing what everyone else in town was saying—that the new Presbyterian parson was unlike any minister they'd seen before. Within a year of his arrival Henry had become a local celebrity.

From the first Beecher made friends with the legislators and lawyers who thronged the capital when the courts and state legislature were in session, strategically targeting sermons to their interests. Soon the Second Presbyterian Church was the darling of the capital crowd, especially among young men looking to establish themselves professionally. Henry's congregation was so pleased that they were now building him a new church on Governor's Circle, right across from the court buildings and legislature. With its rare New England–style belfry, it was considered a "colossal edifice" by the locals and a tourist site by visitors.

As travelers spread stories of the remarkable young fellow they'd heard in the state capital, invitations to preach in neighboring towns flowed in. Henry began preaching regularly throughout the outlying settlements, like a Methodist circuit rider. Henry told stories of "being stalled in the mud, half-drowned in crossing rivers, long, lonely forest rides, camp-meetings, preachings in cabins, sleepings in the open air." With the state's dense forests and everlasting swampiness, Indiana roads were the worst in the nation. "Horrible, abominable, outrageous roads," as Henry complained in his diary. In the woods most were simple bridle paths hacked out of the underbrush, so dark at night that horsemen carried tree-branch torches for light and to ward off wolves. More beautiful but just as frightening were the endless, treeless prairies, where a man could ride for dozens of miles through waist-high wildflowers without seeing any hint of a road. Physically Henry was fairly fearless, but even he was terrified of fording the web of rivers that crisscrossed the state. "In going from place to place the thought of the ford that I would have to cross was a perpetual torment to me."[20] Mud could turn to quicksand, or the tide could sweep the horse from its feet, and several times Henry almost drowned.

The "towns" where Henry preached were often little more than one or two log cabins in a clearing, some so new and raw they had no door, just a wide spot to duck through, and no fireplaces, just an open fire on the floor and a hole in the roof. Most taverns were simply private homes along the road, where for two bits a stranger could eat, sleep, and feed his horse. Beds were often little more than straw strewn in a corner, and even the best corncob mattresses were usually shared by fleas and bedbugs, as well as other travelers or the host's family. The air was thick with the pungent odors of sweat and manure, wet dogs and horse ammonia, whiskey and tobacco fumes, melting tallow candles, drying diapers, and damp wool. Henry preferred to sleep on clean straw in a farmer's barn, or under the stars, or he searched for a roadside house with flowers in the yard. "We were seldom misled," he recalled. "A patch of flowers came to signify kind people, clean beds, and good bread."[21]

But for all Henry's efforts, he found that while he was getting plenty of attention, he wasn't making many conversions. "I can preach so as to make the people come to hear me," he observed to a colleague. "But somehow I can't preach them clear into the kingdom."[22]

Finally he was determined to find out what the difficulty was. Living out of his saddlebags, with only his Bible at hand, he found himself drawn over and over again to the New Testament. "I get along better with the New Testament," he confessed.[23] He especially identified with the Four Gospels—the tales of Christ's twelve disciples traveling the countryside spreading Christ's teachings. Henry studied the apostles until, as he put it later:

> I got this idea: That the apostles were accustomed first to feel for a ground on which the people and the apostles stood together; a common ground where they could meet. Then they stored up a

large number of the particulars of knowledge that belonged to everybody; and when they had got that knowledge, which everyone would admit, then they brought it to bear upon them with all their excited heart and feeling.

He'd made the beginner's mistake, Henry realized, of thinking "the sermon was the *end* and not the *means.*" The point was not to outline "correct" doctrine but to motivate the audience psychologically. With the very next sermon he prepared, the young pastor tried his new approach. "I remember it just as well as if it were yesterday," he recalled.

> First, I sketched out the things we all know, and in that way I went on with my "you all knows," until I had about forty of them. When I had got through that, I turned round and brought it to bear upon them with all my might; and there were seventeen men awakened under that sermon. I never felt so triumphant in my life. I cried all the way home. I said to myself, "Now I know how to preach." I could not make another sermon for a month that was good for anything. I had used all my powder and shot on that one. But for the first time in my life, I had got the idea of *taking aim.*

Immersed in the New Testament, he focused less on the Lord as lawgiver and more on Jesus Christ as soul mate—"a Christ that never was far from me, but was always near me, as a companion and friend, to uphold and sustain me." Henry was increasingly convinced that if God sent Jesus Christ to Earth out of love for mankind, offering salvation to all those who embraced and reciprocated Christ's love, then, as Henry wrote in 1843, "*Love* should be the *Working Principle*" of religion—not blind obedience, abject submission, or cold justice.[24]

This vision of Christ as a lover sent down to ease the burdens of mankind was so effective, said Henry, that it "made metaphysical doctrines and philosophical formulas more repugnant to me than they had ever been before, and I entered into a vow and covenant that if I were permitted to preach I would know nothing but Christ and him crucified among His people."[25]

Calvinist principles still bubbled up in his sermons, of course, and Henry was not above whipping up sectarian controversy if it served his purposes. But his father's theology was losing its stranglehold on him. "*Man* was the thing," he declared. From now on he would be "preaching from sympathy with living men rather than from sympathy with any particular system of thought."[26]

As Henry's confidence grew, so did his independence. "Parson Beecher was a lot diff'rent from most of the preachers at that time," one Hoosier recalled. "He believed in mixin' happiness and a good time with religion. He made a lot of friends with his style of preaching, especially with the young folks." On that score at least, Henry practiced what he preached. Now in his late twenties, youthful vigor seemed to burst from his threadbare seams, spilling out in his bounding stride, rosy complexion, and almost inexhaustible energy. "His vitality was immense, his jollity at times irrepressible," his friend Hugh McCulloch remembered.[27]

Nothing about him seemed ministerial. Instead of the white cravat that marked a Presbyterian minister as surely as a white collar signified a Catholic priest, he wore open-throated shirts, tied loosely with a black stock or tie. He was the first minister in those parts to sport a working-man's soft, wide-brimmed felt hat (and in summer a jaunty straw hat) instead of the stiff top hats of professional men. He usually threw on the clothes he'd tossed to the floor the night before, tucking his pants into muddy work boots worn straight from the garden to the pulpit. Rather than the stovepipe trousers and short, snug "pigeon-tailed" frock coats favored by fashionable young men, he wore an old-fashioned, round-breasted shad-bellied jacket (a Methodist coat, in the lingo of the day) and wide, well-patched pants. It was presumed that he did not even own a dress coat, since no one ever saw him wear one. He tried growing whiskers but soon gave them up—they were neither flattering nor fashionable at the time. Inevitably when he preached a long wavy lock of hair fell in his face, which he brushed back with a dramatic sweep.

Henry seemed to care nothing for decorum or social conventions. He was an enthusiastic member of the volunteer fire company, once halting in midsermon when the fire alarm rang to race to a nearby fire. When the blaze was out, he cheerfully returned, covered in soot and mud, his hands cut and bloody, to finish the service. He shocked the carpenters working on his house by hanging from the exposed joists and "skinning the cat," a country boy's gymnastic trick of drawing his legs up through his arms and over the joist, then pulling himself up until he was sitting on the beam. After church he'd often challenge the young men of the congregation to jump the fence posts around the center circle with him—a game that was awfully hard on the trousers, as Eunice observed, especially when he missed. When passersby occasionally found him lying lazily on the grass, eyes shut, his answer to their surprised inquiries was that he was working on a sermon.

Henry put together the finest choir in the state and introduced the custom of regular church socials. At these he was at his best—joking, singing, teasing, and leading old-fashioned games imported from New England: "Hunting the Key Hole," "Blow Out the Candle as the Jones Family Did," "Dumb Orator" (in which, on one memorable occasion, his dignified friend John Ketcham recited and Henry made the faces and gestures). "I remember in a game of copenhagen at a church picnic he was in no way disconcerted by being rolled over and over down the hill when entangled in the rope," one friend recalled.[28] One little boy became his lifelong admirer when Beecher, amused by the lad's half-baked attempts to build a kite, finally surprised the child by making him a kite bigger than the boy himself.

Henry brought his boyish informality into the pulpit. In private, Hugh McCulloch remembered, Henry would laughingly "mimick preachers who seemed to think that sanctimonious countenances and whining tones were the indications of zealous faith." In contrast to the flowery, formal styles of most popular orators, he spoke with an intimate, almost conversational tone, a "sublime kind of talking," as many observed.[29] After years of practice Henry's voice was incredibly flexible. It could drip with sarcasm or float like an angel's, and shift from the subtle pathos of a whisper to a clap of thunder in the flash of an eye.

His long immersion in the King James Bible and fine English writing gave Henry's phrasing a natural elegance, but he used blunt language and homey images. "Don't whip with a switch that has the leaves on, if you want to tingle," as he liked to say.[30] Henry's overflowing curiosity, his voracious reading, and warm friendships with everyone from ditch-diggers to high-court judges gave him a wealth of everyday anecdotes and illustrations to draw upon.

Henry had an ear for dialects and slang and would often slip into imitations as he told his stories, occasionally sending a guilty titter of laughter through the audience. At these moments, as one observer noted, the young minister invariably "would drift into a channel tender and deep and full of tears," choking up the people who had been giggling only moments before. "If I can make them laugh, I do not thank anybody for the next move; I will make them cry," Henry later said. "Did you ever see a woman carrying a pan of milk quite full, and it slops over on one side, that it did not immediately slop over on the other also?"[31]

The key to this dramatic style, as McCulloch noted, was that Beecher seemed entirely "free from egotism." Not everyone agreed, of course. "There was a good deal more of Henry Ward Beecher in that sermon than there was of Christ," as one visitor noted disapprovingly.[32] But there was no denying that Parson Beecher—with his irreverence, candor, and almost impious aura of happiness—attracted many who never set foot in church otherwise.

Finally Henry was the mirthful minister he'd longed to be. "Some people," he mused, "think that I am not solemn enough in the pulpit, nor staid or reverent enough out of it. I wonder what they would think if I should act just as I feel."[33]

BACK IN MASSACHUSETTS ON AUGUST 8, 1841, Eunice gave birth to a son, naming him Henry Barton. In late July Henry set out to fetch his family home. His friends Sam Merrill and Harvey Bates asked him to take their two girls back East with him to visit relatives and get a dose of culture. It was a thrilling journey for the girls, despite a few bouts of both homesickness and "the Western sickness" (malaria). "I do not think I have forgotten a mile of the way," Julia Merrill told Henry more than forty years later.[34]

While Henry was back East, a full-fledged revival finally broke out in the Second Presbyterian Church. His parishioners were so excited that they asked Lyman Beecher himself to lead the revival in his son's absence, which he did with relish. Unfortunately, by the time Henry returned, the religious fervor had died down. But Henry got his chance a few months later, when a friend, the Reverend Merrick A. Jewett, asked him to travel to Terre Haute, Indiana, to help with a revival-in-progress. Off he went, riding two days through towering beech trees, dazed with nervousness. "How helpless and wretched did I feel when Jewett sent for me," he recalled. "I did not know how to preach in a revival."

But then, said Henry, "Hardly was my saddle empty before Jewett was at my elbow. 'You have done well to come. You must preach to-night.' In a moment the cloud lifted. The reluctance was gone. It has been so all my life."[35]

Beecher plunged into a grueling schedule. Every day after breakfast he rode from house to house, to talk one-on-one with people about the state of their souls, until the daily midmorning prayer meeting started around ten. Then more house visits after lunch, followed by another evening prayer meeting. Within a week religion was the only thing anyone could talk about. Converts poured in, and the town buzzed with praise for this eloquent newcomer.

It was exhilarating to wield so much power and unleash so much passion. Like his father, he quickly became addicted to the adrenaline of the revival experience. For three weeks he prayed and labored "until my heart was on fire." At the end of January, Henry reluctantly headed home. "To go back to the ordinary round of church life from this glowing centre seemed so intolerable that my whole nature and all my soul rose up in uncontrollable prayer," he recalled later. "Through the beech woods, sometimes crying, sometimes singing, and always praying, I rode in one long controversy with God. 'Slay me if Thou wilt, but do not send me home to barrenness.'"[36]

As soon as he arrived home, Henry announced that he would be holding evening meetings every night until they kindled their own revival. The first evening was stormy, turning the icy roads into swamps. The room was only two-thirds full, and the audience was cool. On the second night, again rainy and unpleasant, he asked anyone interested to stay afterward and talk further with him. No one did. The third night, when his lecture was over, he watched in despair as the room emptied out.

"All the children of my friends, the young people that I knew very well got up and went out," until only one person remained, a poor, thin servant girl. "She smelt of the kitchen and looked kitchen all over," Henry recalled. "I remember that there shot through me a spasm of rebellion. I had a sort of feeling. 'For what was all this precious ointment spilled?' Such a sermon as I had preached, such an appeal as I had made, with no results but this!" But then, "The next minute I had an overwhelming revulsion in my soul; and I said to myself, 'If God pleases, I will work for the poorest of his creatures.'"[37]

That night was itself a conversion experience of sorts for Henry. No matter what was said later of his luxurious tastes, high-falutin' friends, and obvious ambition, from this day on Henry made it his special mission to reach the hardest, most despairing of sinners. Cynics would say he was interested only in reaching the masses, the lowest common denominator. But among people who felt marginalized and alone, he made them feel loved and respected. "I always feel most for those who are farthest from grace," Henry confessed, "perhaps because I see in them some likeness to myself."[38]

His vow was rewarded when "two of my sweetest children—not my own, but they were like my own to me—stopped on the next night" (most likely Elizabeth Bates and Julia Merrill, who officially joined the church a few weeks later).[39] Their example quickened interest, especially among the young ladies, who began to pour out their souls to the sympathetic parson. Soon a full-scale revival was rolling through the city's churches.

By April several hundred citizens were clamoring to enter the rolls of heaven. In yet another example of the bitter sectarian squabbling that marked the era, the hot controversy of the day was over the rite of baptism. There were almost as many methods as there were sects—from the sprinkling of holy water on the Presbyterian's forehead to the full-body dunking of the Baptists—with many a good Christian condemning the other to hell for not being doused the right way. Privately Henry could hardly have cared less about the issue, but he was happy to banter the subject around the cracker barrel. When word went round that Henry had been thrown by his horse into the Miami River while traveling, he was immediately razzed by the local Baptist minister.

"Well, Brother Beecher," the Baptist called out as Henry strolled by, "I've heard of your immersion in the river. I thought you would adopt our custom of baptism in the end."

"Haven't adopted it," shot back Beecher. "I was immersed by a horse—not an ass."[40]

So it was considered a great event when Beecher and his fellow ministers decided to hold a cross-denominational "Union Baptism" to celebrate the spiritual harvest. Nearly three-quarters of the city turned out for this rare spectacle on the bank of the Whitewater River. As Beecher waded into the water, he sent a roar through the crowd by announcing that he personally would baptize his new congregants by any method that made them happy, pouring, sprinkling, and immersing as they desired.

Still, Henry was his father's son. As he noted in secret satisfaction, with a haul of one hundred members in three months, he'd made more converts than all the other city churches combined.

LYMAN BEECHER WAS OVERJOYED by his son's unexpected success. After many awkward years, he and Henry were now comrades in arms, keeping up a regular congratulatory correspondence and preaching on the same platform whenever they had the chance. But if it was surprising to see how closely Henry was following in his father's footsteps, the paths of Lyman's more sober-minded sons were even more surprising. Lyman's great plans had not wrought the glories he'd hoped for.

The oldest son, William, had a weak personality that was unsuited to the ministry. One congregation after another sent him packing, including one that literally starved him out by reducing his salary until he was forced to resign just to feed his family. The promising second son, Edward, tried to defer to his father's wishes while fulfilling his own academic desires, taking a job as president of the newly founded Illinois College, but running a college on the hostile frontier brought him little satisfaction and endless hardship.

Far worse, the three youngest boys—Charles, Tom, and Jim—were openly rebelling against the ministry. Charles, who had married and fathered a child, remained snarled in unhappy agnosticism. In desperation Lyman asked Henry to invite Charles to Indianapolis. "My opinion is that there is not an other place in the world as yet where Charles could be safe and happy," Lyman wrote confidentially to Henry.[41] In early 1842 Charles moved his family into a small house next door to Henry and Eunice, becoming the music director and general assistant in Henry's church.

Before long Charles's resistance was softened by Henry's judicious lack of pressure and his lovable vision of Christ. When a revival swept through the church, Henry did not argue or cajole, but one night toward the close of the revival, Henry turned to him, asking, "Charles, have you anything to say?" Warmth flooded Charles's veins, and "from that night I threw off and put aside all the philosphisings in which I had found no end," and dedicated himself to Christ. Henry wrote to Lyman with triumph, *I feel that Charles is safe.*"[42] The following autumn, Charles joined the ministry.

Pressured by Lyman, nineteen-year-old Tom was now studying at Illinois College. But he, too, wanted nothing to do with the ministry. Hoping Henry could repeat his success with Charles, Lyman sent Tom to Indianapolis for the summer. Tom's time in Indianapolis confirmed Henry's new place in the oedipal order; "of all my brothers I think I like Henry the best. He is the most like father of all his sons and as a speaker and writer far surpasses any divine I have ever heard," Tom told Isabella. "And then for warmth of affection, and adaptation for domestic usefulness and happiness he is hardly second to our dear father who on these points I feel by daily experience that he is peerless."[43] As with Charles, Henry's touching vision of Christ's love soon wrought what Lyman could not. Eventually Tom too set his sights toward the ministry.

Finally Lyman sent James, the baby of the family, to Henry. Raised almost entirely in the West, James was hotheaded, with a taste for violent pranks, brawling, gambling, and drinking. Unfortunately James did not fall under Henry's spell. Shipped off to Dartmouth College in 1845, he was a constant troublemaker who graduated only because he was Lyman Beecher's son. Where he would go from there was a grim question.

The only Beecher boy giving Henry a run for his money was George. At the age of thirty-six, he was settled in a prosperous post in Chillicothe, Ohio, and an up-and-coming leader in the antislavery movement, not to mention happily married and the proud father of a new baby. But George's outward success belied inner misery. "He was naturally very high-strung, of very fine fiber," in Henry's words.[44] Nowadays the diagnosis would likely be manic-depressive disorder. But at this time religion was the crucible of his suffering.

George had become obsessed with the controversial doctrine of "perfectionism," which maintained that the Bible commands us not simply to obey God's laws, but to strive toward actual perfection, in every deed, feeling, or thought. "Turned outward on the world, perfectionism supported utopian communities and radical reforms like the abolition of slavery," as the historian Joan Hedrick has observed. But when it turned inward, it placed almost intolerable pressure on individuals to repress every stray impulse that did not focus entirely on God, creating tremendous guilt and self-loathing when, inevitably, one's mind strayed toward worldly matters. George's journals record terrible cycles of irrepressible zeal and harsh self-discipline: "When I am not in a state of religious enjoyment, from bodily weakness, and feel the fear of guilt, Satan takes advantage of it to goad me . . . beyond my strength," he confided to his diary.[45]

His worried family warned George of the risks of perfectionism in their most recent "circular letter"—a sort of chain letter for the far-flung clan, with each member adding his or her own news and then forwarding it on to the next—all except Henry, who jovially dismissed their fears. "As to perfectionism, I am not great troubled with the fact of it in myself or the doctrine of it in you," he joked to George, "for I feel sure that if you give yourself time and prayer you will settle down right, whatever the right may be."[46]

But Henry was wrong.

THE YEAR 1843 BEGAN with glad tidings. For the second year in a row, a revival swept the Second Presbyterian Church, pulling Charles back into the family fold and making it the largest Presbyterian church in the state. At home five-year-old Hattie was the apple of her father's eye, and could often be spotted riding in his wheelbarrow, nestled among the squash, cabbage, and onions he sold at the open-air market. His son, Henry, was a bubbly, healthy toddler.

That summer they decided to take a family holiday. The first week of July, Henry borrowed a carriage and they set off for Jacksonville to deliver the commencement address at Illinois College, while Edward was away with his father on a fund-raising trip back East. It was a wonderful trip, Henry remembered, and on the way home they "were as elated and songful and merry as one can imagine anybody to be." The carriage was within two miles of the city when they ran into one of his Presbyterian elders.

"I suppose you have heard the news?" he asked.

"No," said Henry, "what is it?"

"Why, your brother George has killed himself!"

The whole party was struck dumb. "We rode on," Henry recalled, "and as we rode I could not help thinking, 'Killed himself! killed himself! killed himself!' "[47]

"Henry did not speak, but drove rapidly on," Eunice remembered. "I just glanced at his face. It was like marble, and I can never forget the agony I saw there."[48]

Hundreds of miles to the east, Lyman Beecher was walking down the street when he passed an old friend carrying a newspaper. The man stopped Lyman, asking abruptly, "Have you heard the dreadful news which has come into the city this morning?"

"I said, 'No,' " Lyman remembered.

"Your son George is dead."

The friend handed Lyman the newspaper folded open to the notice of George's death. "The shock was like that of a blow across my breast which almost suspended respiration, and left to me only the power of articulating at intervals, Oh! oh! oh!" said Lyman. He stumbled through the city streets, "bathed in tears, subsiding and anon bursting out again," until he arrived at the room where he was staying, where he poured his grief into a letter to his now-widowed daughter-in-law.[49]

Soon a letter arrived from Harriet telling the story. Catharine Beecher had just arrived for a visit with George the day before. He seemed happier than he had in a long time, Catherine thought, but as dusk came on, the oppressive heat seemed to put George in an unusually

emotional mood. At his evening lecture he spoke tearfully of his eagerness to join Christ in heaven and his strong feeling that these would be
"the last words that many of his church ever heard him speak."[50]

The next morning George awoke before everyone else and stepped
out into his cherry orchard. A deacon walking by the house heard a
blast and saw a flock of birds whirl into the air. Another shot followed,
but he could see nothing through the trees. An hour later the hired girl
went to call George for breakfast and stumbled upon his body, lying
near his favorite sweet cherry tree, with a double-barreled shotgun in
his hand. A bullet had gone through his cheek, shattering the top of
his head.

It was reported as a suicide, although there was no note to confirm
it. It is telling, though, that the Beechers' initial reaction to that theory
was not the disbelief one might expect. Indeed, God's motives seemed
far more mysterious than George's. "*Why* had God spoken to us in so
decided a tone—and wrung our hearts as much by the *manner* of this
event as by the death itself?" Harriet asked in anguish. "Our circle has
begun to break up—who shall say when it shall stop?"[51]

But after learning the details of his death, the family decided it
was an accident. "It is supposed that he fired one barrel at the birds in
his trees and was preparing to recharge the barrel and was blowing the
smoke out for that purpose when he accidentally sprung the lock for
the other barrel," Harriet wrote.[52] The family clung to the belief, for as
Eunice said, "to find that 'killed himself' did not mean suicide seemed
to take away half the sorrow."[53]

Henry retreated into himself. "It was not for several days after the
news that he could utter a word about it, even to his wife,—but he
spent his time mostly in solitude and silence and now, he scarcely ever
trusts himself to speak much about it," Harriet wrote to George's widow,
Sarah.[54] A month passed before Henry could bring himself to write to
Sarah himself.

At first, Henry finally wrote to Sarah Beecher, this anguished question rang over and over in his head: "Oh, what can Christ mean—how
can he afford to take away his Servants from the battle, in the very
height and heat of conflict?"[55] But as he imagined George's glorious
entry into Heaven and his joyous first meeting with Christ, Henry could
not mourn his brother's fate. He consoled Sarah with a vision of unimaginable love and pure faith.

So it would always be. When faced with sorrow in person, Henry faltered every time, but on paper or in the pulpit he made even death an expression of love.

HENRY TOOK A DRAMATIC TURN after his brother's tragic death. Harriet Stowe described it as a new spiritual fervor. "He seems every day to burn with new zeal for that cause of Christ and to be baptized with the spirit of him who has left us," she told George's widow.[56] As if to honor his fallen brother in arms, Henry seemed to set off on a warpath, pursuing one furious crusade after another. Although he continued to preach what he called the "Doctrine of Love," Henry was returning to his belligerent Beecher roots.

Years later Henry occasionally joked about this apparent contradiction in his personality: "I am a peace-man, except when I wish to fight." But there was a bedrock of hubris under his easygoing exterior. Like most of his family, Henry had what he called "a conceited conscience," which would not let him drop an idea he considered important. When pricked, Henry's outrage obliterated his magnanimous feelings and moderate beliefs. He "does sometimes lose the reins of prudence," one friend noted. "He is occasionally like a man who has struck his foot so hard against a stone, that, to save himself from falling on his face, he needs *must* run awhile, though every step be on vipers."[57]

Many of his most thrilling moments as a speaker came in this way, when he and his audience fed off each other's reactions, spiraling to great heights of emotion. Any problems arose only afterward, when Henry's dramatic pronouncements—which seemed so right on stage— had to be explained or sustained. "I have found all my life long that in special emergencies I could come to high states of experience, while the difficulty was to carry those states as small change along with me every day," he confessed ruefully.[58]

Henry's excesses were fed by his time and place. He came of age in a particularly feverish time, as the foundations of the American two-party political system were being laid. We tend to think of Christian political organizing as a late-twentieth-century movement, but in fact religion was one of the most critical divisions between the first modern political parties.

In a country as heterogeneous as the United States, national parties are by necessity constructed as coalitions. And like all coalitions, they are strongest when unified by shared fears. Democrats built their loose but flexible coalition primarily around an egalitarian fear of tyranny, whether by an economic elite, meddlesome churches, or an authoritarian government. In particular they railed against evangelical crusades to unify church and state, and capitalist efforts to use the federal government to promote narrow economic interests.

The Whigs, meanwhile, tended to unite around a dread of disorder, anarchy, and immorality. Known colloquially as the Christian, the Moral, or the Yankee Party, the Whigs were the party of capitalists and evangelical Protestants, who believed that the role of government was to "improve" the nation through economic and moral development. Whigs exploited the techniques of religious revivals, running political picnics and rallies like camp meetings, while insisting that the secular progress of the nation depended on the spiritual discipline of its citizens. Of course plenty of Christians, capitalists, and Yankees voted Democrat, but if a voter was a New England–born Presbyterian wading comfortably in the marketplace, he was almost certainly a Whig. These ideological poles of fear remain potent to this day, but they dominated the politics of the western frontier. As one prominent historian put it, in most campaigns, "the party of order and morality confronted the party of laissez-faire and hedonism."

Indianapolis in the 1840s was a ferociously political city, with voter participation rates consistently above those in the rest of the country, and a distinct "Whig-Presbyterian-evangelical subculture."[59] When Henry arrived in Indianapolis, he immediately fell in with what the Democratic *Indianapolis Sentinel* sneeringly called the "Whig Junto," a set of prominent bankers, businessmen, and politicians, including Sam Merrill, Calvin Fletcher, ex-governor Noah Noble, and his successor, Governor Samuel Bigger. They were the driving power behind most of the city's benevolent institutions. Soon Henry had joined them as an official pillar of the community, helping to establish or aid Wabash College; the Benevolent, the Historical, and the Horticultural societies; the Deaf and Dumb Institute; and a school for the blind; as well as campaigning for a statewide public education system and various "Blue Law" ordinances banning gambling, drinking, Sabbath breaking, and prostitution.

These initiatives, however well intentioned, were not always welcomed by Hoosiers who resented what they saw, quite fairly, as attempts to impose militant Protestantism, higher taxes, and burdensome regulations. For this reason, Methodists—the largest denomination in the state—were regarded as a crucial swing voting bloc. They had the churchmen's love of order and morality but were wary of giving more political power to their Presbyterian rivals. With the upcoming state elections scheduled for August 8, 1843, both parties were carefully cultivating the Methodist vote.

Unfortunately Henry was in no mood to tread lightly. A week or so after George's suicide, Henry rode up to Crawfordsville, Indiana, to speak at the commencement of Wabash College, a Presbyterian-affiliated institution. There he shocked the audience by tossing aside his carefully cultivated ecumenism and launching a nasty attack against Matthew Simpson, the president of Asbury College, Wabash's Methodist rival, who was secretly campaigning for James Whitcomb, the Democratic gubernatorial candidate.

Word of Henry's impolitic speech spread quickly. The Democrats pounced, using Beecher's sectarian screed to turn Methodist voters against Governor Bigger. "The wrath of the Whigs is descending fearfully on the head of Beecher for his Crawfordsville speech," crowed Lucian Berry, the Methodist politico who coordinated the counterattack. "This moment a leading Whig told me if Bigger was defeated it might— and would be ascribed to Beecher. I, of course, believing it to be a fact, have done my best to deepen the impression."

Hoping to control the damage, Henry denied the details of the story in the *Indiana Journal,* the local Whig organ. But since there had been so many witnesses to the speech, this seemed to cast him as a liar. Berry's prediction came true. When Governor Bigger lost by two thousand votes, due largely to Methodist defections to the Democrats, Beecher was blamed. "The indignation of the community never fell as heavily on any man as it does at the present on him," exulted Lucian Berry.[60]

Henry was badly burned, but he seemed to take no cautionary lesson from it. In December he announced that he would deliver a seven-week series of evening lectures on the vices of the capital: gambling, dueling, circuses, theaters, horseracing, idleness, political demagoguery, intemperance, and, most shockingly, prostitution. Many in Beecher's own congregation were indignant that he dared talk so openly about such evils, and some refused to let their women and children attend. But the hue and cry only spurred public interest, and each evening the hall was packed.

Those who came were rewarded with Henry's most spectacular performance yet. The wages of wickedness was a hackneyed topic, but his dramatic illustrations and vitriolic language gave it new life. In each lecture he spun a vivid portrayal of the first, enticing temptations to vice—the harmless wager, the small glass of wine, the comely face—then traced the downward spiral to rack and ruin.

The success of the lectures churned the cloud of controversy. Beecher mentioned no sinners by name, but angry speculation surged among those who thought he was referring to them or suspected political revenge. When a local printer offered to publish the lectures as *Seven Lectures to Young Men*, the slim volume made a big splash. Three thousand copies were printed that first year, and it would go though forty editions over the next fifty years.

As the series wound down in January 1844, the church elders were inspired by Brother Beecher's lectures to clean house, moving to excommunicate a half dozen church members for gambling, fornicating, visiting houses of ill repute, and other sins. This was less to Henry's taste—happy as he was to rail against evil in the abstract, he had little stomach for investigating his friends' personal lives. For the moment his crusading urge seemed sated.

AT HOME, LIFE WENT ON in its usual rhythm. Eunice suffered another miscarriage in the fall of 1843 but was soon pregnant again, exacerbating her mercurial moods. But as more of the family, both Beechers and Bullards, joined them in Indianapolis, her outlook brightened.

Harriet Stowe came for a long visit in the middle of the hot, humid summer of 1844. She and Henry sat up late into the night, just like the old days, talking about everything under the sun. "I love him so much," Harriet told her husband, Calvin Stowe, "it really makes me cry to think of it."[61] But her pleasure was marred when Henry brought home the unnerving news that a Presbyterian minister they knew had been caught in a sex scandal.

This sort of thing was not unheard of. The pastoral relationship was fraught with intimate temptations. Years later one Indianapolis wife recalled how, during Henry's first revival, while tearfully talking over the state of her soul, she became so emotional that she "threw her lovely arms around his neck and cried: 'Oh, Mr. Beecher, save me!' 'You must look to a higher power,' was his grave reply, as putting both hands from about his neck he fell on his knees and said, 'Let us pray.' "[62]

Still, both Harriet and Henry were strangely affected by the story. Henry "seemed so depressed that a horrible presentiment crept over me. I thought of all my brothers and of you," Harriet wrote to Calvin, "and as I am gifted with a most horribly vivid imagination, in a moment

I imagined—nay saw as in a vision all the distress, despair that would follow a fall on your part till I felt weak and sick."

"Well I thank my God that I can stand up as strait as a poplar in the judgment day for all any sin of that kind," Henry declared later. "But," Harriet noted, "Henry looks really heart worn and shocked—who would not! such terrifying things!"[63]

On October 18, 1844, Eunice gave birth to her second son after a long, difficult delivery. He was, Henry wrote to his mother-in-law, "a fine, well formed and healthy boy—George Lyman—who eats and sleeps and cries only by way of pepper and salt—a little only in a good while." Eunice was already recovered enough to be walking around and sitting with them at the dinner table, Henry reported cheerily. But Eunice's postscript contradicts her husband's happy picture. "I am not well enough to write today," she told her mother. "Henry is so hurried with business just now, that you must not scold him for a short letter. He leaves me for Ft. Wayne on Monday to be gone 4 or 5 weeks."[64]

It was a terrible time to leave Eunice, with two small children and a brand-new baby. Perhaps as a way of compensating for her husband's neglect, Eunice insisted that roly-poly baby Georgie was the spitting image of his father and, by her own admission, his mama's favorite child.

BY NOW HENRY COULD SAY with honest pride, "I am a *Western man*."[65] Over the winter of 1844–45, he created a new secular soapbox for himself, becoming the editor of a new bimonthly newspaper, the *Indiana Farmer and Gardener*, a spinoff from the Whig *Indiana Journal*. The paper allowed him to harness his literary ambitions, his infatuation with horticulture, and his passion for scientific knowledge and self-improvement, and gave him a forum to discuss any issue that caught his interest.

The *Indiana Farmer and Gardener* also provided a roundabout path into party politics. Henry launched his very first issue with an assault on whiskey. Temperance, as everyone knew, was one of the Whigs' prime issues; currently the Whigs were pushing the state legislature to regulate liquor sales. But it was also one of the party's great liabilities, stoking their reputation as holier-than-thou evangelical tyrants.

Henry might have gone further with his new crusade, but it was soon overshadowed by national politics. In 1845 the newly inaugurated Democratic president, James K. Polk, moved to annex the Mexican territory of Texas as the twenty-eighth state. Democrats were convinced that only land, land unrestricted by the interference of the federal government and sanctimonious priestcraft, would extend prosperity to everyone. It was, as the *Democratic Review* argued that summer, the "Manifest Destiny" of the United States to extend the empire of liberty from the Atlantic to the Pacific.[66]

Americans had been eyeing Texas for some time—especially Southern planters, whose soil was being depleted by the harsh single-crop farming of cotton, and who looked greedily on the large tracts of rich, untouched land to the west. When rumors spread throughout the South that the British were plotting to turn Texas into an abolitionist stronghold by buying out Texas slaveholders and emancipating their slaves, Southern statesmen demanded its immediate annexation, insisting that the only way to preserve the right to slavery in the United States was through territorial expansion.

Polk's decision ignited a violent clash with Mexican troops along the new, disputed border. Seizing on the specter of foreign aggression, in 1846 the U.S. declared open war on Mexico. Most Whigs were appalled by the Democrats' naked landgrab, especially if it led to the expansion of slavery. They had no desire to interfere with the "peculiar institution" of the South, but they were equally adamant that slavery stay confined where it was. A wide swath of citizens from all parties condemned the invasion as an act of despotism—most famously, Henry David Thoreau, who later penned the essay "On Civil Disobedience" in protest.

HENRY'S FEELINGS ABOUT SLAVERY were evolving in fits and starts. He could see that the antislavery movement was slowly gaining respectability and converts. His closest friends in Indianapolis were strong antislavery advocates, as were a growing number of Indiana's New School clergy. Even his own father was edging toward the antislavery movement. By early 1839 Henry had repudiated the disgraced theory of colonization. In Indianapolis he defied local custom by developing warm friendships with a number of local black families, including an elderly former slave named "Uncle Tom" Magruder and his family, who lived down the street. When his sister Harriet came to visit, Henry took her to meet the Magruders, providing Harriet, it was said, with the namesake of her famous novel of the 1850s.

The question that bedeviled Henry was not the moral status of slavery, but how slavery could be eliminated without tearing apart the Union. He speculated that one solution, perhaps ordained by God, was the interbreeding of the races. After all, Henry noted in his diary, the "Etheopians had mingled with lighter blood," giving "rise to Egypt, mother of art and science." A year later Henry proposed another peaceful solution in his diary: "The cottons and sugars of America have drained Africa of her offspring for slavery and I think ere long the cottons and sugars of Africa and India will drain America of slavery."[67] Radical as his thoughts on intermarriage might seem, his only practical solution was letting the aggregate forces of history take their slow, evolutionary approach. But even these were private thoughts, shared only within the city's tiny circle of antislavery sympathizers.

"It grew on me that it was a subject that ought to be preached upon; but I knew that just as sure as I preached an abolition sermon they would blow me up sky high," Henry said later. "It seemed to me that my church would be shut up, and that I should be deprived of the means on which I depended for the support of my family."[68] Indiana, with its strong Southern roots, was even less hospitable to free blacks and abolitionists than Ohio, and here a drunken mob was easier to raise than a square dance. One of Henry's own church elders had sworn that, "If an Abolitionist comes here, I will head a mob and put him down."[69]

But the pressure on Henry was growing. In 1840 the New School General Assembly passed a resolution requiring every minister to preach at least one antislavery sermon a year—a measure first proposed by George Beecher in 1838. After three years of putting it off, in May 1843 Henry finally announced that he would deliver a sermon on slavery. He chose the date with care. The Indiana Supreme Court convened on May 25, and the church and surrounding area would be crowded with attorneys, judges, and other government officials, mitigating the possibility of violence.

On the appointed Sabbath the pulpit was still empty as the final stragglers were squeezing into their seats, recalled Alfred G. Riddle, an out-of-towner visiting Beecher's church for the first time. When Riddle first spotted the "rather heavy looking young man from the country— decidedly country—of a stout clumsy figure, [in] heavy, coarse, soiled shoes, with baggy trowsers" standing forlornly at the back of the church, he thought it strange that no usher offered the poor greenhorn a seat. When the man rushed up to the platform and sat down, Riddle was appalled that no one told him to move.

Suddenly, to Riddle's surprise, the man stood up and announced the title of the sermon: "The New Testament View of Slavery." The sermon started off jerkily, but then Beecher took hold. "A miracle had been wrought," said Riddle. "The *exuviae* of the country boor had vanished. A man inspired, radiant, glorified, transfigured, face aflame, eyes flashing, voice reverberating, stood instead. His notes a crushed crumple, in the vise of his right hand, were shaken aloft in the intense energy of free, bold action."[70]

The performance was far more dramatic than the message, however. Beecher's solution to the vexed problem of slavery was prayer, sympathy, and calm discussion. But as far as it went, it was a success. The trouble was he'd just have to do it again next year.

Now, in the summer of 1845, as American troops massed on the border of Mexico, slavery's poisonous pot was boiling over with a viciousness unseen since the mid-1830s. Independence Day in the West was a combustible mix of patriotism, whiskey, and wild-eyed stump speaking (Ohio prudently dealt with the problem by exempting all citizens from arrest on July 4). Henry's church was packed that afternoon, while outside in Governor's Circle, the drinking was heavy and the crowd boisterous.

John Tucker, a forty-five-year-old former slave from Kentucky and longtime resident of Indianapolis, was passing by the Circle when a drunk named Nicholas Wood blocked his path and began harassing him. Tucker stood his ground until several of Wood's friends jumped him. When he tried to run, they chased after him with clubs and bricks. They beat Tucker to death while the crowd watched, screaming "Kill the damned nigger, kill him!"

Less than a hundred yards away, the audience in the Second Presbyterian Church could hear the shouts and curses. Finally Beecher and a few other men rushed out to the street. By that time the mob had taken on a life of its own and was looking for other targets, cheering themselves on: "The niggers are getting too cursed thick, and ought to be thinned out!" "I would as lief kill a nigger as an Ox!" "Damn them, I wish every one was shot, and the Abolitionists too!"

The mob roamed the streets, coming upon Henry Depuy, the small, mild-mannered editor of the *Indiana Freeman*, Indianapolis's recently established antislavery newspaper. As the rioters began taunting and pushing Depuy, Beecher ran up and shouted: "Get out! Run! You have no friends here!" Depuy took his advice at top speed.[71]

After the mob dispersed Henry and his friend Calvin Fletcher found Depuy in his office, still bloody and mud stained, feverishly setting type by the light of a single candle for a special extra of the *Freeman*, recounting the terrible violence and linking it to the city's antiabolition culture. Fearing that Depuy would only heap fuel upon the fire, Fletcher and Beecher pleaded with him not to print anything about the matter in his paper, to let the courts deal with it.

No doubt Fletcher and Beecher felt they were saving the city from more bloodshed, but obviously Depuy did not agree. Not only did he publish an account of the riot but also of his conversation with the two men. Depuy's instincts were right. In the end only one of the murderers was found guilty of manslaughter, one was acquitted, and the other hightailed it out of town. But the story of Beecher's attempt to quash the story, with its taint of moral cowardice, was picked up by the Indianapolis and Cincinnati papers.

Henry was himself offered a beating later that year, after the beleaguered Depuy was cursed at by a bartender from one of the local saloons. When Depuy told Beecher of it, the parson said breezily, "Oh, why do you care for the abuse of this low fellow? No one whose esteem is worth having is influenced by him."

Depuy printed Beecher's comments verbatim in the next issue of the *Freeman*. The next time Henry passed the bar, the bartender spotted him. "If it were not for your cloth, Sir," roared the bartender, "I'd give you the damnedest thrashing."

As Henry told it, he whipped off his coat for battle. "Never mind the cloth," Henry shot back. "You are not dealing with Mr. [Depuy] now but somebody who is willing to accommodate you."[72] The bully backed down. Henry had several confrontations like this, and always spoke of them with pride, as if physical and moral courage were one and the same.

Perhaps hoping to compensate for his hesitancy on slavery, in the autumn of 1845 Henry renewed his temperance crusade in the *Indiana Farmer and Gardener*, condemning the owner of a new distillery in Lawrenceburgh that could turn out a remarkable 150 barrels a day. Attacking drunks and grogshop owners was one thing, but distillers were among the region's wealthiest and most respectable men, including this one, Dr. Cornelius G. W. Comegys, a prominent physician, church member, and known temperance man.

Dr. Comegys was shocked by Beecher's attacks, but his reply in the *Indiana Journal* was calm. He rebuked Beecher for his "petty malice, his unmanly and ungentlemanly attacks," but made it clear he wanted no further trouble.[73]

But Beecher would not be placated. His next assault was even more pugnacious. Now Comegys dropped all pretense of respect, detailing in the *Journal* every disparaging rumor ever whispered about Beecher. Back and forth they went for several months, the Christian distiller and the Christian zealot. As usual young Julia Merrill took Henry's side, but even she was "surprised with Mr. Beechers severity in the 'Farmer,'— yet—when I saw Mr. Comegys reply it was merited," she wrote to Elizabeth Bates. "I should think he would sell his distillery at once or else burn it down."[74]

But in other circles Henry was fast using up his goodwill.

AT THE END OF FEBRUARY 1846, a rare blizzard blanketed Indianapolis with a foot of snow, freezing the city for weeks. Shivering in their drafty cottage, seven-year-old Hattie and three-year-old Henry fell ill with malaria for the first time. It was a heart-wrenching experience, Eunice remembered, to watch "a little child, with its tiny chilled fingers, its poor, blue, pinched nose, its anxious eye turned, questioningly, from one attendant to another[.]"[75]

Sitting up with the children at night, nauseous from the early stages of her latest pregnancy, Eunice was exhausted. Henry bitterly invoked the common joke that at least the children's chills seemed to "come on *alternate days, and one will be comparatively comfortable while the other is shaking,* and thus lighten, somewhat, your labor in nursing." In fact, Eunice admitted, it did.

Their anxiety ebbed after a week, as Hattie and Henry made their way back to health. Then, all at once, little Georgie's cheeks turned red and his pulse quickened, marking the onset of the fever. By evening his skin was pale and covered in beads of perspiration. When Eunice tried to hold him, he stiffened into a convulsion.

For eight days Eunice and Henry watched anxiously as the fever rose higher. "I shall not forget while I have conscious being, the look of grief and reproach which my little child gave me, in his anguish," Henry said years later; "why did I not help him? What could I say? What could I do, but stand by and tremble in agony?" Henry prayed to God, begging, bargaining, and promising great sacrifices. When he became too wound up to stay in the sickroom a moment longer, Henry left the house and "at night, under a cold, brilliant, star-studded sky I raced and ran down the long street[.]"[76]

They were beginning to give up hope when suddenly Georgie rallied and he was able to say a few words, as if determined to hold on.

"I shall never forget the amazing uplift of soul that I had," Henry said; "which seemed to fill the whole hemisphere, for the life of my child."

But Georgie's revival was nothing more than the brief, cruel gift of lucidity that often graces the hours before dying. There were no bargains to be made with God or Satan. Little Georgie, the darling baby of the house, passed away before dawn. "It was a double sorrow because I had given him up and then taken him back again," Henry said. "Then came the sudden wrench."

The funeral was held six years, almost to the day, after they buried their stillborn boy. This time it was much harder, Henry recalled:

> We went down to the graveyard with little Georgie, and waded through it in the snow. I got out of the carriage, and took the little coffin in my arms, and walked knee-deep to the side of the grave, and looking in I saw the winter down at the very bottom of it. The coffin was lowered to its place, and I saw the snowflakes follow it and cover it, and then the earth hid it from the winter. If I should live a thousand years I could not help shivering every time I thought of it. It seemed to me then as though I had not only lost my child, but buried him in eternal snows.

Their hard-bitten congregation offered little consolation. "Our people did not know *how* to sympathize," Henry later told Harriet. The struggle to survive went on, Eunice remembered, even "on returning from the grave, right to hard work again. Not a flower, nothing but a cold hard coffin and no money to pay for that for weeks—a cold dark stormy day, the loss is the same in either case but the surroundings do rasp or soothe as they happen to be."[77]

Characteristically Henry turned stoical and silent in his sorrow. "It was not for me to quail or show shrinking," he recalled. "So I choked my grief and turned outwardly from myself to seek occupation." The very afternoon of the funeral he was back in the pulpit, preaching a heart-rending sermon on the consolations of heaven for those left on earth.

"Eunice was heart-broken," Henry later told his sister Harriet. "My home was a fountain of anguish."[78] Always so frank with her sorrows, Eunice blamed the climate, their poverty, their stonehearted parishioners, and herself for not being able to save him. "I have the wildest longings to *look into his grave and see* if he is, indeed there—or if this be not a horrible dream," Eunice told Harriet.

Eight months after the funeral, Eunice gave birth to a little girl they named Catharine Esther. "I did not mean to love her very much, but I can't help it," Eunice confessed to Harriet a few weeks after the birth. "My heart is almost broken by this year's trials, and excepting when my kind husband is near me, I hardly know myself so full of wretchedness and anguish is every thought and feeling[.]"

"If you were to step in," she concluded, "I think you would have some trouble to recognize your sister in the thin faced, grey haired, toothless old woman you would find here."[79]

But Henry's life did not end with his son's. Two weeks after Georgie's death, Dr. Comegys's next reply appeared in the *Indiana Journal*. This time he meant to draw blood. "I could not bear that a man of exceedingly censurable life, should, with a sanctimonious air, be continually flinging at me departures from Christian life," Comegys sneered. Then he pulled out his trump card.

> Let us see! Slavery—That is a rather delicate subject with the gentleman since his church, because it was LEGAL, says it was not sinful to hold them; but slavery is an *evil*, and by its laws men without the exercise of their will or inalienable rights, such as "life, liberty and the pursuit of happiness," are held by *iron law* fast in its chains. Does alcohol do that? Or does the distiller do that? [. . .] His excuse is that he cannot hold still when some principle in religion is attacked, and "may his tongue cleave to his mouth and his right hand lose its cunning" if he hold back—Why is thy tongue still and thy pen idle, when the sentiments of thy brother and thy church on slavery are promulgated? Thou idle boaster—where is thy vaunted boldness?[80]

Weakened by grief and battered by this well-aimed truth, Henry was uncharacteristically speechless. He abruptly dropped the subject.

Beecher's popularity was taking a drubbing. Some congregants responded by withholding their pledged contributions to his salary, adding to his already heavy load of debt. Yet foolishly Henry now borrowed another five hundred dollars to build a larger house in Indianapolis.

But his troubles were not over. On April 3, one month after Georgie's death, the Indianapolis Presbytery passed a new resolution commanding the clergy to preach with new vigor against the sin of slaveholding. Henry had recently spoken against slavery among the more liberal students of Wabash College, but at home he continued to bow to the prejudices of his people. The Presbytery's rebuke to Henry was quiet but clear.

On May 13, 1846, President Polk declared war on Mexico. The next week Governor James Whitcomb called for volunteers to join the fighting, sparking a new wave of violence against the local black population. Finally Henry announced that he would again deliver two sermons on slavery on the Sunday after the Circuit Court opened for the season. Several church elders tried, unsuccessfully, to dissuade him.

That Sunday in May, Henry gingerly took up the slavery issue once more, starting with a history of Roman versus Hebrew slavery and ending with the Presbytery's late resolution. He had harsh words for slaveholders and the warmongers in Texas, and he plainly declared slavery a moral evil, albeit one whose "extinction is to be effected by the gradual action of those laws by which it is regulated."

Ironically—or hypocritically—he also censured the antislavery camp for their bellicose agitation and "provocative language." "The language of rebuke, of invective, the necessarily exaggerated figures of impassioned rhetoric, irony and above all searching denunciation, are the very worst possible instruments of effecting reformation." As for Henry, he ranked himself with those who considered emancipation a moral duty but how it should be accomplished, "they know not." "It is," he concluded, "a subject too mighty for man's handling."[81]

The performance was a triumph, in Henry's opinion. "I had preached two flaming sermons with no reaction by a judicious adaptation to time and circumstance," he exulted. Young Julia Merrill thought they were heroic, but her father was less impressed, noting, "They did not suit the abolitionists nor the other extreme."[82] The only concrete result was to make it even harder for Henry to collect his salary.

PERHAPS IT WAS INEVITABLE that someone would woo Henry Ward Beecher away from the West. His revival riding had stoked his regional fame, and the *Indiana Farmer and Gardener* and *Lectures to Young Men* had extended his name to the East Coast. In the fall of 1846 a New York merchant named William Cutler came through Indianapolis on business. Cutler had attended Lyman Beecher's church in Boston, and he stopped in at Henry's church, curious to see how Lyman's son was faring.

Cutler was impressed and intrigued. He knew a number of wealthy businessmen who were starting a Congregational church in the growing suburb of Brooklyn, New York, and looking for a minister. Young Beecher seemed like he might be just their man. On his way back to New York, Cutler stopped in Cincinnati to ask Lyman Beecher for his blessing.

Lyman Beecher "set his face like flint against it, enquired who he could send to in your state to carry out his plans?" Cutler reported to Henry from New York. "I told him you could do *here* something like the work he accomplished in Boston. Still he felt that you could do more for the king of kings in the West than here."[83] Already Edward Beecher, worn out from the myriad indignities of running a frontier college, had returned to Boston. If Henry went East, Lyman's dream of a western empire would be dead. Nonetheless Cutler asked Henry point-blank if he would consider taking the job.

Henry's response was coy. "A minister, like a maiden, ought not to make the first overtures, nor to be over-eager to have them made to him," he replied. Cutler took this in the spirit intended, promptly repeating the offer, then sweetening it with an irresistible request. Would Henry come to New York in May to speak at the annual Anniversary Week of the benevolent societies, all expenses paid? To see thousands of eager urbanites "crowd the spacious Broadway Tabernacle to hang upon your lips would be a sight worth crossing the mountain to see," Cutler gushed.[84]

On May 10, 1847, Henry and Eunice arrived at the massive New York Tabernacle to address the Home Missionary Society. James L. Corning, a young Brooklynite studying for the ministry, remembered what a peculiar figure Henry cut on stage that day, unkempt and rustic, as if he'd just come from a camp meeting. But Henry wowed the skeptical audience with his blunt, colorful language and dramatic stage presence. The *New York Express* declared it the "best speech thus far of anniversary week."[85]

On Sunday, Henry spoke to the little congregation in Brooklyn, who were visibly moved, Eunice observed with pleasure. As people headed home for their Sunday dinners, word of this curious young preacher spread quickly through Brooklyn. When Henry returned that evening to preach his second sermon, the house was thronged. By Monday, Henry's New York debut was pronounced a smashing success by no less than the *New York Tribune*, arbiter of all things respectable.

For the Brooklynites it was love at first sight. Now the letters came fast and furious, with a wealthy merchant named Henry Chandler Bowen now taking the lead. With the urgency of a jealous lover, Henry

Bowen wrote to Beecher constantly that summer. "Your name was spoken of as the man of our choice—'our first love,' the desire of our hearts," beseeched Bowen.[86] On June 21 the new congregation was officially christened Plymouth Church, in homage to its New England heritage. By unanimous vote the new trustees sent a formal call to Beecher, offering a handsome salary of $1,500 the first year, $1,750 the second, and $2,000 after that.

Brooklyn had many advantages besides financial. Moving to a Congregational church would free Henry from the oversight of the Presbyterian system, and he could shape the infant church to his own tastes. And, as he wrote in his list of pros and cons: "1. If [I] stay I give up a life of writing for one of labor. 2. If I go I start upon a life of writing for now and for future."[87] The incentives to leave were also persuasive. He'd collected many powerful enemies who were openly attacking him in the Democratic papers that spring. The church owed him $940 in back salary, and his own debts around town were even higher.

Meanwhile Henry Bowen continued his letter campaign, flattering, cajoling, and spinning glorious visions of the great metropolis. He pressed his wife, Lucy, to write to Eunice and to add her own notes to his letters. He personally raised enough money to pay off the Beechers' debts and cover their moving expenses, contributing generously from his own pocket. As Bowen put it, "the truth is we are *willing* to do more for you than you ever *dreamed* of—we are in the condition of—of—of— any loving wife like yours or mine willing to do just what 'you say'—for you have 'stolen our hearts.' "[88]

The trump card, everyone knew, was Eunice. The gossip in missionary circles was that no one would blame Henry for abandoning the field if his wife's health was as bad as they'd heard. "Who knows but that God has *providentially* laid the hand of sickness upon your wife in order to *furnish* a *clear* reason for you to come to us," Bowen wrote with sly piety.[89]

In the final clutch Providence did indeed lay the hand of sickness upon Eunice. Suddenly she began suffering convulsions so severe it took several people to hold her down. The convulsions subsided, one female congregant noted, but "the result is just what was feared—yesterday Mr. Beecher address'd a long letter to the session relinquishing his pastoral charge of this congregation, and the reason given is he must go to the sea shore to save the life of his wife." She concluded sourly, "is it not too bad for such a miserable woman we must lose having here so good a preacher."[90]

Sadly no one seemed sorry to lose Eunice. "Mrs. B. has not, I really believe, a real friend in the Church," wrote another member. "Full of large tales, and enormous exaggerations, no one believes a word she says. And I believe the opinion is general that her recent sickness was *for the occasion*."[91]

Plymouth Church was ecstatic. But Henry Bowen's pleasure was tempered when, before Henry's official letter of acceptance even arrived, he received a bill for five hundred dollars to pay part of the minister's debts. Bowen was a businessman before all else, and he was beginning to size up the situation. "We want you to be able to look every man in the face 'square and fair' and say (to yourself) *I owe you nothing*," Bowen admonished Beecher—unaware of how unlikely that was. "If you get into debt when you get here you must 'look *out for yourself*' as I am afraid my agency or the agency of your friends will not be quite so *promptly* responded to a second time for the same thing. But I must say I never collected a subscription which was paid more *promptly* and with more *pleasure* than the one for *your* benefit."[92]

THAT LAST MONTH IN INDIANAPOLIS was a melancholy one for Henry. Eunice left with the children as soon as the decision was final, while Henry stayed on until the end of September to tie up loose ends. Now that he was nearly gone, long-simmering complaints bubbled to the surface. "We have liked him as a preacher but many of the Church as I now learn complain much of him as a Pastor," wrote Samuel Merrill with surprise.[93] Beecher has been "a great man in the pulpit—but woefully deficient in every other respect," observed Merrill's son-in-law:

> Often he has failed to attend prayer meeting without any excuse. Never has been in Sabbath School more than thrice in his residence here of seven years. Visits almost none among his people. Makes appointments for meetings of Session, and half the time forgets them. Always funny and often frivolous. He had the admiration of every body—and I should think that he has been off on preaching and other excursions at least one quarter of his time since he has been our Pastor. Well he always made a noise wherever he went and we were flattered by it and held on. The truth is, we as a *town* feel that we are loosing a valuable citizen; but he has never endeared himself as a pastor to his church—he has not been a pastor at all—only a brilliant preacher—and brilliant he is.[94]

There were other tensions. On the night before Henry's farewell sermon one disappointed church member cried so hard she could not sleep, sending her husband into a jealous rage, according to one story. "Tortured by angry fears," the next morning he accompanied his wife to church, thinking Beecher might somehow take advantage of her. But Beecher preached with such solemn humility that it was said the abashed man instead swore to become a better husband.[95] Of course Julia Merrill and Elizabeth Bates were among the heartbroken. "Oh, we never knew half how happy we were!" Julia lamented to Betty.[96]

Henry Ward Beecher left on a red-letter day in Indiana history. On October 1 the first railroad car of the Madison and Indianapolis Railroad rolled into the city. A huge crowd gathered at the platform to celebrate the "iron horse" with speeches and a show of fireworks. In all the hubbub no one noticed when the Reverend Beecher boarded the first train to leave Indianapolis. Henry went West with the age of the steamboat and left as it passed into the age of the railroad.

"As I sat upon the wharf boat and looked upon the water, I thought of the passage of life," Henry wrote mournfully to Julia Merrill as he made his way from train to boat to stagecoach. "Who knows the fate of that half wilted flower that is flowing past? On what point will it be through, when will it sink? Who that sees these passing objects can have any idea of their destiny, except that they will be wafted down, *no one can tell when*."[97]

What he meant is unknown, although his most attentive biographer suggested that his "half wilted flower" might be a euphemism for Eunice. Julia did not marry for seven more years, but her adoration of Henry never diminished. "How much your love is to me you cannot know, for I can never tell you," she wrote to Henry near the end of his life.[98]

But it was Elizabeth Bates, in Julia's words "the youngest and most intense" of the two girls, who would remain linked to Beecher in the lore of Indianapolis. Betty served as a nurse in the Civil War and never married. Over time she grew bitter, telling Julia that she "shuts all up in a cave and puts a stone over the mouth of it." Elizabeth died a painful, wasting death in 1873. "You come nearer her than any earthly friend," Julia told Henry as Betty lay dying.[99]

Two years after Elizabeth passed away, Henry made national headlines when he was accused of seducing one of his Brooklyn parishioners. As newspapers dug through Beecher's history, Dr. A. C. Stanton, an old Indianapolis resident, was interviewed by the *Chicago Inter-Ocean*, a staunchly pro-Beecher paper, about the relationship between Betty and Henry.

It had been common gossip in evangelical circles back in the 1840s. Like many young ladies, "she became infatuated with the great preacher," Stanton recalled. "It was the most complete unbounded worship I ever knew." Whether Beecher returned her feelings no one knew, but there were whispers of "criminal intimacy." The news that Beecher was going to Brooklyn "froze Miss Bates into a statue." She met Mr. Beecher at least once alone after that and "came from the meeting with a far away look, an icy calmness, a cheerless, hopeless expression that nearly broke the hearts of her friends and gained the pity of all who saw her."[100]

Stanton's story was hotly denied by indignant Hoosiers who insisted that Elizabeth's feelings were like those of a child for a father. Dr. Stanton was frankly surprised at all the hubbub—after all, it was an old and familiar story.

Chapter 7

"A Peculiar Minister Was Needed
for So Peculiar a Church"

From Henry's view on Brooklyn Heights, Manhattan was a man's city. Of course, this wasn't always so. Twenty years before, Manhattan had been an unremarkable port town, lagging well behind Boston and Philadelphia in wealth and influence. It was perhaps most notable as one of the few colonial cities to be founded without any religious mission—a city whose soul was devoted to commerce. The opening of the Erie Canal transformed its destiny. Ships could now pass with ease from the Atlantic Ocean up the Hudson River, all the way to the Great Lakes of the Midwest. By midcentury the Empire City, as it was dubbed, was the nation's major metropolis, the great exchange point between West and East, South and North, America and the rest of the world.

The signs and symbols of New York's rising power could be felt across Manhattan Island in 1847. One could see it on Wall Street, in the splendid neoclassical pillars of the new merchants' exchange, and in the hurried gait of the messengers, copyists, bankers, and speculators who swarmed in the narrow street below. It was evident in the dozens of clipper ships from Europe, China, and the Cotton Kingdom, anchored so close to the city's shoreline that their long bowsprits projected halfway across South Street.

One could feel it in the vigorous life of the Bowery, a bawdy avenue of music halls, opera houses, firehouses, and taverns, where the tough "Bowery B'hoys," in the lingo of the day, and their working-girl companions promenaded the theater district around Astor Place. One could sense it in the great immigrant slums of the Five Points, where the poor and the criminal mingled freely in grog shops, flophouses, and tenements. One could hear it in the cries of the street vendors, the black women calling out "Hot co-o-rn," the men with their buckets of freshly shucked oysters on the half shell, the newsboys shouting the day's headlines, and the ragpickers and knife grinders, who strung their pushcarts with bells.

It was in the dazzle of Broadway, New York's great thoroughfare, where the carriages, carts, and horse-drawn omnibuses were so thick that it could take up to twenty minutes to cross the street. Here were the workshops and showplaces of the city, the great dry-goods emporiums, the eateries and stopping places of Hotel Row, and famous landmarks like the massive Broadway Tabernacle and the curiosities of P. T. Barnum's American Museum. And it was in the suburbs, "above Bleecker," in the phrase of the day, where genteel brownstones were gobbling up the farmland around Union Square, and marble mansions were beginning their march up the empty expanse of Fifth Avenue.

But head back down to the southern tip of the island, and catch the red-trimmed Fulton Ferry to Brooklyn. There on the other side of the East River was an even more remarkable phenomenon: a city ruled by women. Every morning Brooklyn emptied itself of men. From eight to nine, office boys, clerks, and men in rough blue shirts who worked with their hands streamed onto the ferry to Manhattan. From nine o'clock on came the white-collared men of affairs, heading off to run the Stock Exchange, the mercantile firms, and shipping warehouses. After nine the price of a ferry ticket doubled to two cents, but it was a mark of pride to pay it—a sign that a young man was moving up in the world. Until five in the afternoon, a man of working age in Brooklyn seemed as rare as hen's teeth.

With fewer than one hundred thousand souls, one-fifth the size of its sister across the bay, Brooklyn was a quiet, modest place, strident only in its virtues. "It is the home of the married middle people of New York," as one journalist observed; "Manhattan Island being the seat of the very rich, the very poor, and the unmarried."[1] Even at night the gentle sex held the upper hand. Every respectable house was shut up tight by ten, and prayer meetings were the big Friday-night entertainment. There were no theaters, music halls, and few dens of ill repute outside the waterfront area.

Fulton Street was Brooklyn's main artery, splitting the town into the well-to-do west side and the working-class east side. From the ferry landing Brooklyn Heights was a steep, stony walk up Fulton Street, past clapboard shops and ancient, humpbacked Dutch houses, turning onto a grassy bluff overlooking the bay toward New Jersey. Within the last year or so Brooklyn Heights had still been farmland. Now the pastures were parceled into empty lots, with town houses rising up out of the orchards and blackberry brambles. A gutter ran down the middle of each unpaved street, into which people flung household garbage to be collected by oxcarts. Water was supplied by hand pumps on the street corners, and backyard privies still served as bathrooms. Pigs and goats still roamed the streets, cows and sheep could still be met on their way to slaughter.

On weekdays women gossiped at the corner pumps, boys loitered about the stables that lined the side alleys, and children played in the surf of the bay below. On sunny Saturday mornings, ladies took their weekly jaunt down Fulton Street to Journeay & Burnham's Emporium, while men lounged outside on barrels and bales, chatting, whittling, and chewing tobacco. But Sunday was the big day, when the entire town promenaded to church. The churches were so central to social life that Manhattanites returning from a visit to Brooklyn were sure to hear the hackneyed joke: "Oh, did you go to prayer meeting?" So many homesick Yankee transplants found refuge on the Heights that it was nicknamed "Little Boston."

John Tasker Howard was one of those Yankee refugees. At the age of thirty-eight, Tasker, as his friends called him, was a slight, amiable man whose unpretentious appearance and gentle manner belied considerable wealth. Short side-whiskers and fine black hair that was just beginning to thin framed his rosy face, and sympathetic black eyes winked behind his gold-rimmed spectacles. Tasker was born to a well-to-do sea merchant from Salem, Massachusetts, back when Salem was still a center of the Atlantic shipping trade. In 1827, when the import-export business was migrating to New York, Tasker's father followed, resettling his business in Lower Manhattan and his family in Brooklyn.

Life among the Yorkers, as they were called, was faster paced and less bound by tradition than in New England. As an apprentice and then partner in his father's firm, Tasker grafted Yorker vigor and flexibility onto his steady Yankee habits and Calvinist conscience. He developed a keen ability to see the financial possibilities in any situation. He and his father started the first line of steamships to California, earning a small fortune during the Gold Rush of 1848. Later he became a director of the first telegraph company and an early promoter of what would become the Panama Canal. He was a natural facilitator, an expert at introducing capital to opportunity.

But it was Tasker's piety that won him a wife. Susan Raymond was a cheerful, bookish girl from a prominent Brooklyn family. Her father was a well-to-do shoe manufacturer and a pillar of the Baptist church. The two young people met at a prayer meeting in the winter of 1830–31, as the Great Revival was sweeping down the Hudson from upstate New York. Nine months later they married.

Plymouth Church of the Pilgrims was born out of this mixture of Yorker entrepreneurship and Yankee conscience. Tasker was chatting with a friend as he rode the Fulton Ferry to his office in Lower Manhattan when he heard that the First Presbyterian Church on Cranberry Street in the Heights was going up for sale. Tasker leaped at the opportunity and secured an option on the property for 10 percent down, with the plan of establishing a new Congregational church. He had already helped establish one Congregational church on the Heights— New York was traditionally Presbyterian territory—but he wasn't happy with the minister they'd chosen. The Reverend Richard Salter Storrs was intelligent and earnest, but he was too refined, too concerned with theological niceties for Tasker's tastes. He envisioned a church with a more modern, expansive appeal, but for that he would need help.

Tasker approached several pious Yankee-Yorker businessmen— David Hale, Seth Hunt, and Henry Chandler Bowen—who were part of a circle centered around the wealthy evangelical merchants Arthur and Lewis Tappan. The Tappan circle was devoted to combining principle with profit—"Philanthropy plus 5%," as one prominent Brooklyn man phrased it. They were actively backing a movement to bring more progressive Congregational churches to New York, as an alternative to the Presbyterian church's social conservativism. On a practical level, a popular church was an excellent investment. It was exempt from taxes, its revenues were regular, it was unlikely to chisel or default, and it brought up the real estate values of the neighborhood, creating more opportunities for wise investors to make money. The church paid the owners rent or a mortgage with a profitable interest rate, and they could make extra money by hiring out the building for speeches, concerts, meetings, and other entertainments during the week.

After some discussion Seth Hunt agreed to pay the entire purchase price of fifty thousand dollars out of his own pocket. He then sold one-third of the church property to Hale and one-third to Bowen. Now they had to find a minister with enough charisma to fill the pews. In the words of the journalist Matthew Hale Smith, "A peculiar minister was needed for so peculiar a church."[2]

Tasker suggested the name of a young minister from Indiana, whose *Lectures to Young Men* had recently made a splash in the East—a son of Lyman Beecher. He was known in reform circles to harbor firm antislavery sentiments, but carried none of the baggage of a radical abolitionist. The task of wooing young Beecher fell to Henry Chandler Bowen.

HENRY C. BOWEN OFFERED a striking contrast to Tasker Howard. While Tasker was a small man who cloaked his ambition under a gentle exterior, Bowen was tall, energetic, and brusque—"a steam engine in coat and breeches," as one reporter declared. Bowen had a sharply defined face, with deep-set, penetrating eyes and a hairline that even when he was a younger man was receding beyond view. He wore a long beard that gave him, along with his eyes and his height, an air of almost biblical severity. When Lewis Tappan, his future father-in-law, first caught sight of this tall, grave figure, he whispered to the man next to him, "Who is that young man who looks so like a Catholic priest?" Bowen was unabashedly competitive. "His firm mouth can say No, with emphasis," the reporter concluded, "and his magnetic manner can easily persuade others to do his bidding."[3]

Henry Bowen was born in 1813 in the village of Woodstock, tucked away in what is still called the Quiet Corner of Connecticut, near the border of Rhode Island and Massachusetts. At the age of sixteen Bowen left school and went to work in his father's general store and post office. He had a keen head for figures at a time when modern accounting methods were just beginning to spread through the countryside, and a natural talent for bargain making, for evaluating the worth of things and finding the profit in them. Soon his father was sending him alone to Providence, Rhode Island, with wagons full of farm produce to exchange for goods that could be had only in the city.

Like Tasker Howard and so many of his generation, Bowen was converted to Christianity when the Great Revival swept through Woodstock in 1830. When he asked his father's permission to go to college to become a minister, however, the elder Bowen refused. Young Bowen was too valuable to let go. Bowen channeled his disappointment into religion and good works. His fortunes changed at the age of twenty, when his father sent him to New York City to find a clerkship for his younger brother Edward. Through connections Edward obtained an interview at the mercantile firm of Arthur and Lewis Tappan. Arthur Tappan was unimpressed with Edward Bowen, but when Henry appealed to Mr. Tappan, hoping to change the merchant's mind, the merchant was so taken with the bright, serious twenty-year-old that he offered Henry a job on the spot. Again the elder Bowen refused to let him go, but when Tappan wrote the boy's father offering more money, the parsimonious old man finally relented.

The Tappan Brothers' firm was legendary for mixing business and religion. Clerks were not allowed to drink wine or spirits of any kind, to visit houses of ill-repute, to stay out past 10:00 P.M., to go to the theater or befriend people in the theatrical profession, or to engage in any other fast habits. Every Sunday they were required to attend church twice a day, and—to ensure compliance—on Monday morning they were required to report to their supervisors which church, the name of the clergyman, and the texts upon which he preached. All clerks had to belong to an Antislavery Society and make as many converts as possible.

Bowen thrived under the Tappans' rigid regime. At the end of five years Lewis Tappan was so impressed by the young clerk that he invited Bowen to enter into a partnership with him. Instead Bowen went into business with a retired merchant who wished to be a silent investor, and a fellow clerk, Theodore McNamee. The firm of Bowen and McNamee sold silks, cottons, ribbons, fancy dry goods, and sewing notions. The firm flourished from the start, quickly surpassing New York's silk wholesalers in volume of trade. Soon Henry Bowen formed another partnership, with Lewis Tappan's daughter Lucy Maria. She was only nineteen to Henry's thirty-one, but theirs was a genuine love match. He was her "dearie," "my loved Henry," and she was his "Little Lucie."[4]

While Bowen shared his father-in-law's passion for making and giving away money, there was a stark generational divide in their approach to *spending* money. Bowen gave freely to a host of evangelical charities, but he was equally generous with his young wife, lavishing her with silk dresses, jewelry, and a large town house on Brooklyn Heights, around the corner from Lewis Tappan's more humble home. In 1845 their first child arrived, and he began building a gorgeous Carpenter Gothic mansion in Woodstock, Connecticut. Roseland, as Lucy Bowen named it, still stands as a monument to Bowen's ambition. Bowen had it painted in multiple shades of pink with red trimming, and filled it with fine furniture, rich silks, and intricate woodwork, a bowling alley and later a croquet court—neither, of course, to be used on Sundays. Yet, despite his philanthropic instincts, Henry Bowen retained a certain Yankee sharpness. While building Roseland he went through two sets of carpenters, and he squabbled with the local tradesmen. It was said, perhaps unfairly, that no one who worked for Henry Chandler Bowen ever left with a kind word for him.

Luckily Henry Ward Beecher fell into the category of philanthropy. Bowen was determined to bring the young minister to Brooklyn, deluging him with flattering letters and raising the money to pay Beecher's debts and moving costs, contributing the lion's share himself. He pressed his wife to write to Eunice and to add honeyed postscripts to his letters—including Lucy's kind but mortifying offer to give Eunice "a present of *a full set of teeth.*"[5]

"It is not simple prominence, personal regard, kind feeling or anything that can be thus coolly named. It is *deep,* solid *love, Christian* love, emplanted in our hearts by Him who said to his followers, 'love one another,' " Bowen wrote to Henry in Indiana. "We love you finally because (as a wife would say to a beloved husband), you are 'the one of all others' adapted to *us.*"[6]

Surely it was a match made in heaven.

In October 1847 Henry and his family arrived in Brooklyn Heights in typical Beecher fashion—ragged, poor, and hopelessly countrified. The Reverend Beecher was "a dilapidated specimen of a preacher," as one reporter put it. "His hat was shockingly bad, his coat seedy, and his pants darned, his books and his shirts equally out of repair."[7] Although Eunice was only thirty-five, the malarial fevers had caused her to lose most of her teeth, and her full, rosy face had become ashen and thin. The children—Hattie, nine, Henry, six, and the toddler, Kate—were shy and unhealthy. Susan Howard noticed that Hattie, in particular, had the anxious air of a child burdened with adult cares, and spent much of her time tending to her little brother. Lucy Bowen welcomed them into the Bowens' grand four-story town house until they could get settled, and then insisted on buying them all new clothes.

Even in his new store-bought suit, Henry showed up for his first service looking like no minister they'd ever seen. He did not sport the high stiff white collar of a clergyman—perhaps, as some local wits suggested, because his neck was too short and stout to accommodate it. He dressed like a man who worked, from his broad-brimmed hat to the rough gray shawl he wore to stave off the cold weather. His thick brown hair was almost shoulder length and brushed back behind his ears in what was considered a western style, and he had the ruddy complexion and calloused hands of a homesteader. "I noticed the almost contemptuous looks on the strangers present as they watched his face," Eunice recalled with typical distrust.[8]

Henry paid no heed. He was determined not to repeat the mistakes of Indianapolis. Freedom from stifling social conventions was to be the cornerstone of his new ministry. "If I remain here and you come to this church," he announced in his most forcible manner, "it must, at the commencement, be distinctly understood that I wear no fetters, that I will be bound by no precedent, and that I will preach the Gospel as I apprehend it, whether men will hear or whether they will forbear, and I will apply it sharply and strongly to the overthrow of every evil, and to the upbuilding of all that is good." No subject would stand outside his purview, and those who did not wish to see religion applied to real life should not come. He then proceeded to give his opinions on what he called "living issues" of the day: slavery, temperance, the war against Mexico, and the general reform of society.

Liberal-minded though these good people were, they were shocked by Henry's boldness. After the service several came to speak to him with a mixture of kindness and anxiety. "Don't ally yourself to unpopular men nor unpopular causes," they warned him. "There is no need of it. You can have your own notions about abolition; what is the use of preaching antislavery sermons?" Such talk would destroy the fledgling church and ruin his reputation.

"I despised them all, and preached like thunder on those subjects," Henry recounted. "I remember saying, with some discourtesy and with language that I should not use now: 'If you don't want to hear such doctrines, don't take a pew here next time.' "[9] It was a heroic beginning, becoming a little more heroic each time he told the story.

Henry and Eunice found a small, brown wooden house to rent a few blocks from the church. The pastor was one of the few men on the Heights who did not work in Manhattan, leaving him plenty of time to call upon the ladies of the church, inquiring after their health and fussing over their children. He poked around the docks, talking to the sailors and ferry pilots. On Fulton Street he stopped to chat with the local men, absorbing the politics and personalities of Brooklyn. While the other men smoked or "chawed," he picked up the rather undignified habit of eating peanuts as he strolled, littering shells behind him like a newsboy.

At first many of the fellows treated him like a regular clergyman, hastily clamming up when he stopped to say hello. They warmed up once they realized that Henry preferred to talk about almost anything *but* religion. He could tell a man what to do for a head cold, a smoky chimney, a sick horse, a sterile fruit tree, or a mischievous boy. Quick to tease, the pastor was playfully razzed in return. He was a first-class storyteller, regaling his neighbors with tales of the western frontier.

Beecher's friendships crossed the social spectrum. An undertaker, a grain merchant, a grocer, an Irish cartman, and an old English tavernkeeper were all special pals, although none belonged to his church. He loved the grizzled sea captains who settled on the Heights to be near their ships anchored below. Oddly enough he was not very close to other clergymen, with the exception of Richard Salter Storrs (an Amherst man like himself), although he was always cordial.

But it was the men who first brought him there, the wealthy evangelicals and their charming well-bred families, who captured his heart. On Brooklyn Heights he discovered "a circle of friends more refined and gentle and loveable than those with whom I had spent my ministerial life," he told his sister Harriet. For the first time since college, he was surrounded by what he called *"my sort of men"*—intelligent, ambitious, "go-ahead" types, liberal Christians who appreciated art and poetry and lively conversation.[10] With their wealth and urbanity they opened whole new worlds of sophistication to him.

Eunice did not make friends as easily as her husband. Henry Bowen had too hard an edge for her taste, and Lucy Bowen was so young, pretty, and rich that her charity must have been irksome. But Eunice took to Susan Howard instantly. They were nearly the same age and had suffered the same scars of pregnancy, illness, and death. Susan's cheerful equilibrium provided a soothing foil for Eunice's nerves. If the two women quarreled occasionally, as Henry teased Eunice, it was merely because they found it a pleasing pastime. When Eunice became pregnant for the sixth time, Susan, too, was pregnant. William Constantine Beecher was born January 26, 1849, just before Susan's own little boy. When Susan's milk failed after the birth, Eunice nursed the child at her own breast. Susan named her boy Henry Ward Beecher Howard.

Tasker became Henry's chief ally after Henry Chandler Bowen. Unlike Bowen, though, Tasker preferred to remain behind the scenes. The

Beechers' circle soon expanded to include Susan's extended family—her brothers Robert and John Raymond, ministers and educators, her sisters, Helen and Esther, and their broods. The Howards' comfortable home at 150 Hicks Street became a retreat for Henry, a hideaway from critics and fans alike. Long after others had fallen away, the Howards would remain his staunchest protectors.

Henry had one last hurdle to jump before settling in for good: an examination before a board of Congregational ministers. The examination should have been a mere formality. Henry's old professor, Heman Humphrey, the former president of Amherst College, came to New York to serve as one of the examiners, as did Henry's older brother Edward, and the Reverend Horace Bushnell, the famous liberal theologian from Hartford. The Reverends Richard Storrs and Joseph Thompson, of the Broadway Tabernacle, represented his colleagues in New York.

But Henry's patience for the iron cage of orthodoxy had evaporated out West. "During all that time my mind was *intensely* unsettled theologically," Henry confessed to his sister Harriet several months later, "I had dropped so many technical views, through a preference for those more in accordance with my own philosophy, as to produce the vague impression that in time I should serve the remaining views in the same manner."[11]

The moderator of the council, the Reverend Doctor Hewitt of Bridgeport, opened the examination with an easy question. What were Henry's views on the doctrine of election—the belief that certain souls are selected by God for salvation, regardless of their behavior?

To everyone's surprise Henry replied that for the last decade he had been so busy trying to save souls in the West that he had had no time to go into an arithmetical calculation as to the proportions of the elect and the nonelect. Many in the audience were shocked by the pastor's irreverence. But the tone was set: Henry continued on with a breezy nonchalance that would have verged on insolence had he not seemed so warmhearted.

With each technical theological question, Henry blithely returned to his practical experience in the West. Fishing for souls in that rough, rude place, he had almost forgotten the technicalities of theology, he claimed. In kindness, or perhaps desperation, Dr. Humphrey threw his old student a softball. "Do you believe in the perseverance of 'the saints?'" Humphrey asked, referring to the belief that once one was chosen by God, one would remain saved.

"I was brought up to believe that doctrine," Henry replied, "and I did believe it 'till I went out West and saw how Eastern Christians lived when they went out there. I confess since then I have had my doubts."[12]

The grave faces of the ministers began, unwillingly, to crack into smiles. But they quickly righted themselves. Taking another tack, the Reverend Hewitt asked him to describe his religious conversion and his call to the ministry. The story Henry told was so touching that tears rose unbidden to their eyes.

Ultimately, however, the panel was unmoved by Henry's sentimental appeal. By a large majority they voted that they could not, in good conscience, proceed with the evening's installation ceremony. It was Edward who saved the day, tearfully appealing his brother's case. Edward's orthodoxy was unimpeachable, and his arguments were detailed and dogged. Finally the committee gave in. That was the difference between his two sons, Lyman Beecher later observed: "Edward fires forty-pounders, and woe betide the man he hits. Henry fires grapeshot, and kills most men."[13]

But trouble would not be put off so easily. When Henry returned home that evening from his installation, Eunice met him at the door in a panic. Their toddler, Katie, was sick and had taken a sudden turn for the worse. The doctor had come and spoken reassuringly, but Eunice did not believe him. The words were barely out of her mouth when Katie went into convulsions.

Katie lingered unconscious, without apparent pain, for almost a week. The doctors diagnosed it as inflammation of the brain, but they had no real idea of what was plaguing her. She died on November 16, after only sixteen months of life.

The death of a child is always tragic, but some funerals are sadder than others. When little Georgie died in the Indiana forest, the settlers of Henry's congregation were so beaten down by hardship that they had no comfort to give their pastor and his wife. "Our people did not know how to sympathize," Henry recalled. Only a handful of people even came to the burial.

"But two years found me in a different scene," he told Harriet not long after Katie passed away. Though they had known the Beechers for less than two months, the people of Plymouth Church opened their hearts to the newcomers, doing everything they could to ease the chaos of death. On the morning of the funeral, their new friends covered the tiny coffin with flowers, as if to spite the winter cold. The small parlor was filled with mourners. After the service Henry and Eunice carried their third child to the grave.

With Georgie's death it took all Henry's effort to bear the blow, but now Henry asked, "What had I to bear up against? I was held up by increasing love and sympathy on every side."[14] Even Eunice's grief seemed less heartrending, but perhaps that was resignation. "I often think," Henry mused to his father after the funeral, "how large our family is becoming in Heaven."[15]

"Ah! if ever I am called to leave Brooklyn, will it not be to me like rending soul from the body?" Henry sighed to Tasker Howard less than a year after his arrival:

> Heretofore, I have had to labor often up hill; to carry everything, inspire everything, and do everything, besides which there was sorrow in my house and sorrow in my heart. But now I seem to have gone over to the opposite extreme;—what comfort is wanting—how many dear friends who love me far beyond what I deserve—whose kindnesses are ceaseless! Sometimes when I think of all God's mercies to me, my feelings rise and almost suffocate me![16]

IN A QUIET HOUR AFTER DINNER on December 12, 1847, Susan Howard sat down and began a long-delayed letter to her brother John Raymond. A million distractions had kept her from writing sooner. "Were I to reduce them all to the first elements," she explained, "I verily believe they would all come down to Beecher, *Beecher, BEECHER!* He seems to be a subject of universal interest, and he is a curiosity, that is a fact. Don't ask what *I* think of him, I can't tell you, for the life of me. I only know that I am intensely interested."

"Personally," Susan concluded, "I like him, though he is rather rough and 'dreadful homely.' "[17]

Rumors of Henry's unorthodox examination, his controversial opinions, and peculiar appearance only whetted the public's curiosity. After only two months almost every pew on the main floor was reserved. "The house has been over thronged—filled through every nook and corner," Henry informed his father with pride. The crush of Sunday visitors was so great, Susan Howard told her brother, that no pew holders even thought of occupying their own pews unless they arrived an hour early.

"At first the great prosperity of the enterprise in which we are embarked cast a sort of coldness upon the ministerial brethren," Henry told his father.[18] Dire predictions came from every corner: "It is a new thing; people will run after novelties; It won't last long, depend on that. These young guns burst suddenly—vanity charges them too heavily … Oh, it's more the name of Beecher than anything else … Any man that has tact and boldness, and that knows how to swell can draw a crowd for a while."[19] The more the critics carped, however, the more people came to judge for themselves. Speculating about just what made Beecher so fascinating became a kind of parlor game around New York in the winter of 1847–48.

Some of the answer lay in his eccentric, hybrid style. His accent and education were unmistakably Yankee, but his free-and-easy manners were entirely western. He was almost shockingly casual in the pulpit. If a name or date slipped his mind, he asked one of the people near him. If those sitting near the platform had no hymn books, he leaned forward and handed them some from his desk. "I am at home; they are our guests," he explained. "What is proper in my house is eminently proper in the house of the Lord."[20]

Henry had picked up some peculiar habits from those years of raucous western revivals. He was unabashedly theatrical, using his whole body to communicate the full range of human emotion, with dramatic gestures and subtle facial expressions. Audiences were startled by his imitations of a sailor taking a pinch of chewing tobacco and wiping his hands on his pants, of a fisherman casting, or a young girl flirting. "His knowledge of human nature is better than that of any other minister in the city—in fact astonishing," reported the *Brooklyn Eagle* not long after Beecher settled in. "He seems to have sounded the deepest springs of the human heart and brings up, of good and bad, all that is lodged there."[21]

Over time Beecher had fallen into the custom of writing his sermons at the last minute. "Some men like their bread cold," he explained. "I like mine hot." He would muse on a subject during the week but wouldn't write his sermon outline until Sunday morning. Sometimes this made him seem disjointed. As one woman observed, he had, at best, a "somewhat rugged and informal chain of argument."[22] A passionate description of seeing God in a sunset might be followed by an anecdote about a horse trader, and conclude with a ruthless denunciation of corrupt politicians.

But this also meant that his sermons expressed much more of his spontaneous inner feelings; indeed, his sermons are often more revealing than his private letters. Strangers who came for thunder and lighting were sometimes disappointed when the fever was not in him. But when it was, he carried his audience away, largely because he himself was carried away. "I am impetuous," Henry admitted. There are times "when I think things in the pulpit that I could never think in the study and when I have feelings that are so far different from any that belong to the lower or normal condition that I can neither regulate them nor understand them."[23]

Ironically the boy who confided to his diary that he "never could be sincere" was rapidly becoming famous for his emotional soul baring. It was a trick he discovered back in 1835; onstage he seemed to stroll through his thoughts in what he called "mental *dishabille*." "Instead of scoffing at their doubts, he boldly proclaimed his own," as one listener recalled. "He pictured in vivid colors the unhappiness of his thoughts, the terror of his fear, and produced in their minds the impression that Beecher and they were one and the same."[24] This powerful combination of empathy and audacity made him seem incapable of pretense.

Henry wore his huge heart on his sleeve. He cried without shame and picked up the vaguely European habit of kissing his friends hello. It was often remarked—sometimes disapprovingly, sometimes jokingly—that his lush mouth and heavy-lidded eyes gave him a sensual, almost sexual air. Henry preferred extravagant emotions, even when they were dark—"if the occasion is only large and worthy, I am glad to be made sad by a great pain," he declared. "Indeed it is the petty things that vex—but are not large enough to strike deep—that nettle life!"[25]

He was that rare creature who embodied both feminine sensitivity and vigorous masculinity, drawing women and men to him in equal numbers. "There is such *manliness* in Beecher," marveled one acquaintance, "that every one likes him who is not a coward, and at the same time he is one of the kindest-hearted men in the world. The slightest pathos will make his soul run over with tears."[26] His quick logic and emotional perceptiveness smacked of feminine intuition. Yet with his roguish sparkle and boyish vigor, he smashed the stereotype of the wan, effeminate minister.

Those who knew him only by the zealous Beecher reputation were surprised at how sensible and—well—lovable Henry was in person. "He is unpretending, simple, and genuine in his manners. His conversation boils with earnestness and bubbles with playfulness. He says many striking and memorable things; but above all (and this surprised me) is marked by common sense," observed the Unitarian minister Henry

Bellows after spending an afternoon chatting with Beecher on a train; "you may be sure that Beecher is a very prudent man—and that it is prudence winged by genius that carries him so far ahead. He has moreover great sweetness and makes you love him."[27]

Some grumbled that he was too free with slang, that some of his stories were not on the right side of respectable. But one thing truly shocked: The Reverend Beecher was funny. He didn't tell jokes, exactly. He just put human foibles in such an ironic light that people couldn't help giggling. The effect was often so subtle, so dependent on a knowing tone of voice, a roll of the eyes, or a slight shrug of the shoulders, that it is hard to find the humor when reading the sermons on paper.

When people began laughing in church, often in spite of themselves, there let loose a "concerted cry of horror," in the words of one young parishioner, "a symphony of alarm."[28] Newspapers editorialized; readers wrote letters to the editors; fellow ministers, even those who liked Henry personally, denounced his irreverence. One rival announced that the only time he'd ever disgraced the pulpit with a chuckle had been an accident, which he regretted to this day.

But these stylistic eccentricities had a serious aim. Henry was launching an assault on everything he'd ever hated about his father's religion. "I was brought up a Pharisee of the Pharisees," he told his church, referring to the Hebrew high priests in the Bible whose self-righteous obsession with the letter of God's law kept them from behaving in the true spirit of God, leading Jesus to condemn them as hypocrites. "During the whole of my early life, almost, I was brought up to do things because I *must*. I went to church because I *must*," Henry explained. "I kept Sunday, so far as I did keep it, because I *must*."[29] Not once did *"must"* produce a scrap of real faith in him. What had kept him on the straight and narrow was *"want"*—that is, his deep desire for the love of God and his father.

Now he was declaring a crusade against the modern-day pharisees, the hypocritical Christians, who wave their church membership as a substitute for good behavior. He ridiculed the vinegar-faced deacons who strip religion of joy; the merchants who flaunt charity on Sunday and abuse their employees on Monday; the ladies who stint on the collection plate while preening in their Sabbath-day silks. The corrupt local politician and pettifogging lawyer were hit no harder than the local clergymen caught up in nasty sectarian squabbling.

"Mr. Beecher does not seem to have much faith in the perfection of even converted men," the *Brooklyn Eagle* observed, "and while 'showing up' the monstrous wickedness of sinners does not forget the peccadilloes of the saints." Many were shocked by what one reporter described as his "very unlovely analysis of human character, by which he made it appear that men were apt to wear half a dozen characters at the same time."[30] Some Christians complained that he was harder on them than on unbelievers—and Henry agreed. Frankly, he confessed, he preferred the company of an honest infidel to that of a phony Christian.

Picayune theological distinctions, false proprieties, subtle hypocrisies—all such things were barriers to a direct, loving relationship with Jesus. Beecher's innovations seem minor today, but they were startling in the 1850s. The religious papers were aghast when Henry preached with a vase of flowers on his pulpit desk one Sunday, but soon the entire church was brimming with flowers. He brought the Methodist devotion to congregational singing to Plymouth Church, making the shared voice of song one of the most emotionally moving parts of every service. He raised a ruckus by inviting all self-proclaimed Christians to take part in holy communion, whether they were of other denominations or no denomination at all. "That's a quare man, is Beecher," remarked an Irish Catholic cartman who knew Beecher from his strolls around Brooklyn. "When I tell him of a friend of mine that's doin' wrong he niver tells me to sind him to his church; he tells me to thry to coax him to go to confession."[31]

Henry was no wild-eyed radical, no Theodore Parker or Ralph Waldo Emerson, willing to throw out all formal religion. He was too much of a Beecher for that. But he had an instinctive feel for the edge of the envelope, for what would startle and thrill his audience without pushing them over into fear or disbelief. He insisted that he still believed in theology, as one friend noted, but it was "as he believed in the human skeleton; it was useful and necessary in its place, but should be kept out of sight."[32] He retained the mantle of Congregational orthodoxy, but he insisted on redefining its terms to suit himself. He cloaked challenging new ideas in familiar language, to make them easier to swallow, and gave old ideas new resonance with his vivid illustrations and unexpected connections.

Nonetheless Beecher's pulpit pyrotechnics blinded most people to his conservative impulses. Within months of his arrival Old School religious newspapers like the *Evangelist* and the *Observer* were railing against his dangerous laxness. Confused lay people approached him anxiously, asking him to deny the rumors that he was preaching Unitarianism, Universalism, or worse. Even his friends were occasionally perplexed by Henry's broadmindedness. "I should call him a pretty good Methodist," Susan Howard told her brother. "The Unitarians like him because he preaches good works, and calls no doctrine by its name. (I am a little afraid sometimes he don't know their names, nor know them by sight, either—but I won't judge him yet.)"[33]

Henry offered to join hands with anyone who was willing to do good, regardless of their beliefs or motives. He went even further in a speech to the graduating class of Williams College on the sweeping topic: What is the end and purpose of life? "We think we are safe in saying," concluded the local newspaper, "that Mr. Beecher considered this end to be the *doing* of good, rather than the *being* of good."[34]

BY COMMON CONSENSUS there were three sure paths to public acclaim in the nineteenth century: the Pulpit, the Platform, and the Press. Almost overnight Henry had become the rising star of the pulpit. Now, only six months after arriving in New York, he got his first shot at the Platform, when the Boston Mercantile Library invited him to speak on any topic, for the sum of twenty-five dollars plus expenses. Henry was about to enter the newborn entertainment industry.

Up through the 1840s entertainment in America was generally a homemade affair. Brooklynites boasted of their lack of public amusements with the same pride as their lack of crime. Before gaslights and sidewalks were erected in the 1850s, people generally stayed home in the evening, and when they did go out they made their own amusements, like church sociables, spelling bees, parlor musical performances, and the informal Sunday after-church promenade.

Across the river, though, things were changing. Manhattan was awash with young, single men and women living in boardinghouses far from their families. After a ten- to twelve-hour workday, with their wages burning holes in their pockets, they craved excitement and pleasure. But most places of amusement were distinctly unwholesome: billiard rooms blue with cigar smoke, music halls featuring rum and bawdy tunes, and theaters with scoundrels on stage and prostitutes in the third balcony. There was serious money to be made, but to do so one had to broaden the audience to include women and middle-class families. That meant finding a way to offer titillation without the taint of immorality.

Public lecture series—the "lyceum circuit," as it was called—were the vanguard of the new entertainment industry. At first public lectures were sponsored by local civic groups promoting public education during the monotonous winter months. Lectures were the essence of respectable entertainment, open to young and old, men and women, and priced cheaply enough for all but the poorest to attend. But audiences' tastes were growing more sophisticated. Local fellows who knew something about chemistry or European affairs were old hat. Now, with the rise of the railroad and wider newspaper circulation, it was possible to book big names with big-city reputations. A first-class lecturer was like P. T. Barnum's FeeJee Mermaid—something so sensational you just had to see it for yourself.

Boston was the high citadel of the pharisees. Socially and intellectually Boston and New York were poles apart. The cultural life of New York was anchored by hard-driving newspaper editors with little formal education but lots of moxie. In Boston, by contrast, the most exalted opinion makers were genteel scholars and introspective ministers who wrote for weighty journals like the *North American Review*. Boston produced iconoclastic thinkers and truly radical reformers like Bronson Alcott and Henry David Thoreau, but the city's astonishing creativity was offset by stifling social homogeneity and bred-in-the-bone snobbery. It was a tension that produced many of the century's great works of literature: Emerson's "Divinity School Address," Thoreau's *Walden*, Nathaniel Hawthorne's *Blithedale Romance*, and Henry James's *The Bostonians*, to name only a few.

In Indiana, Henry had considered taking a job in Boston but decided against it, knowing how the Puritan legacy would chafe his soul. But the very conformity that disqualified it as a home made it an inviting target. Like his father twenty years before him, Henry was planning a spectacular assault on the City of Pilgrims.

"Amusements," the topic Henry chose, was an unpromising subject. Everyone already knew that gambling, theater, and drinking were bad; hard work, temperance, and prayer were good—what more was there to say? Still, Beecher's reputation was enough to bring out a typical audience on a cold Wednesday night in December—a sprinkling of old folks, slightly deaf and prone to dozing; young men fidgeting in the hard wooden seats in the back; bright, eager women in the front, some looking simply to get out of the house, some for a chance to flirt with the opposite sex. Several newspaper reporters came to cover his debut.

Henry's first blow struck squarely in the face of conventional wisdom. The problem with popular amusements, he declared, was not that there were too many, but too few, for man was not made solely for toil. Indeed, according to one surprised reporter, Beecher's leading idea

seemed to be that "man was made for enjoyment." God gave
the ability to laugh, frolic, love, and make merry, and it was i~
to dam up these natural impulses without doing serious dama~~
mental and physical health. "You accumulate the pent-up stream only
to see it break over the dam with still more sweeping violence," he
declared in almost Freudian terms. "You check the flow for a time, but
you do not decrease the fountain or divert the current to any useful
purpose."[35]

Young people *will* have amusements, so they should have harmless, virtuous ones. Why shouldn't they go bowling, play sports, and
dance? Even billiards or theatergoing might be all right, he admitted,
were it not for the corrupt atmosphere. "The church has been so fearful
of amusements," he noted, "that the devil has had the care of them."[36]
Make good things pleasurable, and make pleasurable things good; tap
people's natural desires to bring them to Christ, and heaven would be
just around the corner.

Today this may seem as trivial as our own endless debates about
whether video games cause violence, or television rots the brain. But
Henry was attempting something far bigger than that—he was overturning the very nature of desire. Pious folks traditionally considered pleasure a distraction from religious duty at best, and a gross sin against God
at worst. Now a man of the cloth—a Beecher no less—was announcing
that pleasure was neither good nor bad in itself, but a powerful lever
capable of good and bad uses. Instead of regarding desire for pleasure as a
selfish impulse to be overcome by anguished prayer and self-denial, why
not use our natural desires to entice us to be more godly?

"I have found in family government that I could break the will of
a child with a stick of candy quicker and with less ado, than with any
other stick, switch, or rod," as he later put it.[37] The same was true, he
insisted, in God's government. If desire was the strongest lever, then
love was always the great stick of candy—and the love of God was the
ultimate reward for good behavior.

When accounts of his "Amusements" speech began to circulate,
Boston seemed to rise up with one voice to denounce him. The *Boston
Puritan* was particularly incensed. Beecher's hometown popularity was
proof, they sniffed, of how low morals had sunk in New York. The outrage of the Boston sheets was picked up by papers around the country,
setting off debate as far away as Ohio. Liberals applauded him, conservatives declared him a viper in the bosom. Even some of his own family
objected to these dangerous ideas.

Henry was unshakable. "If it was a shock to them to hear free and outspoken things—even new ones—it was a shock that they need," he responded to his brother Tom's concern.[38] In ten years his views would be standard thought, he insisted, and even now they would be perfectly acceptable in New York.

In New York a call went up for Henry to repeat the lecture in different venues around town. Each was a smashing success. Rather than downplay the criticism, Henry used it as a foil, reading bits from the hostile Boston Puritan, then demolishing its arguments, sending the audience into a frenzy of applause. As Henry predicted, most of the New York papers pronounced the speech good common sense.

Now lecture committees were swarming "thick as blackflies," in his words, begging him to come speak to their own groups. The Beechers had long been connoisseurs of controversy, but for the first time one had found a way to make it pay: Novelty and controversy were the twin engines of a successful lecturer. The lyceum circuit was enormously lucrative, but it had its own hardships. "It is the hardest thing in the world to fill up a vacant hour before going before such an audience to lecture," he told Eunice. "I cannot read, nor think; my head is a little inclined to be hot—never a good sign—always indicating super excitement."[39] Worst of all was the travel, the arduous hours on hard wooden train seats, long waits in lonely railroad stations in the middle of the night, frigid sleigh rides when the tracks were shut down by snow, bundled up in buffalo robes against the cold. But the money and fame were impossible to resist.

By the next winter Henry was delivering as many as four lectures a week around the Northeast. Railroad tracks were proliferating so fast that he could leave on a Tuesday and return on Friday, having spoken in, say, Boston, Newburyport, and Salem. As the lines spread west, he began touring through upstate New York, and later out to Cleveland, Cincinnati, and other Midwestern towns. Henry became a train buff, befriending the conductors and engineers, who often invited him to ride up in the front engine and gave him free rail passes. By the 1852–53 winter season Beecher had doubled his price, and Eunice had assumed the role of secretary and booking agent. Within a few years Henry Ward Beecher was one of the most popular entertainers in the country.

To Eunice's disappointment this new career was not much different from Henry's days as an itinerant revivalist. The differences, she said sadly, were that out West "I had a far more thorough knowledge of Mr.

Beecher's inner life, his thoughts and feelings, than I ever had after we came East."

Every morning as she watched Henry head out, "it would be difficult to describe or explain the feeling of bereavement and loneliness I felt," Eunice said. "It was impossible to reason away the sense of trouble or alienation between us." Sometimes "when he went out I used to gasp for breath and my eyes would fill with tears, for it seemed as if we had quarreled."

Occasionally Henry would return later in the day and detect the trouble on her face and ask, "What's the matter?"

"Nothing dear; just a little nonsense."

"But what is it? I must know."

"Well, I hardly know myself. It all seems so strange—our life here," she replied. "I know you will call me foolish, but when you have your study at the church we seem so separated. I half feel we have quarreled."

"With one of his real old-time hearty laughs he would reply: 'I imagine we are both foolish, then, for that's just the way I was feeling, and ran round to find out if we really had quarreled!'" Yet, he insisted, there was no help for it, they must simply adapt.

"When I got here to Brooklyn," Eunice later wrote, "the public began to take Henry away from me."[40]

Eighteen forty-eight was the "Year of Revolution," as the history books proclaim. Every day clipper ships arrived bearing the most fantastic tales from Europe. The economic depression of 1847, a relative inconvenience in New York, had cataclysmic effects on the other side of the Atlantic. In England a full-scale rebellion by the working classes was narrowly averted by an adroit combination of humanitarianism and politics. On the Continent, where the ruling aristocracy remained unmoved by the pleas of the suffering, famine and unemployment turned into bloodshed.

In February 1848 revolutionaries stormed Paris and overthrew King Louis Philippe, demanding a constitutional republic. By December the uprising was obliterated, and Louis Napoleon (later Napoleon III) ruled the nation. But events in France detonated a wave of violent revolt against the Austrian Empire, which dominated much of Central Europe. In Hungary and northern Italy serfs-turned-soldiers fought to expel the Austrian forces. In the German provinces the insurrections were led by intellectuals and artisans, but the goal was similar: the establishment of humane and enlightened constitutional monarchy. In Ireland the economic devastation was so complete that a peasant revolution seemed inevitable. American newspapers reported these crusades with tremendous excitement. A cast of romantic foreign heroes was suddenly the talk of the town: John Mitchel, Giuseppe Garibaldi, Giuseppe Mazzini, Lajos Kossuth. It seemed that all the world was straining to follow America's grand democratic experiment.

Henry Ward Beecher was intoxicated by the heady politics of 1848. The democratic revolutions in Europe resurrected all his youthful heroic impulses. The victories of Mazzini in Italy and Kossuth in Hungary moved him to raptures in the pulpit and whetted his ambition. When the great Kossuth came to New York City seeking aid for the cause of Hungarian freedom, Beecher and Henry Bowen threw a huge fundraiser in Plymouth Church. "I was sucked into the political controversies and the moral reformations of the age," Beecher said as soon as he arrived in New York.[41]

In America the only cause that could approximate the romantic appeal of revolution was the antislavery crusade. But while New Yorkers were thrilled by the tales of European uprisings, that did not translate into support for the emancipation of the American slaves. Then as now, New York was a politically schizophrenic state.

Since the religious revivals of the Second Great Awakening, upstate New York had been a hotbed of radical social activism, producing many of the earliest abolitionists. New York City was an entirely different matter. Manhattan had long been the linchpin of the Southern trade. More than $200 million a year flowed into New York from the Cotton Kingdom. The city's banks and financiers provided Southern planters with financial credit and investment, and its shipping industry hauled the cotton and tobacco to the lucrative European market and to Northern manufacturers. Slaves were often used as collateral on loans, making many New York merchants de facto or, in case of foreclosure, actual slave owners. Even those with no direct ties to the slave trade were inclined, as businessmen usually are, to defend the status quo against anything that might disrupt profits. When the London *Times* asked a local editor where they would be without slavery, his answer was blunt: "The ships would rot at the docks; grass would grow in Wall Street and Broadway, and the glory of New York, like that of Babylon and Rome, would be numbered with the things of the past."[42]

At the other end of the social spectrum were New York City's workingmen. The majority were Democrats who resented the meddling reformers who were always trying to shut down the taverns and theaters, and turn Sunday—their one day of recreation—into a morgue. Many were recent immigrants or greenhorns from the hinterlands, working at low-skilled jobs. For them the specter of free blacks flooding the New York labor market represented a terrible economic and psychological threat. Their social superiority over blacks, and particularly over slaves, was the thing that kept them from the bottom of the barrel. In the 1850s the epithet "nigger" was far more commonly heard in New York City than in the South.

In a sea of Southern sympathizers, Beecher's new social circle was a beacon of antislavery activism. Lewis Tappan, Henry Bowen's father-in-law, was William Lloyd Garrison's main rival in the abolition movement. Where Garrison was a propagandist with a gift for vitriol, Lewis Tappan was an organizer, networker, and money man, working quietly behind the scenes. Tappan was more conservative than Garrison, with a businessman's preference for order and stability, but no less devoted to the cause. After "long hesitation" Tappan joined Plymouth Church.[43] Privately Tappan thought that Beecher was a trimmer like his father—trimming his principles to fit the prevailing breeze—but he was pleased by the young preacher's rising reputation as a reformer, and enjoyed his company when they met in Lucy Bowen's parlor.

From the beginning Beecher made the Bowens' house his second home, especially when Eunice and the family were out of town. In summer he vacationed at their country house in Woodstock, Connecticut. While Henry Bowen established himself as the most public pillar of the church, Lucy Bowen quickly became a private pillar for the pastor.

Only twenty-two years old when she met Beecher, Lucy Maria Bowen was, as Lyman Beecher observed, "a beautiful woman."[44] She was petite, with large dramatic eyes set in a pale, oval-shaped face, framed by dark brown hair worn in long girlish ringlets. Well-bred, sensible, and sweetly affectionate, she was extremely pious but had the urbanity of growing up a wealthy, well-connected child in New York.

Lucy Bowen had been deeply shaped by Lewis Tappan's evangelical zeal. She was only nine years old in 1833, when their Manhattan home was ransacked by a mob of men looking to tar and feather her notorious father. The house was destroyed, and everything, including the children's toys, was tossed into the street and torched. Two summers later, while on vacation in upstate New York, Tappan created an uproar when he insisted on seating his children in pews reserved for black wor-shippers. Nonetheless Tappan's daughters inherited their father's liberal sympathies. Lucy's sister Susan married an equally ardent abolitionist, a prominent lawyer named Hiram Barney. When Lucy took a husband, he was very much in her father's mold.

Like his wife, Henry Bowen's antislavery instincts were kindled in childhood. As a little boy he was mesmerized by the stories of an elderly black man named Cuff Fellows, who was famous locally for his strength, his cleverness, and his fine, full set of teeth (at a time when few people had all their teeth). Slavery was still legal in Connecticut when Fellows was a young man, and it was said that any slave trader who could catch and sell Fellows would make a pretty penny.

"One day," Fellows told the rapt little boy, "I was in the field cut-tin' hay, and a gentleman drove up to the fence with a handsome horse hitched to a very handsome chaise. He stopped, took out a big whip which had a big handle to it and marched into the field where I was workin'. I look at him and I feared that he was arter me."

The man walked slowly right up close to Fellows, and growled, "I want you."

"What?" asked Fellows.

"I want you," he repeated, and then whacked Cuff's head with the butt of his whip. Frightened and furious, Fellows grabbed the trader and began biting him in the arms, chest, face, and hands until the driver begged to be let go. Fellows released him with a warning, "Now you go, and if you attempt to ketch me again, I will bite your head off." The story was permanently etched in Bowen's mind.

But it was an incident a few years later that, Bowen claimed, "made me then into a first-class abolitionist—the younger side of 20."[45] A white schoolteacher named Prudence Crandall opened a school for black girls in Canterbury, Connecticut. When Crandall refused demands to shut down this abomination, men mobbed the school. The children fled, but the teacher refused to leave town. The townspeople organized a boycott to starve her out, demanding that all local businesses refuse to sell food to her.

Bowen lived not far from Canterbury, where the news quickly passed through his father's general store. When Bowen joined a temperance organization the year before, he'd begged his father to stop selling rum. His father flatly refused; there was too much money in it. If such a boy-cott spread to Woodstock, there was little chance that his own father would not capitulate. Fearing for her life, Prudence Crandall finally left

Connecticut, but that did not diminish the potent contrast between her courage and his father's lack of principle.

Bowen's antislavery beliefs help land him the job at the Tappans' dry-goods business the next year. In 1834, when the antiabolition mob attacked the Tappan Brothers warehouse, Bowen was part of an ad hoc militia of clerks who helped defend it. As the rioters began smashing windows, a cry went up from inside the building: "The military are inside ready to fire!" The rabble panicked, turned on their heels, and ran—another vivid lesson in the links between commerce, conviction, and cowardice.

The Mexican War officially ended in 1848, opening the question of whether slavery would be allowed in the newly acquired territory. Some in Beecher's circle were actively organizing a new third party, the Free-Soil Party, based on the principle of banning slavery from the federal territories. Encouraged by his new pals, Henry grew bolder in his denunciation of slavery. But his budding radicalism was stymied by that same old stumbling block: the United States Constitution. The crucial question for anyone who sympathized with the slaves was how to follow one's conscience and also preserve the Constitution, which legally protected slavery.

It is easy to forget that in 1848, the United States was barely half a century old. In this nation of immigrants, there were no shared ethnic or linguistic roots, no monarchy, state church, or ancient traditions to bind people together. What united this disparate population into a nation was an almost superstitious faith in the Constitution, as that canny New York politician William H. Seward once observed.

This created an impassable dilemma for many thoughtful people. Northerners who wanted the slaves to be free, as the historian David Potter noted, also "cherished a conflicting value: they wanted the Constitution, which protected slavery, to be honored, and the Union, which was a fellowship with slaveholders, to be preserved. Thus they were committed to values that could not logically be reconciled."[46]

The problem, then, was not a stark choice of alternatives—antislavery or proslavery—but a ranking of values: How much should human liberty be sacrificed out of respect for the Constitution and the Union? The vast array of opinions in the North—those of militant abolitionists, moderate antislavery men, Unionists, antiabolitionists, proslavery men—were divided by how these priorities were ordered.

Some, like William Lloyd Garrison and his silver-tongued colleague Wendell Phillips, had no problem ranking their values. If the Union would dissolve without slavery, then the Union was not worth saving. "The existing Constitution of the United States is a covenant with death, and an agreement with hell," Garrison famously declared. No Union with slaveholders!"[47] Most Northerners, however, were unwilling to make such a stark choice. So they resolved the conflict through the old psychological technique of compartmentalization—putting their opposition to slavery in one context (the individual states) and the respect for the Constitution in another (the nation as a whole).

The abolition of slavery, they maintained, was a matter for individual states to decide. Thus the North eased its conscience by outlawing slavery within its own states. In the federal context, however, most people felt bound by mutual, legal obligation to respect the rights of each state to make its own laws, and thus felt relieved of responsibility.

Yet one question lingers: How could a piece of paper, no matter how sacred, outweigh the suffering of 3 million fellow Americans living in bondage? Fundamentally most white Americans harbored a deep core of what can only be called racism. They feared disturbing the status quo because they were certain that—with white skin—they could never be slaves. The Rights of Man did not apply to those who were not fully men.

Henry Ward Beecher was no William Lloyd Garrison. He hedged on the question of states' rights and was given to sudden reversals of opinion—reranking his values depending on the immediate threats. In general he should be called a moderate. He hated slavery, but he loved the Union more, and he saw no way around the Constitution.

ON THE EVENING OF APRIL 15, 1848, the streets of Washington, D.C., were ablaze. Bonfires crackled, and multicolored lanterns hung from trees lit up the main avenue, where a rowdy torchlit procession marched to Lafayette Park. There thousands were gathered to celebrate the spectacular news from France: The revolution was won, and Paris was now the capital of a democratic republic. From a rough platform cabinet secretaries, senators, and congressmen clamored to address the crowd and offer their congratulations to the French revolutionaries.

Senator Henry S. Foote of Mississippi rose to speak. Foote, a slaveholder and one of the Senate's most notorious champions of the right of white men to own black men, saw no irony as he bellowed of his pleasure that "the age of *Tyrants and Slavery* is rapidly drawing to a close; and that the happy period to be signalised by the universal emancipation of man from the fetters of civil oppression, and the recognition in all countries of the great principles of popular sovereignty, equality, and *Brotherhood,* is at this moment visibly commencing."

In many parts of the United States an abolitionist could be tarred for uttering those words. But his hypocrisy was drowned out by the cheers for good old Foote and universal emancipation. As Harriet Beecher Stowe later remarked, it was hardly surprising that the slaves who peppered the crowd might take Foote and his fellow senators at their word.

As the oratory droned on, three black men quietly made their way around the edges of the crowd, where small clusters of blacks stood watching the spectacle. The men were spreading their own news of liberty: A schooner named the *Pearl* lay waiting at a secluded wharf on the Potomac River. The captain of the *Pearl* was offering to carry North any slave who could get to the wharf by midnight.

One of these men was Samuel Edmonson, the son of Paul and Amelia Edmonson, a free black man and his enslaved wife. The Edmonsons were respected members of the black community in D.C. and founders of a dissident Methodist church. Amelia Edmonson was allowed by her mistress to live with her husband, working at home as a seamstress and washerwoman, but by law all fourteen of their children were born in bondage. Samuel Edmonson persuaded five of his siblings to join the escape, including his sisters Mary, age thirteen, and Emily, age fifteen. Under the cover of a rainy night sky, seventy-seven slaves managed to sneak to the harbor and onto the *Pearl*. It was the largest escape attempt in the history of American slavery.

The voyage went smoothly till daybreak, when a squall arose and the captain was forced to drop anchor in a small cove to wait out the storm. Back on land, the owners awoke to discover their property had disappeared. Fire bells rang the alarm, and a posse was quickly assembled to search the country roads where runaways usually headed. A ship full of defiant slaves was too preposterous to imagine. But the *Pearl's* luck ran out when the posse came across an informer, who told the pursuers everything. By two o'clock the next morning, the fugitives were being towed back to Washington.

Most of the outraged owners promptly sold their runaway slaves to Bruin and Hill, a large slave-trafficking firm in Alexandria, Virginia, who planned to resell them at the lucrative slave market in New Orleans. The trafficker paid $4,500 for the six Edmonson children, plucking them directly from jail. A local who knew the family offered $1,000 for thirteen-year-old Mary, but Mr. Bruin refused, saying he could get double the price at auction for a lovely, light-skinned young girl. Everyone in the trade knew that a pretty, pliant girl made an excellent concubine and brood mare.

One brother was purchased by his already emancipated brother, hoping that together they would earn the money to buy the rest. The other brothers were sold down river. But by September the fate of the girls remained up in the air. After much pleading by Paul Edmonson, Bruin and Hill agreed to sell the girls to their father for $2,250 if he could come up with half the money before the girls were scheduled to be shipped to Louisiana. Friends in D.C. donated some money, but not enough. So Paul Edmonson headed to New York, where there was rumored to be an Anti-Slavery Office filled with generous men. In New York he found support, but still he needed more. The deadline was fast approaching, and he was growing desperate. Finally several Methodist ministers agreed to arrange a fund-raising event on October 24.

Someone suggested that he talk to Reverend Beecher. A few months before, Beecher had spoken at a meeting to raise money to redeem a local Baptist's son from slavery, and he might be willing to do it again. On the morning of the event Paul Edmonson found his way to Beecher's house, but as he mounted the steps to ring the doorbell, his courage failed, and he sank down to wait anxiously on the stoop. There Henry found him.

The pastor was heart-struck by the girls' plight. Henry was not naive, but the bluntness of Paul Edmonson's tale shocked him. He was dumbfounded by the trader's unashamed admission that the girls would be sold for sex. How could anyone sell a young girl—a Christian no less—into a life of rape, beatings, and crushing labor?

Suddenly Henry saw a way of cutting through all the congressional stalemates and Constitutional impasses. Here was a case he could see in his mind's eye and feel in his heart, without the complications of policy or politics. And if he could see it, then he could make others see it.

THAT EVENING THE BROADWAY TABERNACLE was packed with sympathetic faces, including many Plymouth Church folks. The gaslights flickered dramatically as Henry mounted the platform to give the first speech.

Some of you, he began, even those sympathetic to the plight of these young Christian girls, may object to helping them because they ran away, and that seems dishonorable. He put the question to them directly: "Suppose that you, venerable old man, young man, maiden, suppose that you were a slave, I ask you could logic frame an argument strong enough to satisfy you that you ought not to try to escape? Should it not burn in your veins?"

His answer drew forth a thunderclap of applause: "If any son of mine had been captured and did not want to leave his prison and come home to freedom, I would think 'He is no son of mine.' "

Henry then expertly worked the room up to an even bigger response. He took up the next objection, that buying slaves one by one was impractical and only legitimized the selling of human souls. True, true, but focus your mind on these particular girls—Christians! Methodists!—whom the "human flesh-dealers" would sell as prostitutes to any white man with a pocket full of money. Forget principles, law, and prejudice and think only of this: How would you feel if your daughter were kidnapped and sold to a man who would rape her, sell her children for a profit, and whip her if she put up resistance? Then he subtly switched perspectives, vividly depicting the mind of the master looking over the girls for the best bargain, and then finally he assumed the voice of the auctioneer: "And more than all that, gentlemen, they say she is one of those praying Methodist niggers; who bids? A thousand—fifteen hundred—two thousand—twenty-five hundred! Going, going! Last call! *Gone!*"[48]

Henry's appeal to their imagination—to put themselves in the shoes of the outraged Christian, the grief-stricken father, the innocent slave child, the libertine master—electrified the audience and lit up Beecher in return. Susan Howard described the scene in admiration: As he spoke, "he poured forth the breathing thoughts and burning words of indignation, scorn, contempt, and pity, his audience seemed completely in his hands, and the breathless silence, the flowing tear, or thunder of applause gave unmistakable evidence that he made himself understood and felt. He seemed to enjoy the hurrahs!"

Beecher closed with a plea that they be blind to color, that they feel only as they would if they had lost all their other children, and their last daughter was about to be sold into a fate worse than death. But the moment that made Beecher famous came after the speeches were over and a collection was taken up and counted. The tally was six hundred dollars—not nearly enough. A voice from the crowd called out, "Take up another!" "Another collection was made, but still several hundreds were lacking," Susan Howard recalled.

Mr. S. B. Chittenden gave his name for another $50; his brother, Henry Chittenden, another $50; H. C. Bowen, $100; Chittenden, another $25; and so the ball rolled on, the ministers on the platform making short and appropriate remarks, the audience calling out, "How much is wanting now?"

Mr. Beecher seemed to be on his feet and talking all the time, popping about like a box of fireworks accidentally ignited, and going off in all shapes and directions—a rocket here with falling stars, a fiery wheel there, and before you could think, a nest of serpents right in your teeth. [. . .]

When the whole sum was raised but fifty dollars, "Now," said Mr. Beecher, "I never did hurrah in a public meeting, but when this account is closed up, I will join in three of the loudest cheers that ever rang through this old building."

"I'll take the balance," called out Mr. Studwell of Plymouth Church. And then there was a mighty shout! Hats were swung, handkerchiefs waved, mouths were on the very broadest grin, and more ministers than Mr. Beecher joined in the row.[49]

To these earnest Northerners it was as if they were witnessing a live slave auction, and they were the saviors. "I think that of all the meetings that I have attended in my life, for a panic of sympathy I never saw one that surpassed that," Henry recalled, and "I have seen a great many in my day."[50] A few weeks later the girls returned joyously to their parents.

The *Tribune* reported Henry's speech verbatim, and it was picked up by other papers, setting off waves of controversy. Some were shocked at the sexual theme, and his frank references to "Southern sensualists." Abolitionists criticized Beecher for paying ransom to slaveholders. Others carped that the entire event had been sensational and indecorous, particularly Beecher's whipping up of the crowd at the end.

Why all the tumult? True, Henry offered no new solution to the constitutional quandary. Instead he hit upon a strategy that created empathy for actual black people, bridging the alienation of color and bondage and binding the listener to the slave if only for a moment, by the common longings of human nature. He exploited the contradictions of the human heart: What is abstract and far away is never as moving as what is intimate and in the flesh. As Henry later noted with irony, "The very men who give their counsel and zeal and money against the unseen slave *of the South* irresistibly pity the particular fugitive whom they *see* running through the North."[51]

It was a technique that his sister Harriet Beecher Stowe would bring to its highest form a few years later. Twentieth-century critics later belittled both Beechers' antislavery work as sentimental, unsystematic, and pandering to white prejudice. But such criticism misreads the mind of the average American of the nineteenth century. It was a radical thing indeed to persuade free whites to feel a genuine kinship with enslaved blacks (or even free blacks, as Henry later did). This imaginative, emotional exercise was crucial to recognizing blacks as fellow citizens.

This is not mere speculation. The effect could be seen in Beecher's own heart. Stepping into the shoes of Paul Edmonson, the brokenhearted father; and of Samuel Edmonson, the noble fugitive; and donning the mantle of defender of female virtue all solidified Henry's own commitment to the cause.

It could also be seen in Plymouth Church. From this point on Plymouth Church was a steadfast antislavery institution. The congregation adopted the girls as one of their charitable causes and helped Millie Edmonson raise the money to buy herself and two more daughters out of bondage.

Over the next fifteen years the Reverend Charles B. Ray, Brooklyn's most prominent African American abolitionist, journalist, and Congregational minister, worked closely with Lewis Tappan and other members of Plymouth Church to both purchase the freedom of slaves and speed safely those fugitives who stole their own freedom. The basement of the church, it was rumored, was used by New York's antislavery Vigilance Committee as a secret way station on the Underground Railroad that led runaway slaves from Washington, D.C., to New York City and up the Hudson River to Canada.

Just as crucially, Plymouth Church was now an unwavering pro-Beecher institution. Over the next decade, many ministers would lose their jobs after preaching against slavery—including two of Henry's brothers. Not Henry. He was so beloved, it was often said, that if his own church ever let him go, dozens more would clamor to hire him.

THE YEAR 1849 entered snowy and colder than it had been in a decade. Following the old Dutch tradition, on New Year's Day young men made their way from house to house calling on friends, especially those with pretty daughters and liberal punch bowls. In later years the Beecher house would fill with so many well-wishers that Henry came to dread the day. But that year the parsonage was subdued. Eunice was nearing the end of her sixth pregnancy, and her delicate condition made her moody, "irascible—and sensitive to those unskillful with her—tender even to tears toward those she loves," Henry told his father.[52] On January 26 she gave birth to a son with the heroic name of William Constantine, in honor of Henry's oldest brother and his closest childhood friend.

All in all it was an auspicious start to the year. Except for the harsh weather. On January 13 the temperature rose to thirteen degrees Fahrenheit, a comparatively balmy day in that bitter season, but more than cold enough to require the sexton to light the furnace at the church. That afternoon, just as the Brooklyn Eagle was going to press, the editor included a breathless report that as of 2:00 P.M. Plymouth Church was "on fire and likely to be consumed."[53]

When the volunteer firemen got to Cranberry Street the smoke was so dense that all they could do was aim their hoses and crank up the water. After the smoke and vapor cleared, they found that the flames had extended from the basement furnace to the top of the organ gallery, essentially demolishing the church.

As news of the fire spread, local churches rushed to offer Beecher the use of their sanctuaries. Lewis Tappan donated an empty lot on Pierrepont Street, rent-free, where they put up a rough, tin-roofed "Tabernacle" as they called it, while they decided what to do next. The congregation was growing so quickly that the old sanctuary was literally overflowing, but how much more could it grow? The trustees finally concluded that the fire was Providence telling them to raise their spiritual ambitions. Plymouth Church would rebuild on the same spot but would more than triple in size.

"You Plymouth people are spoiling your young minister," one friend warned Susan Howard; "you flatter him by putting up so large a church. It is not possible that he will be able to fill it after a year or two longer; and if he should go away or die, what could you do with that great house?"

"It is you that flatter him," Susan replied hotly. "We think that the same God who made him and sent him to us is able to make another and provide us with another leader when we need one."[54]

Susan Howard was right. The burning of Plymouth Church seemed to deepen both religious fervor and curiosity about the young westerner. People of all persuasions came to the tin tabernacle to see what the fuss was about—Catholics, Methodists, Unitarians, atheists, all Lyman Beecher's old enemies—including, as Henry Bowen recalled, one memorable fellow who was violently opposed to all religion but came because he just liked to hear what Mr. Beecher had to say. From October 1848 to April 1849, 176 new members joined.

If the Lord was telling them to build, then Henry Chandler Bowen was His primary agent and overseer. It was Bowen who pitched the project to his fellow trustees, and Bowen—with his usual canny generosity—who lent the church the money to rebuild, at a tidy profit. The decision to erect a massive new church transformed Bowen's and Beecher's relationship from patron and pastor to a true partnership. In temperament the two men were polar opposites. Where Bowen was sharp, efficient, and tightfisted, Beecher was warm, disorganized, and openhanded. Nonetheless Bowen admired Beecher tremendously. Beecher possessed the college education and moral stature that Bowen had longed for as a young man. The pastor had an easy way with people that the businessman, for all his sharp negotiating skills, would never have. As for Beecher, he relied gratefully on Bowen's personal generosity, financial acumen, and religious vigor.

What the two shared was a rare combination of spiritual and worldly ambition. They were each intensely competitive and politically shrewd. Above all else they longed to be opinion makers, public men who served the cause of heaven on earth. Both men recognized the growing market of consumers eager for stimulation, guidance, and emotional connection, and kept a steady lookout for opportunities to combine propaganda and profit. With Beecher's charisma and Bowen's financial backing, they could accomplish great things for both God and Mammon.

Over the next decade the duo built Plymouth Church into one of the few institutions in America that was popular, prosperous, and unapologetically antislavery. They led a drive to build dozens of Congregational churches in New York and the West and helped raise funds to free a fair number of slaves. Every month brought some new meeting or cause to which Beecher lent his voice and Bowen his formidable resources. It was commonly said that Plymouth Church was run by "two Henrys," as one clergyman teased; "when one fires the shot, the other pays for the powder."[55]

That autumn, as the new Plymouth Church rose from the ashes, Henry Bowen offered Henry yet another opportunity to do God's work while filling his pocketbook. Bowen and his fellow evangelical entrepreneurs had started a new weekly religious paper entitled the *Independent,* and Beecher seemed like a natural choice for a regular columnist. The Reverend Beecher had conquered the pulpit and the platform. He was more than ready to tackle the press.

Chapter 8

"Politics in the Pulpit"

enry Ward Beecher had an astonishing knack for landing at the hot spots of American history—born in Litchfield, Connecticut, when it was one of the most influential villages in the Union; coming of age during the heady cultural experiments of the 1830s; going West when it was still raw frontier. But his canniest move of all was to arrive in New York just as the city was giving birth to what we now call the modern media industry.

When Henry was a boy, "news" for the average person was local, passed along by word of mouth or letters. Most newspapers served either the mercantile community, which needed information about ship arrivals and current prices for commodities and banknotes, or by political parties, which used them to push candidates and platforms. The invention of the steam-driven Hoe press in the 1830s encouraged the first mass readership for newspapers by speeding up the delivery of news and pushing the price down to a single penny. The telegraph, patented in 1844, enabled information to be transmitted in a fraction of the time. By 1850 New York City alone circulated 1.5 million newspapers daily among a population of approximately five hundred thousand. Since most newspapers passed through several hands and were often read aloud around the hearth or the workbench, the number of actual readers was estimated at ten times that.

The rise of the penny press inaugurated the era of the imperial editor. The professional "reporter" had not yet come of age. Instead newspapers were dominated by powerful owner/editors, most of whom got their start as journeyman printers and partisan hacks but who now courted readers with the ardor they once gave to political machines. The old English style of writing—literary, ruminative, written for the ages, as epitomized by the genteel English journal, the *Spectator*—lost favor. In its place came what was loosely called the French style: vigorous, personal, lightly sarcastic, and openly competitive, emphasizing sensational storytelling rather than elegant analysis. In a bid to attract more women readers, editors were now expanding their coverage of cultural events, especially religion, and adding serialized fiction.

Scores of papers were published in New York, all competing ferociously for readers and influence. For workingmen there were the cheap penny papers, led by the wildly popular *New York Sun*. For the well-to-do there were the upmarket sixpenny papers like the *Evening Post*, edited by the poet William Cullen Bryant. Mercantile sheets like *Journal of Commerce* and the *Courier and Enquirer* vied for business readers. Dozens of specialized papers and magazines were devoted to various causes, political parties, and religious sects, with new ones popping up all the time. Then as now, the New York media presumed that their own local doings were inherently fascinating, chronicling editors, writers, and local personalities as if they were national celebrities—thus making them so.

The loudest voices—the ones that would shape Beecher's career— were the *Tribune*, the *Herald*, and the *Times*. James Gordon Bennett's *Herald* and Horace Greeley's *Tribune* were the fiercest rivals. Both the editors and their papers were diametrically opposed in style and politics (ironically, the two papers would later merge to become the *Herald-Tribune* in the twentieth century). Like its boisterous editor, the *Herald* was rabidly Democratic, antiabolition, antireform, and anti-all-isms, and possessed a bloodcurdling appetite for sensation.

The *Tribune* even more closely reflected the idiosyncrasies of its editor, Horace Greeley. Greeley was mythically eccentric, devoting the *Tribune* to the "Progress of Society" and a dizzying array of reform schemes. At the same time Greeley had a common touch, and knew how to appeal to country folk and urbanites aspiring to the respectable middle class. The *Tribune* put out a weekly edition, distributed by rail to over a hundred thousand subscribers across the North. It was considered the most influential paper of the day, even by Greeley's enemies.

The *New York Times* was a latecomer to the scene, arriving in 1851.

The founder, Henry Jarvis Raymond, proposed the *Times* as an antidote to the *Tribune* and *Herald*, a paper that would avoid, in the words
of reporter Augustus Maverick, the "socialistic heresies of one and the
abominable nastiness of the other."[1] A rare college graduate at a time
when most editors started as printer's devils, Raymond would begin to
push journalism away from colorful editorializing toward a focus on accurate fact collecting.

These strong editorial personalities and politics fostered vicious
competition, even occasional violence. James Gordon Bennett alone
was beaten up at least three times by rival editors. Even the religious
papers were prone to decidedly un-Christian personal attacks and petty
backbiting. Done well, however, a successful newspaper united propaganda and profits like no other enterprise.

For several years Lewis Tappan, Henry Bowen, and their coterie
had talked of starting a paper to promote their two pet causes: Congregationalism and abolitionism. For the last two decades the Tappans
had been campaigning to turn American churches against slavery, beginning with their ill-fated endowment of Lane Seminary. But while
antislavery sentiment was slowly spreading in the North, the majority of churches refused this radical reinterpretation of Holy Scripture.
By the end of the 1840s each of the three major denominations—
Presbyterians, Baptists, and Methodists—had experienced devastating
schisms over the slavery question. Many ministers who were personally
sympathetic to the slave refused to broach the subject for fear of alienating their congregations.

Between the conservatism of the clergy and the contradictions of
the Bible, it was starting to seem to many people that humanitarian ethics and traditional Christianity were irreconcilable. William Lloyd Garrison's response was the same as with the Constitution—if Christianity
defended human bondage, then Christianity was not worth defending.
The "Come-outers," as they were called, went a step further, standing
up in the middle of religious services to exhort the stunned congregants
to "come out" of the corrupt churches, citing Revelation 18:4: "Come
out of here, my people, that ye receive not of her plagues."

Evangelical stalwarts like the Tappans were alarmed by this rising
anticlericalism. It cast the pall of atheism over the entire antislavery
movement, turning off respectable folk. Again it was a question of ranking values; if forced to choose between emancipation and the church,
the average American chose the church. Finally Tappan and Garrison

split over these issues of religion and respectability. Tappan established the American and Foreign Antislavery Society (AFASS), a more conservative, church-based antislavery organization headquartered in New York City. Garrison retained control of the Boston-based American Antislavery Society (AASS). Throughout the 1840s, the Garrisonians dominated the discourse, largely because Garrison's paper, the *Liberator*, was such a strong voice. Now the Tappanites saw their chance to reclaim leadership of the movement.

The *Independent* was to be the new standard-bearer of the Christian antislavery movement. It was Congregational not only out of Yankee nostalgia but because the denomination had no Southern wing or ecclesiastical hierarchy to censor it. Once again Henry Bowen took the lead, dividing ownership of the paper among some of the same wealthy dry-goods merchants who first invested in Plymouth Church. Bowen himself wrote a weekly commercial report for the back of the paper, for a popular religious paper was also an excellent way for dry-goods merchants to boost their brand-name recognition. Three prominent Congregational clergymen were hired to share the editor's chair: Joseph P. Thompson, minister of the Broadway Tabernacle; Richard Salter Storrs, Henry's compatriot in Brooklyn; and Leonard Bacon, minister of the First Church of New Haven and an old friend of the Beecher family. The editors were moderates in every sense of the word, the type who took pains to call themselves "antislavery men" rather than "abolitionists," and who put as much emphasis on rescuing the reputation of the church as on demolishing slavery. The venerable reform journalist Joshua Leavitt brought a more strident strain of evangelical abolitionism to the role of managing editor.

The *Independent* debuted in December 1848, garnering good reviews but few subscribers. Slavery stayed on the back burner, crowded out by theological debates and clerical announcements. For the paper to survive, it needed some excitement.

In October 1849 the editors announced that Henry Ward Beecher was joining as a weekly contributor. Unlike the other contributors, he refused a byline, instead signing his column with an asterisk (*) or "star"—which only whipped up curiosity about the author's identity. In tone and topic the columns varied widely: sentimental paeans to nature, rapturous visits to art galleries, essays promoting better church music, bitter screeds against things he disapproved of, and sarcastic rebukes to those who dared attack *him*. When ideas dried up he occasionally wrote book reviews—without always reading the books beforehand, he was once forced to confess. He came into the office when he pleased, if he pleased. He took much the same tack with deadlines.

In fact, taking the ferry over to the Manhattan office was the best part of the job. The *Independent* was located in a narrow warren of offices at 5 Beekman Street, in the heart of Park Row, where New York's publishers, newspaper offices, and print shops clustered. From here it was a short stroll to the wharves, City Hall Park, and the hurly-burly of lower Broadway. Newspapers posted breaking news on bulletin boards outside their offices, ships arrived daily with the latest foreign intelligence, and the Broadway hotels provided a steady influx of gossip and visiting dignitaries. Henry loved to wander the crowded streets, browsing through bookstores and newsrooms, window-shopping while he chatted with local craftsmen, dining at Delmonico's with his new friends. In truth Beecher far preferred the worldly, vigorous company of entrepreneurs and newspapermen to that of his sedate fellow clergymen.

Henry courted controversy right out of the gate. In November 1849 he tossed his first firecracker, roused by the remarks of one Reverend Thomas T. Skinner, who accused the growing band of liberal Congregationalists of plotting to bring down Presbyterianism in New York. One of Henry's Brooklyn rivals chimed in, calling for Presbyterians to show more esprit de corps in the face of these aggressive new competitors—likening them to ecclesiastical "bastards," couching the insult in the Latin term *filius degener.*

Writing under his own signature, Henry excoriated Reverend Skinner for being "filled with witch-blood drawn from the shriveled body of sectarianism" and professed shock that a man of the cloth would describe his fellow Christians as bastards. As for himself, Henry protested sweetly, he had no interest in ecclesiastical quarrels. Others might call for esprit de corps, but he prayed only for an *esprit de Christ.*[2]

Over the years this would become his preferred tactic—a brutal "nonpartisan" attack on other people's partisanship. The *New York Presbyterian* responded in fury, embroiling the *Independent* in the first of many battles. Their strongest argument was that Henry's Latin translation was vulgar and incorrect—probably true, given his terrible command of Latin, but hardly a fatal blow. The *Brooklyn Eagle* picked up the controversy, looking eagerly for a pastoral brawl, but Henry had already moved on to other skirmishes. The Presbyterians simmered with anger, but Beecher and Bowen got what they wanted: Both the *Independent* and its "star contributor" were the talk of the town.

∾ ∾

ON THE FIRST SUNDAY OF 1850, thousands of people streamed down
the narrow streets of Brooklyn Heights toward the new Plymouth
Church. Three large double doors opened onto Orange Street, a shady
block of wood-framed houses. From the sidewalk the broad red-brick
building resembled a barn. As the throngs shoved their way through the
vestibule, they entered a vast open space as plain, white, and unadorned
as a Puritan meetinghouse.

The church had been designed according to Henry's strictly practical specifications. A steep gallery encircled the entire room, with two
extra mezzanines in the back, so that the audience could see itself on
all sides. Some 2,100 people could fit easily in the seats, and hundreds
more could fit on benches along the walls, with others standing in the
back of the room. No columns or other architectural flourishes blocked
the view of the audience, and huge multipaned windows let in a flood
of light. "I think that we have the most *convenient* and well arranged
church that I have ever seen," Henry crowed to his brother Tom, "and a
perfect love of a pulpit—as much as we shall have no pulpit at all."[3]

The pulpit, or lack thereof, was the most innovative feature. When
one of the trustees, a civil engineer, asked Henry how he wanted the
audience located, the pastor's answer was emphatic: "I want them to
surround me, so that they will come up on every side, and behind me
so that I shall be in the center of the crowd, and have the people surge
all about me." Instead of a traditional raised pulpit, Henry insisted on a
wide stage that thrust out into the audience. The front pews came right
up to the stage in a shallow semicircle. When the room was crowded,
children often sat on stairs at the foot of the stage, close enough for the
preacher to tousle their hair. At the back of the platform stood a comfortable armchair and a small side table for his notes.

For many years Plymouth Church was the largest hall in Brooklyn
and one of the best in New York for public speaking. Many weeknights
it was filled with concerts and lecture events, serving as a center of local
social life. Henry later liked to brag that Charles Dickens, after giving a
reading at Plymouth Church, told him never to build a new hall because
this one was perfect. "It is perfect," Henry said, "because it was built on
a principle—the principle of social and personal magnetism which ema-
nates reciprocally from a speaker and from a close throng of hearers."[4]
Even visitors who were unimpressed by Beecher were enthralled when

the audience stood to sing, with thousands of voices reverberating from the walls.

That Sunday of the grand opening, the sanctuary was so crowded that a hundred people were forced to stand. To capitalize on their fresh start the trustees had scheduled the annual meeting to rent pews on the first week of January and hired a professional auctioneer to turn it into a night of entertainment. Some observers called it vulgar, but the auction was a huge success, with Tasker Howard and Henry Bowen taking two of the top seats.

All around New York a sense of infinite possibility hung in the air, like the electricity of an approaching thunderstorm. The world "is in a wonderful state of commotion just now," observed the editor of the *Brooklyn Eagle*. "Society is stirred up from the bottom; men act with new motives, new feelings, new stimuli; they are in a whirl of excitement, and ready for any movement which promises a change. They are aspiring after something without knowing exactly what they want."[5]

New York was leading the nation in an economic revolution. Until the 1840s the United States was a nation of isolated villages and farm regions, each acting in relative economic self-sufficiency. The whirlwind technological advances of the last few years were changing all that. The building boom in railroad lines and toll roads had reduced the journey from, say, New York to Boston from several days to a few hours. Telegraph wires stretched to the Mississippi River, and construction was under way to sink a telegraph cable under the Atlantic Ocean, linking the United States to Europe. Several leading New York newspapers had created the first "Associated Press," to speed up the transmission of foreign news. National networks of credit were proliferating, along with mercantile credit agencies that gathered and sold information about an individual's financial trustworthiness. The Croton Reservoir, part of a system of aqueducts linking the city to upstate New York, ended the city's chronic water shortages and cholera outbreaks with the first modern sewer system. New techniques of mechanized mass production were unleashing a flood of cheap consumer goods.

Interstate trade, which was insignificant in 1800, was three times higher than international trade by 1850. A new regional division of labor ruled. The South produced export crops such as tobacco and cotton. The old Northwest (soon to be the Midwest) was the breadbasket of the country, producing the corn and wheat that fed the South and the burgeoning cities in the East. New England and the mid-Atlantic states were the center of commerce and manufacturing. The nation seemed suddenly smaller, as one newspaper editor observed in wonder, when every tick of the clock or raging of a storm could be instantly registered a thousand miles away.

In actuality the country was growing at a gargantuan rate. In 1845 John C. Frémont completed an overland trek to the Pacific, laying the first American claim to the southwestern lands long settled by the Spanish, and to the northwestern territories held by England. With the help of his brilliant wife, Jessie Benton Frémont, the "Great Pathfinder" captured the public imagination with a bestselling account about his western adventures. With their book as a guide, Conestoga wagons filled with hopeful homesteaders began to beat a steady trail west. Then in September 1848 a settler in Sutter's Mill, California, happened upon a shiny rock that turned out to be gold. Within a month tens of thousands of men were on their way to California.

New York was euphoric from so much good news. Among Henry's personal friends, Tasker Howard was earning a fortune building steamships to carry eager miners to the goldfields of California. Riding the boom in the textile trade, Bowen and McNamee opened a gorgeous new dry-goods emporium on Lower Broadway. It was one of the first marble commercial buildings in Manhattan, with four stories boasting all the latest luxuries, including gas chandeliers, hot running water, and a monstrous five-ton safe. With so much shared good fortune, the *Independent* predicted that 1850 would be the year the slavery question finally died away for good.

But human nature is tricky. The more people were bound by roads, telegraph lines, and credit, the more people chafed against their regional differences—and the thorniest difference of all was slavery. The cultural divide over slavery had remained stable as long as it was under the jurisdiction of individual states. Now the dark side of interdependence was coming to a head. In less than a decade the United States had acquired enough territory to double the size of the nation. Now the question was unavoidable: Would slavery be allowed to spread to these future states?

THIS QUESTION HAD BEEN DOGGING America since the Louisiana Purchase, when it nearly broke the Union in two. Back then the Whig senator Henry Clay had proposed what came to be known as the Missouri Compromise of 1820. In exchange for the admission of Missouri as a slave state, the South agreed that slavery in the territories acquired from France would be legally limited to states south of 36° 30' latitude (Missouri, which lay above the line, was excepted).

But with all this fertile new territory and all that gold, that law now seemed arbitrary and unfair to the South. Part of their reasoning was financial. The plantation system—mass cultivation made economically feasible by cheap slave labor—depleted land quickly. To keep their investments profitable, planters needed to expand into the fertile lands to the west. Slaveholders felt that they were simply defending their right to transport their legal property across state lines.

Yet three-quarters of Southerners didn't own slaves. Why would nonslaveholders so fiercely defend the territorial expansion of slavery? Fear is one answer. Blacks in slave states were approximately a third of the population, and two states (South Carolina and Mississippi) had black majorities, raising the threat of violent rebellion. The West seemed like a natural safety valve for potential trouble.

Political power is another answer. The Northern population was growing at a faster rate than the Southern, as was their influence in Congress. Increasing the number of slave states would maintain the current balance of power, especially in the Senate. It was also a matter of honor. Why shouldn't they have as much right as anyone to live with their own property and traditions in these rich new territories? Southerners—slaveholders or not—believed that they were fighting for their equal rights against rapacious Northerners who cared nothing for the hapless slaves but were simply using them to subjugate the South.

Meanwhile, the vast majority of Northerners were adamant that the territories should remain free. For a few it was a question of principle—to allow the spread of slavery onto national lands would bathe their own hands in blood. Many more Northerners, however, were motivated not by antislavery sympathy but by economic self-interest: White men had no desire to compete with slaves for jobs. In fact, many wanted to ban blacks from the new territories altogether. "Free-soil" sentiment, as it was called, was widespread enough to spawn a new "Free-Soil Party" in 1848, which was remarkably successful for its first campaign, carrying 14 percent of the vote in the free states.

By the middle of 1849 the renowned Quaker poet John Greenleaf Whittier observed to Lewis Tappan that it was almost as hard to find a proslavery man in the North as it used to be to uncover an abolitionist. Yet, he added wryly, "I have scarcely charity enough to suppose that this marvelous conversion is altogether genuine and heartfelt."[6]

Southerners watched these developments with mounting anger. The more the North united across party lines in free-soil feeling, the more zealous they became in self-defense. The rumblings of discontent grew louder and more ominous. Then, to the surprise of almost everyone, President Zachary Taylor sent a message to Congress announcing that gold-rich California would be applying directly for statehood, skipping over the federal-territory stage (thus giving Congress and the Southern politicians no control over its position on slavery). Under the influence of its military governor, John C. Frémont, California would almost certainly adopt a free-state Constitution.

The slave states were stunned. Allowing this to pass would start a domino effect, they feared. First California, then New Mexico, then the vast Oregon Territory would likely become free states, putting slaveholders in an intolerable political minority. Suddenly the South was united as never before. When a violent shoving match erupted on the floor of Congress over the selection of the Speaker of the House, Georgia congressman Robert Toombs shouted the unthinkable: *"I am for disunion!"*[7] The entire Southern delegation cheered and stamped their feet in approval. From Virginia to Texas, rage and defiance poured out like a volcano. A conference was called to consider the viability of seceding from the United States. Suddenly the nation seemed to be splitting asunder.

Out of this chaos stepped the "Great Pacificator," Kentucky senator Henry Clay. In a two-day speech to the Senate, Clay laid out a compromise package with concessions for each side. To the North, Clay offered the prohibition of the slave trade in Washington, D.C., and the admission of California with a free constitution.

To the South he offered ironclad guarantees of their existing rights. Congress would have no power to interfere with the slave trade between states. Human bondage could be abolished in Washington, D.C., only with the consent of the citizens of Maryland, and with financial compensation to the owners. There would be no congressional restrictions on slavery in the territories acquired from Mexico, thus allowing the territorial residents to decide for themselves whether to allow human bondage (this was a fairly empty gesture, since it was assumed by all that slave-based agriculture would not thrive in the arid Southwest). The federal government would strengthen what became known as the Fugitive Slave Laws, requiring Northern citizens to actively capture and return runaway slaves in free states.

Most of the concrete concessions went to the North. But the concessions of principle went to the South. Slaves were reaffirmed as legitimate property, even when in free states. Symbolically the claims of the "Slave Power," as it came to be called, were strengthened and given federal legitimacy, promising, in theory, that the agitation against slavery would fade away.

The response to Clay's Compromise proposal was volcanic. For seven bitter months Congress debated the measures. The capital was literally an armed camp barely containing two hostile forces. Congressmen took to carrying pistols not only on the streets but on the floor of the House. When one legislator unintentionally set off his pistol while fussing with papers on his desk, thirty or forty pistols instantly appeared in the air.

The uproar from Capitol Hill echoed in the streets, barrooms, and newspapers—"our country is now so sympathetically connected, the transmission of news is so marvelously easy and quick, that Congress has become a speaking trumpet," as Henry observed.[8] To the militant abolitionists and the fire-eaters, the Compromise measures were an abomination. But in the vast middle, most prayed fervently that Clay's Compromise would work.

New York City panicked when President Taylor's message hit the presses. The initial prosperity of 1850 vanished. Merchants were deluged with letters from Southern customers telling them their orders would be delayed or canceled due to the agitation in Washington. Wall Street, Broadway, the seaport—all would be wiped out if the South defaulted on its debts and withdrew its trade. The free-soil momentum of the last two years evaporated in the space of weeks as businessmen raced to placate the South.

In the midst of the stampede, a passionate minority stood up against Clay's Compromise. "I was thoroughly roused," Henry said. "It is time for good men and true to gird up their loins and stand forth for God and humanity." He launched an offensive from his new pulpit, condemning the players and the platforms by name. It is hard to say who got the worst end of his contempt: the men behind the Slave Power or the yellow-bellied Northern businessmen, "as anxious for the shame of supple servility as the slave is for the manliness of liberty."[9]

For Henry the Compromise struck directly at the fundamental rift in his personality. His progressive, crusading instinct warred against his conservative tendency to claim the middle ground. The result was a manifesto of moderate antislavery, published in the *Independent* under the title, "Shall We Compromise?"

No lasting compromise was possible between Liberty and Slavery, Henry argued, for democracy and aristocracy entailed such entirely different social and economic conditions that "One or the other must die." The only solution was to allow natural law and God's will to take its course by limiting the growth of slavery. "If slavery is stationary it will be speedily overrun and smothered by the rampant vine of freedom," he wrote. "It must thrust out its roots; it must borrow vigor from fresh soil." Leave slavery alone where it already existed, but don't allow it one more inch of territory. Natural evolution would take care of the rest.

But Beecher drew the line at the Compromise measures that compelled the North to return runaway slaves. Jesus commands us to shelter the suffering and give food to the hungry, he reminded his readers, and even the Constitution could not compel him to disobey Christ. Here Henry found himself echoing the Garrisonians. "If the compromises of the Constitution include requisitions which violate humanity, I will not be bound by them," he declared. "I put Constitution against Constitution—God's against man's."[10]

From our privileged point in history, we may judge Beecher's stance as wishy-washy or hypocritical. He would save the slaves who fled one by one, but seemed perfectly willing to leave three million people in bondage as long as they stayed south of the Mason-Dixon line and east of the Texas border. Beecher's belief in peaceful evolution, that with patience and time liberty would naturally drive out slavery, seems overly optimistic and naive. Certainly Garrison and his crowd thought so.

To the South, however, Beecher's words were incendiary. Moderates like Beecher saw eye to eye with the fire-eaters on this issue: If slavery was not allowed to expand, the insatiable North would overrun the South, destroying their "peculiar institution" and the society that rested upon it. To Southern radicals the free-soil plan was as treacherous as the demand for immediate abolition.

Henry's frank editorial was reprinted in many papers. Nearing death and too weak to read for himself, Senator John Calhoun, the ancient titan from South Carolina, asked his secretary to read aloud the newspaper coverage of the congressional debates. His secretary took up "Shall We Compromise?" When he finished reading Beecher's essay, it was said, Calhoun leaned up in bed saying, "Read the article again." Again it was read to him. After hearing it again the senator asked the name of the author. It was signed with only an asterisk or star. "The man who says that is right," pronounced Calhoun. "There is no alternative. It is liberty or slavery."[11]

∾　∾

THE COMPROMISE DEBATES raged through the halls of Congress as winter turned to spring and spring to summer. On March 4 Senator Calhoun gave his final dramatic speech in the Senate, although he was so close to death that an emissary had to read it for him. Speaking for the extreme slave faction, Calhoun called for more concessions from the North, warning of disaster if they were not forthcoming. On March 7 Daniel Webster, the legendary senator from Massachusetts, long a foe of slavery, rose to speak. The galleries were packed with onlookers anxious to hear whether he would support or derail the Compromise. The suspense ended with his famous opening line. "I wish to speak today not as a Massachusetts man, not as a Northern man, but as an American," he said gravely. "I speak today for the preservation of the Union. 'Hear me for my cause.' " By the time the senator sat down, the tide had turned in favor of the Compromise.

With Webster's capitulation, a howl of outrage went up from the Free-Soilers. "I joined with all Northern men of any freedom-loving spirit in denouncing it and in denouncing him," Beecher recalled. Most of the country hailed Webster as a hero, however. The stock market soared out of sheer relief, and businessmen showered the senator with memorials, gifts, and long petitions of gratitude. Of course the commercial classes supported Webster, Henry sneered. "With such men a moral principle is an abstraction—a thing for philosophic leisure," he wrote in the *Independent*. "Like sick men made delirious, they are more anxious to quiet pain, than to get rid of it by removing the disease."[12]

On March 11 William Seward, a young Whig senator from New York, countered with the last defining speech of the debate. Unlike his illustrious predecessors, he rose to speak to a nearly empty room. Yet it was Senator Seward who let loose the rallying cry that would dog the Compromise for the rest of its existence. There is, Seward proclaimed, a "higher law than the Constitution"—the law of God and of conscience. A *Tribune* correspondent telegraphed an account of Seward's speech back to New York, claiming it would wake the nation. He was right. By the end of the month one hundred thousand copies of the speech had been distributed, trumpeting the idea of "a higher law."

For opponents of slavery, Seward's call for conscience over political expediency perfectly captured the argument they had been making for decades. For those with Southern sympathies, it was a fanatical invitation to lawlessness. For the silent, uncommitted majority of the North, the question of the "higher law" versus the Fugitive Slave Law was the first time they felt truly implicated in the quarrel.

Of all the measures in Senator Clay's bill, the Fugitive Slave Laws were the most inflammatory. For the South, the provisions were a matter of honor as well as money. The number of runaway slaves had been rising over the last decade, which Southerners blamed on the antislavery fanatics. Their anger intensified when many local authorities in the North openly refused to cooperate with federal slave catchers. The Fugitive Slave Laws were as much a reprimand to the North as a tool for retrieving lost property.

The measures of the law were intentionally draconian, stripping away all rights to due process. Suspected fugitives could be arrested without a warrant, based only on the say-so of their alleged owner, and were denied the right to a jury trial. Instead they were turned over to a special commissioner, who received a fee of ten dollars for sending a fugitive back to the purported owner, reduced to five if the fugitive was released. Alleged runaways could not testify on their own behalf, so they could be convicted on nothing more than a white man's claim to ownership. Because the evidentiary requirements were so flimsy, free blacks were as likely to be seized as actual runaways, with little legal recourse.

Compounding the outrage, the measures compelled the North to enforce the obnoxious law. The number of federal marshals would dramatically increase, and any federal marshal who did not arrest an alleged fugitive would be fined one thousand dollars. If called upon, ordinary citizens of free states were required to join posses to help trap the escaped property. Any citizen aiding a runaway with shelter, food, or assistance could be sentenced to six months in prison and a ruinous thousand-dollar fine.

The worst aspect of the Fugitive Slave Laws to most people was that they made it impossible for the North to claim that it was not complicit in the sins of the South. As Henry put it with blunt sarcasm, "the North is to have the guilt and the South the profits of Slavery."[13] But those who would follow God's "higher law" instead ran headlong, once again, into the Bible.

The New Testament specifically takes up the question of how Christians should treat fugitive slaves. In the book of Philemon, a Roman slave and Christian convert named Onesimus runs away from his Christian master and seeks safe harbor with the apostle Paul. Paul must choose whether to aid Onesimus or to return him, according to Roman law. In the end Paul reluctantly sends Onesimus back to his master, with the hope that Philemon will free the bondsman out of love, of his own free will. Under any circumstances, the apostle admonishes Philemon, he must welcome Onesimus with the respect and humanity that he would accord to any fellow Christian, including Paul himself. The analogy to 1850 could hardly be more direct.

Some antislavery ministers countered Onesimus's story with opposing Scripture, such as Deuteronomy 23:15, God's injunction to Moses: "Thou shalt not deliver to his master the servant which is escaped from his master to thee." But most of the clergy followed Paul's ambivalent example, preaching obedience to the Fugitive Slave Laws while admonishing the slaveholders to voluntarily reform. For the first time, however, a significant number of ministers went whole hog for slavery. Dr. Leonard Woods of the Andover Seminary set the bar by publishing an influential tract, *Conscience and Constitution*, arguing that slavery was a divinely sanctioned institution. Woods and his compatriots launched a huge petition drive to persuade fellow ministers to support the Compromise, and urged their fellow ministers to stamp out antislavery agitation in their communities, and to work openly against antislavery clergy.

"Then it was that I flamed," Henry said. The rage he felt toward cowardly businessmen and callous slave owners was dwarfed by his contempt for these clergymen. To the argument that the apostle Paul sanctioned the Fugitive Slave Laws, Henry responded that he might accept that claim—if slaveholders followed Paul's instructions by receiving their runaway servants as Christians and family members, educating them, encouraging them to marry and own property. Of course, Henry noted, that would essentially spell the end of slavery. In one notable speech Henry hammered home the absurdity of the biblical justification with an imitation of a runaway slave sauntering back into his master's house, "with his broad, black, beaming face," and greeting the shocked whites with a warm, "How d'ye do, my brother? and how d'ye do, my sister?"[14]

Henry's scriptural and legal arguments were padded with namecalling, motive impugning, and detailed accusations of hypocrisy and immorality. But he was careful to make a distinction between sin and sinners, between the "Slave Conspiracy" or the "Slave Power"—that is, the legal system of bondage and its major public defenders—and the average citizens of the South. It was a distinction that would remain central to all of Henry's antislavery arguments, although often lost in the vituperation of his language. His exhortations were not always internally consistent but they were colorful, funny, and aimed precisely at the great ambivalent middle. Coming from a man so respectable and personally popular, they were all the more dangerous to the New York establishment.

It didn't take long for Henry to draw the fire of the leading mercantile mouthpiece, the conservative *Journal of Commerce*. The *Journal of Commerce* had been founded twenty years before by Arthur Tappan and David Hale as a Christian financial paper. Under the current editor, Gerard Hallock, the editorial policy retained the Christian rhetoric but took a laissez-faire approach to everything except the promotion of business interests. Hallock freely admitted that slavery was wrong, but he saw no need to do anything about it.

In the middle of March, as the fury over Webster and Seward was reaching a high pitch, Hallock attacked liberal ministers in general, and the *Independent* and its anonymous "star contributor" in particular, "for prostituting their professions and their pulpits and the Sabbath day to the preaching of Free-Soilism" and other poisonous "Ultraisms." How dare these fanatics use the pulpit—which businessmen paid for—to denounce their patrons and preach politics? The role of the clergy was to lead their congregants to personal piety. Period. Anything outside the church door was beyond their purview.

"Clergymen ought to understand that while they attend to the proper duties of their calling they will be respected, honored, and beloved," Hallock concluded, "but that if they descend to the arena of politics, their black coats will most likely be rolled in the dirt." Any congregation that didn't want the filth of politics in their midst ought to fire the troublemakers, he suggested. After all, what would fix a misguided minister faster than snatching away his "bread and butter"?[15]

Nothing raised Henry's wrath like the hint of physical intimidation. His response was no different than when he was a hot-tempered Hoosier, ready to beat up the local tavern owner who insulted him. For three months Beecher and Hallock traded scathing editorials, under the banner "Politics in the Pulpit."

For some time now, Henry had been drifting from theology toward practical moral matters, but the fight with the *Journal* hardened this move into a manifesto. The Holy Gospel, he averred, is merely medicine for the sick soul. "It has no intrinsic value as a system. Its end and value are in its power to stimulate the soul, to develop its faculties, to purify the emotions," he declared.[16] Christianity did not exist for the glory of God, he insisted, but for the pleasure and health of mankind. Nowadays this therapeutic view of religion so thoroughly dominates culture that it is almost impossible to imagine how shocked were by Henry's words.

By contrast, Beecher claimed, the *Journal of Commerce* promoted a "Coward's Ethic." Such men wanted a Gospel "that will snatch away their sins while they are asleep; some chloroform Gospel." Just what, Henry inquired sarcastically, did the *Journal of Commerce* consider a suitable topic for discussion in church? After all, he observed, many modern sins were not mentioned in the Bible. Should we not preach against drunkenness or swindling or gambling simply because they were not specifically forbidden in Scripture?

Perhaps the problem was merely a matter of distance? Men like Gerard Hallock gladly gave money to send missionaries to the Far East, Henry noted, yet "a Turkish harem is a cradle of virgin purity" compared with the slave pens of the American South. "Will the Journal tell us how many leagues off a sin must be before it is prudent and safe for courageous ministers to preach against it?"

Or was it simply bald hypocrisy? After all, Henry observed, the *Journal of Commerce* hailed the Presbyterian *New York Observer* when it preached against free soil, and it loudly praised Dr. Leonard Woods's public support for Daniel Webster. "This is but an new reading of the old maxim," Henry wrote: *"Orthodoxy is MY doxy; heterodoxy is YOUR doxy."*[17]

Back and forth they went, citing Scripture and secular law, with each paper reprinting the entire debate in special supplements. Nasty as it was, the long clash rendered a great public service, challenging common prejudices, laying out statistics, detailing legal ordinances, examining every aspect of the problem. It also gave a well-needed boost to the struggling *Independent*. Subscriptions were increasing at double the previous rate, with hundreds of new readers every week.

The fight catapulted Beecher into the limelight. As the rhetoric heated up, the *Independent* editors, while generally in agreement with their "star contributor's views," were nervous enough to announce several times that these opinions were Henry Ward Beecher's alone. "It is well understood that Brother Beecher is erratic," as one editor, Leonard Bacon, noted. "No discreet person would undertake to be responsible for *all* his sayings and doings."[18]

Suddenly Henry was a genuine celebrity, whose colorful sayings and doings were being picked up by newspapers across the country. Not everyone agreed with Henry Ward Beecher, and nobody agreed with *everything* he had to say. But everyone wanted to hear it.

∾ ∾

ON MAY 7, the opening day of the May Anniversaries when the various national reform groups gathered for their annual meetings, the atmosphere in the Broadway Tabernacle was tense. William Lloyd Garrison's radical Antislavery Society had the morning session, and in the afternoon Henry Ward Beecher was to make his official debut at the meeting of Tappan's moderate antislavery society. For weeks now, the scapegoating of the abolitionists had been growing more frenzied. As the Anniversary Meetings approached, several Democratic papers began urging their readers to stop these lawless fanatics. "What right have all the religious lunatics of the free States to gather in this commercial city for purposes which, if carried into effect, would ruin and destroy its prosperity?" demanded the *Herald*.[19]

The morning meeting began smoothly but descended into chaos when a posse of rough-neck Bowery boys leaped onto the stage during Garrison's speech, cursing, shouting, and shoving. Women and children in the audience screamed and hid, some men jumped up to fight, while others stood on their seats, laughing, the better to view the bedlam. A score of police watched motionless from the wings. Finally an evangelical choir group seated in the gallery, the famous Hutchinson Family singers, struck up a popular hymn. Their singing began to quiet the tumult below. After a few more skirmishes, the meeting concluded without serious violence. But the day was only half over.

Now came Henry's turn to face down the crowd. Tappan's more moderate society usually attracted neither the numbers nor the threats that Garrison's did. But this time the Tabernacle was packed, and a small band of rowdies in the corner gallery kept up a stream of taunts, hisses, and groans.

After Lewis Tappan finished reading a resolution condemning Clay's Compromise, Beecher stepped to the front of the stage. First off, Henry announced, he would address this common objection: If you insist on preaching antislavery, why don't you go down South where the sin is? Henry's answer was to pantomime putting a rope around his neck, then throwing his head back as if he were hanging from a noose.

Beecher then jumped headlong into the bedrock question: Could a slave also be a *man?* He would not even begin, he said, to argue whether slaves were human. "God made man;" he thundered, "slavery made him a *thing.*" Instead, he would argue that "Slaveholders are not half so bad as slave law," for it was the legal system, rather than mere individuals, which perverted God's noble creation. Turning to the law as the crux of the crime, he cleverly skirted the sticky question of dueling Bible verses. By statute it was impossible to act as a Christian. Why, a slave can't even read the Bible, Henry exclaimed, for one cannot "even teach him to read without being sent to the penitentiary."

"That's a lie!" shouted a voice from the audience. A wave of hisses and threats fanned out in approval.

Beecher blanched. He paused, then shot back: "Well, whether it was a penitentiary offence or not," he would not dare to argue it with the gentleman in the corner. "I've no doubt you know, for I'll bet you've been there."

The auditorium erupted with laughter and more booing from the corner gallery. A few minutes later the room exploded when Beecher suggested that the black man might be too good to be equal to the general run of white men. Finally Lewis Tappan stepped forward, begging the audience to settle down, if only for the sake of the ladies.

But Beecher dismissed Tappan's placating words. "Never mind, boys," he taunted the men in the gallery. "I have played at football too often myself to heed a few kicks on the shins or a few tumbles; besides, I like opposition; it stimulates me to more energy and exertion, therefore, I hope you will not permit our friend Lewis Tappan to come it over you so as to make you desist." Several more times the hecklers tried to trip him up, but as the *Tribune* noted, Beecher's retorts brought down the house with laughter at their expense, so they soon gave up.

As the thugs cooled off, the rest of the audience warmed up, with applause and cheers coming faster and louder. Beecher then worked the room up to the grand finale as if this were a camp meeting and he was fighting Satan himself for their souls.

"I know not how long I may live; but as long as I do live, I will not, as one man, cease my endeavors or hold my peace, unless the vile monster is driven from the land," he bellowed, as his calls for peaceful persuasion became a war cry. "Peace!—there be none, until God in his infinite mercy takes us from the face of the earth, or the vile stain is removed from America."[20] The audience went wild with applause, men stamping the floor like thunder, ladies frantically waving white hand-kerchiefs—a veritable blizzard of enthusiasm.

Henry's adroit handling of the hecklers caught the imagination of the press. No less a man than Frederick Douglass, the brilliant former slave who edited the *North Star*, described how Beecher "poured forth one continuous strain of eloquence for more than an hour," riveting the audience despite "the miserable attempts at interruption[.]"[21] The poet Walt Whitman, reporting the event for the Brooklyn *Daily Advertizer,* observed with admiration that "abuse and prosecution are the spears that prick such men as Beecher on." And yet even a rough and ready fellow like Whitman was a little disturbed by Henry's bare-knuckle approach.

"Carried away by his ardor and depth of conviction, on such occasions," Whitman wrote, "Mr. B. is no doubt apt to show too palpably how the wounds smart. In one sense we honor him for it. But still we would, if we might take such a liberty, advise more coolness, even contempt or indifference, towards those who violently assault him."[22]

NOW THAT HENRY WAS EMBRACING the role of outside agitator, he reinterpreted the early history of abolition as heroic protest rather than insane folly. Now Garrison seemed rather like a romantic hero, with his reckless courage and unwavering perseverance in the face of terrible odds. Garrison's great weakness, in Henry's opinion, was one of personality, not principle. He did not temper his outrage with "conciliation, good-natured benevolence, or even a certain popular mirthfulness"—that is, the qualities that Beecher possessed in abundance. Had he only more urbanity, more moderation or piety, Garrison would have been "the man of our age," Henry wrote in the *Independent.*[23] The question now was: Who would be that man?

On May 8 Wendell Phillips was scheduled to address the second day's meeting of the radical Antislavery Society. If Garrison was the intellectual godfather of abolition, Wendell Phillips was its dazzling mouthpiece. Born to a wealthy Beacon Hill family whose ancestors came on the *Arbella* in 1630, Phillips attended the Boston Latin School a few years ahead of Henry before going on to Harvard and a brief career as an attorney.

Like many of the great Boston reformers, Phillips was converted to evangelism by Lyman Beecher. He was only fourteen years old when he returned home from seeing Lyman preach, locked the door to his room, and fell to the floor, committing himself then and there to God's will. After his wife converted him to abolition, he repudiated the church and the bar, and made antislavery activism his full-time career.

Independently wealthy and a genuine Boston Brahmin, Phillips could afford to stand on principle alone. Even hostile audiences were spellbound by the contrast between his aristocratic poise, his lawyerly logic, and his unbelievably incendiary words. He treated his opponents like social and moral pariahs, too lowborn to touch him with their criticism.

After the near riot the day before, the trustees of the Broadway Tabernacle barred the Garrisonians from the premises, and no other venue in Manhattan would have them. They turned to Brooklyn, where the Democrats were less powerful, renting the Brooklyn Institute for Thursday evening. Beecher offered to give the opening prayer. Then, early Thursday morning, a trustee of the institute called to tell Henry that the Brooklyn Institute was rescinding Phillips's engagement for fear of being mobbed.

"If there is anything on earth that I am sensitive to it is the withdrawing of the liberty of speech and thought," Beecher later recalled, and in this he was in utter sympathy with the radicals. This was also a chance for Brooklyn to best Manhattan, and for the Tappanites to offer charity to the Garrisonians. Henry Bowen proposed the solution: "You can have Plymouth Church, if you want it," he told Beecher.

"How?" Beecher asked in surprise.

"It is a rule of the church trustees that the church may be let by a majority vote when we are convened; but if we are not convened, then every trustee must give his consent in writing," Bowen explained. "If you choose to make it a personal matter and go to every trustee, you can have it."[24]

Beecher immediately went to find Garrison's organizers. "Say nothing about your defeat in not getting Lyceum Hall," he told them, "but if you do not hear from me in one hour, get out 5,000 handbills, stating that Wendell Phillips will speak *in my church* to-night. Circulate them everywhere. I would do this much if you were atheists and were propagating atheism *for the right of speech!*"

The minister and the merchant went to work. Bowen personally paid to distribute new posters and handbills, while Beecher went around to every trustee to obtain their signatures, saying, "I want you to do me a personal favor—sign this. Perhaps *you* don't like the idea—*I* do. Oblige me this once and then ask of me a favor."

The trustees protested that their handsome new church would be burned to the ground. Beecher declared scornfully that he'd rather speak on principle and ashes. Then he made it personal. "You and I will break if you don't give me this permission," he told the holdouts. By that evening everyone had signed, each agreeing to attend, armed with a good heavy cane.

"Let us teach New York a lesson!" vowed Henry.[25]

Around seven o'clock the combatants began assembling. Reporters sat at their regular table near the front. Police were stationed in the vestibule. Privately hired plainclothes detectives were sprinkled throughout the audience. Outside a horde of rough-looking men loitered, their gruff voices filtering into the sanctuary.

Henry introduced Wendell Phillips himself, announcing as hisses roiled the audience, "If he were 10,000 times blacker than he is (I mean his belief and not his skin) I would still stand up for his right to speak his own sentiments."[26] Phillips then stepped forward and began his speech in a voice as "sweet as a new-blown rose; in voice, clear and silvery," Henry recalled. Hisses, then jeers, interspersed with a few cheers, accompanied Phillips for the first three-quarters of an hour.

But, "you may depend upon it, by this time the lion was in him," Henry recalled. "I remember at one point—for he was a man without bluster; serene, self-poised, never disturbed in the least—he made an affirmation that was very bitter, and a cry arose over the whole congregation. He stood still, with a cold, bitter smile on this face and look in his eye, and waited till they subsided, when he repeated it with more emphasis. Again the roar went through. He waited, and repeated it if possible more intensely; and he beat them down with that one sentence, until they were still and let him go on." Before long the booing subsided, and the disgruntled men in the street wandered off to look for excitement elsewhere. When he finished, the applause was loud, long, and uninterrupted.

"I never heard a more effective speech than that night," Henry later told the abolitionist Oliver Johnson. "I think scorn in him was as fine as I ever knew it in any human being."[27] Beecher and Phillips would cross paths again.

For Beecher the week was a triumph. "We have vindicated the right of speech and also heaped coals of fire upon the heads of the Garrisonians," he exulted. "They will see that there are churches that are not afraid to stand by liberty!"[28] Unfortunately it was also a victory for the mob; it would be several years before the Garrisonians were again welcome in New York.

The spring of 1850 placed Beecher firmly in the trenches of the antislavery movement. His reputation as an agitator was permanently set, far beyond his own moderate inclinations. But it also radicalized him, introducing him into the society of the great reformers and original thinkers of the century. And as Henry Bowen observed, "It settled the question forever, in Brooklyn, at least, that a man had a right to speak his sentiments."[29]

Then just as the Reverend Beecher was scaling a new peak of fame, he abruptly disappeared. On June 7 Henry sailed for Europe on the steamer *New World*.

IT WAS A SURPRISE TO ALMOST EVERYONE when Henry found himself lying seasick in a stateroom steaming toward Europe. "It was a sudden move," reported the *Independent*. "The day before he started, he had no idea of coming, but made up his mind very suddenly," according to an acquaintance on board the ship.[30]

Why he left so abruptly for Europe is a mystery. A voyage across the Atlantic was still a rare and extravagant thing, which Henry could not afford. The *Independent* reported that friends urged him to go for the sake of his health, and undoubtedly his wealthy friends helped pay his expenses. It is true that Henry had suffered several bouts of throat infections in the last year. But except for the nausea and vomiting of severe seasickness, he reported perfect health on his vacation.

Whatever ailed him in Brooklyn evaporated as he walked down the gangplank in Liverpool. Henry was a ideal tourist—enthusiastic, open-minded, voracious for new experiences. He was so overstimulated by the novelty of everything that he felt at times as if he were having an out-of-body experience.

To Eunice he wrote long, effusive accounts of his adventures. You see, he teased Eunice, "when I am wholly relieved from care and *inward working,* for pulpit purpose—I am as good a correspondent as in courting days; at least in the matter of length." Written with an eye for later publication in the *Independent,* they are not intimate letters but they are some of the most charming, self-revealing essays of his career. "If they have any value," he warned readers, "it must be found in their egotism."

And what feelings he had! His first order of business was to tour several old castles made famous by Sir Walter Scott. He scoffed as he approached Kenilworth Castle that to really enjoy such a place required "the sentiment of veneration," which was not in his personality. As he gazed on the stone ruins, however, he found himself trembling as tears stung his eyes and a welter of emotions rushed through him. "I had never in my life seen an *old* building," he said in wonder. Wandering among the ruins, his imagination ran riot picturing himself as a nobleman, a knight, an epic hero. "Oh, if I had been a Baron, in olden times, and my castle were beleaguered, how I could have fought; how I would have fired my soul within to do deeds of surpassing heroism," he wrote Eunice. "How cheap a thing is *life* before a heroic achievement."[31]

Henry was genuinely surprised by how deeply he responded to the sheer accumulation of history, culture, and beauty in England. "That *I* should be a *hero-worshipper*—a relic hunter, was a revelation indeed." He visited the fortresses, churches, galleries, and homes he'd read about in books. He paid homage to the graves of John Milton, John Bunyan, John Wesley, and to any place associated with Robert Burns. At Stratford-on-Avon, the birthplace of his idol Shakespeare, he could barely eat or sleep for excitement. Tears flowed down his cheeks as he listened to an Anglican mass, picturing his mother praying to the same liturgy as a child.

The pinnacle of the trip came in Paris, when he entered the galleries of the Louvre. "I knew that I had gradually grown fond of pictures from my boyhood," he recalled, and now in New York he regularly visited art galleries and collected art books and prints. Nothing, however, prepared him for the sensuous pleasures of actually seeing the old masters. His first response, he told Eunice, was astonishment, his second was "intense pleasure."

"To find myself absolutely intoxicated," he wrote in wonder, "to find my system so much affected that I could not control my nerves—to find myself trembling and laughing and weeping, and almost hysterical, and that in spite of my shame and resolute endeavor to behave better—such a power of these galleries over me I had not expected." He felt as if transformed; "what a new world has been opened to me," he wrote in wonder, "and what a new sense within myself!"

Henry's taste was remarkably broad-minded for an evangelical American. He was incredulous at the sheer number of religious paintings, and not overly impressed by most of them. Most depictions of Jesus failed to satisfy him—they lacked "that suffusion of love," which was Christ's essence. He was surprisingly open, as he put it, to "French nakedness." Indeed, Henry grew quite discriminating on the subject. The many depictions of Venus left him "agreeably disappointed." They should be more wanton and voluptuous, according to his reading of Greek mythology. Finally, in London's National Gallery, he discovered his perfect

Venus in a painting by Antonio Correggio. Correggio's Venus, "entirely nude, seems—I do not know how, neither arch, nor mirthful, nor voluptuous, but all of them!" Rubens's women were too fat for his taste, but he discovered his ideal women in the paintings of Jean-Baptiste Greuze. "I never saw such sweetness, innocence, or simplicity of character," he wrote Eunice. "They are not all insipid, as innocence usually is, at least on canvas."[32] If Eunice objected to her husband's preference for playful voluptuaries over insipid innocents, we have no record of it.

Europe challenged Henry's presumptions, helping him crystallize many of his more liberal impulses. While visiting Oxford, he was shocked when a fellow cleric offered him a choice of wine or ale with dinner. Instead Henry requested cold water, playfully admonishing his host.

"My dear sir, I am a thoroughgoing teetotaler, and you surely would not have me come to England to lose my good principles?"

"Why, sir, I am not a teetotaler, but I am a temperance man—was never drunk in my life," responded the cleric "—but you surprise me!"[33]

He must have enjoyed this cosmopolitan respectability, however, because upon returning to America, Henry took up wine upon the prescription of his doctor, who recommended it when he felt overworked. But Eunice's disapproval trumped Henry's new sophistication. She soon banished liquor from the house, at least for a while.

Underneath Henry's ecstasy, though, lurked a mysterious melancholy, the "old time sadness," as he called it. Sometimes standing in front of the pictures of Christ filled him with shame, as if all "my secret sins" were exposed to Jesus in the flesh. "I know that he will forgive them—but will he deliver me from them?" Henry asked. "It is not a want of faith in Christ for the past that I lack—but, O, that I might have a Christ who should assure me of rescue and purity in every period of my life to come!"[34]

Despite his moodiness, the vacation served as a tonic to his health. After six weeks abroad, he boarded a Cunard steamer in Liverpool, laden with gifts, souvenirs, and a head full of new notions. On the trip home, however, despite his seasickness, he became embroiled in a dispute between the captain of the vessel and a group of ministers traveling to the United States.

The passengers demanded the right to hold their own Sunday services on board, in addition to the Anglican liturgy allowed by the Cunard management. When the captain refused, the ministers threatened a boycott of the English steam line if he did not capitulate. Finally the owner, E. Cunard, Jr., blew up, telling the shocked parsons that if Americans objected to the policy then they "might go to hell!"[35] Personally Henry had no desire to preach, but now his patriotism was piqued. As soon as he landed, he lambasted the Cunard line in a series of essays in the *Independent,* telling tales of cardplaying, swearing, and gambling on board. The captain responded by accusing him of lying. If he were going to lie, Beecher replied, at least he would not lie in such a ridiculous manner.

It was a surprisingly petty end to the trip. The *Journal of Commerce,* still smarting from its own recent boxing match with Beecher, sniped at the combative clergyman. "Either Mr. Beecher is peculiarly unfortunate in being dragged into every sort of controversy, against his will; or else he has a penchant for such collisions not very common with ministers of the Gospel, and we should suppose not very favorable to their peace of mind."[36]

BUT COMBATIVENESS WAS the temper of the times. Three days before Henry landed in New York, the first of Senator Clay's measures was passed by Congress. Several weeks later President Millard Fillmore signed the final package of bills into law. The bill was more clever horse-trading than a genuine compromise, but it seemed to succeed in its main aim: shutting down the debate. Whatever their opinions beforehand, the vast majority of people breathed a deep sigh of relief. Finally the slavery controversy was permanently settled and the threat of disunion vanquished. The country could get back to business.

The illusion of peace lasted less than two months. In Mississippi, Georgia, and South Carolina the fire-eaters were already campaigning to replace the Southern compromisers with legislators who would torpedo the bill and then lead the South out of the Union. Within a week of the bill's signing, the first fugitive slave was caught in New York City, sending whispers of armed resistance through some African American neighborhoods and extreme abolitionist circles. Both blacks and whites formed vigilance committees to turn away slave catchers, but blacks bore most of the risks. The news stories of their daring escapes and tragic captures fed the public's outrage.

In response Henry tried to straddle "higher law" rebellion and rule-of-law conservatism. "I will both shelter them, conceal them, or speed their flight, and while under my shelter or my convoy they shall be to me as my own flesh and blood," he announced, before tipping his hat to the lower law. "We shall not attempt to rescue, nor interrupt the officers if they do not interrupt us."[37]

Militant abolitionists condemned Henry's apparent hypocrisy—why laud the revolutionaries of Europe yet deny the right to armed resistance to the slaves? But among moderates his words seemed heroic. "It did my heart good to find somebody in an indignant state as I am about this miserable wicked fugitive slave business," his sister Harriet wrote to Henry after reading one of his essays. "I wish I had your chance, but next best to that it is to have you say it, so fire away, give them no rest day nor night."[38]

By contrast, New York's frightened business leaders rushed to reassure their Southern brethren that they were shutting down all antislavery agitation. Led by the clarion call of the *Journal of Commerce* they established a "Union Safety Committee," dedicated to saving "the *Constitution*, the *Compromise* and the *Union*."[39] On October 23 the committee held a monster meeting in Castle Garden, the massive stone fort that still stands off of Battery Park in Manhattan, drawing thousands of conservative Whigs and Democrats. Any leading men who refused to attend or endorse the Castle Garden meeting were placed on the "Black and White List," a blacklist of the city's antislavery merchants. The one significant holdout was the firm of Bowen and McNamee.

Infuriated by the *Independent*'s anticompromise editorials and the refusal of Henry Bowen and his partners to join the Union Safety Committee, the *Journal of Commerce* called for a boycott of their business and sent copies of the *Independent*'s editorials to the *Journal*'s Southern subscribers, in an attempt to ruin their Southern trade.

Bowen asked for Beecher's help in drafting a response. Henry came up with a catchy phrase but soon ran out of ideas and passed it for revision to Bowen's brother-in-law Hiram Barney, a politically savvy attorney. Bowen then sent it to the city papers, which printed it under the banner: "Principles Not for Sale"

The public, including the *Journal of Commerce*, are informed that we are silk merchants, and keep an extensive and well assorted stock of goods which we offer to responsible buyers on reasonable terms.

As individuals we entertain our own views on the various Religious, Moral and Political questions of the day, which we are neither afraid nor ashamed to declare on all proper occasions. But we wish it distinctly understood that our goods, and not our principles, are in the market. The attempt to punish us as merchants for the exercise of our liberty as citizens we leave to the judgment of the community.[40]

Henry's phrase "My goods are for sale, but not my principles" took off as a rallying cry among the dissenters. Henry himself went from store to store to personally buck up wavering merchants. Half of the *Independent*'s six thousand subscribers canceled their subscriptions. S. B. Chittenden and the other nervous co-owners of the *Independent* sold their shares to Bowen at fire-sale prices. But as news of their stand spread, five thousand new subscribers poured in.

Henry took this as proof that the Fugitive Slave Laws and those shameful attempts to put down free speech were backfiring. "Ten thousand Abolition lecturers, sent abroad to every hamlet and village in the land, would have made but a ripple in comparison with that wave of feeling that is rolling across the public mind," he crowed in the *Independent*.[41]

AS HIS SON MOVED ONTO the national stage, Lyman Beecher's dream for the West was dead. Despite two decades of valiant labor, the West was not an extension of New England nor an evangelical empire, but a diverse, lively culture all its own. In retrospect, observed one of Lyman's acolytes, it had been the biggest mistake of his life to leave Boston. "Like a mighty locomotive engine, he had leaped his track in coming West."[42]

In 1847 Lyman was relieved of his duties as pastor of the Second Presbyterian Church of Cincinnati. "For the first time in my public life I have now no pastoral responsibilities and stated preaching on the Sabbath," he wrote sadly to Henry. "What shall I do—a soul without a body?"[43] Lane Seminary was slowly dying, leaving Lyman to survive on the generosity of old friends and the providence of God.

Far worse was the loss of his children. One by one each of Lyman's children turned their faces to the East and headed home. First Edward, worn ragged by his pioneer college, took a church in Boston. Catharine lived a nomad's life, writing books, promoting her educational projects, and tending to her health at various water cures. Isabella and Mary were married to well-to-do Connecticut lawyers, and James was at Dartmouth College. Charles, William, and Tom remained out West but within a few years they, too, would be gone.

Only Harriet remained in Cincinnati, even as Calvin Stowe's salary at Lane dwindled to nearly nothing. Then in 1849 cholera swept through the city, stealing the life of her beloved son Charley. In the depths of her grief, Calvin's alma mater, Bowdoin College in Brunswick, Maine, offered him a professorship. Harriet never looked back. So eager was she to escape the miasma of Cincinnati, that she left half a year before Calvin did.

Stopping in Brooklyn on her way to Maine, Harriet was taken aback by her little brother's new stature. "Henry's people are more than ever in love with him, and have raised his salary to $3,300, and given him a beautiful horse and carriage worth $600," she wrote to her father.[44] Harriet had hoped to rekindle their old warm relationship, but Henry, never much of a letter writer to begin with, was caught up in the whirlwind of his new life. When Henry left for Europe without saying good-bye—and returned without having sent her a single letter—she was so crushed that she finally poured out her pent-up feelings.

Henry's response to Harriet was warmly apologetic, almost confessional, but marked by a new sense of his own limitations. "Every year that I live shows me but the plainer that I am not worth putting trust in by such as one to live by *manifestations* of affection. I am too much a man of moods," he lamented; "so excitable as to be wrought upon by the *present* and to be *used up* by it, so as to have little time or strength for the absent."[45] But his affection was as strong as ever, he insisted, and promised to see her in March, when he came to Maine to lecture.

Henry arrived in Brunswick in the middle of the night, walking from the train station in a blinding blizzard. Harriet was waiting up for him, and the two sat by the fire until dawn, railing about politics. After years of being, in Isabella's derisive phrase, "a father and Mr. Stowe abolitionist," the outrage of the Fugitive Slave Laws had finally pushed Harriet firmly into the antislavery camp.[46] As Henry talked of his protest efforts, Harriet said, "I, too, have begun to do something; I have begun a story trying to set forth the sufferings and wrongs of the slaves." Just as Henry had done with the Edmonson girls, she hoped to create a vivid emotional portrait of slavery that would transcend fruitless constitutional and biblical bickering. After all, as she pointed out, "There is no arguing with *pictures* and everybody is impressed by them, whether they mean to be or not."[47]

"That's right, Hattie," Henry urged. "Finish it, and I will scatter it thick as the leaves of Vallobrosa."[48] He had no idea how little his help would be needed.

The first chapters of Harriet's story began to appear in June 1851, in *The National Era*, an antislavery newspaper published in Washington, D.C. She entitled it *Uncle Tom's Cabin, or The Man That Was a Thing*, partly basing the title character on a former slave who used to work for Henry in Indianapolis. It was meant to run for only a few weeks, but it quickly took on a life of its own, growing from a short sketch into a full-fledged epic.

Uncle Tom's Cabin combined keen-eyed social realism with a sentimental faith in the redemptive power of love. Like Henry, Harriet asks her readers to identify with the humanity of slaves, creating a huge cast of black, white, and mixed-race characters to embody every aspect of the slavery debate. The book is a six-hundred-page emotional roller coaster, climaxing with the murder of the pious slave, Uncle Tom, and the escape of Eliza, the beautiful mulatto slave mother, via the Underground Railroad to Canada. Harriet closed the story with a challenge: What can readers do with this sympathy and indignation overflowing their hearts? "There is one thing that every individual can do," she answers. "They can see to it that *they feel right*."[49] Without a national change of heart, she warned prophetically, God would wreak vengeance on our unrepentant nation.

By the third installment of this odd and fascinating tale, readers were writing to the surprised editor saying they'd never read anything so rich and thrilling. When Harriet missed an installment several weeks later, impatient protests streamed into the *National Era* office. But that was nothing compared to the cry that arose when Harriet killed off the character of Little Eva, the slave owner's saintly daughter, in the December issue. People who scoffed at novels couldn't put the story down. People who believed it vulgar to speak of slavery praised the book from the rooftops. By Christmas besotted readers were besieging her with requests for daguerreotypes and autographs.

It seemed as if everyone was reading it—except Henry. "I have made it a rule of my life to read none of the writings of my relatives, and with two or three exceptions have adhered to that rule," he joked. He certainly wasn't going to torture himself with the suspense of reading it in serial form. "I will not go through the excitement, which it may give me week by week. I prefer to take it all in one dose."

The book appeared in hardcover on March 20, 1852, selling three thousand copies on the first day. Now, Henry declared, he would read it all at once. He began at the breakfast table and was well into the second volume by the time he sent Eunice up to bed without him. "I soon began to cry," said Henry. "Then I went and shut all the doors, for I did not want anyone to see me. Then I sat down to it and finished it that night, for I knew that only in that way should I be able to preach on Sunday." Eunice waited up for him. Finally, as the clock struck three, he came upstairs and threw the book down in front of her, exclaiming, "If Hattie Stowe ever writes another book like that, I'll—well she has half killed me."[50]

Within a year the book, now subtitled *Life Among the Lowly*, had sold 305,000 copies in the United States and a million in England, and was translated into Italian, Swedish, Danish, Dutch, Flemish, German, Polish, and Magyar. It quickly became the first American novel to see more than a million copies in the United States, at a time when the population was less than 24 million. The country was gripped by "Tom Mania," producing hundreds of "Uncle Tom" spin-offs: sheet music, plays, minstrel shows, parodies, knickknacks, handkerchiefs, toys, and lithographs illustrating scenes from the book. A play adapted from the book ran for two hundred consecutive performances at New York's Chatham Theater.

Suddenly Harriet was rich, earning ten thousand dollars in the first three months of sales. Every postal delivery brought fan letters and admiring articles hailing her as a genius. *Uncle Tom's Cabin* would go on to become the single best-selling book in the world, translated into fifty-eight languages. This quiet parson's wife had accomplished the impossible: She took the most unpopular subject in the country and turned it into the most popular book in American history.

Backlash followed quickly. The novel was unofficially banned throughout the South, hate mail streamed in (one envelope brought a bloody brown human ear), and the hostile press excoriated her as a foulmouthed liar, a polluted woman, and "an obscure Yankee school mistress, eaten up with fanaticism."[51] "Mrs. Stowe betrays a malignity so remarkable that the petticoat lifts of itself, and we see the hoof of the beast under the table," wrote the Southern author William Gilmore Simms.[52]

Their animosity had good cause. With her powerful "pictures" Harriet may have done more to undermine slavery in the North than any other single effort to date. "I estimate the value of antislavery writing by the abuse it brings," William Lloyd Garrison congratulated Harriet. "Now all the defenders of slavery have let me alone and are abusing you."[53]

Harriet returned to New York for the May Anniversaries in 1852 as a conquering hero. The parishioners of Plymouth Church immediately adopted her as their own, especially the Howards, who shielded her from the crowds that nearly crushed her at public events. Henry basked in the reflected glow of his sister's celebrity (indeed, many people assumed that *he* was the real author of the book) and inevitably he became entangled in its controversies.

With *Uncle Tom's Cabin* Harriet had launched her own crusade against the pharisees, depicting a cast of spineless Christians who refused, in Harriet's words, "to hurt the feelings of slaveholders[.]"[54] While she was in Brooklyn, Joel Parker, a New York Presbyterian minister, accused her of libeling him in her novel when she quoted by name his assertion that slavery "had no evils but such as are inseparable from any other relations in social and domestic life," as an example of the cold-hearted, cowardly clergy. Parker had, in fact, uttered sentiments to that effect, but he had no desire to see them repeated in the most famous novel in the world. He threatened a twenty-thousand-dollar libel suit if she didn't retract her words.

As Harriet left for Maine she turned the matter over to Henry to resolve. Buoyed by her phenomenal success, Harriet was adamant that she would make no retraction. Henry was about to leave on a lecture tour, but he held a brief, rancorous meeting with Parker to hammer out a statement of reconciliation. Unfortunately Henry—hurried, sloppy, and dismissive—ended up further enraging Parker by publishing a letter of reconciliation under both clergymen's names that Parker had not personally approved or signed. Harriet—righteous, defiant, a little sloppy herself—refused to placate Parker even now.

Seeing an opportunity to strike both Beechers with one blow, the *New York Observer* attacked them as liars, forgers, and heretics. Henry responded with chivalrous indignation at these attacks on a Christian lady. Through the late summer and fall the *Independent* and *Observer* traded blows, reprinting and analyzing the correspondence and documents, with various Beechers tossing in their own two cents, until the public eventually lost interest. Joel Parker never got his reparations. In fact, the fracas only spread his proslavery reputation.

It seems like a tempest in a teapot, but the Parker fight foreshadowed many squalls to come. The secular press judged Henry to be a bit slipshod and impulsive but vastly goodhearted, while his opponents seemed peevish and vindictive, with little left to show for their shouting. As one magazine observed, if the Beecher clan seemed immune to criticism, it was due to their "Yankee prudence, which prevents their advancing without being sure of battalions behind them; and also to a reputation the family has acquired for eccentricity." Indeed, the dustup with Reverend Parker only raised the whole family to a new level of fame. "The Beecher family almost constitutes a genus by themselves," opined the *North American Review*. Or as they said in Boston, "the human race is divided into the Good, the Bad, and the Beechers."[55]

When Eunice gave birth to twins just before Christmas 1851, the press was so captivated by the Beechers' peculiar power that some papers reported that Eunice had given birth to five children in the previous year. The *Brooklyn Eagle* jokingly cited Henry's twins as proof that the "free soilers, women's rights advocates and go-aheaditives of all classes" were planning to take over society through "the multiplication of revolutionary citizens."[56] Perhaps the *Eagle* was right, since Henry had never been as proud as he was of little Alfred and Arthur Beecher.

That same year, at the age of seventy-nine, Lyman Beecher finally came home. He went West a pugnacious Yankee theocrat and returned twenty years later a bona fide national legend: "The father of more brains than any man in America."[57]

Chapter 9

"Courage Today or Carnage Tomorrow"

As he turned forty in 1853, Henry Ward Beecher was more contented than he'd ever been in his life. "Happily, my work is my play," he told his new friend, Emily Drury; "few have so happy a life, and I grow more uniformly happy as I grow older." He had thickened a bit around the middle, but in every other way, marveled a friend, Henry still seemed "like a big boy."[1]

But a closer look revealed significant changes. He still dressed with outward simplicity, but instead of threadbare ill-fitting suits and rough cold-weather shawls, he indulged his taste for expensive wool cloaks and luxurious fabrics—satin, silk brocade, and especially velvet. He kept a fine gold pocket watch and wore his shirts open at the throat, with a rakish air.

Stepping into his house in Brooklyn Heights, the air of prosperity was even more pronounced. His parlor walls were crowded with landscape paintings, old master engravings, and a magnificent stuffed buck's head. A snow-white stuffed owl sat overlooking glass cases crammed with books and bric-a-brac. Down in the basement kitchen were a cook and several Irish or German hired girls. For the first time, Eunice finally had enough help around the house, and Henry had enough money to send his teenage daughter to boarding school.

It wasn't just Henry. New York was booming. Businessmen cited the statistics with glee. Between 1851 and 1854, $175 million in gold came from San Francisco to New York. In nearly the same period the number of banks doubled, as did the value of the city's imports and exports. With more cash flowed more credit, and easy credit fueled an avalanche of shipbuilding, light manufacturing, housing construction, and railroads. The railroad-building boom consolidated New York's position as the commercial capital of the country (and made possible Henry's own lucrative lecturing career). More than 60 percent of New York's population had been born somewhere else, and this influx of labor was as crucial as the influx of cash. This tremendous diversity gave New York a cosmopolitanism and creativity that existed nowhere else in the country.

Brooklyn was growing even faster than Manhattan. It was now the seventh largest city in the Union, with a population of 186,000 in 1854. The changes could be seen in the new sewer system and its boon companion, indoor plumbing; in the twelve hundred new gas lamps that forever changed the nightscape; and in a spate of new civic institutions, including so many new congregations that Brooklyn was now known as the "City of Churches." A new ferry line ran from the bottom of Montague Street, linking Brooklyn Heights directly to the foot of Wall Street in Manhattan, drawing well-to-do bankers, brokers, export and import merchants, and lawyers fleeing the increasingly crowded and commercialized neighborhoods of Lower Manhattan.

As empty lots gave way to brownstones, Brooklyn Heights became more clannish. Alongside the "Beecherites," as some called them, arose an enclave of wealthy Quakers who regarded Beecher with deep distaste. "That he was a great man they did not deny," as Mary Hallock Foote, a young Quaker woman, recalled, "but they saw him too frequently on the street; they were too familiar with his thickset figure and his powerful, unshrinking eye and orator's throat exposed by the backthrown folds of his cape-overcoat. He of course, born conspicuous, the most naturally self-conscious man in the world, took no note of them."[2]

The grandest house on the Heights belonged to Henry Bowen. His new mansion on the corner of Willow and Clark Streets was as notable for its huge yard as for its dramatic facade and opulent trappings. Bowen furnished the whole thing in one swoop, from carpets to chandeliers, showering his wife, Lucy, with luxurious gifts, and later commissioning a bedroom set with all his children's faces carved into it.

More modest, but even wealthier, were the Beecher's new close friends, Moses and Chloe Beach. Moses Sperry Beach, as described by a reporter, had "keen black eyes, is a little below medium height, active, restless, and always smiling."[3] He was just Henry's type of fellow—a "go-ahead" Yankee-Yorker type, wedding Yankee discipline to Yorker ambition, who exuded genuine warmth and good humor.

His father, Moses Yale Beach, a famously canny Connecticut Yankee, had invented the penny press in the 1830s when he founded the *New York Sun*. Born in 1822, Moses Sperry Beach took over the *Sun* in the late 1840s, but his first love was technology (his brother, Alfred Beach, started the magazine *Scientific American*). Moses was an early backer of the Associated Press and the telegraph; he held numerous patents in the printing industry and spent years trying to convince the New York state legislature to let him and his brother build what he called "a Pneumatic Rail Road tunnel" under Broadway, which could carry passengers on an underground train.

Despite his spectacular wealth, Moses Sperry Beach was a genuinely unpretentious man who shunned the spotlight—a rare trait for an editor in that era. As his daughter told him, "you have a way that does not seem a virtue to you perhaps, but it does to most people—of adapting yourself to circumstances and being suited with what you can get."[4] Moses had a joyous appetite for life and loved to travel and entertain, filling his town house on Columbia Heights with beautiful objects and stimulating guests. His wife, Chloe, was quiet but commanding, with a natural grace that charmed everyone who knew her.

After forty years Henry had finally shed the pinched legacy of his childhood, with its self-denial and defiant parochialism. He became an aficionado of classical music, attending all the acclaimed concerts of the day, and sponsoring many musical events in his own church. Art was his obsession, and he was a regular patron of the galleries and art unions that were fast making New York the artistic capital of America. He acquired so many etchings that he could not display them all, and often invited guests to sit with him on the floor as he spread them out for viewing.

He developed a taste for fine horseflesh, as one friend recalled, and "to ride behind a swift stepper for an hour or two seemed to intoxicate him."[5] Some of Henry's well-to-do friends now played cards, put on amateur theatricals, and threw fancy-dress parties with dancing. Even the ban on theatergoing was loosening, as promoters staged adaptations of novels like *Uncle Tom's Cabin* to add the luster of respectability. Henry even considered going to see *Uncle Tom's Cabin*, he said, but decided it wasn't worth the haranguing he would get afterward.

Above all Henry loved to shop. This was the dawning age of the department store. Up and down the "Ladies' Mile" of Broadway, between Ninth and Twenty-third Streets, gorgeous new emporiums were transforming shopping into a tasteful leisure activity. "It is astonishing how one's necessities multiply in the presence of the supply," Henry remarked. "One is surprised to perceive at some bazaar, or fancy and variety store, how many *conveniences* he needs." He bought gifts by the armload for family and friends, always insisting on carrying them home himself, unwrapped so he could appreciate them. He developed a passion for jewels, which he carried, unset, in his pockets, taking them out for comfort when he was tired or in low spirits.

But books were his biggest indulgence. "Alas! Where is human nature so weak as in a book-store!" Beecher asked. "As a hungry man eats first, and pays afterward, so the book-buyer purchases, and then works at the debt afterward."[6] Appleton's famous bazaar of books on Lower Broadway was like a second home to him, and the amount of money Henry spent there is remarkable even in current dollars. In one five-month period in 1854, he bought sixty-five books totaling $905.63, on topics that would have been unthinkable for an evangelical Christian a dozen years before.

Of course it took some doing to fully shed the Calvinist inhibitions against riches, idle pleasure, and free thought. As always Henry worked out his internal conflicts in public. Wealth—its ethics, uses, and abuses—became one of his primary themes in the mid-1850s. He could seem both self-serving and radically democratic, sometimes insisting that true virtue flows up from the bottom of society to the top, at other times arguing that progress would flow from the tiny well-cultivated top down to the broad masses. He made a strong case for using wealth as a source of personal pleasure and uplift, in the arts, architecture, and philanthropy. At the same time no one more frequently or harshly rebuked the abusive boss, the wealthy miser, the unscrupulous speculator, or the indolent rich. Henry lent his voice to campaigns for overworked seamstresses, eight-hour-day regulations, and public relief for the poor just as loudly as he defended the right to spend what one wished on a happy, comfortable home. As he put it, "Everybody knows that wealth, rightly employed, is as the right hand of God."[7]

Beecher lived as he preached, on both counts. With fame came constant appeals for charity, most from strangers ringing his doorbell and filling his mailbox. Beecher was a laughably soft touch who gave money to teary widows, ragged newsboys, clever swindlers, and myriad causes both noble and dubious. He once took off his overcoat and gave it to a particularly persuasive confidence man. "Despite his constant intuitive study, he was easily cheated," said his friend Lyman Abbott. "There is a profound truth in the epigram attributed to Edward Eggleston—'I never knew a person who knew man so well and men so ill as Henry Ward Beecher.' He studied men with a 'charity which thinketh no evil'; looked not so much to see what was in the man today as what were the possibilities for the man in the future."[8]

But in an age of confidence Henry was the perfect apostle. His faith in human progress was unwavering, even in the darkest moments. But this was also the age of the confidence man, a term invented in the late 1840s for a new type of crime that targeted those with a naïve confidence in their fellow man, those who had not yet learned to distrust life in the new metropolis.

THE ONLY THING THAT MARRED Beecher's contentment was the return of death. June 1853 brought an extraordinary heat wave to the city, that left over 350 infants dead throughout New York. Little Arthur and Alfred Beecher, only a year and a half old, contracted mumps. As the temperature rose, so did their fevers. On the Fourth of July Alfred and Arthur passed away.

The death of the twins was the most severe sorrow of their lives, recalled Eunice, tinting Henry with a "shade of sadness" that never quite left him.[9] For years Henry refused to speak of the boys. Three years after their death, Eunice hung a framed photo of the twins, hoping to prompt her husband to say *something*. When he caught sight of the agonizing picture, Henry simply turned on his heel and left. If this seems cold, it is also true that Eunice's grief was often disconcertingly passive-aggressive. "How I wish I knew why [God] took them from us," she wrote to Henry on what would have been the twins' thirteenth birthday. "It must be because He knew I was not good enough to have them, for surely their father was not to blame."[10]

On the day of the funeral, after the service was over, Henry shook off the other mourners and slipped across the river for a consoling trip to Appleton's bookstore. He bought only one book: *Vathek* by William Beckford, a popular Faust-like tale of a sorceress's son, whose hunger for knowledge and experience entices him into friendship with Satan, until, too late, Vathek realizes that vanity and worldliness have corroded his soul. It was a strange choice. Certainly most pious folk would have been shocked to see it on Beecher's bookshelf. A superstitious mind might have called it a bad omen.

SEEKING ESCAPE FROM the sweltering city and their oppressive grief, Henry made his most extravagant purchase yet. In that sad summer of 1853 he and Eunice decided to rent a farmhouse in Lenox, a small village in the Massachusetts Berkshires, about five hours by train from Brooklyn. In September he borrowed money from a few of his wealthy friends to purchase ninety-six hilltop acres and a small farmhouse for $5,500. The view from "Blossom Farm" spanned sixty miles, from Mount Greylock in the north to the dome of the Taconic Mountains in the south.

Once again Henry showed excellent timing. Throughout the late 1830s and '40s, a literary ferment had been brewing in the East, reaching full boil just as the Beechers moved to New York. The years between 1850 and 1855 produced an unmatched number of American masterpieces, including Nathaniel Hawthorne's *Scarlet Letter,* Herman Melville's *Moby-Dick,* Walt Whitman's *Leaves of Grass,* and Henry David Thoreau's *Walden.*

Concord, Cambridge, and Boston were the capitals of this new "American Renaissance." With the coming of the railroad in the late 1840s, the Berkshire Hills became its rural outpost, the place where the literary worlds of New York and Boston met. Here were the summer homes of Oliver Wendell Holmes, the famed physician, author, and raconteur; Catharine Sedgwick, the grande dame of women novelists; and Fanny Kemble, the English actress who was as famous for her divorce from a wealthy slave owner as for her dramatic Shakespearean readings. Hawthorne finished *The House of Seven Gables* here (before being driven out by the harsh mountain winters), and from the window of his study, Melville imagined the profile of his great white whale in the crest of Mount Greylock. A stream of literati came for shorter visits, drawn by the beauty of America's own "Lake District," as Henry dubbed it.[11]

Henry adored Lenox, and it inspired some of his loveliest essays and happiest hours. Sedgwick and Kemble welcomed him warmly into their lively literary salons, and Holmes—the "best talker in Boston"— became an especially close friend. Beecher wrote a charming essay about Holmes's trees, and Holmes returned the favor, penning the limerick:

The Reverend Henry Ward Beecher
Called the hen a most elegant creature.
The hen, pleased with that,
Laid an egg in his hat,
And thus did the hen reward Beecher.

Henry Ward Beecher is not usually associated with the intellectual innovators of the American Renaissance, who sought to free the American mind from the old Puritan shibboleths. In the 1850s, especially around Boston, the Beecher name still conjured images of Lyman Beecher, full of brimstone and "grim with Calvinism," in the words of Theodore Parker, the famed Transcendentalist preacher.[12] Many Yankee intellectuals were surprised to find Lyman's son so irreverent toward the old idols and ideals. When Thomas Wentworth Higginson, the radical Massachusetts reformer and mentor of the poet Emily Dickinson, was invited to tea with the Beechers, he was shocked at how much he had in common with them.

"They were as liberal and friendly as possible," Higginson told his wife, "and I talked all my heresies without fear. I wish you could have heard them roar with laughter when I quoted Mr. Emerson's remark that Evangelical doctrines were like the measles and whooping-cough— important to those who have them and interesting to those who have had them; but not important or even very intelligible to those who have not!"[13]

In fact, Henry had less in common with the anguished former Calvinists like Hawthorne and Melville—those who, in Melville's words, "could not believe but could not be comfortable in unbelief"—than he did with the expansive optimism of Transcendentalists like Ralph Waldo Emerson. When Henry met Emerson around 1850, the two men were the rising stars of the speaking circuit and soon became warm friends and mutual admirers. As angular as New England granite, Emerson was as cool and reserved as the roly-poly Beecher was warm and effusive. But they shared a vibrant curiosity and a genuine joy in unfettered ideas. Emerson appreciated Beecher's genial spirit and his wide-ranging interests, in contrast to the somber, single-minded reformers whom Emerson respected but found personally tedious. Emerson particularly envied Beecher's physical vigor and forceful public personality, so different from his own more inward-looking self.

Then and now, "Transcendentalism" was a much maligned, much

misunderstood term. "When a speaker talked so that his audience didn't understand him, and when he said what he didn't understand himself— that was transcendentalism," the *Brooklyn Eagle* joked in 1853.[14] The Transcendentalists themselves disliked the name, preferring more open-ended terms such as the "Disciples of Newness," the "New School," or "Eclecticism."

Transcendentalists did not share a single philosophical or religious system; instead they shared a liberal habit of thought. It was characterized by an appreciation for provocative new ideas, a fascination with the way the mind works, a determination to throw off the constraints of society and tradition, and a Romantic emphasis on strong, intuitive feeling. Transcendentalism deliberately turned Calvinism on its ear. Where the Calvinists believed in a deep divide between a superior, supernatural God and an innately corrupt human nature, the Transcendentalists insisted that the divine coursed throughout the natural world, and especially the human heart. They had an optimistic faith in mankind's "infinite worthiness," as Emerson put it, in humanity's—and society's— ability to transcend our lower natures by cultivating the sublime within ourselves.

When Henry returned to the East, he was immediately drawn to Emerson's writing. "I think the man who has read his works without deep thankfulness for benefits, is little susceptible to gratitude or too stupid to know when he is blessed," as Henry put it bluntly. When Emerson published *Representative Men*, a volume of essays on great historical figures, Henry filled the page margins with wonder at "this *Platonic* Yankee" who so boldly rejected conventional wisdom, "As naked and impudent as a white house on the top of a hill without a tree or shrub about it." Spurred by Emerson's iconoclasm, Beecher scrawled the back flyleaf with urgent thoughts on his own career challenges: "Whether I can afford to stand alone in this generation that I may have much company in the next? Whether the love of truth and a true benevolence to give it to the world as God gives it to me, is stronger than a love of present applause and a limited present usefulness?"[15]

Emerson bolstered the minister's courage and independence and helped him define his course. Coming from the West, where institutions were weak and individual freedom was sacrosanct, "I insisted upon the indispensableness of authority and of obedience to that authority. I preached every Sunday against individualism, and in favor of association," Henry recalled. But here in the East he found that, "Men were lopped off on every side to make them fit into crowded populations. Society was tyrannical. And ever since I came East I have fought society, and tried to get individual men to be free, independent, and large. I was right both times."[16]

To Emerson's admiring eye, Beecher often seemed to embody the Transcendentalist impulse. "I never knew what people meant by 'Transcendental,'" Emerson confessed in 1850 to a literary gathering attended by the young Rutherford B. Hayes. "They are men who believe in themselves, in their own convictions, and rely upon them," he suggested, "they believe there is something more than this narrow scene in which we are to act. Men who are self-trusting, self-relying, earnest, are called by the name Transcendentalists." Emerson then applied this definition explicitly to Henry Ward Beecher, counting Beecher as "one of the bold, *hopeful* reformers" of their generation. In 1852 Emerson bestowed this great compliment: "Our four most powerful men in the virtuous class in this country are Horace Greeley, Theodore Parker, Henry Ward Beecher, and Horace Mann."[17]

Henry gave a popular voice to many of Emerson's more rarefied ideas. "There is no religion in the Bible, any more than there is a road upon the guide-board," said Beecher, echoing a Transcendentalist truism. "Religion is *in the man*, or it is not anywhere." What Emerson called "self-reliance" Henry called "the great law of Liberty." "Liberty," he claimed, "is the breath of the soul." As Beecher would later put it, Jesus "comes to every heart to make him free—free in thinking, free in choosing; free in tastes and sentiments; free in all pleasurable associations."[18]

The two men shared a tremendous confidence in human nature, seeing people as essentially good but held back from their fullest development by false idols, prejudices, and unnecessary fears. Love was the great glue that could both free individuals to cultivate their unique capacities and bind individuals into a harmonious whole. "The growth of Christian life is to be measured by the growth of *love*; and love itself is to be measured in its progressive states by its restfulness, its undisturbed trust, its victory over every form of fear," Henry declared. "The state of perfect loving is incompatible with distrust."[19]

Perceptive readers recognized many of these parallels. In 1855, when Beecher's collected *Star Papers* was published, his rapturous essays extolling the divinity of nature, the centrality of imagination to faith, and the sublime beauty of ordinary life struck some reviewers as distinctly Transcendental. Others rejoiced that however Emersonian the book might seem in spirit, "There is nothing transcendental about it;

everyday language, such as the common people can understand, and the ideas those with which they can accord."[20]

Beecher himself was careful to avoid the off-putting label of Transcendentalism. Years later, when the two men sat eating lunch together, he asked Emerson, "Do you think a man eating these meats could tell what grasses the animals fed on?"

No, replied Emerson.

"I'm glad to hear it," Henry said jovially, "for I've been feeding on you for a long time and I'm glad my people don't know it."[21]

Their biggest difference was that Beecher was very much a *Christian* Transcendentalist—in many ways less of a theological than a stylistic distinction. Emerson tended toward abstraction. He portrayed Christ as a set of ideal teachings rather than as the actual son of God (a belief Henry called "unsafe and not true" in his 1850 marginal notes). By contrast, Beecher was addicted to, in his words, "the principle of anthropomorphism," clothing ideas in flesh-and-blood images.

" 'This loving God,' you say; 'I can't do it. How can I love infinity—omnipotence?' " Beecher preached. "I might as well try to love a cloud, or to try to embrace in my warm palpitating affections the vast expanse of ether." For Henry the only way fully to experience the divine was through Christ, a real person who was capable of being loved and loving in return. "All that there is of God to me is bound up in that name. A dim and shadowy effluence rises from Christ, and that I am taught to call the Father. A yet more tenuous and invisible film of thought arises, and that is the Holy Spirit."[22]

Beecher's transcendent experience of the divine was not *like* love, it was the *actual feeling of love* that he and Jesus Christ shared. You cannot know Jesus, he maintained, "until you have been intimate with him." And like Christ, a "preacher is in some degree a reproduction of the truth in personal form," as Henry put it.[23]

> To preach the Gospel of Jesus Christ; to have Christ so melted and dissolved in you that when you preach your own self you preach Him as Paul did; to have every part of you living and luminous with Christ, and then to make use of everything that is in you, your analogical reasoning, your imagination, your mirthfulness, your humor, your indignation, your wrath; to take everything that is in you all steeped in Jesus Christ, and to throw yourself with all your power upon a congregation—that has been my theory of preaching the Gospel.[24]

And it worked. When Beecher read the Bible from the pulpit, observed the journalist Matthew Hale Smith, "The idea that Jesus is speaking to them pervades the assembly."[25] Imagine, then, the feelings of love between Beecher and his audience.

Not all the Disciples of Newness agreed with Emerson's assessment of Beecher. When Henry David Thoreau and the philosopher Bronson Alcott attended services at Plymouth Church, Thoreau dismissed the whole thing as "pagan." Thoreau found Beecher's divine confidence overbearing. "If Henry Ward Beecher knows so much more about God than another, if he has made some discovery of truth in this direction I would thank him to publish it in *Silliman's* [Scientific] Journal, with as few flourishes as possible," Thoreau groused in his diary.[26] Alcott was quite impressed by the preacher, but for Thoreau the highlight of the trip was meeting that other notable Brooklynite, the poet Walt Whitman.

Whitman was himself an early admirer of Beecher's. When Whitman first heard the minister speak in 1849, "he hit me so hard, fascinated me to such a degree, that I was afterward willing to go far out of my way to hear him talk." According to the poet, Beecher was given a first edition of *Leaves of Grass,* and Whitman was convinced that the preacher "stole terrifically from it," or, more generously, "that perhaps quite unconsciously he imbibed, accepted, its spirit: molded many of its formulas into his own work." Certainly Whitman's friends thought so, and they often stopped him on the street, saying, "I heard Henry Ward Beecher last night (or the night before) and his whole sermon was you, you, you, from top to toe."[27]

The poet and the preacher were never more than passing acquaintances—although the new humor magazine *Vanity Fair* noted that Beecher was beginning to look like the bohemian poet, with his long hair and open collar revealing just a bit too much chest for good taste. But both men shared a bottomless enthusiasm for New York, with its vast variety and primal energy, and both insisted that love was the only meaningful bond between the heterogeneous human atoms and the great cosmos.

Indeed, there may be no better way of capturing the man Henry Ward Beecher had become than to borrow from Charles Eliot Norton's 1855 assessment of *Leaves of Grass:* "a mixture of Yankee transcendentalism and New York rowdyism and, what must be surprising to both these elements, they here seem to fuse and combine with the most perfect harmony."[28]

∾ ∾

PEACE AND PROSPERITY—these were the long-desired fruits of the Compromise of 1850. But prosperity brought unintended consequences. The irony of the Compromise of 1850 was that it didn't actually answer the burning question of the day: Would slavery be allowed into the new western territories? Clay's Compromise had invalidated the Missouri Compromise's invisible line that limited slavery to the Southern states. But did this mean that the slave owners now had free rein to bring their human chattel into the new territories to the north? Or did it mean that the inhabitants of the territories could now choose for themselves whether to allow slavery, a concept called "popular" or "squatter sovereignty"? Southern politicians claimed the former, while Northern champions of the Compromise claimed the latter.

Greed finally forced an answer. Everyone agreed that there should be a transcontinental railroad linking the Atlantic Coast to the goldfields of California, but there was fierce competition over whether it would be a northern route anchored in Chicago, or a southern route with New Orleans as its hub. Boosters of the northern route faced one huge obstacle: the "Indian Barrier." The vast Nebraska Territory west of the Mississippi River was populated by all the native tribes that had been shoved out of the East. "Why, everybody is talking about a railroad to the Pacific Ocean," said one exasperated congressman. "In the name of God, how is the railroad to be made if you will never let people live on the lands through which the road passes?"[29] (By "people," of course, he meant white settlers.) Before the first rail could be laid, the federal government would have to seize the native lands and organize the territory into states.

On January 4, 1854, Senator Stephen Douglas, the powerful Illinois Democrat, shattered the fragile peace. He introduced a bill to organize the Nebraska Territory into two states, Kansas and Nebraska, allowing the settlers in each state to choose whether to permit slavery. To gain Southern backing for the bill, he threw in a clause declaring the Missouri Compromise officially "inoperative and void." It seemed a small price to pay for the financial bonanza of a transcontinental railway.

But Senator Douglas misjudged the temper of the times. When news of the bill spread, the North exploded in fury. After the bitter debates of 1850, when so many Northerners had placated the South in the name of peace, this was an unimaginable betrayal. Now the Slave

Power was aggressively trying to bring human bondage to the rest of the country. Even those who cared not a fig for the slave were infuriated by the South's insatiable hunger for more land and political influence, admitting that the abolitionists might well be right when they spoke of a great Slave Conspiracy.

The turnaround in the business community was profound. "We went to bed one night, old-fashioned, conservative compromise Union Whigs, and we waked up stark mad Abolitionists," recalled textile magnate Amos A. Lawrence—with only some exaggeration.[30] The religious community joined them in their about-face. Within weeks of the bill's introduction, clergymen from New York and New England delivered more than three thousand anti-Nebraska sermons and signed innumerable petitions.

With the Kansas-Nebraska Act, Henry threw off the airy mantle of the Transcendentalist and took up the cudgel of the New York rowdy. "That Compromise was a ball of frozen rattlesnakes," he thundered at those "Union-savers" who had defended the 1850 Compromise. "We protested and adjured. You persisted in bringing them into the dwelling. You laid them down before the fire. Now where are they? They are crawling around. Their fangs are striking death into every precious interest of liberty! It is your work!"[31]

Beecher, reported the *New York Times,* "rejoiced that the veil was now being removed from the hideous face of Slavery, and that the North would no longer be cajoled by the specious cry of 'regard for the Union.'" Henry implored the public to pour its outrage into letters, protests, and petitions to Congress. "If civil wars are to be prevented, now is the time; courage today or carnage tomorrow." One father wrote to the *Independent* proudly telling how his young son collected 140 anti-Nebraska signatures in two days after reading Beecher's call to arms.[32]

After five months of blistering public debate, Douglas's bill passed with strong support from President Franklin Pierce's proslavery administration. Now the conflict shifted from the halls of Congress to the prairies of Nebraska. Under "squatter sovereignty" settlers would vote whether to proceed with a slave or free constitution. Both sides now raced to send the most settlers before the fall election.

The proslavery forces had the advantage, since Kansas was bordered to the east by the slave state of Missouri. But the Yankees were the first to organize. Within a month of the bill's passage Eli Thayer, a Massachusetts abolitionist, formed the first Emigrant Aid Company, to fund new free-state colonies in Kansas. The rough Missouri frontiersmen seethed as they watched the steamboats full of "the filth, scum, and offscourings of the East," as one Missouri man described them, bound for Kansas.[33] Something must be done to stop them, with the butt of the rifle and the point of the bayonet if need be. In October 1854, during the territory's first election, 1,729 "Border Ruffians," as the Missourians came to be called, swarmed across the border and flooded the polls, forcing the election of a proslavery delegate to represent the territory in Washington. President Pierce did nothing.

Six months later, when Kansans gathered to elect a full territorial legislature, a swarm of Border Ruffians, drunk on corn whiskey and armed to the teeth, again rode into Kansas, swamping the free-state voters at the polls. With 2,905 legally registered voters, 6,307 votes were cast, electing every proslavery candidate but one. Once again Pierce turned a blind eye to the fraud. The new legislature immediately drafted a draconian state constitution requiring the death penalty for anyone caught helping a slave run away, and ten years in prison for anyone concealing a fugitive slave. A fellow could get two years' imprisonment for simply denying the right of slaveholding in the territory, either by speaking, writing, printing, or circulating books or papers.

THE "NEBRASKA INFAMY" sent the political landscape into upheaval. Free-Soil-leaning Democrats streamed out of the party in protest—earning the nickname of "Barnburners" for their willingness to burn down the partisan barn just to get rid of the rats—while Southern Democrats fumed at the frantic backpedaling of Northern politicians. But the Whigs were hit hardest. Already weakened by internal rifts between "Conscience Whigs" and "Cotton Whigs," the party was now wiped out in the South. By 1856 the Whig Party would be extinct.

As the old alliances shattered, voters faced a stunning array of political factions. Some were disgruntled party regulars, infuriated by broken political promises or drawn by the Free-Soil cause. Others mushroomed around a single issue, like the Temperance Party, devoted to antiliquor legislation, and the anti-immigrant American Party (nicknamed the Know-Nothings, from their origins as a secret political society), which opposed the Catholic Irish and German immigrants currently pouring into the United States.

The initial calls for a new fusion "anti-Nebraska" party came from the West. Protestant politicos, in particular, hoped to create a coalition of Temperance men, Free-Soilers, Conscience Whigs, and Barnburner

Democrats by whipping up fears of "Rum, Romanism, and Rebellion"—
essentially fusing the fear of a tyrannical elite ("the Papal Conspiracy"
and "Slave Conspiracy") to the fear of disorder (drunken, dirty immigrants and Border Ruffians). Michigan's Free-Soil coalition was the first
to adopt the name "Republican," conjuring up the liberal democratic
values of Thomas Jefferson and George Washington as well as the antiaristocratic revolutions in Europe. By 1855 the anti-Nebraska forces had
made enough strides to steal control of Congress from the Democrats.
But the "Republican Party" did not become truly national until New
York State, with its deep pockets, valuable political spoils, and diminished but disciplined Whig Party organization, joined the fold. This was
truly something new: the first major party in America formed around a
single principle—the nonextension of slavery—and the first to have no
Southern wing at all.

For years Henry Ward Beecher had cast a secret, longing eye toward
electoral office but was held back by the American taboo against clergymen in government. In fact Henry had no desire to join the old party
machines, which ran on back-room deals, free-flowing booze, and the
unsavory manipulation of political patronage. But the Republican Party
promised to be different—a party of principle and modern Christian
morality, led by many of the Yankee-Yorker reformers and journalists
who were his friends and allies. Without the trappings of traditional
party loyalty or an established "machine," the Republicans' future would
depend almost entirely on the popular appeal of their ideas. It was a
once-in-a-lifetime opportunity for the self-styled "political parson."

Horace Greeley's *Tribune* and the *New York Times* quickly became
the national organs of the party. Beecher liked Greeley, but he was
closer to Henry Jarvis Raymond, the founder of the *Times*, then lieutenant governor of New York and one of the party's key architects. A short,
youthful-looking man, with a chin ringed by a half-moon of whiskers,
Raymond was cut from the same cloth as Beecher; a witty conversationalist and wide-raging intellect who zigzagged between mildly conservative and defiantly progressive positions. Under Raymond the *New York
Times* became the leading defender of both the Republican Party and
the Reverend Beecher.

Beecher had no talent for the backroom dealings that men like William Seward and Henry Raymond excelled at—the horse-trading and
intricate plotting required to bring Whigs, Democrats, Know-Nothings,
and Free-Soilers into a new party structure. But the preacher knew how
to distill complex ideas into rock-bottom principles and then bring them

to life in vivid, emotionally resonant images. Before the first national Republican convention in February 1856, where Raymond was to deliver the keynote address, Beecher and Raymond spent hours debating which ideas could unite everyone from reluctant Democratic defectors to distrustful archabolitionists. Keep the focus on Kansas, Kansas, Kansas, and the treachery of the Slavocracy, Henry counseled, defying both the abolitionists, who wanted a platform of immediate emancipation, and the Know-Nothings, who wanted to focus on immigration and religion.

The fruit of these discussions, Raymond's "Address to the American People," became the manifesto of the new party, guiding the platform for the coming election. "I wrote the address," Raymond confessed, "but for much of its argument and all its conclusions Henry Ward Beecher is quite as much responsible as I. The whole scope was discussed between us before pen was put to paper, and the arraignment of the men then in power for high crimes against the constitution, the Union and humanity, was suggested and all but phrased by Beecher."[34]

The infant party faced impossible odds in the upcoming presidential election. Out on the Kansas prairie, among the shantytowns and sod houses, clashes between the Free Staters and the Border Ruffians were growing more violent. In self-defense the Free Staters begged the eastern emigrant aid societies to send them weaponry, especially the new breech-loading Sharps rifles, which were much more accurate and deadly than the buffalo rifles or army muskets favored by the Missourians. The aid societies sent rifles, bowie knives, revolvers, a howitzer, and a cannon, packed in casks, barrels, and boxes marked "Crockery," "Hardware," or "Books," so they could pass downriver undetected. Meanwhile eastern newspapers dispatched dozens of official "correspondents" to the plains—a new concept in journalism.

In the fall of 1855, the free settlers, enraged by the continuing voting fraud, set up an illegal Free State government. Tensions boiled over when a proslavery man murdered a Free Stater over a land claim, setting off retaliatory series of kidnappings and raids. All through that bitterly cold winter, horrific tales of "Bleeding Kansas" blanketed the eastern papers. Correspondents sent back lurid, and not entirely reliable, stories of armed thugs roaming the plains, robbing wagons, harassing travelers, tarring men, and looting homes. They wrote of a home missionary who nearly had his eyes gouged out after upbraiding a proslavery neighbor for reading his mail, and of Free State women riding innocently past the Ruffians with gunpowder bags secretly hanging under their petti-coats and percussion caps stuffed in their stockings. In January 1856 the *Independent* predicted that without more men, money, ammunition, or firearms, there would be a massacre of the Free Staters by the spring.

For years pacifism had been a cornerstone of both radical abolition-ism and moderate antislavery feeling. But once people were stuffed with a daily diet of Kansas atrocities, their attitudes toward violence began to shift. Many Christians began to see the honor and necessity of fight-ing back in the face of unrepentant lawlessness. Beecher, who preferred a hero to a martyr any day, was a quick convert, weaving a fine web of Scripture and common sense to support the case for Christian self-defense.

"The New Testament declares that malign revenge or hatred are not to be felt toward an enemy. We do not think it touches at all the question of what kind of instruments men may employ. It simply teaches what is the state of mind which is to direct either kind of instrument, moral or physical," Beecher argued. "We know that there are those who will scoff at the idea of holding a sword or a rifle in a Christian state of mind. I think it is just as easy to hold an argument in a Christian state of mind." Frankly, Henry said, "there was more moral power in one of those instruments, so far as the slaveholders of Kansas were concerned, than in a hundred Bibles."

At the end of March 1855, Henry rode up to New Haven, Connect-icut, for a meeting to raise rifles for the Connecticut Kansas Colony, which was about to depart for the frontier. Yale faculty, students, and other ultrarespectable Christians packed the North Church, clapping wildly as he delivered his standard stump speech on the cataclysmic bat-tle between Liberty and Slavery, spiked with spicy stories from the Kan-sas prairies. When Henry finished, a distinguished Yale professor stood up to give the first pledge of a rifle, setting off a cascade of pledges, while Beecher joked and cajoled the audience. When their energy began to flag, Henry announced that if twenty-five rifles could be raised on the spot, he'd pledge twenty-five more from Plymouth Church—enough to arm the entire colony. A Mr. Killam stood to pledge next.

"Killam," Beecher wisecracked, "that's a significant name in con-nection with a Sharps rifle."[35]

By the end of the evening they'd raised enough for twenty-seven rifles at twenty-five dollars each. A few weeks later a company of young men, calling themselves the "Beecher Bible and Rifle Colony," marched through New Haven on their way west, each one the proud owner of a Sharps rifle and a Bible embossed, courtesy of Plymouth Church, with the motto: "Be ye steadfast and unmovable."

The press seized on Henry's sensational remarks, dubbing Sharps rifles "Beecher's Bibles" and Plymouth Church the "Church of the Holy Rifles." Political cartoonists quickly learned how to draw the moon-faced minister with a shotgun in his hand. From all sides—from the ultrapacifist *Liberator* to the proslavery *Observer*—Beecher was lashed for advocating violence. "Why strain at a gnat, and swallow a camel? If every 'border ruffian' invading Kansas deserves to be shot, much more does every slaveholder, by the same rule," taunted William Lloyd Garrison. "Who will go for arming our slave population?" Beecher blithely dismissed all criticism. "There are times when self-defense is a religious duty," he insisted.[36]

On May 21, 1856, a local sheriff led a posse of eight hundred Border Ruffians to the free town of Lawrence, toting five cannons and banners declaring "The Superiority of the White Race!" and "Bibles not Rifles!" At the town line the posse dissolved into a mob. When the landmark Free Soil Hotel withstood their onslaught of cannonballs, the Ruffians ignited kegs of gun powder inside, and finally set the hotel on fire. They destroyed the town's presses, torched several buildings, and "liberated" all the whiskey they could find before arresting the Free Staters' unofficial "governor."

The next day in Washington, D.C., as news of the "Sack of Lawrence" was racing across the wires, Preston Brooks, a young congressman from South Carolina, stepped onto the floor of the Senate. He was in search of Senator Charles Sumner, the brilliant Massachusetts abolitionist who, only two days before, had delivered a blistering diatribe on the "Crime Against Kansas." Sumner singled out Senator Andrew Butler, Preston Brooks's elderly uncle, as a "Don Quixote who had chosen a mistress to whom he has made his vows, and who though ugly to others is always lovely to him, though polluted in the sight of the world is chaste in his sight—I mean the harlot, Slavery."[37] In defense of his family's honor, Congressman Brooks stepped up to Sumner's desk, raised his gold-tipped cane, and began viciously pummeling Sumner's head. The senator crashed to the floor, unconscious and gushing blood.

"Bleeding Sumner" and the sack of Lawrence set the public on fire. Across the North newspapers shrieked of the slaughter in Kansas and the barbarism of the Southern "aristocrats." Defiant Southerners hailed Brooks as a hero, sending him canes to replace the one broken over

Sumner's head. The North took this as only further proof of the depravity slavery bred in whites. "The mask is off, and all disguises are thrown to the winds, and the slave power stands out in its true character, making its last and most infamous demands upon the North," roared Henry in the *Independent*. "All we have to do is say No."[38]

This ghastly parade of violence did more to create the Republican Party than anything else in its history. "Nothing was ever so unlucky," complained one "Old Fogey" Whig. "Providence itself seems to be on the side of the Republican party."[39]

One final episode marked that bloody week in May. Three nights after the attack on Lawrence, John Brown, a grizzled fifty-six-year-old Yankee immigrant with piercing gray eyes, gathered six of his fellow settlers, including four of his own sons, for a secret mission. Around the campfire Brown told them why they were here: God had instructed him to destroy all the proslavery men on Pottawatomie Creek. "I have no choice," Brown said. "It has been ordained by the Almighty God, ordained from eternity, that I should make an example of these men."[40]

Just before midnight on May 24 Brown and his men muscled their way into a proslavery farmhouse. They shot the farmer and then hacked the man's two sons to death with broadswords. They rode on to the next cabin on the creek, where they killed two more settlers, hacking their skulls, slicing off a hand, and driving swords through their bodies. Five died before Brown and his band slipped off to elude arrest.

The Pottawatomie Massacre got little coverage, since the grisly story did not fit the hysterical anti-Southern mood of the day. But when John Brown resurfaced to complete God's mission, it would be front-page news.

ACROSS THE NORTH mass meetings sprang up in volcanic outrage. On the night of a massive pro-Sumner meeting at the Broadway Tabernacle, Henry and Tasker Howard dined in the city and then strolled over to catch the speeches, which were headlined by William Evarts, the famed Whig attorney. It was a conservative lineup, with each speaker handpicked to avoid any taint of antislavery radicalism. As the meeting was breaking up, someone in the audience spotted Beecher's familiar face and began calling out: "Beecher! Beecher!" The audience took up the cry, to the visible annoyance of Evarts, who tried to adjourn the meeting.

Dozens of hands pushed Beecher up to the stage. The minister quieted the raucous audience with a wave of his hand, then pitched into a dramatic retelling of the last five years, climaxing with a heartrending account of Sumner's beating. Evarts had good reason for his chagrin. The press gave short shrift to all the speakers but Beecher, and the Republican Party heelers took note.

By now Plymouth Church had a reputation among African Americans as a stop on the Underground Railroad where they would find a reliable source of money and aid. On many Sundays Beecher announced that a former slave would be standing by the door with an upturned hat as the service let out, to collect money to buy his or her family out of bondage. Occasionally a tenderhearted owner would send a slave to Brooklyn to touch the purse strings directly, knowing, Henry said sarcastically, "that better prices were obtained for slaves that were put up for sale here."

Two day after Henry's debut as a political stump speaker, the parson paused before the final hymn of the Sunday-morning service. "Some two weeks since, I had a letter from Washington informing me that a young woman had been sold by her own father to go South, for what purposes you can imagine when you see her," Henry told his spellbound congregation. The slave trader was so moved by compassion for the girl that he offered her the chance to purchase her freedom. Henry turned and said, "Come up here, Sarah, and let us all see you."

A pretty young woman with light brown skin and long, wavy hair ascended the steps of the platform and then sank down, blushing and embarrassed, into the pulpit chair. "And this," proclaimed the minister, "is a marketable commodity." Then he demanded, "What will you do now? May she read her liberty in your eyes? Shall she go out free? Christ stretched forth his hand and the sick were restored to health; will you stretch forth your hands and give that without which life is of little worth? Let the plate be passed, and we will see."

"Tears of pity and indignation streamed from eyes unused to weeping," as Eunice described the scene. "Women became hysterical; men were almost beside themselves."[41] Coins, banknotes, rings, bracelets, and watches poured into the contribution boxes, and some people threw money directly onto the pulpit. Finally Lewis Tappan stood up and announced that several gentlemen would provide the rest of the money needed. Applause rolled like thunder across the room. A rapturous account of the scene appeared in the *Independent*, written by a young poetess named Edna Dean Proctor.

This was altogether too much for New York's roughneck Democrats. That week, the New York papers reported rumors that a mob of Bowery boys was planning on "cleaning out the damned abolition nest at Plymouth Church" next Sunday. That Sabbath the anxiety was nearly unbearable as Brooklyn's mayor, police chief, a squad of officers in plainclothes, and dozens of congregants armed with pistols and canes watched a score of tough-looking young men skulk into the church and take seats. But Beecher was slow in arriving, and soon the hooligans grew restless and bored. Finally, muttering curses against the "abolitionists and nigger-lovers," they left. Nothing like the discomfort of an old-fashioned stiff-backed pew to drive away the devil.

On June 17, 1856, the first Republican presidential nominating convention opened in Philadelphia—the "Philadelphia Nigger Convention," the *Brooklyn Eagle* sneered.[42] After much maneuvering, the party nominated the Great Pathfinder, John C. Frémont. The forty-three-year-old western explorer was chosen for his handsome face, romantic exploits, moderate antislavery reputation, and lack of political baggage. His inexperience was offset by the canny political instincts of his wife, Jessie Benton Frémont, the brilliant daughter of the powerful Missouri senator Thomas Benton. "Frémont, Free Speech, Free Soil, Free Kansas!" was the rallying cry.

It is a political truism that elections are most feverish when they are framed as a battle of fundamental fears—morality versus debauchery, liberty versus tyranny—rather than mere policy differences. The election of 1856 proves the point. People across the North responded to Frémont's nomination with the "devotion and dedicated zeal of a religious conversion," recalled George Julian, the antislavery congressman from Indiana.[43] Clergymen, Quakers, radical abolitionists, women, children—people who normally avoided politics—united with intellectuals, farmers, and businessmen to push back the Slave Power. Women played a substantial campaign role, establishing Frémont singing clubs, sewing circles, and prayer gatherings (one lady recommended making mammoth wheels of "Frémont Cheese" to exhibit at local county fairs). Massachusetts senator Henry Wilson gave much of the credit to *Uncle Tom's Cabin*, noting "that many votes cast for Frémont were but the rich fruitage of seed so widely broadcast by Harriet Beecher Stowe."[44]

Once again, Beecher was in the right place at the right time. By chance, Tasker Howard had become friends with John C. Frémont when Howard was building steamships to carry miners to California. Later Frémont sought Howard's help in developing the gold mines that lay under his estate in the foothills of the Sierra Nevadas. After Frémont's nomination Tasker volunteered his office at 34 Broadway as Frémont's unofficial headquarters and personally contributed nearly forty thousand dollars to the campaign. Best of all, he recruited the services of his old friend Henry Ward Beecher.

Frémont was Henry's ideal of a hero—dashing but with a manly reserve, calm but intense, untainted by professional politics. Even more important, Jessie Benton Frémont was Henry's kind of woman— intelligent, charming, and strong willed, with a gentility that enhanced rather than suppressed her bold personality and shrewd ambition. Henry admired Frémont, but he had a genuine rapport with Jessie. Plymouth Church became a mighty engine for the Republican cause, raising money, packing rallies, politicking behind the scenes in the labyrinthine world of New York politics. The church trustees even voted Beecher a leave of absence to spend the autumn campaigning throughout the Northeast.

By then the election had settled into a three-man race. The Democrats nominated former secretary of state James Buchanan—"a Northern man with Southern principles," as one antislavery reporter noted.[45] Former president Millard Fillmore, a Whig who took over when President Zachary Taylor died in office in 1850, was nominated by the anti-immigrant American Party, composed of Know-Nothings who had refused to join the Republican coalition.

The Democrats whipped up racist fears of the "Black Republicans," deriding them as "woolley heads" and "nigger worshipers." Southern politicians painted Frémont as an ultraradical who would destroy the sanctity of home and marriage, spreading the motto: "Free Love and Frémont." Yet still Frémont fever spread. Alarmed, the Democrats reverted to the scare tactic that had worked so well in 1850: the threat of disunion. A Southern merchant, writing in the conservative *Journal of Commerce*, put it bluntly: "if Frémont is elected, the South will secede."[46]

Meanwhile the Fillmore forces exploited anti-Catholic, anti-immigrant prejudices, circulating the rumor that Frémont was a secret Roman Catholic. As proof they cited his father's French citizenship (then as now, a sure sign of untrustworthiness) and the fact that when he and Jessie eloped they were married by a Catholic priest. Frémont was Episcopalian, in fact, but at the urging of Henry Raymond and the other party handlers, he refused to discuss such a private matter in public. Henry had long ago repudiated the anti-Catholic bigotry learned from his father, and he openly despised the Know-Nothing movement, often praising immigrants for their vigorous contributions to American culture. Nonetheless, defending Frémont's Protestantism became Henry's primary task in the campaign, and he managed it with aplomb.

"Had we been in Col. Frémont's place," Beecher said gallantly, "we would have been married if it had required us to walk through a row of priests and bishops as long as from Washington to Rome, winding up with the Pope himself."[47]

Through late summer and fall Henry spoke at massive outdoor rallies mesmerizing thousands of listeners for hours, without seats, shade, or amplification. Beecher's most popular routine described his old dog Noble, whom Henry once saw chase a red squirrel into the crevice of a stone wall in Lenox. The squirrel never appeared there again, but the dog couldn't stop obsessing about that hole. "When there were no more chickens to harry, no pigs to bite, no cattle to chase, no children to romp with," said Henry, "he would walk out of the yard, yawn and stretch himself, and then look wistfully at the hole, as if thinking to himself: 'Well, as there is nothing else to do, I may as well try that hole again.'"

He'd forgotten all about Noble until this ludicrous insistence that Frémont was a Catholic. "Col. Frémont is, and always has been, as sound a Protestant as John Knox ever was," Beecher claimed, but the anti-Frémont press, "like Noble, has opened on this hole in the wall, and can never be done barking at it. Day after day it resorts to this empty hole." Why, he couldn't pick up a Democratic paper "nowadays without thinking involuntarily, 'Goodness! The dog is letting off at that hole again.'"[48]

Beecher's "old Noble" speech was the most reprinted of any in the campaign, it was said. Enoch Wood, a young Quaker in upstate New York, wrote of marching with his entire school to a Frémont rally bearing banners "representing 'Dog Noble' barking at the empty hole and the squirrel in the tree above him." Nearly eight thousand people turned out to watch as Beecher "spoke three hours to an almost breathless audience, his speech abounded in side-splitting fun and pathos alternately," Wood wrote in his dairy. "He proved that Frémont not a Catholic, Slaveholder, or Disunionist."[49]

As election day approached, Henry's voice grew ragged, and the mud was slung fast and furious. Pundits denounced "The Rev. Kill 'em Beecher" as leader of the "gun-powder divines," and cartoonists pictured him as the "Rev. Political Buffoon," passing out Sharps rifles and cavorting with other "Black Republicans." In Brooklyn, Democrats paraded with banners bearing the phrase "Henry Ward Beecher had better stick to the pulpit." In the South he was a pariah.

But by now Henry had a skin as thick as buffalo hide. "He says 'if we can only carry this election he shall not care if he only has breath and throat enough left to say, "Now I lay me down to sleep,"' " wrote Susan Howard about Henry. "Well, asks one—'but what if we lose it?'—'lose it?' he replies, 'if we lose it, I shall sleep on it one night, and be up and at them again the next morning.' "[50]

Henry would need his optimism. By October the Democratic fear-mongering was beginning to tip the balance away from Frémont. On the morning of the election the *Brooklyn Eagle* ran one final smear, printing the rumor that Beecher was extorting four hundred dollars for each stump speech. But by now people had made up their minds.[51] An astonishing 83 percent of voters went to the polls in New York, some waiting for hours to cast their ballot.

That evening on Park Row, men crushed around the newspaper and telegraph offices, scanning the bulletin boards for news. At first the results were encouraging. All of New England, the upper Midwest, and New York State went for Frémont. Fillmore took only Maryland. As expected, Buchanan swept the South. It all came down to the border states: Illinois, Indiana, and especially Pennsylvania. In the end Buchanan took them all. In Pennsylvania, where Buchanan won by only three thousand votes, there were cries of fraud, but that changed nothing.

Despite his disappointment Beecher judged the campaign a great success. The fledgling party won approximately 45 percent of the Northern vote and acquired millions of ardent supporters. Better yet, the Republicans sent thirteen senators to Washington and now controlled most Northern state legislatures. They had a beachhead for the fight to come.

Only two days after President Buchanan's inauguration, the Southern-dominated Supreme Court issued a historic ruling. A slave named Dred Scott was suing for his freedom on the ground that for years he had resided with his master in U.S. territories where slavery was prohibited. The Supreme Court's decision was devastating: Not only did they throw out Scott's case, they ruled that slaves had no right to bring legal action, that the U.S. Constitution and the Bill of Rights did not apply to African Americans, that the Missouri Compromise was unconstitutional, and that Congress had no authority to limit slavery in the territories. Chief Justice Roger Taney put it as bluntly as he could: Blacks were "so far inferior that they had no rights which the white man was bound to respect."

The Dred Scott decision, in the joyful words of one Georgia newspaper, "covers every question regarding slavery and settles it in favor of the South."[52] A slave was a slave, whether in Massachusetts or South Carolina. The Supreme Court had officially declared slavery a national institution.

"They have sown the wind," warned Beecher, "and they will reap the whirlwind."[53]

MIRRORING THE CHILL of discouragement that hung over the North, the weather turned foul and frigid after the election. January 1857 was so cold that the Bay of New York froze solid. It was not uncommon to see people walking across the ice between Brooklyn and Manhattan. A few weeks after the New Year, the Brooklyn Eagle ran this startling item: "Henry Ward Beecher, accompanied by a lady (his daughter 'twas said), was seen on Saturday afternoon, about 4 p.m., floating on a detached piece of ice." The two were saved from disaster by the timely arrival of a boat and ladder.[54]

"Henry Ward Beecher never did a more thoroughly characteristic thing in his life, than when he crossed from New York to Brooklyn upon the ice on Saturday night. He acted then precisely as he does always—impulsively, courageously, rashly and successfully," gushed the New York Times in response. "Everybody is constantly scolding him for such desperate ventures—but their anger soon subsides in anxiety for the result, and that in turn merges in exultation at his success. He is always 'crossing the ice'—somewhere or other;—and though he has had some narrow escapes he has never yet 'fallen in.' "[55]

Henry was about due for another scolding. The last frenzied year had taken its toll, personally, professionally, and financially. He'd spent lavishly on his house in Brooklyn Heights and the farm in Lenox, and was well over ten thousand dollars in debt—more than twice his annual salary. His last winter lecture tour through the West had turned into an unprofitable public relations disaster, when the newfangled "lecture agent" who booked his tour doubled the ticket prices, raising the cry of speculator and profiteer.

Strain was showing in Plymouth Church as well. Although he was still tremendously popular, discontent stirred in certain circles of the congregation. Always a lackadaisical administrator, Henry abandoned all church administration while he was off on his political crusade. The congregation had grown to 750 members, far too big to "watch over" in the traditional manner, abetted by Henry's increasingly lax approach to church rules. He entirely gave up pastoral visits, a duty he'd never cottoned to—except among his personal friends, which only aroused jealousy in the rest of the congregation. Some complained that his farm in Lenox was too far from the city. A committee chaired by Lewis Tappan was formed to bring discipline and structure to what was coming to seem like Beecher's personal fiefdom.

These tensions extended to the *Independent*. The fastidious Henry Bowen was increasingly exasperated by Beecher's slipshod ways. Beecher blithely missed deadlines while drawing advances on his salary. He treated Bowen's purse like an extension of his own, volunteering the merchant's charity for his own pet projects. When Beecher asked Bowen and another wealthy deacon to put up money to publish a *Plymouth Collection* of hymns, it became a colossal headache when Beecher insulted a rival hymnbook edited by Leonard Bacon Jr., the son of one of the *Independent*'s editors. The ensuing squabble played out, as always, in the public press, hurting sales of the *Plymouth Collection*. Charles Beecher, who helped assemble the *Collection*, was shocked by the *Independent*'s coverage of it. "I should almost think there was a concealed jealousy, a sort of lurking hostility under the surface," he wrote to Henry. "If I were to prophecy—I should say that there were the germs of an explosion somewhere under the surface of the Independent Lion."[56]

Yet Bowen was in a bind. Beecher's essays and sermons were far and away the most popular items in the paper. Indeed, the *Independent* was routinely referred to as "Beecher's paper," with many readers assuming that Beecher was the editor, annoying the actual editors no end. Bowen was equally dismayed by the cult of personality rising around Beecher in Plymouth Church.

Beecher was just as bound to Bowen. As his lifestyle became more lavish, Henry was increasingly dependent on financial opportunities offered by his wealthy patrons. Seeing a chance to regain the upper hand, after the election Bowen renegotiated Beecher's contract to include both carrots and sticks. Beecher would receive five hundred dollars annually for fifty-two essays, with ten dollars deducted for each missed article, and a one-hundred-dollar bonus for missing no articles. For those occasions when Beecher failed to deliver, Bowen hired a budding young journalist named Theodore Tilton to cull "star papers" from Beecher's sermons and lectures—a ghostwriter, in essence.

With the lifelong instincts of a middle child, Henry abhorred open conflict with friends. Instead his resentment slipped out subtly. Beecher missed most of his deadlines in the month or so after signing the new contract, and soon Henry Bowen and his wife, Lucy, were complaining that he no longer visited the way he had in the early days, when theirs was like a second home to him. Up on the Heights sharp-eyed neighbors peeping through their lace curtains had their own theories: Beecher had found a new refuge in the magnificent home of Moses Sperry Beach and his lovely young wife, Chloe.

BEECHER ENTERED MIDDLE AGE, as a friend recalled, "in the prime of his oratorical vigor. He ripened more in after years, but his impetuosity of delivery was at its best at this period."[57] Older folks still considered Beecher a dangerous young iconoclast, but for the generation just coming of age, he was *the* icon of modern rational religion.

Plymouth Church was packed with young men who had left rural villages to seek their fortune in the city—clerks, apprentices, students, those torn between ambition and homesickness. "It was a common remark in those days that, whereas the average church congregation was made up in the proportion of five women to one man, in Plymouth church the proportion ran the other way," recalled one parishioner, with only slight exaggeration.[58] Most had been raised in the stern Yankee tradition but came of age when the old truths and virtues no longer seemed so self-evident or desirable.

For this new generation the main appeal of "Beecherism" lay in its two interwoven tenets: Liberty and Sympathy, or Freedom and Love. Beecher's "Gospel of Love" maintained that one could be true to one's desires without feeling guilty or alone. He encouraged people to transcend the merely "mechanical" bonds of family and tradition, to embrace our natural "soul-affinities," those people or paths that suit our individual natures. "Jesus felt instantly that there were affinities and relationships far higher and wider than those constituted by the earthly necessities of family life," Beecher preached.[59] "Not those who have your blood in their veins, but those who have your disposition in their soul, are your true kindred. Many and many a one is born sister to you, and is not sister; is born brother, and is no kindred of yours. And many, whose father and mother you never know, are own brothers to you by soul-affinity."[60]

In essence, Love tempers the loneliness of Liberty, while Liberty allows true Love to blossom. Not surprisingly, thousands of listeners and readers felt they shared a "soul affinity" with the preacher. Bushels of letters poured in from strangers, repeating the heartfelt sentiments of one E. W. B. Dakin, who insisted to Beecher that "I don't know your body but I do know your soul."[61]

Theodore Tilton, Beecher's new "assistant," was sure he and Beecher were soul mates. Born in 1835 to a dour New Jersey shoemaker, Theodore was fifteen when he enrolled in the New York Free Academy (later the City College of New York). Here he'd learned the new art of phonography (now called stenography, shorthand, or speedwriting), edited the college magazine, and dreamed of becoming a man of letters. Forced to leave school before graduation, Tilton found work as a stenographer at various newspapers, but he got his first real break through Plymouth Church connections.

Theodore discovered Plymouth Church as many men did—on the arm of a pious young lady. Elizabeth Richards was a petite, dark-eyed brunette from Brooklyn who had gone to school with Beecher's daughter Hattie. Her brother, Joseph, was a schoolmate of young Theodore Tilton. Tilton's parents were, in his words, "extreme and rigid" Old School Presbyterians. "I was brought up to the conviction that all men were miserable sinners," Theodore recalled. But Tilton was soon entranced by the minister's liberal ideas and social activism. In 1853, at the age of eighteen, Tilton joined Elizabeth as a member of the church, serving as a Sunday-school teacher and enthusiastic volunteer. In 1855 he was hired to transcribe a volume of Beecher's collected sermons for publication, which led directly to a job on the *Independent*. Theodore was thrilled when Bowen asked him to help with Beecher's "star papers." "Mr. Beecher was my man of all men," he said.[62]

Henry Bowen introduced Beecher to another unexpected boon that winter: Edna Dean Proctor. Proctor and Theodore Tilton had much in common. Born in 1829 in New Hampshire, Edna Dean Proctor was twenty-three years old when she came to live in the Bowen mansion. She was a beauty, with black, lustrous hair and eyes and the rich, dramatic voice and regal grace of an actress. Like Tilton, she was precocious. By the age of fourteen she was firm in her literary ambitions and progressive political opinions.

She spent a year at Mount Holyoke College before taking teaching posts in Cincinnati, New Haven, and Bowen's hometown of Wood-stock, Connecticut. With his sharp eye for talent, Henry Bowen wooed Miss Proctor away from Woodstock Academy in 1854 and brought her to Brooklyn to serve as a private teacher for his children and a com-panion for his young wife. She began her career as a poet and literary woman in the pages of the *Independent*.

Like Tilton, Proctor was dazzled by the Reverend Beecher. From Bowen's prestigious front pew, she began jotting down pithy passages from his sermons to share with her mother and friends. Early in 1857 Proctor's friends began urging her to turn her sermon notes into a book. Henry Bowen agreed, and when they proposed the plan to Beecher he was delighted. They sold it to one of Boston's leading publishers, with Bowen negotiating on Proctor's behalf.

As their collaboration progressed, Beecher and Proctor grew closer. Henry invited her to join him in his afternoon jaunts through the pic-ture galleries and art studios of New York. She came to his house to view his collection of etchings and met him at Brooklyn Heights soi-rees. Beecher encouraged her poetry and, in turn, savored her obvious admiration.

On occasion Beecher might joke self-deprecatingly about his weak-ness for flattery, but it was true that his "soul-affinity" was often stron-gest with such unabashed young hero-worshipers. His friendships with both Tilton and Proctor could hardly be more mutually advantageous. Beecher got his words into print without effort on his part, and by hitching themselves to Beecher's star both Tilton and Proctor stepped on the fast track to literary fame. Bowen, ever the canny middleman, got notoriety for the *Independent*.

ON APRIL FOOL'S DAY 1857 Herman Melville came down from his Berkshire hillside with a new book titled *The Confidence Man: His Mas-querade*. It was that most unpopular of genres, the political allegory, and readers and reviewers alike hated it. The plot, such as it is, consists of a series of conversations between the various passengers on a steam-boat named the *Fidèle* as it heads down the Mississippi River to New Orleans, into the heart of slave territory. It begins with the appearance of a stranger bearing a slate with the motto "Charity thinketh no evil." He is succeed by a series of nineteenth-century stereotypes—Methodist missionary, frontiersman, country merchant, reformer—one might en-counter on the river. Each seems to be a victim or perpetrator of a vague "confidence game," as well as a parody of various philosophers, politicians, and public men. Although contemporary readers were baffled, later scholars have doggedly identified some of the real-life objects of Melville's satire, among them Ralph Waldo Emerson, Edgar Allan Poe, Henry David Thoreau, and the actress Fanny Kemble.

Melville was beginning the second half of the book in the summer of 1856, just as Beecher began his campaign tour across upstate New York. Abruptly he narrowed the focus of the story to one single character, the genial Cosmopolitan, Frank Goodman. The historian Helen Trimpi makes the strong case that "Frank Goodman," with his rosy, round figure, flamboyant style, and "fraternal and fusing feeling," is a satire of Henry Ward Beecher.[63] Beecher's unwavering faith in the ultimate benevolence of human nature and the progress of society is satirized in the Cosmopolitan's obsessive need for the confidence of others.

"What is an atheist," Goodman demands of one skeptic, "but one who does not or will not see in the universe a ruling principle of love; and what is a misanthrope, but one who does not or will not see in man a ruling principle of kindness? Don't you see? In either case the vice consists in a want of confidence."[64]

The centerpiece of the last half of the book is an extended conversation between the warmhearted Goodman/Beecher and Ralph Waldo Emerson's cooler character, Mark Winsome, satirizing the coldness of Transcendental principles when put into actual practice. But the ending of the Confidence Man, with Goodman/Beecher quietly extinguishing the light and leaving the passengers to a fitful sleep, is deliberately ambiguous. Is Beecher a fool, a rogue, or a prophet for peddling such confidence?

It hardly mattered, since no one read the book. Coming after the crushing failure of Moby-Dick a few years earlier, Melville's disappointment was so deep that he never published another novel in his lifetime. Still, The Confidence Man was not a good sign for Beecher's prospects.

FOR THE TIME BEING, BEECHER'S natural confidence served him well. He retrenched his finances, reluctantly selling the Lenox house and upping his lecture schedule, speaking more than thirty times that winter. Plymouth Church raised his annual salary to five thousand dollars. Soon he was back to his spendthrift ways. He bought a lot on Columbia Street, the finest street on the Heights, with fantastic views of New York Bay, and began erecting a "first-class house," filled with expensive "modern conveniences"—coal furnace, gaslights, gas cook-stoves, hot and cold running water, and a full bathroom and laundry. He made plans to send his daughter Hattie to Europe for "finishing." One congregant summed up the prevailing opinion of Beecher: "Three thousand dollars a year is, as far as his own interest is concerned, just as good as ten thousand; for he has nothing, now, when the end of the year comes; and he would have no more then."[65]

The first inklings of trouble came in the spring of 1857. Initially most people dismissed it as a little tightening in the financial markets. Then on August 24 one of Wall Street's most respected financial insti-tutions, the Ohio Life Insurance Trust Co., defaulted on five million dollars in loans. Their failure set off a domino effect, as its creditors called in debts in the desperate hope of covering their own obligations. By the end of October the banks of nearly every major American city had closed their doors, and the nation was engulfed in a full-scale finan-cial panic.

The causes were far-flung—ranging from the end of the Crimean War in Europe causing a drop in demand for American grain, to the rising interest rates in England that drained English investment from American securities—and so complex that it would take economists fifty years to untangle them. But it was clear that American credit net-works had become overextended and underregulated, as people rushed to get in on the gold rush, the railroad boom, and western land specu-lation. As with all economic bubbles, people had put too much confi-dence in their own confidence.

Now the bubble burst. Construction projects stopped dead, goods piled up in warehouses, bankruptcies and unemployment skyrocketed. As the weather turned colder, thousands of unemployed workers turned out for "hunger meetings" in New York, demanding "work or bread" from the government, and clashing with the police. Reluctantly the City Council allocated funds for a massive work-relief project, an im-mense "Central Park" to be carved out of the rocky ledges and squatters' shacks above Fifty-ninth Street.

On Brooklyn Heights things looked especially gloomy. "*Bowen* has suspended; so has Henry Chittenden; and everybody is going heels over head, apparently," Henry told Eunice. "The better off people have been, the worse they are now, if they have notes to pay."[66] Henry suffered along with his patrons, as church donations and lecture fees evaporated.

That fall he poured his own anxiety into a series of brilliant sermons on the mysterious causes of the Panic. Some people declared it was divine punishment for the sins of slavery, others for the sins of Mammon, still others blamed the telegraph for spreading bad news like a contagion. Some blamed the ladies, for wasting so much of the nation's wealth on extravagant dresses and bonnets. The South blamed the North, the West blamed the East, and everyone blamed the speculators and confidence men in New York.

Henry assigned some fault to greedy speculation, some to God's wrath at America's "dollar-worshipping" society, but his explanation was more psychological than economic or theological. "There is money enough, property enough, and need for goods and manufacturing," Beecher exhorted, "but men are all paralyzed to-day chiefly by fear of each other. But why should there be this sudden cessation of confidence?" As soon as men begin to trust themselves and each other again the world would right itself. "It is the faith of man in man" that is needed. "It is mutual trust, it is confidence."[67]

Yet Beecher also insisted that the Panic was a sign of America's strength. "Adventurousness and speculation is the source of our prosperity as well as our occasional downfall. We owe everything to those pioneers and speculators, the ruined men of the community who make the prosperous men," he told his congregation. "It does not hurt a sanguine man, full of spring and hope to be destroyed, like cutting a worm in pieces only multiplies it."[68]

Henry did not just counsel confidence, he radiated it. And in their despondency and fear, people flocked to him as they never had before. "I am ashamed of myself, positively, to be an object of more faith than my Savior," Beecher declared during one particularly packed meeting. "How eagerly they believe every statement I make; how they hang upon my sympathy, and hope I will let them come again tomorrow. With half the faith you come to me with, you might be rejoicing in half an hour."[69]

Then something peculiar happened. Down on Fulton Street, only a few steps from Wall Street, a former businessman began holding an interdenominational noon prayer meeting in the old Dutch Reformed Church. Shell-shocked bankers, clerks, and stockjobbers trickled in, looking for comfort and guidance. The trickle swelled to a steady stream, and soon prayer meetings began popping up all over the city. Starved for good news, the New York papers began reporting on this spontaneous religious awakening in the very capital of Mammon. Driven by the breathless newspaper coverage, prayer meetings mushroomed in countinghouses and factories, even on city sidewalks, across the nation.

Soon the steamroller had a name: the "Prayer Meeting Revival" or the "Businessman's Awakening."

As they read of the miracle in Manhattan, Plymouth Church people began pressing Beecher to start a revival in his own church. To their surprise he flatly refused, saying he didn't believe in "got-up" revivals. In fact, said one parishioner, he "appeared almost to discourage the meetings."[70] At this stage of his career he had no need for the hard work of revivalism.

Suddenly, out of nowhere, a rumor raced through Brooklyn Heights: The Reverend Beecher was leaving immediately for California, for his health. No one knew the source of the rumor. In fact, noted the *Eagle*, the preacher seemed not only healthy but notably "hopeful and cheery."[71] All they knew was that one evening Henry Chandler Bowen called a sudden ad hoc meeting to propose that Beecher take a leave of absence immediately. Even stranger, Beecher himself didn't attend the meeting. In fact no one had heard him express any desire to go to California. Then, just as abruptly, the gossip disappeared. The rumors were groundless, reported the *Eagle*, although it offered no explanation for Bowen's peculiar presentation.

Just as the *Eagle* was retracting its story, Beecher announced that he was ready for a revival. Daily morning prayer meetings were instituted, and soon the church was in the throes of a "love feast." Perhaps it was the hand of God, or perhaps it was a return of his old childhood cycle of sin, anxiety, and relief (which he recalled in a sermon that spring), or maybe it was just his instinct for the popular mood, but Henry was on fire.

As the revival was reaching its climax, one more odd bit of news appeared. On April 1, 1858, the *Eagle* reprinted an article from the *Milwaukee Daily Wisconsin*. It was the familiar urban tale of a young woman seduced and abandoned, who turns to drink and prostitution. But *this* young woman claimed to be a protégé, an "adopted child," of Henry Ward Beecher's. The Beechers had taken her in and sent her to school in Brooklyn, where she'd been considered a bit wayward but bursting with literary talent. Then she fell in love with a Brooklyn man who returned her love but was already married. The emotional trauma caused a "violent brain fever" in the girl, and she became addicted to the "stimulants" prescribed to ease her pain.[72] It was a swift downward spiral until that winter, when an old schoolmate from Brooklyn found her begging door-to-door in Chicago. When friends offered help, she squandered their money on rum and then vanished.

As a rule Henry ignored personal aspersions, but this time he responded with lightning speed, sending an uncharacteristically harsh letter to the *New York Times* and the *Brooklyn Eagle*. Yes, she'd been a member of Plymouth Church, but she was never his "adopted child." "I have reason to think that from her first coming to this country from Ireland, she was profoundly deceitful," he wrote. "Her downfall did not begin with an unrequited romantic attachment. That was but one of hundreds of tales, which, at times, she employed with singular power, to excite the compassion and secure the contributions of the benevolent."[73]

Nasty gossip of this sort was easily dismissed as the smear tactics of Beecher's foes or a misreading of his tremendous personal warmth. But the leading men of Plymouth Church took it very seriously. If the public lost confidence in Beecher, they personally stood to lose a great deal, spiritually, socially, and financially. But Beecher paid no heed. At the May communion service, 186 new members joined the church, including Harriet Beecher Stowe; Henry's own son, Harry; and the son of his late brother George. The next month 166 more people joined the harvest. By the end of 1858 Plymouth Church had admitted 442 new members, three times any previous year, and by all accounts more than any other church in the country.

Henry's celebrity was now unrivaled, except perhaps for that of his own sister Harriet. In the spring he and Edna Dean Proctor finished the manuscript for *Life Thoughts*, and it came out that summer to rave reviews and stellar sales. "It was evidently done *con amore*," noted one reviewer.[74] Miss Proctor, the once-poor poetess, was now a minor literary star. At the urging of their publisher, Henry and Edna agreed that Edna would quit teaching and devote herself full-time to assembling a sequel.

Beecher's name was now commercial gold. In the shopwindows of Broadway, photo studios and art galleries used Beecher's famous visage to advertise their wares, and newspapers filled their pages with reports, anecdotes, and unauthorized copies of sermons. Entrepreneurs asked him to endorse products, impudent young men asked him for lectures they could deliver under his name, and budding writers inundated him with manuscripts. So much mail came to the house that Eunice took over his correspondence, saving the fan letters and gifts and tossing out the love letters, hate mail, charitable requests, and dubious business propositions. Like a modern-day movie star, Henry sent out hundreds of small, inexpensive photos of himself, called cartes de visites, in response to the fans' requests.

Plymouth Church was now one of New York's most popular tourist attractions—the Brooklyn ferries were nicknamed "Beecher boats," and "Follow the crowd" was the standard direction to Plymouth Church. "I have known visitors to spend Saturday night in gambling hells and other wicked places," said one Manhattan hotel clerk, "and then sit up for hours, so as to be sure to be in time to hear Mr. Beecher."[75] Only strangers with the stamina to wait at least an hour and possessing elbows sharp enough to push through the throngs got into "Beecher's theater."

In June *Harper's Weekly*, the literary bible of the middle classes, pronounced Beecher "the most celebrated preacher and the most popular orator in the country."[76] Topping the parade of honors, the trustees of Plymouth Church announced plans to build a new Plymouth Church, with a gargantuan seating capacity of six thousand. Henry's friend Moses Beach promised that he would personally raise $100,000 of the estimated $160,000 required.

More than one person wondered how Henry could possibly retain any sense of modesty amid all this adulation. Even his sister Harriet was shocked by the boxes of flowers that arrived from utter strangers. "One would think you were a *prima donna*," Harriet said. "What does make people go on so about you?"[77]

Walt Whitman, an unapologetic admirer of the minister, was equally alarmed by the phenomenon he dubbed "Beecherroyalty." "Mr. Beecher is doubtless a very able and sincere teacher of the people," Whitman wrote in the *Brooklyn Times* that September. Yet given the public's extraordinary infatuation with him, "we may well doubt whether he is not making people Beecherites instead of making them Christians, and teaching them to worship him instead of that Creator whom he so eccentrically defines as 'a dim and shadowy effluence.' "[78]

THE GREAT REVIVAL OF 1857–58 was Lyman Beecher's last. At eighty-three, Lyman was still spry, but his mind was losing its sharpness. His younger sister, Aunt Esther, passed away in 1855, and two years later Lyman and his wife, Lydia, moved to Brooklyn Heights. Lyman became a regular at Plymouth Church, basking in his son's remarkable success and occasionally reminding bemused admirers, "If it hadn't been for me, you'd never have had him!"[79]

No one took more pleasure in the Great Revival than Lyman Beecher. "I waited to see *one more revival*," Lyman said with joy. "I have seen it—a glorious one." But the revival also revealed how much religion had changed in the last twenty-five years. Gone were the fire and brimstone and the devastating pressure to "repent, repent." Instead these revival meetings were deliberately upbeat and nondenominational, dwelling on love, consolation, and practical piety instead of divisive theological arguments. "Is not the whole of this talk about a plan of salvation a mess of sheer ignorance, not to say nonsense?" was Henry's typical comment. When asked, "What about 'original sin'?" he brushed it off. "There has been so much actual transgression that I have not had time to go back on to that."[80]

Proud as he was of his son, such talk set Lyman's teeth on edge. "He had no business to tell sinners of the love of God without telling them of the wrath of God," Lyman snapped after one of Henry's sermons. "I cannot tell you how much the motive of helping men that would not listen to anything but such like preaching has to do with Henry."[81]

For once Lyman's Old School enemies agreed. No one was more responsible for the decline of Calvinism than the Beecher children, sneered the *Princeton Review* in 1857. They had a point. For thirty years Lyman's children had struggled publicly to reconcile the image of a benevolent, righteous God with the harsh dogma of their father's faith. In the 1850s Edward, Catharine, Charles, Harriet, and Henry each stirred controversy by publishing their own gentle reinterpretations of orthodoxy. (Indeed, Henry openly ridiculed "vinegar-faced evangelicals"!)[82] It is no small irony that in the end the children judged God by the standard of Lyman Beecher, assuming that a perfect God would be no less unconditional in His love than their own beloved father.

But, of course, it was unfair to lay all the blame on the Beechers. Others would say that Calvinism was doomed to irrelevance by the rising faith in free will. In his classic poem "The Deacon's Masterpiece," Henry's friend Oliver Wendell Holmes named the very day Calvinism died: November 1, 1855. On this day, joked Dr. Holmes, that marvelous, all-encompassing theological machine ("built in such a logical way / It ran a hundred years to the day") on which Lyman Beecher had labored so long, finally fell apart—each joint, each argument, steadily weakening until the system could no longer be sustained. In Dr. Holmes's words:

> You see, of course, if you're not a dunce,
> How it went to pieces all at once,
> All at once, and nothing first
> Just as bubbles do when they burst.

∾ ∾

Henry Ward Beecher had what he wanted: influence, independence, wealth, and, not least, the unbridled love of hundreds of thousands of hearts. Yet something was wrong. Sometime after 1856, Henry later testified, he was beset by "violent" but "elusive" symptoms he eventually attributed to "excessive cerebral activity and fatigue-over-action of the mind." He had difficulty sleeping and sometimes felt he would faint in the street or in the pulpit. Even casual observers noted that he seemed more distracted, "more often in a brown study."[83]

Undoubtedly many people laid the blame on his home life. At the age of forty Eunice became pregnant for the last time, giving birth once again to twins in the summer of 1854. Only one twin survived the difficult labor. Again Eunice was devastated by the loss. "Poor little one!" she crooned to her baby boy, whom she named Herbert. "He will never know that one dreadful blow has closed his mother's heart to all strong love—for any but his father."[84]

After this, Eunice seemed "cold and changed," in Harriet Stowe's words. She quarreled constantly with Henry's family, and was so unaccountably rude to his sisters, that Isabella and Harriet began staying at the Howards' house when they came to Brooklyn, which only infuriated Eunice all the more. Her jealousy was now legendary on the Heights—she was "one of the most jealous women that ever lived," as Henry's friend Oliver Johnson put it. Then again Henry's flirtatiousness was equally notorious—"he is very susceptible, and much given to such frivolities—a clerical weakness, perhaps," as their friend John Raymond admitted.[85] They were now entrenched in the classic marital cycle. The more his wife nagged and complained, the more time Henry spent away from the house, and thus the more she nagged.

These tensions had existed since they were newlyweds, but by 1858 something had changed in their marriage. That May, Eunice took the children up the Hudson River to Mattawan, New York, where they'd rented a farmhouse for the summer. Immediately she began sending Henry plaintive letters. When Henry did not write in return, Eunice's petulance grew. She finally exploded when their teenage son, Harry, returned from the city with the news that Plymouth Church had offered the minister an extra month of vacation to rest up after the long revival. She was hurt that not only had Henry refused the offer but he hadn't

even mentioned it to her. "If you would only write me one word!" she
wrote from Mattawan:

> I do, assuredly, know after twenty years trial that you are *not* given
> to letter writing but up to last summer you *always have* written me,
> at least *once* a week a few words and now you write not at all—and
> I feel all that time that you do not love me or are angry at some-
> thing and life is very dark. I know your duties and fatigues, but I
> must think even if you disagree with me that there are *some duties*
> beside public ones. And yet I should not like you to write *just from*
> *duty.*[86]

If Beecher responded, even once that summer, the letter did not survive.

EUNICE WAS NOT THE ONLY unhappy woman in Brooklyn Heights.
At the end of 1858 Edna Dean Proctor had nearly finished compiling
the sequel to *Life Thoughts*, when she opened her mail to find a publisher's circular advertising upcoming releases. Proctor was shocked to see
that another publisher was offering a carbon copy of her own book, entitled *Timely Thoughts of Henry Ward Beecher*, edited by Augusta Moore,
a well-known parishioner of Plymouth Church.

Proctor was stunned. How could Mr. Beecher have agreed to a rival
book? Worse yet, why had he not told her? With "great grief and excitement," as she described it, Edna informed Henry Bowen of the betrayal.
She recalled that he "felt more aggrieved, so to say, than I did, and considered that it was a very great breach of faith on Mr. Beecher's part." In
an "indignant, excited state of mind," Edna penned a furious letter to
Beecher, accusing him of being "abusive and treacherous" and closing
with a vague but ominous threat.

The very next day Henry sent back a half-conciliatory, half-
defiant letter of defense, explaining that over the summer Miss Moore
had beseeched him for permission to publish a book of his sayings to
earn money to feed and clothe her two orphaned brothers. He'd given
in only, he said, "when I found that she was on the brink of despair and
sliding down helplessly after years of heroic suffering." Why he had not
mentioned this philanthropic decision he did not say. Instead he urged
her to think of it as a compliment to her own work, rather than a humiliation or "eternal disgrace."

"Really, Miss Proctor," wrote Henry, "when you think of the close of your letter, the intimation of some dark future; some leaving of town; some, I don't know what, of fantastic and imaginary awfulness into which you dare not look, you do not think that you have carried your feelings a little in the direction of extravaganza?"[87]

Proctor was somewhat placated by Beecher's response. The two remained friendly, although they did not see each other as often as before. But it soon became clear that Beecher had lost interest in the sequel to *Life Thoughts*. Finally the project fizzled—a significant loss for the young poet.

Years later there would be much dispute over precisely what Edna Dean Proctor told Henry Bowen in her anger and disappointment and how Beecher responded to the accusation. At first she complained only of Beecher's perfidy with the book, but over time she spilled out a shocking story. In the words of Henry Bowen, Edna Dean Proctor made a "full and explicit confession of adultery with Mr. Beecher."[88]

According to two accounts, sometime in late 1856 or early 1857, when the rest of the family was gone, the minister paid a call on Proctor at the Bowen mansion. As Beecher stood to leave, to his surprise she leaned forward and gave him what Beecher later described as a "paroxysmal kiss." As Bowen told it, Beecher then took Proctor "in his arms by force, threw her down upon a sofa, accomplished his deviltry upon her and left her." (For those readers picturing an impassable barrier of petticoats and pantaloons, it should be noted that most nineteenth-century women's underpants consisted of two fabric legs joined together only at the waist and left open at the crotch.)

It was "no less than rape," Bowen claimed angrily, "the rape of a virgin" or at least, "something very nearly like ravishment." When it was all over, Edna rose from the sofa and rushed out of the room. A few moments later she came back "very much flustered, saying: 'Oh I am covered with blood!' "[89]

When asked about these accusations years later by a worried friend, Henry protested hotly he had "never committed any violence upon any woman, and God knew that he had committed no violence upon that woman."[90] He was sure, Henry said, that Edna had been lying about the bloody evidence that he had taken her virginity, "feeling convinced that she had had other and previous experiences of the same sort."[91] But he did not deny that they had sex.

In the immediate aftermath of their alleged encounter, Henry seemed genuinely remorseful, explaining that he'd been overcome by a sudden, uncontrollable passion. He swore it would never happen again. A few days later Beecher returned, Edna told Bowen, proclaiming his love and insisting that their intimacy had only deepened his passion for her. He'd always been unhappy in his marriage, he told her, and wished that Edna were his wife. His sweet words must have been persuasive, because again they allegedly had sex.

The first two times, asserted Bowen, Beecher exerted superior strength against her protests, and she was so paralyzed with fright that she lost consciousness. But for more than a year after that, according to Bowen, they had sex frequently, in both her house and Beecher's, and in his study at Plymouth Church, usually after the morning prayer meetings were over. He gave her a key to the study, telling her to go in, lock the door, and not open it to anyone until he gave the special signal.

Edna had heard rumors of Beecher's flirtations with other women, of course, but thought little of them until the day she saw a well-known female member of the congregation going into the side door of the church when the building was empty. She followed the woman, watching as she entered Henry's study and shut the door. Edna tried the handle. Finding it locked, she waited outside the church until the woman left. The relationship ended not long after that, a year or so before Edna made her confession. Over the next few years, Edna poured out a series of passionate poems about star-crossed lovers that were published in 1866, bringing her literary stardom and financial security. Edna never married.

Beecher, too, seemed preoccupied with the anguish of love and the strange psychology of self-deception. Suspicious minds could (and later did) easily read his sermons from this period as a series of secret confessions—as if he were *The Scarlet Letter*'s Reverend Dimmesdale come to life. "Every man is living two lives—an external one and an internal one. They are not always or often either parallel or morally alike," Henry proclaimed in a typical sermon:

Men often wish to deceive themselves. It is very strange how much a man may do that is beautiful and right, and yet how many things wounding and depressing to the whole moral character will begin to rise in his imagination, or in his affections, as mists, and low places and valleys, rise at evening or morning, and grow we scarcely know how, out of the air, until the whole is covered and enshrouded. [. . .]

They try to cover it up and get rid of it, but are conscious that there still remains that same weakness. And though a man may say to himself a hundred times, "I have forsaken the wrong, I will cover it up for evermore," there it is, down at the bottom of his heart. He knows that when the same circumstances, the same pressures with temptation, come again, he will promise the same course of wickedness.[92]

As for Henry Bowen, he was thunderstruck by Proctor's tale. This was a tricky situation for the close-fisted Connecticut Yankee. Bowen was genuinely devoted to the path of righteousness, but he had a lot of money tied up in Beecher. Just as Beecher was breaking Edna's heart, Bowen was negotiating a new contract with the minister, offering him a share of the Independent's profits in exchange for his weekly sermons and "star papers." Under such circumstances it would be unwise to say anything about Proctor's accusation.

Three days after Beecher and Bowen nailed down their new agreement, the minister signed a second contract. Robert Bonner, the publisher of the New York Ledger, the most popular magazine in the country and an indirect rival of the Independent, offered Beecher a weekly column, paying three times more than Bowen. Beecher happily decided to write for both papers. After years of gifts, loans, and hospitality, Bowen was surely livid. Not long after this came Proctor's confession.

"I then halted, waited and watched him," as Bowen said later. "At last he found out, or seriously suspected, that I knew his guilt and from that day to this he has been both a secret and open enemy."[93]

Chapter 10

"GIVE ME WAR REDDER THAN BLOOD
AND FIERCER THAN FIRE"

*A*merica had never been as divided as in 1859. For ten years the Slavocracy had won one symbolic victory after another for "Southern Rights," but to their chagrin each victory only brought more vituperation from the North without adding one square mile of actual slave territory. After years of antagonism Southern spokesmen had shifted from a reluctant defense to a defiant celebration of slavery and a loathing of all things Yankee. As the *Richmond Examiner* wrote:

> We have got to hating everything with the prefix free, from free negroes down and up through the whole catalogue—free farms, free labor, free society, free will, free thinking, free children, and free schools—all belonging to the same brood of damnable isms. But the worst of all abominations is the modern system of free schools, which has been the cause and prolific source of the infidelity and treasons that have turned [Northern] cities into Sodoms and Gomorrahs, and her land into the nestling places of howling Bedlamites.[1]

Up North such talk only strengthened the belief that any further compromise with the Slave Power was futile.

But brinkmanship was good for the lecture business. Abolitionist orators were suddenly drawing crowds who came for the sparks that were sure to fly between speaker and audience. Beecher was in constant demand on the lecture circuit, and it was a rare day when his name didn't appear somewhere in the press. "It is probable that there is not another man in the United States who is so much heard and read as Henry W. Beecher, unless the other man be Wendell Phillips," observed the journalist Frederick Hudson.[2] Their every utterance was recorded by stenographers, then reviewed, reproduced, and argued over in newspapers from New York to San Francisco.

While Wendell Phillips used his new notoriety to call for disunion from the pestilent South, Beecher was trading his in for cold cash. It was a lesson he learned from his new editor, Robert Bonner, whose weekly family paper, the *New York Ledger*, was the least political and most read magazine in the country. Conflict brought attention, but the real money came from being broad-minded, inclusive, and decidedly uncontroversial. Henry's charming essays for the *Ledger*, on everything *but* politics and religion, were bringing him a whole new audience. In the spring he was flush enough to send his daughter Hattie on a grand tour of Europe, and to purchase a thirty-seven-acre farm in Peekskill, New York, about fifty minutes up the Hudson from New York City.

His widening fame had a distinct downside, however. Beecher was constantly inundated by beggars, autograph hounds, critics, reporters, do-gooders, and cranks. "Your affairs are everybody's business," Beecher complained in the *Ledger*. "What you do, or say, or do not do or say; what you wear, where you go, with whom you walk, when you get up and when lie down; what it costs you to live and how you get your means to pay for your living; who makes your coats or boots, who shaves your face, all are diligently observed and reported."[3]

By appealing directly to the "sovereign public," Beecher had liberated himself from the institutional middlemen he'd always found so irksome, only to replace them with the tyranny of public opinion.

TWENTY-TWO-YEAR-OLD THEODORE TILTON saw none of this. He saw only the waves of love and admiration that engulfed the minister, and he yearned for his share. Like Beecher, Tilton possessed a curious combination of burning ambition, passionate idealism, and deep-seated vanity. He was a talented writer and principled to the point of zealotry. "I love you for the utter recklessness of consequences with which you adhere to what you believe to be just, and the valor with which you defend the irresistible conclusions of right reasoning," the Republican politician Matthew Carpenter told him.[4] Close friends often spoke of his exuberant charm and genuine warmth, but with less intimate colleagues he had an unctuous, self-conscious air; his letters reveal a mixture of extravagant flattery and calculated self-deprecation that can seem insecure and insincere. In the small world of Park Row, he was an easy target for his journalistic rivals, who ridiculed him for his affected accent, self-righteous politics, and unabashed self-promotion.

Indeed, Theodore Tilton had an inborn instinct for the art of networking and publicity. Despite their youth and anonymity, when the Reverend Beecher married Theodore and Elizabeth Richards in October 1855, their wedding in Plymouth Church attracted an astounding one thousand guests and a rare write-up in the *New York Times*. They were "one of the fairest pairs that I ever married," Beecher remembered. "I had strong sympathies for their future."[5]

Mr. and Mrs. Tilton cut a striking contrast. Theodore was fair, with blond locks and a strong, handsome face, and tall enough to tower over most men. Elizabeth Tilton was a tiny brunette who stood a full foot shorter than her husband. She was pretty enough, if not beautiful, with a bow-shaped mouth and large dark eyes, fringed by long lashes, which glowed with sweetness and sympathy. "Libby," as he called her, was an ideal companion to Theodore: pious, well educated, well connected, and devoted to her darling "Dory." It was through Elizabeth's family connections that Theodore landed his job at the *Independent* as assistant editor. Starting at the slim salary of seven hundred dollars a year, he did not earn enough for them to rent their own home, so they lived in a Brooklyn boardinghouse run by Elizabeth's eccentric, sharp-tongued mother.

Young Tilton, with his quick mind, progressive political views, and "epigrammatic and yet somewhat poetical style," became an instant favorite of Henry Bowen's.[6] Bowen immediately began grooming the young man to replace the aging antislavery warhorse Joshua Leavitt as managing editor. Six months later Bowen asked Tilton to serve as Beecher's unofficial assistant and ghostwriter. Over the next few years Tilton carved at least thirty "star papers" out of Beecher's sermons when the minister missed his deadlines.

Tilton was "dazzled" by the opportunity to work next to his idol. "I thought he was the most charming man I ever saw," said Tilton when asked about Beecher years later. "I loved him, sir, next to my father."[7] Tilton began imitating Beecher's dramatic writing style and appearance,

$\mathcal{P}$anoramic view of the village of Litchfield, Connecticut, from Chestnut Hill in the 1820s.

$\mathcal{L}$yman Beecher as a young minister and father in 1806.

$\mathcal{S}$alem Street in Boston's North End, where Henry played as a young teenager.

$\mathcal{H}$enry's alma mater, Amherst College, in 1830.

$\mathcal{H}$enry's high school, Mount Pleasant Classical Institution, Amherst, Massachusetts, in 1828.

*A*n unusual cartoon depicting a brawl spilling out of a one-room schoolhouse, very much like the one Henry sparked while working as a schoolteacher during college.

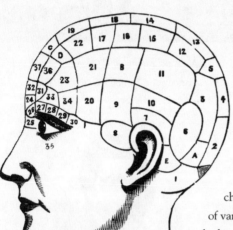

A phrenological chart showing the locations of various character traits on the human skull. This was Henry's introduction to the concept of psychology.

Names of the Faculties.

1. AMATIVENESS —Sexual love, affection
A. CONJUGAL LOVE.—The pairing instinct, oneness of affection
2. PARENTAL LOVE.—Love of offspring, and all young
3. FRIENDSHIP —Sociability, gregariousness
4. INHABITIVENESS.—Love of home and country
5. CONTINUITY. — Application, consecutiveness
E. VITATIVENESS.—Desire to live
6. COMBATIVENESS.—Defence, courage
7. DESTRUCTIVENESS.—Executiveness
8. ALIMENTIVENESS.—Appetite for food, etc.
9. ACQUISITIVENESS. — Desire to get, economy
10. SECRETIVENESS.—Self-restraint, policy
11. CAUTIOUSNESS.—Guardedness, fear
12. APPROBATIVENESS.—Love of praise
13. SELF-ESTEEM.—Self-respect, dignity
14. FIRMNESS.—Stability, perseverance
15. CONSCIENTIOUSNESS.—Sense of right
16. HOPE.—Expectation, anticipation
17. SPIRITUALITY.—Sense of the unseen

18. VENERATION.—Worship, respect
19. BENEVOLENCE —Sympathy, kindness
20. CONSTRUCTIVENESS.—Ingenuity, tools
21. IDEALITY.-*Taste*,love of beauty,poetry
B. SUBLIMITY.—Love of the grand, vast
22. IMITATION.—Copying, aptitude
23. MIRTH.—Fun, wit, ridicule, facetiousness
24. INDIVIDUALITY.—Observation, to see
25. FORM.—Memory, *shape*, looks, persons
26. SIZE.—Measurement of quantity
27. WEIGHT.—Control of motion,balancing
28. COLOUR. — Discernment and love of colour
29. ORDER.-*Method*, system. going by *rule*
30. CALCULATION.— Sense of numbers
31. LOCALITY.— Memory of place, position
32. EVENTUALITY.-Memory of facts,events
33. TIME.—Telling *when*, time of day,dates
34. TUNE.—Sense of sound, music
35. LANGUAGE.— *Expression* by words
36. CAUSALITY.—Thinking, originating
37. COMPARISON.—Analysis, inferring
C. HUMAN NATURE.—Sagacity, intuition
D. SUAVITY.—*Pleasantness*, blandness

*T*he famed Public Landing on the Ohio River in Cincinnati, Ohio.

A daguerreotype of
Henry Ward and
Lyman Beecher
in the
mid-1840s.

*L*ane Seminary,
where Lyman Beecher
served as president
and Henry studied for
the ministry.

*B*uilding of the *Indiana
Journal*, where Henry spent
many leisure hours and
edited the *Indiana Farmer
and Gardener*.

A minister being dragged from his pulpit
for preaching against slavery—Henry's great fear out West.

*B*owen & McNamee's
magnificent marble
palace for dry goods,
on Broadway near
Pearl Street
in Manhattan,
in the 1850s.

*H*enry's Presbyterian
church on Governor's Circle
in Indianapolis, well known
for its Yankee-style steeple.

*P*lymouth Church
on a typical
Sunday morning.

The view of Brooklyn Heights from Manhattan in 1851.

The view of Manhattan from Brooklyn Heights in 1851.

Henry and Eunice Beecher, around the time they moved to Brooklyn Heights.

*E*unice Beecher holding her twins Arthur and Alfred, who died in 1853, not long after this was taken. In his suppressed grief, Henry refused to look at this photo when Eunice had it framed.

*T*he Beecher family's final reunion in New York, photographed by the famed Mathew Brady in 1859. FROM LEFT TO RIGHT, STANDING: Thomas, William, Edward, Charles, and Henry. SEATED: Isabella Beecher Hooker, Catharine, Lyman, Mary Perkins, and Harriet Beecher Stowe. INSET: James and George, both of whom are believed to have committed suicide.

The *Heroes of Liberty* in the antebellum struggle against slavery, including, among others, Beecher, William Lloyd Garrison, Wendell Phillips, Theodore Tilton, and Horace Greeley.

THE UNITED STATES IN 1856

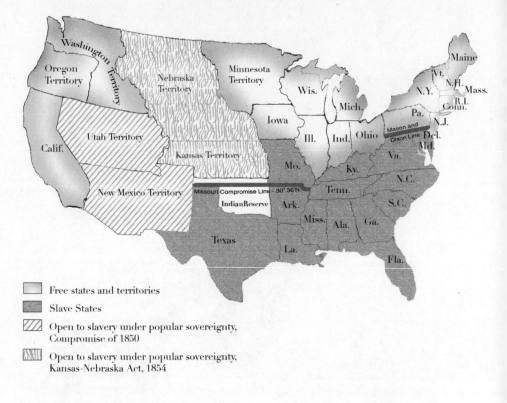

Free states and territories

Slave States

Open to slavery under popular sovereignty, Compromise of 1850

Open to slavery under popular sovereignty, Kansas-Nebraska Act, 1854

The United States in 1856, after the passage of the Kansas-Nebraska Act—slave states, free states, and federal territories.

The Freedom Ring, by Eastman Johnson. "Pinky," later known by her free name, Rose Ward, was the slave girl "auctioned" to freedom at Plymouth Church on February 5, 1860. The next day Henry took Rose to Johnson's studio to have this portrait painted of her gazing at the ring given to her to symbolize her liberty.

COL FREMONT'S LAST GRAND EXPLORING EXPEDITION IN 1856.

"*Col. Fremont's Last Grand Exploring Expedition in 1856.*" In this satire on the Republican presidential campaign of 1856, Henry carries an armload of rifles, saying, "*Be heavenly minded, my brethren all. / But if you fall out at trifles / Settle the matter with powder and balls / And I will furnish the rifles.*" Presidential candidate John C. Frémont rides an "Abolition nag" led by William Seward, U.S. senator and Republican wire-puller from New York, and sporting the face of Horace Greeley, editor of the powerful *New York Tribune*. A Kansas ruffian ridicules them.

The poetess Edna Dean Proctor in the early 1860s, not long after she coauthored a book and had an alleged affair with Henry.

"*Kansas Crusader.*" Quoting Henry's infamous pledge to send rifles to the settlers in "Bleeding Kansas": "*Well, sir, in regard to Rifles I propose to compromise. We will keep the weapons ourselves, but give you the contents.*" This is a rare image of Henry with a beard, which he sported very briefly in the early 1850s.

VOL. 7. NO. 167.

VANITY FAIR

Saturday, June 20
1863.

THEODORE TILTON

EDITOR OF THE INDEPENDENT: A YOUNG GENTLEMAN WHO MAY BE SAID TO POSSESS A BLACK EYE FOR COLOR.

Theodore Tilton in the 1860s. With his long blond locks, tall good looks, and constant crusades, he was hailed as both a romantic radical and a narcissistic zealot.

"*A young gentleman who may be said to possess a black eye for color.*" Theodore Tilton on the cover of *Vanity Fair,* whose editors delighted in mocking him as "Tilt-on" or "Slasher Tilton."

VOL. 5. NO. 122

VANITY FAIR

Saturday,
APRIL 26,
1862.

"*The Rev. Henry Ward Beecher. Taken in one of his moments of inspiration at Plymouth Church (just before the applause came in).*" Henry protested to the editors that this cover made him seem homely, while his family complained that it captured him all too well.

THE REV. HENRY WARD BEECHER.
TAKEN IN ONE OF HIS MOMENTS OF INSPIRATION AT PLYMOUTH CHURCH, (JUST BEFORE THE APPLAUSE CAME IN.)

RESIDENCE OF THEODORE TILTON.

The Tiltons' house on Livingston Street in Brooklyn Heights, where Henry was a frequent visitor in the late 1860s.

Henry Chandler Bowen, Beecher's patron and later his nemesis, in the 1860s.

"Beecher's American Soothing Syrup."
A British cartoon depicting Beecher's famous "English speeches" in 1863. Henry is feeding the British Lion a bowl of brimstone mixed with sweet treacle.

" BEECHER'S AMERICAN SOOTHING SYRUP."

Chloe Beach's husband and Henry's
good friend, Moses Sperry Beach,
in the 1860s.

Henry's close friend Chloe
Beach with her daughter
Violet in the late 1860s.
Violet Beach may have been
the illegitimate daughter of
Henry Ward Beecher.

Henry Ward Beecher
with Violet Beach in
the early 1870s.

Leading woman suffrage reformers Elizabeth Cady Stanton and Susan B. Anthony in 1870, when they became entangled in the Tiltons' accusations of adultery.

Victoria Woodhull, stockbroker, reformer, and clairvoyant, in 1872, as she was running for president of the United States and upending Henry's life.

Violet Beach as a teenager in the early 1880s.

The interior of Plymouth Church during its "Silver Jubilee" in October 1872, just before Victoria Woodhull dropped her "bombshell."

Frank Moulton and Henry, seated in a typical posture, while tearfully discussing the infamous "Letter of Contrition."

Elizabeth Tilton declares her innocence in court, only to be ignored by the lawyers and judges.

Early in the trial Elizabeth Tilton shakes hands with Henry, her alleged paramour, while his wife, Eunice, glowers in the crowded courtroom.

A rare photo of the passionate and pious Elizabeth Tilton.

"*Mr. Beecher says he d-d-doesn't believe in hell—(and then he shivers).*" A cartoon parodying Henry's conveniently timed repudiation of the concept of hell in 1877.

Cartoon quoting Henry's views on the Great Railroad Strike of 1877: "*The man who can't live on bread and water is not fit to live.*" Henry was ridiculed for the hypocrisy of criticizing the railroad strikers while living in luxury himself.

"*The Great Brooklyn Race—The Second Heat. Who will win?*" Theodore Tilton and Beecher, carrying a satchel of incriminating letters, during the Scandal Summer of 1874.

Henry Ward Beecher and Harriet Beecher Stowe in 1868 at the height of their celebrity. On seeing this portrait, Harriet's daughters were mortified by her eccentric outfit.

Henry Ward Beecher not long before his death in 1887, at the age of seventy-three.

growing his blond curls to his shoulders and taking up Beecher's trademark wide-brim slouch hat and flowing cloak.

Beecher was charmed by Tilton's untempered adoration, and soon the two were thick as thieves. They could often be seen strolling up Broadway arm in arm, poking through shops and galleries, talking of politics, paintings, books, every topic under the sun. Beecher introduced the young man around New York and encouraged his ambitions. "I had loved him much," Beecher later recalled; Theodore "seemed like a son to me."[8] As the relationship between Henry Bowen and Henry Beecher cooled, Tilton served as a buffer, earning them the nickname "Trinity of Plymouth Church."

After a decade of red ink, Henry Bowen was eager to make the *Independent* profitable. For that he needed more controversy and more advertising. Standing in the way, however, was the paper's trio of mild-mannered editors. With the secret blessing of Bowen, Theodore sent out a flurry of sycophantic letters to the leading antislavery radicals, introducing himself and inviting them to write for the *Independent*. Most refused his offer, but Theodore gained a reputation as a "fine young man," in William Lloyd Garrison's words, "who is beginning to take a vital interest in radical abolitionism."[9] By the end of 1856 Tilton was inviting Garrison himself to stay with him in Brooklyn. In 1857 he got his first taste of notoriety by attempting to "abolitionize" the Brooklyn YMCA.

Yet even as Tilton was sliding toward Garrison's more militant views, Beecher remained his first loyalty. Tilton was thrilled when Wendell Phillips invited him to make his speaking debut at Garrison's antislavery association at the May Anniversaries in 1859. But when Tilton stood to speak, it was to defy Phillips's recent attack on the minister for refusing to repudiate the corrupt American church. Why, it was Henry Ward Beecher's teachings that had made him the antislavery man he was today! Tilton protested heatedly.

ON OCTOBER 16, 1859, in a Maryland farmhouse just over the border from what is now West Virginia, John Brown, of Pottawatomie infamy, gathered together the "Provisional Army of the North." Composed of five black and sixteen white men, Captain Brown's "army" set out after dark in a wagon loaded with pistols, pikes, rifles, and broadswords. They followed the Potomac River into Virginia, then headed toward the federal armory at Harpers Ferry. By early morning they had captured the armory and rifle works and sent scouts to the surrounding plantations, hoping to ignite a spontaneous slave uprising.

John Brown's coup was short-lived. Brown had not actually told any local slaves of his plan, so his imagined backup army failed to appear. Instead, local and federal militia poured into Harpers Ferry. The battle was brief and bloody, taking fourteen lives, including those of two of Brown's sons. By dawn the following day, federal troops led by one Colonel Robert E. Lee had retaken the armory and arrested the severely injured ringleader.

Everyone on both sides of the Mason-Dixon line was stunned by the stories racing out of Virginia. This was the South's worst nightmare and most paranoid fantasy come to life. Just as Northerners had taken "Bleeding Kansas" as definitive evidence of the secret treachery of the South, the massacre at Harpers Ferry was regarded as undeniable proof that abolitionists were plotting a major slave rebellion.

North and South united in denouncing Brown as a murderer and a madman. But over the next six weeks, as Brown lay wounded in jail awaiting his singularly swift trial, the public mood began to change. The newspaper coverage of Virginia's hysteria, of Brown's dignity and calm composure in prison, and his own eloquent defense of his actions in a series of public letters and testimony, turned many Northerners from revulsion to reluctant admiration. By the time John Brown received his death sentence, the murderer had deftly recast himself as martyr.

On December 2, 1859, John Brown was hanged. In the North black crepe was hung, church bells tolled, massive protest meetings were held, prayers intoned, memorials printed, and pictures of Brown were hawked for a dollar apiece. Wendell Phillips, speaking in the Plymouth Church lecture series a few weeks after the raid, praised Brown as a revolutionary hero and called for a genuine slave revolution, as in Europe in 1848. As always Phillips was the extreme, but as the *Eagle* noted, he got more cheers than hisses from the Brooklyn crowd.

One might suppose that John Brown's selfless if foolhardy courage would appeal to Beecher's heroic aspirations. When he finally preached on Brown, he did praise the old evangelist as "Bold, unflinching, honest, without deceit or dodge, refusing to take technical advantages of any sort, but openly avowing his principles and motives, glorying in them in danger and death as much as when in security[.]" But the longer he spoke, the more uneasy Beecher seemed. Undoubtedly he was being politically pragmatic; all would be lost if Republicans were branded the party of madmen and murderers. But his discomfort went deeper. Although Henry had had nothing to do with Brown, Southerners and Democrats—even the lawyers for the defense—happily gave him a share of blame, with his "Beecher's Bibles" and call to arms. Even he might have felt that his words were turned to blood.

So it was not surprising to hear Beecher publicly disavow Brown's "mad and feeble schemes." Beecher's observation that a half-baked in- surrection would be as bad for blacks as for whites had the virtue of common sense. And his insistence that Northerners ought to look first to their own disgraceful treatment of free blacks was admirable. But Beecher's logic dissolved into a jumble of racist backpedaling when he returned to the question he once thought he'd settled: When is it right to take up arms against an oppressor? Beecher offered this startling statement:

> The right of a race or nation to seize their freedom is not to be
> disputed. It belongs to all men on the face of the globe, without
> regard to complexion. But according to God's word, so long as man
> remains a servant, he must obey his masters. The right of the slave
> to throw off the control of his master is not abrogated[.]

What, then, was the slave's path to liberty? Here his answer was even more unexpected. "It is the low animal condition of the African that enslaves him. It is moral enfranchisement that will break his bonds," Beecher said. "Teach him to be an obedient servant, and an honest, true, Christian man. These virtues are God's step stones to liberty."[10] Exactly how obedience would led to freedom, he did not say.

After Henry Ward Beecher's death it became fashionable to dismiss him as a soft-headed sentimentalist, whose Gospel of Love ignored harsh realities. But these critics misunderstand the nature and dangers of sen- timentalism. It has been said that the fundamental difference between "sentimentalism" and "realism" in the nineteenth century is that real- ists held that "the redemption of the individual lay in the social world," while sentimentalists believed that "the redemption of the social world lay in the individual."[11] For the most part Beecher was a consummate realist who preached the consolations of love precisely because he was so keenly aware of the world's inevitable pain and alienation.

But Beecher allowed sentimentalism to overtake intellectual and moral rigor in moments such as this, when he turned away in fear or uneasiness from the real-life implications of his ideals. Often he could *see* the excellent outcome—the happy homes, the free and honorable citizens, the cheerful laborers—when he could not quite pick out the path to get there. Here his remarkable ability to translate complex ideas into vibrant images betrayed him. As the *Tribune* observed after the Harpers Ferry sermon, "Mr. Beecher, when he find himself occasionally in a logical maze, is very apt to dash through the obstructions on a steed of far more eccentric paces than the regular roadster on which he approaches them. In a word, he often trusts to his feelings and his imagination to picture a truth that it would be difficult or impossible to enunciate in logical form."[12]

As the *Brooklyn Eagle* put it: "His reasonings are oftener wrong than his conclusions."[13]

Beecher's words on Harpers Ferry were widely reprinted and debated. Everyone could find something to like and to hate in his mishmash of sentiments. A *Herald* reporter smuggled a copy to old John Brown himself as he lay in jail. As Brown read through the sermon, marking up the margins, his frustrated responses mirrored Henry's mixed messages. For every *"Truth!!"* or "So say I!" that Brown scrawled, there was a "False assumption" or "Another vile assumption." By the time Beecher declared that religious education is the solution to slavery, Brown broke into open sarcasm. "Why don't Beecher come South to preach?" he jeered. "Come on, Beecher." Nonetheless Brown closed with an entirely sincere: "Amen! So says old Brown; Amen!"[14]

So readers chose their own emphases. Moderates found it, in the poet John Greenleaf Whittier's words, "the right word from the right place." Democrats delighted in Beecher's backtracking. In an editorial entitled "Mr. Beecher in 1856 and in 1859," the *Eagle* declared it a bad sign for the Republicans that Beecher should "undergo such a perfect and instantaneous transformation from the outspoken anti-slavery orator of the Frémont campaign, to a very malleable 'dough face.' "[15]

Old-line abolitionists were offended, if not entirely surprised, by Beecher's sermon. A few weeks after Brown's execution, the abolitionist writer Lydia Maria Child huffily refused Theodore Tilton's request to write for the *Independent*, citing specifically Beecher's contradictory course over the last few years. What does Beecher mean, she demanded, by "sending rifles to Kansas, and then denying that the *slaves* have a right to insurrection? I should like to know who *has* a right to fight, if the *slaves* have not? There you have, in brief, my reasons for not wishing to write for the Independent."[16]

∾ ∾

THE HARPERS FERRY MASSACRE turned out to be Theodore Til-ton's big break. While herds of reporters vied to cover the trial, Tilton snagged a genuine scoop: the only interview with John Brown's wife, soon to be a widow. Tilton's morbid good fortune continued two weeks later, when he scored a private interview with another of his heroes, Washington Irving, the grand old man of American letters. Irving died a week after the interview appeared in print, boosting interest in the young firecracker at the *Independent*.

At the tender age of twenty-four, Tilton's ambitions began overflow-ing the narrow channels of assistant editor and admiring acolyte. He leaped at any opportunity to speak in public, his poetry began appearing more often in the *Independent*, and he began a starstruck correspon-dence with England's most celebrated poet, Elizabeth Barrett Browning. After his run-in with Wendell Phillips in May, Tilton began cultivating the silver-tongued Brahmin as a mentor, and when Phillips spoke at the Plymouth Church lecture series praising John Brown, Tilton proudly introduced him.

That autumn Tilton announced his candidacy for the New York state legislature. Tilton's decision to introduce Wendell Phillips sank his prospects, but he buried his disappointment in newfound militancy. "I must tell you that the watch-word and warning, in the polls, was— 'Vote against a wild Abolitionist!'" he wrote to Phillips. "And I had the immense satisfaction of being for one brief winter's day at least!—the town-talk of all the politicians."[17]

As his reputation grew, so did Tilton's discontent. Embarrassed to still be living at his mother-in-law's boardinghouse, he decided over the objections of his wife to rent a house in Brooklyn where he could en-tertain his new friends in style. Inspired by the Come-outers who railed against the racism and hypocrisy of the American church, Theodore also began questioning his religious beliefs.

It may have been the stark contrast between Phillips's fiery defense of Brown and Beecher's cautious sidestepping. Or perhaps it was the natural disillusionment of the hero-worshipper viewing the object of his admiration up close. Whatever the cause, the more Tilton drifted toward the radicals the less impressed he was with Beecher; "as I enlarged my acquaintanceship among public men, here and there, one rose around me to a greater height than Mr. Beecher," Tilton later testified.[18]

Tilton began 1860 with a subtle blow at his old mentor. He sent a letter to Henry Bowen asking to be paid for thirty or so "star papers" he'd ghostwritten under Beecher's name—a loaded request, given the tensions between the two men. Bowen was angered to find that not only had he paid the minister for Tilton's work, but Beecher was way overdrawn on his salary.

A few weeks later Tilton openly attacked Beecher for the first time. Lewis Tappan had embroiled Plymouth Church in a dispute over whether to stop their donations to the American Board of Commissioners for Foreign Missions. For years the stodgy American Board had resisted pressure to recall its missionaries to the Choctaw and Cherokee tribes because they practiced slavery. Plymouth Church was split on the matter, so a debate was scheduled, with Henry Bowen presiding. The debate raged for five frosty evenings in January, to a packed audience. To the surprise of almost everyone Beecher passionately defended the American Board. Just as surprising, Lewis Tappan had young Tilton leading the offensive.

Beecher began affably, arguing that the Board was slowly moving toward antislavery ground, and to give it "kicks and cuffs" was "a poor reward for its conversion."[19] Far more shocking, after years of demolishing those who would try to mitigate the evil of slavery, Beecher now claimed that slavery was not inherently evil. "There was nothing bad or good *per se*," Beecher argued, applying one of his favorite concepts. "Anything bad in its consequences was bad, and vice versa, and all things were to be judged by their tendency to good or bad," as he put it.

> If in any single case a man can prove that, though he holds the legal relation of slaveholder, it is against his wish and without his moral consent; that he is doing all that the laws of the peculiar circumstances of trust in which he is placed will allow, to give his slaves their rights; and that he is preparing them for liberty and training them as free;—then we hold that this man, in so far as slaveholding is concerned, is worthy of confidence and religious fellowship.

The American Board, he argued, was now having a *good tendency*, for at least it now discriminated between good slave owners and bad slave owners. Then he fell back on his old standby: free speech. "He would not be a bigot for Antislavery," Beecher declared, according to the *New York Times*.[20] He would protect the right to self-expression for those who supported slavery just as he would protect the rights of abolitionists.

As in his Harpers Ferry speech two months earlier, his discomfort surfaced in his muddled logic. "Mr. Beecher did not treat this subject in his usual plain-spoken manner," the *Eagle* noted, "but showed rather metaphysically and obscurely that immediate emancipation was impracticable." Even more uncharacteristic, Henry went out of his way to make this "a distinct personal issue, and stated that it would be an expression of want of confidence in himself if the Church decided against the side of the question he has espoused."[21]

On the fifth day, then, when Tilton began his rebuttal, it was clear that he was not simply speaking against the Board but against Beecher personally. For nearly two hours Tilton skillfully tripped up the minister with his own words, peppering him with subtle mockery and personal gibes at Beecher's notorious inconsistency, using his disciple's knowledge, in his words, to "quote Beecher against Beecher!"

The pivotal question of the debate was one that Beecher had seemed to settle back in 1850—could a slaveholder be a Christian, allowed in Christian communion? "In 1855, Mr. Beecher would bar out the slaveholder, in 1860 he would let him in," Tilton observed.

> Wherever I go, whether in the stage, in the railroad cars, in the ferryboat, or on foot up and down the streets, I am perpetually accosted with the question: "Is the Pastor of Plymouth Church changing his views? Is Mr. Beecher becoming more conservative?" I have always answered these salutations with an emphatic No; and until Monday night I always believed No. But what am I to say if my friend puts up the bars in 1855, only to let them down in 1860?

Then Tilton dramatically unfurled a map of the Nebraska Indian territory. There the Board would allow slavery, and yet it had been saved for freedom by the agitation of the North. "And who was it that saved it?" The audience stared as Tilton picked up a lumpy green sack and pulled out a Sharps rifle. "I wish to remind Mr. Beecher how he helped to make Kansas a free state."

The room exploded with applause. Someone called out, laughing, "Is it loaded?"

"No! Only with an argument," shot back Tilton, to more laughter. "It is not; and it has done good work in Kansas, having been 3 months in the possession of John Brown," he added, to more applause, frayed with hisses. "I ask him to remember his heroic appeals of '56, and now," said Tilton.[22]

Tilton's pyrotechnics were brilliant, but he won no converts among the Beecherites. After a raucous vote Beecher's side won handily. Publicly Beecher insisted that his views had not changed, but privately, he told his friend Emily Drury, "It seems very queer to me to be on the side of *hold back*. I always knew that I was largely conservative when the time should come."[23] Why this was so he did not say.

The small, gossipy world of New York journalism took note of the conflict between Beecher and his protégé, and the new humor magazine *Vanity Fair* parodied the pugilism of "Bully Beecher" and "Tilton Slasher." Now everyone was speculating on Beecher's conservative turn. Some blamed pressure from the church's wealthy merchants, anxious about losing their Southern trade. Others credited their own editorializing and speechifying for bringing the preacher to right. Perhaps, still others suggested, Beecher was held hostage by the plans for a massive new six-thousand-seat church, out of fear of alienating conservative donors. For several years the project had languished, dogged by rumors of internal conflicts.

Odd confirmation of this theory came a few months later, when the trustees, in Beecher's absence, refused to allow Wendell Phillips to lecture again in the church, citing just that reason, according to Tilton. When Tilton told Beecher of the decision, the minister publicly denounced the trustees for their cowardice. A few days later, after several trustees resigned, Beecher retracted his angry accusations, explaining lamely that he had been misinformed, that the whole thing had been a mistake of technicalities. Clearly *something* was bedeviling Henry.

One week after the brouhaha in Plymouth Church, Beecher stood on the stage of Manhattan's new Cooper Institute (later renamed the Cooper Union) next to Lucy Stone and Robert Dale Owen, two of America's most famous radicals, to demand the vote for women—the most ultra of isms, by many lights!

Two days later the minister held another mock slave auction in Plymouth Church.

Nine-year-old "Pinky" was being sold by the man who was likely her father, a Virginia physician who traded Pinky's mother and sisters downriver but gave in to her grandmother's tearful pleas that he send the girl north to be bought by Mr. Beecher's church. The congregation went wild as Beecher brought the flaxen-haired girl onto the platform, throwing more than $1,000 worth of cash and jewelry into the collection boxes. As he drew the scene to a close, Henry plucked a delicate ring from the pile, donated by one of his literary lady friends, the author Rose Terry, and placed it on the little girl's finger, saying, "Now remember that this is your freedom-ring."

Beecher was so charmed by this image that the next morning he took the girl to the Manhattan studio of Eastman Johnson, the famed genre painter, who painted Pinky gazing in awe at her "freedom ring." Others were more cynical. She was so light-skinned that the *New York News* declared her a hoax, a free white girl come to con the congregation out of their money. Meanwhile, the *Eagle* derisively observed that the pandering preacher had "quite regained the confidence of the ultra portion of his congregation whose faith in him had been somewhat shaken by his recent outspoken conservative views on slavery."

Whatever Henry feared, it was not the hobgoblin of foolish consistency. As the *Tribune* remarked disapprovingly, lately Brother Beecher "seems to us to savor of unusual eccentricity."[24]

On February 8, 1860, three days after her husband's sensational "slave sale," Eunice took seven-year-old Herbie out for a morning drive. Eunice had become awfully independent of late. She drove herself everywhere and spent much of her time up in Peekskill running Beecher's "gentleman's farm." She held the family purse so tightly that Henry was shocked to discover he needed her signature to write a check—after that he kept his lecture fees in a separate account as his own "pin money." Still, Eunice did not share her husband's new taste for women's rights. "What is the ability to speak on a public platform of the wisdom that may command on a judge's bench compared to that which can insure and preside over a true home?" as she put it.[25]

Eunice was driving down Hicks Street when a noise sent her skittish young horse galloping onto the sidewalk, overturning the chaise and dashing them onto the stone steps of the Long Island Bank on Fulton Street. Herbie suffered only bruises, but Eunice landed face and shoulder first, knocking her unconscious. The evening papers reported that she was near death. So Plymouth Church folks were surprised when the pastor appeared at the Wednesday prayer meeting later that evening. As they crowded around asking about his wife, Henry responded impatiently, "It would have been serious with any other woman."[26] Harsh but true. Eunice would soon recover.

If Henry seemed distracted, however, he had good reason. Besides that unpleasantness with Miss Proctor in December 1859, rumors were now swirling around the Heights about his relationship with Chloe Beach. In the last several years his friendship with Moses and Chloe Beach had blossomed into an intimacy that eclipsed other friendships. While Henry appreciated Moses's generosity and good humor, it was Chloe who, as one church member put it, exercised a "powerful influence with Mr. Beecher."[27]

Moses Sperry Beach met Miss Chloe Buckingham in 1843, when he was twenty-one and she was a sixteen-year-old orphan from a good Connecticut family. "I consider her as quite plain looking—almost homely in the common acceptation of the term," Moses confided to his diary after meeting her, "but in an intellectual point of view she appears extremely bright. Although she has seen little of the world she is well informed and highly intelligent and her plain looking features are quite overlooked in dwelling upon her glowing intellect. Apart from this she is elegant, tender, modest and confiding and seems to posses many if not all the good qualities of an affectionate wife." Although initially put off by her uninspiring appearance, Moses soon found "something so substantial, so heartful" about her that "my *first impressions* were speedily worn away and the rhapsody in which I indulged while describing them appeared as it does even now, extremely laughable and ridiculous."[28]

The girl's quiet graciousness and moral earnestness seemed to wreathe her plain features with an angelic glow. "She seldom talked," recalled one of Chloe's admirers, "she spoke to the point, a sentence at a time. She never fussed, yet nothing escaped her."[29] Moses married Chloe in the fall of 1845 and soon proved to be an unusually affectionate and kindhearted family man, who delighted in spoiling both his children and his beloved wife.

Moses and Chloe had been married for about five years when they began crossing the river to hear Beecher preach. Both were Episcopalians, but while Moses enjoyed Beecher's progressive ideas, Chloe couldn't help feeling these trips "to be sinful and wrong," in her husband's words. In 1854 Moses moved the family to Brooklyn Heights and joined Plymouth Church. He soon became a good friend of the pastor and a major benefactor of the church. As his relationship with the Bowens cooled, Henry began to spend more time in the Beaches' elegant brownstone—made easier by the fact that Chloe, unlike many women, went out of her way to be kind to Eunice. Eunice grasped gratefully at Chloe's quiet affection and discreet generosity.

Not long after moving to the Heights, Moses began to notice in his wife, "though with a careless eye, the existence of a warm regard for you," he later wrote to Henry. Knowing of Chloe's religious reservations, "I smiled, inwardly, at the little evidences of regard for you which were from time to time manifested. They will soon pass by, I reasoned, and my happiness remained undisturbed." But those unmistakable signs of infatuation "did not pass by. They increased and strengthened and finally I was being taken captive."[30]

Moses was not the only one who noted their growing closeness. Eunice noticed, but she was so touched by Chloe's kind attentions to *her*, that her natural jealousies were disarmed. But in the hothouse of Brooklyn Heights, inevitably others would mark how free Beecher was in the Beaches' house.

"Often he came in the evening, letting himself in with a latchkey, and went down the hall into the library unannounced and he might remain there thinking or reading by himself for hours. He came frequently to escape from guests in his own house; he was pursued by cranks and enthusiasts and men with axes to grind," recalled Mary Hallock Foote, a friend of the Beaches' daughters:

> He might and occasionally did fall asleep over his reading and not wake till after midnight. It might occur when no one ever knew that he was there, but if it were known it was understood; it was deemed a compliment to the library and an honor to the house that he should use it as if it were his own. But if you were a Quaker lady from the country, sitting up perhaps with a sick person in one of the opposite (and opposition) houses on that block, and saw Mr. Beecher, that unmistakable figure, let himself out of Moses Beach's house hours after the house was dark, you thought it "strange" and if you were something of a gossip, as many Quaker ladies were, you mentioned it to a friend in awed whispers—and Quaker ladies were not the only gossips: Mr. Beecher laid himself open a hundred ways; he was the center of legend in a world not made of angels.[31]

Moses watched in agony as his wife fell more and more under the spell of her pastor. Finally he could stand it no longer. "Absence for a time will remove the cause I then reasoned," recalled Moses. So in 1860 he quietly made plans to sell the *Sun* and move out of Brooklyn, to an estate on the Hudson River near Poughkeepsie.[32]

For some time now, said Henry Bowen, the leading men of the

church had been "troubled about the extremely suspicious relations of Mr. Beecher with certain ladies of the church. It was a matter of common talk, and excited the gravest apprehensions." By early 1860 "so serious were the reports, so extreme seemed the danger that half a dozen leading members met on Sunday and deputized one of them to call on Henry Ward Beecher and tell him about the rumors frankly."

The next day the gentleman returned to Bowen and told him "that Mr. Beecher was greatly embarrassed at what he had to say, and acted, as it appeared to him, like a guilty man. He also said that Mr. Beecher promised that there should be no further occasion for such scandal, and that he would use his influence to have the lady remove to a distant part of the country. This gentleman said that he earnestly advised Mr. Beecher never to admit or deny anything on this subject but to be absolutely silent."[33]

The Sunday after Eunice's accident Henry delivered a truly strange sermon. Again he preached on his belief that it is far worse for one's soul to be an uncharitable judge than a weak-willed sinner. But this Sunday he spoke with a bitter tone unheard before, as he worked up to a furious crescendo, picturing packs of vicious hyenas hunting down a public man for a single moment of weakness. "Revenge is almost invariably cloaked under the guise of moral indignation," he thundered.

> But multitudes of men collect every particle of such filth, and treasure it up, as a soil out of which revenge is to grow. They lie back, they note down and remember, they read up the account frequently, and ponder a settlement with full interest. If the day delays, yet patience, oh my soul, it will be all the sweeter when it comes! At length the victim trips with a public downfall. Instantly the air is full of poisonous speeches, flying in a myriad swarm, to cover the wretch and sting him to madness!

Then, abruptly, Beecher lurched to the point of view of the public man's victim, spinning a gothic vision of the public man as "seducer."

> Playing upon the most sacred affections, he betrays innocence. How? By its noblest faculties; by its trust; by its unsuspecting faith; by its tender love; by its honor. The victim, often and often, is not the accomplice so much as the sufferer, betrayed by an exorcism which bewitched her noblest affections to become the suicides of her virtue! The betrayer, for the most intense selfishness, without

one noble motive, without one pretense of honor—by lies; by a devilish jugglery of fraud; by blinding the eye, confusing the conscience, misleading the judgment, and instilling the dew of sorcery upon every flower of sweet affection—deliberately, heartlessly damns the confiding victim! [. . .]

Surely, society will crush him. They will smite the wolf, and seek out the bleeding lamb. Oh, my soul! Believe it not! What sight is that? The drooping victim is worse used than the infernal destroyer! He is fondled, courted, passed from honor to honor! And she is crushed and mangled under the infuriated tramp of public indignation. On her mangled corpse they stand to put the laurels of her murderer's brow! When I see such things as these I thank God that there is a judgment and that there is a hell![34]

The sermon was so vivid, yet so uncharacteristic, that it stuck in people's memories. "The Seducer," as it came to be known, would return to haunt him.

TWO WEEKS LATER, on Saturday, February 25, Henry Bowen lingered in his office at the *Independent*, finishing up the week's business before the Sabbath. A rap was heard at the door. Expecting a messenger boy, Bowen said "Come in" without looking up.

A voice asked with hesitation, "Is this Mr. Henry C. Bowen?" Absorbed in his writing, Bowen replied yes, but still he did not lift his eyes from the paper.

"I am Abraham Lincoln."

Bowen swung around. "I faced a very tall man wearing a high hat and carrying an old-fashioned, comical-looking carpet bag," Bowen recalled. "His clothes were travel stained and he looked tired and woebegone, and there was nothing in my first hasty view of the man that was at all prepossessing." Abraham Lincoln was, to speak plainly, a homely man with deep-set gray eyes, hollow, weatherbeaten cheeks, and a sharp brow topped by wiry black hair. With his battered black stovepipe hat, he was nearly seven feet tall.

Bowen had never met Lincoln before, although his dry-goods firm had once retained the attorney on a legal matter out West. "My heart went into my boots," Bowen remembered. *This* was the man the Plymouth Church Lecture Series had invited to speak?

"Mr. Bowen, I'm just in from Springfield, Illinois," said the stranger, "and I am very tired. If you have no objection I will lie on your lounge here and you can tell me about the arrangements for Monday night."

What the merchant had to say, Lincoln already knew. To take the White House, Republicans needed a candidate who could draw the border states that had gone to the Democrats in 1856. New York's William Seward was the obvious front-runner, but he suffered from an undeserved reputation as a radical abolitionist, and strong local opposition, led in part by Bowen's brother-in-law Hiram Barney. In 1858 Abraham Lincoln had garnered a national reputation as a moderate antislavery Republican during a series of debates with the infamous Illinois senator Stephen Douglas. He was invited to New York in the hope of discovering the perfect alternative to Seward. "No event in his life had given him more heartfelt pleasure," Lincoln told a friend, than the invitation from the Plymouth Church Committee.[35]

As he watched the ungainly stranger splay his long legs over the couch, Bowen scrambled for words. "I felt sick at heart over the prospect," recalled Bowen, "and could not greet my visitor with any warmth of manner although I tried very hard to suppress any manifestation of my thoughts."

The merchant explained that the venue had been changed from Plymouth Church to the Cooper Institute in Manhattan in hopes of attracting a larger audience. As they talked Bowen began warming up to his visitor's gentle, unself-conscious dignity. When Lincoln rose to leave, Bowen invited him to join his family at church services the next day. Although Lincoln was not much of a churchgoer himself, his wife was a subscriber to the *Independent,* and his law partner, William Herndon, was an avid fan of Henry Ward Beecher—it would hardly do for him to leave New York without seeing the famous preacher.

The next day Lincoln followed the crowds across the river to the church and made his way to Bowen's pew. The Illinois lawyer had missed the big show two weeks before, when Beecher auctioned a slave girl out of bondage. By contrast, that Sunday's sermon was staid, and his introduction to Beecher afterward unmemorable.

After the service Bowen asked Lincoln to join his family for dinner, but as they started up the imposing front steps of Bowen's mansion, the awkward westerner stopped abruptly. "Mr. Bowen," Lincoln said with some agitation, "I guess I will not go in."

"My good sir," Bowen replied in surprise, "we have arranged to have you dine with us, and we cannot excuse you."

"Now, look here, Mr. Bowen, I am not going to make a failure at the Cooper Institute tomorrow night, if I can possibly help it," Lincoln replied. "Please excuse me and let me go to my room at the hotel, lock the door, and there think about my lecture." With that, Lincoln turned and headed back to the ferry.[36]

The next day Lincoln sat for a portrait at the studio of the famed photographer Mathew Brady before heading over to the Cooper Institute. On the dais sat an array of Republican bigwigs: the lawyer David Dudley Field; the poet and editor of the *Evening Post*, William Cullen Bryant; Horace Greeley of the *Tribune*; John A. King, the former governor of New York; and—surprisingly—Theodore Tilton, once again exhibiting his remarkable talent for attaching himself to important people. Beecher was not there.

Abraham Lincoln stepped out under the gaslights, shifting uncomfortably in his ill-fitting new suit. "The first impression of the man from the West did nothing to contradict the expectation of something weird, rough and uncultivated," recalled one audience member.[37] As Lincoln began to speak, stumbling a bit, in his thick western accent, recalled another listener, "I said to myself, 'Old fellow, you won't do; it's all very well for the wild West, but this will never go down in New York.' "[38]

Within moments, however, Lincoln's awkwardness disappeared. "His eye kindled, his voice rang, his face shone and seemed to light up the whole assembly," recalled another observer. "For an hour and a half he held the audience in the hollow of his hand." Lincoln's speech was vehement in tone but moderate in policy. Republicans had no wish to stir up slave insurrections or forcibly remove slavery from where it already existed, he insisted vigorously. But make no mistake, nothing would ever satisfy the South except "this, and this only: cease to call Slavery *wrong* and join them in calling it *right*." He ended with a ringing call for courage: "Let us have faith that right makes might, and in that faith, let us, to the end, dare to do our duty as we understand it."[39]

The audience went wild, stomping feet, throwing hats in the air, frantically waving handkerchiefs. Dignitaries crowded the platform to shake hands with this remarkable orator from the West. Newspapermen gave the speech banner coverage. Horace Greeley published the full text in the *Tribune*, then distributed it as a campaign pamphlet, illustrated by Mathew Brady's photo. Within days Lincoln was swamped with telegrams from New England inviting him to speak before he returned to Illinois. Lincoln accepted, delivering nine speeches in twelve days—what Greeley called "the most systematic and complete defense yet made of the Republican position with regard to slavery."[40]

Ultimately Lincoln's speech at the Cooper Institute turned the course of the election. Five months later at the Republican convention, the New England states threw their support to the "prairie statesman," awarding Lincoln the presidential nomination over William Seward. "Brady and the Cooper Institute made me president," declared Lincoln.[41]

Coming through New York after finishing his ad hoc speaking tour of New England, Lincoln stopped again at Plymouth Church, quietly slipping into the gallery after services had begun. One of the ushers took note of this odd-looking stranger. "As Mr. Beecher developed his line of argument, Mr. Lincoln's body swayed forward, his lips parted, and he seemed at length entirely unconscious of his surroundings—frequently giving vent to his satisfaction at a well-put point or illustration, with a kind of involuntary Indian exclamation—'ugh!'—not audible beyond his immediate presence, but *very* expressive!"[42]

Francis B. Carpenter, the artist who famously chronicled his six months in the White House spent painting President Lincoln's portrait and eavesdropping on his conversations, said that Lincoln more than once expressed "profound admiration for the talents of the famous pastor of Plymouth Church." Lincoln once remarked, said Carpenter, that "he thought there was not upon record, in ancient or modern biography, so *productive a mind* as had been exhibited in the career of Henry Ward Beecher."[43]

THE FORTUNES OF THE POLITICAL PARTIES had reversed since 1856. Now the Republicans stood united behind a moderate candidate while the Democrats disintegrated into sectional factions. The Southern fire-eaters made no secret of their desire to split the Democratic vote and hand victory to the Republicans, which would then force the South to secede. When the Democrats nominated Senator Stephen Douglas for the presidency, the southern wing of the party bolted. Taking the name "National Democrats," they nominated Vice President John C. Breckinridge of Kentucky, as the secessionist candidate. Pro-Union Southerners nominated John Bell, a slaveholding senator from Tennessee, under the banner of a new "Constitutional Union Party."

This time the Republicans tried to minimize the slavery issue, but in the South there was only one issue: disunion. Most Southerners had no desire to secede, but nearly all believed that a Republican victory would unleash a tidal wave of violence and political repression in the

South. In the North, "doughface" conservatives frantically responded by calling for federal protection of slavery to save the Union, while Horace Greeley and some militant abolitionists cried "Let the South go!" But for most Northerners, the Slaveocracy had played the disunion card too often for it not to seem like a bluff.

Henry Ward Beecher actively supported Lincoln, but he never warmed to the homespun westerner as he had to the handsome and heroic but much less astute John C. Frémont. Beecher's tastes no longer ran to the rustic after a decade in New York. Besides, Henry seemed preoccupied. When he wasn't preaching politics, his sermons had a melancholy, even morbid air. As he told the Howards in March, "more this winter than ever before, I think I have had a *sense* and premonition of the end. I do not mean that I really expect to die early, but only that life seems to me more than ever void, brief, and of little worth, relatively."[44]

His sense of foreboding lingered through August, when Moses Beach sold the *Sun* and promptly left Brooklyn. Beecher gave a rousing speech at the farewell dinner, but as soon as they left, he checked himself into a water cure in upstate New York for several weeks—something he'd never done before.

As election day drew closer, the South's warnings grew more apocalyptic, drawing panic from New York's mercantile community as stock prices plunged. Thousands jammed the steps of Plymouth Church the final Sunday before the election, hoping for a spectacle of political fireworks. They were not disappointed. Beecher loudly mocked those who believed the Union would be torn in two. "Some dear timid men will say, Oh! My! What *will* happen? What will happen! Well, I'll tell you—" here Beecher leaned forward, putting both hands on his knees, his eyes sparkling. "Well, I'll tell you—NOTHING!!"

A murmur went up in the audience. "Oh! Why don't you run home, jump into your cradles and let your grandma's rock you?" Beecher snapped. "For shame, let babies fear fairy tales and run from the Black Douglas—but let not *men* act so. Take my word for it—all the barking will be done before the election and there will be no biting afterward."[45]

Henry's optimism was only half right. The Slave Power had overplayed its hand. Lincoln carried all eighteen free states except New Jersey, giving him a clear majority of electoral votes. In Democrat-dominated Manhattan, Lincoln claimed only 34 percent of the vote, but he got a respectable 43 percent in Brooklyn. "The power of the slave-interest in Washington is broken," proclaimed the ecstatic *Independent*, and "the crisis is over."[46]

The joy was nearly as great in the Palmetto State. Long before election day South Carolina's politicians had vowed to leave the Union if Lincoln won. Now liberty was at hand. "The tea has been thrown overboard; the revolution of 1860 has been initiated," declared the *Charleston Mercury*.[47] On December 20, after a decade of blustering threats, South Carolina seceded. Mississippi, Florida, Alabama, Georgia, and Louisiana soon followed. One week before Lincoln took the oath of office, Jefferson Davis, former senator from Mississippi and U.S. secretary of war, was inaugurated as president of the Provisional Government of the Confederate States of America.

That winter panic reigned. New York's mercantile community, facing ruin if the South defaulted on its debts, begged for new concessions to King Cotton. Manhattan mayor Fernando Wood proposed, unsuccessfully, that New York City secede to form its own independent state. As business plummeted, the abolitionists again became the scapegoats. Several times police were called to Plymouth Church, after rumors that Beecher would be mobbed. Talk of assassination was so loud that Lincoln's inaugural train to Washington was sent by a secret route to foil attacks.

While New York was hysterical, Washington was paralyzed. Congress frantically tried to appease the slaveholders, but it was too late. Emboldened by President Buchanan's inaction, the Rebel states began seizing federal forts and arsenals. One of the last garrisons to retain federal troops was Fort Sumter on the South Carolina coast, the heart of "secesh" country. Without more supplies the troops would be starved out.

The country waited breathlessly to see what the new president would do. Abraham Lincoln faced a nearly impossible task. While the upper North demanded that he use full force to crush the rebellion, he had to avoid antagonizing the border states of the upper South, which still remained, tenuously, in the Union. If war was inevitable, however, he wanted the South to fire the first shot. Lincoln ordered unarmed federal troops to resupply Fort Sumter and then he informed the Confederates, explaining that federal warships would enter the harbor only if the supply ships were attacked. The Rebels opened fire on the fort on April 12 at 4:30 in the morning. Thirty-four hours later Union forces surrendered their flag. The bloodiest war in American history had begun.

The next day Lincoln issued a proclamation calling for 75,000 volunteers for ninety days to put down the insurrection. Two days later

Virginia voted to secede—joined by Texas, Tennessee, Arkansas, and North Carolina—and offered Richmond as the new capital of the Confederacy. Of the slave states only Delaware, Maryland, Kentucky, and Missouri remained in the Union.

The attack on Fort Sumter galvanized the North. All talk of appeasement evaporated, replaced by patriotic indignation. Recruiting offices opened overnight, red-white-and-blue bunting blossomed on buildings, and mass meetings seemed to spring up spontaneously. Once again New York City reversed course, raising $150 million for the Union cause in three months and sending more volunteers than any other city. In Brooklyn mobs now marched on the *Eagle* and other Democratic papers, forcing them to hang American flags to prove their loyalty.

Henry Ward Beecher was in Cincinnati, preparing to lecture, when he heard of Sumter's fall. Fearing riots, the lecture committee tried to cancel, but Beecher persuaded them to go on, declaring that he'd speak in the street if forced to. But fear ran so high that almost no one showed up.

Back in New York, Beecher's nineteen-year-old-son, Harry, dropped everything when he heard the news and headed home. On the way Harry stopped impulsively at an army recruiting station and enlisted, before catching the ferry to Brooklyn. He must have kept this a secret, for when his father returned, Eunice forbade him to leave the house afraid that he would sign up. The moment Beecher stepped through the door, young Harry blurted: "Father, may I enlist?"

"If you don't I'll disown you," replied Beecher.[48] Clearly Eunice had no say in the matter.

Henry was energized, even elated, by the rebellion. "War at last! It could be no other way," he wrote to his friend Emily Drury. "When men fall among wolves, it is not with the *men* to say whether there shall be peace."[49] He had prayed this day would not come, but now that it had, his only regret was that he was too old to fight.

"So far as I myself am concerned, I utterly abhor peace on any such grounds. Give me war redder than blood and fiercer than fire," he told his congregation the first Sunday after Sumter fell. "The War is terrible, but that abyss of ignominy is yet more terrible."[50]

The North labored under a number of obvious disadvantages. Politically Lincoln walked a narrow tightrope between the upper North's rage to crush the traitors and the border states' reluctance to take up arms against their neighbors. One false step and whole swaths of the Midwest might throw down their arms or join the Confederacy.

Lincoln was also hamstrung by the federal government's military unpreparedness. In 1861 the U.S. Army had only fifteen thousand soldiers, most without battle experience, and was dominated by Southern officers, many of whom defected to the Confederacy. The procedures for calling up new troops were Byzantine. Private citizens recruited volunteers, elected officers, gathered resources (volunteers supplied their own horses and basic supplies), and then presented their potential regiment to the state governor for approval and mustering. The state then offered the regiment to the federal government for inclusion in the military campaign. These new recruits had no military training, lacking even the basic discipline of following officers' orders.

But no matter—everyone knew that the Rebellion would be smashed by summer. There were so many eager volunteers aching to see battle that the new secretary of war, Simon Cameron, was turning away entire regiments. When Plymouth Church boys were unable to get into the oversubscribed New York regiments, Beecher began recruiting his own regiment, the First Long Island or Sixty-seventh New York Volunteers—the "Brooklyn Phalanx," as it was known, or, more derisively, "Beecher's pets." His son Harry was elected second lieutenant in the regiment, and Beecher donated or raised the money for the regiment's supplies, including rifles, bowie knives, blankets, and other sundries. When Secretary Cameron refused the regiment, saying he had no need for more soldiers, Henry personally went to Washington and got it accepted.

While hotheaded young men worried that the war would end before they saw fighting, the abolitionists were equally worried that the war would end before slavery was vanquished. Both fears were dashed on July 21 at the Battle of Bull Run, Virginia, the first major assault of the war. After suffering terrible casualties, the poorly trained Union soldiers turned and fled, leaving eight hundred men dead. The humiliation at Bull Run sobered and divided the North. Voices ranging from Horace Greeley to the governors of Kentucky and Ohio abruptly called for an armistice. Lincoln's fragile coalition was already fraying.

But Beecher's faith was unshaken. Bull Run "is that humiliation which shall teach us not to rely so much on words and cheers and newspaper campaigns. A defeat just sufficient to make us feel that we must fall upon the interior stores of manhood," he assured his congregation.[51] Henry's complaint was that Lincoln was being too cautious. The way to crush the Rebellion was through an immediate, aggressive show of power.

Although fearful for her son, Eunice shared her husband's zeal. She led the church ladies in making bandages, knitting socks, sewing uniforms, and sending packages to the "Plymouth boys." On occasion Plymouth Church pews served as makeshift beds for regiments passing through New York on their way to the front. Beecher's home became a storehouse for military goods and a place to hear the latest news from Washington.

Trouncing the Confederacy was not the same thing as emancipating the slaves, of course. Beecher loudly insisted that it was a battle to liberate America from slavery, but he was in a minority. An even smaller number of abolitionists argued that as commander in chief in a time of war, Lincoln could free the slaves under the rubric of military necessity. Most foes of slavery, including both Beecher and Lincoln, believed that emancipation by presidential decree would be struck down by the federal courts.

But the major barrier to emancipation was not legal but political; if this became a crusade to free the slaves, the loyal slave states and large portions of the North would be lost. Here Lincoln's ranking of priorities was crystal clear. "My paramount object in this struggle *is* to save the Union, and is *not* either to save or to destroy slavery," he told Horace Greeley. "If I could save the Union without freeing *any* slave I would do it, and if I could save it by freeing *all* the slaves I would do it; and if I could save it by freeing some and leaving others alone I would also do that."[52]

After Bull Run, though, the slavery question suddenly seemed more urgent. Was this blood sacrificed merely to preserve a coalition of state governments? Why preserve the Union at all if it did not stand for something noble?

The best hopes and worst fears of the abolitionists were confirmed a month after Bull Run. General John Frémont was in charge of the Department of the West, headquartered in St. Louis, Missouri. Frémont chose Tasker Howard's son, John Raymond Howard, and his nephew, Rossitor Raymond, to serve on his staff, and he asked Tasker, unofficially, to help him acquire badly needed supplies. Officially Missouri was loyal, but it was riddled with Confederate sympathizers. Hoping to excise this festering cancer, on August 30, 1861, General Frémont issued a proclamation freeing all bondsmen owned by Missouri citizens who resisted the U.S. government. Antislavery forces were wild with joy. But Missouri's slaveholders and the other loyal slave states furiously demanded its retraction. Blindsided by Frémont's unilateral act, Lincoln asked the general to rescind the proclamation. When Frémont refused, Lincoln countermanded it himself.

The backlash from the antislavery sympathizers was swift and severe. Petitions, letters, memorials, resolutions, and editorials denounced Lincoln's capitulation. Yet Henry Ward Beecher did not join them. His personal sympathies lay with Frémont; indeed, Frémont's proclamation was written by the hand of John R. Howard, who considered it a personal tribute to Beecher's years of agitation. When Lincoln stripped Frémont of his command in November—due to his continued insubordination and to complaints about unorthodox military contracts with cronies like Tasker Howard—Henry invited Jessie and General Frémont to Plymouth Church, where he honored them in a rousing sermon.

But at the same time Beecher was indirectly but profitably bound up with patronage of the Lincoln administration through Henry Bowen and his power-broking brother-in-law Hiram Barney. Although he rarely asked for anything for himself, Beecher was constantly making introductions and seeking favors on behalf of friends and parishioners. In the fall of 1861, as Frémont was being ousted, Beecher's interest in Lincoln's good graces suddenly became much more personal. Beecher's son Harry, stationed outside D.C., was caught in a serious moral infraction and dismissed from his regiment in disgrace. His "crime" was hushed up, but judging by his mother's reaction, it likely took place in one of Washington's notorious bawdy houses, where booze, prostitutes, and politicians mingled freely.

Theodore Tilton came to Beecher's rescue. When Beecher finished telling Harry's shameful story, Tilton asked for Henry's pocketbook, took out fifty dollars, and caught the next train for D.C., where Tilton wangled an interview with Secretary of War Cameron. He returned with a commission for Harry in the federal Army of the Potomac. The minister wept tears of gratitude, according to Tilton, but Eunice was furious at Theodore: first for keeping her son in harm's way, and later for bragging incessantly about it, at Harry's obvious expense. After this, Tilton claimed, Eunice barred him from the house whenever she was home.

Whether it was Beecher's gratitude for his son's commission, or his own natural prudence, his Thanksgiving sermon was an enthusiastic endorsement of Lincoln's cautious path. "We who boast of our Constitution must not violate it ourselves in putting down those who violate it. We must not by congressional legislation declare political emancipation. I wish we could. I wish Adam had not sinned," he added; "but that does not change the matter." Yet Beecher was certain that the destruction of war would bring about emancipation, even if was not yet clear how. "What legislation cannot do, the sword can and will do."[53]

As usual the abolitionists were baffled by Henry's conflation of strict legalism, vulgar politics, and pure faith, while Henry's foes gloated over anything that got the goat of the abolitionists. "I see all the pro-slavery journals are copying his ill-timed, ill-digested, absurd, and practically pro-slavery sentiments, with 'thanksgiving,' " wrote Garrison in outrage.[54]

Ralph Waldo Emerson tried to persuade Beecher to change his views. "I said it is our business to write the moral statute into the Constitution, and give the written only a moral interpretation," the philosopher wrote in his journal after their conversation.

" 'Tis very well for you and me to say this in lectures, but, when it comes to practice, we can only go to the Constitution," Beecher responded. "We might have bought our land with a different line, or ought to have bought more, or less; but all this is foreign to the subject, we have only to refer to the deeds."

Emerson considered the point. "I answer: Any right of land from written deeds is an imperfect right,—a right only of agreement and convenience; but the right to freedom is a perfect right, and any invasion of it noxious to human nature, and invalid therefore."[55] It was a peculiar combination—Beecher's almost naïve reverence for the power of the written document and the way he routinely broke or reinterpreted any rule that didn't suit him. It would not always serve him so well.

IT WAS HARD TO MUSTER much gratitude that Thanksgiving. New York was economically devastated by the coming of the war. The number of coastal ships coming into port was cut in half, and the dry-goods industry was nearly destroyed when southern customers reneged on $160 million of debts, sending hundreds of firms into bankruptcy. Plymouth Church was especially hard hit, with so many of its members in the dry-goods and shipping businesses. In January 1861, at the height of the secession crisis, Plymouth Church's trustees decided to abandon plans for a huge new church, selling the lots they'd already purchased at a substantial loss. Publicly, they blamed the stagnant economy and the ballooning cost of construction. Privately, however, Henry Bowen laid the blame on the minister.

From the beginning the project had been fraught with conflict. Beecher quarreled with the trustees over the location—they wanted the most economically advantageous spot to get a good return on their investment, but Beecher insisted on a more prestigious (and expensive) plot on Montague Street near the Wall Street ferry, where the spire of the new church would be visible in Manhattan. Beecher won that battle.

Moses Beach and Henry Bowen had been the prime backers of the project until Beach moved away. Bowen agreed to lead the fund-raising on the condition that the minister would personally accompany Bowen and the other trustees on their appeals until every last penny was received. Bowen and Beecher set off, raising pledges of nearly thirty thousand dollars on their first foray. The next day he was to accompany another trustee, but Beecher never showed up. Week after week Beecher put off the unpleasant task of dunning the donors, until war broke out and the project fell through, at a loss of almost twenty-five thousand dollars to the early investors. "It was enough to make even an angel provoked to have any kind of business with Mr. Beecher," as Henry Bowen's son later testified.[56]

By now Bowen had a long list of grievances against the pastor. His financial diary over the last decade was scrawled with angry comments, noting each time Beecher reneged on his financial commitments. In May 1861 Bowen discovered that, behind his back, Beecher was telling everyone that Bowen owed him money. In retaliation the merchant notified Beecher that he owed him the hefty sum of five thousand dollars, most of it spent on supplies for the Brooklyn Phalanx, and demanded that Beecher retract his slanderous statements. Beecher then threatened to withdraw from the *Independent* altogether. Facing open warfare, they agreed to let a mutual friend arbitrate the matter.

But Bowen could no longer contain his rage. Crossing on the Brooklyn ferry with Theodore Tilton one day, Bowen's secret spilled out. Beecher is an adulterer, Bowen told his astounded assistant editor, and he had enough proof to drive the preacher out of Brooklyn any time he chose. "From that time onward your references to this subject were frequent, and always accompanied with the exhibition of a deep-seated injury to your heart," Tilton later reminded Bowen.[57]

Yet—and many would later find this strange—neither Tilton nor

Bowen said a word to Beecher. Money seemed to motivate the silence. By December 1861 Bowen and McNamee were heading toward bankruptcy. Bowen was determined to make the *Independent* the cornerstone of his financial recovery. It had steadily grown in subscribers and influence, especially among the middle classes, who were the core of the Republican Party. Now that Republicans held the purse strings of power, Bowen could use the *Independent* as leverage to get his hands on New York's profitable political spoils.

In the mid-nineteenth century, before civil-service reform defined it as corrupt, spoilsmanship was considered a legitimate, even crucial, part of politics. In New York's bustling port, the spoils were particularly rich. Henry Bowen had strong ties to the Lincoln administration through Hiram Barney, an early backer of Lincoln who shrewdly lent Salmon P. Chase a substantial sum of money just before Chase was made secretary of the treasury. Secretary Chase rewarded Barney with the best patronage plum in the country—the job of collector of the Port of New York (second in power only to postmaster general). Barney now controlled millions of dollars in fees, taxes, contracts, and jobs. Every ship that entered the harbor passed under his authority, creating abundant opportunities for personal profit. But the patronage game worked both ways, with government employees expected to kick back money and support to the party in power. It wasn't hard for Barney to make the case that Bowen, as publisher of an influential Republican sheet, should share in his good fortune.

That December, as bankruptcy loomed, Bowen signed over ownership of the *Independent* to his father-in-law, in a successful effort to elude his creditors. He also used this tactic to force the resignation of the paper's stodgy coeditors, Bacon, Thompson, and Storrs, who were resisting Bowen's and Tilton's efforts to jazz up the paper. But Bowen couldn't afford to lose Henry Ward Beecher. If he left or, as the rumors had it, started a rival religious journal, the *Independent* would die a quick death.

By the time Lewis Tappan handed the paper back to Bowen in January 1862, the hardheaded publisher had made his most surprising decision yet: He invited Beecher to become the editor in chief. Just as surprisingly, Beecher agreed, on the condition that Theodore Tilton would be elevated to assistant editor, to relieve Beecher of all the day-to-day editorial work. It should have been a win-win-win situation, with each man getting what he longed for.

As they say, there's nothing more dangerous than getting what you want.

～ ～

As 1862 entered Lincoln was determined to make a fresh start. After the disaster at Bull Run, General George B. McClellan—a proslavery Democrat but an organizational genius—had taken command of the bedraggled Army of the Potomac. In a matter of months he whipped 150,000 untrained boys into a disciplined fighting force. But as 1861 wore on, General McClellan seemed strangely reluctant to send his well-polished army into harm's way, engaging only in a series of indecisive skirmishes. The Union's apparent weakness fed the political ambitions of its foreign rivals, and the possibility that England might offer diplomatic recognition and military aid to the Confederacy was rising with every setback.

Lincoln began 1862 by firing Secretary of War Cameron, replacing him with a vigorous if ill-tempered Ohio attorney, Edwin Stanton. In the Treasury Department, Secretary Chase initiated two controversial proposals to refill the empty government coffers: a raise in federal taxes and a national system of paper currency. At the end of January, frustrated by General McClellan's unaccountable caution, Lincoln directly ordered the military to launch an aggressive coordinated attack on the Confederacy.

By February 1862 the Union's fortunes were looking up. Out in Tennessee, General Ulysses S. Grant won the Union's first significant victory, opening a corridor into the Confederate heartland. Admiral David Farragut led an assault up the Mississippi River, conquering New Orleans, the gateway to the Mississippi. Then on April 6 forty thousand Rebel soldiers surprised General Grant at Shiloh, Tennessee. Grant's forces held the field, but the price of victory was beyond belief. Out of sixty-three thousand Union soldiers, thirteen thousand perished, as did eleven thousand Confederates. Desperate parents and wives crowded around New York's newspaper offices waiting for the casualty lists to be posted, in shock at the bloody toll.

Back on the eastern front, McClellan still lingered in his winter camp, oblivious to the demands of Congress, the press, and the president that he make a move. After much badgering by Lincoln, McClellan's one hundred thousand men headed into Virginia, getting as far as Yorktown by May 4. But when they were turned back at Williamsburg, McClellan lost his momentum. Mired in Virginia, still unscathed by battle, young Harry Beecher was exasperated. "The more I desire to participate in a battle the more remote seems the prospect," he complained to his parents.[58]

These Union victories, such as they were, forced the fate of the slaves into the open air. As federal troops recaptured territory in the South, thousands of slaves seized their freedom, slipping behind Union lines or simply staying put as their frightened owners fled. What should be done with them? For antislavery folks the answer was obvious: To send slaves back to serve the Confederacy was both morally and militarily absurd. Opponents argued that the government was legally bound to return this legitimate property. General Benjamin Butler offered a temporary solution, declaring liberated slaves the "contraband of the war," like a horse, rifle, or other military tools that could legally be confiscated from enemy combatants.

Politically Lincoln was in a hard spot. To advocate wholesale emancipation might torpedo the fragile war coalition at a time when the administration was desperate for fresh recruits. At the same time the receding hope of easy victory strengthened the hand of those who believed that emancipation would strike a fatal blow to the Confederate war effort.

In March 1862 Lincoln called for Congress to award financial aid to any state that adopted gradual emancipation, with compensation to slave owners. Abolitionists dismissed it as an empty gesture, but the *Independent* called it a "masterly stroke." "No more crutches, no more staves and bandages, no more stimulants or medicines," gloated Beecher. "Slavery must lie in its own filth and find remedies for its own diseases. Its bounds are fixed. It cannot travel for its health."[59]

Meanwhile a core of "Radical Republicans," as they were becoming known, pushed a series of antislavery measures through Congress. In March they prohibited military officers from returning fugitive slaves. In April they abolished slavery in the District of Columbia, and at Lincoln's request they pledged money to any state that undertook gradual, compensated emancipation. In May, Major General David Hunter, commander of the Department of the South, issued an order freeing all slaves in the recaptured areas of South Carolina, Georgia, and Florida, and began recruiting them as soldiers. And in June, Congress prohibited slavery in all U.S. territories.

Back at the *Independent* the "Trinity of Plymouth Church" was making its own fresh start. Putting aside the tensions of the last few years, Theodore Tilton, Henry Bowen, and Henry Ward Beecher were transforming the *Independent*. Dry doctrinal essays and sectarian screeds were replaced by fresh, lively editorials on the burning topics of the day, especially politics. Tilton did most of the heavy work, but he and Beecher shared the task of writing the unsigned lead editorials. After so many years of working together, their styles were nearly indistinguishable. Soon new subscriptions were pouring with in with every mail.

The two were as close as they'd ever been, and Henry confided in the young man. The preacher "used to pour in my ears unending complaints against his wife, spoken never with bitterness, but always with pain," Tilton recalled. "He said to me one day, 'O Theodore, God might strip all other gifts from me if he would only give me a wife like Elizabeth and a home like yours.' "[60] Small wonder that Eunice so disliked Theodore. But he was a brilliant protégé, and Beecher delighted in his precocity. "We have here the most brilliant and eloquent young man I have ever known," Beecher told a lecture committee that winter. "An original thinker, and a fervent and electric speaker—and he's one of my chickens!"[61]

Tilton's feelings were more conflicted. He basked in Henry's affection and was jealous of his other intimacies. He often urged the preacher to visit him at home, in part as a mark of pride, in part to please his wife, Elizabeth, who was awestruck by the pastor. "He would often speak in extravagant terms of his wife's esteem and affection for me," Henry recalled. "He urged me to bring my papers down there and use his study to do my writing in, as it was not pleasant to write at the office of the *Independent*."[62]

Yet as the months passed, doing all the work while Beecher got the credit no longer seemed like such a lucky break. And then there were Bowen's vague but insidious accusations. "As I grew older and mingled with the world and saw other men, the fine gold of my idol gradually become dim," Tilton later put it. "I saw that he was not the greatest man in the world, nor the pleasantest man in the world, nor the frankest man in the world."[63]

The *Independent* was swiftly becoming one of the most influential papers in the country. Bowen captained the financial page, making it a billboard for Secretary Chase's policies on greenbacks and taxation, while Tilton and Beecher filled the editorial page with praise for Lincoln's policies. Given free reign, Bowen, who was secretly maneuvering to be appointed to the lucrative post of collector of internal revenue for the city of Brooklyn, would have turned the paper into Lincoln's house organ. Tilton would have tied it to the rising Radical wing of the Republican Party. But Beecher's moderation ruled the editorial page.

Beecher supported the president's cautious proposals for gradual emancipation, his diplomacy in Europe, his calls for more soldiers and more taxes, and kept up a steady drumbeat of confidence in the Union cause. Even when, at the end of May 1862, Lincoln reversed Major General Hunter's edict of emancipation in deference to the protests of Kentucky and the other loyal slave states, Beecher remained sanguine.

"The president moves deliberately, and will only act as he is compelled," Beecher responded; "but when compelled he will use all the power of this Government—the strongest Government in the world—to exterminate their rebellion, root and branch."[64] In the *Independent's* opinion, the war would be over by September.

BUT BENEATH HIS PROFESSIONAL OPTIMISM Beecher seemed troubled. In January 1862 Chloe Beach returned to Brooklyn Heights, only sixteen months after moving to a grand estate on the Hudson River. Publicly her husband, Moses Beach, said they returned because the new owners of the *Sun* went bankrupt. But privately, Moses wrote in a sorrowful letter to Beecher, "the new home had no charm and most evidently—as I saw from a thousand indirect manifestations—because you were not there. One excuse and another were found to get back to the old spot—to get back to you."[65]

But if Chloe's return brought Henry pleasure, it did not show in his sermons, which again sank into melancholy. "I think that the attempt in this life to build a character upon moral sensibility and conscientiousness is an attempt to build a hell on earth," Beecher mused in February. Worse yet, Beecher was realizing that he'd made a terrible mistake in accepting the editorship of the *Independent.* Whether or not Beecher knew of Bowen's suspicions, the tension between the two men had become intolerable. The job, as Eunice noted, was making him "at times irritable and peevish to a strange degree."[66] On May 16 he resigned as editor, giving Bowen six months' notice.

Bowen responded with a conciliatory note. "In the relations which now exist between us, there is no want of cordiality, respect or sympathy," he entreated Beecher. "If we either of us make one or two or 'seventy times seven' mistakes, if we have the right spirit we shall forgive each other and work on for God and humanity."[67] Beecher seemed placated, but a month later he was even more desperate. Just as things were mounting to a crisis, the crush of history once again swept Henry's personal troubles under the rug.

In May 1862 the engine of emancipation stalled. The newspapers told of fresh outrages: of slave catchers roaming the streets of Washington, D.C., seizing the runaways (and random blacks) who flooded in once slavery was abolished; of the military governor in the recaptured zone of North Carolina who disbanded the new "contraband" schools in deference to the old state law forbidding the education of blacks.

Things were even worse in the field. In June the increasingly impatient president again prodded McClellan into action. For seven days the two armies clashed around Richmond. With their superior numbers the Yankees hammered the Rebels, but at the last moment, instead of pursuing them into the Confederate capital, McClellan ordered a retreat, insisting that he didn't have enough men to press on. A week later Lincoln issued a call for three hundred thousand more volunteers, but this time there were no crowds at the recruiting stations. This meant a draft.

After these bitter reversals, the *Independent* abruptly changed tune. "The Government seems to us to be in the position of men who don't know what to do, and are afraid that the people will find it out," Beecher now wrote. "Mr. Lincoln is good man: a consistent, prudent, honest politician. But not a spark of genius has he; not an element of leadership, not one particle of heroic enthusiasm."[68]

In August, for the first time, Beecher went on record demanding *"immediate and universal emancipation!"* Until then he'd seen no way out of the constitutional impasse, *"But slavery has become a military question. One year has changed all things."* Abolition, he wrote, "would push away at one stroke a thousand hindrances, give simplicity and unity to our plans, and distinctness to our policy. It would end all threat of foreign intervention. Above all, it would give to the American armies that pillar of smoke by day and fire by night by which God the Emancipator led forth his people from bondage to liberty."[69]

Week after week that summer, the *Independent* pounded away at Lincoln. Someone—probably one of Bowen's patronage rivals—stuffed the harsh editorials in an envelope and mailed them to the president. One rainy Sunday, Lincoln took them from his desk. "One or two of the articles were in Mr. Beecher's strongest style, and criticized the President in no unmeasured terms," recalled the artist Francis B. Carpenter, who was painting Lincoln's portrait at the time. As Lincoln finished reading, his face flushed with indignation. "Dashing a packet to the floor, he exclaimed, 'Is thy servant a *dog,* that he should do this thing?'"

"The excitement, however, soon passed off, leaving no trace behind of ill-will toward Mr. Beecher; and the impression made upon his mind by the criticism was lasting and excellent in its effects," recalled Carpenter.[70] Despite his eccentricities Beecher was a bellwether. If he was saying it, plenty of people were thinking it.

It was becoming increasingly clear to the president that emancipation was inevitable, for both political and military reasons. On July 12 Lincoln summoned a delegation of border state politicians to plead once again for them to accept his offer of compensated emancipation. They dismissed Lincoln's appeal, haughtily reminding the president to "confine yourself to your constitutional authority."[71]

A week later, Lincoln announced to his cabinet that he had decided to issue a preliminary Emancipation Proclamation, on his authority as the commander in chief in a time of war. The shocked silence was broken only by a few tentative comments. Finally Secretary of State Seward suggested that the proclamation be delayed until the Union forces had some sort of military success, so that this would not seem like a gasp of desperation. The president agreed.

But he would have to wait some time for a victory.

WHEN BEECHER RETURNED from his annual summer vacation at the end of September 1862, he studiously avoided the offices of the *Independent*. He continued to write some of the lead editorials, but now Tilton's more militant views dominated the paper.

On September 17 Confederate forces led by the former U.S. colonel, now Confederate general, Robert E. Lee invaded Maryland only fifty-two miles from Washington, D.C. After a day of ferocious fighting McClellan turned back the Rebels, but allowed them to retreat unmolested back into Virginia. The battle at Antietam was the bloodiest day in U.S. history, claiming more than twenty-three thousand lives in all. It would be the last Union victory in the East for a long while.

This was all Lincoln needed. On September 22 the president served notice that on January 1, 1863, he would declare "then, thenceforward, and forever free" all slaves in states still in rebellion. Loyal slave states and any Rebel states that returned to the Union would be exempt from this edict, and he pledged support for gradual, compensated emancipation in loyal states and the colonization in Africa of former slaves. With one rhetorical stroke Lincoln swept aside the constitutional barrier to abolition.

"I have been in a bewilderment of joy ever since yesterday morning," Theodore wrote to William Lloyd Garrison. "I am half crazy with enthusiasm! I would like to have seen whether *you* laughed or cried on reading it: *I* did both."[72] Privately Garrison, like most of the abolitionists, thought it a feeble halfway measure that might yet be derailed, but publicly almost all agreed that it was a great victory.

Opponents of the administration savagely attacked it as an act of unconstitutional tyranny and predicted an epidemic of violent slave uprisings. In fact there was little more legal standing for Lincoln's Emancipation Proclamation than there had been for Frémont's or Hunter's, but the press of war now dwarfed such objections. Certainly it was enough to quell Beecher's objections. Now, he assured the people, we will have "the *Union as it was meant to be*. A Union so perfect that you shall lay it on the Constitution and it shall not anywhere bulge or shrink away."[73]

But still the *Independent*'s criticism did not end. Honest, Abe might be, but by the *Independent*'s lights, "The country is going toward disunion and toward despotism, because one of the most honest men that ever held the Presidential chair is not a man of affairs."[74] The editorials were so vitriolic that Beecher's siblings wrote to him, "with great pain," urging him to ease up.

"At a time when we need all the elasticity, all the vigor and courage that mortal men can feel, you are doing all you can to discourage and weaken, you make every man's heart lead in his bosom," his sister Mary wrote. Harriet implored him to come with her to Washington, to speak to the president himself, "and see if you can't throw out a few notes of encouragement."[75]

Henry's brother Tom, who was recruiting soldiers up in Elmira, New York, told Henry he didn't blame Lincoln for ignoring Beecher's advice. "I am satisfied that the day you succeed in writing your magnificent principles on our national banner, you will have only a flag and a sentiment; the army, the men with one consent will say, 'We ain't going to fight for the Niggers,' " Tom wrote. "You remember Indiana. Do you soberly think that those fighting Hoosiers would hurry to enlist for the sake of freeing the slave? Will negro hating Illinois that now gives nigh half her men to the war, consent to fight for the slaves she despises? I can answer for rural New York. The more emancipation you talk, the less recruits you can enlist."[76]

Tom was right. Among antiwar Democrats Beecher's name was a synonym for warmongering, self-serving, disunionist demagogue, often strung with other abolitionist names into a single epithet used to designate all "nigger lovers." On Thanksgiving, when he offered Plymouth Church to a regiment of soldiers from Maine who had nowhere to sleep, vandals slathered the front of Beecher's house with a dark mixture of "lampblack, petroleum oil, liquid nastiness and odorous filth."[77]

But Henry had stood too long in the public whirlwind to heed such threats. When he heard that the president had complained of the *Independent's* harshness, he was pleased. Henry "thinks it capital both as showing that he reads them and that the arrow is well directed," his sister Isabella told her husband.[78]

Henry Bowen, on the other hand, immediately wrote to Lincoln, dissociating himself from the minister's essays. "I have frequently of late regretted the appearance of Editorials censuring you, but it was out of my power to do anything," Bowen told Lincoln. "If once the proprietors should attempt to control the Editors, as far as Henry Ward Beecher is concerned, there would be another 'rebellion.' "[79]

Despite his cool facade, Henry had never felt so low. His sermons were filled with long disquisitions on the mysterious promptings of the unconscious and the secret desires that plague the best people. Henry was so strangely preoccupied that he forgot to write to his daughter when she gave birth to his first grandchild that fall. "I have been swamped with work, even for me, and many things have troubled me," he told Eunice. "I confess to more fear than I have ever had, and, fear is not apt to be my state of mind."[80]

THE SUSPENSE HAD GROWN UNBEARABLE over the last two months. Would the president go through with the Emancipation Proclamation? On New Year's Day President Lincoln spent several hours shaking the hands of well-wishers and then slipped off to his office and laid out the proclamation. When he picked up his pen, his hand shook so badly that, "I paused and a superstitious feeling came over me which made me hesitate," Lincoln said later. Was this a divine sign that he was making a mistake? Then he remembered "that I had been shaking hands for hours, with several hundred people." Slowly he formed his signature, then gave a quiet laugh, and said, "That will do."[81]

Across the North that evening, huge crowds gathered anxiously to await word. Hours passed, orators droned, but still no news. Finally the telegraph brought the glorious tidings—it was done. Lincoln's proclamation freed only those slaves in states still in rebellion, leaving slavery untouched in the border states and many Union-occupied areas, but all references to financial compensation or colonization had disappeared. "The proclamation may not immediately free a single slave," Beecher wrote, "but it gives liberty a moral recognition."[82]

That same day, recalled Theodore Tilton, "on the first of January, 1863—Mr. Lincoln's immortal day—the negroes were emancipated from their bondage and Mr. Beecher was emancipated from his editorship. The first of these events was celebrated by the *Independent* with joy and rejoicing; the other was not even so much as whispered by its columns to the passing breeze."[83] Under Beecher subscriptions had risen to a spectacular 70,000, twice that of any other religious weekly by their own estimate. No need to mention that Tilton was taking the reins.

That New Year's Day Bowen was too ill to make the traditional round of visits. From his sickbed he sent a brief note to the preacher, wishing him a happy new year. That evening Beecher replied.

> My Dear Bowen,
> Your words go right to my heart. I feel the love which I had the first eight years of our intercourse—and may God grant that it may beat again—and forever without intermission! One of these days, when you shall have been assured of my affection for you, I may have some things to say in explanation of things to you strange— but not now.
> With the new year will you take my heart and hand and pledge of a brother's love? I say the truth before God, if their dark passage be again illumined with full confidence, it will take from my heart a load which I have borne with many sighs. [. . .]
> I am, with true love,
> Your old friend, Henry Ward Beecher[84]

Whatever Beecher intended, Bowen felt triumphant. Finally here, Bowen would later insist, was the preacher's confession and repentance! For what *strange things* did Beecher mean, if not adultery?

LYMAN BEECHER DID NOT JOIN the celebration on that historic New Year's Day. Over the last several years, the old man had slowly succumbed to senility. When the family gathered at Henry's house for a reunion in 1859, Lyman was still cognizant enough to pose for a family photo in Mathew Brady's studio. But by the beginning of the war, he no longer recognized the faces of his beloved children. Lyman would sit in

Plymouth Church listening to his son with confused admiration, saying, "I never expected to sit in a pew and hear myself preach."[85]

Over Christmas 1862, Lyman slipped into a sort of coma, waking occasionally to take a little broth. In a rare lucid moment as death beckoned, he called to his stepdaughter as if she were his best-loved first wife, Roxana: "Mother, mother, come and sit beside me; I have had a vision of heaven. I think I have begun to go. Oh, such scenes as I have been permitted to behold! I have seen the King of Glory himself."

"Did you see Jesus?" she asked. But Jesus Christ was the passion of a younger generation. Lyman's eyes were trained higher.

"All was swallowed up in God himself," he choked out.[86]

When the doctor warned that the end was near, Henry stopped at the telegraph office to cancel his engagements for the week, then went around to Lyman's house on Willow Street. "As he stepped in the door," Eunice told her daughter Hattie, "grandfather's last breath went out so peacefully and quietly that no change was apparent save that one could see that no other breath followed the last, not a quiver or gasp or contraction of any muscle. Nothing could be gentler."[87]

"The old oak finally fell," said Henry, on January 10 at the rare old age of 87.[88]

Lyman Beecher's legacy was complex. In his later years Lyman admitted that perhaps the religious training of his children was "not the best." Looking over six decades of family letters, Catharine sadly observed, "What anxiety, perplexity, disappointment and agonizing fear are there recorded on the part of the father, and what suffering and vain efforts on the part of the children!"[89] By the time of his death, not one of the children could be called a good Calvinist.

Yet Lyman remained undaunted to the end. In one of his last public moments, standing in the comfortable gaslit lecture room at Plymouth Church, he stuttered at first, then gathered steam. "If God should tell me that I *might* choose—that is, if God said that it was *his* will that I *should* choose whether to die and go to heaven, or to begin my life over again and work once more, *I would enlist again in a minute*."[90]

EARLY ON THE MORNING OF MARCH 25, 1863, the Bowens discovered that Lucy Bowen was dying. Lucy was only thirty-eight years old, but after giving birth to her tenth child a month before, her body seemed simply to wear out. Her soul slipped away at 9:30 A.M. The Reverend Beecher arrived soon after and led the weeping family in prayer.

The following Sunday, Beecher was visibly shaken as he baptized Lucy's newborn baby and then led her funeral service. Lucy Bowen had been his first friend in Brooklyn, and "no calamity outside of his own family, he said, could come so near to him as the death of this Christian woman." Later that night, as he delivered his regular Sunday-night sermon, Beecher seemed exhausted and stopped several times to apologize, finally concluding, "you cannot trust men; but do not distrust God. Man's love is blurred with selfishness: there is not a seam in the love of God."[91]

In their shared grief, it seemed that Lucy's death might wipe away the strife between Bowen and Beecher. Not long before her death, they settled their longstanding financial dispute, with Beecher paying a reduced claim of one thousand dollars. On April 2, the day Beecher's obituary for Lucy appeared in the *Independent*, Bowen wrote the minister a grateful letter, referring pointedly to their recent reconciliation.

"From that time until I went into the country, I scarcely saw Mr. Beecher to speak to him. He appeared to avoid me, to be afraid of me. He seemed always conscious of guilt in my presence," Bowen later recalled. "I made no allusion to the past when I met him, and was always cordial, but here seemed to be a great guilt between us." When Bowen retreated to his house in Connecticut that spring, "I was struck through with the belief that Mr. Beecher was not to be trusted, and I was more and more afraid that his repentance was not sincere."[92]

It was now obvious to everyone that Beecher was depressed. Three weeks after Bowen's letter the Plymouth Church trustees held a special meeting to discuss Beecher's low state. They voted unanimously to send him to Europe, all expenses paid, and then walked over to Beecher's house to surprise him with the news. Beecher agreed on the spot.

"His trip will be mainly for recreation," the *Independent* reported, but still the gossip mill churned. Some whispered that the government was sending him on a secret mission, for diplomacy or espionage, but as Beecher joked, after his criticism of Lincoln no one would send him anywhere. Listening to his final farewell in Plymouth Church, one might be forgiven for thinking that Beecher was mortally ill, as he dwelled on his recent premonitions of death. He wasn't sick, Henry said later, "but certainly I was jaded."[93] On May 30 more than eight hundred friends and parishioners, accompanied by a huge brass band, gathered to see Beecher off—frustrating Eunice, who longed for a private, romantic good-bye.

With Beecher gone, Theodore Tilton stepped into the limelight as editor of the *Independent*. He enticed Wendell Phillips, Frederick Douglass, and William Lloyd Garrison to contribute to the paper, and courted relationships with powerful politicians like Senator Charles Sumner, Massachusetts governor John A. Andrew, and Secretary Chase. He edited a volume of Elizabeth Barrett Browning's poetry (writing such a self-aggrandizing introduction that reviewers ridiculed him) while churning out his own poetry, heavy on the heroic couplets.

Tilton was almost giddy with his new fame. He seemed as delighted when he was caricatured on the cover of *Vanity Fair* as when he was quoted in the *New York Times*. He spent the summer publicly urging Lincoln to call a national draft, but when he himself was drafted in July, he paid three hundred dollars to a Prussian soldier to take his place at the front. He caught hell for his hypocrisy, but even this seemed to please him. "I have been so abused for being drafted that I have come to possess a *national reputation*!" Theodore wrote to Henry. "But out of the dung of abuse I hope to blossom like a lily!"[94]

Beecher's tour through Italy, Switzerland, Germany, France, and Belgium served as a tonic to his shot nerves, although depression settled on him in quieter moments. But up in Woodstock, Connecticut, Henry Bowen remained mired in anger at Beecher. In June, Bowen poured out his feelings to Tilton.

> When I think of the continued troubles in Brooklyn, of those which will surely be more severe, in all probability, my heart sickens. I sometimes feel that I must break silence, that I must no longer suffer as a dumb man, and be made to bear a load of grief most unjustly. One word from me would make a revolution throughout Christendom, I had almost said—and you know it.

"You have just a little of the evidence from the great volume in my possession," Bowen concluded. "I am not pursuing a phantom, but solemnly brooding over an awful reality."[95]

Tilton shared none of this with Beecher, however, and neither did Bowen. When the preacher wrote him a long, warm letter from Europe, the merchant responded with yet another plea for reconciliation. For, as Bowen wrote, "not a moment have I ever seen when I have not loved you as I have never loved a man on earth before." And yet, he added, "I cannot help saying that I have been a bereaved, sorrowing, and tongue-tied sufferer for nearly six years, but never have I by act or word injured a hair of your head. Your reputation was even as dear to me as my life, and I have been willing to wait God's time for a lifting of the clouds."[96]

Ten years later both Tilton and Bowen would insist that he was referring to Beecher's infidelity. Others would seize upon this letter as evidence that Beecher had seduced Lucy Bowen. Both Theodore Tilton and Henry Bowen vehemently denied this, but by then there had been so many vague accusations and ominous threats that no one knew what to believe.

WHEN BEECHER LEFT FOR EUROPE, critics taunted him for abandoning the nation in its lowest depths. In the first six months of 1863, the Rebels scored a string of brilliant victories, lowering the North's already low morale. Desperate for more soldiers, Lincoln called a draft that summer, sparking vicious antiblack riots in New York. But the manpower and resources of the Confederacy were dwindling. If the Yankees stayed the course, they could eventually outlast the South. This made Europe the pivotal factor; if they threw their weight behind the Rebels, all bets were off. England had sworn neutrality in the conflict, but economic pressures were pulling it Southward. The "cotton famine" caused by the Union blockades had thrown thousands of Manchester's textile laborers out of work, while Liverpool's shipbuilders were secretly supplying the Confederate navy with warships. Were this a moral war against slavery, the British government would have been hard pressed to act against the North, but Lincoln's wavering robbed Washington of that diplomatic leverage. Jealous of America's rising power, and impressed by the military might of the Rebels, England seemed to be on the verge of intervention.

When Henry arrived in Liverpool, he was met by eager lecture committees, entreating him to speak on behalf of the Union cause. Uncharacteristically, Beecher refused all invitations. His self-protective instincts were dead on. As he traveled, he found Europe teeming with self-exiled Southerners and their aristocratic sympathizers, who behaved abominably to Beecher and his friends. To speak now would court humiliation.

But over the Fourth of July the war took a dramatic turn. On the eastern front, Robert E. Lee's second invasion of the North was turned back at Gettysburg, Pennsylvania. In the West the Rebel defeat at Vicksburg, Mississippi, gave Ulysses S. Grant control of the Mississippi River, effectively cutting the Confederacy in two. Suddenly, Henry noted, all those arrogant Southern exiles were nowhere to be seen. Bursting with patriotic energy, Beecher now agreed to end his trip with a two-week speaking tour through Manchester, Glasgow, Edinburgh, Liverpool, and London.

Conditions were not auspicious. After twenty weeks of vacation—the longest he'd gone without speaking since the 1830s—his throat was out of shape, and already his opposition was organizing mobs to shout him down. At his first speech in Manchester, Henry was escorted past hostile crowds and bloodred posters violently denouncing him, into a huge hall packed with furious people, hissing, shoving, pounding feet and waving umbrellas. "I have seen all sorts of camp meetings and experienced all kinds of disturbed meetings in New York City, and they were all of them as twilight to midnight compared with an English hostile audience," said Henry later.[97]

Right after his introduction as "the Reverend Henry Ward Beecher Stowe," the audience began its barrage. Henry tossed aside his intended speech and focused on the reporters seated in the front, saying, "It will be in sections, but I will have it connected by-and-by." Tailoring his speech to Manchester's industrial base, he was explaining how using free rather than slave labor creates American consumers for English goods when his eye drifted toward the back of the room, where "a large, burly, red-haired, red-whiskered man was sitting, who was particularly vociferous, shouting, clapping his hands, pounding his feet, and throwing himself back in his chair."

Twenty minutes into the tempest, the red-haired man threw himself back so violently that he burst through the door behind him and tumbled down the stairs outside. Beecher burst into loud, spontaneous laughter. The astonished members of the audience turned to look and began to laugh themselves. Beecher deftly interjected a joke, then grabbed their attention with a pithy story, and soon he had smooth sailing. "I was never more self possessed and never in more perfect good temper," said Henry afterward.[98]

The shipbuilding center of Glasgow was less openly violent, but still the jeers were so loud that he declared he would "sit down and rest until they got the hissing over with." Again he threw out his speech, speaking in volcanic bursts punctuated by heckling. There he shamed the working-class audience for building ships to cast down those who earned their living by the sweat of their own brows rather than the backs of others.

"We don't sympathize with slavery, but we go for the South because they are the weaker party," one Scotsman called out.

"Go, then, and sympathize with the devil—he was the weaker party also when he rebelled and was turned out of heaven," Henry hooted.[99]

After this the press began to soften toward Beecher, admiring his pluck if not his arguments. Edinburgh was relatively civilized, but "Liverpool was worse than all the rest put together," said Henry, requiring a brace of bodyguards. "I thought I had been through *furnaces* before," he wrote to Tilton. "But this ordeal surpassed all others."[100]

Back in London, Beecher's speeches were the talk of the men's clubs and newsrooms. By the time Henry returned to America in late November, it was clear that England would remain neutral, cutting off all arms shipments to the Confederacy. Beecher was hailed as the hero who had turned the tide for the North. "It is no exaggeration," said the *New York Times,* to say that these five speeches "have done more for our cause in England and Scotland than all that has been before said or written."[101]

Others, like Charles Francis Adams, America's minister to England and the son and grandson of two presidents, scoffed at this claim, noting that the British government's decision was certainly not based on popular opinion, especially in a country where the vast majority of men could not vote. The preacher modestly agreed, rightly attributing England's reversal to the military victories at Gettysburg and Vicksburg. "It was my happy fortune to be there to jar the tree," he noted. "The fruit that fell was not of my own ripening."[102]

True enough, but any farmer would testify that timely picking makes all the difference between a rich or rotten harvest. Beecher's speeches revealed how divided were British attitudes toward the United States since the Emancipation Proclamation, making it harder for the Southern-sympathizing aristocracy to enact pro-Confederate policies. No less an authority than Robert E. Lee, according to his aide Roger Pryor, believed that were it not for *Uncle Tom's Cabin* and Beecher's speeches, the Confederacy would have secured diplomatic recognition by England and France, whose material and moral aid would have tipped the war to the Rebels.

President Lincoln agreed, telling his cabinet "that if the war was ever fought to a successful issue there would be but one man—Beecher—to raise the flag at Fort Sumter, for without Beecher in England there might have been no flag to raise."[103]

～ ～

WHATEVER ELSE THEY ACCOMPLISHED, Henry's British speeches swept him to international fame. New York welcomed Beecher home with a series of massive receptions, the literary lions of Boston feted him in their clubs, and in Washington politicians like Secretary of War Edwin Stanton aggressively cultivated his friendship. Stanton sent him regular telegrams with the latest war news—a valuable favor when the public was so starved for information from the front. There was even talk of sending Beecher to the U.S. Senate.

"Pray for me," he told his congregation, "not so much that I shall have strength for outward work, as that I may not be seduced from the work of the ministry, that I love nothing better than this work."[104]

As Henry was basking in the glorious noon of his career, the war was entering its bloodiest phase. General McClellan was long gone, replaced by General Grant, who was leading a steady push to Richmond, while General William Tecumseh Sherman's forces were marching into Georgia. In the seven weeks between May 5 and June 30, 1864, more than 61,000 Union soldiers died. After years of longing for decisive action, the citizens of the North were sickened by its costs.

On the home front, however, New York City was booming. The city plowed its capital, ingenuity, and industrial might into the war effort, giving birth to what would later be called the military-industrial complex. Brooklyn was particularly prosperous, laying claim to both the Brooklyn Navy Yard, which built the Union's steam engines, "ironclad" warships, and its first submarine, and the early pharmaceutical industry, churning out bandages, splints, ether, and artificial eyes and limbs. Brooklyn's factories produced millions of cheap boots, uniforms, blankets, tents—much of it "shoddy" work that fell to pieces on the field, while minting new millionaires back in Brooklyn Heights. Plymouth Church, said the *Eagle* in disgust, was a citadel of this nouveau-riche "Shoddy Aristocracy."

Hoping to exploit the racist fears raised by emancipation, several Copperhead reporters seized on an 1863 speech by Theodore Tilton that suggested that mingling white and black blood would create a more powerful nation. They coined a new term—"miscegenation"—for the old fear of interracial sex, and then printed up hoax publications to make it seem as if antislavery Republicans were promoting "the beastly doctrine of miscegenation." By March, observed the *Brooklyn Eagle*, "All leading men and journals are ranging themselves on either side in the battle between decency and lust."[105]

Meanwhile a growing number of Radical Republicans, frustrated by Lincoln's halfway measures on slavery, began secretly searching for an alternative candidate. A Massachusetts faction was pushing General Frémont, while a cabal of New Yorkers, including Horace Greeley and Theodore Tilton, was secretly promoting Treasury Secretary Salmon P. Chase. It was a dangerous business, ousting a sitting president from his own ticket during wartime, especially for Henry Bowen, who depended upon government patronage delivered through Chase but awarded ultimately by Lincoln. But Bowen allowed Tilton to go ahead. Although an admirer of both Frémont and Chase, Beecher wisely kept himself out of this internecine battle.

It was well that Beecher maintained his good relations with the administration, for in May 1864, Tasker Howard's oldest son was arrested for treason. As city editor of the *Brooklyn Eagle*, Joseph Howard and a friend crafted a false presidential proclamation declaring a day of penitence and calling for a new draft of four hundred thousand men. He then sent out what would later be dubbed the "Bogus Proclamation" on Associated Press stationery to all the major papers, hoping that the currency market would panic, driving up the price of gold and allowing them to make a killing.

In no time flat, Joe Howard and his accomplice found themselves in the military prison at Fort Lafayette in New York. The press, of course, pounced on his close ties to Beecher. Bowen urged Beecher to stay out of the matter, and Beecher promised to follow his advice, according to Bowen. But a day or two later Beecher began quietly calling on his Washington contacts to plead for Joe's release. Henry Bowen took this as yet another betrayal.

"I very much wish to oblige Henry Ward Beecher, by releasing Howard," Lincoln told Secretary Stanton.[106] Lincoln pardoned the young man, but it was said that nothing he did during the war pained him so much as that act. The president told an associate of Bowen's that "no other man but Henry Ward Beecher could have induced him to be guilty of pardoning Joe Howard."[107]

If wrong on principle, Lincoln was right politically. He had two big problems with the voters—General Sherman's stalemate outside Atlanta and General Grant's outside Petersburg. Lincoln's hopes for reelection were fading with every dispatch from the field. "Mr. Lincoln is already beaten," the *Tribune* declared in August. "We must have another ticket to save us from utter overthrow."[108] In such dire times Lincoln was especially grateful for Beecher's powerful voice.

Henry Bowen lost his risky wager in July, when Chase's secret candidacy was revealed and the president accepted his resignation from the cabinet. Deprived of Chase's protection, Bowen's brother-in-law Hiram Barney was removed from his lucrative patronage job one month later. Despite this blow, Tilton continued his intriguing with the Radicals.

Suddenly the tide began to turn. Just after the Copperhead Democrats nominated former general George McClellan for the presidency, stunning news came from the front. On September 3 General Sherman captured Atlanta. Then came reports that General Philip Sheridan had whipped the Rebels in the Shenandoah Valley.

On the first Sabbath of October, Henry announced that he would preach on politics every Sunday until the election, so those who didn't like it should stay away. "We shall expect to see him on election day, flying round the polls, clamoring for a vote for Lincoln, and guaranteeing as the reward for it, a place, not in the Custom House or the Navy Yard, but in the kingdom of the blessed," jeered the *Eagle*. "May we ask Mr. Beecher to what he owes his sudden conversion to the present administration?"[109]

On election day Henry voted early and spent the day calling on friends and checking the returns. When the polls closed, people gathered at the Cooper Institute to hear the results but Henry stayed home, presuming that "it would be best for *him* to keep quiet."[110] He got the verdict with the morning papers: four more years for Father Abraham.

Bowen and Tilton instantly sent letters of congratulations to the president and his staff. The campaign, Tilton wrote with melodramatic hypocrisy, *"half killed* me—speaking as I did, so often and laboriously that on the Saturday night before election I *fainted on the platform."*[111] Sore Democrats banged the miscegenation drum one last time, publishing another fraudulent "abolition" pamphlet titled *What Miscegenation Is! and What We Are to Expect Now that Mr. Lincoln Is Re-elected*, dedicated in honor of Henry Ward Beecher.

THE END OF THE WAR WAS IN SIGHT, and with it the end of slavery. On January 31 Congress passed the Thirteenth Amendment to the Constitution, forever prohibiting slavery in the United States. Henry was in Baltimore delivering his first speech in a former slave state at a fund-raiser for the freedmen, as the liberated slaves were called, when he heard the glorious news. The amendment would be ratified within the year—a certain sign of how much the crucible of war had recast America.

From Baltimore, Beecher headed to Washington to see if he could obtain a more prestigious military commission for his son Harry. The preacher was rewarded with a late-night interview with Lincoln. Four years had taken its toll on the prairie statesman. "His hair was 'every way for Sunday'; it looked as though it was an abandoned stubble field," Henry remembered. "He had on slippers, and his vest was what was called 'going free.' He looked wearied and when he sat down in a chair looked as though every limb wanted to drop off his body."[112]

Beecher asked anxiously about the recent rumors that the president was considering a negotiated peace with the Confederacy and about his plans for reconstructing the nation. Lincoln was reassuring, bolstering his points with three funny stories, Henry told his friend Robert Bonner, "two of which I forget, the third won't bear telling." ("How is it that you remembered the bad one—the one that would not bear telling?" asked Bonner.)

"I do not know that I ever saw him after that," Henry said of the president.[113]

On April 2 Beecher was just finishing his morning sermon when someone handed him a telegram from Secretary Stanton. He opened it, then said, "The congregation will turn to 'America' while I read the following telegram."

As they opened their hymnbooks, Henry read with trembling voice that Grant's army had finally shattered Lee's lines at Petersburg, forcing the Confederates to retreat, leaving Richmond defenseless. After a moment of stunned silence, the members of the congregation rose to their feet, tears streaming down their faces, and sang with one voice, "My country, 'tis of thee!" The beginning of the end had come.

One week later, at the president's request, Beecher set off for Fort Sumter to speak at the raising of the flag, four years to the day after the fort fell. He was accompanied by his wife and children, the Howards, Chloe Beach, and a specially chartered second steamer entirely filled with Plymouth Church folk.

By the time Beecher returned, the Confederates had surrendered and President Lincoln was dead. "It was," Henry said, "the uttermost of joy and the uttermost of sorrow—noon and midnight without a space between."[114]

Chapter 11

"MY HEART IS WITH THE RADICALS,
BUT MY EMOTIONS ARE WITH THE ORTHODOX"

*H*enry Ward Beecher was euphoric in the spring of 1865. His first stroke of unexpected fortune arrived in the shape of a letter from Robert Bonner, his good friend and editor of the *New York Ledger*. "I have a proposition to make to you; and, whether you accept or decline it I wish the *compensation part of it kept secret*," Bonner wrote. If Beecher would write a novel for the *Ledger*, Bonner would pay him the staggering sum of twenty-four thousand dollars![1]

"A clap of thunder would not have been more astounding to me," Beecher said later. "I laughed as I read the dispatch. I refused at first, but he continued to talk to me about it, until finally I agreed to do it."[2] How could he not? Twenty-four thousand dollars was nearly double his annual salary.

The second stroke of luck came in April, when President Lincoln asked Beecher to speak at the flag raising at Fort Sumter. Robert Bonner took particular pleasure in Beecher's success at Fort Sumter, and not just because it was good for business. "I am, *personally*, very much pleased that you delivered such a splendid oration because some of your *so-called* friends (I allude particularly to Tilton) have in a Pecksniffian way been regretting that you were on the decline. Tilton has said to me within two months that you reached the culminating point in your career when you were in England, that your discourses were not what they used to be, etc. etc.," Bonner told Beecher confidentially.

"I can only say (and I will stake my life on it) that Tilton is not a real friend of you or yours. If he is, he has a queer way of showing it," Bonner continued. "Every one knows that he owes his position to you. *You may not care anything about such a matter as this*; but *I* hate to see a man constantly following you—hanging on to your coat-tail—identifying himself with you as your right-hand man and co-laborer—and behind your back endeavoring to boost himself up at your expense."[3]

Beecher blithely batted away Bonner's warning about Tilton. "I hope that his utterances are but the effusion of a heated moment," he replied mildly. "I cannot remember a year for fifteen years in which I have not been told that I had reached the end of my influence."[4] Beecher wrote with the confidence of a man who was, in fact, at the peak of his influence. For him 1865 seemed like the fulfillment of a prophecy—the beginning of a Golden Age of Liberty and Progress.

Perhaps it was inevitable that after two decades of promoting "Free Soil, Free Labor, Free Press, and Free Speech," Beecher would now take up "Free Thought." After his death Beecher gained a reputation for unthinking emotionalism, for preaching a "Gospel of Gush." But during his lifetime Beecher was considered a great, if erratic, intellect. He kept up with the latest thinkers, using his constant train travel to consume dozens of journals and a steady stream of new books. He was vitally interested in science of all kinds, especially the emerging fields of psychology and sociology. Above all he loved the "scientific method" of thought—freely experimenting with new ideas to find the ones that work best, holding no idea too sacred to test against practical experience.

It was the scientific method, as much as any particular scientific discoveries, which so alarmed America's orthodox. Religious orthodoxy in the late nineteenth century was as much an ingrained obedience to traditional authority, especially the authority of the Bible, as it was a set of specific religious beliefs. In the postwar period Beecher was determined to bridge the divide between rational thought and Christian faith. "My heart is with the radicals, but my emotions are with the orthodox," as he put it.[5] To him religion was the emotional, and science was the rational, response to the world. As the journalist James Parton observed:

No matter how fervently he may have been praying supernaturalism, he preaches pure cause and effect. His text may savor of old

Palestine, but his sermon is inspired by New York and Brooklyn; and nearly all that he says, when he is most himself finds an approving response in the mind of every well disposed person, whether orthodox or heterodox in his creed.[6]

The most important intellectual influence on Beecher in this period was Herbert Spencer, the famed British social thinker who originated the term "survival of the fittest." Spencer had a talent for stitching together ostensibly unrelated facts and phenomena into broad, overarching structures—Beecher's favorite sort of thinking. He was one of the earliest American fans of Herbert Spencer's "conception of gradual development"[7]—the theory that everything—nature, society, individuals—evolves and, if left alone, progresses. Spencer's all-encompassing, laissez-faire theory of evolution predated Charles Darwin's *On the Origin of Species*, but in its raw form it was just as shocking to people raised to believe that truth was eternal and identity was fixed.

After the war Beecher was increasingly open about his religious liberalism. In 1867 Ralph Waldo Emerson noted with surprise that "Beecher told me, that he did not hold one of the five points of Calvinism in a way to satisfy his father." By 1870 Beecher was campaigning to drop the concept of hell, or divine punishment, from the official creed of Plymouth Church. "Love, with its freedom, has taken the place of authority, and of obedience to it," he argued. For those who had "ripened" to a "nobler plane," desire was a far more effective motive than fear.[8]

Those worried that such freedom might be sacrilegious, corrupting, or chaotic were reassured by the example of Beecher's own homey common sense. "He was one of those men," as the writer Edward Eggleston noted appreciatively, "who connect the past with the future, and make of themselves a bridge for the passage of multitudes."[9] Henry was often accosted by strangers, like the young man who sat down by him on a train, asking: "Mr. Beecher! Must I believe every word in the Bible, to be a Christian?"

"No!" replied Beecher.

"Well—what then?" asked the bewildered boy.

"You must believe the *truth* that is in the Bible."

The boy pondered this for a moment and then asked "Now, about the Incarnation? Why do I need to believe in that?" Beecher quickly sketched his views.

"I see, now what about Conversion?" They talked until the train reached the station. The young man took his leave, saying, "Mr. Beecher, you have laid my ghosts to rest."

"I hope they will never rise again," replied Beecher.[10]

THE GOLDEN AGE OF LIBERTY was not without challenges. At the end of the war two questions hung ominously over the landscape: What would happen to the Rebel states? What would happen to the former slaves? Making peace with hostile Southern whites while empowering Southern blacks promised to be a Sisyphean task.

President Lincoln had intended to navigate these contradictory demands with the same combination of principle and pragmatism that carried him through the Rebellion. At the end of 1864 a coalition of conservative Republicans led by Secretary of State William Seward brokered a deal to pass the Thirteenth Amendment, abolishing slavery throughout the country, in exchange for the promise of a speedy reconciliation with the Rebel states. Lincoln made both justice for the freedmen and generosity to the former Confederacy the cornerstones of his famous second inaugural address—"With malice toward none, with charity for all," in his immortal words. But Lincoln's assassination threw all such plans into the whirlwind.

No one knew what to expect from Lincoln's successor. Andrew Johnson was an antiaristocratic populist who had worked his way up from poverty through the ranks of the Tennessee Democratic Party. When Tennessee seceded, Johnson was the only U.S. senator from a Confederate state to remain loyal to the Union. When Tennessee was reconquered in 1862, Lincoln appointed him military governor of the recaptured territory, and in the presidential race of 1864, Lincoln asked him aboard to balance the Union ticket. During the election the Republican press had applauded Johnson's vicious denunciations of the Slavocracy. But reporters were literally dumbfounded when Johnson arrived at his own vice-presidential inauguration ceremony so drunk he could barely take the oath.

Henry Ward Beecher and Theodore Tilton eagerly threw themselves into the debate over how to reconstruct the Union. Both strongly supported universal suffrage, for women as well as black men, and were active fund-raisers for various freedmen's aid organizations. But from the first the two pundits disagreed about Andrew Johnson. Tilton was appalled by Johnson's drunken inaugural escapade, and his opinion of the Tennessean declined rapidly. Beecher, by contrast, was one of many Republicans who were secretly pleased to see a firebrand at the helm. "Johnson's little finger was stronger than Lincoln's loins," declared Beecher only hours after learning of Lincoln's death.[11]

But their differences sank deeper. Since returning from England, Beecher had ensconced himself in what was now called the "Conservative Republican" camp, led by men like Secretary Seward and *New York Times* founder Henry J. Raymond. Meanwhile Tilton had attached himself to the "Radical Republican" wing, represented by Wendell Phillips, Pennsylvania congressman Thaddeus Stevens, and Senator Charles Sumner. The two factions clashed bitterly over the readmission of the Confederate states.

Tilton and the Radicals advocated onerous concessions from the Rebels and strict federal protections for the freedmen. To the surprise of those who remembered only his fiery war sermons, Beecher (like his fellow Conservatives) advocated a generous and quick reconciliation with the South. Even before the assassination, Thaddeus Stevens ridiculed Beecher's magnanimous message at Fort Sumter, accusing Beecher of misusing the Bible to persuade Northerners to embrace "the impenitent and unwashed traitors whose garments are still dripping with the blood of my relatives, neighbors, friends and countrymen."[12] Instead Stevens quoted the Old Testament's demand that the righteous smite those who have offended the Lord. Lincoln's murder only made the calls for retribution more clamorous.

It soon became obvious that, unlike his predecessor, Johnson was a pugnacious ideologue and an unreconstructed racist. "This is a country for white men and, by God, as long as I am president it shall be a government for white men," he vowed on more than one occasion.[13] As soon as Congress recessed for the summer, Johnson seized control of the Reconstruction process. He offered blanket amnesty to all but the very highest-level Rebel leaders and ordered all land in federal hands returned to its former owners, evicting the freedmen who'd been settled on them and sparking a series of violent confrontations. Johnson gave each state free rein to begin reconstituting their governments, requiring only that they repudiate secession, abolish slavery, and forfeit all Confederate debts.

The North was incensed by Johnson's apparent about-face. By the time Congress returned to Washington in the winter of 1865, a powerful coalition of Radicals and moderate Republicans was determined to wrest control of the Reconstruction process from the president. Theodore Tilton eagerly leaped into the breach, turning the *Independent* into a Radical mouthpiece.

Yet many people were surprised to find Beecher's faith in the president and his policies unshaken. When Beecher spoke against the death penalty for Jefferson Davis, even such gentle Christians as Calvin Stowe objected. "If such a man deserves to be treated and eulogized as a generous and magnanimous foe then let the Devil have full credit for such magnanimosity and generosity," Calvin admonished Henry.[14]

HENRY'S REASONS RESTED ON BOTH morality and expediency. Henry genuinely believed that sin was itself a form of suffering, making further punishment cruel and unnecessary, a belief borne out by the terrible devastation he witnessed in Charleston. Politically he believed that delay would only deepen Southern resistance to the new regime, and he feared the expansion of federal power and the use of it to compel behavior, even for a just cause. "Unless we turn the government into a vast military machine, there cannot be armies enough to protect the freedmen while Southern society remains insurrectionary," Beecher said.[15] "However humane the end sought and the motive, it is, in fact, a course of instruction preparing our government to be despotic and familiarizing the people to a stretch of authority which can never be other than dangerous to liberty."[16]

Here was the first challenge to the Golden Age of Liberty—was it possible to have freedom without the compulsion of law? At bottom this was a conflict over human nature itself. The Radicals took what might be called the pessimistic view, insisting that the only way to redeem the South was to punish its evil mistakes and force it to reform.

Beecher claimed a more realistic understanding of human psychology. It was foolish to believe that Northern coercion could force either slaves or their owners instantly to abandon the bad habits of generations. "It is hard enough to take a kid out of a lion's paw; and to insist that the lion shall take the kid into his den, and make him an equal, and call him a lion, is too much for a lion to bear." After watching the Slave Power dominate the federal government for three decades, Henry had good reason to fear the further concentration of power in Washington. And while there is something distasteful in it, he wasn't entirely wrong in insisting that "the welfare of the freedmen depends far more upon the good will of their white neighbors than it does upon northern philanthropy or Governmental protection," as he wrote to President Johnson.[17]

But underlying these caveats was the sort of reckless optimism that Herman Melville satirized in *The Confidence Man*—now bolstered by Herbert Spencer's theories of laissez-faire evolution. Henry genuinely believed that with love, patience, and goodwill toward the Rebels, "the great normal, industrial and moral laws shall work such gradual changes as shall enable them to pass from old to the new." Theodore Tilton offered a more cynical interpretation. Mr. Beecher "never was willing to see any one punished for anything he had done," he told a friend flatly.[18]

By the autumn of 1865 Beecher and Tilton were clashing openly, egged on by the anti-Radical press. When Beecher delivered a sermon on his reluctant willingness to delay black suffrage in pursuit of peace, Tilton was certain it was "aimed at the *Independent*," and replied with a zinging editorial.[19] Beecher responded the next week with another veiled reference to Tilton. For every magnanimous sermon from Henry printed on page 2 of the *Independent*, Theodore countered with a harsh editorial on page 4.

By December it was clear that Beecher's view of human nature was overconfident. Left by Johnson to their own devices, the Southern states quickly resurrected the old white-supremacist regimes. They established "Black Codes" that kept blacks from voting, owning land, accessing the legal system, and making free labor contracts. They restored the old planter elite to power, electing scores of former Confederate leaders to state and federal offices. Instead of blocking them from taking office, Johnson began issuing pardons by the fistful.

Privately Beecher urged Johnson to do more to protect the freedmen, but publicly his support for the president was unwavering. Beecher was equally poor in judging President Johnson's personal character. Even as Johnson was making enemies in every corner, Beecher wrote to compliment the president on how "enlightened and statesmanlike" he seemed.[20]

This battle between justice and mercy roused that apostle of ambivalence, Herman Melville, from his literary exile, inspiring one last meditation on misplaced confidence. *Battle-Pieces*, a volume of war poetry accompanied by an essay on Reconstruction, appeared in 1866. But this time he concurred with Beecher. "Nor should we forget that benevolent desires," wrote Melville, "after passing a certain point, can not undertake their own fulfillment without incurring the risk of evils beyond those sought to be remedied."[21]

Unsurprisingly, the *Independent*'s review of *Battle-Pieces* excoriated Melville—"this happy optimist"—warning that "gentlemen of Mr. Melville's class are mischievous men in these troubled times. Only absolute justice is safe. Peaceable, by all means peaceable, in God's name; but *first pure*, in God's name, also."[22]

As 1866 ENTERED, Beecher was firmly on the wrong side of public opinion. Speaking at the Brooklyn Academy of Music, Frederick Douglass, America's premier black intellectual, summed up prevailing opinion on the preacher. He was reminded, Douglass said, of a speech Beecher gave back in 1852, declaring that he'd rather wait twenty-five years to have slavery abolished through Christ than see immediate emancipation without Christ. "If he had been the slave of a man and I had had a decent sort of a slave whip in my hand and stood over him I could have changed Mr. Beecher's opinion," Douglass thundered. "I think he would have been in favor of abolishing slavery whether the church were ready for it or not."[23] Cheers and laughter rolled through the hometown audience.

Reconciliation between Congress and the president still seemed possible that spring, when even the Conservatives supported federal action to nullify the heinous "Black Codes" sweeping the South. In March, Congress passed the Civil Rights Act of 1866, granting equality before the law to all American citizens and making it a federal crime to deprive citizens of their civil rights. Privately Beecher urged Johnson to sign it. "I have strongly and to my own personal inconvenience (for the present) defended your wisdom, in most things, and your *motives*, and I feel most profoundly how the signing of this bill will strengthen the position that I have defended in your behalf," Beecher wrote.[24] But when Johnson vetoed the bill and then compounded the insult with a shockingly racist veto message, Beecher made no public protest.

Tilton, by contrast, went to D.C. to help lead the successful fight to override the veto. The evening the override passed, Gideon Welles, the Conservative secretary of the navy, ran into an exultant Tilton and could barely suppress his contempt. "Theodore Tilton, as full of fanatical, fantastical, and boyish enthusiasm as of genius and talent, but with no sensible ideas of the principles on which our government is founded or accurate knowledge of our republican federal system, or of the merits involved in pending questions, was boisterous over the result in the Senate," Welles wrote with disgust in his diary that evening.[25]

Johnson's veto of the Civil Rights Bill set off a political war that raged through the brutally hot summer of 1866. In Washington, Johnson vetoed every Reconstruction measure passed by the Congress, and Congress overrode nearly every veto. In the South it was increasingly clear that white Southerners were determined to strip blacks of any semblance of legal equality. As the fall midterm congressional elections approached, the battle shifted to a series of political conventions.

The first—and worst—was a convention of black and white Republicans in New Orleans to promote a black suffrage amendment to the Louisiana constitution, held at the end of July. The North was horrified when white rioters, including policemen and former Confederate soldiers, attacked the convention with clubs and guns, killing 40 Radicals of both races and wounding 140.

Two weeks later the president's supporters called a National Union Convention in Philadelphia. It was to be a formal burying of the hatchet, featuring both Northern and Southern states, as well as Republicans and Democrats, Copperheads and Unionists. But when the ceremonies opened with a grand procession into National Hall, in which the delegates from Massachusetts and South Carolina paraded arm in arm down the aisle as a symbol of national reconciliation and social equality, the hypocrisy was so rank that the press broke into open ridicule.

Johnson compounded the bad publicity by spending the next two months taking what became known as the "Swing 'Round the Circle," a speaking tour in support of his policies and candidates. Riled by alcohol and anger, the president delivered a series of venomous stump speeches, in which he wildly accused the Radicals of instigating the New Orleans massacre and of plotting to assassinate him, and jokingly suggested executing their leaders. By September even Johnson's strong supporters were beating a hasty path away from him.

Meanwhile, back in Philadelphia, a second convention was assembling, gathering together Southern loyalists and Radical Northern Republicans. But the Radicals proved only that hypocrisy was nonpartisan. When Frederick Douglass arrived as a delegate from upstate New York, the convention nearly shut down rather than seat him. And during their own grand procession, marching two abreast into National Hall, the delegates refused to come near Douglass. As Douglass was about to march alone down the aisle, Theodore Tilton rushed up and locked arms with him, in imitation of Johnson's Philadelphia convention.

Onlookers cheered, but privately the delegates were furious at Tilton for giving fodder to their racist opponents. "Why it was done I cannot see except as a foolish bravado," lamented Thaddeus Stevens, the leader of the Congressional Radicals. The convention finally broke down when, under Tilton's leadership, the New York delegation passed a resolution calling for black suffrage, leading the border state delegations to withdraw in a huff. So much for the City of Brotherly Love.

Cleveland, Ohio, hosted the last ill-starred convention of the summer. The National Convention of Soldiers and Sailors was called to support Johnson's policy of prompt reconciliation with the South, and they invited Beecher to serve as chaplain to the convention. Beecher, suffering from his annual end-of-summer hay fever, declined their invitation but wrote a warm letter restating the views he'd been preaching for the last year and a half. But Henry had not bargained for the hostility created by the slaughter in New Orleans and Johnson's disastrous "Swing 'Round the Circle."

When the so-called Cleveland Letter appeared in the press, Beecher was enveloped in a tempest of anger. "To think of a man like H. W. Beecher lending himself to the unprincipled schemes of that tippling traitor, that boozy boaster, that devilish demagogue! What can be his motive?" demanded the abolitionist Lydia Maria Child in her inimitable way.[26] Whatever the motive, wrote Tilton in the *Independent*, Beecher "has done more injury to the American republic than has been done by any other citizen except Andrew Johnson."[27] His family was furious, and for the first time Plymouth Church was on the verge of open rebellion.

Beecher quickly backtracked. His first effort, an agree-to-disagree letter read aloud to his congregation, did little to placate the outrage, however. So he followed it with an appearance at the Brooklyn Academy of Music on October 25. This time he read a carefully written speech that reaffirmed his loyalty to the Republican Party and repudiated Andrew Johnson. He dissented only in personal philosophy and practical policy, he patiently explained, not on fundamental principles. Although Beecher had not actually changed his position, it sounded enough like an apology that most people grudgingly accepted it.

But not Theodore Tilton. "The spectacle at the Academy of Music had in it a touch of humiliation which even the noblest passages of the address did not redeem," Tilton wrote in the *Independent*. "Something of true moral grandeur is wanting to the position of a veteran who, after 25 years of service as a pioneer of political opinion, has nothing nobler to say in the present juncture than simply: 'I am not a Democrat.' "[28]

∾ ∾

Radical Reconstruction allowed Tilton to combine with remarkable success his passionate idealism and personal ambitions. By minimizing religious sectarianism and maximizing partisan politics and social reform, Tilton turned the *Independent* into one of the most influential journals of the postwar period and catapulted to the top of the editorial profession. He parlayed the popularity of the *Independent* into a lucrative career as a public lecturer. By 1866 Tilton was prosperous enough to purchase an airy, three-story house at 124 Livingston Street, about six blocks from Plymouth Church.

Nonetheless, in the winter of 1866–67 Theodore was deeply discontented, and much of it seemed strangely centered on Beecher. When Sarah Putnam, a close friend of Elizabeth Tilton, visited the Tiltons' house in October, just after the uproar over the Cleveland Letters, she was surprised to find that they had turned their small plaster bust of Henry Ward Beecher to face the wall.

Why? asked Mrs. Putnam in surprise, knowing of Elizabeth's warm devotion to Beecher.

"Theodore says that our pastor has proved himself a traitor to the Republican party," Elizabeth replied dutifully, as Theodore looked on.

Nonetheless Theodore denied that the *Independent*'s attacks had strained his relationship with the preacher. "Mr. Beecher was too magnanimous a man to lay up anything against anyone that expressed his honest sentiments," he told Sarah Putnam.

Didn't he think that Mr. Beecher's feelings might be hurt? she asked.

Theodore replied, rather smugly, that he "presumed it had, but Mr. Beecher would never show it." Besides, he added, "Mr. Beecher had a very peculiar constitution of mind; if anyone wanted to enlist Mr. Beecher in his behalf, the best way to do it was to abuse Mr. Beecher."

Like his former mentor, Tilton was increasingly drawn to freethinkers, social radicals, and men of the world. But unlike Beecher, he seemed unsettled by these new associations. Theodore was a man who thrived on absolutes; it was his gift and his curse. Deprived of his old certitudes, he swung wildly between self-complaisance and self-loathing. As Bessie Turner, the Tiltons' hired girl, put it, "he would be apparently very happy some part of the day, and then in about an hour, it may be, he would be so cross and ugly that nothing or nobody could please him." He regretted his dark moods, he told Sarah Putnam, but they were "the penalty that genius had to pay."[29]

Elizabeth bore the brunt of his ill temper, but what worried her most was Tilton's growing contempt for organized religion. Theodore admitted that his declining "religious conviction was a great source of tears and anguish to her; she said to me once that denying the divinity of Christ in her view nullified our marriage almost."[30] But he seemed to enjoy goading her, speaking scornfully of the Bible, and bragging about attending the theater, playing billiards, and bowling on Sunday. He told friends that if he had his way he'd forbid his children to attend church. "He used to say that a man and wife should not live together longer than they took pleasure in each other's company," recalled one friend with surprise.[31]

Under Tilton's direction the *Independent* now featured essays satirizing the orthodox, bashing Conservatives, advocating women's rights, and promoting radical new thinkers. A council of seven Congregational ministers led by Edward Beecher called Bowen onto the carpet, insisting that he get rid of Tilton or give up any religious pretensions. Bowen soothed them, but Tilton's rising fame and considerable talent made him too valuable to fire. When the council of seven admonished Tilton directly, he defiantly told them that his views were exactly the same as those of the eminent pastor of Plymouth Church.

Edward Beecher immediately wrote to his brother, demanding to know if this was true. "I fear Tilton more and more. His advice to young men to read Emerson's essays and especially Herbert Spencer's first principles as 'awakeners' is dangerous and may be ruinous," Edward warned. "If things come to this issue, you will not be able to uphold Tilton but he will sink you."[32]

Henry replied to his brother with unusual speed and harshness. Carefully sidestepping his own affection for Spencer and Emerson, he vigorously disavowed the *Independent*; "it is well known that I am in positive antagonism with the whole general drift of the paper," he told Edward. "Mr. Bowen will scarcely recognize me in the street and feels bitterly about my withdrawal from all part or lot in the paper." But everyone, he noted with uncharacteristic nastiness, had noticed that the *Independent* still advertised Edward Beecher as a contributor. "How is that?" Beecher gibed. As for Theodore, "I am an old man—Tilton a young man—The question is not whether I agree with him, but how far he agrees with me!"[33]

With Beecher off the *Independent* and Theodore out of the church, their fraught relationship ought to have cooled. But the two men seemed locked in a strange antagonistic embrace. Beecher couldn't stand breaking openly with anyone, and Tilton couldn't bear losing such a famous friend. But there was something more.

Fed by Bowen's bitter whisperings, Theodore had become obsessed with the perennial rumors of Beecher's sexual indiscretions. Theodore began "to talk to me about Mr. Beecher's wrong-doings with ladies which he had heard from Mr. Bowen," Elizabeth Tilton recalled, "night after night, and day after day he talked about Mr. Beecher[.]" In November 1865 Tilton shocked Charles Judson, a Plymouth Church congregant, by hinting that he knew the dark truth behind the rumors of Beecher's infidelity. When Judson protested, Tilton only moaned several times, "I have lost my faith in man."

Appalled, Judson went directly to Beecher with these accusations. Yet when Beecher confronted Theodore, the editor denied it all, and then sent Beecher a long, sycophantish letter of "recuperated love," signing himself "your unworthy but eternal friend."[34] For a man who hated hypocrisy above all, it was a strange performance.

In November 1866 Theodore set off on a four-month lecture tour through New England and across the Midwest. He departed, as he told Elizabeth, with "unusual disquiet of mind—something akin to bitterness of spirit."[35] Despite his hostility, before Theodore left he told the minister, "I wish you would look in after and see that Libby is not lonesome or does not want anything."[36]

Beecher, with exquisite passive-aggression, did just that.

THEODORE TILTON WAS NOT THE ONLY ONE obsessed with Beecher's roving eye. For Moses Beach, his wife's infatuation with her minister was becoming intolerable. After Chloe Beach accompanied Beecher on his trip to Fort Sumter in 1865, the two had grown more intimate than ever. Jealous beyond endurance, Moses sold their Brooklyn Heights town house to his brother and moved the whole family out of the city, trying once again "to cut off the associations which were constantly dragging me into a mire of unhappy thought and depriving me of an affection which it had been the one aim of my life to cherish and nourish."

To no avail. In his deepening depression, Moses fell desperately ill. The cause, ostensibly, was typhoid fever, but as he later wrote to Beecher, "you know enough of the human mind to be aware that a mind afflicted not unfrequently brings affliction to the body; and this, more than anything else, as I then thought and have ever thought, brought affliction to me."

All through the winter of 1865–66, Moses lingered on the edge of death. "For myself I would then, most cheerfully, have passed away," Moses told Henry. "But one object for life remained—that I might still keep watch and ward for her—one hope for happiness; that she would return with me to our wonted days of confidence and perfect happiness." When his health finally returned, Moses was determined "to add every whit to her happiness, though I should thereby be dragged to yet lower depths of mental misery. I did hope to awaken those dormant feelings of attachment by this sacrifice of self. And so, came back the old home again—so, came back the opportunities, which I too well knew were coveted, for association with you."

So Moses repurchased the house on the Heights and returned to his private hell. Chloe seemed blind to the neighbors' whispers as well as her husband's pain. She had eyes only for Henry. Mary Hallock Foote, a young friend of the family, remembered being scolded by Mrs. Beach one evening when Beecher was holding forth to a room full of people. As Mary quietly rose to slip out, Mrs. Beach said sharply, "Mary Hallock, sit still!"

"Mr. Beecher was in and out of the house every day," recalled Mary with surprise; "and still he was sacrosanct: to leave the room where he was in full tide of speech was an incredible offence against that homage everyone was supposed to pay him."[37]

In April 1866, while Moses was still feeble from his long illness, Chloe Beach became pregnant. Moses was an unusually warm and devoted father, but this pregnancy only deepened his despondency. "I had over estimated my own power of endurance," he told Beecher. "I gave way and tried to hide from it by informing you what I observed," hoping that the minister might cool his relationship with Chloe. Not long after that conversation, Moses sailed for Germany with his son, hoping for some change. But when he returned in December 1866, he found that Chloe and Henry were more tightly entwined than ever. "I felt little less than crazed to observe that my absence had been improved—if such things can be called improvements—and that the goal I wished was vanishing from even hope."[38]

Chloe's thoughts on these or any other subject are a mystery. In the gossipy world of Brooklyn Heights she was an unusually private woman who hated writing letters. Eunice Beecher considered Chloe her dearest friend in the world, writing her hundreds of notes over the years, but at some point before death, the two women must have returned each others' letters, for barely a scrap of Chloe's handwriting exists among thousands of Beecher documents.

HENRY, TOO, ENTERED THE WINTER OF 1866–67 in a low mood. The uproar over his Cleveland Letters on Reconstruction rattled him more than he cared to admit. And then there was the looming deadline for his novel, *Norwood*. The book was more than a year late and his publisher, Robert Bonner, was becoming impatient. Paralyzed by inexperience, insecurity, and chronic procrastination, Henry had written almost nothing. "I am like a young wife for the first time with child," Henry complained to Bonner. "Sometimes I imagine there is nothing— then I am sure there are *twins*, and next I am *perfectly* sure that 'I never shall live to get through.' "[39]

Normally Henry would have turned to Chloe Beach for encouragement, but that uncomfortable conversation with Moses Beach, Chloe's blossoming pregnancy, and her husband's return from Berlin only further strained his overwrought nerves. Feeling beleaguered and sorry for himself, Beecher found comfort in the parlor of Elizabeth Tilton.

Beecher began stopping by 124 Livingston Street as soon as Theodore left for his long winter lecture tour, seeking, Henry said, a refuge "where people could not find me."[40] He often brought his latest chapter of *Norwood* to read aloud to Elizabeth. "In the earlier chapters I was almost in despair," Henry admitted. "I needed somebody that would not be critical, and that would praise it, to give me courage to go on with it."[41]

The relationship between Elizabeth and her pastor blossomed along with his novel. After he read a passage glorying in the trailing arbutus, "like the breath of love,"[42] he presented her with a watercolor of a trailing arbutus. *Norwood*'s heroine, Rose Wentworth, "the woman of nature and simple truth," bore an increasing resemblance to Elizabeth. Years later she would adopt his description of Rose's secret love as her own:

> It would seem as if, while her whole life centered upon his love, she could hide the precious secret by flinging over it vines and flowers, by mirth and raillery, as a bird hides its nest under tufts of grass, and behind leaves and vines, as a fence against prying eyes.[43]

Henry brought toys for the children and gifts for Elizabeth—flowers, books, perfumes, fancy soaps, stationery, and pictures of himself, most of which she locked in her bedroom closet. They talked of Theodore's growing irreligiosity and Eunice's coldness, and of spiritual and literary matters. "It was entering into her life, and, in a sense, giving her an interest in mine," Henry said.[44]

Unlike Chloe Beach, Elizabeth wore her heart on her sleeve. She and Theodore wrote each other nearly every day, long letters overflowing with high-toned language and extravagant emotions. As Elizabeth blossomed under Beecher's attention, she tried to share her feelings with Theodore—in part from sheer enthusiasm, in part, as she explained later, because "when Mr. Beecher came to see me, Mr. Tilton immediately began to have suspicions."

Theodore hotly denied this. "I am not jealous," Tilton told Elizabeth. "I think any man is a fool who is jealous[.]" Still, Beecher's visits weighed on his mind. That winter Theodore was electrified by the bestselling novel *Griffith Gaunt*, by Charles Reade, the story of a devout woman who becomes so infatuated with her priest that her jealous husband abandons her. "Go to the bookstore, buy a copy, and read it," he instructed Elizabeth. Two weeks later, when Elizabeth put off his request to meet him in Chicago for a few days, Tilton blamed Beecher. "Now that the *other* man has gone off lecturing (as your letter mentions), you can afford to come to *me*," Theodore wrote with barbed humor. "Leave home, children, kith and kin and cleave unto him to whom you originally promised to cleave. You promised the *other* man to cleave to *me* and yet you leave *me all alone* and cleave to him. 'O Frailty! Thy name is woman.' "

Elizabeth's efforts to be, as she put it, "perfectly transparent" in her feelings about Beecher worked all too well. Theodore could hardly have been comforted by letters like the one she wrote at the end of December.

> I have been thinking of my love for Mr. B considerably of late, and those thoughts you shall have. I remember Hannah Moore says: "My heart in its new sympathy for one abounds towards all." Now, I think I have lived a richer, happier life since I have known him. And have you not loved me more ardently since you saw another high nature appreciated me? [. . .]
>
> But to return to Mr. B. He has been the guide of our youth, and until the three last dreadful years, when our confidence was shaken in him—we trusted him as no other human being. During

these early years, the mention of his name, to meet him, or, better still, a visit from him, my cheek would flush with pleasure—an experience common to all his parishioners of both sexes. Is it not strange, then, darling, that on a more intimate acquaintance my delight and pleasure should increase? Of course I realize what attracts you both to me is a supposed purity of soul you find in me.

Years later Theodore said that Elizabeth had been trying to save Beecher from himself. "She had been much distressed with rumors against his moral purity and wished to convince him that she could receive his kindness, and yet resist his solicitations," Theodore testified. She wanted to give him "an increased respect for the chaste dignity of womanhood."[45] As the winter wore on, however, Elizabeth's confidence faltered. Exactly what occurred is unclear, but by mid-January, Elizabeth suddenly gave full credence to rumors of the minister's philandering.

"You, my beloved, are higher up than he; this I believe," Elizabeth wrote of Beecher in a teary letter to her husband.

Oh let us pray for him. You are not willing to leave him to the evil influences which surround him. He is in a delusion with regard to himself, and pitifully mistaken in his opinion of you. [. . .] Why I was so mysteriously brought in as actor in this friendship, I know not, yet no experience of all my life has made my soul ache so keenly as the apparent lack of Christian manliness in this beloved man.[46]

Others also noticed the pastor's unusual attentions to Mrs. Tilton. Joseph Richards, Elizabeth's brother and the former publisher of the *Independent,* had heard enough of Bowen's gossipmongering to feel uneasy—especially after he stopped by the house and found Beecher and Elizabeth in the front parlor, his sister making, as he later described it, "a very hasty motion, and with highly flushed face, away from the position that Mr. Beecher occupied."[47]

But like Chloe Beach, Elizabeth was so artless and so goodhearted that she was oblivious to these ill winds. As she told Theodore on January 28, 1867:

Mr. B called Saturday. He came tired and gloomy, but he said I had the most calming and peaceful influence over him, more so than anyone he ever knew. I believe he loves you. We talked of you.

He brought me two pretty flowers in pots, and said as he went out, "What a pretty house this is; I wish I lived here." It would make me very happy if you could look in upon us without his knowing it.[48]

THREE DAYS LATER, ON JANUARY 31, Chloe Beach gave birth to a little girl she named Violet. It is a fearsome thing to suggest, but there is reason to think that Violet might be Henry Ward Beecher's daughter. In the absence of modern DNA testing, the evidence is circumstantial but provocative.

When Violet was conceived, around April 1866, sexual relations between the Beaches would have been minimal at best. Not only had the Beaches' marriage reached a new nadir, but Moses was barely recovered from the painful rashes and intestinal distress of typhoid fever. Knowing how feeble Moses was, Chloe coyly tried to push back her due date. The biggest challenge for a woman seeking to hide the paternity of her unborn child is to make sure the date of conception matches her opportunities to conceive. Eunice, an experienced nurse, was extremely surprised when, on January 25, Chloe told her that her baby was due in mid-February. No doubt Eunice was far more surprised when the baby arrived only four days later, with no evidence of premature birth.

Then there is the Beaches' uncharacteristic behavior. Not long after Chloe's pregnancy became apparent, Moses finally confronted Henry about his relationship with Chloe and then fled the country in despair. While there is no sign that Moses questioned Violet's paternity, he took little pleasure in her birth, spending almost the entire first year of Violet's life either up at their farm on the Hudson, while Chloe and Violet remained in the city, or traveling abroad. By contrast, for the rest of her life, Chloe favored Violet over her other children; "you are dearer than the others," Chloe explained to Violet, "perhaps because your love for me is deeper, perhaps that you have not been in health like them, maybe that you are the youngest, and perfection seems to be in the younger one usually."[49]

But Henry's role is the most telling. First there was Violet's name. Flowers were a shared passion of Chloe's and Henry's, and they often communicated through gifts of flowers. Like many Victorians, he believed that flowers had their own personalities and symbolism, and that there were strong "analogies between plants and thoughts and sentiments," as he wrote in *Norwood*.[50] The violet was one of his favorite flowers. A small, fragrant blossom that blooms in shady, sheltered spots, in the common language of flowers the violet symbolizes a hidden gem and innocence slightly eroticized. In Roman mythology the goddess Diana turned the nymph Ion into a violet to save her from the lustful attentions of the god Apollo.

Henry adored children, but his devotion to Violet went beyond normal boundaries. Unlike the other Beach children, Violet called him "Grandpa," and came and went in the Beechers' house as if it were her own. When she was as young as four, Violet would scamper over to Henry's first thing in the morning to play with him at breakfast. In fact Henry seemed closer to Violet than to his own grandchildren. As she got older he took her on outings, wrote her warm letters, showered her with gifts, and accompanied Chloe to the train station when Violet went away to boarding school.

But the most compelling evidence is the photographs. When she was around six, Violet and Henry posed together for a formal studio portrait—then as now a very unusual thing for a man and his neighbors' daughter to do. Already her face shows hints of Henry's moon shape and ample mouth. By the time she is a teenager the resemblance between Violet and Henry—the large, heavy-lidded eyes, the broad chin, and wide, thin lips—is so pronounced that even today some casual viewers assume they are close relatives.

Of course there is something tawdry in such speculations. All we know for certain is that Moses Beach spent decades agonizing over his wife's increasing infatuation with her minister, and that from 1866 until Henry's death the Beach and Beecher families were deeply intertwined beyond the conventional bonds of friendship. We also know this: Had Henry not spent that winter seeking consolation in the company of Elizabeth Tilton, no one would ever have entertained such a vulgar idea.

Whatever conflagration Beecher had feared from the Beaches, it did not come, and within a few weeks of Violet's birth Henry was feeling quite jolly again. Even Theodore was in good spirits when he returned in early March, and feeling generous toward the parson. "In view of his kind attentions to you this Winter, all my old love for him has revived, and my heart would once more greet him as of old," he told Elizabeth. "I sometimes quarrel with my friends on the surface, but never at bottom."[51]

Only Elizabeth was disappointed that spring. For now that Theodore was back, the only time she saw the Reverend Beecher was in the pulpit.

IN JANUARY 1867 a thirty-one-year-old writer named Samuel Clemens arrived in New York. Sam Clemens joined the bohemian journalists swarming the city; drinking, smoking, and swearing were his pleasures, and sarcasm was his stock-in-trade. Under the pen name Mark Twain, Clemens had made a splash out West with his humorous essays and lectures, and now hoped to hit the big time in the East.

The last time Twain had been in New York was 1853, and he was astonished by how much the city had changed. In '53 *Uncle Tom's Cabin* had been the big box-office smash. Now risqué "Model Artists Shows," which had been banned in '53, were all the rage. One current smash, *The Black Crook*, featured "70 beauties arrayed in dazzling half-costumes; and displaying all possible compromises between nakedness and decency," marveled Twain. Even women on the street looked racier as the wide-hooped crinoline dresses of the fifties were replaced by form-fitting ankle-length dresses that, as Twain noted with approval, exposed "the restless little feet. Charming, fascinating, seductive, bewitching!"

Frank as this new generation of New Yorkers was about sex, they were even more blunt about money. "The old, genuine, traveled, cultivated, pedigreed aristocracy of New York, stand stunned and helpless under the new order of things," observed Twain. "They find themselves supplanted by upstart princes of Shoddy, vulgar and with unknown grandfathers. The incomes which were something for the common herd to gape at and gossip about once, are mere livelihoods now—would not pay Shoddy's house-rent." If things get much worse, Twain concluded, "I fear I shall have to start a moral missionary society here."

Like all tourists, Twain made Plymouth Church one of his first stops. It was well worth the frigid ferry ride and sitting jammed into a spot "about large enough to accommodate a spittoon," he declared. As Beecher "went marching up and down the stage, sawing his arms in the air, howling sarcasms this way and that, discharging rockets of poetry, and exploding mines of eloquence, halting now and then to stamp his foot three times in succession to emphasize a point, I could have started the audience with a single clap of the hands and brought down the house. I had a suffocating desire to do it," wrote Twain. "Mr. Beecher is a remarkably handsome man when he is in the full tide of sermonizing, and his face is lit up with animation," Twain concluded, "but he is as homely as a singed cat when he isn't doing anything."

Casting about for fresh subjects, Twain stumbled on something new under the sun: America's first luxury cruise. Captain Charles Duncan, a deacon of Plymouth Church and close friend of Beecher's, was leading the steamer *Quaker City* on a five-month pleasure cruise through the Mediterranean to the Holy Land. It was to be both deluxe (costing an exorbitant $1,250 at a time when a round-trip first-class fare to Paris was $200) and pious, with all passengers required to present character references. Rumor had it that the Civil War hero General William Tecumseh Sherman and the Reverend Beecher would be going. The passenger list was already half filled with Plymouth Church folk.

Twain finagled the editors of a California paper into paying his fare, but from the outset he struggled against the piety part. Twain and a reporter from the *Tribune* he called Smith were unshaven and a little tipsy when they arrived in Captain Duncan's office. Smith made it worse by introducing Twain as a Baptist missionary just returned from the Sandwich Islands (now known as Hawaii). Twain then asked, with mock solemnity, about the rumor that Beecher would be coming and whether he might allow a Baptist to preach on board.

"I am only a Baptist, you see, but I'd like to have a show," Twain explained, barely suppressing his laughter.

" 'Oh, d——it!' Smith whispered, 'you'll ruin everything with that slang.' Then aloud: 'Yes, my friend is a Baptist clergyman, and we feared that inasmuch as Mr. Beecher is a Universalist, he—' " This subtle dig at Beecher's free and easy salvation had the gratifying effect of flummoxing Captain Duncan.

" 'Universalist! Why, he is a Congregationalist. But never mind that,' " Duncan protested. " 'I have no doubt he would be sincerely glad to have Mr. Twain assist him in the vessel's pulpit at all times—no doubt in the world about that.'

"I had to laugh out strong, here—I could not well help it," Twain recalled. "The idea of my preaching time about with Beecher was so fresh, so entertaining, so delightful." Twain returned the next day to apologize and pay his fare.

But the captain could not afford to be picky, as it turned out. By the time the *Quaker City* left New York, both General Sherman and Beecher had withdrawn from the passenger list. With Beecher out, most of the Plymouth Church people stayed home as well. The one major exception was Moses Beach. He had returned from Berlin in time to see Violet born but was so miserable in Brooklyn that he jumped at the chance to escape again. This time he took along his seventeen-year-old daughter, Emma.

The night before the *Quaker City* shipped off, Moses Beach hosted an elegant reception for the passengers, with Beecher as a featured guest. What the passenger list had lost in selectivity they made up for in self-righteousness. One passenger, "a solemn, unsmiling, sanctimonious old iceberg that looked like he was waiting for a vacancy in the trinity" as Twain described him, asked the captain if the ship would stop sailing on the Sabbath. Even Captain Duncan was taken aback by that suggestion.[52]

Twain's shipboard essays soon turned from an exotic travelogue into a biting satire of his sanctimonious shipmates, with their daily prayer meetings, petty prejudices, and shipboard bans on dancing and other sins. The final straw came when the whole group toured the Pyramids and refused to travel on Sunday, stranding everyone in the scorching desert. "Such was our daily life on board the ship—solemnity, decorum, dinner, dominoes, prayer, slander," wrote Twain. "The advertised title of the expedition—'The Grand Holy Land Pleasure Excursion'—was a ghastly misnomer. 'The Grand Holy Land Funeral Procession' would have been better—much better."[53] He ridiculed the Holy Land as dirty and uncivilized, Europe as overrated, and Americans as pretentious and parochial. This was not Beecher's gentle irreverence. This was the unadulterated impudence of a new generation, mocking the very idea that anything could be sacred.

But Twain appreciated Moses Beach, who was adventurous, enthusiastic, and a Christian of the best sort. When the *Quaker City* ran across forty destitute Yankees who had been lured to Palestine by a confidence man claiming to be a prophet, Beach personally paid for their passage back to New England. Twain took a special shine to seventeen-year-old Emma Beach, who became his regular chess partner.

After the *Quaker City* returned in the fall of 1867, Mark Twain continued his flirtation with Emma Beach. Through the Beaches he was invited to Beecher's house for dinner one Sabbath. "We had a tip-top dinner, but nothing to drink but cider," Twain wrote to his mother. "I told Mr. Beecher that no dinner could be perfect without champagne, or at least some kind of Burgundy, and he said that privately he was a good deal of the same opinion, but it wouldn't do to say it out loud."

The two men hit it off handsomely. "Henry Ward is a brick," declared Twain in the superlative slang of the day. A few weeks later, as

Twain was negotiating with a Hartford publisher to turn his *Quaker City* essays into a book, Beecher took the young man aside, saying, "Now, here, you are one of the talented men of the age—nobody is going to deny that—but in matters of business, I don't suppose you know more than enough to come in when it rains. I'll tell you what to do, and how to do it."

Following Beecher's advice, Twain made a savvy deal that turned into a small fortune when the book, *Innocents Abroad, or, the New Pilgrim's Progress*, became a best-seller. Suddenly endowed with wealth and respectability, Twain moved to Hartford's Nook Farm neighborhood, a literary enclave where his close neighbors were Henry's sisters, Isabella Hooker and Harriet Stowe. A year later he was married by Tom Beecher to Olivia Langdon, a close friend of the Hookers.

"Puritans are mighty straight-laced and they won't let me smoke in the parlor, but the Almighty don't make any better people," Twain decided after an evening at Isabella's.[54] If any of them noticed the irony of a Beecher advising an avowed heathen on how to profit by parodying self-righteous Christians, it went unrecorded.

FOR MOSES BEACH the *Quaker City* trip turned out to be a grave mistake. "That my continued absence would continue the evil was a matter of course," Moses realized when he returned to Brooklyn.[55] With Eunice up at the farm in Peekskill, Henry had spent most evenings with Chloe, and when Henry moved upstate to Peekskill for his summer vacation, Chloe made plans to join them.

Once again Moses repressed his bitterness. In a supreme act of self-effacement he brought a magnificent gift to Beecher—an entire olive tree from the Holy Land, which he had crafted into a pulpit chair and desk that he presented to Beecher on New Year's Day 1868. That same day Moses gave up the *New York Sun* for good, selling it to Charles Dana, a former editor at the *Tribune*. His bed might be cold, but at least he now had full freedom to flee when he could no longer bear it. That summer he again left for several months, taking Emma on a long trip to California.

In 1870, in honor of her forty-third birthday, Moses bought Chloe, as he told her, "thirty acres of the land you have so much and so long coveted—adjoining that of Mr. Beecher in Peekskill."[56] That "a residence should be obtained in your immediate neighborhood did not surprise me though it did and does embitter my thoughts and feelings.

Other reasons were given for that residence and much I wish they had been the true ones," Moses wrote to Beecher. "One less infatuated would have devised ways to avoid the heart-woundings then and on previous occasions given."

This reluctant sacrifice finally pushed Moses to his limit. Unable to sleep one midnight not long after this, he rose from his bed and composed a heartbreaking letter to Henry. Out poured the story of the last decade, watching his wife fall in love with the pastor:

> During all this time you have been stealing the affections of one dearer to me than life itself. That you have not done it with intent I most fully believe, but that you have done it ignorantly I cannot feel so confident, for the reason that, in my crude, uncertain way I once strove most fiercely to make you aware.[. . .]
>
> And if you yet question the truth of my complaint, ask your own heart for a reply. Have you no feeling, a thought more tender in the direction where lies my wound than in others of your many associations? If not why should I have heard the intimacy remarked upon by those who I knew were strangers to my own thoughts and feelings—remarked apparently, to draw attention to it?[. . .]
>
> But what can I do? you will ask, possibly. And I shall but echo the question back again. I come to you because I can do nothing else. I come that you may know what is the result to me of the constant intercourse and how deeply I am being wounded at every turn—how that, more and more, I am being left in a sea of mental trouble, by one whose right it is but whose pleasure I more and more feel it is not, to sympathize with and help me to rise above and overcome all that assails me, and whose duty it is to be watchful against acts or thoughts calculated to give me pain.
>
> If you can see light any whither lend me your eyes that I also may look. I would suggest your verbal influence but that I fear an evil result from the fresh awakening of a naturally self-sufficient and self-reliant disposition. And thus I wait the judgment of more mature and more experienced heads than my own.[57]

There is no sign that Moses ever sent this anguished letter. If he did, it had little effect. After Violet was born, Chloe became, essentially, a second, unofficial wife to Henry, especially now that Eunice spent half the year in Peekskill and would soon begin wintering in Florida. Indeed, Eunice depended upon Mrs. Beach almost as much as her husband did.

A day rarely passed without Eunice's asking Chloe for some intimate favor, from searching Henry's bureau for clean shirts to secret loans of money. "I shall feel always sure that he is comfortable and *at home* when I know he is with you," Eunice told her gratefully.[58]

IN MAY 1867 the first installments of *Norwood* appeared in the *New York Ledger*. Bonner's bet paid off handsomely as readers rushed to see what sort of novel a clergyman—a Beecher, no less!—would write.

The plot of *Norwood*—the tale of a boy much like young Henry, growing up in a village much like Litchfield—was thin. But it was redeemed by the deftly drawn characters who gave voice to Beecher's various theories. The village doctor becomes the vehicle for Beecher's beliefs in the spirituality of nature and the natural law of evolution, while the village parson is the butt of Henry's jokes about dour Yankee theology. The heroine, Rose Wentworth, entertains two suitors, one Yankee, one Virginian, who become friends while competing for her heart, dramatizing Beecher's generous vision of Reconstruction. (Beecher was still Yankee enough to kill off the Southern suitor in the Battle of Gettysburg, while the Northern suitor became a Union general and married the heroine.)

The critics were kind, if not ecstatic. In the *Atlantic Monthly* William Dean Howells complained of "the ruthlessness with which the author preaches, both in his own person and in that of his characters, spinning out long monologues and colloquies upon morals, religion, and the whole conduct of life." But only one reviewer spied the freethinking heresies hiding beneath the sentimental sermonizing. "The author, though nominally a Christian, professedly a Congregational preacher, is really a pagan, and wishes to abolish Puritanism for the worship of nature," wrote Orestes Brownson in the *Catholic World*. "Beecherism," Brownson concluded with genuine anger, "resolves the Christian law of perfection into the natural laws of the physicists."[59] Still, the novel was a popular success and was quickly adapted for the stage.

Beecher took it all with good humor. "People used to accuse me of being the author of *Uncle Tom's Cabin*," he joked, "until I wrote *Norwood*." Whatever its literary merits, Henry exulted, "*The book has taken me entirely out of debt. The farm is my own. The house and its contents in Brooklyn is my own*."[60]

Ever on the lookout for new paths to profit, a group of investors from Plymouth Church led by Tasker Howard set up a publishing firm to milk the insatiable market for all things Beecher. The first act of J. B. Ford and Co. was to give Beecher a ten-thousand-dollar advance for a two-volume novelistic biography of Jesus called *The Life of Christ*. Soon they were churning out Beecher's sermons and prayers by the ream and planning their own weekly paper. Even Eunice got to indulge her long-suppressed literary ambitions, taking the helm of a short-lived magazine called *Mother at Home*.

THEODORE TILTON OUGHT TO HAVE BEEN content in the winter of 1867–68. In December 1867 Elizabeth gave birth to a son named Paul and was recovering nicely. He could boast of a national reputation as a political crusader and an editorial wunderkind, and personal friendships with many of the era's great thinkers and doers. The Fourteenth Amendment to the Constitution, granting citizenship to African American males, would soon be ratified. And after nearly two years of demanding Andrew Johnson's ouster, Congress was moving to impeach the president. As Elizabeth wrote to her husband, "Now, I say to myself—with Andy removed, and your wife restored, and your debts most paid, what remains but to be happy?"[61]

But always he felt the dampening shadow of Beecher. While Beecher was earning the magnificent sum of thirty thousand dollars (including a six-thousand-dollar bonus) for his mediocre novel, Theodore published a book of leaden poetry to caustic reviews. Every word Beecher uttered was packaged and repackaged for sale, but Tilton was that winter publicly humiliated when *Demorest Magazine* bought some of his poems and then sued him when they discovered he'd already published the poems elsewhere. Beecher's flirtations with free thought only extended his popularity, while Theodore's unorthodoxy endangered his very livelihood.

In fact, Beecher took ten times the public criticism that Tilton did. But unlike the resilient preacher, Theodore felt every blow and seethed with resentment. He was too high-minded to hedge his views yet too proud to be a pariah. He yearned for fame and adulation but was disgusted by his own desires. He disdained the pursuit of wealth, but the trappings of bohemian gentility—art, books, salonlike entertaining—kept him in perpetual debt. Capping his contradictions, that winter he spent five hundred dollars ("more money than I could afford," he admitted ruefully) commissioning his friend William Paige to paint a portrait of Henry Ward Beecher![62]

The sharpest point of rivalry was Elizabeth. "I think she regarded Mr. Beecher almost as though Jesus Christ himself had walked in," Theodore said bitterly.[63] The further Theodore drifted from orthodoxy, the more her faith, especially her faith in Beecher, aggravated him, and the more he harped on Beecher's alleged infidelities. Elizabeth brushed them off. "I attributed those criticisms from Theodore to Mr. Bowen's criticism," she said.[64]

As soon as Theodore departed for his annual winter lecture tour, Beecher again began to appear at the house on Livingston Street. He took Elizabeth on outings and read her the first chapters of his new *Life of Christ*. He frolicked with her children and rocked baby Paul to sleep. But this winter Elizabeth was more uneasy.

"About 11 o'clock today, Mr. B called. Now, beloved, let not even the shadow of a *shadow* fall on your dear heart because of this, now, henceforth or forever. He cannot by *any possibility* be much to me, since I have known you. I implore you to believe it and look at me as in the Day of Judgment I shall be revealed to you. Do not think it audacious in me to say I am to him a good deal," she wrote to Theodore in a typical letter.

Soon the gossip mill was churning loudly enough that even Elizabeth's best friend, Mattie Bradshaw, was worried. "I think she feels a little care that Mr. B visits here," Elizabeth confided to Theodore. "She said: 'Lib, I heard through Mrs. Morrill that Mr. B called on you Wednesday. I believe he likes you ever so much.'"[65]

But Theodore was too busy to pay much attention. When he returned from his western tour, the impeachment of Andrew Johnson was well under way. Tilton spent most of the spring in the capital, caucusing and scheming with the Radical congressmen. Tilton led the frantic, last-minute negotiations and, according to Navy Secretary Gideon Welles (no fan of the Radicals or Tilton), it was his "sanguine representations" that spurred the Radicals to call for the final vote. Despite his efforts, President Johnson was acquitted by one ballot.[66]

The loss was crushing. For Theodore it amounted to a midlife crisis. "I became editor of the *Independent* when I was quite young, and my hands were immediately filled with public questions—the antislavery movement, the prosecution of the war, the reconstruction of the Union," Tilton later explained. "But, when slavery was abolished and the war was over, my occupation in a certain sense, was gone."[67]

His petulance became unbearable. Bessie Turner, a teenager who lived off and on with the family as a mother's helper to Elizabeth Tilton, recalled how, unable to sleep, Theodore would roam around the house at night, rehanging pictures, or switching from bed to bed, looking for one that suited him, with his groggy wife following behind. He was increasingly irritable with Elizabeth, berating her for her spending, her grammar, her religiosity, even her small size. He began drinking more and occasionally staying out all night without warning.

On August 25, 1868, their one-year-old son, Paul, died of cholera. Beecher rushed down from Peekskill to officiate at the funeral. When Tilton's friend and fellow reformer, Susan B. Anthony, arrived for the service, she was surprised to find the Tilton house filled with sunlight and Elizabeth dressed entirely in white rather than the typical black of mourning. "I expected to find her overwhelmed with grief," recalled another friend, "as when her little daughter died, she was inconsolable for months; but instead, she was lifted up into a rapt, spiritual state of communion with the invisible world."[68]

But Theodore was inconsolable, his grief untempered by the faith that sustained his wife. He was filled with regret at how little time he had spent with Paul—indeed, Beecher had spent nearly as much time with the boy as he had.

NOW THAT ANDREW JOHNSON'S FATE was settled, all political eyes turned to the upcoming presidential election. The Democrats offered New York governor Horatio Seymour, who ran on a platform of rabid, unreconstructed racism. The Republicans nominated the closest thing to a sure bet: the great hero of the Union army, Ulysses S. Grant.

Beecher was an unabashed admirer of Grant, despite the general's lack of political experience. "Solid, unpretentious, straightforward, apt to succeed and not spoiled by success, wise in discerning men, skillful in using them, with the rare gift (which Washington had in an eminent degree) of wisdom in getting wisdom from other men's councils," Beecher declared. "I confidently anticipate that, great as his military success has been he will hereafter be known more favorably for the wisdom of his civil administration."[69] Sadly, Beecher was as wrong about Grant as he had been about Andrew Johnson. Grant's administration would go down as one of most corrupt in history, precisely due to his lack of wisdom "in discerning men."

But Beecher could hardly be blamed. Even the venerable Ralph Waldo Emerson clambered onto Grant's bandwagon. Emerson's daughter Ellen was a huge fan of Beecher's (although she exhibited almost no interest in her father's work) and in April, Ellen dragged her father to Plymouth Church. Emerson enjoyed the service, noting with approval how few Calvinists there were in the audience. ("He could always tell them by sight," Ellen said, and Methodists too. "Methodists were very different, but equally marked.") But the big thrill came as they were heading to the ferry, when a shout electrified the crowd: "Why! it is General Grant!"

"Father and I joined madly in this pursuit, and ran along, now in the street, now out, like little boys beside the trainers, and one way and another succeeded in seeing his head and shoulders, and, now and then, an interrupted glimpse of his face," Ellen said. They chased the poor ex-soldier all the way to the ferry landing. "Then Father, saying, 'We have nabbed him now; he can't get to the boat without our seeing him,' manned the small gate, and posted me in an advantageous position behind him. But we were outwitted. General Grant went in at the horse-gate. Father quickly discovered his intention, rushed to the gate and saw him very well, so did I."[70] They stared unashamedly at the general until the ferry arrived in Manhattan.

The year 1868 brought another ugly election. The Democrats denounced Grant as a drunk and a military dictator, and promised to roll back Radical Reconstruction. Republicans branded Democrats as the party of Copperheads, Rebels, and drunken Irishmen. Beecher "waved the bloody shirt" with gusto, setting aside all talk of charity for the former enemy. Democrats assailed him with the old "nigger-lover" attacks, and tried to trip him up with his Cleveland Letters, but Beecher deftly threw off all comers.

On October 9, 1868, after the regular Friday-night prayer meeting, Beecher and a bevy of parishioners, including Elizabeth Tilton, walked over to the Brooklyn Academy of Music, where Beecher was to speak at a mammoth Grant rally. Eunice was gone for several weeks, visiting their son Harry, his young wife, and their brand-new baby up in Albany, and then heading on to Connecticut to see their daughter Hattie, who had just given birth to a baby boy—named, at Eunice's insistence, Henry Ward Beecher Scoville.

The Academy of Music was packed to the rafters and eager for excitement. Just as Beecher stepped out onto the stage, a huge canvas backdrop unrolled dramatically from the ceiling. On it the renowned illustrator Thomas Nast had painted Governor Seymour sitting dejectedly on the steps of the White House next to a lamppost with a black man hanging from the crossbar, and General Grant being led up to the front door by Columbia, the goddess of liberty. "It is said that General Grant is a drunkard. I do not believe a word of it," Beecher thundered. "But if it were so, I had rather have General Grant a drunkard than Horatio Seymour sober!" The audience roared with approval.[71]

The next day Elizabeth Tilton made her way over to Beecher's house to congratulate him on his enthralling performance the night before. She was one month pregnant and still in a "tender state of mind" from the death of her baby, Paul.

What happened that day in Beecher's brownstone would become a matter of international debate. According to Theodore Tilton, Henry, "after long moral resistance by her and after repeated assaults by him upon her mind with overmastering arguments, accomplished the possession of her person;" in other words Elizabeth and Henry allegedly made love.[72]

All we know of this encounter comes secondhand, from people who swore they heard it from Elizabeth's own lips. In her diary she described it simply as "A Day Memorable."[73] We do know that Henry immediately canceled his plan to go see Hattie's new baby. Instead he told Eunice that he'd forgotten an engagement and she should stay in Connecticut for another week until he could come get her. The following Saturday evening, according to later testimony, Henry came to the Tiltons' house on Livingston Street, where he and Elizabeth again made love.

By the very nature of seduction and adultery, no one but Elizabeth and Henry can know for certain what actually happened that October. But nearly everyone could agree on this: Religion, not lust, was Elizabeth's downfall. Beecher "took advantage of her orthodox views to make her the net and mesh in which he ensnared her," Tilton claimed bitterly. "They were years courting each other by mutual piety." "God would not blame them," he said the minister assured her, for theirs was a "a high religious love," a sacred outgrowth of their love for Christ, which transcended vulgar impulses and conventional morality. Their sexual intimacy was as "natural and sincere an expression of love," said Elizabeth, according to another friend, "as words of endearment."[74]

After Theodore left for his annual lecture tour in the winter of 1868–69, Beecher visited Elizabeth at least a dozen times and, according to Theodore, continued to press her for sex. The visits slackened when Theodore returned, but that summer, when Elizabeth gave birth to a baby named Ralph, Beecher came bearing armloads of flowers. She and the preacher continued their alleged affair through the spring of 1870, having sex at her house and his, and at other unnamed places.

Elizabeth seemed to regret nothing but the deceit. For even though Beecher "repeatedly assured her that she was spotless and chaste," he insisted that they must be cautious, for lower minds would persecute them if their secret was revealed. *"Nest-hiding,"* he called it.[75]

THE ELECTION OF ULYSSES S. GRANT signaled the beginning of the end for both the Radical Republicans and the nation's interest in the fate of the slaves. The Republican Party's original social activism was fast fading. Within a decade it would be the party of big business and laissez-faire policies. February 1869 marked the last great battle of the abolitionists, the passage of the Fifteenth Amendment to the Constitution, stipulating that voting rights cannot be denied on the basis of race, color, or previous condition of servitude. "Reconstruction is nearly concluded, and the great principle on which the party rests is that of equal suffrage," wrote Tilton in the *Independent*. "It is the last step taken, or to be taken."[76] But "equal suffrage" was a misnomer. The one category entirely excluded was women.

The women's rights movement had been active for two decades, but like many of the reforms that mushroomed in the 1840s, it was placed on the back burner during the Rebellion, as reform-minded women threw their energies into the war effort and emancipation. The abolition crusade had sharpened the skills and ambitions of women like Susan B. Anthony, Elizabeth Cady Stanton, Lucy Stone, and Julia Ward Howe. Now with the Radicals in control of Congress, and all the talk of equality, natural rights, and radical social change, the time seemed ripe to resurrect their cause.

As a result many women activists felt angry and betrayed when they read the wording of the Fourteenth Amendment, which defined U.S. citizens specifically and solely as "male"—the first use of the word "male" in the Constitution. Their Radical allies placated the women, explaining that political realities made it impossible to pass both woman and black suffrage. This was "the Negro's Hour," but their time would come soon. Now they were again bitterly disappointed to find that the Fifteenth Amendment specifically excluded women from the right to vote. Again they were offered reassurance. Having delivered the crowning blow to slavery, some of the bolder male reformers were now ready to embrace the women's cause.

Henry Ward Beecher was an early and enthusiastic advocate of expanding women's rights, and had converted many friends to the cause, including Theodore and Elizabeth Tilton. He was one of the few Republicans who had not told the women to wait their turn. "If you have any radical principle to urge, any higher wisdom to make known, don't wait until quiet times come, until the public mind shuts up altogether," he had told the first meeting of the American Equal Rights Association two years earlier in 1867.[77] That same year Beecher made his first and only run for political office, unsuccessfully campaigning to be a delegate to the New York State Constitutional Convention in hopes of persuading the convention to extend voting rights to all adult citizens. Now he took up the women's cause in earnest.

With Henry in the lead, the Beecher sisters began to prick up their ears, particularly his youngest sister, Isabella, or Belle as she was nicknamed. Instead of following Catharine and Harriet into public life, Isabella had taken her sister Mary's example, marrying a well-to-do Connecticut lawyer and focusing on her family. But as her children grew older, Isabella began to chafe at the limitations of the domestic sphere, and the comparisons with her famous siblings—"everywhere I go—I have to run on the credit of my relations—no where, but at home can I lay claim to a particle of individuality," she complained to her husband, John.[78] Now in her mid-forties, Isabella decided to make her debut as a public woman and reformer by becoming a leader in the women's movement.

In May 1869 Isabella accompanied Henry to the third annual gathering of the Equal Rights Association in New York, along with Elizabeth Tilton and a who's who of major reformers—a convention of "long-haired men and short-haired women," in the phrase of the day. Intended to rally support for a proposed Sixteenth Amendment, giving women the right to vote, the meeting was a disaster. Not only did it degenerate into a mudslinging match over the Fifteenth Amendment, but a new fissure erupted along the old Boston/New York fault line. The New York faction, led by Susan B. Anthony and Elizabeth Cady Stanton, wanted to move beyond suffrage, to take up a wide range of economic and social issues, including abortion, birth control, prostitution, divorce reform, financial independence, and the double standard that turned a blind eye to the sexual foibles of men while destroying any woman who dared speak of sexual matters. The more conservative clique of Boston women, led by Lucy Stone, were disgusted by these taboo topics and feared that such talk would derail their campaign for the vote. Henry wisely stayed above the fray.

Two days after this acrimonious meeting, Stanton and Anthony broke away and founded the National Woman Suffrage Association (NWSA), turning their newspaper, the *Revolution*, into its official organ. Unfortunate as the split was for the cause, it was wonderful for Isabella's ego. Both the conservative Bostonians and the radical New Yorkers immediately began to compete for her loyalty. Not only would it be a coup to catch a Beecher but Isabella might bring along her famous sisters, who, despite their own unconventional careers, had stayed aloof from women's reform.

At the outset, Isabella's Yankee propriety prejudiced her against Susan B. Anthony and Elizabeth Cady Stanton. But that summer, Isabella was won over by their charismatic personalities and bold intellects. She tried to use her newfound influence to bring the factions together, but that went nowhere. She was, however, pulling in her sister Harriet Stowe, who was considering writing an *Uncle Tom's Cabin*–style novel about the injustices suffered by women. By late 1869 Harriet and Isabella were negotiating with Stanton and Anthony to take over as editors of the *Revolution*.

Catharine was a tougher nut to crack. She was a heroic pioneer in the field of women's education and employment. But Catharine had long relied on the rhetoric of traditional femininity to smooth her path and bolster her arguments. It was too late now for her to start dismantling those prejudices. That summer of 1869, she began a personal crusade against woman suffrage as demeaning and unnatural—"the Beecher idea against the Stanton idea," as the *New York Times* termed it.[79]

LURKING BEHIND ALL THESE CONFLICTS was the pungent aroma of sex. Just as racism was made more potent by linking it to interracial sex, so it worked with those who wanted to enforce the hierarchy of gender. Victorians were no more or less sexual than any other generation. But just as in our own time, because sexuality was so deeply personal and so inextricably linked to shame and taboo, any attempt to challenge sexual mores—whether it be interracial marriage, the recognition of female desire, or legalizing divorce—brought with it a firestorm of discomfort and disgust.

Yet there was no denying that New York, like many cities, was teeming with sex. Prostitution, casual and organized, seedy and high class, was second only to the garment trade in employing female workers. They plied their trade on street corners, in saloons, in dance halls, and in the elegant brothels that lined the finer regions of Broadway.

Before the war it was estimated that there was one prostitute for every sixty-four men in New York, and the disruptions of the Rebellion vastly increased their numbers and visibility. In 1868 the city was home to an estimated twenty thousand prostitutes and six hundred bawdy houses, many helpfully listed in A Gentleman's Guide for tourists. Venereal disease was rampant, with philandering husbands often infecting their faithful wives, and abortionists openly advertised their services in the city papers.

People were beginning to acknowledge sexuality as not only a matter of public morals but of public health. But attempts to address the situation were shut down by the ironclad double standard that ruled Victorian America. Those who called for more liberal divorce laws, controlling childbirth, or better sex education were accused of promoting "free love," a dangerous variant of "free thought."

This double standard, in turn, depended on a conspiracy of secrecy. While it was a known fact that many of the nation's public men patronized bawdy houses or kept mistresses, anyone speaking openly of such matters would be cast out of respectable society. The penalty was double for women. Ministers and reformers might occasionally speak out against prostitution or abortionists, at their own peril, but a true woman should not even know of such things.

This deplorable situation pressed itself on Beecher's attention in June 1869, when his close friend, the editor of the New York Times Henry J. Raymond, died of a heart attack. Beecher delivered a glowing eulogy, but as he rode back from the funeral with John Bigelow, another friend and former Times staffer, he whispered to Bigelow the real circumstances of Raymond's death. While his wife was in Europe, Raymond had been carrying on a torrid affair with Rose Etynge, a popular dark-eyed actress. When his wife returned, Raymond tried to end the affair, but his recalcitrant mistress was using his love letters to blackmail the editor. Blackmail was fairly common in the back rooms of nineteenth-century New York; it was the price men paid to keep the double standard intact. The night of his death, Raymond told his wife that he was going to a political meeting, but instead headed to Etynge's apartment, where they had "a very stormy time."[80] Late that evening two men in a carriage brought Raymond's body home and threw it on the hall floor of his house, and then disappeared. The next morning a servant stumbled upon him, still alive but barely breathing, and he died soon after. Beecher did not seem the least bit shocked by the story.

Just as Henry was eulogizing his wayward friend, his sister Harriet was writing an article on the infamous libertine Lord Byron for the *Atlantic Monthly*. In her travels abroad Harriet Beecher Stowe had become friends with Byron's widow, who confided to Harriet that the reason she had left her marriage to Lord Byron was that he had committed incest with his half sister, Augusta. Lady Byron had been much abused for abandoning her husband before her recent death. Now that she was gone, Harriet was determined to tell the true story.

Friends warned Harriet that the story would cause a commotion, but after the furor over *Uncle Tom's Cabin* she felt that nothing could shake her. Harriet was wrong. When the article appeared at the end of August, the outcry was immediate and unforgiving from all sides. Many were mystified at her sudden debauchery, suggesting the whole thing was a hoax, or that if she had truly written it, perhaps she'd been possessed by the devil. Nearly all insisted that even if such sordid filth were true, it should never have been uttered, especially by a woman. Henry Bowen ostentatiously announced that he was canceling his subscription to the *Atlantic Monthly*, a move followed by many shocked readers. Subscriptions to the *Atlantic* dived from fifty thousand to thirty-five thousand, and Harriet's book sales plummeted.

Henry made light of Harriet's latest controversy. "You have stirred up the annual family row—sometimes it is one, sometimes another of those Beechers, that keep people in hot water. Now it is *your* kettle that has boiled over," he wrote to her.[81] But he was careful to keep out of it publicly. He was working steadily on the *Life of Christ*, and, after years of plotting, he and the Howards were starting his own weekly religious paper. But his turn in the hot water would come quicker than he thought.

The conservative Boston wing of the women's rights movement quickly absorbed the lesson of the Bryon flap—any association with sexual reform would surely sink the suffrage campaign and tar the women's movement. So in November 1869, five months after Anthony and Stanton formed the NWSA, the Boston wing retaliated by founding the rival American Woman's Suffrage Association. The AWSA's first act, before they even drafted a constitution, was to invite Henry to serve as their first president. He agreed and was elected unanimously.

Why he chose this path is unclear. Henry had close ties to both camps, not to mention a long aversion to joining organizations. Whatever the reason, he would soon regret it. Intensifying the rivalry between the organizations, within months the NWSA had set aside their rules requiring all officers to be female, and elected Theodore Tilton the president of *their* organization! By March 1870, reported Susan B. Anthony with pleasure, Beecher was swearing that "if he can get out of this—he'll never be so big a fool again as to give his name to any dividing party or movement."[82]

The regret of the Bostonians would come even faster. Less than a week after Beecher accepted the presidency of the conservative AWSA, Beecher hoisted the ladies by their own proper petards.

ON NOVEMBER 30, 1869, a messenger was sent to bring Beecher to the Astor Hotel on Broadway. There Beecher found the journalist Albert Richardson on his deathbed. Albert Richardson came to fame as an undercover war correspondent for the *Tribune* who spent two years in a Confederate prison camp before making a daring escape and turning his story into a best-selling book. After the war Richardson fell in love with an actress named Abby Sage McFarland, whose life was being destroyed by her drunken, abusive husband, Daniel McFarland. With Richardson's help she moved to Indiana, a state known for its liberal divorce laws, and she had just returned to New York, divorce decree in hand. On November 25 her enraged ex-husband hid behind a pillar in the *Tribune* office and shot his rival at close range.

Now, with Abby by his side and his life ebbing away, Richardson asked Beecher to marry them. Beecher was a great admirer of Richardson's career, and the case touched his romantic instincts. So after asking a few questions, he performed the brief ceremony. Richardson died the next morning.

As with Harriet, both press and public descended upon him instantly. Byron and McFarland may have been beastly, but their private crimes paled in comparison to the Beechers' combined assault on public decency. Not only did Beecher seem to be sanctioning adultery, home wrecking, and easy divorce, but it turned out that Indiana divorces were not recognized in New York State, making Abby McFarland a bigamist. "Yes," sneered the *New York Sun*, "it is the pious, the popular, the admired, the reverend Henry Ward Beecher, who comes boldly and even proudly forward, holding by the hand and leading Lust to her triumph over Religion!"[83]

Beecher defended his actions and gave the eulogy at Richardson's funeral, but he didn't sound entirely sure of himself. "I took every statement of every kind respecting the affair," he told the *Sun*. "Was that a time for sifting evidence?" He'd been told that Daniel McFarland had been guilty of adultery himself, thus making her "legally and morally free from her husband," but if further investigation proved that Beecher was mistaken, he would "make such reparation to McFarland as I can." To his outraged parishioners Beecher explained that he'd acted "as a magistrate," not as a minister, but despite all that he'd since learned, he said he would do it again if asked. As the *Brooklyn Eagle* observed, he gave a "Dutchman's answer": If his foresight were as good as his hindsight, he'd do a lot of things better.[84]

Henry also rushed to shore up his commitment to traditional marriage, although it was not the most inspiring message. "Men must overcome the causes of unhappiness within the household, or else endure them," he told an audience in Hartford; "two hearts are to be shut up, and forbidden to go out until they have adjusted all their differences—and then they will not wish to go out."[85] Knowing observers could hardly fail to think of Beecher's own famously strained marriage.

To Theodore Tilton's credit, he defended both beleaguered Beechers. He printed Elizabeth Cady Stanton's defenses of both Henry and Harriet, and wrote his own editorials reviewing the Bible on fornication and calling for more liberal divorce laws.[86] But the support of such known radicals only tarred the Beechers blacker. Fearing for what was left of her reputation, Harriet abandoned her plan to edit the *Revolution* and began to backpedal from the women's movement. But Isabella was radicalized by the scandals.

Longtime Beecher watchers professed no surprise over the McFarland flap. Really, pointed out the *Eagle*, it was one more example of Beecher's notion of "higher law," which they'd first seen during the Fugitive Slave Law debates. "Beecherism—or the higher law," said the *Eagle*, "means merely that each man is to believe and do in all things about as he feels like doing, regardless of all recognized moral codes or legal provisions."

"Being a personally pure and good man, Beecher's higher law delusion does not lead him into worse errors than those of the tongue. But his preaching guides others," warned the *Eagle*. If it isn't the Richardsons turning it into an "excuse for captivating other men's wives," it's the "Republican politicians" using it to justify the military occupation of the South.[87]

But Beecher dismissed such anxieties as the chimeras of those who had not yet evolved to a higher sphere. As he preached only one week after that *"Day Memorable"* when he and Elizabeth allegedly first made love: "Those who are on the lower plane—namely the plane where they act from rules—are strongly inclined to believe that those who go higher and act from principles are," as he put it, "abandoning right and wrong."[88]

Others offered a simpler explanation. "It seems a rule that these popular sensational 'free-thinkers' of the pulpit and the platform, such as Beecher," mused the famous Manhattan diarist George Templeton Strong; "have a screw loose somewhere. They are brilliant, clever, astute talkers, efficient in business—'men of the world' and of affairs, far more than ordinary clerics; yet every now and then their common sense gives way and lets them down, with a grievous fall, into some flagrant disastrous blunder, like this one."[89]

Chapter 12

"I Am Reliably Assured That Beecher Preaches to Seven or Eight Mistresses Every Sunday Evening"

*T*he Golden Age of Liberty was turning out to be, in Mark Twain's famous phrase, the "Gilded Age"—in which a thin veneer of virtue covered a host of shoddy work. People would come to use the phrase "Grantism" to refer to the stunning array of scandals that erupted under the two terms of Ulysses S. Grant's presidency. In the South the utopian promises of Reconstruction were shattered by violence, bigotry, and neglect. In the North massive corporations were mushrooming without any regulation or check on their powers, and their enormous pools of money often went to defrauding investors and bribing legislators. Government, too, had grown exponentially since the war, creating new opportunities for graft, greed, and partisan profiteering. The scandals are familiar to any student of the period—the Whiskey Ring, Crédit Mobilier, Black Friday, the Indian Ring, Boss Tweed's Tammany Hall, the Panic of 1873, and many lesser disgraces.

As the 1870s began, it seemed that Americans had too much liberty and that freedom had invited corruption, just as the Calvinists warned. In fact, despite the twentieth-century stereotypes of rapacious robber barons and prudish moral hypocrites, Victorians were no more greedy, lustful, or insincere than any other generation. Rather, they were living in a period of such rapid change that the devices of virtue could not keep pace with the innovations of sin. The ethical standards governing politics, business, journalism, and law that we take for granted did not yet exist.

Nowhere was this more true than in Brooklyn. This once-bucolic village had matured into the nation's third-largest city and a major industrial center. (Brooklyn remained a separate city until 1898, when it was absorbed into the City of New York.) And no Brooklynite took greater advantage of the blurry ethical lines among government patronage, economic opportunity, and moral stewardship than Henry Bowen. "Everything in this world, to Henry Chandler Bowen, is something to be bought, something to be sold, or something to be haggled for. He is always in the market," wrote the *Brooklyn Eagle* in one of its kinder moments.[1]

At the age of fifty-eight, Henry Bowen's beard was graying and his head balding, but his ambition was as sharp as the day he arrived in New York. Bowen was deeply involved in the federal spoils system; first as a collector at the New York Custom House, where he awarded sweetheart contracts to himself and his allies, then as a federal tax collector, where a number of his appointees were accused of taking bribes. He gladly accepted $50,000 in bonds and $460,000 in stock from the fantastically corrupt Northern Pacific Railroad. In exchange he agreed secretly to promote Northern Pacific and its bonds in the pages of the *Independent*. (So, too, did a number of prominent writers and editors, including Henry Ward Beecher, Harriet Beecher Stowe, Horace Greeley, and others, although they did not reap the censure Bowen did when it all came out.) Among journalists he was notorious for his unscrupulous advertising policies, stuffing the *Independent* with ads for dubious patent medicines, baldness cures, and other fraudulent products.

But Bowen had suffered a number of reversals. Tilton's incessant attacks on President Andrew Johnson had helped oust Bowen from his appointment as tax collector, drastically undermining his influence with the local Republican Party. The *Independent* was losing subscribers due both to Tilton's increasingly radical social theories and the competition from Henry Ward Beecher's new magazine, the *Christian Union*.

Bowen was determined to regain power. As his first step, in January 1870 he purchased a controlling interest in the local Republican organ, the *Brooklyn Union*. He would use the *Union* to shoehorn his own candidates into office, who would then reinstate Bowen as tax collector or at least reward him with a larger bite of the spoils flowing through Brooklyn's waterfront warehouses and flourishing Naval Yard. Reestablishing at least the appearance of rapprochement with Henry Ward Beecher was critical to Bowen's plans. He wanted Beecher's sermons back in the *Independent* and Beecher's political influence back in his pocket.

How much influence Beecher actually had is hard to say. Both Andrew Johnson and Ulysses S. Grant had good reason to thank the Reverend Beecher for his public support, at a time when gratitude looked a good deal like nepotism. Certainly people believed he had pull. Beecher was constantly approached by friends and strangers looking for help in getting government jobs or contracts, and he was constantly writing letters of recommendation, introduction, and advice to politicians and their backers.

But Beecher no longer needed Bowen. The trustees of Plymouth Church had just offered to raise his annual salary to the magnificent sum of twenty thousand dollars, but he was so flush from his various publishing projects, lecture fees, and product testimonials that he refused the raise as unseemly. Within Plymouth Church a crowd of younger men was taking power, and their loyalty to Beecher was rock solid.

Enraged by this snub, Bowen began hinting menacingly within select circles on the Heights that he *knew something* about Beecher, something that would shake all of Brooklyn if it became public. Beecher's supporters grew alarmed. Finally a mutual friend brokered a private meeting between the two men in February. Beecher was conciliatory when they met, by Bowen's account. But when Beecher asked if they could renew their old friendship, the merchant exploded. "I said, 'Mr. Beecher, you have done a great wrong, and you know it and I know it. You know what I refer to.'" Presumably he meant the long-simmering accusations of adultery.

"Mr. Beecher then trembled like a leaf," Bowen later testified; "he drew his chair up to me, turned it so that the side fronted toward me, got into it on his knees, resting his left arm on the back of it, and then made such an appeal to me as I never heard before. He said the past must be buried, buried forever; that he loved me tenderly; that no other man in the world had been so good to him, or such a friend as I had been; that he could not live without my confidence and affection."

Bowen did not spell out his accusations, but "Mr. Beecher, I know, fully understood me, and I know I as fully understood him." They talked for three hours, until Beecher "with tears streaming down his cheeks like rain," agreed to Bowen's various demands, including reinstating his sermons in the *Independent* and apologizing to Bowen in front of Plymouth Church.[2]

Beecher's account matches Bowen's generally, without the tears. Yet because Bowen never actually said the word "adultery," Beecher later insisted that the merchant's grievances "were *all* either of a business nature of or my treatment of *him personally.*"[3] Sex never came up, Beecher said.

Thinking that all was resolved, Beecher then asked Tasker Howard to meet with Bowen "to remove the little differences between *them.*" But when the two men met, Bowen spitefully told Tasker that he personally possessed evidence that, if he chose to use it, "would drive Mr. Beecher out of Brooklyn." Tasker demanded to know what Bowen could possibly mean.

Bowen refused to say more but challenged Tasker to ask Beecher about it, assuring him that "*Mr. Beecher would never* give his consent that he (Bowen) should tell Mr. Howard this secret."[4] If Tasker did quiz Henry, there is no record of it.

IT IS SURELY NO COINCIDENCE that within weeks of this encounter with Bowen, Elizabeth Tilton and Beecher tried to break off their relationship. The pressure on them was mounting, not only from Bowen but from Theodore.

The Tiltons' marriage had been deteriorating steadily for the past two years. When Theodore returned from his annual lecture trip at the beginning of 1870, he found Elizabeth so absorbed in Beecher that all pretense of harmony evaporated. He interrogated their oldest daughter, Florence, about Beecher's visits, and everything she said fed his fury. Now old suspicions came flooding back to him. He remembered Elizabeth sitting on a stool in Beecher's library, as the minister spread out his collection of engravings on the floor, and being almost certain that he saw Beecher reach "very slyly" under Elizabeth's skirt and caress her ankle and calf. When Theodore got home and asked her about it, at first, he recalled, "she was a little confused and denied it; and then said it was so, but that she had said, 'You must not do that,'" to Beecher.

"I was very young in those days and utterly unsuspicious of such things," Theodore said, and it was "blotted out of my mind."[5]

On another occasion Theodore recalled returning to the house in the early afternoon, and being surprised to find the bedroom door locked. When he knocked, Elizabeth opened the door, and behind her was Beecher looking startled, "with his vest unbuttoned," said Tilton, "his face colored like a rose when I saw him."[6] Again Elizabeth explained it away, saying they had only wanted to talk privately, away from the noisy children.

The Tiltons were trapped in the classic cycle of jealousy—he interrogating, she trying to prove her fidelity with small confessions and copious innocuous details, each of them growing ever more paranoid; "whenever I was alone with him, I used to make a memorandum and charge my mind with all the details of the conversation that passed between us, that I might repeat them to Mr. Tilton," said Elizabeth of the preacher's visits.

> I never had a visit from Mr. Beecher that I was not questioned; Theodore would question me till I thought I had told him all that we talked about, and, perhaps, a day or two afterward, I would throw out a remark which Mr. Beecher had made, and Theodore would say, "You didn't tell me that yesterday;" I would say: "Oh, yes, I did mean to tell you, but I forgot it;" for 2 or 3 years I tried faithfully to repeat to my husband everything that I said and did till I found it made him more suspicious than ever.[7]

Theodore became obsessed with the idea that their strained marriage would improve if only she would admit the affair, Elizabeth later testified. He swore he would forgive her if she would just tell the truth.

It was a miserable spring on Livingston Street. Theodore was openly cruel to Elizabeth, harassing her at home and ignoring her in public. He threw all his energy into the women's movement, hoping to be the savior who would reunify the splintered suffragists. But his obvious rivalry with Beecher—whom he now "alternately snubs and patronizes," noted the *New York Times*—only undermined his already doomed efforts, earning him the ridicule of the press and the enmity of many former friends.[8]

Finally in June 1870, broken in health and spirits, Elizabeth fled to a friend's house in the country. On the sweltering hot evening of July 3 she unexpectedly took the train back to Brooklyn. According to Theodore's account of that night, she said she had something to tell him, but only if he would promise not to do anything or tell anyone. He promised. Then, said Theodore, she confessed to having an affair with Beecher.

As he pressed her, the details spilled out. At first she had resisted Beecher's passes, but over time:

she had been persuaded by him that, as their love was proper and not wrong, therefore it followed that any expression of that love, whether by the shake of a hand or the kiss of the lips, or even bodily intercourse, since it was all an expression of that which by itself was not wrong, therefore that bodily intercourse was not wrong; that Mr. Beecher had professed to her a greater love than he had ever shown to any woman in his life; that she and I both knew that for years his home had not been a happy one; that his wife had not been a satisfactory wife to him; that she wished—that he wished to find in her—Elizabeth—the consolation, the help to his mind, and the solace of life which had been denied to him by the unfortunate marriage at home; that he had made these arguments to her during the early years of their friendship, and she had steadfastly resisted; that he had many times fondled her to the degree that it required on her part almost bodily resistance to be rid of him; that after her final surrender, in Oct. 1868, he had then many times solicited her when she had refused; that the occasions of her yielding her body had not been numerous, but that his solicitations had been frequent and urgent, and sometimes almost violent.[9]

Their sex had not come, she told Theodore, "out of low or vulgar thoughts either on her part or his, but always from pure affection and a high religious love." Even now, according to Theodore, she still "felt justified before God in her intimacy with him, save the necessary deceit which accompanied it, and at which she frequently suffered in her mind."[10]

When asked about this evening several years later, Elizabeth denied saying any such thing, but by that point Elizabeth and Theodore had contradicted each other and themselves so often that no one was quite sure what to believe. However, Theodore's salacious story was the one that came to be whispered in dim parlors and trumpeted in headlines. Henry and Elizabeth were left to reinterpret or rebut Tilton's accusations, as best they could—something to keep in mind in the pages that follow.

Despite his long-held suspicions Theodore said he was stunned by Elizabeth's confession. After a long night of arguments and tears, he agreed to keep her secret and to help "restore her wounded spirit."[11] The next morning, Independence Day, he wandered over to his office in a daze. Unable to work, his anger mounted at Beecher. "That man is growing old," Theodore said to himself. "I will punish him only to this extent—Elizabeth shall go and tell him that I know from her own lips which pattern of Godliness he is, and that I am a living, suffering sacrifice for his children." Tilton was so inspired by his own nobility that "for two weeks I lived a kind of ecstasy."[12]

That same day, at Henry Bowen's annual Fourth of July celebration in Woodstock, Connecticut, Beecher and Bowen were enjoying the first fruits of their rapprochement. President Grant was there, along with a host of dignitaries, a testament to their combined influence. During the picnic the original Plymouth triumvirate of Beecher, Bowen, and Tasker Howard competed in a footrace—surely a good sign. Some of the partygoers whispered that Bowen had bent his strict temperance principles, in deference to the president. Beecher's oration was so wild and disjointed that many listeners suspected that he had joined the old general in his cups.

ELIZABETH TRIED TO TELL Beecher that something had happened between her and Theodore. In August she sent an urgent note summoning the preacher from Peekskill. "I found her lying in the upstairs, second story front room," Beecher remembered. She was "very much depressed in spirits, and she seemed to me like one who wanted to talk and didn't. I prayed with her and cheered her as best I could."[13] He returned the next day, but she was too ill to see him. Not long after this, she discovered she was pregnant.

But if Elizabeth didn't keep her promise to tell Beecher of her confession, neither did Theodore hold his tongue. His magnanimous high soon gave way to a smothering rage. Forgetting his pledge of forgiveness, he spent hours haranguing his wife, accusing her of seducing other men, and insisting that only three of their four children were his. Within a month of her alleged confession, Theodore had told the terrible story to Elizabeth's best friends, Andrew and Mattie Bradshaw, and Oliver Johnson, the managing editor of the *Independent*. He had hinted so broadly to Elizabeth's family that they guessed his secret. "Theodore, Theodore!" pleaded Elizabeth in a letter:

> Do you not know, also, that when in any circle you blacken Mr. Beecher's name—and soon after couple mine with it—you blacken mine as well? When by your threats, my mother cried out in agony to me, "Why what have *you* done, Elizabeth, my child?" Her worst suspicions were aroused, and I laid bare my heart then—that from

my lips and not yours she might receive the dagger into her heart! Did not my dear child [their daughter Florence] learn enough by insinuations, that her sweet, pure soul agonized in secret, till she broke out with the *dreadful question?* I know not but it hath been her death blow.

When you say to my beloved brother—"Mr. B. preaches to forty of his mistresses every Sunday," then follow with the remark that after *my* death you have a dreadful secret to reveal, need he be told any more ere the sword pass into *his* soul?[14]

One evening, as that wretched summer passed into fall, the Tiltons planned to meet Elizabeth Cady Stanton, Susan B. Anthony, and Laura Curtis Bullard, the new editor of the *Revolution*, for dinner. Through some misunderstanding Theodore, Stanton, and Bullard ended up dining separately, leaving Anthony and Elizabeth alone at the house on Livingston Street. That night at dinner Theodore told the two women the story of the affair. "We were reformers," Stanton later explained. "He gave us the story as a phase of social life."[15]

When he arrived home around eleven o'clock, the ladies rebuked Theodore for his rudeness. This sparked a passionate argument between Elizabeth and Theodore, with each accusing the other of infidelity. Appalled, Susan B. Anthony withdrew to a guest room. A few minutes later, Elizabeth rushed up the stairs and into Anthony's room, hastily bolting the door while Theodore pounded to be let in. Anthony refused, and Theodore finally retreated. Sobbing and distraught, Elizabeth spent the night in Anthony's room, spilling out the whole story of her affair with Beecher. When Anthony and Stanton next saw each other, they found they had both heard the same terrible tale.

Elizabeth again fled, spending a month at a friend's house in Ohio. The day she returned to Brooklyn, Elizabeth and Theodore fought so viciously, according to Bessie Turner, the Tilton's hired girl, that Elizabeth took Bessie and the children to stay with Elizabeth's mother, Johanna Morse.

That summer Theodore made the colossal mistake of telling Mrs. Morse of their troubles—for she was, by every account, crazy. She had recently separated from her second husband after trying to choke him in a murderous rage. She had long disliked Theodore, but now she set out to ruin him. Without telling Elizabeth, Mrs. Morse consulted a divorce lawyer, and then she sent Bessie Turner to Beecher's house, instructing the girl to tell the pastor that Elizabeth had left her husband, and he should come immediately. Astonished and alarmed, Henry hustled to Mrs. Morse's house. Once he got there, Elizabeth's mother did most of the talking, telling of Theodore's cruelty but not of his allegations of adultery. It fell on his ears, Henry later testified, "like a nightmare dream."[16]

Beecher's response could hardly have been more humiliating or hurtful to poor Elizabeth. "This is a case, it seems to me, where a woman is needed, and if you will allow me I shall bring my wife and let her hear," said Beecher. Eunice had hated Theodore for years, nonetheless the next day both Beechers showed up. First Eunice and Elizabeth went upstairs to talk privately, then Mrs. Morse and Eunice conferred, leaving Elizabeth and Henry alone for the first time in months. "I have a recollection of only one single thing that I said to Mrs. Tilton," he later testified. " 'How is it,' I said, 'that I have been so long with you and you never alluded before to me about distress in your household?' " She was despondent, Henry recalled, and replied that she had "sought to conceal, in the hope that the difficulty would pass away[.]" Elizabeth could not bring herself to tell him of her confession.[17]

The next day Eunice returned for another excruciating consultation. "I was not greatly helped in my mind by that interview with Mrs. Beecher," Elizabeth admitted; "my talks with Mrs. Beecher were long and painful, and I cannot recall all that was said."[18] Eunice left Brooklyn some days later to spend the winter at Harriet Stowe's new house in Florida, but before departing she advised Elizabeth, in no uncertain terms, to officially separate from her husband.

Elizabeth ignored Eunice's surprising advice and returned several days later to the desolate house on Livingston Street. Theodore wasn't around much, often sleeping at the home of Frank Moulton, an old friend from school who was now a merchant in Brooklyn. That Christmas Eve, 1870, Elizabeth suffered a miscarriage—"*a love babe* it promised, you know," Elizabeth told a friend.[19]

As always, just as matters were reaching a crisis, politics intervened to make everything worse. "Republicanism was brought together from chaos by the question of slavery," observed the *New York World* with typical Democratic derision. "Its leaders were carried into power by using the negro as their hobby horse. Now that he can carry them no longer, their differences of opinion are more clearly shown."[20]

The *World* was right. After ten years of ascendancy, the Republicans had gone from a minority party of progressive reformers to the party of entrenched power, beholden to the massive corporations that now dominated the postwar economy. Under the careless eye of President Grant, bribery, fraud, and outright thievery were thriving, labor strife was spreading across the North, and the South was still embroiled in often-violent racial clashes. Before, the Conservative and Radical wings of the party had split over government expansion and equal rights. Now the line of division was shifting. A new "Liberal" coalition of disillusioned Radicals, reformers, intellectuals, dispossessed politicians, and laissez-faire moneymen arose to challenge the Republican "Regulars" who still supported Grant and his federal policies. To the Liberals it seemed as if the country had tipped too far toward equality, giving the reins of government to ignorant masses who were easily manipulated by demagogic politicians and rabble-rousers, and had fallen into deep disorder. Gripped by the twin specters of corrupt power and class warfare, the Liberal Republicans argued for a government limited in size and ambition, and run only by the "best men."

Among Brooklyn Republicans, Henry Bowen fell squarely among the Regulars who were eager to preserve their privileges and patronage. For Theodore Tilton, his disgust with "Grantism" overwhelmed his egalitarian instincts, and he took up with the Liberals. That fall the two men clashed over the editorial policies of Bowen's new newspaper, the *Brooklyn Union*. As editor in chief, Tilton not only refused to endorse President Grant and Bowen's handpicked candidate in the U.S. congressional race, he openly attacked the man as a corrupt spoilsman. "If anybody in King's County expects to see the *Union* consenting to be chained like a coach dog to the Republican or any other party, he is woefully mistaken," wrote Tilton.[21] Bowen's candidate did not win.

Theodore's stridency was also becoming a distinct liability to Bowen at the *Independent*. On December 1, 1870, the *Independent* published Theodore's most inflammatory editorial yet, on "Love, Marriage and Divorce." "Marriage without love is a sin against God—a sin which, like other sins, is to be repented of, ceased from and put away,"[22] wrote Tilton, an argument sure to bring howls from orthodox readers. But Bowen could not afford to act precipitously.

Bowen's weakened role within the Republican Party was directly linked to his declining influence in Plymouth Church. Bowen's long dominance of Brooklyn's political spoils was being challenged by an upstart faction led by Benjamin Tracy, a relative newcomer to Brooklyn Heights. Ben Tracy was Brooklyn's district attorney and a ruthless political schemer who burnished his reputation for rectitude by joining Plymouth Church and striking up a friendship with Beecher. On December 21, at a meeting of the local Republican Committee, Tracy officially accused Bowen of defrauding the city when he was tax collector. Both sides began shouting. The packed room descended into pandemonium when one of Bowen's friends clouted one of Tracy's men in the face. The next day Bowen was ousted from the governing committee.

Bowen needed to regain control fast, and that meant ridding himself of Tilton. For the last year or two, a cloud of unseemly rumor had swirled around the editor, but Bowen had no specific proof of immorality with which to nail him. Then, the day before Christmas 1870, Bowen opened his mail to find a hysterical letter from Tilton's mother-in-law accusing Theodore not only of practicing free love but of planning to elope to Europe with Laura Bullard, the editor of the *Revolution*. Bowen summoned Tilton to his mansion on Willow Street and confronted him with, in Tilton's words, "an avalanche of accusations."[23]

Yet when Tilton angrily challenged him to provide evidence, Bowen quickly dropped the subject and brought up the *Brooklyn Union*. He wanted Tilton to devote more space to Plymouth Church, and noted that Tilton himself hadn't been in church for a long while.

"I never again should cross the threshold of Plymouth Church," Tilton replied hotly.[24] When Bowen pressed him, Theodore told him of Elizabeth's confession.

Here, finally, was Bowen's long-awaited opportunity to destroy Beecher without any risk to himself. "You ought to proceed against him instantly. Don't let him preach another Sunday!" the publisher roared, setting off into a long tirade against the minister. Tilton asked why Bowen didn't hit Beecher himself. Bowen explained that in February 1870 Beecher had confessed to adultery and tearfully begged Bowen's forgiveness, which was granted. Thus, Bowen concluded, "I cannot open a settled quarrel." But if Tilton was willing to put his charges in writing, Bowen would back him up and personally carry the letter to Beecher. After much heated conversation, with Bowen egging him on, Tilton penned the following:

December 26, 1870, Brooklyn
Sir: I demand that, for reasons which you explicitly understand, you immediately cease from the ministry of Plymouth Church, and that you quit the City of Brooklyn as a residence.
                                                            Theodore Tilton

Bowen tried to get Tilton to add the phrase "and cease editing the *Christian Union*," but Tilton vetoed that as nakedly self-serving. Bowen then took the letter, promising to deliver it immediately.[25]

A LITTLE LATER THAT DAY, Tilton's old friend Francis D. Moulton stopped by. Frank Moulton was a prosperous Brooklyn exporter, a junior partner in the firm of Woodruff and Robinson, marked by gentlemanly manners, quiet common sense, and bushy, bright red hair and mustache. Although Moulton had no interest in religion, and had only met Beecher a few times, his wife, Emma, was a devoted member of Plymouth Church. Moulton was appalled when Tilton told him of the arrangement with Bowen. Moulton, said Tilton, "told me with great emphasis that I was a fool" to trust the wily merchant. "You have made your demand all alone," Moulton said. "What if he leaves you to support it all alone?" The best they could do now was to create some sort of record, so Moulton immediately wrote the following memo:

Brooklyn, Dec. 26, 1870. T.T. informed me today that he had sent a note to Mr. Beecher, of which Mr. H. C. Bowen was the bearer, demanding that he (Mr. Beecher) should retire from the pulpit and quit the City of Brooklyn. The letter was an open one. H. C. Bowen knew the contents of it, and said that he (Bowen) would sustain T. in the demand. 3:45 p.m.[26]

Moulton's prediction was correct. At five o'clock that same day Bowen delivered the letter to the minister, acting as if he had no idea what Tilton had written. "Why, this man is crazy, this is sheer insanity!" cried Beecher as he scanned the paper. Bowen asked innocently if Beecher had any answer to send. Now it was Beecher who tried to turn the tables, asking calmly, "Are you friendly with me, Mr. Bowen?"

"I am," replied Bowen. "We have settled all our differences. I have no unfriendly feeling toward you."

According to Beecher, "Mr. Bowen fell in at once with me and commenced talking about Mr. Tilton, and not favorably."[27] Ever the opportunist, Bowen seemed to be manipulating the former friends into destroying each other, while keeping his own hands unbloodied.

The next day, December 28, Tilton decided he would personally confront Beecher with the full array of evidence, and sent a note to Bowen telling him of this plan. Not long after the note arrived, Bowen

burst into Tilton's office, his face white with fury. He began screaming that if Tilton told the minister anything that Bowen had said, he
would fire Tilton and call the police to toss him into the street. Bowen
slammed out of the office, leaving Tilton in a confused panic.[28]

He turned again to Frank Moulton for advice. With no idea what
Bowen was plotting or what he'd said to Beecher, Frank and Theodore
decided that the only way to save himself and his family from ruin was
to have his wife sign a written confession. Elizabeth, still weak and bedridden from her miscarriage, was barely able to sit up in bed. When
Theodore told her what he and Bowen had done, she was beside herself.

Beecher would have no idea what the letter meant, she told him,
since she had never told him of her confession last summer. If Beecher
resigned, she said sobbing, "Sooner or later everybody will know the
reason why and that will be to my shame and to the children's shame,
and I cannot endure it."[29] She then begged him to send for Beecher, so
the three could defuse the situation. Theodore finally agreed to meet
with him in person. In exchange she and Theodore wrote up a letter
informing Beecher of her confession.

On the night of December 30, as a snowstorm descended on the city,
Theodore gave Frank Moulton Elizabeth's written confession to take to
Beecher. The preacher was about to go to the regular Friday-evening
prayer meeting when Moulton met him. Beecher protested, "this is
prayer meeting night; I cannot go see him." But as soon as Moulton
mentioned the letter sent by Bowen, the minister hastily arranged for
someone to take his place at the church. Together the red-haired agnostic and the preacher headed out into the sleet and snow.

"What can I do? What can I do?" Beecher asked in panic as soon as
they were outside.

"I don't know," said Moulton. "I am not a Christian. I am a heathen, but I will try to show you how well a heathen can serve you. I will
try to help."

As they walked, Moulton told him of Bowen's accusations of adultery, which seemed to surprise Henry. "This is a terrible night. There is
an appropriateness in this storm," Beecher groaned.[30]

Tilton was waiting for Beecher at Moulton's house on Remsen
Street. Moulton left the two men together in an upstairs parlor. "You
have been guilty of adultery with numerous members of your congregation ever since your Indianapolis pastorate, all down through
these twenty-five years, you are not a safe man to dwell in a Christian

community," Theodore declared as he entered. For nearly an hour he barraged Beecher, repeating Bowen's tales and accusing him of seducing Elizabeth. He read aloud Elizabeth's declaration of guilt—which he had copied onto the back of an envelope from the original in Moulton's possession. As they talked, Theodore nervously tore the envelope to pieces. Neither Moulton nor Tilton ever actually showed a copy of the confession to Beecher.

This turned out to be a critical misstep, for Beecher would later insist that that evening Tilton charged him only with making "improper advances," saying, as Beecher put it, that "I had corrupted Elizabeth, teaching her to lie, to deceive him, and hide under fair appearances her friendship to me," but mentioning nothing about sex—at least not "strictly and literally speaking." (For a while Moulton retained the original confession for safekeeping, but later returned it to Elizabeth, who burned it before the scandal broke.)

Either way, Beecher admitted, his words "fell like a thunderbolt on me."[31]

Theodore ended by announcing that he would no longer insist that Beecher quit the church, and he would not join forces with Bowen, but only because his wife had begged him to be merciful. Beecher's face had become so bloodred that Theodore feared he might have a heart attack. "This is a dream," Beecher burst out. "I don't believe Elizabeth could have made charges so untrue against me."[32]

Theodore unlocked the door to the room, saying stiffly, "You are free to retire." Beecher did not move. Again Theodore pointed to the door. As he rose to go, one of them (they disputed which) insisted that Beecher go see Elizabeth to confirm the truth of her confession. Henry staggered down the stairs and out of the house, muttering, "This will kill me."[33]

He made his way to Livingston Street in a daze. The visiting nurse led the minister into Elizabeth's sick chamber. "Mrs. Tilton lay upon her bed, white as marble, with closed eyes, as in a trance, and with her hands upon her bosom, palm to palm, as one in prayer," Beecher recalled.[34] At first she refused to open her eyes or speak, as he pressed her to explain. Finally, according to Beecher's testimony, she opened her eyes and, in a feeble voice clogged with tears, began to explain how much pressure she'd been under, and how she'd hoped a confession would solve everything.

" 'But,' I said to her, 'Elizabeth, this is a charge of attempting improper things. You know that is not true.'

" 'Yes, it is not true,' she says, 'but what can I do?'

" 'Do! You can take it back again.' She hesitated, and I did not understand her hesitation. 'Why can you not take it back? It is not true.' She said something about—she would be willing to do it if it could be done without injury to her husband, which I did not at all understand. 'But,' I said, 'you ought to give me a written retraction of that written charge.' "[35]

After making him promise that he would not use it to harm her husband, Elizabeth then wrote the following note:

> Wearied with importunities, and weakened by sickness, I gave a letter inculpating my friend, Henry Ward Beecher, under assurances that that would remove all difficulties between me and my husband. That letter I now revoke. I was persuaded to do it, almost forced, when I was in a weakened state of mind. I regret it and recall its statements. E. R. T.

At the bottom she added a postscript:

> I desire to say explicitly, Mr. Beecher has never offered any improper solicitation, but has always treated me in a manner becoming a Christian and a gentleman.
>
> Elizabeth R. Tilton[36]

After leaving Elizabeth, Beecher returned to Moulton's. He begged the exporter to "be a friend to him in this terrible business," in Moulton's words, but neglected to mention the retraction in his pocket.[37]

The eventful night was not yet over. When Tilton returned to his home around midnight and spoke with Elizabeth, discovering what Beecher had done, he was livid. Finally Elizabeth agreed to retract her retractions.

> December 30, 1870—Midnight
> My Dear Husband:
> I desire to leave with you before going to sleep a statement that Mr. Henry Ward Beecher called upon me this evening, asked me if I would defend him against any accusation in a *council of ministers* and I replied solemnly that I would in case the accuser was any other but my husband. He (H.W.B.) dictated a letter, which I copied as my own, to be used by him against any other accuser except

my husband. This letter was designed to vindicate Mr. Beecher against all other persons save only yourself. I was ready to give him this letter because he said with pain that my letter in your hands addressed to him, dated December 29, "had struck him dead and ended his usefulness." You and I both are pledged to do our best to avoid publicity. God grant a speedy end to all further anxieties.

Affectionately, Elizabeth[38]

THE NEXT DAY, the last of that terrible year, Elizabeth summoned Frank Moulton to her bedside and begged him to retrieve all the letters she had written the night before. That evening Moulton stopped by the warehouses of Woodruff and Robinson and then headed once again to Beecher's house, to rebuke the minister for his sneakiness and to take back Elizabeth's retraction so it could be burned along with the original confession.

As Beecher was reluctantly digging it out, Moulton, who regularly carried a pistol on his trips down to his warehouses on the rough New York docks, took off his coat and took the pistol from his pocket, assuring Beecher that he would protect the document "with my life." Later Beecher's allies would cite the "Pistol Incident," as it came to be known, as proof that Moulton was blackmailing the preacher with physical threats. Both Moulton and Beecher denied this, but they disagreed sharply on what came next.

After being scolded for treating both Tiltons so disgracefully, according to Moulton, Beecher "with great sorrow, weeping," defended himself. He explained "that he had loved Elizabeth Tilton very much" and that "the expression, the sexual expression of that love, was just as natural in his opinion—he had thought so—as the language that he had used to her." It was the first but not the last time, said Moulton, that Beecher admitted his sin. "I throw myself upon your friendship," cried Beecher, and he begged Moulton to save him from "the brink of a moral Niagara."[39]

"Such language is simply impossible to me," Beecher would later retort, despite a lifetime of evidence to the contrary.[40]

Just as Moulton was retrieving Elizabeth's letter, two notices from Bowen arrived at Livingston Street, officially dismissing Tilton from both the *Independent* and the *Brooklyn Union*. Theodore hightailed it to Moulton's, arriving just as he returned from his conference with

Beecher. The two friends spent that New Year's Eve walking the streets, searching for some way to save the Tiltons from disaster.

For the first time in seven years, the next afternoon Henry Bowen stopped by the New Year's Day reception at Beecher's house on Columbia Heights. Bowen pulled Beecher aside, whispering that he'd fired Tilton. Beecher murmured his approval, but over the next several hours of shaking hands and kissing cheeks, he began to worry. Surely Theodore would blame him for this mortifying blow.

That evening when the guests dispersed, Beecher hurriedly requested Moulton to return. As they discussed Tilton's plight—now without a job or any prospects of respectable work—Beecher paced the room weeping with regret and self-pity.

"I felt that my mind was in danger of giving way. I walked up and down the room, pouring forth my heart in the most unrestrained grief and bitterness of self-accusation," Beecher later admitted.

Finally Moulton suggested that a written apology would go a long way to placating Theodore. Beecher was too distraught to write it himself, so he asked the merchant to take down his words as he dictated them. Although he did not know it then, Beecher's fate would rest on this "Letter of Contrition," as it became known.

> In trust with F.D. Moulton
> My dear friend Moulton:
> I ask through you Theodore Tilton's forgiveness, and I humble myself before him as I do before my God. He would have been a better man in my circumstances than I have been. I can ask nothing except that he will remember all the other hearts that would ache. I will not plead for myself; I even wish that I were dead. But others must live and suffer. I will die before anyone but myself shall be inculpated. All my thoughts are running toward my friends, toward the poor child lying there and praying with her folded hands. She is guiltless, sinned against, bearing the transgressions of another. Her forgiveness I have. I humbly pray to God that He may put it in the heart of her husband to forgive me. I have trusted this to Moulton in confidence.[41]

Beecher then hastily signed the paper, and Moulton delivered it to Theodore.

The next day Theodore and Henry accidentally ran into each other at Moulton's house. There, Tilton later claimed, Beecher finally admitted that he had seduced Elizabeth. Beecher, in Tilton's words, "wept again and again, and his face assumed a very peculiar redness," as an avalanche of excuses, pleas, confessions, and explanations poured out of him. He begged for mercy not for himself but for Elizabeth and both their families.

"She was not to blame," Beecher said over and over by Tilton's account. "I was altogether at fault." He said they'd only had sex during the last year or so, and even then he'd been gone on vacation for part of it; he said the sex had "been through love, and not through lust," and that he'd originally sought "companionship in her mind." He offered to resign if that would fix things, but pleaded for Tilton to tell anybody but Eunice, "for she is not only your enemy but may very well become mine." He added that it was Eunice, not him, who had told Bowen all that malicious gossip. If Tilton ever decided to reveal his crime, please, Beecher begged, "give me notice in advance of your intention to do so in order that I may either go out of the world by suicide, or else escape from the face of my friends by a voyage to some foreign land."[42] Finally Moulton asked Theodore to leave so he and Beecher could talk privately. For the moment Theodore seemed placated.

Although Moulton was Theodore's friend and an avowed agnostic, he was also an exceptionally decent man who genuinely believed that if Beecher's secret were revealed it "would tend to undermine the very foundations of social order," a conviction shared by everyone who heard the story. At considerable risk to himself, Moulton agreed to help them cover up the scandal.

"The Mutual Friend," as Moulton came to be known, shuttled between the two men, soothing tempers, ferrying messages, and serving as the repository for the bushels of official and unofficial written statements they produced, in a fruitless attempt to establish definitive truths. In politics Beecher had always wavered between a defiant belief in the higher law of individual choice and its polar opposite, an almost superstitious Constitutionalism, as if ink and paper could of themselves command power. He'd had a weakness for legalistic "official documents" since high school, when he and his friend Constantine Fontellachi Newell signed a five-point "friendship covenant." Henry brought these paradoxical impulses to the cover-up. They produced reams of documents—raw emotional letters, quasi confessions, declarations of friendship, pleas for forgiveness, contemporaneous notes from meetings, formal accusations, official denials, secret agreements, and public statements, with all copies going to Moulton's vault. But Beecher's political foes were right—the authority of contract and the authority of emotion cannot coexist. Of course if Elizabeth had had her wish, every scrap of paper would have been burned.

For more than two years Beecher saw Moulton nearly every day, usually at Frank's house where prying eyes would not notice him, and Henry grew to love him. "I never doubted his professed friendship for me," Beecher said later. "My confidence in him was the only element that seemed secure in that confusion of tormenting perplexities."[43]

Their first task was to find Theodore a job. Bowen refused to reinstate him, so Moulton raised the money to start a new weekly paper for Tilton to edit, the *Golden Age*. Beecher invested five thousand dollars of his own money, a fact kept secret from Theodore and Eunice. They secured a written statement from Bessie Turner denying Mrs. Morse's tales, and then Beecher paid to send her away to school in the West. Then there was Bowen's alleged evidence that Beecher had raped Edna Dean Proctor back in the 1850s. Proctor was still unmarried and now living with another wealthy Plymouth Church family in Brooklyn. Moulton asked about Bowen's allegation, and Beecher furiously insisted that the affair with Proctor had been consensual. So Moulton sent Beecher to ask the poetess for a written statement denying any impropriety—since, as Moulton noted archly, he was so good at that sort of thing.

At first the fragile cover-up seemed doomed. Elizabeth's crazy mother, Johanna Morse, exasperated everyone by sending harassing letters to Bowen, Tilton, and Beecher. The rumor that Theodore had run off with Laura Bullard appeared in the *Eagle*, provoking Tilton's already frayed temper. Then Theodore summoned Beecher to his house and demanded to know if he was the father of his son Ralph—which both Beecher and Elizabeth denied. But as Tilton focused on founding his new magazine, his mood improved. A few weeks after their blowup over Ralph, at Moulton's suggestion Henry, Elizabeth, and Theodore met for a meeting of "amnesty and amity." The conversation between Henry and Theodore was so gratifying, Beecher later testified, that "I came up to him and sat down on his knee," causing Elizabeth to burst out laughing. When they rose to leave, said Beecher, "I kissed him and he kissed me, and I kissed his wife and she kissed me, and I believe they kissed each other."[44]

Things seemed on an upward swing. But their desperate attempts at contractualism were constantly undermined by their emotional impulsiveness. For all his promises, Theodore continued to tell tales of

Beecher's infidelity to his friends in the press, who gleefully repeated his line that "Beecher preaches to seven or eight mistresses every Sunday evening." The gossip spread quickly through the network of female reformers and Beecher's inner circle, including the investors in the *Christian Union* and J. B. Ford and Co., and the bondholders of Plymouth Church. Beecher complained that church members were constantly asking him, with a concerned air, "Well, brother Beecher, how is your soul today?"

"None of your business," Beecher testily told his Friday-night prayer meeting. "It is a kind of familiarity that I don't relish."[45]

Similarly, although Moulton had forbidden Henry and Elizabeth to see each other without his prior approval, as the atmosphere thawed they exchanged warm clandestine letters (it was "safe," Beecher told her, since Eunice was in Florida).[46] For the first time in more than a year, Elizabeth's spirits soared. But Elizabeth's feelings for Henry were dashed, by one account, when she learned with "certainty that, notwithstanding his repeated assurances of his faithfulness to her; he had recently had illicit intercourse, under the most extraordinary circumstances, with another person."[47] It seems hardly believable that Beecher would behave so recklessly, were it not so similar to Edna Dean Proctor's story back in 1859.

By May it seemed to sink in for Elizabeth that Beecher had no intention of resuming their special relationship; he meant only to keep her placated and quiet. "My future either for life or death would be happier could I but feel that you *forgave* while you forget me," she secretly wrote to him. "In all the sad complications of the past year my endeavor was to entirely save from *you* all suffering; to bear myself alone, leaving you forever ignorant of it. My weapons were love, a larger untiring generosity and *nest-hiding!* That I failed utterly we both know. But now I ask forgiveness."[48]

Despite her emotional ups and downs, Elizabeth was easily controlled. Eunice was in Florida till May, and even Mrs. Morse was, for the moment, quieted by Elizabeth's pleas. Then a magnificent wild card entered the game.

VICTORIA CLAFLIN WAS BORN in 1838 in Ohio, the seventh child of a small-time confidence man and his slatternly wife. Although raised in squalid poverty, Victoria was marked by her pretty face, unusual intelligence, and mystical visions of angels, devils, and spirits. Married in her teens to an alcoholic named Canning Woodhull, she and her family scraped up a living by running séances, telling fortunes, peddling patent medicines and makeshift contraceptive devices fashioned out of vinegar and sponges, and a bit of casual prostitution. Soon Victoria Woodhull divorced her first husband (but kept his name) and married Colonel James Harvey Blood, a radical anarchist. In 1868 she settled in New York City with Colonel Blood; her sister, a curvaceous fellow medium named Tennie C. Claflin; an assortment of illiterate relatives; and her first husband, who was too broken down by drink to support himself.

In New York, Victoria Woodhull drifted among the city's demi-monde—including high-class prostitutes and the "female doctors" who provided them with opium and abortions—but she had higher aspirations. Spiritualism, the belief that it is possible to communicate with the dead, was a hot topic in the postwar period. In a world where words could fly over telegraph wires, why shouldn't they also descend from heaven? Although riddled with hoaxes and charlatans, spiritualism gained many respectable adherents over time, including nearly half of Henry's siblings, particularly Harriet and Isabella. Harriet attributed "the sudden increase of spiritualism" to the millions of grieving families created by the war. "It is the throbbing of the severed soul to the part of itself that has gone within the veil."[49]

By 1870 Colonel Cornelius Vanderbilt, a fantastically wealthy railroad mogul who took an ardent interest in both spiritualism and sex, had taken Victoria and Tennie under his wing. It was a mutually beneficial relationship. The high-toned gentlemen who frequented Manhattan's brothels often gossiped in front of the prostitutes, boasting of business plans and telling other men's secrets. It was believed that Victoria collected valuable information from the working girls and passed it on to Vanderbilt as being "from the spirit world," and he used it to outmaneuver his rivals. Vanderbilt rewarded Victoria and Tennie by setting them up as the country's first female financial brokers—the "Bewitching Brokers" of Wall Street, as the fascinated press dubbed them.

But Woodhull's ambitions were manifold. Not long after her Wall Street triumph, she decided to enter politics. A bill proposing the sixteenth amendment, giving the vote to women, had been languishing in Congress for a year. Woodhull moved to Washington temporarily, where she developed a cozy relationship with Massachusetts senator and former Union general Benjamin Butler, a Radical Republican famed for his backroom dealing, "the smartest damn rascal that ever lived," as Lincoln's private secretary called him.[50] Butler arranged for Victoria

to testify—entirely on her own initiative, unbeknownst to the suffragists—in favor of woman suffrage to the House Judiciary Committee in
January 1871, making Woodhull the first woman to address Congress.

By chance Isabella Beecher Hooker had volunteered to organize a
national woman suffrage conference in the capital in January 1871. On
New Year's Day, just as her brother was descending into his personal
purgatory, Isabella was shocked to discover that Mrs. Victoria Woodhull
was going to address Congress on the opening day of their conference.
None of the suffragists had met her, but some had heard tales of her
multiple marriages and unconventional lifestyle. Their odor was nasty
enough that Isabella nearly didn't go to hear her speak.

When Woodhull expressed anxiety about her reputation among the
female reformers, Ben Butler bluntly told her to ignore any snubs from
the NWSA women, especially from Isabella Hooker. Overhearing this,
a Radical congressman commented with a smirk, "It would ill become
these women and especially a Beecher to talk of antecedents or to cast
any smirch upon Mrs. Woodhull, for I am reliably assured that Beecher
preaches to at least twenty of his mistresses every Sunday."[51] Woodhull
filed away this information but said nothing.

Woodhull's fears were unnecessary. Isabella and her compatriots
were bowled over by Woodhull's beauty and ladylike bearing, as well as
her incisive testimony (written by Butler, it was later said). "All the past
efforts of Miss Anthony and Mrs. Stanton sink to insignificance beside
the ingenious lobbying of the new leader and her daring delegation,"
declared the *Tribune*.[52] Suddenly Victoria Woodhull was the rising star
of the women's movement. She brought not only a magnetic presence,
but just as important, her own money and contacts, even a brand-new
newspaper backed by Cornelius Vanderbilt named *Woodhull & Claflin's
Weekly*.

Isabella was Mrs. Woodhull's most ardent convert. She "impressed
me profoundly, and in a manner I could never describe, with the conviction that she was heaven sent for the rescue of women from her pit
of subjection," wrote Isabella.[53] Her more conservative sisters, Catharine and Harriet, recognized Woodhull's talents but were uneasy about
the rumors of free love and other immoralities that dogged her. Isabella
urged them to meet her. Together, she hoped, the Beecher sisters might
persuade Woodhull to drop some of her more outlandish views.

In February 1871 Catharine met Woodhull for the first time in
Manhattan, sharing a carriage ride in Central Park. As they trotted
along, Catharine began to lecture her about the natural subordination

of women and the dangers of social equality. Suddenly, as Woodhull told the story, she saw a vision of a band of devils with rat tails dancing around Miss Beecher's head.

"You are misguided," Woodhull finally burst out. "Many great people have already accepted and are living my theories of social freedom though they are not ready to become its avowed advocates, as I am. You speak of Free Love with derision while your own brother, Henry Ward Beecher, the most powerful preacher in America, openly practices it. I do not condemn him, I applaud him. Would that he had the courage to join me in preaching what he practices."

"Evil!" Catharine exclaimed. "I know my brother is unhappy but he is a true husband. I will vouch for my brother's faithfulness to his marriage vows as though he were myself."

"But you have no positive knowledge that would justify your doing so," said Victoria.

"No . . . no positive—" stammered Catharine. "I know he is unhappy. Mrs. Beecher is a virago, a constitutional liar and a terrible woman altogether, so terrible his friends and family seldom visit. But unfaithful—no. I will hear no more of it."

"You will hear," said Victoria. "In concubinage with his parishioner's wife—it is common knowledge. And if you were a proper person to judge, which I grant you are not, you should see that the facts are fatal to your theories."

"Victoria Woodhull, I will strike you for this. I will strike you dead!"

"Strike as much and as hard as you please. Only don't do it in the dark so I cannot know who is my enemy."

"Stop!" Catharine cried, then climbed out and stalked away.[54]

Catharine's version of the interview was much the same, minus the whirling rat-tailed devils. Catharine, Isabella wrote with amusement, "saw Victoria and, attacking her on the marriage question, got such a black eye as filled her with horror and amazement. I had to laugh inwardly at her relation of the interview and am now waiting for her to cool down!"[55] But it was too late. The Beecher sisters, Catharine, Harriet, and Mary, now declared war on Victoria Woodhull.

The sisters began digging up the spiritualist's sordid family history as fodder for a steady stream of public and private attacks. They inundated Isabella and her husband with letters begging him, in Mary's words, to bring Isabella "back to God and away from that harlot."[56] Harriet satirized Woodhull in her current serial novel, My Wife and I, which was appearing in Henry's paper, the *Christian Union*, characterizing her as a shameless hussy named Audacia Dangereyes. Isabella was torn; "my prevailing belief is in her innocence and purity," she wrote to Susan B. Anthony, yet her sisters "have nearly crazed me with letters imploring me to have nothing to do with her."[57] Couldn't they investigate Woodhull to discover the truth?

Anthony's response to Isabella was blunt. "When we begin to search *records, past* or *present*—of those who bring brains or cash to our work for enfranchising women—it shall be with those of *the men—not the women,* and *not a woman—not Mrs. Woodhull*—until every insinuation of gossip of Beecher, Pomeroy, Butler, Carpenter shall be *fully investigated,* and each of them shall have proven to *your* and our satisfaction—that he never flirted or trifled with or desecrated any specimen of Womanhood," wrote Anthony, naming a number of prominent Republicans.[58] It was most likely the first time Isabella had heard the gossip about her brother put so plainly.

BY MAY 1871 the free-love attacks were savaging Woodhull's reputation. But Victoria was a dangerous opponent. On May 3, the same day that Elizabeth Tilton was writing her "nest-hiding" letter to Henry, Elizabeth Cady Stanton told Woodhull the story of the Tiltons' night of mutual confessions. Two weeks later Woodhull published the following notice in the *New York World*.

> I advocate free love in its highest purest sense as the only cure for the immorality, the deep damnation by which men corrupt and disfigure God's most holy institution of sexual relation. My judges preach against "free love" openly, and practice it secretly; their outward seeming is fair, inwardly they are full of "dead men's bones and all manner of uncleanness." For example, I know of one man, a public teacher of eminence who lives in concubinage with the wife of another public teacher of almost equal eminence. All three concur in denouncing offenses against morality. "Hypocrisy is the tribute paid by vice to virtue." So be it. But I decline to stand up as "the frightful example." I shall make it my business to analyze some of these lives, and will take my chances in the matter of libel suits.

The morning the notice appeared in the paper, she sent a note to Theodore, whom she had never met, demanding to see him. He hustled to her brokerage office, where she handed him a copy of the *World*. "I read, sir, by the expression on your face, that it is true?" she asked, before launching into a full recitation of all she knew of the scandal. Her story was, as Theodore described it, "extravagant and violent" but basically correct.[59]

Tilton hurried back to Brooklyn to confer with Moulton and Beecher. The way to keep her quiet, they decided, was to place her under "social obligation" by befriending her, a task which Henry left mostly to Theodore. Soon Theodore, too, had fallen under Woodhull's spell; compared with his own web of hypocrisy, Woodhull struck Theodore like a beacon of moral courage. Later she claimed that for three months "we were hardly out of each other's sights, and he slept every night in my arms."[60] Theodore denied having sex with her, but they were unquestionably intimate. He spent many late nights at her house that summer talking over their shared passion for social freedom and political justice, and preparing a biography of Victoria for his new magazine, the *Golden Age*.

Beecher spent almost the entire summer sequestered at the farm in Peekskill, as far from the city as he could get. His mood on vacation was almost manic. As Eunice observed, he is "just as full of fun and mischief and high spirits as a wild colt."[61] But behind his merry facade, the stress was taking a toll. He progressed from taking an occasional glass of wine "for the stomach" to drinking with gusto; he was eating like a stevedore and putting on weight. All work on the second volume of the *Life of Christ* was at a dead stop. The financial costs of the cover-up—including sending the talkative Bessie Turner away to school and a hefty investment in Theodore's new paper—were mounting, and were exacerbated by the need to keep these expenditures a secret from Eunice.

Unfortunately Theodore's contradictory mission of placating Woodhull while shoring up his own reputation was aggravated by his ill-advised zealotry. When Theodore's biography of Woodhull came out in September 1871, it was so extravagant in its flattery and so rapturous in his description of her seedy childhood, multiple marriages, communings with the spirit world (especially her patron spirit, Demosthenes), and anarchistic social views, that everyone—friend or foe—was appalled. "Too ridiculous almost, even to ridicule," wrote one of Tilton's friends. An "incredible specimen of highfalutin' idiocy," declared the author Bayard Taylor, who harbored nothing but scorn for the editor. "Such a book is a tomb from which no author again rises," wrote Julia Ward Howe, the leader of the Boston suffragists.[62]

"I urged him to make a prompt repudiation of these women and their doctrines," Beecher later said.[63] But their new "social obligation" worked both ways. Woodhull's reputation had sunk low enough that only the imprimatur of a man like Beecher could redeem her. In November, Victoria wrote to Henry, demanding that he introduce her upcoming lecture on "The Principles of Social Freedom."

"Two of your sisters have gone out of their way to assail my character and purposes, both by means of the public press and by numerous private letters written to various persons with whom they seek to injure me and thus to defeat the political ends at which I aim," Woodhull wrote to Beecher. "I repeat that I must have an interview tomorrow morning, since I am to speak tomorrow evening at Steinway Hall; and what I say or shall not say will depend largely upon the result of the interview."

Beecher hastily agreed to see Victoria at Tilton's house the next evening. They had met once or twice before, briefly, but Henry had explicitly avoided her all summer. Now, in typical fashion, he did his best to convey mutual sympathy without committing to anything concrete. "Marriage is the grave of love," he told Victoria, by her account. "I have never married a couple that I did not feel condemned."

"Why then do you not preach that conviction?" she asked.

It was one of the first lessons he'd learned from Lyman Beecher, and the bedrock of his career—a public teacher could only go as far as his people would support him. "If I were to do so I should preach to empty seats," he told her. "Milk for babies, meat for strong men."

When she pushed him further, according to Woodhull, the preacher "got up on the sofa on his knees beside me, and taking my face in between his hands, while the tears streamed down his cheeks, he begged me to let him off." It would all sound preposterous were it not the exact pose he'd taken when asking Bowen's forgiveness, a story unknown to Victoria.

Victoria rose to leave, in disgust. "Mr. Beecher, if I am compelled to go on that platform alone, I shall begin by telling the audience why I am alone and why you are not with me."[64]

The next day was one of the longest of Beecher's life. Theodore and Frank urged him to reconsider, but he refused. At the last minute the two friends nervously rushed over to Steinway Hall, and Theodore stepped in to introduce her. "It may be that she is a fanatic," he said to the audience, "it may be that I am a fool. But, before high heaven, I would rather be a fanatic and a fool in one than to be such a coward as would deny a woman the right to free speech."

Sadly, Theodore was indeed made the fool, when midway through the lecture, Victoria lost her temper at some hecklers. When one cried out, "Are you a free lover?" Victoria furiously proclaimed: "Yes, I am a free lover. I have an inalienable, constitutional and natural right to change that love every day if I please."[65] The line was gleefully reprinted in all the New York papers.

Now Tilton was truly ruined. Subscribers fled the *Golden Age*, his winter lecture tour was beset by canceled engagements, withdrawn invitations, and nasty comments in local papers, and he was on the verge of bankruptcy. He and Victoria were in the same sinking boat, watching resentfully as Beecher seemed to sail smoothly on.

BY FEBRUARY 1872, more than one year into the cover-up, Beecher was a wreck. Woodhull was actively peddling the story to newspaper editors, who so far had declined to take her bait. Pressure was growing in Plymouth Church to investigate Theodore's incessant rumormongering, despite Beecher's efforts to sweep it under the rug. He was under terrible pressure from his publishing firm, but he could not focus enough to write. Meanwhile Theodore's bitter tone was becoming ominous. When Elizabeth sent him a secret letter warning of Theodore's volatility, Beecher could stand it no longer. On February 5, 1872, he wrote Moulton what came to be known as the "Ragged Edge Letter."

No man can see the difficulties that environ me unless he stands where I do. To *say* that I have a church on my hands is simple enough—but to have the hundreds and thousands of men pressing me, each one with his keen suspicion, or anxiety, or zeal; to see tendencies which, if not stopped, would break out into a ruinous defense of me; to stop them without seeming to do it; to prevent anyone questioning me; to meet and allay prejudices against T. which had their beginning years before this; to keep serene as if I were not alarmed or disturbed; to be cheerful at home and among friends when I was suffering the torments of the damned; to pass sleepless nights often, and yet to come up fresh and full for Sunday—all this may be talked about, but the real thing cannot be understood from the outside, nor its wearing and grinding on the nervous system. [...]

If my destruction would place him all right, that shall not stand in the way. I am willing to step down and out. No one can offer more than that. That I do offer. Sacrifice me without hesitation, if you can clearly see your way to his safety and happiness thereby.

I do not think that anything would be gained by it. I should be destroyed, but he would not be saved. E. and the children would have their future clouded.

In one point of view I could desire the sacrifice on my part. Nothing could possibly be so bad as the horror of the great darkness in which I spend much of my time. I look upon death as sweeter-faced than any friend I have in the world. Life would be pleasant if I could see that re-built which is shattered. But to live on the sharp and ragged edge of anxiety, remorse, fear, despair, and yet to put on all the appearance of serenity and happiness, cannot be endured much longer. I am well-nigh discouraged. If you too cease to trust me, to love me, I am alone. I have not another person to whom I could go.[66]

When overwhelmed by such self-pity, Beecher turned to Frank Moulton and increasingly to Frank's gracious, sensible wife, Emma. Emma Moulton was "very sympathetic," as Henry said, "without being sentimental." Although deeply disappointed in her pastor and not entirely trusting of Theodore, like her husband she took a realistic view of the whole mess. In dark moods Beecher would lie on the sofa in her sitting room, moaning about his sorrows. "I was groaning and saying it did not seem to me that I could live and I didn't want to live," said Beecher of a typical visit. "Hmmm," responded Emma dryly; "you come and you are going to die, but I notice you like to live well enough."[67]

"You are the best friend I have in this world," Henry once told her; "you are dearer to me than any sister I have, for you, knowing all the truth, knowing that I am guilty, still stand by me, while they believe I am innocent."[68]

Yet he was just as headstrong as Theodore. Beecher was nearly sixty and easily could have retired from the pulpit or taken a long journey to the Holy Land to do research for the *Life of Christ*, as Moulton suggested. But for all his anxieties, Beecher was incapable of giving up the adulation and the money.

By April 1872 Tilton was in dire financial straits. Moulton—along with several alarmed investors in Beecher's publishing ventures who had caught hints of his troubles—pressured Bowen to settle Tilton's claim for the broken contracts with the *Independent* and the *Brooklyn Union*. On April 2 Tilton, Beecher, and Bowen signed a secret "Tripartite Agreement," in which Tilton was awarded seven thousand dollars—enough to keep him afloat for a while. In exchange the three men swore to withdraw and never repeat "all charges, imputations, and innuendoes," and "resume the old relations of love, respect and reliance."[69] For a brief moment they were buoyed by their misbegotten faith in written contracts.

Then the letters from Isabella began arriving. Isabella's attachment to Woodhull had only grown more steadfast, despite the disapproval of her family and friends. By now Isabella had heard the tales of her brother's alleged affair from Elizabeth Cady Stanton and received indirect confirmation of them from Woodhull. By her own observation of Henry's marriage, Isabella was inclined to accept them as true. With remarkable naïveté, she first wrote to Tilton for more information.

When he did not reply, she questioned Henry directly. Although the practice of free love "at present is revolting to my feelings and my judgment," Isabella told Henry, she would be open-minded. "The only reply I made to Mrs. Stanton was that, if true, you had a philosophy of the relation of the sexes so far ahead of the times that you dared not announce it, though you consented to live by it."[70]

"Of some things I *neither talk nor will be talked with*," Henry calmly replied to Isabella. "The only help that can be grateful to me, or useful is *silence*, and a silencing influence on others. A day may come for converse—it is not *now*. Living or dead, my dear sister Belle, *love me* and do not talk about me or suffer others to in your presence."[71]

Internally, however, he was panicked. For several weeks he suffered "spells" of dizziness so severe he could not preach. "I fear they are keeping something from me," fretted Eunice from Florida to Susan Howard.[72]

Then arose that old devil politics, to stir the pot again at just the wrong moment. The presidential elections of 1872 were an unappetizing stew. President Grant's administration was beginning to erupt in a series of spectacular scandals. Beecher remained an unapologetic Grant man, campaigning vigorously for the old general. Theodore Tilton, to no one's surprise, rushed to the head of the oppositional Liberal wing of the Republican Party, announcing that the party "needs the thorn of the doctrinaire in its side."[73] That summer when the Liberal Republicans split off from the party and nominated Horace Greeley of the *Tribune* for the presidency, Tilton served as campaign manager. Greeley's candidacy had the feel of a fool's errand, but if he won Tilton would reclaim both public stature and the moral high ground.

But the most astounding turn came when Victoria Woodhull, determined to claim her place in the public eye, announced in May that she would be the first woman to run for president, on the ticket of her brand-new People's Party. After Cornelius Vanderbilt dumped her, she had added socialism and labor reform to her other causes, printing the first American edition of Karl Marx's *Communist Manifesto* in *Woodhull & Claflin's Weekly* and giving speeches excoriating Vanderbilt and his fellow robber barons.

Frank Moulton carefully monitored the situation to keep Tilton and Beecher from clashing on the stump, but he had no control over Woodhull, who was furious when Theodore refused to support her candidacy. As he was leaving for the Liberal Republican convention, Theodore called on Woodhull, explaining that he was going merely as a reporter.

"Theodore, you are lying again," hissed Woodhull. "You are going to Cincinnati to nominate Mr. Greeley, and I see, clairvoyantly, a coffin following you, in which you will be responsible for putting him, because it will result in his death."[74] Theodore left without saying a word and never spoke to her again, ending all pretense of any mutual "social obligation."

Woodhull was now frantic. Her presidential campaign was stillborn, Cornelius Vanderbilt had withdrawn his financial backing, she was evicted from her house, and no respectable landlord would rent to her. By now Isabella Hooker was one of the very few suffragists who still stuck by her. In desperation Woodhull sent another threatening letter to Beecher in June, asking for help.

But Beecher sent no reply. Instead he gave the letter to Moulton for safekeeping, asking if Frank could not make her "understand that I can do nothing? I certainly shall not, at any and all hazards, take a single step in that direction, and if it brings trouble—it must come."[75]

By September, Woodhull was determined to strike. On September 12, 1872, a motley collection of psychics and seers, radical social reformers, random eccentrics, and curiosity seekers gathered in Boston, Massachusetts, for the annual convention of the American Association of Spiritualists. The hall was growing restless when all of a sudden, from a side door, a small, dark-haired woman flashed onto the platform. Her delicate features were pale and twisted into a tragic expression. Her blue almond-shaped eyes shone with what one observer called a lurid light. A sort of electric shock swept over the assembly, striking them into dead silence, as if they had seen a streak of lightning and were waiting for the thunderclap.

Woodhull paused, tossing her curls with a dramatic flourish. Then she began, as one audience member, Mrs. Elizabeth Meriwether, wrote, to "pour out a torrent of flame." One by one she named some of the most powerful men in the country, following each name with a horrifying list of sins and hypocrisies—cheating, lying, swindling, committing adultery, visiting prostitutes. "It was, in fact, a declaration of war against those men," Mrs. Meriwether said. "It made our flesh to creep and our blood to run cold."

But the king of free love, Woodhull declared, was the Reverend Henry Ward Beecher. The audience shuddered in astonishment. For years this legendary minister had been carrying on an affair with his best friend's wife, a poor defenseless woman named Elizabeth Tilton. There was no question the story was true, she claimed, for she had heard it directly from Elizabeth Tilton, her husband, Theodore, and from Henry Ward Beecher himself.

Nor was Tilton the only one, Woodhull cried, her pale cheeks now crimson. Every Sunday morning Henry Ward Beecher stood in his Brooklyn pulpit and preached to a dozen of his mistresses, every one of them *"members of his church sitting on their pews robed in silks and satins and high respectability!"*[76]

Then Woodhull disappeared from the platform, slipping out the side door of the auditorium. Afterward she remembered little of her speech. "They tell me that I used some naughty words on that occasion. All I know is, that if I swore, *I did not swear profanely,*" she said later. "*I swore divinely.*"[77]

BACK IN BROOKLYN, Plymouth Church prepared for a week-long Jubilee, celebrating Beecher's twenty-fifth year as pastor. The organizers, chaired by the indefatigable Moses Beach, called it their Silver Wedding Anniversary, marking the marriage of "Church and Pastor—Man and Wife!" Eunice Beecher remarked tartly that half the people thought it was the anniversary of her own long marriage to Henry.

Beecher seemed unusually moved by the ceremonies. The emotional climax of the grand jubilee came when the Reverend Richard Salter Storrs, the other Congregational titan on the Heights, stood to pay tribute to his old friend and fellow worker. When Storrs finished Beecher stood, "with tears, and trembling from head to toe, arose and placing his hand on Dr. Storrs' shoulder, warmly kissed him on the cheek." The hushed audience erupted into tears and applause. "I want to say something, but I am unable to," said Beecher, his voice choked with emotion. Instead they closed the evening with a favorite hymn, "Jesus, Lover of My Soul."[78]

Woodhull read the glowing accounts of the Silver Jubilee with disgust. By contrast, the few papers that reported her Boston speech noticed it only to further insult her. "Very well," she declared. "I will make it hotter on earth for Henry Ward Beecher than Hell is below."

On October 28, just in time for election day, Woodhull published a new edition of *Woodhull & Claflin's Weekly*, bearing the startling headline "The Beecher-Tilton Scandal Case." Inside she recounted many of the details of the affair and cover-up, adding some dramatic flourishes and presenting it all as solid fact. She listed Isabella Beecher Hooker, Elizabeth Cady Stanton, and other well-known reformers as her sources, and claimed that both Theodore and Henry adhered to "free love theories" but were too cowardly to avow them publicly. "I intend," she wrote, "that this article shall burst like a bomb-shell into the ranks of the moralistic social camp."[79]

Within hours of its release, scores of newsboys were hawking the paper, and by evening the ten-cent papers were selling for $2.50 a copy. Within days 150,000 copies of *Woodhull & Claflin's Weekly* were sold, with secondhand copies going for as much as twenty dollars apiece. Now, after two years of seething in silence, Henry Bowen pounced. A little after midnight on the twenty-eighth, Bowen and his Brooklyn rival, District Attorney Benjamin Tracy, contacted Anthony Comstock, the eager young spearhead of the YMCA's antipornography campaign. The next morning Comstock instructed two of Bowen's clerks to buy and mail copies of the paper to a designated address. When the papers arrived at their destination on November 2, police arrested Woodhull and her sister Tennie for violating an 1865 law that forbade sending obscene materials through the U.S. mails. It was obvious, observed the *Brooklyn Eagle* when they discovered Bowen's machinations, that he engineered the arrest to draw attention to Woodhull's accusations.

And it did. All the respectable papers that would not reprint Woodhull's articles gladly reported the details of her arrest, including all her accusations. Rumors, puns, dirty jokes, and cartoons about Henry and his paramours ran wild through the city.

Beecher was outwardly unperturbed. "For myself I have not a word to say. Twenty-five years must speak for me—or else *Character* is worthless," he told one supporter. Plymouth Church rallied around him with unwavering support. "They act nobly—as I knew they would," Beecher said.[80]

But as soon as he could slip away, Beecher ran to Moulton's. Theodore didn't see Woodhull's bombshell until election day, when he returned from the campaign trail. "As soon as I entered the house Mrs. Tilton, with great distress, put into my hands a copy of *Woodhull & Claflin's Weekly*," said Tilton.[81] He too headed to Moulton's. There the three men nervously recommitted themselves to the "policy of silence."

Tilton's wager on Greeley ended disastrously. Theodore's connection to Victoria Woodhull made him a laughingstock and a liability to the campaign. Greeley alienated voters in both parties when he took Tilton's advice and accepted the nomination of the Democratic Party, after years of vilifying them as the enemy of all things good and holy. Tilton joined the Liberal Republicans in repudiating the commitment to universal suffrage by calling for literacy tests for voters, banning women's rights from the campaign, and actively courting former Confederates, while declaring that there was no more need for federal measures to protect the former slaves. Tilton had lost his idealism; nothing was left of his old zeal but self-righteous anger.

The loss crushed Greeley. He was ruined in fortune and health. At the end of November he sank into a coma and then died. His final instructions seemed almost prophetic: "Be kind to Tilton—he is foolish—but young."[82]

"At last the blow has fallen," Isabella wrote to their brother Tom, asking him to help her bring things right. "At present, of course, I shall keep silent, but truth is dearer than all things else and if he will not speak in some way I cannot always stand as consenting to a lie."

Over the decades the formerly close brothers had drifted apart as Tom, who inherited both his mother's melancholy and his father's rigor, realized he could not share Henry's sanguine view of human nature. Tom responded coolly to Isabella's plea. Victoria Woodhull "only carries out Henry's philosophy, against which I recorded my protest twenty years ago, and parted (lovingly and achingly) from him, saying, 'We cannot work together,'" he told Isabella. "In my judgment Henry is following his slippery doctrines of expediency, and in his cry of progress and the nobleness of human nature has sacrificed clear, exact, ideal integrity." Tom wanted nothing to do with the matter, and advised her to do the same. Even a court of law would never reveal the whole truth, he reminded her. "Perjury for good reason with advanced thinkers is no sin."[83]

But still Isabella pleaded with Henry to make a clean breast. Finally she decided to do it for him. "I can endure no longer. I must see you and persuade you to write a paper which I will read, going alone to your pulpit, and taking sole charge of the services," she wrote to Henry before Thanksgiving. She would take the train from Hartford to New York on Friday, to discuss her plan and to meet personally with Mrs. Tilton. "I feel sure," she added, "that words from her should go into that paper and with her consent I could write as one commissioned on high."[84]

"This is a disaster!" groaned Beecher to Moulton when he brought the stack of Isabella's letters to Remsen Street, away from Eunice's prying eyes. "Is there no end of trouble and complication?"[85]

Henry met his sister at the train station. Over a long dinner, he did his best to convince her of her mistake. After Henry went home, Isabella told her husband, John, "I sent for Tilton and he spent all the evening in trying to blind my eyes—declared that his wife solemnly assured him that she never confessed anything of the sort to Susan [B. Anthony]—and Henry told me the same thing." The next morning Theodore told his co-conspirators that he'd broken Isabella to the point of tears, by threatening to accuse *her* of adultery and criminal insanity.

"Bravo!" responded Beecher, clapping his hands with delight.

The highlight of Isabella's strange trip to New York turned out to be Horace Greeley's grand public funeral at the Church of the Divine Paternity at Forty-fifth Street and Fifth Avenue. Beecher was to give the eulogy, so he got Isabella an invitation to the crowded ceremony. "When we came to fall in line to walk to the church I found myself side by side with *Mrs. Tilton,* who looked up in my face with a sweet smile," wrote Isabella with surprise. "I drew her hand in mine, under my shawl pressed it close to my heart and we walked in silence to the church and sat close together through the service and at its close we spoke together a moment and instinctively our lips met in a long kiss of love and trust and she grasped my hand holding it till she passed out of the pew to join her husband and go to the grave."

As he entered the pulpit and gazed over the audience, Henry was horrified to spot the two of them sitting together. With heart pounding and head swimming, he thought he might collapse then and there. As he told Isabella afterward, "he felt he was going just as Greeley did." His voice was so choked by anxiety that the audience could barely hear the eulogy. The next day he met with Isabella again. Writing to her husband, Belle captured the cascade of charm, flattery, and self-pity Henry used in a fruitless attempt to regain her loyalty. He said that

> for two years he had been utterly alone—no woman to counsel or help and he feared he had lost me at one time—but now he took a long breath and would try to live to do the things His God would have him. There are no clouds between me and him he said and no lies. *He* [Christ] knows all and when He tells me to do what you ask I shall do it—but I can't go any faster than I can see my way—don't be discouraged keep on telling me what you feel and think—if I could only have you near me all the time—but that is impossible. I have always loved you more than any of my brothers and sisters and needed you at my side—but it can't be even now—do you know I was away lecturing and Ma [Eunice] got hold of your first letters and *read them all,* etc.

Ironically Eunice "was drawn to him by my accusation but I suppose she would kill me if she had the opportunity," Isabella concluded wryly.[86]

The only thing Henry did not do was deny committing adultery. Isabella returned to Hartford feeling that her worst fears had been confirmed. But Isabella's continued loyalty to Woodhull made her a pariah. Her sisters, the Howards, her Hartford neighbors—all shunned her. Even that genial infidel Mark Twain informed his wife, as his sister put it, that she "shall not cross Mrs. Hooker's threshold and if he talks to Mrs. H. he will tell her in plain words the reason."[87]

Henry took his own precautions. On Sunday he stationed his sister Harriet in the front pew of Plymouth Church in case Isabella suddenly appeared. A few weeks after Greeley's funeral, the *Tribune* reported that Henry Ward Beecher and his family feared that Mrs. Hooker's friendship with Victoria Woodhull was a sign of insanity, and were consulting with doctors. Henry received no more letters from his sister.

Chapter 13

"It Is the Letters—the Letters, Only the Letters"

*T*heodore Tilton's commitment to the cover-up was crumbling fast. "For the last four or five weeks, or ever since I saw the Woodhull libel, I have hardly had a restful day, and I frequently dream the whole thing over at night, waking the next morning unfit for work," he wrote to a friend. Everyone was blaming him, Theodore complained, when in fact it was "Bowen's assassinating dagger drawn against Beecher" that fouled Brooklyn's air.[1]

Increasingly eager to defend himself, that winter Theodore wrote up a lengthy "True Story" of the scandal, which he had copied and leather bound, to show to his "personal friends." Unfortunately most of his personal friends were journalists. He also published a trumped-up "Letter To A Complaining Friend," explaining that, while he could not truthfully deny all of Woodhull's story, "I shall try with patience to keep my answer within my own breast, lest it shoot forth like a thunderbolt through other hearts."[2] As if this were not enough, in the spring of 1874 Theodore published *Tempest Tossed*, a novel clearly based on his troubled marriage.

Worst of all, Theodore went to consult with Henry's friend the Reverend Richard Salter Storrs, whose Congregational church stood only a few blocks from Beecher's. Like the "Letter to the Complaining Friend," it was a disingenuous move, as Theodore's relationship with Storrs was cool at best ("that iceberg," Theodore called him).[3] He offered a coy explanation of his troubles, framed as a miniconfession that he wrote up and had Elizabeth sign: "In July, 1870, prompted by my duty, I informed my husband that Rev. H.W. Beecher, my friend and pastor, had solicited me to be a wife to him, together with all that this implies."[4]

Storrs seemed to assume that she had refused the solicitation, and Theodore didn't say otherwise. "Oh, Theodore, of all the men in the world, I wish you had kept clear of Dr. Storrs!" groaned Beecher when he heard of the visit.[5] Beecher had spent too much time among heresy hunters to not smell danger. Besides, it hurt his pride to be put "in the position of a man who had solicited favors from a woman, and be put in the position of one who had been rejected by her," he told Frank![6]

Enough people knew enough details that the story now took on a life of its own. Victoria Woodhull was out of jail and was running regular updates on the Brooklyn scandal in *Woodhull & Claflin's Weekly*. The *Eagle*, prodded by Tilton's "True Story," was hammering Henry Bowen, their journalistic rival. Nearly every issue featured some scurrilous slam, accusing Bowen of ruthless moneygrubbing, using bankruptcy to cheat his creditors, political double-dealing, appointing corrupt tax collectors, running fraudulent ads, filing lawsuits to threaten his rivals, and slandering his own pastor.

The more people read of Bowen's perfidy, the less explicable they found Beecher's silence, and the more they clamored for him to speak. And yet, as papers as far away as the *Cincinnati Post* noted with growing suspicion, "Of all those whose names were given in the Woodhull publication, not one, from Beecher to Tilton down, has so much as uttered the word 'False!' "[7]

"I think the silence of the Beechers is a hundred-fold more of an *obscene publication* than that of the Woodhulls and the said silence is a thousand-fold more potent in convincing people of the truth of that scandal than the evidence of fifty Woodhulls could be," said Mark Twain, summing up the public's growing anxiety. "You will find presently that the general thought of the nation will gradually form itself into the verdict that there is *some* fire somewhere in all this smoke of scandal."[8] By April of 1874 newspapers were running a steady stream of letters to the editor, demanding an end to the "policy of silence."

BOTH PHYSICALLY AND MENTALLY Henry was a wreck. He was startlingly thin, his hair had turned snow white, and he had a resurgence of the dizziness and psychosomatic near-paralysis he'd suffered during the

Proctor troubles in the late fifties. Running into him that winter, one friend was shocked at the minister's appearance. "I found him a gray, haggard old man. His face shows time and bitterness of spirit," wrote Moses Coit Taylor, an editor at the *Christian Union*. "Perhaps it was my imagination, but I thought I had seldom seen eyes and a face expressing greater wretchedness. It was indeed the countenance of a great soul in desolation."[9] With Tilton's magazine, the *Golden Age*, on the verge of bankruptcy, Beecher mortgaged his house for five thousand dollars, carrying the check directly from the bank to Frank Moulton, who delivered it to Theodore. This had a "beatific" effect on Theodore's mood, said Henry. "I recollect thinking that $5,000 was very mollifying."[10]

Henry had one comfort: Eunice was in Florida all that winter, far from the urban press. He would not speak of the subject with her, so Eunice turned to Chloe for news. "You will see him every day, do keep me a little informed," she begged; "if only to tell me how he is—how he looks."[11]

In April, Moses Beach took his daughter Emma and her friend Nellie to northern Europe for the summer, leaving Chloe and the younger girls in Brooklyn. Even in the middle of the Atlantic, however, it was impossible to escape the growing scandal. After Henry came to the ship to say good-bye, Moses unhappily noted that "Emma and Nellie overheard—of necessity—the comments of some of the passengers upon the conduct of Rev. Henry Ward Beecher who had been seen to kiss two of the lady passengers. To be sure they *might* be relatives but when so much of scandal was afloat he ought to be more circumspect."[12]

Undoubtedly Chloe, like most of Beecher's friends and parishioners, believed in his innocence. The preacher's well-known flirtatiousness only made it easier to attribute these rumors to misunderstanding, jealousy, or the unrequited infatuation of a foolish woman. But as the scandal mushroomed over the summer, Chloe seemed to go into shock. Traveling through Norway and Russia, Moses heard nothing about the scandal, but Chloe's letters began to worry him. "I cannot tell why it is, but you seem to write as though in pain or sickness which you were trying your best to conceal," he wrote. "Indeed you *must* tell me how *you* are when writing after you receive this."[13] Chloe laughed off his concerns, but said nothing. Would that everyone had been as discreet as Mrs. Beach.

Beecher's financial backers, who knew the story and suspected its truth, were desperately worried. Sam Wilkeson, publicity man for Jay

Cooke's Northern Pacific Railroad, brother-in-law of Elizabeth Cady Stanton, and a major investor in Beecher's publishing ventures who had personally put up the ten-thousand-dollar advance for Beecher's *Life of Christ*, was one of the first to hear about the scandal. "This will knock the 'Life of Christ' higher than a kite," he told Stanton with alarm.[14] Back when Bowen first fired Tilton, Wilkeson tried to quell the conflict by offering him a job promoting the Northern Pacific, which the high-minded editor refused. Now Wilkeson, in consultation with Tasker Howard and other investors, but *not* with Tilton and Moulton, decided that the best path would be to shift all blame onto Bowen. In the *New York Times* of May 30 they published in the paid columns a copy of the "Tripartite Agreement"—in which Beecher, Tilton, and Bowen repudiated their mutual rumormongering—as well as an old document of Theodore's detailing all Bowen's original accusations from as far back as 1863.

Theodore's beatific mood evaporated. Why, that agreement made it seem as if *he* shared Bowen's villainy, and that Beecher had pardoned *him!* In retaliation, he threatened to publish Beecher's "Letter of Contrition" of January 1, 1872. The next day, Sunday, Henry was too despondent to preach. Instead he composed what came to be known as the "Day of Judgment Letter." "I have determined to make no more resistance. Theodore's temperament is such that the future, even if temporarily earned, would be absolutely worthless," he wrote to Frank. "With such a man as T.T. there is no possible salvation for any that depend upon him." He had his letter of resignation ready to hand to Plymouth Church if Theodore went forward.

On Monday, Henry showed up at Frank's house, saying he wanted to talk to his wife Emma. She "has been to me as one of God's comforters," he told Frank.[15] Over the last two years the sympathetic yet sensible Emma had become one of Beecher's closest confidantes. "This is probably my last conversation with you," he said with self-pity, according to Emma; "if that letter of apology is published, I might as well go out of life; it is useless to try to live it down."

"Mr. Beecher," she replied, "there is something better for you than that. I think that would be a very cowardly thing for you to do. Go down to your church and confess your crime; they will forgive you."

"No; that I can not do; I should be—my children would despise me. I could not go back to my home, and my church would not forgive me, they would not deal with me as you have done. There would be nothing left for me to do. My work would be finished. It would be better that I should go out of life than to remain any longer in it."

"You could write for your paper. You could go to your farm and write."

"No," Beecher said tearfully; "if they would not listen to hear me preach, they certainly would not read anything that I should write. Besides, my position in life is that of a spiritual and moral teacher. If I can no longer hold that position there is nothing left for me, and I am resolved to take my life. I have a powder at home on my library table which I have prepared, which I shall take, and shall sink quietly off as if going to sleep, without a struggle." Back and forth they went for four hours, she urging confession, he dreaming of the rest of death.[16]

As usual, his suicidal urge passed. That same day the papers printed Beecher's first public statement on the scandal, briefly denying that Tilton was "the author of the calumnies" but saying nothing else.[17] Eunice regarded the statement as a dreadful mistake. "I can hardly think of anything else," she told Chloe Beach. But Henry was treating her with that tight-lipped silence that he always had during times of trouble, so she could say nothing to him. She begged Chloe "to collect and keep for me everything that you see about this matter. If Henry won't talk with me I *must* know somehow."[18]

ON JUNE 21, 1873, that noble old abolitionist Lewis Tappan died. He had long ago left public life, and his death might have passed without much comment were it not for his unscrupulous son-in-law, Henry Bowen. One week later the *Eagle* reported that Bowen attended Tappan's funeral, where he appeared deeply moved by Beecher's eulogy. As soon as the service was over, Bowen and several other prominent businessmen went directly to Victoria Woodhull's house to demand that she hand over any incriminating letters from Henry Ward Beecher.

It was too much to believe—some of the richest men in New York consulting with the nation's most notorious strumpet about their pastor's debauchery! This was the last straw—Beecher could no longer remain silent. On June 30 he published a letter to the editor in the *Eagle* declaring that "the stories and rumors which have for some time been circulated about me, are grossly untrue, and I stamp them in general and in particular as utterly false."[19]

"I tell you," remarked Susan B. Anthony to Isabella after reading her brother's statement, "when God shall take up his old plan of punishing *liars*—there will be a good many people struck dead in Gotham and its suburbs."[20]

Across the country the press went mad. After a year of being held back by Beecher, the Examining Committee of Plymouth Church declared it would wait no longer: These slanders must be investigated. Beecher tried again to put them off but to no avail. The preacher was a master of emotional compartmentalization, but that summer the chasm between his inner turmoil and his serene public facade grew so wide that he began having hallucinations. Every night, he told his doctor, he was awakened around four o'clock in the morning

> by hearing my name called; and I lie awake, hearing, distinctly and with apparent reality, voices calling me in the sweetest and most inviting tones. Nothing of terror is experienced; on the contrary, my moral state is the most blissful and entrancing. I seem to be on the very borders of Heaven. Now, while this is the case my judicial reasoning self lies there perfectly aware that this is all hallucination, and the outworking of an overwrought and overstrained brain. I seem to have a double existence, as if another self were beside me in the bed.

It was as if, Henry said, "Each separate part of me was an individual, and all in discord." The doctor prescribed "Cannabis Indica, or Haschish as it is called in the East," and the hallucinations faded.[21]

NOW EVENTS CAME thick and fast. In October 1873 Plymouth Church finally brought Theodore Tilton before its Examining Committee. Henry thought he had arranged it so that the meeting would merely give formal confirmation to Theodore's decision to leave the church several years before. So Theodore was surprised when the committee announced it was charging him with slander. With a look of barely repressed contempt, Theodore turned dramatically toward the minister and declared "that if he had slandered him he was there to answer to the man he had slandered; that if Beecher had aught to say against him, if he would say it, he would answer him as God was his judge."

Everyone turned to look at Beecher. The piercing silence was broken only by a few muffled sobs rising from the audience. Beecher stood and said calmly, "Mr. Tilton asks if I have any charge to make against him. I have none. Whatever differences have been between us have been amicably adjusted and, so far as I am concerned, buried. I have no charges."[22] Nonetheless Theodore Tilton was formally dropped from Plymouth Church by a vote of 210 to 13.

Angry at once again being made the villain, Theodore sought the help of Dr. Storrs, who called a council of local Congregational churches to investigate the unusual excommunication procedures of Plymouth Church. Beecher and Plymouth Church refused to participate, citing the historical independence of individual congregations. Still, the council treated its premier preacher gingerly, concluding with a slight slap on the wrist for his church's ecclesiastical irregularities.

Just as it seemed the worst had passed, Beecher's overzealous parishioners again stirred the embers. Plymouth Church's clerk, Thomas Shearman, a corporate lawyer notorious for his shady corporate clients, ruthless tactics, and ardent admiration for Henry Ward Beecher, told the Brooklyn Union that Elizabeth Tilton was given to "mediumistic fits" and her husband was insane—infuriating Theodore anew. "Is there no end of trouble?" Henry asked Moulton in despair. "Is wave to follow wave in endless succession? I felt like lying down and saying, 'I am tired—tired—tired of living or trying to resist the devil of mischief.' "[23]

Even worse, in April 1874, just after the Congregational council drew to a close, its moderater, the Reverend Leonard Bacon, gave a lecture at Yale Seminary calling Theodore Tilton a "knave" and a "dog," adding, "I think Beecher would have done better to have let vengeance come on the heads of his slanderers."[24] Unfortunately a Tribune correspondent was there and reported it in full. Bacon followed this insult with a series of critical editorials in the Independent.

Finally Theodore was done. Forced to sell the Golden Age to pay its debts, with no prospect of employment, his wife estranged, and his reputation destroyed, he had nothing left to lose. On June 21 his reply to Leonard Bacon appeared in all the major New York papers, alleging that Beecher had committed an unnamed crime against his family, and refusing any longer "to sacrifice my good name for the maintenance of his."[25] Four days later, with Theodore's permission, the Eagle published its own version of "Tilton's Story." Although it did not specifically mention adultery, it explained that Theodore had left Plymouth Church because he suffered an "offense" at Beecher's hands. It offered many incriminating details, including a recent offer by Beecher's friends to send the Tiltons to Europe until the scandal blew over, and an explosive extract from Beecher's original "Letter of Contrition":

I ask through you Theodore Tilton's forgiveness, and I humble myself before him as I do before my God. He would have been a better man in my circumstances than I have been. I can ask nothing except that he will remember all the other hearts that would ache. I will not plead for myself; I even wish that I were dead.

The cover-up was officially over. Frank urged Henry to at least speak with Theodore, but he refused. "The crisis is at hand," Beecher wrote to Frank. "When I say, will not, I mean cannot. Events are masters, just now. There is no earthly reason for conference with Mr. T. It makes nothing better; everything worse. The matter is in a nutshell. No light is needed, only choice."[26]

The day after "Tilton's Story" hit the press, Henry came down from Peekskill to confer with his cabal, including Tasker Howard, Ben Tracy, Tommy Shearman, and Moses Beach. They reluctantly appointed an investigating committee composed of his staunchest supporters, including several who had been serving as intermediaries in the cover-up, but held off announcing it publicly. Even now Beecher was frantically meeting with Frank Moulton in hopes of a miracle, or at least some clarity. "I shall make a clean breast of it," he declared at the last minute. "I shall tell the whole truth, I shall take the blame on myself. I shall vindicate Theodore and Elizabeth."[27] But once again he could not bring himself to do it.

Meanwhile Henry's counselors, Shearman and Tracy, had already begun their machinations. Beecher's lawyers were the most distasteful characters in the whole lurid story, bearing out their wide reputation for rascality. Before the investigation was even announced, they secretly lured Elizabeth into testifying before the handpicked committee.

The last two years had been hellish for Elizabeth; "my little miserable body is so tired, so tired, dear that I cannot even love," she told her worried friend Sarah Putnam in May.[28] With every word her husband released to the press, Elizabeth grew more humiliated and angry, and his public assault on Leonard Bacon pushed her to the breaking point. "I have always been treated as a nonentity—a plaything—to be used or let alone at will; but it has always seemed to me I was *a* party not a little concerned," she told her brother, Joseph. Now she was ready to act on her own behalf.

It was not hard, then, for Beecher's lawyers to convince her that if she did not take Beecher's side he, her family, her church, and all

Christendom would fall. Ben Tracy went over her testimony with her, and then gathered the investigating committee at the house of one of Elizabeth's close friends. The committee asked her directly: "Was there any improper intercourse between Mr. Beecher and yourself?" Did he "make any improper overtures to you?"

No, she said with passion, never, "in thought, or deed, nor has he ever offered me an indecorous or improper proposal."[29]

In a later examination they probed further. If Beecher never propositioned her, why then had she told her husband that Mr. Beecher made improper advances?

It was Theodore's constant harassment, she replied; "a mesmeric condition was brought to bear on me." "I was pretty nearly out of my mind, and my attitude was that I shan't be here very long anyway, so if you want me to do this, I will do it," she said. "I thought it would some way serve Theodore and bring peace to his household."[30]

What about Susan B. Anthony's claim that she heard Elizabeth confess the affair? Elizabeth admitted that she'd told Anthony of Theodore's accusations against her and Reverend Beecher, but she'd never explicitly told Anthony that Theodore's allegations were false; "it never occurred to me to do it; I took them to be reasonable persons, and I never thought of their wondering if it was so."[31]

The committee asked her to describe Theodore's erratic behavior, his irrational jealousy of Beecher, and their troubled marriage. She willingly obliged. Theodore "laid the cornerstone of free love" in their home, she said stoutly, "so that the atmosphere was not only godless but impure for my children." His "hatred to Mr. Beecher has existed these many years, and the determination to ruin Mr. Beecher has been the one aim of his life."[32]

As for her own relations with the pastor, "With Mr. Beecher I had a sort of consciousness of being more," Elizabeth told the committee; "he appreciated me as Theodore did not; I felt myself another woman; I felt that he respected me; I think Theodore never saw in me what Mr. Beecher did."[33]

LATE THAT EVENING Elizabeth returned to Livingston Street and informed Theodore that she had just testified before a committee of investigation, fully acquitting Beecher of all wrongdoing. Theodore, who had had no idea of the investigation, was livid. Over the next few days they fought viciously. Finally, very early one morning, said Elizabeth, "I rose quietly and having dressed, roused him only to say, 'Theodore, I will never take another step by your side. The end has indeed come.' "

Theodore Tilton tried to persuade her to stay, but Elizabeth was truly done with him. Mr. Tilton's "idea of truth-loving is self-loving," as she told the committee with disdain.[34] She went to stay with close friends from the church.

Embittered by the theft of his wife, Theodore prepared a full assault. When he appeared before the committee, there was no more talk of "improper advances"; now it was "criminal seduction." He read a long written statement, taking the story from their wedding in 1855 through the horrible Christmas week of 1870, up to the troubles of the last year, quoting from Beecher's and Elizabeth's various letters to support his claims. In his own way he defended his wife. "If Mr. Beecher held the same religious views I did, he never could have made any approach to her. I do not believe in point of moral goodness that there is in this company so white a soul as Elizabeth Tilton," he concluded.[35] Theodore then submitted to a full cross-examination, in which the committee did its best to make him out as a lout and a libertine.

The committee proceedings leaked out almost as fast as they occurred. Theodore's statement hit the press the day after he gave it— probably provided by Theodore himself. As soon as they saw the papers the panicked committee telegraphed Beecher to come quickly from Peekskill. Henry released a very brief statement in response in which he, too, praised Elizabeth: "One less deserving of such disgrace, I never knew," he insisted. "I cherish for her a pure feeling, such as a gentleman might honorably offer to a Christian woman, and which she might receive and reciprocate without scruple."

Then Beecher explained the crux of the conflict. When problems arose in the Tilton marriage, he explained, "it was to my wife that she resorted for counsel; and both of us, acting from sympathy, and, as it subsequently appeared, without full knowledge, gave unadvised counsel, which tended to harm." Theodore was angry when he found that Mrs. Tilton's "reliance upon my judgment had greatly increased, while his influence had diminished, in consequence of a marked change in his religious and social views which was taking place during those years."

Believing that he had unconsciously hurt their marriage, "I gave expression to my feelings in an interview with a mutual friend, not in cold and cautious self-defending words, but eagerly taking blame upon myself and pouring out my heart to my friend in the strongest language, overburdened with the exaggerations of impassioned sorrow." After all, had he been the "evil man" that Tilton claims, he would have been far more crafty. More to the point, Henry concluded, it was absurd to think that Theodore could possibly have remained so friendly had he really seduced his wife.[36]

Now the floodgates were open. Interviews, statements, and documents proliferated. Many of the most sensational items emanated from the radical female reformers. Isabella's damning letters to Henry appeared in the press, Victoria Woodhull announced that she and Theodore had been lovers for six months, and Elizabeth Cady Stanton recounted to a reporter the lurid details of the Tiltons' night of mutual confessions. Susan B. Anthony, an honorable exception, refused to comment on Stanton's story. "If I did say it, it was very ungracious of them to repeat it," she told a reporter. "If I did not, it was worse to make it up."[37]

When Anthony scolded her fellow-worker for her indiscretion, Stanton apologized, although her anger and disgust continued to boil over. "The whole odium of this *scandalum magnatum* has, in some quarters, been rolled on our suffrage movement as unjustly as cunningly; hence I feel obliged just now to make extra efforts to keep our ship off the rocks," Stanton explained to Anthony. "When Beecher falls, as he must, he will pull all he can down with him. But we must not let the cause of woman go down in the smash."[38]

Of course the Beecher siblings were right in the thick of things. Isabella fled to Europe when the scandal broke, so she missed hearing Thomas Shearman accuse her of insanity, hallucinations, and, he implied, a lesbian attraction to Woodhull. The rest of the family defended their brother, sometimes rather comically. Catharine sent the *Tribune* a backhanded defense of Henry's marriage, insisting that Eunice had always been "civil" to the family. William, the oldest brother, put it another way. "If Henry were in the habit of running after women," he told a reporter, "why should he choose an old, faded, married woman? There are plenty of young girls that he could have had if he had been so inclined." Harriet kept up a steady barrage of private attacks, reserving special venom for "the free love roost of harpies generally."[39]

"We can recall no one event since the murder of Lincoln that has so moved the people as this question whether Henry Ward Beecher is the basest of men," declared the *Herald*.[40] During the "scandal summer," through the fall of 1874, the *New York Times* alone ran 105 stories and thirty-seven editorials about the uproar in Brooklyn—and that was one of the more circumspect papers. Pamphlets, broadsides, cartoons, and doggerel—ranging from serious to satirical to pornographic—poured off the presses, as well as cheap books with titles like *The Beecher-Tilton War* and *The Romance of Plymouth Church*.

"It is the topic of the breakfast table, on the cars and on the Exchange," marveled the *Boston Post*. "Mothers complain that the girls and boys get up before breakfast, watch the newspaper men, seize the paper and devour the scandal before the family is stirring. The newspaper offices in Brooklyn are having a second edition of war times. The bulletin boards are mammoth and crowds surge round the office for the latest editions."[41] Papers west of the Alleghenies generally stood with Tilton, with the eastern papers tending to side with Beecher. Some, like the *Eagle* and the *Herald*, which had spent years disparaging Beecher, became his strongest defenders, apparently deciding that the minister was the lesser of the devils. Others, like the *Sun* and the *New York Times*, which had long backed the minister, turned against him as more evidence came out.

Tilton's bid to revive his reputation by casting himself as innocent victim was an utter failure. The press, even when unconvinced of Beecher's innocence, was vicious and unrelenting toward his accuser, condemning his morals and speculating on his sanity. Power brokers in the Republican Party, fearing a fatal conflagration, called in Senator Ben Butler, that old Radical schemer, to try to negotiate a settlement. But Tilton had long ago burned his partisan bridges. "There is great pressure brought to bear to keep matters hushed up," noted Butler's daughter when Frank Moulton met with Beecher at the senator's house. "Poor Tilton will be sacrificed and Beecher sustained."[42]

"Beecher's own people say it is Tilton that is on trial. I like the idea of a man insulting my wife and then I being tried for the heinous offense of complaining about it," observed Mark Twain in a letter to his close friend Reverend Joseph Twichell, who was also the pastor to several of Henry's siblings in Hartford. Twain's early faith in Beecher's innocence was fading fast. "But I have no sympathy with Tilton. He began by being a thundering fool and a milksop, and ends by being a hopeless lunatic and a lunatic of that poor kind that hasn't even spirit enough to be interesting. Mr. Tilton never *has* been entitled to any sympathy since the day he heard the news and did not go straight and kill Beecher and then humbly seek forgiveness for displaying so much vivacity."[43]

Yet even those who believed that Theodore was a fiend had one hesitation: What did Beecher mean in all those letters, especially that "Letter of Contrition"? Perhaps they were fakes, but if not, what then?

Many readers shared the ambivalence expressed by Lydia Maria Child, who knew the main characters better than most.

"I sometimes veer to one side, and sometimes to the other, according to the conflicting testimony. I have, for several years, considered Tilton an unprincipled, unscrupulous man; and, for the sake of public morals, I am painfully anxious to have Beecher's reputation cleared beyond a shadow of a doubt," Child wrote to a friend. "And yet he seems to me to give a very unsatisfactory explanation of that letter which he wrote to Tilton, saying: 'I humble myself before you as before my God. I wish I was dead.' And was it not *very* strange that Mrs. Tilton, with all her professed reverence for her pastor, should sign a paper accusing him of such a grievous misdemeanor as would blight him utterly if believed?"[44]

Everyone clamored for Frank Moulton to release the original documents, but he refused, saying he'd sworn to keep them "in trust." Instead, in what was becoming a habit, Tilton arranged for a reporter to publish 201 of the Tiltons' love letters in a special supplement of the *Chicago Tribune*, carefully excerpted to show how the libertine preacher had destroyed their once-great romance!

NOT FOR ONE MOMENT did Eunice Beecher doubt her husband. Indeed she rejoiced that he had finally come to share her long hatred of Tilton and Bowen. While herds of reporters stalked the streets of Brooklyn, she stayed at the house on Columbia Street, ever the vigilant "Griffin," as Elizabeth Tilton once called her. There Eunice remained, as she told her daughter, Hattie, "hunting, searching for papers, etc., and keeping watch and ward that no one gets access to father or *interviews* anyone."

"Aunt Hattie Stowe is here and makes my work much harder," Eunice wrote to her daughter; "she has the greatest longing to talk with just the ones she must not. 'Oh let me go, I'll soon settle it,' she explains, when she hears me badgered by reporters as I stand in the door preventing their entrance. She'd make another *Byron muddle* if she could. I wish she'd go home, but she is father's sister."

What baffled Eunice was the same thing that stumped so many of Henry's followers—how could he have trusted Frank Moulton (not even a Christian!) enough to give him all his private letters for safekeeping? "*Safekeeping,* as if he, the infernal villain, would be a safer repository than I, father's wife," Eunice wrote. "It is the *letters—the letters,* only the letters. That is all they ask for."[45]

Meanwhile Henry retreated to Peekskill, huddling with Tommy

Shearman as they composed his statement to the committee. He seemed distracted, depressed, and, for the first time, as old as his sixty-one years.

On August 13, 1874, Beecher finally appeared before the committee. Now his tactics had changed entirely. All defense of Elizabeth was tossed aside, he was saving only himself. His retelling of the story was detailed—reinterpreting every point Tilton touched—but simple. Beecher was the victim of a treacherous former friend, his conniving henchman, his weak-willed wife, and Beecher's own trustfulness. "I suffered much, I inquired little," as he put it.[46] His former "respect" for Elizabeth was abandoned. Now, he said, she thrust upon him her "excessive affection for me," and concocted the affair in response to Theodore's "own alien loves." Frank Moulton was no longer the "Mutual Friend," but a "blackmailer" who had used the Tiltons' problems to extort money from the gullible minister.

As for the emotional language in his "Letter of Contrition" and other documents, Henry explained, "I am one upon whom trouble works inwardly, making me outwardly silent, but [for] the reverberations in the chambers of my soul, and, when at length I do speak it is a pent up flood, and pours without measure or moderation."[47] He'd felt terrible when he learned of Elizabeth's infatuation, and of how hurt Theodore felt when he and Eunice advised them to separate. Repentant and worried that Tilton's irrational anger would bring odium upon all their families and this great church, he tried to contain the cesspool of gossip.

> I can now see that he is and has been from the beginning of this difficulty a selfish and reckless schemer pursuing a plan of mingled greed and hatred, and weaving about me a network of suspicions, misunderstandings, plots and lies, with which my own innocent words and acts—nay, even my thoughts of kindness towards him— have been made to contribute. These successive views of him must be kept in view to explain my course through the last four years.

"I chose the wrong path and accepted the disastrous guidance in the beginning," he concluded. "But I cannot admit that I erred in desiring to keep these matters out of sight."[48] The committee's gentle cross-examination of him only drew out these themes in more vivid detail.

As soon he finished, Beecher and his family left for his annual August vacation at the Twin Mountain House in New Hampshire, followed, of course, by a pack of hungry reporters.

Deeply hurt by Beecher's betrayal, Moulton finally renounced his loyalty to the minister and broke his silence. "Why, I've kept the doors of Plymouth Church open for the last four years," he raged to a reporter.[49] Soon Moulton's "Full Statement," including every last scrap of writing in his possession, was blanketing the nation.

OVER THE PAST YEAR of ominous silence, even the minister's closest friends had grown increasingly nervous. With the publication of Beecher's statement they breathed a sigh of relief, even if it made Henry look foolish. "It furnishes an hypothesis of innocence to those who must have one of innocence, at the expense of Beecher's supposed good sense, knowledge of human nature, penetration, foresight, or moral courage," as one of Beecher's friends observed.[50]

But those who were not diehard partisans found Beecher's testimony decidedly disappointing. "This delay was, in fact, the crowning blunder of a series of blunders," charged the renowed editor E. L. Godkin in the *Nation:*

> His audience last week was by no means as indulgent as it would have been a month earlier, and the explanation which he has finally produced is not the kind of explanation which people are disposed to excuse a man for not producing hastily. It is neither a cold careful narrative of facts, nor a technical or closely-knit argument. It is an impassioned, pathetic, somewhat effusive, and highly-wrought history of four miserable years, full of confessions of weakness and folly, of appeals *ad misericordiam,* and of descriptions of states of feeling—of the kind, in short, which is most effective when it is fresh, and over the composition of which the world does not permit a man to linger.[51]

Before the committee even rendered its decision, Theodore Tilton swore a complaint in Brooklyn City Court against Beecher charging him with having willfully alienated and destroyed his wife's affection and demanding one hundred thousand dollars.

That the investigating committee labored for more than a week before announcing its findings only added to the growing skepticism. "The amount of Beecher's innocence must be uncommonly great if one may judge by the time and trouble it takes to prove it," as Beecher's good friend and Republican colleague John Bigelow wryly observed.[52] Still, no one had any doubt what the verdict would be.

A tremendous crowd gathered in Plymouth Church on the evening of August 28, 1874, to hear the committee's final report. People spilled into the streets, straining to hear through the open doors and windows. Tasker Howard opened with a prayer, and Susan Howard's brother Robert Raymond began to read the report, making off-the-cuff jokes and pausing for waves of laughter and applause. Suddenly Frank Moulton strode in through the side door, brazenly taking a seat up front. The room crackled with tension. A few moments later Raymond lashed out at the interloper, declaring that Moulton had poisoned the minds of Beecher's defenders with his infamous lies.

Moulton leaped to his feet shouting, "You are a liar, Sir; you are a liar!"

The audience descended into confusion. Men rushed up, yelling "Put him out!"

"You dare not put me out! You dare not do it!" cried Moulton, as hisses rose around him.

"Brethren, brethren, let him keep his seat," implored the assistant pastor, Samuel Halliday.

"Yes, I will keep my seat, whether you want me to or not."

Now the whole room rose, some brandishing pistols, others repeating their cries, "Put him out!"

Police quieted the crowd, and Robert Raymond resumed the report to loud cheers, concluding with "a word or two on the subject of blackmailers."

Joe Howard yelled, "Give the blackmailer a shot!"

People say that one can't be blackmailed without being guilty of something, but, Raymond explained, "People can be blackmailed by appealing to their finer feelings, and a man can be induced to give from generosity what threats could not extort from him."

"What about the pistol!" came a cry from the crowd, in reference to the notorious "Pistol Incident" at the beginning of the cover-up.

"Yes, how about it?" called out Moulton.

No one said Moulton was going to shoot the pastor, Raymond replied. "The significance of the pistol is just this—that it reveals the character of the man who goes to call on a minister with a pistol." Another round of huzzahs filled the room.

After praise for the pastor, punctuated by insults for his accusers, the final resolution was read, declaring that there was "nothing whatever in the evidence that should impair the perfect confidence of Plymouth Church or the world in the Christian character or integrity of Henry Ward Beecher."[53]

In the vote to affirm the resolution, only Moulton stood to say "Nay," as a storm of jeers and hisses broke over the church.

When he tried to object, he was shouted down. The congregation began to sing the Doxology: "Praise God from whom all blessings flow." As Moulton began to make his way out, men surged around him, shoving, pulling, shaking their canes, and shouting, "Give it to him!" "Lay him out!" Blue-coated policemen hustled him into a waiting carriage, which took off for Remsen Street with the mob trailing behind for several blocks, screaming its righteous anger.

THE CIVIL TRIAL, *Theodore Tilton v. Henry Ward Beecher, Action for Criminal Conversation*, was set to begin on January 11, 1875. In the lull, lawsuits proliferated. Henry Bowen alone filed at least three accusations of libel against various newspapers, including one against the *Brooklyn Argus* for reporting that his late wife, Lucy Bowen, had been seduced by Beecher. Theodore Tilton filed two libel suits against newspapers, and was himself arrested for libeling Beecher. (The charges were later dropped.) The most sensational was Edna Dean Proctor's brief libel suit against Moulton, despite the fact that her name never appeared in any of the documents. (Moulton amiably agreed to settle.) By now so much of the scandal was known that there were few surprises to be had. More than with most trials, the verdict would depend largely on which side spun the evidence into the most believable story.

Meanwhile a journalistic gold rush hit Brooklyn, as hundreds of reporters from across the country descended. Many a young reporter cut his professional teeth on the Beecher-Tilton trial. Like modern-day paparazzi, they staked out the haunts of anyone who had anything to do with the scandal, climbing trees to peek in windows, hiding behind bushes to eavesdrop, collaring people on their way to church. They dug up the old stories from Indiana about Betty Bates, who had mercifully passed away just as the scandal was breaking. They reported, without evidence, that on her deathbed in 1863 Lucy Bowen had confessed to an affair with her pastor, leading Beecher to flee to Europe. The *Eagle* turned its wrath on Henry Bowen, detailing every dubious business deal he'd made since the 1840s.

When the trial began, the plaza in front of the Brooklyn City Courthouse was packed with spectators, with thousands turned away every day. Tickets were issued but were so hard to get that a lottery was instituted. They were scalped for five, even ten dollars each. Friends and strangers had the bad taste to ask Beecher and the other participants for tickets, and he was generous enough to provide them. A steady parade of dignitaries stopped to see the show, and several score of reporters crammed the press tables.

At one point the crowding was so great, and the testimony so seamy, that Judge Joseph Neilson tried to ban female visitors but was defeated by the determined ladies of the church. When Neilson forbade people to stand in the back and aisles, people got around it by bringing their own camp stools. The judge did succeed in banning the daily bouquets of flowers that were turning the attorneys' tables into fragrant jungles.

The lawyers for both sides were stellar. The star of Beecher's seven-member team was a ringer: William Evarts, the attorney who saved Andrew Johnson from Tilton's crusade to impeach the president, and former U.S. attorney general. Evarts was backed by Benjamin Tracy and Thomas Shearman, who were notorious in New York for both their unscrupulous legal careers and their stalwart support of Beecher. Led by William Fullerton, Tilton's team of five was less well known but equally sharp, and notable for including Roger Pryor, a former Confederate officer. Times truly had changed.

Eunice Beecher was perhaps the most crucial piece in the defense's strategy. She came nearly every day, even when Henry did not, clad in a plain black silk dress adorned with simple jewelry—all gifts from her husband—her white hair pulled into a severe bun at the nape of her neck. Her face was stern, impassive, and dignified, relieved occasionally by a dry, scornful smile. Had she wavered even a little, all might well have been lost.

Her daughter, Hattie Scoville, was horrified at the public humiliation her mother had to bear, but Eunice strode through the vulgar crowds with flinty Yankee fortitude. Nearly every day Moses Beach or another family friend took her by carriage to the courthouse, where she descended into a teeming crowd of loafers, lawyers, frantic tourists, concerned parishioners, ticket scalpers, organ grinders, sandwich vendors, and reporters, kept in order by a cordon of police. "I have not given it a thought and walk through the streaming, reeking, masses of tobacco, bad breath and foul air as calmly as if I was in the parlor at home," she assured Hattie.

Hour after hour Eunice sat stoically behind the defense team's table, listening to one witness after another speak of her abysmal marriage and philandering husband. In the evening, sitting around the parlor talking over the day with family and friends, only "then do I begin to realize where I have been. I wonder why I have not shrunk from it, but the next day all is forgotten but the one great subject. Yet after all it is not so formidable as one might suppose."[54]

Elizabeth Tilton, wearing black velvet and a short veil as if in mourning, also attended most sessions, in which she was shamelessly gawked at for hours. She no longer attended Plymouth Church, however. Beecher's strategists urged the church to treat her like a virtuous victim, but the ladies of Plymouth Church were too horrified by the previous summer's revelations to feel any warmth toward Elizabeth. " 'I pity her and forgive her—but don't let us lose all moral distinctions, and call black white because we are sorry for her,' " as Susan Howard characterized their response.[55]

By contrast, Henry wore the good cheer of a man going to a party. He smiled and cracked jokes, occasionally with the opposing attorneys, and stood around chatting at the end of the sessions, shaking hands as if church had just let out. Even after the judge banned bouquets from the courtroom, he carried a nosegay he would occasionally hold to his nose as if trying to block the fetid smell of the testimony. Beecher's sunny mood, his total repression of all anxiety or pain in public (except during dramatic moments of testimony), astonished even his most besotted fans. As the *Herald* wrote with genuine bafflement, Beecher "presents for the investigation of scientific men, a psychological problem which they must despair of solving."[56]

Beecher's friends and family formed a united front, with a few exceptions. Isabella, still convinced of Henry's guilt, hid herself in Europe. Harriet Beecher Stowe fled to Florida, unable to bear the attacks on her baby brother, but beseeched the family to send her all the newspapers. Edward Beecher, who had retired to Brooklyn when the scandal broke, defended all the ecclesiastical and theological parapets. Perhaps most surprising, given his own feelings about Beecher, Moses Beach drove Henry and Eunice to court most days, often remaining to watch.

Frank Moulton was the first key witness, and essentially recapped the story told in the church investigation. The papers made much of his tufted red hair and mustache and his worldly yet gentlemanly demeanor. As the former evidence depository, he had the advantage of vivid precision. Still, it was hard for viewers to reconcile his calm, concise testimony with the vile business he described, as in one widely quoted exchange:

Beecher's attorney: "Didn't you say that Mr. Beecher was a damned perjurer and libertine?

Moulton: "I don't know whether I said he was a damned perjurer and libertine. I may have said he was a perjurer and libertine—as he is."[57]

But if Moulton really believed Elizabeth was an adulteress and a deceiver, how could he justify defending her to the world? The explanation Frank offered to the press was as insightful as it was harsh.

> We respected her even after her fall because we had studied Beecher out and knew him to have a fine mind, a powerful animal nature, and between the two he has got his power. He never could have preached the sermons he has, addressing the weakness of the flesh, but for the animality which drew him into libertinism and was followed by self-reproach. The fact is he has been sifted out of the little principle that he possessed, by the flattery of mankind. Everybody took care of him, paid his bills, wanted his society, and encouraged his selfishness. He has had bursts of emotion and tenderness, but they are not reliable, and he was too mean to lose his fame.[58]

Tilton was next, spending eleven painful days on the stand, going over much the same ground. He began with a certain stern righteousness, enlivened by occasional sarcasm. But as he was systematically savaged in the cross-examination and by later witnesses, he began looking peaked and bedraggled. The defense portrayed him as a free lover, an abusive husband, a blackmailer, and a dangerous social radical who was viciously jealous of his former mentor; not hard to do when Theodore admitted under oath, "My object was to strike him right to the heart, Sir." The defense attorneys' message was simple and effective: The very story Tilton had to tell made him seem so monstrous that he could not be trusted. "This testimony of Tilton's is an outrage on human decency," Harriet sputtered from Florida, after reading the day's transcript in the *Tribune*. "They might believe something less but anything like *that* is a nightmare creation of insanity and unnatural lust and indecency."[59]

The prosecution's best witness was Frank Moulton's lovely wife, Emma, whose demure grace and candor gave a powerful boost to Tilton's case. "Both Mrs. Tilton and Mr. Beecher admitted in language not to be mistaken that a continued sexual intimacy had existed between them, and asked advice as to the course to be taken because of it," she stated unequivocally. She described in vivid detail Beecher's tearful confession and threats of suicide. Adding to her persuasive power were Beecher's letters to Frank, praising "the great-hearted kindness and trust which your noble wife has shown, and which have lifted me out of despondencies often, though sometimes her clear truthfulness has laid me out pretty flat."[60]

Yet as with her husband, to many minds, Emma's gentility put the lie to her testimony. "Gentlemen, you have seen for yourselves, that Mrs. Moulton is naturally a lady," Ben Tracy told the jury. "She could no more have made that coarse and vulgar speech to her pastor, at that time than she could have cut off her hand." That is to say, she was such a respectable lady that she must be a liar! The defense team's great weapon was the inane paradox of the sexual double standard: Anyone base enough to speak of such sordid sexual matters was, de facto, too immoral to trust. In this, Beecher had a decided advantage, for he had built a career by peddling paradoxes. As court let out when Emma Moulton finished, Henry was overheard calmly telling Emma's uncle, a member of Plymouth Church, that her testimony was "In foundation the truth; but in effect a lie."[61]

"The evidence begins to pinch Monsignor Beecher very hard. He is probably ruined by his utterly fatuous confidences and confessions," the indefatigable diarist George Templeton Strong observed after Emma's testimony. "But," Strong added in disgust, "Plymouth Church is a nest of 'psychological phenomena,' *vulgo vocato* lunatics, and its chief Brahmin is as moonstruck as his devotees. Verily they are a peculiar people. They all call each other by their first names and perpetually kiss one another. The Reverend Beecher seduces Mrs. Tilton and then kisses her husband, and he seems to acquiesce in the osculation."[62] The press agreed. Even the rabidly pro-Beecher *Eagle* was taking a more temperate tone, as if covering its bets.

Finally, on February 24, Benjamin Tracy began the opening statement for the defense. It lasted more than a week and set the bar high. "It is a miracle if he was guilty," Tracy told the jury. Perforce Tilton's lawyers "must produce sufficient evidence to convince the jury that a miracle has happened in our midst."[63] A stiff task for theologians, let alone attorneys.

Apparently all the defense lawyers had to prove was that the Moultons and Tiltons were unscrupulous scoundrels. Beecher's side called more than a dozen witnesses to testify to their combined instability, immorality, and untrustworthiness. As the defense slogged through its long list of witnesses, the suspense grew unbearable. Readers were driven to tears, psychosomatic illness, public arguments, and private anguish; others were driven quite literally to distraction, as in the cases of two women and one man who were reported to be sent "to the asylum for the insane, having gone crazy over the Beecher trial."[64] When would Beecher defend himself?

Finally, on April Fool's Day, Beecher strode to the stand, carrying a nosegay of wild violets. The clerk offered him a Bible to swear on, but Beecher waved it away, saying, "I have conscientious scruples against swearing on the Bible." A murmur went through the courtroom, and the lawyers squabbled over whether he could swear in the "New England custom"—"by the uplifted hand." Finally he was allowed to swear "in the presence of the ever living God."[65]

Henry's direct examination by his defense lawyers was masterful— warm but dignified, dramatic but modest, abounding in self-deprecating good humor. When he defiantly denied everything, from "undue familiarity" to "carnal intercourse," the room broke into applause. For Beecher's admirers the relief was palpable. "I feel that today's testimony practically ends the trial," wrote John Bigelow after watching the proceedings. "Beecher has wakened up at last, and begins to shake the dogs off right and left who are baiting him."[66]

The cross-examination by Tilton's attorneys was another matter. Now Beecher's answers were clipped, vague, and forgetful. One observer counted almost nine hundred instances where Henry could not recall an answer or evaded a direct question. Tilton's attorney, William Fullerton, easily tripped him up, forcing him to recant many of the claims made in the church investigation. Most damaging, Beecher admitted that he'd never believed that Moulton and Tilton were blackmailing him until his lawyers bullied him into it, telling him he was simply naïve, and even now he "waxed and waned" on it. As the *New York Times* noted, "Every theory which he put forward to account for his conduct *before* the trial was expressly contradicted by himself or his counsel *upon* the trial."[67]

But transcending contradiction was Beecher's forte. Why, pressed Fullerton, would Beecher have continued consulting with Moulton in the summer of 1874, even as his lawyers were convincing him that Moulton was a knave and a blackmailer? Beecher hemmed, then hawed. Fullerton kept pushing. Just as Beecher seemed cornered, he dramatically stood up in the witness box and turned to the judge, asking in a dignified voice, "Your Honor, am I under the rebuke of the Court?"[68] Judge Neilson said no with bemusement, and the examination resumed, but Fullerton had lost both his momentum and the sympathy of the audience, making it seem as if he was hounding the poor witness.

The major weakness in the defense was Beecher's slippery explanation of Tilton's original charge. Tilton and Moulton insisted that it was clear from that first December day in 1870 that they were accusing him of adultery, and that Beecher's "Letter of Contrition" and later documents were admissions of and apologies for seducing Tilton's wife. Beecher insisted that he had understood the charge to be causing dissent in their marriage. But then, later, the charge became "improper advances," which he somewhat assented to as well. Working against Beecher's argument was the extravagantly sorrowful language of the "Letter of Contrition," as well as his later threats of suicide as given in his woeful "Ragged Edge" and "Day of Judgment" letters, and the damning testimony of Frank and Emma Moulton.

As Fullerton quizzed him, Beecher put him off with jokes or forgetfulness. Even on little details, Beecher seemed at a loss. When Fullerton asked Beecher about Elizabeth's reference to "nest-hiding," Beecher couldn't remember ever hearing the phrase before. After the lawyer refreshed Beecher's memory by reading aloud from *Norwood*, Henry quipped, "It is beautiful, I think, whoever wrote it, I am willing to own it." Fullerton asked why the minister would send clandestine letters to Elizabeth, informing her that his wife had just left for Florida. "Well, just at that time it was the most interesting fact, almost, that I had, and I naturally would impart it to a friend," Beecher responded lamely.[69]

Mark Twain, who took an intense interest in the case, came to Brooklyn with his friend Joseph Twichell to see Beecher testify on the day he was interrogated about his guilt-laden "Letter of Contrition." Beecher's oldest son escorted them to court, and Twain's fame won them great seats by the reporters' tables. "The excitement was such as to be painful," wrote Twichell in his diary. Beecher "appeared well— innocent—unafraid—at ease, and yet his bearings and style of answering did not somehow come up to my idea." The next day the *Sun* reported that many in the audience mistook Twain for Frank Moulton, both sporting thick shocks of red hair and handlebar mustaches. "This was a good joke on Mark Twain," laughed Twichell in his diary, "who had been greatly disappointed in Moulton's appearance and *disliked* his looks exceedingly."[70]

After three weeks Fullerton brought Beecher's testimony to an abrupt end by reading from a sermon delivered only four days before that *"Day Memorable,"* when Elizabeth and Henry allegedly consummated their love. "Conscience," Beecher told his church that Sunday,

> frequently leads men to make the most injudicious confessions, and to make them to the most injudicious persons. I do not think we are bound to confess crimes in such a way that they will overtake us and fill us with dismay and confusion and destruction; and not only us but those who are socially connected with us.

Fullerton then turned to the judge, saying: "There is generally not much done sir, after the sermon but the benediction."

"There has been no collection taken up!" Beecher called merrily from the witness box.[71]

AFTER BEECHER, Henry Bowen took the stand but produced little of interest. Now the public clamored for the last two big guns—Victoria Woodhull and Elizabeth Tilton. Both sets of attorneys, however, saw them only as loose cannons with an even chance of backfiring. Finally Woodhull, with a thick veil covering her face, made a brief dramatic appearance in court. As she entered, Eunice stood, her face filled with scorn, and left the room. But everyone else was disappointed when Woodhull was asked only to hand over a packet of letters. An enterprising reporter cornered her later that day, asking what she thought of Theodore's repudiation of her. "I believe Mr. Tilton would make quite a man if he should live to grow up," she replied coolly.[72]

Shy, tiny Elizabeth Tilton made a more spectacular appearance. Theodore Tilton had waived any spousal objection to Elizabeth's testifying, and Elizabeth wanted to take the stand. But after so many confessions and retractions, neither team of attorneys trusted her enough to risk putting her under oath. On May 1 the defense concluded its testimony. The next day in court, Elizabeth suddenly rose from her seat and, in the words of the court reporter, "cried out in her low voice, a little tremulous from embarrassment."

"Your honor, I have a communication which I hope your Honor will read aloud." She handed the judge a piece of paper. He glanced at it but did not read it, and bade her sit. As usual, a few days later her statement appeared in newspapers across the nation:

I have been so sensible of the power of my enemies that my soul cries out before you, and the gentlemen of the jury, that they beware how, by a divided verdict, they consign to my children a false and irrevocable stain upon their mother! For five years I have been the victim of circumstances, most cruel and unfortunate; struggling from time to time only for a place to live honorably and truthfully. Released for some months from the *will* by whose power unconsciously I incriminated myself again and again, I declare solemnly before you, without fear of man and by faith in God, that I am innocent of the crimes charged against me. I would like to tell my *whole* sad story *truthfully*—to acknowledge the frequent falsehoods wrung from me by compulsion—though at the same time unwilling to reveal the secrets of my married life. . . . I assume the entire responsibility for this request unknown to friend or counsel of either side.[73]

Those in the know derided it as one more maneuver by Beecher's lawyers.

The closing arguments went on for twenty-five days, with both sides claiming a monopoly on all things decent and good. In the end the choice came down to a question of human nature. Was it possible for a man to seem one way his whole life and yet behave in an entirely different way in private? Was it possible for a husband to hear his wife confess that she'd betrayed him and yet forgive her and continue to live with her, however unhappily? The irony is that for more than twenty years, Beecher had been saying yes, it is possible; that everyone has mixed motives and conflicting desires, that people often fool themselves without realizing it, that even the high and mighty can have secret sins, thus people should be judged by what they do rather than who they are. Now, of course, his lawyers were arguing the opposite. "I prefer," stated William Evarts, "to find in character the refutation of false evidence."[74]

Letters of sympathy and support poured into Beecher's mailbox, confirming that this challenge to human nature was not theoretical but a matter of great anguish for thousands of Americans. "I have said and say now if you fall, *no more humanity for me,*" wrote one J. O. Smith in a typical passage. "If you should prove guilty of the charges made against you I should never place confidence in any mortal being and *I would not.*"[75]

Others took precisely the opposite view. Beecher "evidently fails to see, what most other thinking people see, that the calamity which has overtaken him and bid fair to cloud his declining years, is the not un-natural result of his philosophy of life," wrote Godkin in the *Nation*.

"He had long held a theory, and has, we believe, honestly tried to live up to it, that it is a man's duty, as he expresses it 'to look at the world as God looks at it,' " Godkin explained. "As his God is wholly love, and is no respecter of persons, attempts to imitate Him result simply in the deliberate and systematic suppression of all discrimination touching character and conduct, and the cultivation of a purely emotional the-ology, made up, not of opinions, but of sighs and tears and aspirations and unlimited good-nature. As God loves and forgives the sinner, why should not we?"[76]

Henry's friend John Bigelow was more blunt. "Though all the par-ties, witnesses and medley in the case were educated in his church and were or had been members of it, I have yet to hear of one who seemed to have any more hesitation in lying than in picking his teeth."[77]

AFTER SIX MONTHS of testimony, eight days of debate, and fifty-two ballots, worn down by exhaustion and ill health, the jury finally gave up. Neither the Tiltons nor Henry were in the courtroom when the jury filed in, but Eunice was at her usual spot, waiting impassively, joined by her oldest son, Edward Beecher; Susan and Tasker Howard; and a retinue of attorneys.

"Have you a verdict?" asked the clerk.

"No, we have not, I regret to say. We cannot," replied the foreman. "We ask to be discharged." Equally exhausted, the judge agreed.[78]

Eunice's face did not even flicker with emotion. The attorneys looked stunned. The reporters leaped to chase down the jurymen as they gathered up their things to leave. Quickly the final tally was re-vealed: 9 to 3 in favor of Beecher. By the next day the papers had full analyses of the deliberations, broken down by each juror's occupation, religion, family life, social status, and personality. In the end, though, they simply could not agree on who was telling the truth. "The mass of reading material helped rather than hindered the breach," reported the *World*, with "every man finding only support for his own opinion among its many pages."[79]

"It can hardly be said that this is a victory for anybody," concluded E. L. Godkin, "but this is something very like a defeat for Mr. Beecher." Even those who believed him innocent had seen too much of Beecher's weaknesses and poor judgment. The London *Daily Telegraph* echoed the opinion of many, maintaining that the minister had "acted with an imbecility that would have disgraced an uneducated girl."[80]

The next day, the Beecher house on Columbia Heights was jammed with well-wishers. Henry looked as if he'd returned to youth, and Eunice was treated like a hero, especially by the women. "She accepted this as common sense and a matter of course, calling for no more exaltation than anything right and true," the *Eagle* noted. The next evening Plymouth Church was overflowing with well-wishers, gathered to hear Beecher deliver a tender plea for forgiveness. "Don't believe that all men are bad because you have seen some of their weaknesses, or even their sins. Of all the saints I know, stone throwing saints are the most unworthy," he concluded.[81] In response the church trustees voted to increase Beecher's salary for the year to one hundred thousand dollars so he could pay his legal bills.

The scene repeated itself in Peekskill a few days later, when the town, accompanied by horse-drawn fire engines and the local militia, hiked up to Beecher's farm to offer their congratulations. Standing on his porch with Eunice, Chloe Beach, and their various children nearby, Henry responded with an impromptu speech. "I have no new course to take. I am too old to change my position. I shall go on trusting men. I have pursued that doctrine all my life and only once in forty years have I made a mistake. I shall love men; I shall not stop to think of their faults before I love them."[82]

"Mr. Beecher answered it beautifully," wrote Chloe's middle daughter, Ella, in her diary after the day's tributes. "It made Violet feel very badly for she leaned over to Mamma and said, 'Mamma do you know what a good man Grampa is'—all the time she was crying very hard."[83]

The scandal continued to ripple through Brooklyn. Plymouth Church quickly purged the handful of parishioners who had dared to express the conviction that Beecher was guilty, including Henry Bowen and Emma Moulton. Bowen was not done yet, though. He devoted an entire issue of the *Independent* to the case, concluding, "The Rev. Henry Ward Beecher, without even the shadow of doubt in my mind, is guilty of the awful crimes of adultery, perjury, and hypocrisy."[84] He insisted on a hearing before the church, where he brought out all his old accusations, but they were old news now and did nothing to change his fate.

Emma Moulton was removed from the rolls of Plymouth Church without even a hearing. In outrage she called for a Congregational council to investigate this "clerical kangaroo court," early in 1876.

In hopes of heading off any more ecclesiastical challenges, Plymouth Church itself decided to call its own "National Advisory Council" of Congregational clergymen to review the evidence (none were invited from New York or Brooklyn, however). Nearly all of them arrived with serious doubts about Beecher's innocence, but Plymouth Church aggressively worked to win them over, paying their travel expenses and hosting them in the finest private homes on the Heights.

No new evidence or charges were submitted; all the ministers wanted was an explanation that would quiet their doubts. For eight full days the ministers peppered Brother Beecher with questions, and Beecher's off-the-cuff answers were far often more revealing than his controlled trial testimony. Asked at one point why the public did not accept his explanations, Henry burst out: "I don't know—as long as God knows, and my mother, how it is, I have come to about the state of mind that I don't care for you or anybody else. Well, you knew that is not so: I do care and I don't and I do again and then I don't just as I happen to feel. I am tired of you; I am tired of the world; I am tired of men that make newspapers, and men that read them."[85]

When the Hartford minister Joseph Twichell asked Beecher how he could have endured such stress, Beecher replied "that when he was in the pulpit he felt strong and dauntless, but that when he was out of the pulpit he felt—as he expressed it—'like a humbug.' "[86] Twichell was taken aback by this oddly damning answer but finally decided that Beecher meant that "his ordinary sense of himself was the reverse of proud and self-sufficient." Still, Twichell noted, "We thought how this observation could have been twisted by an enemy."

But by the end Twichell and his colleagues were as charmed by Beecher as the earlier Congregational council had been. "He *seemed* like a good man, and I know that many delegates as they listened to him and watched him were conscious of ceasing to doubt his integrity," Twichell wrote in his diary. " 'What a pity that all the world cannot come in personal contact with him!' was a frequent remark."[87]

Who could resist such a lovable man, however flawed? "When you shall find a heart to rebuke the twining morning-glory, you may rebuke me for misplaced confidence," Beecher declared in his closing remarks to the council, "for loving where I should not love. It is not my choice; it is my necessity. And I have loved on the right and on the left, here and there, and it is my joy that today I am not ashamed of it. I am glad of it."[88] At the end of February the council gave Beecher a full vote of confidence.

∾ ∾

IN THE AFTERMATH of the scandal Theodore Tilton scraped together a living by lecturing on current events. When the audiences dwindled he moved to Paris, where he lived a quiet, bookish life. With her reputation beyond repair, Victoria Woodhull also left America in 1876 to remake herself once again, this time as the respectable wife of a wealthy English banker. Bowen continued his pursuit of wealth for another two decades, bestowing his largesse on Reverend Storrs's rival church on the Heights. Over time Isabella Beecher Hooker gingerly reconciled with most of her siblings—Henry excepted—and enjoyed an impressive career as a women's rights advocate and an avocation as a spiritualist medium. But as Elizabeth Cady Stanton had feared, the gathering momentum and stature of the women's movement was dealt a severe blow by its entanglement in the scandal. Another generation would pass before the suffragists gained enough public respect to win ratification of the Nineteenth Amendment to the Constitution in 1920.

Elizabeth Tilton lived with her mother and children in Brooklyn, quietly keeping out of the public glare until April 16, 1878. There in the morning papers was one final retraction (or confession) from Mrs. Tilton. It was addressed to her lawyer:

> A few weeks since, after long months of mental anguish, I told, as you know, a few friends whom I bitterly deceived, that the charge brought by my husband, of adultery between myself and the Rev. Henry Ward Beecher, was true, and that the lie I had lived so well the last four years had become intolerable to me.
>
> That statement I now solemnly reaffirm, and leave the truth to God, to whom also I commit myself, my children, and all who must suffer.
>
> I know full well the explanations that will be sought for this acknowledgment: desire to return to my husband, insanity, malice—everything save the true one—my quickened conscience, and the sense of what is due the cause of truth and justice.

The opinion of the press was unanimous—at that stage nothing that that erratic woman could say would change anyone's mind. Beecher's only public comment was: "She is the strangest combination I ever knew. You see her one time and you would think her a saint on earth;

at another time she is a weak, irresponsible being and anything but a saint."[89]

Down with the Stowes in Florida, Eunice was horrified by Elizabeth's confession. She begged Chloe Beach for some word from her husband. "I am so lonely, so heartsick for a word from him, only *three letters* in nine weeks!" she wrote to Chloe. "Be good and tell me if Mr. Beecher ever speaks as if he wished I could come home," she added. "I only wait hoping for a word from my husband—if not from him, from some who will know if it is best *for him*—no matter about me—for me to come at once."[90] But Eunice was no longer needed, so no letter came.

On June 10 the Plymouth Church Examining Committee summoned Elizabeth Tilton. Once again her testimony was unequivocal, and once again she flatly contradicted her prior statements. "I now repeat and affirm that the acknowledgment of adultery, with the Rev. Henry Ward Beecher, Pastor of Plymouth Church was the truth and nothing but the truth; and that having previously published a false statement denying the charges, I desired to make the truth as world wide as the lie had been."

"I had a lie ready for every question they asked me," she told one horrified friend. "If anyone wants any lying done send them to me."[91] The examining committee unanimously voted to excommunicate Elizabeth Tilton for slandering the pastor.

With his typical astringency Frank Moulton interpreted Elizabeth's final confession for the puzzled *New York Times*:

> She is a religious fanatic, and so long as she believed she was protecting a saint she could say things that were not true. She is not unlike Mr. Beecher in this respect. She believes in God and the angels, and when she speaks she feels that God is looking right at her. Mr. Beecher will swear by God and the angels, but knows that God and the angels won't touch him.[92]

Epilogue

"WHAT A PITY, THAT SO INSIGNIFICANT A MATTER AS THE CHASTITY OR UNCHASTITY OF AN ELIZABETH TILTON COULD CLIP THE LOCKS OF THIS SAMSON"

Henry Ward Beecher survived an ordeal that might well have killed a lesser man. Plymouth Church remained as strong as ever in the aftermath of the trial. Surprisingly few church members left during the scandal years, and new members continued to flood in, keeping pew rents as high as ever. But Beecher, as one old-timer noted, "never recovered his old buoyancy."[1] "I see that the last two years which he has been gentle and forbearing to his foes has given him at home a colder, more abrupt way of speaking—less tender and loving," Eunice complained to her daughter in 1876. "It is not strange, but I long for the old tones—the old cheery smiles."[2]

Financially Beecher was decimated. His publishing firm, J. B. Ford, went bankrupt, involving him in more legal tangles. The *Christian Union* was sold and downsized, although it retained Beecher as the nominal editor at a token salary. No respectable papers would pay for his essays, so the fastest and surest way to make money was lecturing. In early 1877 his new lecture agent, James B. Pond, accompanied him on a major lecture tour through the West, where even those who believed Beecher guilty were willing to pay for the opportunity to judge the great libertine for themselves.

It worked. Beecher lectured forty times in seven weeks, to nearly seventy thousand people, and preached every Sunday but one. In Cleveland disappointed viewers were offering ten dollars for standing-room spots. In Chicago, two hundred people lined up before dawn for tickets, and so many people turned out to hear Beecher preach that a wooden sidewalk gave way beneath the throng. "In the balmiest days of my life, I never had such audiences," Beecher told a friend.[3] Two state legislatures and innumerable schools and churches asked him to speak. Everywhere he went people came to scoff and stayed to shake his hand. Beecher was winning back his reputation, one night at a time.

"The old scandal is hardly thought of," Beecher wrote to the Howards; "one hears no allusion to it, and the papers do not touch it."[4] That wasn't entirely true. Plenty of the time Beecher had to push his way through screaming, spitting crowds at train stations, hotels, and lecture halls. In Iowa, where Beecher was forced by scheduling mishaps to book a private railcar, an angry crowd rushed the car when it stopped outside Decatur. James Pond saved Beecher from a thorough beating by grabbing a red-hot poker from the fireplace and slicing it across the face and arm of the first man to come barreling through the door. The mob turned and fled to the sound of sizzling flesh. Beecher continued on and lectured that evening as if nothing had happened. In general, however, the hint of danger and sin only boosted ticket sales.

Beecher took in $41,530 from that tour alone, most of which he poured into the grand mansion he was constructing in Peekskill. "I have a pride in building the house," he told a friend, "and earning every penny that pays for it, without a cent of debt, and that after the world, the flesh, and the devil conspired to put me down."[5] The house—Boscobel, he christened it—was the fulfillment of all his aesthetic fantasies, with ornate woodwork, many windows framing the gorgeous view across the Hudson River, wallpapers so exquisite that he could not bear to hang pictures over them, cozy nooks, wide verandas, and a "cold room," with cupboards constructed from paper treated with oil and paraffin, a rack for ice, and a drain to catch the melt. He surrounded it with elaborate landscaping, including three hundred varieties of trees and shrubs and a full croquet court.

While he was away, Chloe Beach supervised the construction from her own house next door. Henry urged Violet Beach, "my dear wee little housekeeper," to send him updates on the work. "Tell me about every bird, and mouse, and cricket, and stone, and tree and shovel full of dirt outside of the house and every scrap and particle inside of the house!" he wrote to Violet. "For I am like a lover, and could sit and hear every curve and feature, and smile of my house described hour by hour! But of course that figure throws no light on the subject to *wee little House-*

keeper, and you must refer it to the *Chief Housekeeper* who knows both the figure doubtless and the application."[6]

Eunice, unfortunately, hated Henry's fancy design—the spectacular views didn't make up for the dark, small closets and inefficient layout. When Henry ignored her complaints, Eunice urged Chloe to use her influence. "*Rub* in what I have said, and perhaps even yet he may wake up to his mistakes and in some degree modify them. He is crazy to have you like his *planning* and let him design *your* house," Eunice told Chloe. "I told him if I owned $20,000 *myself* I'd hand over every cent of it to Mr. Beecher if he'd let me *knock out all the inside and remodel it throughout.*"[7]

But building Boscobel only exacerbated their financial obligations. The following year Beecher decided to turn over their townhouse on Brooklyn Heights to his oldest son, Harry, and his wife, Hattie. He and Eunice would live with them, paying for board, when they were not up in Peekskill. Eunice was literally hysterical when she heard of Henry's plan. The great pride and power of her life was as the head of the Reverend Beecher's house. Without that she felt she had lost everything. "Oh Chloe dearest!" Eunice wrote in the spring of 1878. "You can't tell what a horror my *probable position* in the new house will be! If Hattie is to take my place I'd better die. Everything is so dark! Living is so hard!"[8]

That summer James Pond scheduled another lecture tour for Beecher, this time in the Far West. For the first time Henry brought Eunice along, hoping to ease her wretchedness. But after years of longing to travel with her husband, Eunice was disconsolate. Every day she begged Henry to reconsider his decision, but he refused. As they made their way across the plains, Henry and Eunice kept up separate, and unusually frank, streams of letters to Chloe. "Tho' on the whole the trip has been serviceable," wrote Henry about Eunice, "yet the insatiable longing, which only death will cure, of attracting sympathy by representing herself as a martyr, sometimes to sickness, sometimes to hard times, sometimes to misusage—is still strong and operative."

Worse yet, Eunice insisted on telling everyone they met, even strangers, about her martyrdom. In Grinnell, Iowa, they made the mistake of staying with acquaintances rather than in a hotel. "Before half a day had passed the women of the family had heard her story and were saying 'I wonder that the woman is alive'! I do not think she spoke of the housekeeping, though I do not know but she did, but my money matters, my new house, the mortgages, her unwillingness to have me build, the extravagance of everybody, her holding a tight reign and preventing ruin, etc., etc." Henry told Chloe, "This morbid craving for sympathy over fictitious woes seems like the appetite of the inebriate."

By the time they reached Minnesota, Henry had flatly announced to Eunice, in his words, "that *my married life had been a failure in making my wife happy*." This had one good effect, he told Chloe: "It has stirred her, and she is collecting evidence that she has been happy!"[9]

Like most people who wallow in misery, Eunice found it deeply unflattering to be called miserable. She, too, turned to Chloe for support. "Please tell me in your next if during all our acquaintance you have been accustomed to view me—or think of me, as an *unhappy woman*—making all my friends and family sad—because with such blessings all about me I could not be made happy?" wrote Eunice. *"He says he has it from all quarters*—I tell him I *have been very* unhappy since I was *displaced*, but *never* before. Do you know of anyone saying such things?"[10]

Chloe wisely claimed that she never received Eunice's letter. ("It is singular that *my* letters, when away, and only mine or those written to me, ever fail," Eunice noted with suspicion.)

Eunice was certain that the heartache would kill her before they reached Brooklyn. "Henry doses me with tonics," Eunice complained to Chloe. "Ah, one small sentence—'You shall be the head of my house when we return' would do more to build me up than all the tonics in the world! My heart is killed. Why can't he see it?"[11] By the time they reached San Francisco, Henry and Eunice were at an impasse. "I have but one course left me—silence and patience!" he told Chloe. "There is an utter end of communion."[12]

Of course Eunice did not die. Nor did she make good on her threat never again to set foot in Brooklyn, although chances are good that her daughter-in-law wished that she had.

As Beecher rehabilitated his reputation, he gingerly waded back into public affairs. He kept a relatively low profile during the disastrous presidential election of 1876. In what was a kind of forerunner to the disputed election of 2000, the Democratic nominee, Samuel J. Tilden, led in the popular vote, but the final count from four states was disputed. The Republicans accused the Democrats of stuffing the ballot boxes, and the Democrats charged the Republicans with deliberately miscounting the votes. By the end of December there was still no official victor, so Congress appointed a special electoral commission to break the deadlock. The commission cut a deal—Hayes would become president, and in exchange, all federal troops would be withdrawn from the former Confederacy, in effect abandoning any hope of racial equality and Republican influence in the South. It was a dingy end to a noble dream.

This wasn't just a failure of the South. All across the country public support for popular democracy was waning in the face of staggering stories of government corruption and increasing labor strife. After forty years of working to expand the rights of the common man (and woman), many progressives now regretted giving the ignorant, unwashed masses so much power. Increasingly reformers focused on protecting taxpayers' pocketbooks rather than ending inequality and oppression.

Henry's faith in Herbert Spencer's laissez-faire social theories served him both well and ill in this new era. Unlike many reformers Beecher never backed away from universal suffrage and his belief that "it is safe to give liberty to an intelligent common people."[13] Beecher loudly and unequivocally condemned the artificial barriers of bigotry, whether turned against Chinese railroad workers, Irish Catholic schoolchildren, or Jewish businessmen, as well as deplorable American policies toward Mexicans and native Indians.

But during the depression of the late 1870s, when large labor unions aggressively challenged the growing power of corporate monopolies, leading to massive strikes and their violent repression, Beecher was much less certain. For years Beecher had been a friend to the workingman, publicly supporting legally limiting the workday to eight hours and the right of workers to organize. But the spread of socialist and anarchist ideas alarmed him. Henry was too much of an idealist to cotton to the new rhetoric of class warfare, and too much of a realist to believe in the possibility of a classless society. This was not his idea of "free labor."

In July 1877 disgruntled workers in towns and cities across the country rose up in a spontaneous national strike against the railroad conglomerates that were slashing wages to starvation levels. The clash turned spectacularly bloody as strikers attacked railroad property, and state and federal militia troops were sent out to reopen the rails. More than a hundred people died. "The Great Railroad Strike of 1877" brought forth from Beecher the same mishmash of abhorrence of disorder and sympathy for the underdog as had John Brown's attack on Harpers Ferry. Justice was one thing, anarchy another thing entirely. He condemned the strikers and especially the "foreign element" and their socialist theories for interfering with the natural laws of capitalism and evolution. "I do not say that a dollar a day is enough to support a working man," he thundered. "Not enough to support a man and five children if a man would insist on smoking and drinking beer," he added. "But the man who cannot live on bread and water is not fit to live."[14]

Beecher stirred up a hornet's nest in the press with his surprisingly insensitive words. As usual he immediately backtracked when the newspapers castigated him as callous and hypocritical (it was easy, as they noted, for a man now earning more than forty thousand dollars a year to talk of living on bread and water). He pointed out, quite rightly, that the press had focused on the most controversial passages in his sermon, leaving out his biting if less picturesque attacks on rapacious corporations and greedy businessmen. So it had been throughout his career—while his diagnoses of social problems strove to be systematic and scientific, his solutions were usually individualistic and sentimental. He gave ammunition to all sides.

It was Charles Darwin's theory of biological evolution that softened Beecher's views. Charles Darwin came much later to America than did Herbert Spencer, and it wasn't until the early 1880s that Beecher began seriously to study Darwin's ideas. His grasp of Darwinism was crude but enthusiastic, and reconciling Darwin with evangelical religion became one of the main goals and great accomplishments of Beecher's last years. He began lecturing on "Evolution and Religion," publishing his ideas in a book of the same title. "A cordial Christian evolutionist," he called himself. His belief that the natural world was God's way of expressing himself might sound like what is now called "intelligent design." Unlike the promoters of intelligent design, however, Henry treated the Bible as spiritual inspiration, not as a scientific rival. He admitted that God's apparent desire to grow men from monkeys was mysterious, but that had no effect on his faith in God's love. "I would just as lief have descended from a monkey as from anything else—if I had descended far enough," he quipped.[15]

Unlike the ideas of Herbert Spencer, Darwin's theory of evolution or "natural selection"—that over time species adapt in response to their environments—was explicitly amoral. "Progress" for one species or group might well mean the voracious obliteration of other, less-well-adapted species, rather than harmonious prosperity for all. It was an explicit challenge to the idea that unfettered opportunity and economic growth would "lift all boats" equally. The recognition that pure liberty does not always provide justice did much to reconcile Beecher to the labor movement, although he never lost faith in the inevitability of progress. "This vast combination of laboring men is at once a thing to be rejoiced over, and to be dreaded," he wrote in 1883. "But it will work out in the end for good."[16]

OF COURSE THE SCANDAL lingered in people's minds. Many still watched Beecher's public pronouncements for clues to his guilt or innocence. The scandal actually made Beecher bolder, theologically. He no longer felt the need to cover himself with the mantle of orthodoxy. In 1882 he officially renounced all forms of Calvinism and withdrew from the New York Congregational Association. Some saw his explicit repudiation of hell and original sin as further confirmation of his personal immorality, but few people were shocked by his views at this late stage.

Once again, and for the last time, it was politics that shook Beecher's equanimity. Over the years Beecher had managed to meld party, principle, and personal profit—he campaigned for Republican presidential candidates, and in return, received his share of favors, usually in the form of political appointments for his friends and relatives. But now Republican reformers were attacking the old political spoils system, which had served Beecher so well. When he was faced with the choice of backing an antipatronage "Independent" Republican candidate ("Mugwumps," as they were nicknamed) or a "Regular" Republican (the "Stalwarts"), Beecher's public reputation as a reformer clashed with his personal desire for party influence.

Beecher made his way through this minefield unscathed until the 1884 election. He had planned on backing the current president, Chester A. Arthur, for a second term, but was thwarted when the Republican nomination went to Congressman James G. Blaine of Maine, one of the most powerful, least scrupulous men in the party. Not only was Blaine deeply implicated in railroad graft, but it was rumored that Blaine and Beecher had suffered a bitter falling-out in the 1880 election.

Like many fed-up Republicans, Beecher refused to back Blaine, despite the congressman's entreaties. But he was reluctant to join the independent Mugwumps in supporting the Democratic candidate Grover Cleveland, the former governor of New York. By early fall, however, he'd decided to buck the controversy and stump for Cleveland. The Republican Party had lost the love of liberty, betraying the "rights of labor as against combined capital, and the defense of the individual against the despotism of corporate bodies," he declared.[17]

Just as he announced his startling switch, rumors suddenly arose that Cleveland was an immoral carouser who had fathered a child out of wedlock in upstate New York. Plymouth Church and most of Henry's friends were already aggravated by his political drift. Now they were beside themselves.

Beecher hurriedly sought out Governor Cleveland, through various back channels, and was assured that he was no scoundrel. As Cleveland's friends told it, he had been merely a green young man who faced his mistake honorably, fully supporting the illegitimate child for the last fourteen years. Annoyed by the pressure from the church, and stirred by what he saw as the injustice of condemning a good man for one night of sin, Beecher defiantly threw all his weight behind Grover Cleveland. "I will imitate the noble example set me by Plymouth Church in the day of my own calamity," he declared.[18]

It was a nasty campaign, famous for the catchy political ditty:

> Ma! Ma! Where's my pa?
> Gone to the White House,
> Ha! Ha! Ha!

Even to casual observers it seemed that Henry was using the Cleveland campaign to vindicate his own past. His argument was much like the one he'd used in 1866 in advocating leniency toward the South, indeed, toward all sinners. Shunning Governor Cleveland served no moral purpose, he explained, for "Cleveland has already suffered loss, mortification and damage for the commission of a grievous sin." As the campaign grew uglier, his rhetoric grew more reckless, At one point he literally shouted, "If every man in New York State tonight who has broken the seventh commandment voted for Cleveland, he would be elected by a 200,000 majority!"[19]

The campaign came to a head at the end of October, at a rally in Brooklyn, in which Beecher brought the crowd to its feet when he refuted the rumors that Cleveland was a heartless libertine by comparing them to his own adultery scandal:

> When in the gloomy night of my own suffering I sounded every depth of sorrow, I vowed that if God would bring the day star of hope I would never suffer brother, friend, or neighbor to go unfriended should a like serpent seek to crush him. That oath I will regard now. Because I know the bitterness of venomous lies, I will stand against infamous lies that seek to sting to death an upright man and magistrate. Men counsel me to prudence lest I stir again

my own griefs. No! I will not be prudent. If I refuse to interpose a shield of well-placed confidence between Grover Cleveland and the swarm of liars that nuzzle in the mud, or sling arrows from ambush, may my tongue cleave to the roof of my mouth and my right hand forget its cunning![20]

Many in Plymouth Church were livid—some because Henry was repudiating their beloved Republican Party and others because the comparison implied they had stood by him in guilt, not innocence. "The greatest mistake of my life has happened twice, as I have been informed," Henry said dryly, making reference to the 1866 flap over his letters to the Cleveland political convention. "Twice I have stumbled on Cleveland!" Even Henry's colleagues on the campaign trail were put off by his manic enthusiasm. Beecher "is the only man I have spoken with in public of whom I felt ashamed," wrote the old abolitionist Thomas Wentworth Higginson. "There was a coarse jauntiness in his way of treating the attacks on Cleveland that disgusted me."[21]

When Grover Cleveland swept to victory in November it seemed to Henry like a personal vindication. To his critics it only confirmed what they already knew.

IN THE SUMMER OF 1886 Pond arranged one last tour of England for Henry, this time accompanied by Eunice. This trip was a fine success. From July 4 to October 24, 1886, when they boarded the ship to return to America, Beecher preached seventeen times and gave nine addresses and fifty-eight lectures. He wasn't the sensation in England that he had been back in 1863, but he turned out respectable middle-class Christians in droves.

Best of all, the Beechers finally discovered the theater. Whether it was the independence of age or the distance of an ocean, Beecher finally stopped bowing to evangelical prejudices and gorged on the glories of London's West End. Their first show was *Faust*, a story long close to his heart, with the famed Miss Ellen Terry in the lead. When Miss Terry called on Eunice, eventually becoming warm friends with James Pond and the Beechers, they were all thrilled. Eunice, Henry noted with pleasure, "is happy as a child and makes everywhere the best impression." For the rest of his life, he said, "I clasp hands with my fellow-actors as often as I can."[22]

His enthusiastic reception in England stirred Henry's old ambition.

When they returned to New York, Beecher put off lecturing and threw himself into writing, turning out articles for magazines and newspapers, and chipping away at the long-deferred second volume of *The Life of Christ*. In February 1887 Beecher signed a contract with Mark Twain's Hartford publishing company, which advanced him five thousand dollars for an autobiography and "to resurrect Henry Ward Beecher's *Life of Christ*."[23] Twain thought the deal foolish, since Beecher had a terrible track record and *The Life of Christ* seemed genuinely cursed, but his business partner refused to heed Twain's prophetic warnings. Once the contract was signed, Twain forgot his doubts and rosily predicted blockbuster sales.

The winter of 1887 was a sedentary one, and Henry often seemed tired, although he dared not complain for fear Eunice would nag him to stay home for his health. He could still be seen strolling the streets of Brooklyn, but age had given him heavy jowls and a stout outline. His hair had long ago drifted from dark brown to silver gray to pure white, but he still wore it long and loose like a young man.

Sadly, Chloe Beach seemed to be dying. In the last year or two she'd become an invalid, secluding herself up at the farm in Peekskill to protect her easily agitated heart. She and Moses rarely saw each other nowadays, and Violet was in boarding school at Miss Porter's Academy in Connecticut, leaving Chloe alone with her middle daughter, Ella. Every day that he was in Peekskill, Henry came to the house he had designed for Chloe, usually bearing a gift, and quietly talked with her as she lay in bed or sat on the piazza in her wheeled invalid's chair.

Still, Henry was in excellent spirits. That spring he was choosing books from his library of more than nine thousand volumes to donate to the Old Soldiers' Home in Leavenworth, Kansas—filling two wheelbarrows full of books. On Wednesday, March 2, he returned from Peekskill burdened by a dull headache but gave it little thought. The next morning he and Eunice went into Manhattan to purchase new furniture for the church's social parlors. It was a wonderful day, Eunice said. Henry was warmer than usual, reminiscing about old times and old friends.

That night he woke up feeling nauseated, as if suffering from the flu. He threw up and then fell back into a deep sleep. He slept most of Friday, waking long enough to nibble some toast and complain that his head ached and his feet were cold. He kept his eyes closed as he ate his toast and, in a drowsy voice, told Eunice that he just dreamed that he was a duke and she was a duchess, and he'd had to figure the interest on a hundred thousand British pounds a year and doing all that math had given him his headache. By Saturday it was clear that he'd suffered some sort of stroke, or apoplexy, as they called it. He was paralyzed on his left side and could barely be roused. But as he slept his mouth moved and his right arm gestured wildly, as if he were giving an endless speech.

The family was in shock—there had been no sign of illness to prepare them for this. They sought first one and then another physician for a second opinion. As Eunice stood by the bed talking with the doctor, she finally asked if there was any hope. The doctor offered none. Suddenly Eunice whispered intently, "I believe that he understands what we are saying."

"Ask him if he does," said the doctor.

"Henry, do you understand what we are talking about?"

Eyes still shut, his head moved slightly forward and back with great difficulty. "Henry, Henry," pleaded Eunice, bending over and speaking loudly into his ear, "do you know what we said about you?"

His breath rasped heavily as he struggled to open his mouth. His right hand clasped and unclasped convulsively. A slow whisper escaped his lips. "You—were—saying—that—I—could—not—recover," he stammered.

"Then a strange thing happened," according to one chronicler. "The words seemed as if spoken in a dream, but the shadow of a smile fluttered across the mobile mouth, only to vanish into an expression almost of indifference. The intonation of Mr. Beecher's voice expressed absolute indifference, as if he spoke of the chance of life or death for an entire stranger. There was neither hope nor hopelessness, neither gladness nor sorrow, neither confidence nor despair."[24] He never spoke again.

Henry lingered in a coma from Sunday through early Tuesday, his face becoming ashen and gaunt. Eunice kept watch at his bedside while the family waited, shattered and silent, in the darkened house. It was not what Henry would have wanted, but he was no longer there to jovially chide them for their lack of faith. Reporters kept a twenty-four-hour watch from the street, waiting for the doctor's regular updates. "It is the talk on the cars, and by every body," said J. B. Pond, who rushed to Brooklyn as soon as he got the telegram from Henry's son. "Henry Ward Beecher's name was on everybody's lips."[25] A stream of close friends and family came to pay their respects. Isabella tried to visit, but Eunice refused to let her enter the house. Belle lingered on the sidewalk with the reporters for some time, giving interviews and gazing up at the silent brownstone.

On Tuesday, March 8, Henry's breathing became labored. The weeping family was called to his bedside to say good-bye, joined by Pond and the family doctor. As they watched, Henry's breathing slowed and then slowly ceased. At 9:30 in the morning the doctor turned and said, "His pulse is stopped. He is breathing his last. He is gone!" The doctor leaned over, kissed the great man on the cheek, and then went to tell the newspapers that Henry Ward Beecher was dead. It was quick and relatively painless, just as Henry had wished. "I would rather die with the harness on and be dragged out by the heels," he'd insisted, than go as his father had, slowly losing his mind to senility and his body to old age.[26]

As soon as the announcement came, the bells of Plymouth Church and Brooklyn City Hall began tolling. Within an hour, all the flags in the city, including those on the riverfront and ferryboats, were struck at half mast, and workers began draping City Hall in black bunting. Telegrams and letters of condolence poured in. On Thursday a private funeral service was held at the house, as cheerful as the family could muster. "I would not have a semblance of mourning about my grave," Henry had declared many times.[27] Instead of the traditional black crepe on the front door, there was a huge wreath of roses and lilies of the valley tied with satin ribbon.

An honor guard from the Thirteenth Regiment of Brooklyn bore his body to the church, where it lay in state under a blanket of flowers. On Friday a public funeral was held at Plymouth Church, with simultaneous services at three other Brooklyn churches. The City Council adjourned, and businesses across Brooklyn closed for the day. Representatives from New York City's Jewish, Catholic, Chinese, and African American communities marched in the procession to Green-Wood Cemetery—while street peddlers hawked pictures of the deceased minister at ten cents apiece.

Most of Henry's siblings were at the funeral. Not Catharine, the oldest, who had died of a stroke in 1878. Nor James, the troubled youngest, who died in the summer of 1886 by shooting himself in the mouth with a rifle, just as his brother George had four decades before. Eunice banned Isabella from the family service, so Belle joined the fifty thousand public mourners who waited in line for hours to view his casket. Thomas Beecher attended, but as the family assembled to follow the hearse to the graveyard, Tom refused to get in the carriage, saying with a typical lack of sentimentality, "I'm not going to traipse all over Brooklyn behind a corpse."[28]

Henry's simple granite gravestone remains in Greenwood Cemetery.

Back in the hot-tempered 1850s Henry had sworn that his tombstone would read: "He scorned and spit upon the Fugitive Slave law."[29] But peace won out for posterity. His epitaph reads: "He thinketh no evil." It was chosen from 1 Corinthians 13, Beecher's favorite chapter of the Bible, but by serendipity or clairvoyance, these were the very words Herman Melville had used to introduce his marvelous *Confidence Man* thirty years before.

Around the country newspapers paid their tributes, and pastors devoted their Sunday sermons to Beecher's death. Mark Twain choked up when reading the sermon on Beecher delivered by Joseph Twichell, minister to most of Nook Farm. Twain's feelings reflected those of most Americans. "What a pity," he wrote to Twichell, "that so insignificant a matter as the chastity or unchastity of an Elizabeth Tilton could clip the locks of this Samson and make him as other men, in the estimation of a nation of Lilliputians creeping and climbing about his shoe-soles."[30]

There was still money to be made from Beecher, even in death. Within six months an array of tributes and cheap fan biographies appeared, many from Henry's old associates looking to make a quick dollar, including his own widow and children. Eunice was furious when the "official" biography she was working on with her sons was preempted by a competing volume written by Joe Howard.

Frankly Eunice needed the money. Henry earned well over a million dollars in his lifetime, but his spendthrift ways left little inheritance. He had twenty-five thousand dollars in life insurance but no savings to speak of. The house in Brooklyn Heights had been sold several years before, and Eunice was forced to sell the grand house in Peekskill and auction off its beautiful contents, including nearly ten thousand books and a thousand pieces of art, ranging from etchings to silks to ceramics.

Eunice was crushed by Henry's death, although she bore up bravely. "I am happy to say that she is softened, refined, purified by her great trial, and will I hope be finally saved by it," Harriet Stowe wrote of Eunice a few months after Henry's death. "The church gathers around her as *all* they have left of their past and she enjoys all the homage and praise rendered to his memories."[31]

Eunice's public stature only rose as the honored widow. But privately she had few satisfactions, shuttling between her children's homes and slighted by the old friends who did not come around the way they used to when Henry was alive. Even Chloe Beach, ostensibly her dearest friend in the world, abandoned her after Henry's death, writing rarely and visiting even less. "It seems as if when Mr. Beecher left me everything was shattered and all dear ties broken," Eunice complained to Chloe in the fall of 1888. "How very little I have seen of you for the last two years."[32] In the ten years after Henry's death, Eunice saw Chloe less than a dozen times—sad proof of the nature and object of Chloe's love.

Over Christmas of 1896, Eunice fell and broke her hip, triggering a decline from which she never really recovered. She died in the home of her daughter, ten years almost to the minute, after her beloved husband left her. Elizabeth Tilton followed her to Greenwood Cemetery one month later, where she was buried not far from Henry and Eunice. Her estranged husband, Theodore, died in 1907 and was buried in Paris.

The famous Beecher clan was dwindling. Harriet Beecher Stowe succumbed to her father's fate, growing increasingly senile until her death in 1896. Edward and William Beecher had gone on before her and Tom was too frail to travel, but Eunice and Isabella attended Harriet's funeral in Hartford, where they studiously avoided each other. None of Lyman's grandchildren achieved the notoriety or influence of their parents, but after all that had passed, that might well have been intentional. (The quiet sister, Mary Beecher Perkins, produced the one exception in her granddaughter, the pioneering female economist and author Charlotte Perkins Gilman.)

Henry Ward Beecher's own legacy has been uneven. Plymouth Church still stands, looking much the same as when he trod its stage. His greatest talent was oratory, that most transient of arts, so he will never be judged by his best work. But his charming combination of wit, empathy, and uncommon common sense still shines through some of his best essays and extracts. In recent years his pithy epigrams have become Internet staples, quoted by thousands of people who have no idea who he once was.

Was Beecher a great man? Certainly many of his peers thought so, even those who disagreed with nearly everything he said. There is a famous anecdote, told by Henry W. Bellows, the famed Unitarian minister, of an 1855 gathering of prominent Northern intellectuals, including Henry James, Sr., George Ripley, Horace Bushnell, and Frederick Law Olmsted. James had just heard Beecher's antislavery lecture in Boston, "and was bitterly disappointed" by him.

> He pronounced him shallow and vulgar. Ripley thought his coarseness the chief source of his success and defended it as a well chosen

weapon. Bushnell, who hated his style, attributed his influence to his heart which he said was as big as that of an ox.

Beecher's gift, Bellows concluded, was "a very high sentiment and a very low manner—the union of moral philosopher and comedian; his passion and his desire to do good united."[33] At his best, Beecher represented what remains the most lovable and popular strain of American culture: incurable optimism; can-do enthusiasm; and open-minded, open-hearted pragmatism.

What Beecher brought to American culture in an era of bewildering change and fratricidal war was unconditional love so deep and so wide that the entire country could feel his warmth, like it or not. For fifty years he tried to persuade the nation, from the top of his lungs, that love was what God wanted for all of us. In that sense, his reputation has been eclipsed by his own success. Mainstream Christianity is so deeply infused with the rhetoric of Christ's love that most Americans can imagine nothing else, and have no appreciation or memory of the revolution wrought by Beecher and his peers.

In the same way, Beecher's efforts to spread the habits of rational thought, ecumenical generosity, and progressive government seem neither as shocking nor as inspiring now that they have become the cornerstone virtues of American civic culture (even when they are honored more in the breach than in fact). But they were not forgotten by those whom he touched directly. Forty years after Beecher's death and sixty-seven years after Plymouth Church purchased her freedom in one of his sensational mock-slave auctions, the former slave girl "Pinky" returned to Brooklyn Heights at the age of seventy. Her name was now Rose Ward Hunt, taken from Henry's middle name and the name of Rose Terry, the author who donated the "freedom ring" he placed on the girl's finger as the congregation wept and cheered. Rose Hunt returned on Plymouth's eightieth anniversary to give back that same freedom ring, in honor of the man and the institution that had not only obtained her liberty but paid for her schooling so she could become an educator of other African Americans. Who would not be moved by such testimony?

But what of the allegations of adultery? Do they not deny Beecher's claims to greatness?

To answer, first one must decide whether he was indeed guilty of infidelity. Of course, outsiders can never know for certain what happened in the secrecy of the study and the sitting room. But it is indisputable that Beecher had a lifelong pattern of deep intimacies with women other than his wife, intimacies that damaged his friends' marriages, triggered jealousy and discord in his own marriage, and, by his own testimony, filled his heart with agony, guilt, and suicidal desires.

Does it matter whether these infatuations were accompanied by sexual intercourse? Opinions differ even today, but at minimum it is hard not to cry hypocrisy when a clergyman dances so close to temptation. Yet, if Henry preached anything, it was the contradictory complexity of human nature and the presence of secret sin in even the sweetest of saints. "I should be sorry to think that everybody was a hypocrite who was different at one time from what he was at another," as Henry put it. "Men are inconsistent, often, who are not insincere. They are untrue to their own highest ideal, and they act in ways that are contrary to their purposes."[34]

Taken from this angle, the connection between the scandal and Beecher's historical impact is easier to assess. One cannot view Beecher's career without thinking of the many charismatic men who were driven to heady heights by their unquenchable longing for approbation and who risked their legacies by letting this longing shade into lust—men of indisputable stature such as Martin Luther King, Jr., John F. Kennedy, and Bill Clinton. Like them, what made Beecher larger than life was his ability to transform his flaws into a powerful force of empathy and ambition. His struggles with his secret desires brought a new emotional candor to public life. His painful awareness of his own weaknesses and his ongoing battle to overcome them were the wellspring of his great and lasting contribution to American life: the all-forgiving Gospel of Love. As Beecher would have said, without sin there can be no saving grace.

Acknowledgments

It is a terrible cliché, yet the most indisputable thing I ever uttered: This book could not have been written without the librarians. This project was born in the bowels of the Robert Frost Library at Amherst College, and was finished nearly two decades later in the tower of Sterling Memorial Library at Yale University. In between I relied upon the generous stewardship of dozens of archives and libraries, and watched in grateful awe as thousands of manuscripts, books, periodicals, and newspapers relating to the Beechers were digitized by ambitious librarians over the last ten years. "There never can be too many libraries," Henry Ward Beecher said in the *Independent* of March 9, 1854, and I heartily agree.

This is very much a book in the American Studies tradition, from root to bud. I was born to an enthusiastic English major and an earnest graduate student in history, and my book-loving parents tilled the soil for this project with their unfailing encouragement. It was well-manured, as it were, by the remarkable American Studies, journalism, and public-speaking programs at Clackamas High School in Clackamas, Oregon. The seed was planted in the Amherst College Archives, where I discovered Beecher under the watchful eyes of Daria D'Arienzo, John Lancaster, Debby Pelletier, and Thomas Stratford, and blossomed into an American Studies senior thesis, with sage counsel from Professors William Pritchard and Robert A. Gross, in particular. An internship under Jack Larkin at Olde Sturbridge Village (not far from where Beecher worked during his own college summers) settled my career path, without me even realizing it. Like Beecher, my fellow alumnus, I thrived amid Amherst's intellectual and financial generosity.

Beecher helped get me into graduate school in American Studies, where he became the subject of my dissertation. Yale University nurtured the project with unstinting financial support, a genial department, and a first-class library, including, providentially, most of Henry Ward

Beecher's papers. I give special thanks to the Yale librarians, especially those of the Beinecke, the Divinity School, and Sterling's Manuscripts and Archives. Many people shaped my thinking and smoothed my path, but the project was directly aided by my adviser, Alan Trachtenberg; my dissertation reading group, Christina Klein and Kathleen M. Newman; my compatriots, Kirk Swinehardt, Abraham Zablocki, and Thomas and Debra Thurston; and Professors Harry Stout, David Montgomery, Ann Fabian, Michael Denning, Michael Holquist, Richard Brodhead, and John Mack Faragher. Richard Wightman Fox, who was beginning his own book on Beecher as I began my dissertation, offered me both substantive advice and an inspiring example of academic generosity.

It was Johnny Faragher who led me to my literary agent, Susan Rabiner. There might well have been a book without Susan, but it would have been a poor book, indeed. Susan took me, fresh out of graduate school, entirely on faith and taught me how to write something people might want to read. In the seven long years it took to complete this manuscript, her confidence was unwavering, her advocacy heroic.

Many institutions aided me over the next seven years. At Harper-Collins, Terry Karten's early investment allowed me to begin writing in earnest. The New York University Biography Seminar aided my transition into the genre. Through the auspices of the Harriet Beecher Stowe Center, especially Dawn Adiletta, I enjoyed two delightful afternoons, one with Henry Ward Beecher's great-granddaughter Alice Scoville Barry, and the other with Henry Chandler Bowen's great-grandson Alexander H. Rotival and his wife, Edith S. C. Rotival. At Historic New England/SPNEA, Susan Porter provided a last-minute dramatic twist, discovering astonishing new material about Beecher's alleged adultery. Chandler B. Saint, founder of the Beecher House Society, topped even that, unearthing a rare, privately held photo of Elizabeth Tilton just before this book went to press. I give great thanks to the owner.

The two most spectacular moments in the book's long gestation came not in public archives but in private collections. While I was working on my dissertation, Mary Schlosser gave me a copy of a startling letter from Moses Sperry Beach, describing his despair over his wife's infatuation with Beecher. This led me, through several years of detective work, to Brewster Beach, Moses S. Beach's great-grandson, and the equally startling photos of his Aunt Violet. With unusual generosity and open-mindedness, Brewster and Sandra Beach let me spend hours in their home, searching for family secrets. I have tried to repay

Mrs. Schlosser and Dr. Beach by treating their sensitive material with discretion and respect.

My editor at Doubleday, Gerald Howard, entered late in this overlong tale, but he swept in like a hero at the dramatic climax, armed with shrewd insight and a finely tuned ear. His kindness and confidence made the final year of darkening deadlines and late-night prose-making almost pleasurable.

As I neared publication, friends and patrons proliferated in many of Beecher's most beloved places, including Lois Rosebrooks and Frank Decker of Plymouth Church; Tony Seideman and his fellow preservationists in Peekskill, New York; Michael Stubbs, historian of the "Beecher's Rifle Colony" in Kansas; and Cara and Bryan Bowers and the Brooklyn Historical Society in Brooklyn Heights. Scores upon scores of friends from Amherst College—who have cheered on my fascination with Beecher since its beginnings as a seminar paper in Pond Dormitory twenty years ago—turned out in full force for the books debut.

Robert Gross, David Montgomery, and Richard Wightman Fox not only advised me throughout the last fifteen years (twenty in Bob's case) but they each read my eight-hundred-page manuscript and powerfully improved it, as did the eminent Beecher biographer, Joan Hedrick. Jose Celso Castro Alvez competently and calmly led me through the final thicket of endnotes. Stan Tamarkin, Beth Dixon, and Sandra Luckow soothed my vanity as they took my author photos. Ann Lundberg, Bruce Fellman, Rachel Pace, and other kind souls counseled me on the mysteries of marketing. Generous history mavens, most notably Lawrence Stetler, sent corrections and emendations which polished the text. My old Clackamas pal, Paul Thompson, created the book's website: www.henrywardbeecher.com. (I'm sure Henry would be delighted to have his own website even 120 years after his death.) My dear friend, the historian John Gable, passed away before the book was completed, but his pleasure in those first few chapters—the last thing he ever read—meant the world to me.

I owe a deep debt to the many friends and family members, too numerous to name, who brought me encouragement, commiseration, and distraction. Jeff Coombs's technical expertise saved me many times from nervous breakdown. My in-laws, the Tulgans and Ostheimers, particularly Henry and Norma Tulgan, supported this book from its inception with warm pride and cheerful patience. I give the greatest thanks for my family—Julie, Paul, Shan, Tanya, and Frances Applegate—whose un-

conditional love and enthusiatic eccentricities surely shaped my interpretation of Beecher as much as they shaped me. I only wish that Franny
had cast her spell to make me finish faster a couple years earlier.

This book is dedicated to Bruce Tulgan, my partner in all things of
the heart, head, and soul. I met Bruce just before I met Beecher, and in
the intervening years we have become so deeply, uncannily intertwined
that I would not recognize myself without him. I certainly would not
have written this book without him. His faith, generosity, passion, perseverance, optimism, and wisdom, and the greatest of these, his fathom-
less love, suffuse every word in this book and every moment in my life. I
will spend the rest of my days trying to be worthy of his great gifts.

Now at the end, as my gratitude overflows and I long to be most
eloquent, all words fail me except these: I love you beyond measure,
Bruce, and I always will.

Notes

Abbreviations Used in the Notes

Auto HWB Henry Ward Beecher, *Autobiographical Reminiscences*, ed. T. J. Ellinwood
(New York: F. A. Stokes, Co., 1898)

BL Beinecke Rare Book and Manuscript Library, Yale University, New Haven, Conn.

BS William Beecher and Samuel Scoville, *A Biography of Rev. Henry Ward Beecher* (New York: Charles Webster, 1888)

CB Catharine Beecher

CU *Christian Union*

EB Eunice Beecher

HBS Harriet Beecher Stowe

HBSC Harriet Beecher Stowe Center, Hartford, Conn.

HCB Henry Chandler Bowen

HWB Henry Ward Beecher

IBH Isabella Beecher Hooker

IHS Indiana Historical Society

LB Lyman Beecher

LC Library of Congress, Washington, D.C.

BP-SML Beecher Family Papers, Sterling Memorial Library, Yale University, New Haven, Conn.

TT v. HWB *Theodore Tilton v. Henry Ward Beecher: Action for Crim. Com.* (New York: McDivitt, Campbell, 1875).

Introduction

"He Was the Favorite by All Odds: the Best Loved Man in Sumter that Day"

1. Rugoff, *The Beechers*, 370.
2. *Independent*, 13 Feb. 1926.
3. BS, 95.
4. Eunice Beecher to Henry Ward Beecher, 20 Dec. 1865, BP-SML.
5. London *Times*, cited in *New York Times*, 28 May 1865.
6. *Harper's Weekly*, 29 Apr. 1865.
7. *Liberator*, 1 Jan. 1847.
8. *Scribner's Monthly* 4 (Oct. 1872): 752–53; Badeau, *The Vagabond*, 283.
9. Emanuel Hertz to William C. Beecher, 10 Dec. 1926, BP-SML.
10. *Independent*, 11 May 1865.
11. Ibid.
12. Ibid., 4 May 1865.
13. *New York Times*, 18 Apr. 1865.
14. *Independent*, 4 May 1865.
15. Ibid., 11 May 1865.
16. Griswold, *Sixty Years*, 150.

17. BS, 454.
18. Liberator, 5 May 1865.
19. French and Carey, The Trip of the Steamer Oceanus, 54.
20. Theodore Parker and Leonard Bacon, cited by Rugoff, The Beechers, preface.
21. BS, 80.
22. Independent, 13 Jan. 1859; HWB, Royal Truths, 285.
23. Independent, 11 May 1850.
24. Doyle, Plymouth Church, 415.
25. Howard, in Patriotic Addresses, 137, 141.
26. Atlantic Monthly 13, no. 75 (1864): 107.
27. Bok, Beecher Memorial, 13.
28. Conant, Narratives of Remarkable Conversions, 383.
29. Atlantic Monthly 19, no. 111 (1867): 43.
30. Bok, Beecher Memorial, 64, 49.
31. French and Carey, The Trip of the Steamer Oceanus, 80.
32. Independent, 27 Apr. 1865.
33. Ibid., 11 May 1865.

Chapter 1

"Damned If You Do, and Damned If You Don't"

1. HWB, CU, 3 Jan. 1872.
2. LB, Autobiography of LB, 1:57.
3. Auto HWB, 87.
4. HWB, CU, 18 Nov. 1874.
5. Grant, The Miracle of Connecticut, 3.
6. HBS, Oldtown Folks, 9.
7. Dix, Transatlantic Tracings, 43.
8. LB, Autobiography of LB, 1:403.
9. Ibid., 1:259.
10. CB, Educational Reminiscences, 16.
11. LB, Autobiography of LB, 1:220.
12. BS, 41; Roxana Foote Beecher to Harriet Foote, 22 July 1813, BP-SML.
13. Howard, HWB: A Study, 23; CB, Moral Instructor, 137.
14. IBH to John Hooker, 9 Sept. 1843, HBSC.
15. CB, Educational Reminiscences, 14; IBH to John Hooker, 2 Dec. 1839, HBSC.
16. LB, Autobiography of LB, 1:87.
17. Roxana Foote Beecher to LB, 13 Aug. 1798, BP-SML; LB, Autobiography of LB, 1:209.
18. BS, 47.
19. LB, Autobiography of LB, 1:215–21.
20. BS, 49.
21. LB, Autobiography of LB, 1:244.
22. HBS, Men of Our Times, 510.
23. Vanderpoel, More Chronicles, 171.
24. LB, Autobiography of LB, 1:266.
25. HWB, CU, 7 Feb. 1872.
26. LB, Autobiography of LB, 1:268, 271–73.
27. HWB, Lecture Room Talks, 204–6.
28. BS, 50.
29. BS, 77; Lucy Jackson White notes, HBSC.
30. HWB, Lecture Room Talks, 157.
31. Auto HWB, 114.
32. BS, 66.
33. Ingersoll, The Works of R. G. Ingersoll, 12:419–24.
34. HWB, Star Papers, 406.
35. HWB, Evolution and Religion, 239.
36. Lucy Jackson White notes, 31 Dec. 1859, HBSC.
37. HWB, CU, 11 Dec. 1872.
38. Auto HWB, 79–80; Independent, 27 Apr. 1862.
39. Auto HWB, 98–99; HWB, Lecture Room Talks, 205.
40. HBS, Oldtown Folks, 26.
41. Charles Beecher to HWB, 12 Apr. 1857, BP-SML.
42. HWB, Lecture Room Talks, 231.
43. HBS, Men of Our Times, 511.
44. Charles Beecher, Redeemer and Redeemed, vi.
45. HBS, Oldtown Folks, 305, 318.

46. BS, 80.
47. HWB, *Lecture Room Talks*, 83.
48. LB, *Autobiography of LB*, 1:318.
49. *Auto HWB*, 72–75.
50. HWB, *Yale Lectures*, 2:244.
51. HWB, CU, 18 June 1873.
52. *Auto HWB*, 102.
53. BS, 95.
54. HWB, *Star Papers*, 398.
55. BS, 52; HWB, *Star Papers*, 400.
56. Charles Beecher to William C. Beecher, 17 Apr. 1887, BP-SML; HWB, *Lecture Room Talks*, 163; BS, 138.
57. T.S.K., *Universalist Quarterly and General Review*, Jan. 1854.
58. LB, *Autobiography of LB*, 2:340.
59. White, *History of Litchfield*, 34–35.
60. *Auto HWB*, 164.
61. BS, 78.
62. *Auto HWB*, 93–95.
63. *New York*, 5 May 1980.
64. HWB, *Lecture Room Talks*, 69.
65. LB, *Autobiography of LB*, 1:343, 356.
66. Ibid., 1:355–60.
67. HWB, lecture room extracts, 10 May 1878, BP-SML.
68. HBS, *Men of Our Times*, 514–15.
69. LB, *Autobiography of LB*, 1:20; BS, 74; Scoville lecture notes, BP-SML.
70. BS, 79.
71. HWB to George Beecher, 1 Dec. 1825, BP-SML.
72. *Auto HWB*, 84; BS, 67.

Chapter 2

"I Shall Have the Boy in the Ministry Yet"

1. *Eagle*, 12 March 1890.
2. Scoville lecture notes, BP-SML.
3. LB, *Autobiography of LB*, 1:42.
4. Ibid., 2:35.
5. Sherwin, *Prophet of Liberty*, 30.
6. BS, 83–84.
7. Ibid., 90–92; HWB, *Norwood*, 159
8. BS, 86.
9. *Auto HWB*, 42.
10. Piper, *Lives of the Leaders*, 720.
11. *Auto HWB*, 34; Harding, *Certain Magnificence*, 225.
12. *Auto HWB*, 135.
13. Mansfield, *Personal Memories*, 139.
14. LB, *Autobiography of LB*, 2:53,
15. Ibid., 1:126.
16. HBS, *Men of Our Times*, 516–17; BS, 92.
17. Shenstone, *Anecdotes*, 30–31.
18. HBS, *Men of Our Times*, 518–19.
19. Whicher, *This Was a Poet*, 5.
20. *Mount Pleasant Catalogue*, 1828, American Antiquarian Society.
21. BS, 93; HWB to HBS, Nov. 1829, BP-SML.
22. HWB to HBS, Nov. 1829, BP-SML; BS, 97.
23. *Auto HWB*, 153.
24. BS, 94–95.
25. *Auto HWB*, 152.
26. BS, 100.
27. HBS, *Men of Our Times*, 536; BS, 93, 115.
28. HWB to EB, 17 May 1849, BP-SML.
29. BS, 106.
30. Ibid., 95.
31. HWB, autobiographical notes, BP-SML.
32. Shenstone, *Anecdotes*, 159.
33. BS, 97.
34. Ibid., 100.
35. Ibid., 109–10.
36. HWB to HBS, 1 Mar. 1830, BP-SML.
37. Ibid.; *Auto HWB*, 147.
38. HWB, *Lecture Room Talks*, 60–61.
39. *Independent*, 15 May 1862.
40. BS, 101.
41. Shenstone, *Anecdotes*, 43.
42. HWB to HBS, 1 Mar. 1830, BP-SML.
43. BS, 105.
44. LB to Heman Humphrey, 30 Sept. 1830, Amherst College Archives.
45. BS, 90–92.

Chapter 3

"If You Wish True, Unalloyed, Genuine Delight, Fall in Love with Some Amiable Girl"

1. BS, 111.
2. HBS, *The Mayflower*, 169.
3. BS, 112.
4. *Century Illustrated Monthly Magazine*, Nov. 1889; Emerson, "Historic Notes on Life and Letters in New England," *American Transcendentalists*, 5.
5. Allmendinger, *Paupers and Scholars*, 2.
6. Rand, *Village of Amherst*, 54.
7. Tyler, *History of Amherst College*, 164–65.
8. BS, 119.
9. O. S. and L. N. Fowler, *Phrenology Proved*, 256.
10. HWB to HBS, 8 Mar. 1832, BS-SML.
11. BS, 164.
12. HWB to George Beecher, 13 Dec. 1830, BP-SML.
13. BS, 119.
14. *Auto HWB*, 155.
15. BS, 164.
16. *Auto HWB*, 31.
17. Ibid., 183; BS, 164.
18. BS, 120.
19. Ibid., 114.
20. HWB to HBS, 15 Feb. 1831, BP-SML.
21. *Auto HWB*, 88.
22. BS, 103.
23. HWB to HBS, 5 Dec. 1831, BP-SML.
24. HWB to George Beecher, 13 Dec. 1830, BP-SML.
25. EB, Reminiscences, BP-SML.
26. BS, 123.
27. HWB, Reminiscences, BP-SML.
28. HWB to Chauncey Howard, 8 Sept. 1831, HBSC.
29. BS, 90–92.
30. LB, *Autobiography of LB*, 2:170.
31. Barnes, *Antislavery Impulse*, 8.
32. LB, *Autobiography of LB*, 2:167.
33. BS, 604.
34. *Independent*, 27 July 1865.
35. HWB to Chauncey Howard, 8 Sept. 1831, HBSC.
36. HWB to Chauncey Howard, 17 May 1832, HBSC.
37. HWB to HBS, 5 Dec. 1831, BP-SML.
38. HWB to HBS, 15 Feb. 1831, BP-SML.
39. BS, 124–27.
40. HWB to Chauncey Howard, 28 June 1833, HBSC.
41. HWB to William Beecher, 1832, BP-SML.
42. HWB to HBS, 8 Mar. 1832, BP-SML; BS, 113.
43. BS, 113.
44. HWB to S. H. Hanks, 24 Mar. 1857, HBSC.
45. Shenstone, *Anecdotes*, 35.
46. Rugoff, *The Beechers*, 126.
47. HWB to HBS, 8 Mar. 1832, BP-SML.
48. HWB to HBS, 28 Mar. 183[3], Amherst College Archives; HWB to George Beecher, 28 Nov. 1831, HBSC; HBS, *Men of Our Times*, 538.
49. HWB to HBS, 8 Mar. 1832, BP-SML.
50. EB, Reminiscences, BP-SML.
51. HWB to Chauncey Howard, 17 May 1832, HBSC.
52. Hitchcock, *Religion of Geology*, 498.
53. HBS, *Men of Our Times*, 529.
54. HWB, *Yale Lectures*, 1:94.
55. *American Phrenological Journal*, 1 May 1849, 137; HWB, *Yale Lectures*, 1:94.
56. HWB to Chauncey Howard, 20 Dec. 1832, HBSC.
57. HWB to William Beecher, 1832, BP-SML.
58. HWB to Chauncey Howard, 20 Dec. 1832, HBSC.
59. HWB, *Yale Lectures*, 1:143.
60. EB to Olivia Bullard Hill, 23 June 1834, HBSC; BS, 127.
61. HWB, autobiographical notes, BP-SML.

62. BS, 133.
63. HWB to HBS, 5 Apr. 1832, BP-SML.
64. EB to HWB, 27 Sept. 1865, BP-SML.
65. EB to Joseph Bullard, Nov. 1835, HBSC.
66. HWB to Chauncey Howard, 28 June 1833, HBSC; EB to Joseph Bullard, June 1833, HBSC.
67. HWB to Chauncey Howard, 28 June 1833, HBSC.
68. HWB to Chauncey Howard, 26 Sept. 1833, HBSC.
69. HWB, Diary, 30 Mar. 1836, BP-SML.
70. Faculty Minutes, 21 Nov. 1833, Amherst College Archives.
71. White, Reminiscences of LB, 8.
72. Mary Perkins scrapbook, HBSC.
73. Congregational Quarterly, July 1864.
74. Johnson, Garrison and His Times, 44.
75. Liberator, 1 Jan. 1831.
76. Fuess, Amherst, 120–21.

Chapter 4

"It Was a Fearful Thing to Pull Up a New England Oak by the Roots at a Ripened Age and Transplant It to the Soil of the West"

1. Pierson, Tocqueville and Beaumont in America, 566.
2. LB, Autobiography of LB, 2:200.
3. White, Reminiscences of LB, 10.
4. Power, Planting Corn Belt Culture, 12.
5. Cincinnati Chronicle & Literary Gazette, 3 Aug. 1833.
6. LB, Autobiography of LB, 2:241.
7. U.S. Constitution, art. 1, sec. 2; art. 4, sec. 2.
8. Thomas, Theodore Weld, 70.
9. Barnes and Dumond, Letters of Weld, 1:132.
10. Tappan, Life of Arthur Tappan, 233.
11. HBS, Oldtown Folks, 324.
12. Johnson, Garrison and His Times, 177.
13. Finney, The Memoirs, xxxiii.
14. Liberator, 3 Jan. 1835.
15. IBH, Connecticut Magazine 9 (1905): 288.
16. HWB to Chauncey Howard, Nov. 1834, HBSC
17. HWB to Chauncey Howard, 20 Mar. 1835, HBSC.
18. IBH to John Hooker, 2 Dec. 1839, HBSC.
19. HBS to Elizabeth Lyman, fall 1835, HBSC.
20. White, Reminiscences of LB, 11; HWB to Chauncey Howard, Nov.
1834, HBSC.
21. HBS, Men of Our Times, 537.
22. HBS, Oldtown Folks, 381.
23. Cincinnati Journal, 9 Jan. 1835.
24. HBS, Men of Our Times, 538.
25. LB, Autobiography of LB, 2:218.
26. Stowe, Saints, Sinners and Beechers, 52.
27. BS, 605.
28. Rourke, Trumpets of Jubilee, 154.
29. HBS, Men of Our Times, 536; Calvin Stowe to HBS, 20 Aug. 1836, HBSC.
30. BS, 605.
31. HWB Diary, 27 June 1835, BP-SML; BS, 144.
32. Cincinnati Journal, 10 July 1835.
33. Stowe, Life of HBS, 82.
34. William Jones to Peter T. Washburn, 23 Feb. 1837, Ohio Historical Society.
35. HWB to Chauncey Howard, 20 Mar. 1835, HBSC.
36. HWB, Personal Diary, 23 Sept. 1835 and 18 Dec. 1836, BP-SML; Hibben, HWB, 75.
37. HWB, Personal Diary, 14 Sept. 1835, BP-SML.
38. Ibid., 29 Oct. 1835, BP-SML.
39. Ibid., 21 Mar. 1837, BP-SML.
40. HBS, Men of Our Times, 535.

41. LB, *Autobiography of LB*, 2: 269, 270.
42. HWB, Personal Diary, 11 May 1836, BP-SML.
43. HWB to Chauncey Howard, 20 Mar. 1835, HBSC.
44. *Cincinnati Journal*, 11 July 1836, 21 July 1836.
45. Stowe, *Life of HBS*, 84–85, 105.
46. Wilson, *Crusader in Crinoline*, 189–90; *Cincinnati Journal*, 11 Aug. 1836.
47. White, *Reminiscences of LB*, 26; HWB to William Beecher, 4 Oct. 1836, Schlesinger Library.

48. BS, 167.
49. HBS, *Men of Our Times*, 539.
50. HWB, Personal Diary, 21 Mar. 1836, BP-SML.
51. HBS, *Men of Our Times*, 540.
52. Barrows, *HWB*, 66.
53. BS, 590.
54. *Auto HWB*, 90.
55. Emerson, *Conduct of Life*, 162.
56. Mary Wright to IBH, 12 Aug. 1837, HBSC.
57. Emerson, *Selected Essays*; 97; *Appleton's Cyclopaedia*, 345.

Chapter 5

"Humph! Pretty Business! Son of Lyman Beecher, President of a Theological Seminary, in This Miserable Hole"

1. HWB, CU, 6 Dec. 1871
2. HWB, Personal Diary (1835–44), 4 May 1837, BP-SML.
3. Ibid., 15 June 1837, BP-SML.
4. HWB to Chauncey Howard, 20 June 1837, HBSC.
5. HWB, Personal Diary (1835–44), 27 July-Aug. 1835, BP-SML.
6. HWB, Personal Diary (1835–44), 4 May 1837, BP-SML.
7. EB, *Dawn to Daylight*, iii, 23.
8. HBS to Elizabeth Lyman, [fall] 1835, HBSC.
9. HWB, Personal Diary (1835–44), 21 May 1836, BP-SML.
10. EB to Edward Bok, n.d., HBSC.
11. HWB, Personal Diary (1835–44), 3 Aug. 1837, BP-SML.
12. BS, 170–71.
13. EB, *Dawn to Daylight*, 45–47.
14. HBS to EB, June 2, no year, BP-SML; Charles Beecher to IBH, Sept. 1837, HBSC; Mary Wright to IBH, c. 1838, HBSC.
15. EB, *Dawn to Daylight*, 51.
16. HBS, *Men of Our Times*, 541.
17. EB, *Dawn to Daylight*, 51; *Indianapolis Daily Sentinel*, 28 May 1882.
18. BS, 176.

19. EB, *Dawn to Daylight*, 52, 54.
20. HWB, Personal Diary (1835–44), 23 Oct. 1837, BP-SML. *Auto HWB*, 153.
21. HWB, *Yale Lectures*, 1:17.
22. HWB, Personal Diary (1835–44), 4 May 1837, BP-SML.
23. BS, 178.
24. HWB, *Yale Lectures*, 1:145–46, 205.
25. Derby, *Fifty Years*, 450.
26. BS, 179.
27. HBS to EB, 1838, BP-SML.
28. EB to George and Sarah Buckingham Beecher, 25 June 1838, BP-SML.
29. HWB to Lucy Bullard, 17 May 1838, BP-SML; EB to George and Sarah Buckingham Beecher, 25 June 1838, BP-SML.
30. Charles Beecher, *Life of Edward Beecher*, 128.
31. BS, 165–66.
32. HWB to George Beecher, Oct. 1838, BP-SML.
33. HWB to Thomas [Brainerd], HWB, Personal Diary (1835–44), Oct. 1838, BP-SML.
34. HWB to IBH, 11 Jan. 1839, HBSC.

35. HWB to George Beecher, Oct. 1838, BP-SML.
36. HWB, Personal Diary (1835–44), 27 Sept. 1838, BP-SML.
37. Charles Foote to Caty Foote, 8 May 1839, Schlesinger Library.
38. HWB, Working Diary (1837–40), 2 Dec. 1838, BP-SML.
39. HWB, Personal Diary (1835–44), 18 Feb. 1839, BP-SML.
40. HWB, Working Diary (1837–40), 17 June 1838, BP-SML; HWB, Personal Diary (1835–44), 18 Feb. 1839, BP-SML.
41. HWB, Personal Diary (1835–44), 4, [9], May 1839, BP-SML.
42. Ibid., 4 May 1839.
43. Undated clippings, BP-SML.
44. HWB, Yale Lectures, 1:11; LB to Lydia Jackson Beecher, 26 May 1839, HBSC.
45. Lawrenceburgh Political Beacon, 13 July 1839.

Chapter 6

"I Am a Western Man"

1. Julia Merrill Moores to HWB, 21 June 1883, BP-SML.
2. Ladies' Home Journal 9, no. 1 (1891): 21.
3. Derby, Fifty Years, 456.
4. Howard, HWB: A Study, 134, 156.
5. HWB, Working Diary (1837–40), 4 Aug. 1839, BP-SML.
6. HWB, Personal Diary (1835–44), 14 Sept. 1839, BP-SML.
7. Stowe, Saints, Sinners, and Beechers, 266.
8. Samuel Merrill to Hazen Merrill, 14 May 1839, Samuel Merrill Papers, IHS.
9. HWB, Personal Diary (1835–44), Dec. 1839, BP-SML.
10. CB to John Hooker, 27 Nov. 1839; IBH to John Hooker, 2 Dec. 1839, HBSC.
11. Ladies' Home Journal 9, no. 1 (1891): 11.
12. HWB, Personal Diary (1835–44), 11 Mar. 1840, BP-SML.
13. HWB, Yale Lectures, 1:145.
14. HWB, Life Thoughts, 234.
15. HWB, Personal Diary (1835–44), 11 Mar. 1840, BP-SML.
16. Elsmere, HWB, 114; Ketcham, "Reminiscences of Jane Merrill Ketcham," IHS, 69–71.
17. Samuel Merrill to David Merrill, Samuel Merrill Papers, 14 Nov. 1840, IHS.
18. EB to Edward Bok, 26 May 1887, HBSC.
19. Indianapolis Daily Sentinel, 28 May 1882.
20. BS, 208; HWB, Personal Diary (1835–44), 4 May 1839, BP-SML; HWB, Auto HWB, 145–46.
21. HWB, Eyes and Ears, 154.
22. BS, 187.
23. HWB, Yale Lectures, 1:101.
24. Howard, HWB: A Study, 42; HWB, "Notes on Lafayette Revival," 12 Mar. 1843, BP-SML.
25. BS, 193.
26. Ibid., 188; HWB, Yale Lectures, 1:42.
27. Johnson, A Home in the Woods, 228–29; McCullough, Men and Measures, 144.
28. BS, 184.
29. McCullough, Men and Measures, 144; Derby, Fifty Years, 474.
30. HWB, Yale Lectures, 1:229.
31. Knox, Life and Work, 82; Howard, HWB: A Study, 74.
32. McCullough, Men and Measures, 147; Shenstone, Anecdotes of HWB, 55.
33. McCullough, Men and Measures, 144.
34. Julia Merrill Moores to HWB, 21 June 1883, BP-SML.

35. BS, 191.

36. HWB, *Yale Lectures*, 1:46–47; BS, 191.

37. HWB, *Yale Lectures*, 1:46–48.

38. *Independent*, 1 Apr. 1858.

39. HWB, *Yale Lectures*, 1:46–48.

40. Stowe, *Saints, Sinners and Beechers*, 262.

41. LB to HWB, 8 Dec. 1842, BP-SML.

42. Charles Beecher to William C. Beecher, 17 Apr. 1887, BP-SML; HWB to LB, 18 Mar. 1843, Schlesinger Library.

43. Thomas Beecher to IBH, 4 Oct. 1842, HBSC.

44. HWB, lecture talks, 22 June 1877, BP-SML.

45. Hedrick, *HBS*, 147–54; George Beecher, *Biographical Remains*, 83.

46. LB, *Autobiography of LB*, 2:311.

47. Derby, *Fifty Years*, 451–52; BS, 204–5.

48. *Ladies' Home Journal* 9, no. 2 (1892): 5.

49. LB, *Autobiography of LB*, 2:345.

50. HBS to "Dear Brothers and Sisters All," 4 July 1843, BP-SML.

51. HBS to Sarah Buckingham Beecher, 6 June 1843, HBSC.

52. HBS to "Dear Brothers and Sisters All," 4 July 1843, BP-SML.

53. *Ladies' Home Journal* 9, no. 2 (1892): 5.

54. HBS to Sarah Buckingham Beecher, 23 Sept. 1843, HBSC.

55. HWB to Sarah Buckingham Beecher, 9 Aug. 1843, Cincinnati Historical Society.

56. HBS to Sarah Buckingham Beecher, 23 Sept. 1843, HBSC.

57. Kirk, *Beecher as a Humorist*, 78; Howard, *HWB: A Study*, 143; HWB, *Notes from Plymouth*, xxviii.

58. *Auto HWB*, 162.

59. Formisano, *Birth of Mass Political Parties*, 163, 120.

60. Lucien W. Berry to Matthew Simpson, 26 July 1843, Matthew Simpson Papers, LC.

61. HBS to Calvin Stowe, 3 Sept. 1844, Schlesinger Library.

62. *Chicago Tribune*, 6 July 1874.

63. HBS to Calvin Stowe, 19 July 1844, Schlesinger Library.

64. HWB to Lucy Bullard, 30 Oct. 1844, BP-SML.

65. HWB to LB, 13 Sept. 1844, Schlesinger Library.

66. *Democratic Review*, July 1845.

67. HWB, Personal Diary, 2 Jan. 1839, 28 Feb. 1840, BP-SML.

68. HWB, *Sermons by HWB*, 1:193; *Auto HWB*, 157–58.

69. Barrows, *HWB*, 95–96.

70. Riddle, *Magazine of Western History* 5 (1887): 854–57.

71. *Indiana State Journal*, 23 July 1832.

72. McCulloch, *Men and Measures*, 145–46

73. *Indiana State Journal*, 14 Jan. 1846.

74. Julia Merrill to Elizabeth Bates, Julia Merrill Moores Papers, 28 Jan. 1846, IHS.

75. EB, *Dawn to Daylight*, 305.

76. *Auto HWB*, 118, 115.

77. BS, 205–6; EB to Harriet Beecher Scoville, 12 Dec. 1869, BP-SML.

78. HWB to HBS [c. 1848], BP-SML.

79. EB to HBS 27 Dec. 1846, BP-SML.

80. *Indiana State Journal*, 4 Mar. 1846.

81. HWB, Sermons, 6 May 1846, BP-SML.

82. Knox, *Life and Work*, 215; Samuel Merrill to David Merrill, 31 May 1846, Samuel Merrill Papers, IHS.

83. William T. Cutler to HWB, 8 Dec. 1846, BP-SML.

84. HWB to William T. Cutler, 15 Dec. 1846, BP-SML; William. T. Cutler to HWB, 12 Feb. 1847, BP-SML.

85. *New York Express*, 11 May 1847.

86. HCB to HWB, 20 May 1847, BP-SML.

87. HWB, Notebook vol. 2, Henry Ward Beecher Papers, LC.

88. HCB to HWB, 21 July 1847, BP-SML.

89. HCB to HWB, 20 May 1847, BP-SML.

90. Kinnie Graydon to Mary Ellen Graydon Sharpe, 12 Aug. 1847, Mary Ellen Graydon Sharpe Papers, IHS.

91. John L. Ketcham to David Merrill, 18 Aug. 1847, Samuel Merrill Papers, IHS.
92. HCB to HWB, 16 Sept. 1847, BP-SML.
93. Samuel Merrill to Hazen Merrill, 5 Sept. 1847, IHS.
94. John L. Ketcham to David Merrill, 18 Aug. 1847, Samuel Merrill Papers, IHS.
95. *Chicago Tribune*, 6 July 1874.
96. Julia Merrill to Elizabeth Bates, 6 Sept. 1847, Julia Merrill Moores Papers, IHS.
97. HWB to Julia Merrill, 21 Oct. 1847, Julia Merrill Moores Papers, IHS.
98. Julia Merrill Moores to HWB, 16 May 1873, BP-SML.
99. Ibid., 21 June 1883; 16 May 1873.
100. *Chicago Inter Ocean*, 11 Aug. 1874; Elsmere, 302.

Chapter 7

"A Peculiar Minister Was Needed for So Peculiar a Church"

1. Murphy, A *Treasury*, 54.
2. Smith, *Successful Folks*, 851.
3. *Packard's Monthly*, July 1868; Bowen, *The Lineage*, 154.
4. Lucy Bowen to HCB, 1843, Brooklyn Historical Society.
5. HCB to HWB, 4 May 1847, BP-SML.
6. HCB to HWB, 6 Aug. 1847, BP-SML.
7. Smith, *Successful Folks*, 851–52.
8. *Ladies' Home Journal* 9 (1892): 4.
9. BS, 218–19.
10. HWB to EB, 11 Aug. 1850, BP-SML.
11. HWB to HBS, 25 July 1848, BP-SML.
12. Derby, *Fifty Years*, 470.
13. Bungay, *Crayon Sketches*, 129.
14. HWB to HBS [c. 1848], BP-SML.
15. HWB to LB, 14 Dec. 1847, Schlesinger Library.
16. Raymond, *Life and Letters*, 170.
17. Howard, *Remembrance of Things*, 26.
18. HWB to LB, 14 Dec. 1847, Schlesinger Library.
19. HWB, *Notes from Plymouth*, xxxiv–xxxv.
20. Shenstone, *Anecdotes*, 87.
21. *Eagle*, 10 May 1848.
22. Rugoff, *The Beechers*, 370; Murray, *Letters from the U.S.*, 146.
23. Howard, *HWB: A Study*, 140.
24. Knox, *Life and Work*, 82.
25. Undated clippings, BP-SML.
26. *Liberator*, 23 Aug. 1850.
27. H. Bellows to Eliza T. Bellows, 10 Oct. 1855, Bellows Papers, Massachusetts Historical Society.
28. Corning, *Personal Recollections of HWB*, 20.
29. HWB, *Lecture Room Talks*, 204.
30. *Eagle*, 10 May 1848, 7 Feb. 1851.
31. Shenstone, *Anecdotes*, 90–91.
32. Howard, *Eagle and Brooklyn*, 284.
33. Howard, *Remembrance of Things*, 26.
34. *Eagle*, 22 Aug. 1848.
35. Ibid., 27 Dec. 1848, 18 Dec. 1848.
36. HWB, *Life Thoughts*, 185.
37. Undated clippings, BP-SML.
38. HWB to Thomas Beecher, 29 Jan. 1849, Cornell University Archives.
39. HWB to EB, 11 Jan. 1851, 8 Jan. 1851, BP-SML.
40. *Ladies' Home Journal* 9, no. 1 (1891): 21.
41. Howard, *HWB: A Study*, 68.
42. Foner, *Business and Slavery*, 4.
43. Lewis Tappan's Diary, 2 Nov. 1856, Lewis Tappan Papers, LC.
44. LB to Lydia Beecher, 11 Aug. 1848, HBSC.
45. *Independent*, 10 Dec. 1908.
46. Potter, *Irrepressible Conflict*, 45.
47. *Liberator*, 7 July 1854.
48. BS, 293.
49. Abbott, *HWB: A Sketch*, 146–48.

50. *BS*, 293.
51. *Independent*, 26 Dec. 1850.
52. Thomas Beecher and HWB to LB, 5 Dec. 1848, HBSC.

53. *Eagle*, 13 Jan. 1849.
54. Susan Howard, Reminiscences, 21 Aug. 1897, HBSC.
55. *Independent*, 21 May 1857.

Chapter 8

"Politics in the Pulpit"

1. *New York Times*, 18 Sept. 1901.
2. *Independent*, 22 Nov. 1849.
3. HWB to Thomas Beecher, 29 Jan. 1849, Cornell University Archives.
4. HWB, *Yale Lectures*, 1:73–74.
5. *Eagle*, 19 June 1849.
6. Tappan, *Life of Arthur Tappan*, 238.
7. *Journal of Commerce*, 19 Dec. 1850.
8. *Independent*, 26 June 1856.
9. Ibid., 21 Feb. 1850, 24 Jan. 1850.
10. Ibid., 21 Feb. 1850.
11. *BS*, 236.
12. Ibid.; *Independent*, 21 Mar. 1850.
13. HWB, *Patriotic Addresses*, 175.
14. *BS*, 236, 253.
15. *Journal of Commerce*, 12 Apr. 1850.
16. *Independent*, 23 May 1850.
17. Ibid., 11 May 1850. Full debate reprinted in *Journal of Commerce Supplement*, 8 June 1850.
18. Bacon, *Leonard Bacon*, 356.
19. *Journal of Commerce*, 10 May 1850.
20. *Independent*, 9 May 1850.
21. *North Star*, 16 May 1850.
22. Whitman, *Uncollected Poetry*, 1:235.
23. *Independent*, 14 Nov. 1850.
24. *BS*, 246.
25. HWB, "Wendell Phillips: A Commemorative Discourse," 10 Feb. 1884, *Plymouth Pulpit*, ser. 7, no. 20; *Liberator*, 23 Aug. 1850.
26. *Eagle*, 11 May 1850.
27. HWB, "Wendell Phillips"; Martyn, *Wendell Phillips*, 231.
28. *Liberator*, 23 Aug. 1850.
29. HCB's Silver Anniversary Speech, HCB scrapbook, HCB Papers, American Antiquarian Society.
30. *BS*, 339; *Liberator*, 23 Aug. 1850.
31. HWB to EB, 11 Aug. 1850, BP-SML; *Independent*, 23 Jan. 1851.

32. HWB, *Star Papers*, 23, 85.
33. HWB to EB, 11 Aug. 1850, BP-SML.
34. HWB, *Star Papers*, 83.
35. *Independent*, 26 Sept. 1850.
36. *Journal of Commerce*, 28 Sept. 1850.
37. *Independent*, 3 Oct. 1850.
38. HBS to HWB, fragment, n.d., BP-SML.
39. *Proceedings of the Union Safety Meeting Held in Castle Garden*, 30 Oct. 1850, 21.
40. *New York Tribune*, 28 Oct. 1850.
41. *Independent*, 14 Nov. 1850.
42. White, *Personal Reminiscences of LB*, 16.
43. LB, *Autobiography of LB*, 2:405.
44. Stowe, *Saints, Sinners, and Beechers*, 130.
45. HWB to HBS, fragment, n.d., BP-SML.
46. IBH to John Hooker, 30 June 1852, HBSC.
47. Hedrick, *HBS*, 208.
48. Stowe, *Life of HBS*, 475–77.
49. HBS, *Uncle Tom's Cabin*, 631.
50. Derby, *Fifty Years*, 457; EB, Reminiscences, BP-SML.
51. *Southern Literary Messenger*, July 1853.
52. *Southern Quarterly Review* 8 (1853): 226.
53. Stowe, *Life of HBS*, 61.
54. *BS*, 259.
55. *Fraser's Magazine*, cited in *New York Times*, 17 Nov. 1852; *North American Review*, cited in *New York Times*, 9 Oct. 1854; *Scottish Review*, Oct. 1859.
56. *Eagle*, 6 Jan. 1853.
57. Theodore Parker, quoted in *Indiana Free Democrat*, 14 April 1853.

Chapter 9

"Courage Today or Carnage Tomorrow"

1. HWB to Emily Drury, n.d., Schlesinger Library; TT v. HWB, 1:478.
2. Foote, A Victorian, 69–71.
3. Standard, 2 Oct. 1872, clipping from Moses S. Beach Papers, New York Historical Society.
4. Emma Beach to Moses S. Beach, Moses S. Beach Papers, LC.
5. Knox, Life and Work, 254.
6. HWB, Star Papers, 250.
7. Independent, 26 Jan. 1860.
8. Abbott, HWB, 114.
9. Ladies' Home Journal 9, no. 2 (1892): 3.
10. EB to HWB, 20 Dec. 1865, BP-SML.
11. HWB, Star Papers, 181.
12. Parker, The World of Matter, 147–48.
13. Higginson, Letters and Journals, 47.
14. Eagle, 8 Jan. 1853.
15. HWB's copy of Emerson, Representative Men, BL.
16. Howard, HWB: A Study, 52.
17. Hayes, Diary and Letters, 1:301–3; Emerson, Journal and Miscellaneous, 13:49.
18. Branch, The Sentimental Years, 333; HWB, Patriotic Address, 403–21. HWB, CU, 9 Oct. 1872.
19. HWB, Life Thoughts, 241.
20. National Era, 17 Jan. 1856.
21. McAlleer, R. W. Emerson: Days of Encounter, 546.
22. Independent, 13 Jan. 1859.
23. HWB, Yale Lectures, 1:113, 3;
24. BS, 595.
25. Smith, Sunshine and Shadow, 92.
26. Alcott, Journals, 288; Thoreau, Journals, 11:438.
27. Traubel, With Walt Whitman, 2:471, 3:456.
28. Putnam's Magazine, Sept. 1855.
29. Potter, The Impending Conflict, 151.
30. O'Connor, Civil War, 14.
31. BS, 274.
32. New York Times, 10 Feb. 1854; BS, 276; Independent, 6 Apr. 1854.
33. Parrish, David Rice Atchison, 161.
34. Howard, Life of HWB, 273.
35. Abbott, HWB, 211; New York Tribune, 8 Feb. 1856.
36. Garrison, William Lloyd Garrison, 3:439; Independent, 9 April 1856.
37. Potter, The Impending Conflict, 210.
38. Abbott, HWB, 202.
39. Stampp, America in 1857, 11.
40. Nichols, Bleeding Kansas, 113.
41. BS, 298; Van Pelt, Leslie's History of Greater New York, 220.
42. Eagle, 19 June 1856.
43. Julian, Political Recollections, 163.
44. Wilson, History of the Rise, 2:519.
45. Halstead, Trimmers, Trucklers, 35.
46. Eagle, 19 June 1856; Richmond Enquirer, 13 Sept. 1856; Journal of Commerce, 25 Sept. 1856.
47. New York Tribune, 4 July 1856; BS, 290.
48. Independent, 7 Aug. 1856.
49. Enoch Wood to Lewis Palmer [Oct. 1856], Swarthmore College Archives.
50. Susan Howard to the Stowe daughters [fall 1856], HBSC.
51. Eagle, 4 Nov. 1856.
52. Potter, The Impending Conflict, 275. Foner and Mahoney, A House Divided, 60.
53. Independent, 26 Mar. 1857.
54. Eagle, 20 Jan. 1857.
55. New York Times, 20 Jan. 1857.
56. Charles Beecher to HWB, 29 Dec. 1856, BP-SML.
57. Horatio C. King, "Recollections of HWB," Dickinson College Archives.
58. Howard, in Patriotic Addresses, 61.
59. HWB, "Moral Affinity the Ground of True Unity," 6 Dec. 1868, Plymouth Pulpit, ser. 1, 285; Waller, Reverend Beecher, 112–17.
60. Independent, 27 Dec. 1866.
61. E. W. B. Dakin to HWB, 22 Feb. 1876, BP-SML.
62. TT v. HWB, 1:456–57, 420.
63. Trimpi, Melville's Confidence Men, 244–45.

64. Melville, *The Confidence Man*, 211.
65. HWB, *Notes from Plymouth*, xxxvii.
66. HWB to EB, 9 Oct. 1857, BP-SML.
67. HWB, *New Star Papers*, 90–92.
68. *Eagle*, 27 Nov. 1857.
69. Conant, *Narratives*, 383.
70. Abbott, *HWB*, 93; *Memorial of the Revival*, 9.
71. *New York Times*, 19 Oct. 1857.
72. *Eagle*, 1 Apr. 1858.
73. Ibid., 2 Apr. 1858.
74. *National Era*, 13 May 1857.
75. Knox, *Life and Work*, 294.
76. *Harper's Weekly*, 17 July 1858.
77. Stowe, *Life of HBS*, 478.
78. Whitman, *I Sit and Look Out*, 84–85.
79. HWB, *Norwood*, xvi.
80. HWB, *Notes from Plymouth*, 1:xlvii–viii; Howard, in *Patriotic Addresses*, 67.
81. Lucy Jackson White notes, 29 Jan.

1860, HBSC.
82. *The Biblical Repository and Princeton Review*, Oct. 1857.
83. TT v. HWB, 3:127; HWB, *Notes from Plymouth*, xxx
84. EB to HWB, 6 May 1855, BP-SML.
85. HBS to EB, 26 July 1857, BP-SML; *Chicago Tribune*, 1 Aug. 1874; John Raymond to Cornelia Raymond, 2 Sept. 1863, Vassar College Archives.
86. EB to HWB, 7 June 1858, BP-SML
87. *New York Times*, 10 Dec. 1874.
88. Ibid., 3 Mar. 1876.
89. Marshall, *True History*, 314; *Daily Graphic*, 11 Sept. 1874.
90. TT v. HWB, 1:403.
91. *Daily Graphic*, 11 Sept. 1874.
92. *Independent*, 8 Dec. 1859.
93. Ibid., 10 Feb. 1876.

Chapter 10

"Give Me War Redder Than Blood and Fiercer Than Fire"

1. Cole, *Irrespressible Conflict*, 51.
2. Hudson, *Journalism in the U.S.*, 301–2.
3. *New York Ledger*, 6 Aug. 1859.
4. *Woodhull & Claflin's Weekly*, 7 Oct. 1871.
5. TT v. HWB, 2:839
6. *Independent*, Dec. 1908.
7. TT v. HWB, 1:478.
8. Marshall, *True History*, 260.
9. Garrison, *Letters*, 4:415.
10. HWB, *Patriotic Addresses*, 214, 219.
11. Warren, *Black and White*, 75–76.
12. *New York Tribune*, cited in *Eagle*, 27 Jan. 1860.
13. *Eagle*, 10 Dec. 1868.
14. Hinton, *John Brown*, 433.
15. Whittier, *Letters to Whittier*, 2:438; *Eagle*, 4 Nov. 1859.
16. Child, *Lydia Maria Child*, 335.
17. Theodore Tilton to Wendell Phillips, 10 Nov. 1859, Houghton Library.
18. TT v. HWB, 1:479.
19. HWB to Charles Beecher, 2 Feb. 1860, BP-SML.

20. *New York Times*, 24 Jan. 1860.
21. *Eagle*, 24 Jan. 1860.
22. Tilton, "Speech of Theodore Tilton in Plymouth Church, Brooklyn, January 25, 1860," 37, 15, 49–51.
23. HWB to Emily Drury, n.d., BP-SML.
24. *Eagle*, 6 Feb. 1860; ibid., 7 Feb. 1860; *New York Tribune*, cited by *Independent*, 2 Feb. 1860.
25. *New York World*, 19 Apr. 1896.
26. Griswold, *Sixty Years*, 175.
27. J. L. Corning to Chloe Beach, 7 Mar. 1865, Moses S. Beach Papers, LC.
28. Moses S. Beach Notebook, 17 Oct. 1843 and 23 Aug. 1845, Private Collection of Brewster Beach.
29. Foote, *A Victorian*, 75.
30. Moses S. Beach to HWB, n.d., Private Collection of Mary Schlosser.
31. Foote, *A Victorian*, 75.
32. Moses S. Beach to HWB, n.d., Private Collection of Mary Schlosser.
33. *New York Times*, 3 Mar. 1876.
34. *Independent*, 23 Feb. 1860.
35. Freeman, *Abraham Lincoln*, 37.

36. Ward, A. Lincoln: Tributes, 28–29.
37. Freeman, Abraham Lincoln, 83.
38. Rankin, Intimate Sketches, 186.
39. Freeman, Abraham Lincoln, 86; Basler, Collected Works, 4:38.
40. New York Tribune, 6 Mar. 1860.
41. New York Times, 7 Feb. 1960.
42. Carpenter, Inner Life, 135.
43. Ibid.
44. Howard, Life of HWB, 533.
45. New York Times, 5 Nov. 1860.
46. Independent, 8 Nov. 1860.
47. Potter, Irrepressible Conflict, 485.
48. BS, 310.
49. HWB to Emily Drury, Apr. 1861, Schlesinger Library.
50. BS, 311.
51. Ibid., 320.
52. New York Tribune, 25 Aug. 1862.
53. New York Times, 29 Nov. 1861.
54. Garrison, Letters, 5:48.
55. Emerson, Journal and Miscellaneous 15:346.
56. New York Times, 3 May 1875.
57. Marshall, True History, 313.
58. Henry Barton Beecher to EB, 9 Apr. 1862, BP-SML.
59. Independent, 13 Mar. 1862.
60. Marshall, True History, 568.
61. Crofut, An American Procession, 66.
62. Beecher-Tilton Investigation, 109.
63. TT v. HWB, 1:478.
64. Independent, 22 May 1862.
65. Moses S. Beach to HWB, n.d., Private Collection of Mary Schlosser.
66. Independent, 27 Feb. 1862; EB to Samuel Scoville, 4 Apr. c. 1862, BP-SML.
67. HCB to HWB, 16 May 1862, Beecher Papers, LC.
68. Independent, 10 July, 7 Aug. 1862.
69. Ibid., 14 Aug., 24 July 1862.
70. Carpenter, Six Months, 230–31.
71. Guelzo, Lincoln's Emancipation, 183.
72. Theodore Tilton to W. L. Garrison, 24 Sept. 1862, William Lloyd Garrison Papers, Boston Public Library.
73. New York Times, 29 Sept. 1862.
74. Independent, 30 Oct. 1862.
75. HBS and Mary Perkins to HWB, 2 Nov. 1862, BP-SML.
76. Thomas Beecher to HWB, 10 Aug. 1862, BP-SML.
77. New York Times, 1 Dec. 1862.
78. IBH to John Hooker, 19 Nov. 1862, HBSC.
79. HCB to Abraham Lincoln, 2 Dec. 1862, Abraham Lincoln Papers, LC.
80. HWB to EB, Oct. 1862, BP-SML.
81. Guelzo, Lincoln's Emancipation, 109.
82. New York Times, 6 Jan. 1863.
83. Independent, 20 Dec. 1869.
84. Eagle, 2 Mar. 1876.
85. HWB, lecture room notes, 24 Nov. [1877], BP-SML.
86. LB, Autobiography of LB, 2:418.
87. EB to Harriet Beecher Scoville, 11 Jan. 1863, BP-SML.
88. Wilson, Crusader in Crinoline, 491.
89. CB, Religious Training, 340–45.
90. LB, Autobiography of LB, 2:414.
91. New York Times, 30 Mar. 1863; Independent, 16 Apr. 1863.
92. New York Times, 3 Mar. 1876.
93. Independent, 30 Apr., 26 Nov. 1863.
94. Theodore Tilton to HWB, 24 Sept. 1863, BP-SML.
95. TT v. HWB, 1:68.
96. HCB to HWB, 31 July 1863, BP-SML.
97. HWB, Patriotic Addresses, 643.
98. Abbott, HWB, 255–56.
99. Knox, Life and Work, 192.
100. Abbott, HWB: Sketches, 254; HWB to Theodore Tilton, 18 Oct. 1863, HBSC.
101. New York Times, 4 Nov. 1863.
102. Independent, 26 Nov. 1863.
103. Stowe, Saints, Sinners, and Beechers, 293.
104. New York Times, 18 Nov. 1863.
105. Eagle, 29 Mar. 1864.
106. Basler, Collected Works, 7:512–13.
107. New York Times, 30 May 1875.
108. New York Tribune, 14 Aug. 1864.
109. Eagle, 4 Oct. 1864.
110. HBS to Stowe daughters, 8 Nov. 1864, Schlesinger Library.
111. Theodore Tilton to John Nicolay, 12 Nov. 1864, Lincoln Papers, LC.

112. Rice, *Reminiscences*, 249–50.
113. HWB to Robert Bonner, 3 Feb. 1865, NYPL; Robert Bonner to HWB, 8 Feb. 1865, BP-SML; Rice, *Reminiscences*, 250.
114. Knox, *Life and Work*, 180.

Chapter 11

"My Heart Is with the Radicals, but My Emotions Are with the Orthodox"

1. Robert Bonner to HWB, 25 Jan. 1865, BP-SML.
2. Derby, *Fifty Years*, 471.
3. Robert Bonner to HWB, 22 Apr. 1865, BP-SML.
4. HWB to Robert Bonner, 22 Apr. 1865, NYPL.
5. Moses Coit Tyler, *Diary of M. C. Tyler*, 77.
6. *Atlantic Monthly* 19, no. 111 (1867): 43.
7. Fiske, *Edward Livingston*, 104.
8. Emerson, *Journals and Miscellaneous*, 15:72; *Auto HWB*, 75; HWB, "Through Fear to Love," *Plymouth Pulpit*, 16 Feb. 1873, ser. 5, 451–61.
9. Bok, *Beecher Memorial*, 64.
10. Marshall, *True History*, 605.
11. Sandburg, *Abraham Lincoln*, 724.
12. Thaddeus Stevens, Speech at Court House, 10 Apr. 1865, Thaddeus Stevens Papers On-line, Furman University, Greenville, S.C.
13. Trefousse, *Andrew Johnson*, 236.
14. Calvin Stowe to HWB, 28 Oct. [1865], Schlesinger Library.
15. BS, 465.
16. *New York Herald*, 2 Sept. 1866.
17. HWB to Andrew Johnson, 23 Oct. 1865, Andrew Johnson Papers, LC.
18. *Independent*, 6 July 1865; *Eagle*, 4–6 Apr. 1875.
19. *Chicago Tribune*, 13 Aug. 1874.
20. BS, 460.
21. Melville, *Collected Poems*, 465.
22. *Independent*, 10 Jan. 1867.
23. *Eagle*, 30 Jan. 1866.
24. HWB to Andrew Johnson, 17 Mar. 1866, Papers of Andrew Johnson, LC.
25. Welles, *Diary*, 6 Apr. 1866, 478.
26. Thaddeus Stevens to William D. Kelley, 6 Sep. 1866, Thaddeus Stevens Papers, LC; Child, *Lydia Maria Child*, 463.
27. *Independent*, 6 Sept. 1866.
28. Ibid., 25 Oct. 1866.
29. TT v. HWB, 2:161.
30. *Beecher-Tilton Investigation*, 84.
31. *Eagle*, 8 March 1875.
32. Edward Beecher to HWB, 23 Dec. 1867, BP-SML.
33. HWB to Edward Beecher, 27 Dec. 1867, BP-SML.
34. TT v. HWB, 2:738.
35. *Chicago Tribune*, 13 Aug. 1874.
36. Marshall, *True History*, 257.
37. Foote, *A Victorian*, 75.
38. Moses S. Beach to HWB, n.d., Private Collection of Mary Schlosser.
39. HWB to Robert Bonner. 8 Apr. 1865, Robert Bonner Papers, NYPL.
40. TT v. HWB 3:59.
41. TT v. HWB 2:742.
42. HWB, *Norwood*, 21.
43. TT v. HWB, 3:74.
44. *New York Times*, "Review of the Beecher Case," 11.
45. Doyle, *Plymouth Church*, 262.
46. *Chicago Tribune*, 13 Aug. 1874.
47. *Official Report of the Trial of HWB*, 2:712.
48. TT v. HWB, 1:488.
49. Chloe Beach to Violet Beach, n.d., Private Collection of Brewster Beach.
50. HWB, *Norwood*, 202.
51. *Chicago Tribune*, 13 Aug. 1874.
52. Twain, *Mark Twain's Travels*, 84–88, 106, 92–93, 114–15, 276.
53. *Herald*, 20 November 1867.
54. Smith and Bucci, *Mark Twain's Letters*, 2:165, 178, 401–6.

55. Moses S. Beach to HWB, n.d., Private Collection of Mary Schlosser.
56. Moses S. Beach to Chloe Beach, 29 Aug. 1870, Private Collection of Brewster Beach.
57. Moses S. Beach to HWB, n.d., Private Collection of Mary Schlosser.
58. EB to Chloe, Mar. 1871, BP-SML.
59. *Atlantic Monthly* 21, no. 128 (1868): 761; *The Catholic World* 10, no. 57 (1869): 399–400.
60. Derby, *Fifty Years*, 456–57; HWB to Emily Drury, 12 Mar. 1868, Schlesinger Library.
61. *Chicago Tribune*, 13 Aug. 1874.
62. Marshall, *True History*, 517.
63. Ibid., 160.
64. Doyle, *Plymouth Church*, 377.
65. *Chicago Tribune*, 13 Aug. 1874.
66. Welles, *Diary*, 357.
67. TT v. HWB, 1:629.
68. *Chicago Tribune*, 31 May 1875.
69. *New York Times*, 11 July 1868.
70. Rusk, *Life of R. W. Emerson*, 436.
71. *New York Times*, 10 Oct. 1868.
72. Marshall, *True History*, 114.
73. *Brooklyn Union*, 26 Aug. 1874; Marshall, *True History*, 523.
74. *Chicago Tribune*, 31 Aug. 1874; Doyle, *Plymouth Church*, 266; Marshall, *True History*, 114–17, 479.
75. Doyle, *Plymouth Church*, 266.
76. *Independent*, 25 Feb. 1869.
77. Harper, *Life and Work*, 276–77.
78. IBH to John Hooker, 24 July 1860, HBSC.
79. *New York Times*, 6 June 1869.
80. Bigelow, *Retrospections*, 4:289–90.
81. HWB to HBS, 24 Aug. 1869, HBSC.
82. *Against an Aristocracy*, 2:312–14.
83. *New York Sun*, 2 Dec. 1869.
84. *New York Times*, 13 Dec. 1869; *Hartford Courant*, 8 Dec. 1869; *Eagle*, 11 Dec. 1869.
85. *Hartford Courant*, 15 Dec. 1869.
86. *Independent*, 23 Dec. 1869.
87. *Eagle*, 13 Dec. 1869.
88. HWB, "The Strong to Bear with the Weak," *Plymouth Pulpit*, 25 Oct. 1868, ser. 1, 118.
89. Strong, *Diary of George Templeton Strong*, 4:262.

Chapter 12

"I Am Reliably Assured that Beecher Preaches to Seven or Eight Mistresses Every Sunday Evening"

1. *Eagle*, 21 April 1873.
2. *New York Times*, 3 Mar. 1876.
3. TT v. HWB, 2:785.
4. Marshall, *True History*, 319–20.
5. Ibid., 154.
6. Doyle, *Plymouth Church*, 326–28.
7. Ibid., 337.
8. *New York Times*, cited in *Eagle*, 21 Apr. 1870.
9. Shaplen, *Free Love*, 62.
10. *Beecher-Tilton Investigation*, 30.
11. Ibid.
12. Ibid.; Shaplen, *Free Love*, 63.
13. TT v. HWB, 2:741.
14. Marshall, *True History*, 535.
15. Doyle, *Plymouth Church*, 355.
16. TT v. HWB, 3:12–15.
17. TT v. HWB, 2:749.
18. *Beecher-Tilton Investigation*, 93.
19. Marshall, *True History*, 49–50.
20. *New York World*, 26 Jan. 1869.
21. *Independent*, 26 Sept. 1870.
22. TT v. HWB, 1:464.
23. *Official Report of the Trial of HWB*, 2:350.
24. Ibid., 2:355.
25. TT v. HWB, 2:717–18.
26. Ibid.
27. TT v. HWB, 2:759.
28. *Official Report of the Trial of HWB*, 2:360.
29. Ibid., 2:125.
30. TT v. HWB, 1:61.
31. Marshall, *True History*, 261–62;

TT v. HWB, 3:86; *Beecher-Tilton Investigation*, 111.

32. TT v. HWB, 3:28.
33. Ibid., 1:62.
34. *Beecher-Tilton Investigation*, 112.
35. TT v. HWB, 3:31.
36. Ibid., 1:75.
37. Ibid., 1:63.
38. Ibid., 1:75.
39. Ibid., 1:188.
40. Ibid., 2:768.
41. Ibid., 1:65; BS, 505.
42. *Official Report of the Trial of HWB*, 2:145.
43. *Beecher-Tilton Investigation*, 112.
44. Ibid., 3:72.
45. *New York Times*, 11 Feb. 1871.
46. TT v. HWB, 1:84.
47. *Woodhull & Claflin's Weekly*, 2 Nov. 1872, reprinted in *The Woodhull Reader*.
48. TT v. HWB, 1:83.
49. HBS to George Eliot, 8 Feb. 1872, NYPL.
50. Underhill, *The Woman*, 96–97.
51. *Woodhull & Claflin's Weekly*, 2 Feb. 1872.
52. *New York Tribune*, 16 Jan. 1871.
53. IBH to Anna Savery, 12 Nov. 1871, HBSC.
54. *Woodhull & Claflin's Weekly*, 2 Feb. 1872.
55. Harper, *Life and Work*, 379.
56. Mary Perkins and HBS to John Hooker, 2 Mar. 1871, HBSC.
57. IBH to Susan B. Anthony, 11 Mar. 1871, HBSC.
58. Susan B. Anthony to IBH, 21 Mar. 1871, HBSC.
59. TT v. HWB, 1:413.
60. *Eagle*, 17 July 1874.
61. EB to Harriet Beecher Scoville, 26 Aug. 1871, BP-SML.

62. Ellen W. Garrison to Martha Coffin Wright, 27 Sept. 1871, Smith College Archives; Taylor, *Selected Letters*, 378; Goldsmith, *Other Powers*, 289.
63. Marshall, *True History*, 274.
64. *Woodhull & Claflin's Weekly*, 11 Feb. 1872.
65. Woodhull, " 'And the Truth Shall Make You Free': A Speech on the Principles of Social Freedom," *Woodhull Reader*, 23–24.
66. *Beecher-Tilton Investigation*, 53.
67. TT v. HWB, 2:858.
68. *Official Report of the Trial of HWB*, 2:737.
69. TT v. HWB, 1:237.
70. Doyle, *Plymouth Church*, 505.
71. *Beecher-Tilton War*, 78.
72. EB to Susan Howard, 18 Apr. 1872, BP-SML.
73. *Golden Age*, 9 Sept. 1871.
74. Doyle, *Plymouth Church*, 102.
75. Ibid., 266.
76. *Memphis Sunday Appeal*, 17 Nov. 1872.
77. *Woodhull & Claflin's Weekly*, 2 Feb. 1872.
78. Thompson, *The History of Plymouth Church*, 233.
79. *Woodhull & Claflin's Weekly*, 2 Feb. 1872.
80. HWB to S. B. Chittenden, 2 Nov. 1872, BP-SML.
81. TT v. HWB, 1:422.
82. Hale, *Horace Greeley*, 352.
83. Doyle, *Plymouth Church*, 508–12.
84. Ibid., 513.
85. TT v. HWB, I:424.
86. IBH to John Hooker, 4 Dec. 1872, University of Rochester Archives.
87. Smith and Bucci, *Mark Twain's Letters*, 5:230.

Chapter 13

"It Is the Letters—the Letters, Only the Letters"

1. Doyle, *Plymouth Church*, 555–57.
2. *Eagle*, 27 Dec. 1872.
3. *Eagle*, 8 Mar. 1875.
4. Marshall, *True History*, 559.
5. TT v. HWB, 1:427.
6. Ibid., 1:91.
7. *Cincinnati Post*, cited in *Woodhull & Claflin's Weekly*, 15 Feb. 1873.
8. Smith and Bucci, *Mark Twain's Letters*, 6:235–36.
9. Tyler, *Diary of M.C. Tyler*, 77.
10. Marshall, *True History*, 302.
11. EB to Chloe Beach, 23 Feb. 1873, BP-SML.
12. Moses Beach's Diary, 16 Apr.–21 May 1873, Moses S. Beach Papers, New York Historical Society.
13. Moses Beach to Chloe Beach, 22 July 1873, Private Collection of Brewster Beach.
14. *Eagle*, 13 Mar. 1875.
15. Doyle, *Plymouth Church*, 546–47.
16. TT v. HWB, 1:721.
17. *Eagle*, 2 June 1873.
18. EB to Chloe Beach, 8 June 1873, BP-SML.
19. Marshall, *True History*, 329.
20. *Against an Aristocracy of Sex*, 2:618.
21. W. S. Searle, "Beecher's Personality," *North American Review* 144, no. 366 (1887): 494.
22. TT v. HWB, 1:434.
23. Ibid., 1:104–5.
24. Davis, *Leonard Bacon*, 235.
25. Doyle, *Plymouth Church*, 165.
26. *Eagle*, 12 Sept. 1874.
27. TT v. HWB, 2:727.
28. *Eagle*, 8 Mar. 1875.
29. Doyle, *Plymouth Church*, 288–89.
30. *Beecher-Tilton Investigation*, 84–85; *New York Times*, 5 Aug. 1874.
31. *Beecher-Tilton Investigation*, 90.
32. Ibid., 47–48.
33. Ibid., 81.
34. Ibid., 49.
35. Doyle, *Plymouth Church*, 308.
36. *Beecher-Tilton Investigation*, 45.
37. *New York Times*, 1 Aug. 1874.
38. Stanton and Blatch, *Elizabeth Cady Stanton*, 145–46.
39. *Chicago Post and Mail*, 24 July 1874; HBS to Mary Claflin, 22 Aug. 1874, HBSC.
40. *New York Herald*, 23 July 1874.
41. *Boston Journal*, cited in *New York Herald*, 4 Aug. 1874.
42. Ames, *Chronicles*, 1:708.
43. Smith and Bucci, *Mark Twain's Letters*, 6:202.
44. Child, *Lydia Maria Child*, 525.
45. EB to Harriet Beecher Scoville, 9 Aug. 1874, BP-SML.
46. Doyle, *Plymouth Church*, 144.
47. *Beecher-Tilton Investigation*, 113.
48. Marshall, *True History*, 254.
49. *Daily Graphic*, 29 Aug. 1874.
50. Tyler, *Diary*, 84.
51. *Nation*, 20 Aug. 1874.
52. Bigelow, *Retrospections*, 5:151.
53. *Beecher-Tilton Investigation*, 127.
54. EB to Samuel and Harriet Beecher Scoville, 13 Jan. 1875, BP-SML.
55. Susan Howard to HWB, 22 Feb. 1875, BP-SML.
56. *New York Herald*, 21 March 1875.
57. TT v. HWB, 1:281.
58. *Chicago Tribune*, 23 Aug. 1874.
59. Shaplen, *Free Love*, 238; HBS to Mary Perkins, 28 Feb. 1875, Schlesinger Library.
60. Marshall, *True History*, 479; TT v. HWB, 1:118.
61. *Official Report of the Trial*, 2:935; *Eagle*, 19 Feb. 1875.
62. Strong, *Diary*, 4:522
63. Tracy, *Case of HWB*, 91.
64. *Boston Post*, cited in *New York World*, 17 April 1875.
65. *Eagle*, 1 Apr. 1875.
66. Bigelow, *Retrospections*, 5:196, 198.
67. *Beecher Trial: A Review of the Evidence*, 22.
68. *Eagle* 19 Apr. 1875.
69. TT v. HWB, 3:80.

70. Joseph Twichell's Journal, 13–15 April 1875, vol. 1., BL.
71. *Eagle*, 21 Apr. 1875.
72. Sach, *The Terrible Siren*, 233.
73. TT v. HWB, 3:323; *Chicago Tribune*, 5 May 1875.
74. TT v. HWB, 3:654.
75. J. O. Smith to HWB, n.d., BP-SML.
76. *Nation*, 20 Aug. 1874.
77. Bigelow, *Retrospections*, 5:151.
78. *Eagle*, 2 July 1875.
79. *New York World*, July 3, 1875.
80. *Nation*, 8 July 1875; Shaplen, *Free Love*, 258.
81. *Eagle*, 3 June 1875; *New York Times*, 3 July 1875.
82. *Chicago Tribune*, 14 July 1875.
83. Ella Beach's Diary, 12 July 1875, Moses S. Beach Papers, New York Historical Society.
84. *Independent*, 10 Feb. 1876.
85. BS, 548.
86. Joseph Twichell's Journal, 23 Feb. 1876, vol. 2, BL.
87. Ibid., 15 Feb. 1876, vol. 1, BL.
88. BS, 548, 554.
89. *New York Times*, 19 Apr. 1878.
90. EB to Chloe Beach, 23 Apr. 1878, BP-SML.
91. Report of the Plymouth Church of the Pilgrims Examining Committee, 301, 303, Brooklyn Historical Society.
92. *New York Times*, 17 Apr. 1878.

Epilogue

"What a Pity. That So Insignificant a Matter as the Chastity or Unchastity of an Elizabeth Tilton Could Clip the Locks of This Samson"

1. Griswold, *Sixty Years*, 96.
2. EB to Harriet Beecher Scoville, 16 Jan. 1876, BP-SML.
3. HWB to Mary Claflin, 11 Mar. 1877, Rutherford B. Hayes Library.
4. Howard, *Life of HWB*, 247.
5. HWB to EB, 20 April 1877, BP-SML.
6. HWB to Violet Beach, 24 Sept. 1877, Moses S. Beach Papers, LC.
7. EB to Chloe Beach, 17 Nov. 1877, BP-SML.
8. Ibid., 23 Apr. 1878.
9. HWB to Chloe Beach, 6 Aug. 1878, BP-SML.
10. EB to Chloe Beach, 24 July 1878, BP-SML.
11. Ibid., 2 Aug. 1878, BP-SML.
12. Ibid., 2 Aug. 1878; HWB to Chloe Beach, 5 Sept. 1878, BP-SML.
13. Howard, *Patriotic Addresses*, 289.
14. *New York Times*, 30 July 1877.
15. HWB, *Lectures and Orations*, 323, 318.
16. HWB, *Life of HWB*, 559.
17. HWB, *Lectures and Orations*, 311.
18. BS, 577–78.
19. *Eagle*, 23 Oct. 1884; *New York Sun*, 29 Oct. 1884.
20. HWB, *Lectures and Orations*, 311.
21. *Eagle*, 28 Nov. 1884; Higginson, *Thomas Wentworth Higginson*, 310.
22. Howard, *Life of HWB*, 562; Knox, *Life and Work*, 515.
23. Twain, *Autobiography of Mark Twain*, 186.
24. Shenstone, *Anecdotes of HWB*, 281–83.
25. Pond, *Eccentricities of Genius*, 72.
26. BS, 681.
27. Shenstone, *Anecdotes*, 336.
28. Thomas Beecher, "My Brother Henry," in *Notable Sermons*, 13–14.
29. *Auto HWB*, 130.
30. Mark Twain to Joseph Twichell, 14 Mar. 1887, Joseph Twichell's Journal, 5:121, BL.
31. HBS to Mary Beecher Perkins, July 1887, Schlesinger Library.
32. EB to Chloe Beach, 2 Sept. 1888, BP-SML.
33. H.W. Bellows to C. A. Bartol, 20 Jan. 1855, Bellows Papers, Massachusetts Historical Society.
34. HWB, *Plymouth Pulpit*, ser. 2, 420.

Bibliography

A Word About Sources

For reasons of space, I have regretfully limited citations to direct quotations. Because Henry Ward Beecher was so widely written about, many quotations and anecdotes appear in multiple publications, often varying slightly in wording. For example, three different trial transcripts were published, in addition to the daily transcripts printed in newspapers across the country. I have tried to peg my citations to the most accurate and accessible versions, referring to digitized copies whenever possible.

In the long course of preparing this book, I have profited from an array of scholars, too many to include in even the most thorough of bibliographies—early-twentieth-century antiquarians, mid-twentieth-century synthesizers, bottom-up social historians, and postmodern new historicists. I am particularly indebted to a long line of Beecher scholars, including Lyman Abbott, Joseph and John Raymond Howard, Paxton Hibben, William McLoughlin, Clifford Clark, Marie Caskey, Jane Shaffer Elsmere, Robert Shaplen, Milton Rugoff, Kathryn Kish Sklar, Altina Waller, Vincent Harding, Joan Hedrick, and Richard Wightman Fox.

Readers seeking further scholarly discussion might turn to Waller's social history of Plymouth Church, McLoughlin's intellectual history of Beecher's ideas, Rugoff's full family portrait, Hedrick's definitive life of Harriet Beecher Stowe, or Fox's extensive bibliographic essay which dissects the rumors and facts of the scandal. The Brooklyn Daily Eagle On-line, courtesy of the Brooklyn Public Library, and the Making of Modern America Web site, courtesy of the University of Michigan and Cornell University, offer free, word-searchable access to many primary sources about or by the Beechers. My own working notes, arranged as a detailed chronology of Beecher's life, will be available at the Amherst College Archives, in the hope of encouraging further scholarship and debate.

Archives

American Antiquarian Society, Worcester, Mass.
Archives and Special Collections, Amherst College, Amherst, Mass.
Boston Public Library, Boston, Mass.
Brooklyn Historical Society, Brooklyn, N.Y.
Brooklyn Public Library, Brooklyn, N.Y.
Cincinnati Historical Society, Cincinnati, Ohio
Cornell University Archives, Ithaca, N.Y.

Archives and Special Collections, Dickinson College, Carlisle, Penn.
Harriet Beecher Stowe Center, Hartford, Conn.
Harvard University, Cambridge, Mass.
    Houghton Library
    Schlesinger Library, Radcliffe Institute
Hennicker Historical Society, Hennicker, N.H.
Historic New England/SPNEA (Society for the Preservation of New England
    Antiquities), Boston, Mass.
Huntington Library, San Marino, Calif.
Indiana Historical Society, Indianapolis, Ind.
Library of Congress, Washington, D.C.
Litchfield Historical Society, Litchfield, Conn.
Massachusetts Historical Society, Boston
Museum of the City of New York, New York, N.Y.
New Hampshire Historical Society, Concord, N.H.
New York Public Library, New York, N.Y.
Olde Sturbridge Village, Sturbridge, Mass.
Ohio Historical Society, Columbus, Ohio
Rutherford B. Hayes Presidential Center, Fremont, Ohio
Sophia Smith Collection, Smith College, Northampton, Mass.
Friends Historical Library, Swarthmore College, Swarthmore, Penn.
Rare Books and Special Collections, University of Rochester, Rochester, N.Y.
Archives and Special Collections, Vassar College, Poughkeepsie, N.Y.
Yale University, New Haven, Conn.
    Beinecke Library
    Sterling Memorial Library, Manuscripts and Archives

Books and Articles

Abbott, Lyman. *Henry Ward Beecher*. Cambridge, Mass.: The Riverside Press, 1903.
———. *Henry Ward Beecher: A Sketch of His Career: With Analyses of His Power as a Preacher, Lecturer, Orator and Journalist, and Incidents and Reminiscences of His Life.* Hartford, Conn.: American Publishing Company, 1887.
———. *Henry Ward Beecher as His Friends Saw Him.* Boston: Pilgrim Press, c. 1904.
Against an Aristocracy of Sex, 1866 to 1873: The Selected Papers of Elizabeth Cady Stanton and Susan B. Anthony, 2 vols. Edited by Ann D. Gordon, Tamara Gaskell Miller, Susan I. Johns, Oona Schmid, Mary Poole, Veronica A. Wilson, and Stacy Kinlock Sewell. New Brunswick, N.J.: Rutgers University Press, 2000.
Alcott, A. Bronson. *The Journals of Bronson Alcott.* Edited by Odell Shepard. Boston: Little, Brown, and Company, 1938.
Allmendinger, David F. *Paupers and Scholars: The Transformation of Student Life in Nineteenth-Century New England.* New York: St. Martin's Press, 1975.
Ames, Blanche Butler. *Chronicles from the Nineteenth Century: Family Letters of Blanche Butler and Adelbert Ames.* Clinton, Mass.: 1957.
Antislavery Almanac. New York: Anti-Slavery Society, 1839.
Appleton's Cyclopedia of American Biography. New York: Appleton & Co., 1887–89.
Bacon, Theodore D. *Leonard Bacon, A Statesman for the Church.* New Haven: Yale University Press, 1931.
Badeau, Adam. *The Vagabond.* New York: Rudd & Carleton, 1859.

Barber, John Warner. *Historical Collections*. Worcester, Mass.: Dorr, Howland & Company, 1839.

Barnes, Gilbert H. *The Antislavery Impulse, 1830–1844*. New York: D. Appleton–Century Company, 1933.

Barnes, Gilbert H. and Dwight L. Dumond. *Letters of Theodore Dwight Weld, Angelina Grimké Weld and Sarah Grimké, 1822–1844*. 2 vols. New York: D. Appleton–Century Company, 1934.

Barrows, John Henry. *Henry Ward Beecher: The Shakespeare of the Pulpit*. New York: Funk & Wagnalls, 1893.

Basler, Roy P., and Christian O. Basler, eds. *The Collected Works of Abraham Lincoln. Second Supplement, 1848–1865*. New Brunswick, N.J.: Rutgers University Press, 1990.

Beecher, Catharine E. *Educational Reminiscences and Suggestions*. New York: J. B. Ford and Company, 1874.

———. *The Moral Instructor*. Cincinnati: Truman & Smith, 1838.

———. *Religious Training of Children*. New York: Harper & Bros., 1864.

Beecher, Charles. *Redeemer and Redeemed: An Investigation of the Atonement and of Eternal Judgment*. Boston: Lee and Shepard, 1864.

———. *Life of Edward Beecher*. Unpublished manuscript. Illinois College Library, Jacksonville, Ill.

Beecher, Eunice White. *Dawn to Daylight*. New York: Derby & Jackson, 1859.

Beecher, George. *The Biographical Remains of Rev. George Beecher: Late Pastor of a Church in Chillicothe, Ohio, and Former Pastor of a Church in Rochester, New York*. New York: Leavitt, Trow and Company, 1844.

Beecher, Henry Ward. *Autobiographical Reminiscences*. Edited by T. J. Ellinwood. New York: Frederick A. Stokes & Company, 1898.

———. *Evolution and Religion*. Enlarged Edition. New York: Fords, Howard & Hubert, 1886.

———. *Eyes and Ears*. Boston: Ticknor & Fields, 1862.

———. *Lecture Room Talks*. New York: J. B. Ford & Company, 1874.

———. *Lectures and Orations*. Edited by N. D. Hillis. New York: Fleming H. Revell & Company, 1913. Reprint, AMS Press, 1970.

———. *Life Thoughts, Gathered From the Extemporaneous Discourses of Henry Ward Beecher by One of His Congregations*. Boston: Phillips, Sampson and Company, 1858.

———. *New Star Papers; or, Views and Experiences of Religious Subjects*. New York: Derby & Jackson, 1859.

———. *Norwood; or, Village Life in New England*. New York: C. Scribner, 1868.

———. *Notes from Plymouth Pulpit: A Collection of Memorable Passages from the Discourses of Henry Ward Beecher*. Edited by Augusta Moore. New York: Derby and Jackson, 1859.

———. *Patriotic Addresses in America and England, 1855–1885*. Edited by John R. Howard. Boston: Pilgrim Press, 1887.

———. *Plymouth Pulpit: Sermons Preached by Henry Ward Beecher*. New York: J. B. Ford & Company, 1869–75.

———. *Royal Truths*. Boston: Ticknor & Fields, 1866.

———. *Star Papers; or, Experiences of Art and Nature*. New York: J. B. Ford & Company, 1873.

———. *Yale Lectures on Preaching*. New York: J. B. Ford & Company, 1872–73.

Beecher, Lyman. *The Autobiography of Lyman Beecher*. 2 vols. Edited by Barbara M. Cross. Cambridge, Mass.: Belknap Press of Harvard University Press, 1961.

Beecher, Thomas K. *Notable Sermons*. Elmira, N.Y.: Osborne Press, 1914.

Beecher, William, and Samuel Scoville, assisted by Mrs. Henry Ward Beecher. *A Biography of Rev. Henry Ward Beecher*. New York: Charles Webster, 1888.

Beecher-Tilton Investigation: The Scandal of the Age. Philadelphia: Barclay & Company, 1874.

Bigelow, John. *Retrospections of an Active Life*. 4 vols. New York: Baker, 1909.

Bok, Edward. *Beecher Memorial: Contemporaneous Tributes to the Memory of Henry Ward Beecher*. Brooklyn, N.Y.: Privately PrintedBowen, Edward A. *The Lineage of the Bowens of Woodstock, Connecticut*. Cambridge, Mass.: Riverside Press, 1897.

Branch, Edward Douglas. *The Sentimental Years: 1836–1860*. New York: D. Appleton–Century Company, 1934.

Brockett, L. P. *Men of Our Day*. Philadelphia: Zeigler, McCurdy & Company, 1869.

Bungay, George. *Crayon Sketches and Off-hand Takings*. Boston: Stacy and Richardson, 1852.

Carpenter, Francis B. *The Inner Life of Abraham Lincoln: Six Months in the White House*. New York: Hurd and Houghton, 1874.

Carter, Robert. "The Newness." *Century Illustrated Monthly Magazine* 39, no. 1 (1889).

Caskey, Marie. *Chariot of Fire: Religion and the Beecher Family*. New Haven, Conn.: Yale University Press, 1978.

Child, Lydia Maria. *Lydia Maria Child, Selected letters, 1817–1880*. Edited by Milton Meltzer and Patricia G. Holland. Amherst, Mass.: University of Massachusetts Press, 1982.

Cist, Charles. *Cincinnati in 1841: Early Annals and Future Prospects*. Cincinnati: Charles Cist, 1841.

Clark, Clifford E. *Henry Ward Beecher: Spokesman for a Middle-Class America*. Urbana: University of Illinois Press, 1978.

Cole, Arthur Charles. *Irrepressible Conflict, 1850–1865*. New York: Macmillan Company, 1934.

The Common School Almanac. New York: American Common School Society, 1839.

Conant, William C. *Narratives of Remarkable Conversions and Revival Incidents*. New York: Derby and Jackson, 1858.

Corning, Edward. *Personal Recollections of Henry Ward Beecher*. Brooklyn: Eagle Press, 1903.

Crofut, William A. *An American Procession, 1855–1914; A Personal Chronicle of Famous Men*. Boston: Little, Brown, and Company, 1931.

Davis, Hugh. *Leonard Bacon: New England Reformer and Antislavery Moderate*. Baton Rouge: Louisiana State University Press, 1998.

Derby, James C. *Fifty Years Among Authors, Books and Publishers*. New York: G. W. Carleton; London: S. Low, 1886.

Dix, John. *Transatlantic Tracings; or, Sketches of Persons and Scenes in America*. London: W. Tweedie, 1853.

Doyle, John Edward Parker. *Plymouth Church and its Pastor; or, Henry Ward Beecher and His Accusers*. Hartford, Conn.: Park Publishing Co., 1874.

Elsmere, Jane Shaffer. *Henry Ward Beecher: The Indiana Years*. Indianapolis: Indiana Historical Society, 1973.

Emerson, Ralph W. *The Conduct of Life*. Boston: James R. Osgood & Company, 1878.

———. "Historic Notes on Life and Letters in New England." *American Transcendentalists, Their Prose and Poetry*. Edited by Perry Miller. Garden City, N.Y.: Doubleday, 1957.

———. *Journal and Miscellaneous Notebooks of Ralph Waldo Emerson*. Edited by Linda Allardt. Cambridge, Mass.: Belknap Press of Harvard University Press, 1982.

———. *Selected Essays*. Edited by Lazar Ziff. New York: Penguin Books, 1982.

Finney, Charles. *The Memoirs of Charles G. Finney: The Complete Restored Text*. Edited by Garth Rosell and Richard A. G. Dupuis. Grand Rapids, Mich.: Academie Books, 1989.

Fiske, John. *Edward Livingston Youmans, Interpreter of Science for the People*. New York: Appleton, 1894.

Foner, Eric, and Olivia Mahoney. *A House Divided. America in the Age of Lincoln*. New York: Norton; Chicago: Chicago Historical Society, 1990.

Foner, Philip. *Business & Slavery*. Chapel Hill: University of North Carolina Press, 1941.

Foote, Mary Hallock. *A Victorian Gentlewoman in the Far West: The Reminiscences of Mary Hallock Foote*. Edited by Rodman W. Paul. San Marino, Calif.: Huntington Library, 1972.

Formisano, Ronald P. *The Birth of Mass Political Parties, Michigan, 1827–1861*. Princeton, N.J.: Princeton University Press, 1971.

Fowler, L. N. *The Illustrated Phrenological Almanac for 1852*. New York: Fowler and Wells, 1852.

Fowler, O. S., and L. N. Fowler. *Phrenology Proved, Illustrated, and Applied*. Assisted by Samuel Kirkham. New York: Printed for the Authors by W. H. Coyler, 1837.

Fox, Richard Wightman. *Trials of Intimacy: Love and Loss in the Beecher-Tilton Scandal*. Chicago: University of Chicago Press, 1999.

Freeman, Andrew A. *Abraham Lincoln Goes to New York*. New York: Coward-McCann, 1960.

French, Justus Clement, and Edward Carey. *The Trip of the Steamer Oceanus to Fort Sumter and Charleston, South Carolina*. Brooklyn, N.Y.: Union, 1865.

Fuess, Claude Moore. *Amherst: The Story of a New England College*. Boston: Little, Brown, and Company, 1935.

Garrison, Wendell Phillips, and Frances Jackson Garrison. *William Lloyd Garrison, 1805–1879: The Story of His Life, Told by His Children*. 4 vols. New York: Negro Universities Press, 1969.

———. *The Letters of William Lloyd Garrison*. Edited by Walter M. Merrill. 4 vols. Cambridge: Belknap Press of Harvard University Press, 1971–1981.

Goldsmith, Barbara. *Other Powers: The Age of Suffrage, Spiritualism, and the Scandalous Victoria Woodhull*. New York: Alfred A. Knopf, 1998.

Grant, Ellsworth. *The Miracle of Connecticut*. Edited by Oliver Jensen. Hartford: Connecticut Historical Society, 1992.

Griswold, Stephen. *Sixty Years with Plymouth Church*. New York: Fleming Revell Company, 1907.

Guelzo, Allen. *Lincoln's Emancipation Proclamation: The End of Slavery in America*. New York: Simon & Schuster, 2004.

Hale, William. *Horace Greeley: Voice of the People*. New York: Harper & Brothers, 1950.

Harding, Vincent. *Certain Magnificence: Lyman Beecher and the Transformation of American Protestantism, 1775–1863*. Brooklyn, N.Y.: Carlson Pub., 1991.

Harper, Ida Husted. *Life and Work of Susan B. Anthony*. New York: Arno, 1969.

Hayes, Rutherford B. *Diary and Letters of Rutherford B. Hayes*. Edited by Charles R. Williams. 5 vols. Columbus, Ohio: Ohio State Archaeological and Historical Society, 1922–26.

Hedrick, Joan. *Harriet Beecher Stowe: A Life*. New York: Oxford University Press, 1994.

Hibben, Paxton. *Henry Ward Beecher: An American Portrait*. New York: George Dornan, 1927.

Higginson, Mary P. Thacher. *Thomas Wentworth Higginson: The Story of His Life*. Boston: Houghton Mifflin & Company, 1914.

Higginson, Thomas W. *Letters and Journals of Thomas Wentworth Higginson, 1846–1906*. Edited by Mary Thacher Higginson. New York: Houghton Mifflin Co., 1921.

Hinton, Richard J. *John Brown and His Men*. New York, Arno Press, 1968.

Hitchcock, Edward. *The Religion of Geology and its Connected Sciences*. Boston: Phillips, Sampson, and Company, 1854.

Hooker, Isabella Beecher. "The Last of the Beechers: Memories of My Eighty-third Birthday." *Connecticut Magazine* 9 (1905).

Horowitz, Helen Lefkowitz. *Campus Life: Undergraduate Cultures from the End of the Eighteenth Century to the Present*. New York: Alfred A. Knopf, 1987.

Howard, Henry Ward, ed. *The Eagle and Brooklyn: The Record of the Progress of the Brooklyn Daily Eagle*, Brooklyn, N.Y.: Brooklyn Daily Eagle, 1893.

Howard, John Raymond. *Henry Ward Beecher: A Study of his Personality, Career and Influence in Public Affairs*. New York: Fords, Howard & Hulbert, 1887.

———. *Remembrance of Things Past: A Familiar Chronicle of Kinsfolk and Friends Worth While*. New York: Thomas Y. Crowell, 1925.

Howard, Joseph, Jr. *Life of Henry Ward Beecher*. Philadelphia: Hubbard Brothers, 1887.

Howe, Henry. *Historical Collections of the Great West*. Cincinnati: H. Howe, 1851.

Hudson, Frederick. *Journalism in the United States, from 1690–1872*. New York: Harper & Brothers, 1873.

Ingersoll, Robert Green. *The Works of Robert G. Ingersoll: In Twelve Volumes*. New York: Dresden Publishing Company, 1902.

Johnson, Oliver. *A Home in the Woods: Oliver Johnson's Reminiscences of Early Marion County, as Related by Howard Johnson*. Indianapolis: Indiana Historical Society, 1951.

Johnson, Oliver. *William Lloyd Garrison and His Times: or, Sketches of the Anti-Slavery Movement in America, and of the Man Who Was its Founder and Moral Leader*. Boston: B. B. Russell & Company; New York: C. Drew, 1879.

Julian, George. *Political Recollections, 1840 to 1842*. Chicago: Jansen, McClurg & Company, 1884.

Kirk, Eleanor, ed. *Beecher as a Humorist*. New York: Fords, Howard and Hulbert, 1894.

Knox, Thomas W. *Life and Work of Henry Ward Beecher*: Syracuse: Bible Publishing House, 1887.

Linscott, Robert Newton. *State of Mind: A Boston Reader*. New York: Farrar, Straus, 1948.

Mansfield, Edward D. *Personal Memories, 1803–1843*. Cincinnati: Robert Clarke & Company, 1879.

Marshall, Charles F. *The True History of the Brooklyn Scandal*. Philadelphia, 1874.

McAleer, John J. *Ralph Waldo Emerson: Days of Encounter*. Boston: Little, Brown, 1984.

McCullough, Hugh. *Men and Measures of Half a Century*. New York: C. Scribner's Sons, 1889.

McLoughlin, William G. *The Meaning of Henry Ward Beecher: An Essay on the Shifting Values of Mid-Victorian America, 1840–1870*. New York: Alfred A. Knopf, 1970.

Melville, Herman. *Collected Poems of Herman Melville*. Edited by Howard Vincent. Chicago: Chicago, Packard, 1947.

———. *The Confidence Man: His Masquerade*. New York: Oxford University Press, 1989.

Memorial of the Revival in Plymouth Church. New York: Clark, Austin & Smith, 1859.

Murat, Halstead. *Trimmers, Trucklers and Temporizers.* Madison: State Historical Society of Wisconsin, 1961.

Murphy, Mary Ellen. *A Treasury of Brooklyn.* Edited by Mary Ellen, Mark Murphy, and Ralph Foster Weld. New York: W. Sloane Associates, 1949.

Murray, Amelia M. *Letters from the United States and Canada.* New York: Putnam, 1856.

Nichols, Alice. *Bleeding Kansas.* New York: Oxford University Press, 1954.

O'Connor, Thomas H. *Civil War Boston: Home Front and Battlefield.* Boston: Northeastern University Press, 1997.

Official Report of the Trial of Henry Ward Beecher, with Notes and References by Austin Abbott; 2 vols. New York: George W. Smith, 1875.

Parker, Theodore. *World of Matter and the Spirit of Man; Latest Discourses of Religion.* Edited by George Willis Cooke. Boston: American Unitarian Association, 1907.

Parrish, William Earl. *David Rice Atchinson of Missouri, Border Politician.* Columbia: University of Missouri Press, 1961.

Pierson, George Wilson. *Tocqueville and Beaumont in America.* New York: Oxford University Press, 1938.

Piper, Ferdinand. *Lives of the Leaders of Our Church Universal.* Edited by Henry Mitchell MacCracken. Philadelphia: Reformed Church Publication Board, 1879.

Pond, James Burton. *Eccentricities of Genius. Memories of Famous Men and Women of the Platform and Stage.* New York: G. W. Dillingham Company, 1900.

Potter, David. *Impending Crisis, 1848–1861.* Edited by Don E. Fehrenbacher. New York: Harper & Row, 1976.

Power, Richard Lyle. *Planting Corn Belt Culture; The Impress of the Upland Southerner and Yankee in the Old Northwest.* Indianapolis: Indiana Historical Society, 1953.

Proceedings of the Union Safety Meeting Held in Castle Garden, October 30, 1850. New York: 1850.

Rand, Frank Prentice. *The Village of Amherst, a Landmark of Light.* Amherst, Mass.: Amherst Historical Society, 1958.

Rankin, Henry Bascon. *Intimate Character Sketches of Abraham Lincoln.* Philadelphia and London: J. B. Lippincott Company, 1924.

Ray, C.A.B. *Sketch of the Life of Reverend Charles B. Ray.* New York: Press of J.J. Little & Company, 1887.

Raymond, John R. *Life and Letters of John Howard Raymond.* New York: Fords, Howard, & Hulbert, 1881.

Rice, Allen Thorndike, ed. *Reminiscences of Abraham Lincoln by Distinguished Men of His Time.* New York: North American Publishing Company, 1886.

Riddle, Alfred G. "Discovery of Henry Ward Beecher." *Magazine of Western History* 5 (1887).

Rourke, Constance. *Trumpets of Jubilee.* New York: Harcourt Brace & Company, 1927.

Rugoff, Milton. *The Beechers: An American Family in the Nineteenth Century.* New York: Harper & Row, 1981.

Rusk, Ralph L. *The Life of Ralph Waldo Emerson.* New York: Columbia University Press, 1957.

Sachs, Emanie. *The Terrible Siren: Victoria Woodhull, 1838–1927.* New York: Harper and Brothers, 1928.

Sandburg, Carl. *Abraham Lincoln: The Prairie Years and the War Years.* New York: Harcourt Brace, 1954.

Shaplen, Robert. *Free Love and Heavenly Sinners.* New York: Alfred A. Knopf, 1954.

Shenstone, N. A. *Anecdotes of Henry Ward Beecher.* Chicago: J. C. Buckbee, 1887.

Sherwin, Oscar. *Prophet of Liberty: The Life and Times of Wendell Phillips*. New York: Bookman Associates, 1958.

Smith, Matthew Hale. *Successful Folks: How They Win. Illustrated in the Career of Eight Hundred Eminent Men*. Hartford, Conn.: American Publishing Company, 1878.

———. *Sunshine and Shadow in New York*. Hartford: J. B. Burr and Company, 1868.

Stampp, Kenneth M. *America in 1857: A Nation on the Brink*. New York: Oxford University Press, 1990.

Stanton, Theodore and Harriot Stanton Blatch, eds. *Elizabeth Cady Stanton as Revealed in her Letters, Diaries and Reminiscences*. New York: Harper & Bros., 1922.

Stanwood, Edward. *Boston Illustrated*. Boston: J. R. Osgood, 1886.

Stowe, Calvin. "Sketches and Recollections of Dr. Lyman Beecher." *Congregational Quarterly* 6 (1864).

Stowe, Charles E. *Life of Harriet Beecher Stowe, Compiled from Her Letters and Journals by Her Son, Charles Edward Stowe*. Boston: Houghton Mifflin & Company, 1890.

Stowe, Harriet Beecher. *The Mayflower; or Sketches of Scenes and Characters Among the Descendants of the Pilgrims*. New York: Harper & Brothers, 1843.

———. *Men of Our Times; or, Leading Patriots of the Day*. Hartford, Conn.: Hartford Publishing Company; New York: J. D. Denison, 1868.

———. *My Wife and I*. New York: J. B. Ford & Company, 1872.

———. *Oldtown Folks*. Boston: Fields, Osgood & Company, 1873.

———. *Poganuc People*. New York: Fords, Howard & Hulbert, 1878.

———. *Uncle Tom's Cabin; or, Life Among the Lowly*. New York: Modern Library, 1996.

Stowe, Lyman Beecher. *Saints, Sinners, and Beechers*. Indianapolis: Bobbs-Merrill Company, 1934.

Strong, George Templeton. *Diary of George Templeton Strong*. Edited by Allan Nevins and Milton Halsey Thomas. 4 vols. New York: Macmillan, 1952.

Tappan, Lewis. *The Life of Arthur Tappan*. New York: Hurd and Houghton, 1870.

Taylor, Bayard. *Selected Letters of Bayard Taylor*. Edited by Paul C. Wermuth. Cranbury, N.J.: Bucknell University Press, 1997.

Theodore Tilton v. Henry Ward Beecher: Action for Crim. Con. Tried in the City Court of Brooklyn, Chief Justice Joseph Neilson, Presiding: Verbatim Report by the Official Stenographer. New York: McDivitt, Campbell, 1875.

Thomas, Benjamin. *Theodore Weld: Crusader for Freedom*. New Brunswick, N.J.: Rutgers University Press, 1950.

Thompson, Noyes L. *The History of Plymouth Church*. New York: G. W. Carleton & Company, 1873.

Thoreau, Henry D. *The Journal of Henry D. Thoreau*. Eds. Bradford Torrey and Francis H. Allen. 14 vols. Boston: Houghton Mifflin and Company, circa 1949.

Tilton, Theodore. "Speech of Theodore Tilton in Plymouth Church, Brooklyn, January 25, 1860." Reported by William Henry Burr. New York: John A. Gray, 1860.

Tracy, Benjamin F. *Case of Henry Ward Beecher. Opening Address by Benjamin F. Tracy, of Counsel for the Defendant*. New York: G. W. Smith & Company, 1875.

Traubel, Horace. *With Walt Whitman in Camden*. Boston: Small, Maynard, 1906–64.

Trefousse, Hans L. *Andrew Johnson: A Biography*. New York: W.W. Norton, 1989.

Trimpi, Helen. *Melville's Confidence Men and American Politics in the 1850s*. Hamden, Conn. Academy of Arts and Sciences, 1987.

Twain, Mark. *Mark Twain's Letters, 1867–1868*. Edited by Harriet Elinor Smith and Richard Bucci. Los Angeles: University of California Press, 1990.

———. *Mark Twain's Travels with Mr. Brown*. Collected and Edited by Franklin Walker and G. Ezra Dane. New York: Alfred A. Knopf, 1940.

Tyler, Alice Felt. *Freedom's Ferment: Phases of American Social History from the Colonial Period to the Outbreak of the Civil War.* 2d ed. New York: Harper & Row, 1962.

Tyler, Moses Coit. *Selections from His Letters and Diaries.* Edited by Jessica Tyler Austen. Garden City, N.Y.: Doubleday Page, 1911.

Tyler, W. S. *History of Amherst College During Its First Half Century, 1821–1871.* Springfield, Mass.: C. W. Bryan, 1873.

Underhill, Lois Beachy. *The Woman Who Ran for President: The Many Lives of Victoria Woodhull.* Bridgehampton, N.Y.: Bridge Works Publishing Company, 1995.

Vanderpoel, Emily Noyes. *More Chronicles of a Pioneer School: From 1792 to 1833.* New York: Cadmus Book Shop, 1927.

Van Pelt, Daniel. *Leslie's History of Greater New York.* New York: Arkell Publishing Company, 1898.

Waller, Altina. *Reverend Beecher and Mrs. Tilton: Sex and Class in Victorian America.* Amherst: University of Massachusetts Press, 1982.

Ward, William Hayes, ed. *Abraham Lincoln: Tributes from His Associates.* New York: Thomas Y. Crowell, 1895.

Warren, Kenneth W. *Black and White Strangers: Race and American Literary Realism.* Chicago: University of Chicago Press, 1993.

Welles, Gideon. *Diary of Gideon Welles.* Boston: Houghton Mifflin & Company, 1911.

Whicher, George Frisbie. *This Was a Poet: A Critical Biography of Emily Dickinson.* New York: C. Scribner's Sons, 1938.

White, Alain C. *The History of the Town of Litchfield, Conn., 1790–1920.* Litchfield, Conn.: Litchfield Historical Society, 1920.

White, James C. *Personal Reminiscences of Lyman Beecher.* New York: Funk & Wagnalls, 1882.

Whitman, Walt. *I Sit and Look Out: Editorials from the Brooklyn Daily Times.* New York: AMS Press Inc. 1966.

Whittier, John Greenleaf. *The Letters of John Greenleaf Whittier.* Edited by John G. Pickard. Cambridge, Mass.: Belknap Press of Harvard University Press, 1975.

Wilson, Forrest. *Crusader in Crinoline: The Life of Harriet Beecher Stowe.* Philadelphia: J. B. Lippincott Co., 1941.

Wilson, Henry. *History of the Rise and Fall of the Slave Power in America.* Boston: Houghton Mifflin & Company, 1872–1877.

Wilson, James G. and John Fiske, eds. *Appleton's Cyclopaedia.* New York: D. Appleton and Company, 1887–89.

Woodhull, Victoria. *The Woodhull Reader.* Edited by Madeleine B. Stern. Weston, Mass.: M & S Press, 1974.

Illustration Credits

Title page
Daguerreotype of Henry Ward Beecher. Yale University Manuscripts and
    Archives.

Page xii
Fort Sumter. Private collection of the author.

Page 1 of insert
(Top) Litchfield, Connecticut. Litchfield Historical Society.
(Middle left) Salem Street. Stanwood, *Boston Illustrated*. Courtesy of
    Kellscraft Studio.
(Middle right) Lyman Beecher. Shenstone, *Anecdotes*.
(Bottom left) Mount Pleasant Classical Institution. Mount Pleasant
    Catalogue, 1828. Amherst College Archives.
(Bottom right) Amherst College. Barber, *Historical Collections*. Amherst
    College Archives.

Page 2 of insert
(Top) Schoolhouse in chaos. *The Common School Almanac*.
(Middle) Phrenological chart. Fowler, *The Illustrated Phrenological Almanac for
    1852*.
(Bottom) Public Landing of Cincinnati. Cist, *Annals of Cincinnati*.

Page 3 of insert
(Top) Henry Ward and Lyman Beecher. Schlesinger Library.
(Middle) Lane Seminary. Cist, *Annals of Cincinnati*.
(Bottom) Indiana Journal. Bass Photo Collection, Indiana Historical Society.

Page 4 of insert
(Top) Minister dragged from his pulpit. *Antislavery Almanac*.

(Middle left) Second Presbyterian Church. Bass Photo Collection, Indiana
Historical Society.
(Middle right) Bowen & McNamee's. Museum of the City of New York.
(Bottom) Plymouth Church exterior. Shenstone, *Anecdotes*.

Page 5 of insert
(Top) View of Brooklyn Heights from Manhattan. *Gleasons Pictorial Drawing
Room Companion*, June 14, 1851.
(Middle) View of Manhattan from Brooklyn Heights. *Gleasons Pictorial
Drawing Room Companion*, August 31, 1851.
(Bottom left and right) Henry Ward and Eunice Beecher. Beinecke Library.

Page 6 of insert
(Top) Eunice Beecher with twins. Harriet Beecher Stowe Center.
(Bottom) The Beecher family. Harriet Beecher Stowe Center.

Page 7 of insert
"Heroes of Liberty." Brockett, *Men of Our Day*.

Page 8 of insert
(Top) Map of United States in 1856. Created by Martie Holmer.
(Bottom) Eastman Johnson, *The Freedom Ring*. Hallmark Fine Arts
Collection.

Page 9 of insert
(Top) *"Col. Fremont's Last Grand Exploring Expedition in 1856."* Huntington
Library.
(Bottom left) Edna Dean Proctor. Historic New England/SPNEA.
(Bottom right) *"Kansas Crusader." Young America*, 1 (1856). American
Antiquarian Society.

Page 10 of insert
(Top left) Theodore Tilton cartoon. *Vanity Fair*, June 20, 1863.
(Top right) Theodore Tilton photo. Harriet Beecher Stowe Center.
(Bottom) Henry Ward Beecher cartoon. *Vanity Fair*, April 26, 1862.

Page 11 of insert
(Top) Tiltons' house. Doyle, *Romance of Plymouth Church*.
(Middle) Henry Chandler Bowen. Historic New England/SPNEA.

(Bottom) *"Beecher's American Soothing Syrup." Punch, or the London Charivari,* October 31, 1863.

Page 12 of insert

(Top left) Chloe and Violet Beach. Private collection of Brewster Beach.

(Top right) Moses Sperry Beach. Private collection of Brewster Beach.

(Bottom) Henry Ward Beecher with Violet Beach. Private collection of Brewster Beach.

Page 13 of insert

(Top) Elizabeth Cady Stanton and Susan B. Anthony. Schlesinger Library.

(Middle) Victoria Woodhull. Sophia Smith Collection, Smith College.

(Bottom) Violet Beach as a teenager. Private collection of Brewster Beach.

Page 14 of insert

(Top) Plymouth Church interior. *Harper's Weekly,* October 12, 1872.

(Middle left) Henry kneeling. *Frank Leslie's Illustrated,* February 20, 1875.

(Middle right) Elizabeth Tilton in court. *Frank Leslie's Illustrated,* May 22, 1875.

(Bottom) Shaking hands in court. *Frank Leslie's Illustrated,* January 30, 1875.

Page 15 of insert

(Top) Elizabeth Tilton. Private collection.

(Middle) Henry Ward Beecher and Hell. *Puck,* February 6, 1878.

(Bottom left) *"The man who can't live on bread and water." Puck,* August 8, 1877.

(Bottom right) Henry and Theodore footrace. *Daily Graphic,* August 12, 1874.

Page 16 of insert

(Top) Henry Ward Beecher and Harriet Beecher Stowe. Harriet Beecher Stowe Center.

(Bottom) Henry Ward Beecher in 1880s. Yale University Manuscripts and Archives.

Index

Abbott, Lyman, 269
Adams, Charles Francis, 348
African Americans:
  Black Codes, 115, 359, 360
  and Fifteenth Amendment, 383
  and Fourteenth Amendment, 378, 383
  and Reconstruction, 356–62, 383, 391, 460
  as slaves, *see* slavery
  and Thirteenth Amendment, 351, 356
  voting rights for, 361, 362
  see also individual African Americans
Alcott, Bronson, 216, 275
American and Foreign Antislavery Society (AFASS) "Tappanites," 235, 249–51
American Antislavery Society (AASS) "Garrisonians," 128, 235, 249, 251–53, 309
American Board of Commissioners for Foreign Missions, 314–17
American Colonization Society, 105–6
American Equal Rights Association, 384
American Home Missionary Society, 157
American Party (Know-Nothings), 278, 280, 286–87
"American Renaissance," 270–71
American Revolution, 21–22
American Woman Suffrage Association (AWSA), 387–88

Amherst College, 73–74, 77–81, 91–98, 102–3
  slavery debated in, 106–7
  commencement ceremonies of, 107–8
  literary clubs in, 91–92, 102
  temperance societies in, 78, 81, 99
Amherst, Massachusetts, 60, 107–8
Anderson, Robert, 1–2, 10
Andrew, John A., 345
Anthony, Susan B., 380
  and sex scandal, 398, 414, 430, 434, 436
  and women's rights movement, 383, 384–85, 387, 388, 412
antislavery movement:
  backlash against, 115–16, 128–31, 153–54
  and Civil War, 328, 329–31, 338–39
  and colonization, 105–6, 186, 339, 342
  and Fifteenth Amendment, 383
  and free speech, 128, 130–32, 252–54, 259, 314–15
  Garrison on, 5, 105–7, 112, 128, 221, 223–24, 234–35, 243, 249, 251–53, 262, 282, 309, 331, 340
  and "Great Postal Campaign," 128
  Henry's ambivalence about, 106–7, 118, 129, 131, 186–89, 192–93, 223, 224, 242–43, 310–12, 314–16, 317, 331, 360
  Henry's promotion of, 5–7, 15, 246–48, 249–51, 253–54,

A Note About the Author

© BETH DIXON

DEBBY APPLEGATE is a summa cum laude graduate of Amherst College and was a Sterling Fellow at Yale University, where she earned her Ph.D. in American Studies. She has written for publications ranging from the *Journal of American History* to the *New York Times*, and has taught at Yale and Wesleyan universities. She lives in New Haven, Connecticut, with her husband, Bruce Tulgan.